ISBN 978-1-5279-5721-3
PIBN 10924104

1 MONTH OF
FREE
READING

at
www.ForgottenBooks.com

By purchasing this book you are eligible for one month membership to ForgottenBooks.com, giving you unlimited access to our entire collection of over 1,000,000 titles via our web site and mobile apps.

To claim your free month visit:
www.forgottenbooks.com/free924104

MARCH, 1925

Bulletin of the University of Georgia

Vol. XXV   Number 4

University of Georgia

SUMMER SCHOOL

THE OLD CHAPEL

ATHENS, GEORGIA

June 22nd to August 1-21st

1925

THE UNIVERSITY SUMMER SCHOOL

CALENDAR

SATURDAY, JUNE 20TH: Dormitories open.
Faculty Meeting 5 P. M., at Memorial Hall.

MONDAY, JUNE 22ND: Registration 8:30 to 6:00.

TUESDAY, JUNE 23RD: Classes begin as scheduled.

JUNE 29TH TO JULY 4TH: Public Health and Welfare Week, conducted by National Child Health and Commonwealth Clinic and the State Board of Health.

JULY 6TH TO 11TH: Woman's Club Institute.

JULY 13TH TO 18TH: County and City Superintendents' Week.

JULY 20TH TO 25TH: Music Festival Week.

JULY 27TH TO 31ST: Vocational Agricultural Teachers' Short Course.

AUGUST 3RD TO 15TH: Boys' and Girls' Short Course.

AUGUST 21ST: Closing of Nine Weeks Term.

SUMMER SCHOOL BOARD

DAVID C. BARROW_____Chancellor
JERE M. POUND_____President State Normal School
CHARLES M. SNELLING_____Dean of the University
ANDREW M. SOULE_____President Agricultural College
THOMAS J. WOOFTER_____Dean Peabody School of Education
N. H. BALLARD_____State School Superintendent

State Normal Scene

SUMMER SCHOOL FACULTY

ADMINISTRATIVE COUNCIL

CHAS. M. SNELLING, Dean.   ANDREW M. SOULE,   JERE M. POUND,

D. C. BARROW.

JOSEPH S. STEWART_____Director of Summer School
THOMAS W. REED_____Registrar and Treasurer
H. I. REYNOLDS_____Physician to the Summer School
LUCILLE EPPS_____Secretary to the Director

ALFRIEND, KYLE T., A.B., A.M._____Education
    Dean, Bessie Tift
ALLEN, RUTH_____Demonstration School
    Macon, Ga., Public Schools
ANDREWS, WILLIE DEAN, B.A., M.A._____Health
    Physical Educator Athens Child Health Demonstration
ARCHER, FRANCES R._____Librarian, Library Methods
    Librarian, State Normal School
BALLARD, N. H., A.M., State Supt._____Lecturer
    State Superintendent of Schools, Atlanta
BARROW, D. C., LL.D._____Lecturer
    Chancellor University of Georgia
BAUM, EDNA LUCILLE_____Aesthetic and Folk Dancing, Festival
    Instructor Pestallozzi-Froebel Teachers College, Chicago
BENNETT, LOUISE, A.B._____Voice
    Professor of Voice, Shorter College
BENNETT, F. W., B.S.A._____Animal Husbandry
    Associate Professor of Animal Husbandry
BENNETT, U. J., A.B._____High School Mathematics
    Superintendent of Schools, Fitzgerald, Ga.
BITTICK, ELLEN, A.B._____Demonstration School
    Whiteford School, Atlanta, Ga.
BLACKSHEAR, A. LAURA E._____Poster Designing
    Ilustrator, Agricultural College
BLACKMON, BESSIE_____Accompanist, Physical Training
    Teacher in New Holland Schools
BOCOCK, WILLIS H., A.M., LL.D._____World War Studies
    Dean of the Graduate School
BRINSON, F. A._____High School Science
    Superintendent of Schools, Millen, Ga.
BRITTAIN, M. L., LL.D._____Lecturer
    President Georgia Tech
BROCKMAN, CHAS. J., A.M., Ch. Eng._____Chemistry
    Instructor in Chemistry
BROOKS, R. P., Ph.D._____Economics
    Professor of Banking and Finance
BROWN, PETER F., A.B._____Elementary Language, Grammar
    Professor of English, State Normal School
BURKHART, WALTER CLINTON, D.V.M._____Veterinary Medicine
    Associate Professor of Veterinary Medicine, Agricultural College
BURLEIGH, T. D., B.S., M.S._____Forestry
    Associate Professor of Forestry
BURNET, DUNCAN_____Librarian
    Librarian, University of Georgia
BURSON, SUSIE, B.S.H.E._____Home Economics
    In charge of Teacher Training Work
CAREY, BERNARD W., M.D._____Public Health
    Head Commonwealth Clicinc, Athens
CARREKER, H. B., A.B._____High School English
    Superintendent of Schools, Dublin, Ga.
CARTER, L. M., B.S._____Agricultural Chemistry
    Professor of Agricultural Chemistry

CHANCE, CLAUDE, A.B._____Spanish
    Instructor in Spanish. University of Georgia
CHAPMAN, PAUL W., B.S.A._____Vocational Journalism
    State Supervisor of Vocational Agriculture
CHAPMAN, ANNIE_____Demonstration School
    Atlanta Public Schools
CHILDS, R. R., B.S., M.S._____Cotton Grading
    Professor of Agronomy, in charge of Cotton Industry
CLEGG, W. A., B.S.A._____Agricultural Engineering
    Associate Professor of Agricultural Engineering
CORNETT, WALTER G., LL.B._____Law
    Professor of Law
CLEMENT, GLENN C._____Piano
    Granberry Piano School, Carnegie Hall, New York
COBB, JUDGE A. J., A.B., LL.D._____Law
    Professor of Law
COBB, CAROLYN, A.B._____Expression
    Reader and Teacher of Dramatic Art, Atlanta
CRABB, GEORGE A., B.S.A._____Soils
    Professor of Agronomy in charge of Soils
CRESWELL, MARY E., B.S.H.E._____Vocational Home Economics
    Director Department Home Economics
CRESWELL, EDITH, B.S.H.E._____Home Economics
    Adjunct Professor in Home Economics
CUMMING, FORREST, A.B._____Mathematics
    Instructor in Mathematics
DIXON, ELLIS H., A.B._____Physics
    Instructor in Physics
DOWDLE, LOIS P., B.S.H.E._____Food Preservation
    State Agent Girls' Club Work
EARNEST, DAVID L., A.M._____Elementary Science, General Science
    Professor of Natural Science, State Normal School
FURRY, W. D., Ph.D._____Philosophy, Education
    Dean Shorter College
GANNON, ARTHUR F., B.S.A._____Poultry Husbandry
    Adjunct Professor in Poultry Husbandry
GRANBERRY, GEO. F._____Professional Music Course, Piano
    Director Granberry Piano School, Carnegie Hall, New York
GRANBERRY, MRS. GEO. F._____The Organ
    Organist and Instructor in Organ, New York
GROTE, ERNESTINE_____Physical Education
    Professor of Physical Education, Wesleyan College
HARRALSON, KATE LEE_____Public School Music
    Supervisor Public School Music, Atlanta. Ga.
HECKMAN, HAROLD M., B.S.C., A.M._____Business Law, Accounting
    Professor of Accounting
HENDREN, L. L., Ph.D._____Physics
    Professor of Physics and Astronomy
HICKS, KATE E._____Demonstration School
    Principal of State Normal Training School
HOLLIDAY, ANNIE M._____Color Work and Blackboard Sketching
    Department of Manual Arts, State Normal School
HOOPER, WILLIAM D., A.M., Litt.D._____Latin
    Professor of Latin
HUNTER, H. REID, A.M._____City Administration, High Schools
    Assistant Superintendent, Atlanta, Ga.
HUTCHINSON, GEO. A., Ph.D._____Sociology
    Professor of Philosophy and Education
JACK, ALTA, A.M._____French
    Professor of French, Bessie Tift
JONES, ROBERT W., D.V.M._____Veterinary Medicine
    Associate Professor of Veterinary Medicine
KELLOGG, C. E., B.S._____Animal Husbandry
    Associate Professor of Animal Husbandry
KEENER, R. L., B.S.A._____Horticulture
    Adjunct Professor of Horticulture

KRAFKA, JOSEPH, JR., Ph.D._____Zoology
    Associate Professor of Zoology
LAND, F. E., A.B._____Lecturer
    State Superintendent Elect
LANIER, W. B., B.S._____High School Latin and History
    Superintendent Public Schools, Sparta, Ga.
LOWE, W. C._____Penmanship
    Director Penmanship, Atlanta
LUSTRAT, JOSEPH, BACH. ES LETT., LETT.D._____French
    Professor of Romance Languages
LYLE, SAMUEL P., B.S., M.S._____Household Mechanics
    Professor of Agricultural Engineering
MACLAREN, GAY_____Dramatic Impersonator
    New York City
MELTON, W. F., Ph.D._____Literature
    Professor of English, Emory University
MOTE, J. H., B.S._____Physics
    Assistant in Physics Laboratory
McCABE, FRANCIS J., B.L.I._____Pramatics, Public Speaking
    Instructor in Emerson School of Oratory
McHATTON, T. H., B.S., Sc.D._____Horticulture
    Professor of Horticulture
McPHERSON, J. H. T., Ph.D._____History, Government
    Professor of History and Political Science
McWHORTER, R. L., A.M., LL.B._____Law
    Instructor in Law
NEWTON, CATHERINE, B.S.H.E., M.S._____Home Economics
    Associate Professor of Foods and Nutrition
OSTERMAN, F. J., A.M._____Typewriting
    Instructor State Normal School
PARK, ROBERT E., Litt.D._____English Literature
    Professor of English Literature
PATRICK, J. R., B.A._____General Psychology
    Instructor in Psychology
PAYNE, W. O., A.M._____History
    Professor of History
PIGUERON, MARY CRAIG_____Concert Vocalist
    New York
POUND, JERE M., LL.D._____Lecturer
    President, State Normal School
PROCTOR, ERNA, B.S._____Health
    Health Educator Athens Child Health Demonstration
PURDOM, T. LUTHER, Ph.D._____ _____Educational Psychology
    Instructor University of Michigan
RATHBONE, ROSALIE VIRGINIA, B.S._____Home Economics
    Associate Professor of Clothing and Textiles
READE, JOHN M., Ph.D._____Botany
    Professor of Botany
REESE, NELLE M._____Librarian
    Librarian, State College of Agriculture
REITZ, W. W., M.S._____Agricultural Education
    Associate Professor of Agricultural Education
RICHARDSON, ALBERT G. G., D.V.M._____Veterinary Medicine
    Professor of Veterinary Medicine
RITCHIE, HORACE B., A.M._____School Management and Administration
    Professor of Psychology and Pedagogy, State Normal School
SANFORD, STEADMAN V., A.M., Litt.D.____English Literature, Journalism
    Professor of English Language and Journalism
SCHWEPPE, EMMA, A.M._____History and the Social Studies
    The Lincln School of Teachers College, New York
SCOTT, RHEA C., B.S._____Institutonal Economics
    Associate Professor of Institutional Economics
SELL, E. SCOTT, M.S._____Elementary Agriculture
    Professor of Agriculture, State Normal School
SELOVER, MRS. C. L._____Lecturer
    Cleveland, Ohio

SEVERIN, J. E., D.V.M._____*Veterinary Medicine*
  Associate Professor of Veterinary Medicine
SHAW, MRS. OPAL_____*Demonstration School*
  Lee Street School, Atlanta, Ga.
SHEFFER, LAFAYETTE M., B.S._____*Agricultural Education*
  Associate Professor of Agricultural Education
SIMMONS, JAMES H., A.M._____*English Composition, Literature*
  Professor English, Brenau College
SIMPSON, MRS. IDA, B.S._____*U. S. History and Civics*
  Instructor Hunter College, N. Y.
SNELLING, CHAS. M., A.M., Sc.D._____*Lecturer*
  Professor of Mathematics, Dean
SOLOMON, MAGGIE_____*Elementary School Methods*
  Supervisor Elementary Schools, Atlanta, Ga.
SOULE, ANDREW M., Sc.D., LL.D._____*Lecturer*
  President Agricultural College
STEPHENS, A. M., A.B._____*Assistant in Sociology*
  Superintendent Schools, Toccoa
STEPHENS, R. P., Ph.D._____*Mathematics*
  Professor of Mathematics
STEWART, J. S., A.M., Ped.D._____*Director of Summer School*
  Professor of Secondary Education, High School Inspector
SUTTON, WILLIS A., A.M._____*Lecturer*
  Superintendent City Schools, Atlanta
TABOR, PAUL, M.S.A._____*Farm Crops*
  Associate Professor of Agronomy
THOMAS, F. W._____*Football Coaching*
  Assistant Coach University of Georgia
TIGNER, MARY_____*Handicrafts*
  Instructor of Handicrafts, Columbus, Ga.
UPSON, STEPHENS CUMMINS, LL.B._____*Law*
  Professor of Law
VANCE, CAROLYN, B.L.I._____*Elementary Dramatics, Story Telling*
  Department Oratory, State Normal School
VERMONT, ADOLPHE, Ph.D._____*Lecturer*
  Professor of French, Converse College
WATKINS, MRS. ARTHUR C._____*Parent Teachers' Course*
  Executive Secretary, National Parent-Teachers' Association
WHEELER, JOHN T., B.S._____*Agricultural Education*
  Professor of Agricultural Education
WIGHT, AUSTIN J._____*Violin*
  School of Violin Playing, Athens, Ga.
WIGHT, MRS. AUSTIN J._____*Assistant in Violin*
  School of Violin Playing, Athens, Ga.
WILDER, C. N., B.S.A., M.S.A._____*Qualitative Analysis*
  Associate Professor of Agricultural Chemistry
WILLINGHAM, RUBY_____*Kindergarten*
  Director of Kindergartens, Columbus, Ga.
WISE, HENRY A., Ph.D._____*Education*
  Professor of Education, Converse College
WOOD, JAMES H., B.S.A._____*Poultry Husbandry*
  Professor of Poultry Husbandry
WOODBERRY, ROSA_____*Parliamentary Law*
  Principal Woodberry School, Atlanta, Ga.
ZEIGLER, MAY, A.B., A.M._____*Psychology*
  Instructor in Child Study and Psychology, State Normal School

GENERAL INFORMATION

The University Summer School was authorized by the General Assembly in 1903. It is an integral part of the University, the Agricultural College, and the State Normal and its courses coordinate with these as indicated in the outline of courses.

There will be two terms, one for six weeks and the other for nine weeks. They both begin on June 22nd, the first ends on August 1st, and the longer term on August 21st.

The laboratories, libraries, gymnasium, dormitories and other equipment of the three institutions and of the Lucy Cobb Institute are available during the summer. Nearly every department offers courses in the summer, undergraduate and a number of graduate courses, equal in quality and valued in terms of the regular year.

LOCATION

Athens, a city of over 20,000 people, is situated in the Piedmont Region of North Georgia. The climate is excellent. The University and Agricultural College are situated on one body of land of over 1,000 acres and the Normal School has about 50 acres. This gives ample opportunity for walks, rides and picnics.

Excursion parties will be organized for the purpose of visiting points in and near Athens. Excursions will be run every other Saturday to Tallulah Falls about fifty miles distant and into the heart of the Blue Ridge Mountains at Franklin, N. C.

SPECIAL OPPORTUNITIES IN THE SUMMER SCHOOL

In addition to the regular undergraduate work in the three institutions opportunities are offered:

(1) High School teachers who wish to advance in special lines of work.

(2) Candidates for State certificate who need special courses in Education and other subjects.

(3) Teachers who wish to work towards a degree.

(4) Directors of physical training and coaches of athletics in the high schools and playground work.

(5) Supervisors and teachers of Music, Oratory, Home Economics, Agriculture and other special lines of work.

(6) County Superintendents who desire to study problems of Rural School Organization and Management.

(7) Principals of Elementary and High Schools who wish to acquaint themselves with recent progress in education or to study special problems.

(8) Pre-Law and Pre-Medical students who wish to save time in preparation for these courses.

(9) Graduates of college who wish to specialize in some field of work and study for a Master's Degree.

(10) Members of P.-T.-A. and Woman's Clubs and other Social workers who wish to better prepare for their duties.

(11) Librarians and teacher-librarians who wish to better fit themselves to conduct school libraries and small public libraries.

(12) Serious minded men and women in any occupation who wish to broaden their culture and use part of their vacation to secure it while enjoying the delightful associations among a student body of over 2,000.

REGISTRATION

The regular time for registration for both terms will be Monday, June 22nd. All students of the Summer School should register on that day. Registration after June 30th for credit will not be permitted except by vote of the Council.

Registration will be limited to those (1) who meet the regular admission requirements of fifteen units secured by graduation from an accredited four year high school, or through examination; (2) who hold regular state certificate; (3) who are applicants for state certificate and have completed sufficient high school work to prepare for a provisional certificate; (4) special students who are not candidates for a degree nor applicants for first grade state certificate, but who are prepared to carry forward certain courses in the Summer School.

Applications, including certificate of high school work, for admission to under-graduate courses should be sent in advance to Prof. W. D. Hooper, Chairman of the Entrance Committee of the University, or to Pres. J. M. Pound if entrance to the Normal School is contemplated. If advanced credit is desired, the official record at the college attended should be filed with the department concerned. For instance, if Agricultural credit, the applicant should advise with Dr. John R. Fain; Home Economics, with Miss Mary Creswell; Education, with Dean Woofter; Normal School, with Pres. Pound; graduate work, with Dean Bocock; etc.

Dr. L. L. Hendren, Chairman of the Advanced Credit Committee of the University, or President Pound for the Normal School will be glad to rate credits from other institutions in terms of the institutions here.

By consulting the catalog, the applicant can determine to whom she should write for advice. In case of doubt, the **Director** will be glad to forward correspondence to the proper committee.

It will greatly facilitate Monday registration, if candidates for degrees or advanced credit would have all preliminary credits passed upon by the proper committee or Deans between now and the opening date.

Full instructions showing places of registration and the order of procedure in registration will be furnished each applicant on the opening date.

Students desiring college credit, or credit towards a state certificate, will be required to pass examinations during the closing week of the term on scheduled dates.

In courses giving one hour credit, the student must attend not less than 26 days; for one and a half hours credit not less than 43 days; 3 hours credit not less than 86 class periods. No student will be given credit for a course for which he has not been officially registered.

ENTRANCE REQUIREMENTS

No student can become eligible for a degree from the University unless one year has been spent in residence.

For the present the Faculty has ruled that the minimum residence requirement may be, under special conditions, fulfilled by attendance on 30 weeks of college credit work in the Summer School.

CREDITS

In order that the Summer School work may be maintained at the same standard as the work of the regular session, the following regulations will be strictly enforced:

(a). For students staying only six weeks the maximum credit possible is four hours, while the normal is three hours. Additional physical training may be permitted.

(b). For students staying nine weeks the maximum credit possible is seven hours provided one of the subjects is a science with laboratory, while the normal is four and one-half hours.

(c). Any work in excess of "the normal" is classed as extra hours.

No student will be registered for extra hours except in the following cases:

(a). His average for the preceeding year must be 80 or above.

(b). He must be repeating a course on which he has failed or on which he has partial credit.

(c). He must be more mature than the usual student or must have several years teaching experience.

(d). For extra hours to count toward a degree at the University the student must maintain a "standing of 2"; i. e. must make all grades of 80 or above or for every grade of 70 to 79 he must make an equal number of hours with grade of 90 or above.

Work for college credit may be applied on the State Normal School Diploma or towards the University, Agricultural College or State Normal School degree, according to the requirements of these degrees in the regular catalog. Work may also be credited towards a state certificate according to the requirements of the State Board of Education.

FEES

1. Registration fee (payable by every student on registration) $3.00.

2. Tuition fees: The fees are $12.00 for six weeks courses or hours as indicated in catalog; total fees for six weeks, $15.00.

There are no charges for any lecture, concert or entertainment for registered students.

The fee for the nine weeks courses is $25.00. The fee for the professional music course, two periods daily, 6 weeks is $30.00. There is an extra fee for the athletic coaching. The fee for a graduate course is $15.00 for one minor or two half minors, total $60.00 for the degree. There are also special fees in some courses in music, oratory, etc. There are also certain fees in laboratory courses to cover cost of material. These will be indicated in connection with each course.

RETURN OF FEES

Where students report at the office of the Registrar on or before July 1st, that they have discontinued any course for which extra fee was paid, such fee is returned. When reported after that date, no rebate for credit of fees is allowed. Exception to this rule may be made only in case of those who for serious personal illness, certified by the Medical Officer, are obliged to withdraw entirely from the Summer School. Any rebate will be reckoned from the date the Registrar receives the Medical Officer's report. No fees will be returned after the second week of the session.

MONEY

University bills may be paid by check in exact amount. Money orders, express or travelers' checks should be carried for emergency purposes. It would be advisaable for students to bring their money in this form and deposit it in a local bank.

Students should come prepared to pay fees on the day they register. Registration will not be complete until fees are paid.

LIVING EXPENSES

The effort is made to make all expenses for the stay in Athens as small as possible, consistant with the teachers' desired standards.

At the University. Rooms in the Dormitories are $5.00 per person per term of six weeks. Meals in the University dining hall for the six weeks will be $30.00; nine weeks $45.00; for one week, $6.00; for less than one week, 40 cents each meal. No extra charge is made for rooms the last three weeks except actual cost of lights, water, etc.

College of Agriculture. Room rent in Soule Hall for six weeks $10.00 per student, two in a room. A room reservation fee of $5.00 to be refunded when the room is surrendered in good condition is required and should accompany application. Board in the College Cafeteria is $35.00 per student for six weeks.

At the Normal School. Room and board, $32.50 for six weeks.

At Lucy Cobb Institute. Room and board six weeks, $40.00.

At the Chapter Houses. Room rent six weeks only, $8.00.

In Private Homes. Room rent from $6.00 to $12 a month. Table board may also be had in private homes, cafeterias and tea rooms at from $6.00 to $8.00 a week.

TIME AND PLACE OF RECITATIONS

Recitations will be given in all courses, Tuesday, June 23rd at 8:30 A. M. The six weeks courses must run thirty-one days and the nine weeks courses fifty. There will be no classes on every other Saturday. The first Saturday will be a class day.

DORMITORIES

The effort has been made this year to increase the dormitory facilities to accommodate as many as may come and add to their pleasure and comfort.

State Normal School. At the State Normal School five dormitories are available which will furnish superior accommodation for 550 women. These are Bradwell, Gilmer, Senior, Winnie Davis, and Miller Halls. One dormitory reserved for men and wives.

University of Georgia. At the University, Old College, New College, Candler Hall and John Milledge Dormitory will be available, which will accommodate 400 women.

College of Agriculture. Soule Hall at the College of Agriculture will accommodate 70 women, and the College Cafeteria will accommodate 150 men and women.

Lucy Cobb Institute. The Lucy Cobb Institute dormitories and dining hall will accommodate 100 men and women.

Chapter Houses. A number of fraternity houses will be open for the six weeks term, some for men and some for women, accommodating 250 students.

Many prefer private homes or private board. Arrangements have been made to accommodate as many as desire to live in private homes.

Students should have their mail addressed to the dormitory in which they have made reservation.

DINING HALLS

In addition to the dining halls of the Unitervity, Agricultural College, State Normal School and Lucy Cobb Institute, some of the Chapter Houses will run their table and furnish board for the first six weeks. Athens is abundantly supplied with excellent cafeterias and tea rooms, where delightful food may be had at reasonable prices.

APPLICATION FOR ROOMS

Application for rooms at the University, Chapter Houses and private homes should be made to T. W. Reed, Registrar, Athens, Ga. A fee of $5.00 should accompany the application for reservation, except where applicant wishes to room in a private home. This fee will be refunded and room will be released for good reasons, prior to the opening of the school, in other cases it applies on room rent.

Applications for room and board at Lucy Cobb Institute should be made to Miss Mildred Mell, Principal. The music students and French students and others live here.

Application for rooms in the Soule. Hall, State College of Agriculture, should be made to Miss Mary E. Creswell, Athens, Ga., and a fee of $5.00 should accompany the application.

Application for rooms at the State Normal School should be made to A. Rhodes, Registrar of the State Normal School.

Students occupying rooms in any of the dormitories should bring with them at least the following articles: 1 pillow, 2 pairs of pillow cases, 2 pairs of sheets, 2 counterpanes, half dozen towels.

SELECTION OF DORMITORY

It is important that those making application for reservation of rooms keep in mind the fact that courses for primary and elementary work will be given at the State Normal School and all teachers who register for these primarily should take rooms there. Likewise for home economics take the Agricultural College dormitory; for Music take the Lucy Cobb, for University courses select the University dormitories or chapter houses, though students may live at any of these places and be accessible to their work.

RAILROAD RATES

A round trip rate of a fare and a half has been granted by. the railroads on the identification certificate plan. These certificates may be obtained from the Director and must be presented to the ticket agent when ticket it purchased or no reduction will be granted. The selling dates are June 19-24 inclusive, June 28-July 1st inclusive, July 5, 7, 12, 14, 19, 21, 26, 28,; August 2, 5, 9, 11, 16, 21; with final limit August 30.

GEORGIA CO-OPERATIVE ASSOCIATION

A co-operative store for the University is in successful operation on the University Campus where books, etc., may be secured.

In connection with the "Co-op" is a University post-office in which there are about 700 call-boxes.

Baggage. Trunks and other baggage should give the dormitory and room number where reservation has been made prior to coming to the Summer School. In other cases baggage should be left at the railway station until a residence is secured.

Residence. Unless reservation has been made, application for room list should be made at the Residence Bureau in Demosthenian Hall.

Absences. Absences are not excused unless certified by the Summer School Physician.

Weekly Bulletins. Announcements for each week are made in the University Items which is provided for free distribution in all of the buildings, and is edited by the class in Journalism.

BOOKS AND MATERIALS

Students of the Summer School will be expected to provide themselves with all books and materials required for their individual use in the courses pursued. Most of the texts to be used are announced in connection with the description of the various courses. Students may procure their books before coming to the Summer School, or they may get them at the Co-op Book Exchange, at the usual market prices.

Those expecting to pursue courses in Primary School Methods or Grammar School Methods or to take advantage of the observation work in the demonstration classes, may save considerable expense by bringing with them such of the State-adopted books as they have at home.

Students are requested to bring any string or any other musical instrument upon which they play, so that a Summer School orchestra may be organized, and thus add to the pleasure and profit of the Summer School. They should also bring any personal equipment for athletics, or other physical training, such as gymnasium and swimming suits, tennis rackets, ball equipment.

PLAY AND RECREATION

Recreation and play is an important part of summer school life. All forms of athletics will be carried on during the summer. The tennis lover will find several courts at all four institutions. There are basketball courts on each campus, and provision for quoits, indoor baseball, volley ball and other games for women. Sanford Field provides ample facilities for track, baseball, football, basketball and other games for men. The Cloverhurst Golf Club opens its links to teachers in the Summer School, for a nominal fee. Clubs, racquets, suits, etc., should be brought from home.

All three gymnasiums are open to regularly registered students during the session, under the control of competent instructors. No fee is charged for the use of the gymnasium and it is hoped that all will come prepared to avail themselves of this training. The swimming pools and baths will be at the service of the students, certain hours and days being set aside for each sex. Swimming suits may be purchased in Athens or brought from home. A small fee is charged for service.

Arrangements have been made for competitive rifle practice and target shooting and horseback riding.

DAILY GENERAL ASSEMBLY

Daily from 9:20 to 10:00 at the State Normal School and from 11:00 to 11:40 at the University there will be a period in which the students may have the privilege to assembly for devotional exercises, song service, short addresses on topics of current and general interest, or some other interesting exercise. The Assembly music at the University will be under the direction of Mr. Geo. F. Granberry, at the Normal, of Miss Harrison.

ENTERTAINMENTS AND LECTURES

Care has been given in providing the best of entertainments and lectures. Almost every evening on one of the campuses, students will gather on the lawn, the weather permitting, or in one of the assembly halls for songs and games or lectures and other entertainments.

During the first three weeks the National P.-T.-A. course will bring many prominent women to the summer school and frequent public lectures and conferences will be given by these.

During the second week the Georgia Club Women will hold their Annual Institute and many attractive features have been arranged for and by these ladies.

Dr. M. L. Brittain, Supt. Willis A. Sutton, Dr. Adolphe Vermont, Dr. W. M. Melton, Prof. D. L. Earnest and others will deliver lectures.

The fifth week will be devoted to a great Musical Festival, directed by Mr. Granberry, assisted by several concert artists from New York.

The Oratory Department will give a number of dramatic readings and short one act plays.

The Womans' Club Institute during the second week will bring a number of prominent women of national reputation connected with this association for lectures.

There will be many departmental lectures by members of the faculty and outside speakers, followed by a social hour.

Arrangements have been made with the Palace Theatre, probably the most beautiful picture theatre in the state outside of Atlanta, by which each registered summer school student will be given a ticket for one entertainment a week for the six weeks. This feature proved quite popular with the students last summer.

Excellent Radio equipment will be at the services of the summer school students at the University and the State Normal School under the direction of Mr. Earnest and Mr. Dixon.

The program for the afternoon lectures will be announced each week in the Summer School Items.

On the first Friday evening there will be a general assembly of the student body and faculty in the Octagon followed by a social hour and refreshments on the lawn.

On the third Friday evening there will be a general assembly at the Agricultural College in the out-door amphitheater when a patriotic pageant will be presented.

On the fourth Friday evening there will be a general assembly at the State Normal School, with an entertainment presented by the students living here, followed by a social hour.

Gay McLaren of New York will again render two plays in her unexcelled way.

The Coffer-Miller Players of Chicago, will offer two dramatic performances, one of Sheridan's plays and one of Shaw's or Moliere's.

All of these entertainments are free to registered students.

CERTIFICATION OF TEACHERS

I. GENERAL ELEMENTARY

Much of the work of the Summer School has been arranged to meet the new requirements of the State Board of Education relating to the certification of teachers. The University will accept only those with such high school training that they will be able to prepare for the first grade certificate.

Practically all of the work at the **State Normal** may be applied towards meeting professional requirements of 18 semester hours necessary for **State Professional Elementary Certificate.** Any of the educational courses at the University or Agricultural College may also be so applied.

Many teachers have not graduated from an accredited school and have had trouble in securing their high school credits necessary for a state elementary certificate. The summer school has arranged with four prominent Superintendents to conduct **review courses in high school subjects.** Teachers may thus validate their high school work. Over sixty teachers found these classes very helpful last summer.

II. HIGH SCHOOL GRADUATES

Graduates of accredited high schools may begin the study of the required 18 semester hours in Education and Methods this summer and receive a provisional elementary certificate good for three years. By the expiration of this provisional certificate they can complete the professional subjects and be granted a Professional Elementary Certificate good for seven years. The provisional certificate is not renewable.

There are practically 5,000 teachers with provisional certificates. These must complete the required 18 semester hours during the life of their provisional certificates if they wish to continue to teach. Georgia is insisting on professional preparation of the teachers. The summer school makes it possible for them to secure this preparation without loss of time from their schools and at minimum cost. Eight semester hours may be completed each summer in the six weeks courses, or twelve semester hours in the nine weeks courses. Teachers should check up what credits they have so as not to duplicate work this summer.

III. NORMAL CERTIFICATES

These certificates are based upon two years of Normal or College work beyond graduation from a four year high school.

The work must include at least 18 semester hours in education. If it does not a **Provisional Normal Certificate** may be granted, good for three years only.

Teachers may work each summer for this certificate and earn it in five summers while still teaching, or they may complete college or normal courses which they were forced to discontinue. Twelve semester hours may be earned in nine weeks. This certificate enables the holder to teach in a high school.

Teachers may submit a High School certificate and Normal or College work and then complete the two years of work by Summer School attendance and certain correspondence courses with the required residence.

IV. COLLEGE CERTIFICATES

A graduate of an approved college who did not include the eighteen semester hours in education preparatory to Teaching, Supervision and Administration will find under the division of Education all of the courses necessary for compliance with the state regulation converting a provisional college certificate into a professional one, by passing up eighteen semester hours in professional subjects.

These provisional certificates are good for only three years. The state expects every holder of one to convert it into a professional certificate at the end of that time by offering 18 semester hours in Education and Methods.

Many teachers in the high schools have probably neglected, in cation plan no teacher should neglect to apply and secure from the state a certificate. It gives an official rating that cannot be overlooked. The Summer School can help where extra preparation is needed.

Many high school teachers have a general certificate, but the State Board now makes it possible for them to secure a special subject certificate. Study at the Summer School will make possible an application for such a certificate. The time is passed in our high schools when a teacher will offer to teach any subject in the curriculum. She should begin to specialize in one or at most three departments.

There are many teachers of special subjects that have not secured certificates. By concentrating on these special subjects (music, art, physical training, etc.) they will be eligible to apply to the State Department for a certificate to teach, or these subjects may be listed on the general certificate.

Teachers who have taught ten years and can show professional improvement by attendance on Summer Schools, Normal Schools or Colleges and have 18 semester hours in Education may be granted Life Professional Certificates, either Elementary, Normal or College.

Opportunity is thus afforded the teachers in Georgia to secure a certificate, either provisional, professional or life professional, and have his or her record recorded in the State Department of Education.

The Summer School welcomes the opportunity to cooperate with the State Department in this forward step and has endeavored to make available to the teachers the resources of the institutions cooperating in the Summer School.

Do not be satisfied with one of the old county licenses, but work to convert this into a **State Certificate**, good anywhere.

NOTICE

A number of other college courses listed in the general catalog may be offered in the Summer School, provided as many as ten students apply for the same. The Council reserves the right to withdraw any course for which eight do not register, to limit the enrollment in any course or class section, or to fix the time of meeting. Where less than eight register for a course, it may be approved, provided those desiring it make up the cost with the professor to the equivalent of eight. The individual instructors must refer such matters to the Council. The Summer School will not be responsible for bills contracted without written authority of the management.

Leaflets explaining the new certificate plan may be obtained from the State Department of Education or from your superintendent.

Vocational Agriculture Class

ELEMENTARY SCHOOL COURSES

AT THE STATE NORMAL SCHOOL

The work at the State Normal School for the summer of 1925 has been arranged to meet the needs of teachers of first six grades and the kindergarten. **It will be a technical or professional school for teachers of these grades.** The work is arranged primarily for those who have had academic training equal to that of a high school and are now seeking additional training, particularly to qualify for the eighteen (18) semester hours in Education and Methods, required for a professional state certificate.

The work centers about the Demonstration School of six grades and the kindergarten. There will be technical courses in the presentation and problems of each elementary subject with observation in the Demonstration school and practice teaching in the classroom with fellow students.

There will be a dozen pedagogical courses dealing in the large with problems of elementary education in county and city schools. At least half of the eighteen (18) semester hours should be selected from these. With these as a pedagogical and psychological basis, the selection of applied courses in methods, with observation and practice, should give teachers opportunity for real improvement.

I. ARTS AND CRAFTS

S-1. Art in the Primary Grades—N. 1 hr., 6 weeks. Miss Holiday.
This course is planned to help teachers of the first four grades with their art work. It includes methods of teaching art, discussions of courses of study, and practice in primary drawing, painting and designs. Fee, $1.50.

S-2. Blackboard Drawing—N. 1 hr., 6 weeks. Miss Holliday.
Directions and practice in using white and colored chalks and charcoal in drawing on the board. This type of drawing is suitable for teachers of elementary grades who wish to illustrate themes, make borders or calendar panels. Fee, $1.50.

Poster Designing (At Agricultural College.)
Art Structure and Costume Designing (At the University.)
S-5. Handicrafts for Grades—N. 1 hr., 6 weeks. Miss Tigner.
5-A. Handicraft for First, Second and Third Grades.
Including paper folding, paper cutting, toy making, school room borders, rafia work, cardboard construction.

5-B. Handicraft for Fourth, Fifth and Sixth Grades.
Including paper cutting, toy making, paper flowers, basketry, construction of marionette theatres and costumes, doll millinery.
A small fee to cover cost of material is charged.

S-3. Penmanship—N. 1 hr., 6 weeks. Mr. Lowe.
To accomplish this, four classes will be given, two at the Normal and two at the University, each offering the same course. This will enable students to more easily adjust their schedules so as to take penmanship.
The work done in each class will comprise both the technique of handwriting and methods of teaching. Instruction will combine the best from the leading systems of muscular movement writing, and hence, principles and methods will be stressed rather than systems.
During the last two weeks of the term, demonstration lessons will be given by members of each class under the supervision of the instructor.

II. EDUCATION AND METHODS

S-4. Rural Sociology and Education—N. 1 hr., 6 weeks. Mr. Sell.
This course includes a study of rural social conditions in communities and the causes which underlie social and economic changes. The in-

II. EDUCATION AND METHODS

fluence of such factors as production, farm tenancy and educational organizations will be carefully considered. Much of the work will be devoted to the survey of the home community in order that the teacher may be able to correctly evaluate social and economic conditions in the community and thereby better serve society.

5-6. Methods in Agriculture—N. 1 hr., 6 weeks. Mr. Sell.

This is a course in elementary agriculture and the object is to prepare the students for teaching the subject in rural schools. Laboratory exercises, field trips and other teaching material in the community will be used to supplement the state adopted text book. The emphasis in the course will be placed on the methods of teaching the topics of vital concern to the people of Georgia.

S-7. Methods in Arithmetic—N. 1 hr., 6 weeks. Mr. Earnest.

Methods in Intermediate and Advanced Arithmetic, in Theory and Practice. How to use drills for efficiency and exercises in number for the development of logical thinking. Practical and Cultural Arithmetic.

S-1. History of Education—C. 1 hr., 6 weeks. Mr. Ritchie.

A study of the development of ideals, conceptions, organization, and methods of teaching. The work will begin with the transition to modern times and will place emphasis upon the modern periods. The doctrines of Rousseau, Pestalozzi, Froebel, Herbart, Spencer, Mann, Page, Dewey and other moderns, will be interpreted in a practical way to make this course helpful to teachers of any grade.

S-50. School Government and Efficiency—C. 1 hr., 6 weeks. Mr. Ritchie.

A course in modern school efficiency from the standpoint of order, discipline, penalties, reports, supervised study and play, playground equipment and management, interest, attention, and other phases of easy control and highest efficiency. Text; Sears Classroom Organization and Control.

S-13. Intelligence and Educational Measurements—C. 1 hr., 6 weeks. Mr. Ritchie.

An examination of the various achievement tests in the several school subjects, both elementary and secondary. These will be studied from the standpoint of the actual school room problem. The theory of measurement and the administration of the tests will be stressed. Students will purchase a sample set of the most important tests.

S-1. Introduction to Psychology—C. 1 hr., 6 weeks. Miss Zeigler.

Discussion of habit, mind and body, imagery, association, memory, thinking, reasoning, feelings, sentiments action and behavior.

S-52. Child Life—C. 1 hr., 6 weeks. Miss Zeigler.

Home Study: Portions of Parker's books, and others assigned. Discusses the development of the original nature during childhood and adolescence, play activities, social training, laws of heredity.

S-4. Psychology of Elementary School Subjects—C. 1 hr., 6 weeks. Miss Zeigler.

This course is designed to give the psychology of learning as applied to the language arts, handwriting, reading, spelling, arithmetic, supervised study.

S-8. Elementary School Methods—N. 1 hr., 6 weeks. Miss Solomon.

In this course the main emphasis will be laid upon the principles which affect the development of sound methods of teaching and upon the application of these principles in teaching the various school subjects. Attention will be given to such topics as the following: teaching how to study, project method, socialized recitation, testing and measuring, pupil activities that will lead to good habits of work. There will be two sections of this, the first for the first, second and third grades and the second section for the fourth, fifth and sixth grades.

S-9. Methods in Kindergarten—N. 1 hr., 6 weeks. Miss Willingham.

Play Materials in the Education of Young Children: Selection and methods of use of play materials such as toys, building blocks, picture books, pictures, etc.

17

II. EDUCATION AND METHODS

Beginnings of Music for Young Children: Study of musical needs of young children; methods of presentation, etc.
Observation in Kindergarten required.

S-10. Methods in Physiology— . 1 hr., 6 weeks. Mr. Earnest.
The beginner and the more mature need different treatment according to age, maturity, sex and disposition.
This course will show the use of specimens, charts, outlines, microscope, stereopticon, radiopticon and other helpful devices, keeping in mind the preservation and improvement of health—Personal, Domestic and Civic Hygiene.

S-11. Methods in General Science—N. 1 hr., 6 weeks. Mr. Earnest.
Science is not in books but in proper thinking about things. Books help when rightly used, hinder in the development of the scientific spirit if slavishly followed. How to us the life around, the objects, laws and forces of nature as a means of establishing the scientific habit and spirit is the aim of this course. Its importance is established by understanding that we are living in an age of science. To know the method of science and to direct the attention so as to give at least a scientific attitude is indispensible to a life efficient in present day affairs. This is a study of the methods by which this may best be undertaken. Helpful course for teachers of Geography.

S-12. The Teaching of Geography in the Elementary Grades. Mrs. Ida Simpson.
In this course special attention will be given to the organization of material for home geography, for the extension from the home region to distant regions and for a study of the distant regions. Practical and effective methods in the teaching of the subject is the other important element in the course. Text: Smith, E. Ehrlick: Teaching Geography by Problems.

S-14. Methods in Language Lessons and Literature—N. 1 hr., 6 weeks. Mr .Brown.
This is a methods course for teachers in the elementary grades. The consideration of the material best suited for language lessons and the proper method of presenting this material, the relation and coordination of oral and written work, and the devices to be used in fixing habits of correct speech in the minds of children will be the subjects of discussion.
Texts: Modern Course in English, Book I and Language Work in Elementary Schools by Leiper.

S-15. Methods in Composition and Grammar—N. 1 hr., 6 weeks. Mr. Brown.
This is a methods course for teachers of the sixth, seventh, and junior high school grades. The proper relation of composition and grammar will be discussed, and the best methods of teaching these two closely related subjects will be presented and illustrated. A graded course in literature will be planned and lessons in it taught.
Texts: Modern Course in English, Book II, and the Teaching of English by Chubb.

III. ORATORY AND DRAMATIC ARTS

S-2. Story Telling—N. 1 hr., 6 weeks. Miss Vance.
Not for the professional entertainers, but rather a course planned to meet the daily demands made upon teachers in presenting effectively, virtually every subject taught in the primary and grammar grades. More and more does modern pedagogy call upon trained teachers to employ this ancient but invaluable art. In addition to a thorough study of the child mind, program making, attractive style and methods of presentation, and correlation with prescribed studies, there will be a practical "Story Hour" conducted by students of this class. This course includes an exhaustive list of stories classified for all the grade and all occasions.

S-3. Educational Dramatics—N. 1 hr., 6 weeks. Miss Vance.
Methods of coaching plays for and with children from the dramatized reading lesson to a finished performance. Appropriate plays for all occasions will be studied from the point of casting, staging, and costuming. This course is especially valuable in handling problems of reading and speech in primary grades.

III. ORATORY AND DRAMATIC ARTS

S-4. Expression for the Teacher of Reading—N. 1 hr., 6 weeks. Miss Vance.

With special emphasis on the proper use of the Voice. Just how great an asset a well-modulated, pleasing and expressive voice is to a class room no one knows quite so well as children who have had to listen to the harsh, hoarse, monotonous, breathy, rasping, nasal, high-pitched tones of untrained teachers' voices.

This new course offers an excellent and unusual opportunity, meeting a real need so widely recognized by efficient teachers. The material used for voice training will include appropriate and varied reading for each grade and month with program suggestions for all special holidays. A working knowledge of the underlying principles of reading and voice culture will be of two-fold benefit to the teacher; improving her own reading powers, and aiding her in handling the reading problems of her own students.

S-15. The Teaching of Reading—N. 1 hr., 6 weeks. Miss Solomon.

This course will consider the aims and principles underlying the teaching of reading from first through the sixth grade. Various methods of teaching will be discussed.

IV. HISTORY

S-1. Reorganized Courses in Social Studies—N. 1 hr., 6 weeks. Miss Schweppe.

This course is planned for teachers and administrators who desire to be put in touch with the new movements in the field of social studies. An analysis of current practices and the innovations which curriculum-makers are proposing in methods of collecting, organizing, and presenting materials are given in this rapid survey.

Text: The Twenty-Second Yearbook of the National Society for the Study of Education, 1923. Part 11. Gambrill, J. M.: Experimental Curriculum Making in the Social Studies. The McKinley Publishing Company, Philadelphia.

S-2. General World History, a Survey Course for Teachers in the Elementary Schools—N. 1 hr., 6 weeks. Mrs. Simpson.

This course is a rapid survey of World History designed to direct a review which will help teachers who are planning to teach a like course to children. Suggestions on the selection and organization of matrials for a course offered to elementary school classes will be given.

Text: Webster, Hutton: World History. D. C. Heath. 1923.

S-3. The Teaching of History and Civics in the Elementary Grades —N. 1 hr., 6 weeks. Mrs. Simpson.

This course includes a detailed presentation of practical effective methods of teaching history in the grades; the place and treatment of biography; and the selection and organization of materials for class room instruction.

Text: Wayland, John W.: How to Teach American History. The Macmillan Company, New York. 1924.

V. PHYSICAL TRAINING

S-1. Technique and Games—N. 1 hr., 6 weeks. Miss Grote.

Games suitable for play grounds, elementary and junior high school, ranging from simplest primary school games up through the grades, with demonstrations and practice in Demonstration School and with adult classes or groups.

See also Physical Training under University for Aesthetic Dancing, folk dancing, horseback riding, swimming, etc. These classes are all open to elementary teachers.

VI. MUSIC

PUBLIC SCHOOL MUSIC

S-1. Public School Music Course for Grades 1-6—N. 1 hr., 6 weeks. Miss Haralson.

The work requires observation, the preparation of lessons. plans and practice in teaching a class:

VII. DEMONSTRATION SCHOOL

1. Practice in the choice, singing and presenting of rote songs
2. Material and plan for teaching the first steps in notation.
3. Sight-singing, study of fundamental problems in pitch and rhythm.
4. Music appreciation, the use of the phonograph and material for each grade.
NOTE:—See other music courses at the University.

VII. DEMONSTRATION SCHOOL

State Normal School

As abstract theories may be meaningless without concrete illustrations of them, the Demonstration Department of the Summer School was organized in order that teachers might observe the practical application of the most approved educational theories.

This department will consist of Kindergarten, and first, second, third, fourth and sixth grades. Experienced, well trained teachers will be in charge of each grade. In addition to the fundamental subjects which will be taught by the regular teachers, Music, Drawing, Physical Education, Dramatization and Handicrafts will be taught by the teachers of the special departments.

The schedule will be changed daily in order that students may observe the teaching of all subjects. If desired a student may observe the same grade for the entire session, or the time may be divided among all the grades. The latter plan is preferable and students are strongly advised to adopt it as greater inspiration is obtained by observing the teachers of all the different grades.

Portions of the observation periods will be devoted to discussions and reports of the teaching observed. In the teaching and in the conferences the following topics will be emphasized: Project Teaching, Group Work, How to Study, Silent Reading, Care and Decoration of Classrooms, Sand Tables and School Exhibits.

Teaching Staff

Principal—Kate E. Hicks, Normal School.
Kindergarten—Miss Willingham.
First Grade—Ellen Bittick, Atlanta.
Second Grade—Mrs. Opal Shaw, Atlanta.
Third Grade—Ruth Allen, Macon.
Fourth Grade—
Fifth Grade—
Sixth Grade—Annie Chapman, Atlanta.
Playground Director—Miss Grote, Miss Andrews.

Special Teachers

Music—Miss Haralson.
Drawing—Miss Holliday.
Handicrafts—Miss Tigner.
Dramatization—Miss Vance.
Reading—Miss Solomon.
Normal credit, 1 hour, will be given to all students who observe daily, take part in all conferences, make required reports and write required papers. Students not desiring credit, may register for the course and observe the teaching without doing the above additional work.

VII. DEMONSTRATION SCHOOL

S-1. Health—N. hr., 6 weeks. Misses Proctor and Andrews.
Methods of teaching health and physical education in the elementary school. Methods, materials, and demonstrations with children, in teaching health through physical education, health knowledge and practice, and the correlation of these with other subjects in the curriculum. Lectures and demonstrations daily. Prerequisites: High School graduation or its equivalent or acceptable experience as a teacher.

TYPEWRITING DEPARTMENT

Private Lessons

The following courses are offered to those who are specializing to become teachers in the Kindergarten, the Elementary, the Junior High or the High Schools of the State. They are not commercial courses, but instead, they are of a type that hundreds of teachers are demanding.

1. **Course A.**
   Offered to those who have no knowledge of the touch method of typewriting. This is a basic course in correct practice of advanced material at the outset.
2. **Course B.**
   Candidates who can write thirty words per minute, without errors, are eligible. Stress is placed on the vital importance of typewriting as a tool in the hands of student, teacher or social worker. A certificate is issued to all students who pass examinations satisfactorily and can write sixty words per minute. College credit can be arranged for this course.
3. **Course C.**
   Prerequisite: Course B. The psychology of learning and teaching of typewriting (method), the learning curve and transfer values are presented. Regular practice in the use of the dictaphone is introduced throughout the entire course.
   Each course represents, on the average, fifty hours of intensive and pleasant work under very highly controlled conditions. A small fee of $12.00 ($6.00, if you supply your own machine), per course is required, payable in advance.

COURSES OF INSTRUCTION
AT THE UNIVERSITY AND AGRICULTURAL COLLEGE

The courses listed below are regular college courses with credit toward a degree as outlined in the General Catalog. They are based upon the regular college entrance and work completed may be applied towards a degree or normal certificate or the professional courses may be applied towards the eighteen semester hours required for a State Professional Certificate.

I. AGRICULTURE

AGRICULTURAL CHEMISTRY

S-1. Organic and Biological Chemistry—C. 3 hrs., 9 weeks. Mr. Carter.
A systematic study of the compounds of carbon and their relation to plant and animal life. (See general catalogue for full description.) Prerequisite: Inorganic Chemistry 1 or 2 with laboratory. Fee. $7.50; breakage deposit, $3.50. Junior-Senior elective. Required of Sophomore Veterinary Medicine and Junior Home Economic students.

S-2b. Qualitative Analysis—C. 3 hrs., 9 weeks. Mr. Wilder.
Prerequisite: Inorganic Chemistry 1 or 2, with laboratory. Fee, $7.50; breakage deposit, $3.00.

Or

S-3. Quantitative Analysis—C. Mr. Carter and Mr. Wilder.
An elementary course in fundamentals of quantitative chemical analysis. Gravimetric and volumetric methods will be developed. 6 hrs. for 9 weeks. Prerequisites: Chemistry 1 and 2b. Fee, $7.50; breakage deposit, $5.00.

AGRICULTURAL ENGINEERING

S-20. Household Mechanics—C. 1 hr., 6 weeks. Mr. Lyle.
Selection, installation, operation and maintenance of mechanical equipment in the modern home. Laboratory fee, $2.00.

AGRICULTURAL EDUCATION

S-1. Vocational Education and Vocational Guidance—C. 1 hr., 6 weeks. Mr. Wheeler.
This course presents the field of vocational education in its several phases, and shows the place of vocational education in a scheme of education. The philosophy of vocational education and guidance runs throughout the course showing its educational values and implications. Vocational guidance, educational guidance, vocational tests, vocational counseling, occupational analysis, self analysis, and the psychological basis of interest, aptitude and vocational abilities will be considered. Juniors and Seniors. Elective.

S-2. Administration of Vocational Education—C. 1 hr., 6 weeks. Mr. Chapman.
A course designed to meet the needs of school officials, superintendents, principals an dteachers, who are interested in the development of vocational education in the schools of the state. This course deals with the organization of our National Vocational Education Program, and the administration of vocational education within the state and local schools. Juniors and Seniors. Elective.

NINE WEEKS COURSES

S-10. Introduction to Vocational Education—C. 1 hr., 9 weeks. Mr. Reitz.
Educational aims and values: the theory and practice of vocational education.

I. AGRICULTURE

S-12. Introduction to Education—C. 1 hr., 9 weeks. Mr. Reitz.
The characteristics of the learning process; application of the principles of education to the practice of teaching, etc.

S-13. Vocational Psychology—C. 1 hr., 9 weeks. Mr. Reitz.

S-14. Methods and Materials in Vocational Agriculture—C. 2 hrs., 9 weeks. Mr. Wheeler.

S-11. Agricultural Education Administration—C. 1 hr., 9 weeks. Mr. Sheffer.

S-16. Community Problems—C. 2 hrs., 9 weeks. Mr. Reitz.
Further considers problems arising in connection with courses 11 and 14.

S-17. Rural Journalism—C. 1 hr., 9 weeks. Mr. Chapman.

SPECIAL COURSES GIVEN TO TEACHERS IN SERVICE WEEK OF JULY 26TH TO 31ST, 1925

This will be a professional improvement course for our vocational teachers. All will be required to attend and transportation expenses will be paid by the State Board for Vocational Education. The course given will deal with the problems of the teachers.

The complete program for this week will be issued later. For information regarding this course, the applicants should write to Mr. Paul W. Chapman, State Supervisor of Vocational Agriculture, Athens, Georgia. He has already engaged eight lecturers for different phases of work to be brought to the attention to the Vocational teacher.

FORESTRY

S-4a. Tree and Shrub Identification—C. 1½ hrs., 6 weeks. Mr. Burleigh.
A systematic study of the local flora, with emphasis placed on practical field identification. The work will be entirely in the open where the various species of trees and shrubs will be observed under natural conditions, and their characteristics pointed out in more or less detail. Species found in other parts of the State and added from time to time to the college arboretum will be included in this course. The text book will be the booklet issued recently by this institution, "Common Forest Trees of Georgia." Six laboratory periods two hours each. Fee, $1.50.

ANIMAL HUSBANDRY

S-7, 14. Animal Husbandry—C. 3 hrs., 9 weeks. Mr. Bennett.
A study of milk production and various phases of manufacture and marketing. Fee, $3.50.

S-9. Animal Husbandry—C. 3 hrs., 9 weeks. Mr. Kellogg.
A study of the underlying principles of animal nutrition and the commoner feeding stuffs.

AGRONOMY

2. Forage Crops—C. 3 hrs., 9 weeks. Mr. Tabor.
A general study of the forage crops of this country with especial attention to those adapted to the cotton belt. Prerequisite: Farm Crops 1 and Botany 1. Laboratory fee, $3.50.

6. Seeds and Weeds—C. 3 hrs., 9 weeks. Mr. Tabor.
One-half the time will be devoted to the study of weeks and one-half to seeds. Prerequisites: Farm Crops 1 and Botany 1. Laboratory fee, $3.50.

SOILS

1 and 2. Principles of Soil Management—C. 3 hrs., 9 weeks. Mr. Crabb.
Origin, formation and physical properties of soils. Factors in crop production. Drainage and tillage practices. Commercial fertilizers and maintenance of soil fertility. Prerequisite: Chemistry 1. Laboratory fee, $3.50.

I. AGRICULTURE

3. **Soil Formation—C.** 3 hrs., 9 weeks. Mr. Crabb.
Rock disintegration and geological agencies relating to origin and formation of soils. Soil provinces, series an dtypes, of the United States. Practice of soil survey and preparation of maps and reports. Prerequisite: Soils 1 and 2. Laboratory fee, $5.00.

COTTON INDUSTRY

S-9, 10. **Cotton Industry—C.** 3 hrs., 5 weeks. Mr. Childs.
A study of cotton grading, warehousing, and marketing. Experimental cotton breeding. For whole course, prerequisite: Cotton Industry 3 and 4. There is no prerequisite for the grading section of the course. Five hours of laboratory work per day for five weeks. Laboratory fee, $15.00.

HORTICULTURE

S-1, 2, 3. **Horticulture—C.** 3 hrs., 9 weeks. Mr. McHatton, Mr. Keener.
This is the course in Horticulture required of all agricultural freshmen. (See general catalogue for description.) Parallel reading of various Horticultural texts is required. One lecture period and one laboratory period daily. Laboratory fee for the course, $3.50.

S-4, 6, 10 or 5, 7, 9. **Horticulture—C.** 3 hrs., 9 weeks. Mr. McHatton, Mr. Keener.
These are Junior courses required of students specializing in Horticulture and may be used as a general elective in agricultural courses. 4, 6 and 10 may be used as a 3 hour requirement in Group 2 in the agricultural degree. (For further description see the general catalogue.) 4, 6 and 10 is a lecture course requiring parallel reading of various horticultural texts. 5, 7, and 9 is a laboratory course with a laboratory fee attached of $3.50. Mature and special students may be permitted entrance into these courses. General Horticulture 1, 2 and 3 or its equivalent is required as a prerequisite. 4, 6 and 10 has two lecture hours per day. 5, 7 and 9 is a laboratory course with one 4 hour period per day. Fee, $3.50. Both of these courses will not be offered, the professors in charge having the privilege of giving the one for which there is the greatest demand.

POULTRY HUSBANDRY

S-20, 21, 22. **Poultry.** 3 hrs., 9 weeks. Mr. Wood, Mr. Gannon.
Work to consist of lectures and laboratory exercises. Laboratory fee, $2.00.

S-20. **General Poultry.**
Study of breeds and varieties, selection and judging, poultry house construction, feeding, parasites and diseases. Required of freshmen. Laboratory fee, $2.00.

S-21. **General Poultry.**
Mating and breeding, incubation and brooding, care of young stock, fattening, killing and marketing. Required of freshmen. Laboratory fee, $2.00.

S-22. **Utility Judging.**
Entire time devoted to judging and culling for egg production. Junior and Senior elective. Laboratory fee, $2.00.

S-3, 4, 25. **Poultry.** 3 hrs., 9 weeks. Mr. Wood, Mr. Gannon.
Laboratory fee, $2.00. Prerequisite: Poultry Husbandry 20-21. Junior and Senior elective. Work to consist of lectures and laboratory practice.

S-3. **Incubation and Brooding.**
Embryology of the chick, theory and practice of incubation; types and construction of incubators and brooders, and their operation; care and management of baby chicks. Laboratory fee, $2.00.

S-4. **Poultry Marketing.**
Candling, grading, packing and marketing eggs, fattening, killing, picking and dressing fowls; caponizing; study of markets and cooperative marketing. Laboratory fee, $2.00.

S-25. **Standard Judging.**
Entire term to be devoted to studying the Standard of Perfection and practice work in judging and placing birds for standard requirements. Laboratory fee, $2.00.

I. AGRICULTURE

VETERINARY MEDICINE

S. **Bacteriology 1 and 2, 3 or 5—C.** 3 hrs., 9 weeks. Dr. Burkhart.

Bacteriology 1 and 2—General and pathogenic bacteriology for second year students in veterinary medicine.

Bacteriology 1 and 3—General and dairy bacteriology for agricultural students.

Bacteriology 1 and 5—General and household bacteriology for students in home economics.

Bacteriology 1 and 2. Fee, $10.00: breakage deposit, $10.00.
Bacteriology 1 and 3. Fee, $10.00; breakage deposit, $10.00.
Bacteriology 1 and 5. Fee, $10.00; breakage deposit, $10.00.

S. **Bacteriology 4. Infection and Immunity—C.** 1½ hrs., 9 weeks. Dr. Burkhart.

Required of Senior students of veterinary medicine. Fee, $5.00; breakage deposit, $5.00.

S. **Pathology 1. General Pathology—C.** 4 hrs., 9 weeks. Drs. Richardson and Jones.

Required of Junior students of veterinary medicine. Fee, $5.00.

S. **Pathology 4. Parasitology—C.** 2 hrs., 9 weeks. Dr. Richardson.

Required of Junior students of veterinary medicine. Fee, $3.50.

S. **Surgery 3. Clinics—C.** 1½ hrs., 9 weeks. Dr. Severin.

Required of Senior students of veterinary medicine.

S. **Surgery 2. Surgery—C.** 3 hrs., 9 weeks. Dr. Severin.

Required of Senior students of veterinary medicine.

II. ARTS AND CRAFTS

S-4. **Poster Designing—C.** 1 hr., 6 weeks. Miss Blackshear.

Posters for Visual Instruction and Advertising.

Governments, educators and sellers of merchandise realize the power of the poster to carry messages to their people, pupils and buyers. Advertisers realize the power to sell commodities and they pay large sums for artistic advertisements, hence, our billboards and street cars are filled with posters which shout their messages. This course in poster making includes the "advertising idea" as related to teaching any subject or selling a commodity; the technique of composition; drawing, color and lettering. Through problems and lectures suggestions and arrangements are given, for its application to various subjects, and for professional work where the posters, or other graphic forms, may be used.

The "Hambidge Theory of Design" is taught and used in connection with the composition of this work.

Five two-hour periods a week for six weeks, 7th and 8th periods. A fee to cover cost of materials will be charged.

PENMANSHIP

S-1. **Penmanship—N.** 1 hr., 6 weeks. Mr. Lowe.

The penmanship course has two objects in view. First, to improve the handwriting of the teacher, and, second, to instruct the teacher in the best method of presenting the subject of penmanship to her pupils.

The work done in each class will comprise both the technique of handwriting and methods of teaching. Instruction will combine the best from the leading systems of muscular movement writing, and hence, principles and methods will be stressed rather than systems.

During the last two weeks of the term, demonstration lessons will be given by members of each class under the supervision of the instructor.

S-22. **Art Structure and Design—C.** 2 hrs., 6 weeks. Miss Holliday.

In teaching the underlying principles of art, our aim is to learn to recognize and appreciate things of artistic worth. To accomplish this aim, opportunity is provided for the creation of designs based upon these principles and built up by the use of the three elements of art language—line, dark and light and color. Opportunity is provided for the applicant of design in the actual working out of some of the problems of handwork suitable for grammar grades and high school. Double periods.

A fee to cover cost of material will be charged.

For elementary drawing and blackboard sketching, see Normal School Division.

BOTANY

See Science Division.

III. COMMERCE

COMMERCE

S-5, a, b, c. Principles of Economics—C. 3 hrs., 6 weeks. Mr. Brooks.

This course in economic theory is the foundation on which all advanced courses in the School of Commerce rest. It deals with the production, exchange, distribution and consumption of goods and with the usual problems illustrative of the principles.

S-20, a, b, c. Business Law—C. 3 hrs., 9 weeks. Mr. Heckman.

This course in Business Law consists of a case and text study of the main subjects of law which arise in the commercial field. The branches studied are contracts—their formation and interpretation; Agency; Bailments; Sales; Negotiable Instruments; Partnerships and Corporations. The case and text method of study is employed.

S-6. Elementary Accounting—C. 3 hrs., 9 weeks. Mr. Heckman.

This is an introductory course designed ot give the general business student a thorough knowledge of the fundamental principles of accounting. The course begins with the study of the principles underlying the simple balance sheet and profit and loss statements, and proceeds to the development of the theory of debits and credits as applied to ledger accounts, books of original entry and adjusting and closing entries. A comprehensive study is made of partnership problems—partners' capital and drawing accounts, interest on investment, division of profits, closing of partnership and dissolution. Controlling accounts are studied carefully and problems peculiar to the corporation, joint ventures, single entry bookkeeping, and consignments are worked in class.

IV. CONFERENCES AND SHORT COURSES

Third Week
Georgia Federation of Women's Clubs

CLUB INSTITUTE
Tuesday, July 7 to Saturday, July 11

Club Institute Committee, University of Georgia. Chairman, Mrs. C. M. Snelling, Athens; Program, Mrs. S. V. Sanford, Athens; Publicity, Brs. G. A. Johns, Winder; Registration, Mrs. H. B. Ritchie, Athens; Exhibits, Mrs. W. F. Wilhoit, Warrenton; Mrs. W. D. Beacham, Mrs. Jeptha Rucker.

PROGRAM

Only the general outline of the program can be given in this issue of the Bulletin. A detailed program will be issued at a later date.

Tuesday, July 7

American Citizenship:
(a) Making our influence count in party councils; (b) Getting out the vote; (c) How delegates to the county convention are elected; (d) Importance of the primaries. University chapel exercises.

Legislation:
(a) What legislation should the club foster? (b) To what extent should we aid in securing the passage of the measures endorsed? (c) National vs. state legislation.

Parliamentary drills. Public speaking. Round table: Club organization.

Wednesday, July 8

The American Home:
(a) Better homes: 1. Mothercraft; 2. Nutrition; 3. Budget; 4.

IV. CONFERENCES AND SHORT COURSES

Textiles; 5. Insurance. (b) Home economics; (c) Home demonstration. University Chapel exercises.

Public Welfare:
   (a) Problems of delinquency; (b) Problems of industry.
   Parliamentary drills. Public speaking. Round table: Club relationships.

Thursday, July 9

Applied Education:
   (a) Public instruction; (b) Community service; (c) State federation loan funds and endowments; (d) Forestry; Memorial tree planting and highways. University Chapel exercises.

Press and Publicity:
   (a) What the newspaper wants; (b) How to prepare the news; (c) How every woman may be a reporter.
   Parliamentry drills. Public speaking. Round table: Club ethics and other problems.

Friday, July 10

Fine Arts:
   (a) Arts and crafts, with special reference to the Federation School at Tallulah; (b) Community singing; (c) Community drama; (d) Music in our public institutions. University Chaped exercises.
   The Tallulah Falls School—The ideal plan to promote interest in Federation work.
   Parliamentary drills. Public speaking. Round table: Our most pressing problems.

Saturday, July 11

The Club Institute:
   (a) What is has accomplished; ,b) What should be the program next summer. University Chapel exercises. What real service can we render our State? Business session. Adjournment.

Registration fee is two dollars. Registrants may also elect any two courses in the Summer School without extra charge and have free admission to all lectures, concerts, and other entertainments during the week. Certificates will be issued to those who register, by order of the Executive Board of the Georgia Federation of Women's Clubs.

Hotel Georgian offers a rate of one dollar to one and half dollars a day. Cafeterias offer a rate of one dollar a day for three meals.

The Athens Woman's Club will serve tea every afternoon for the visitors. Social functions will be announced later.

The sessions of the Club Institute will be held in Memorial Hall on the University campus.

A beautiful loving cup is offered by Mrs. W. W. Stark of Commerce for the best exhibit; another beautiful loving cup will be offered for the largest attendance by a district.

Many distinguished club women will have a prominent part on the program. Mrs. C. S. Selover, National Chairman of Club Institutes, General Federation of Women's Clubs, and Mrs. A. P. Brantley, President of Georgia State Federation of Women's Clubs are expected to be present during the entire session.

All club women are cordially invited to cooperate in making the third annual Club Institute successful from every point of view. The completed program will be sent to every club in the Federation. Reduced rates on all railroads.

IV. CONFERENCES AND SHORT COURSES

Second Week
PUBLIC HEALTH SHORT COURSE AND CONFERENCE
June 30 to July 4

The Commonwealth Fund Clinic located at Athens for the next five years studying health conditions under the direction of Dr. Carey, will, in connection with the State Organization, conduct a health week during the Summer School. A number of men of National reputation have been asked to attend this conference and give lectures and demonstrations. The full program will be issued later.

Fourth Week
COUNTY AND CITY SUPERINTENDENTS CONFERENCE
July 13 to 18

This short course will be arranged, as in former years, to meet the practical needs of county and city superintendents, with special emphasis on the county superintendents.

The State Superintendent, several of the supervisors and a number of county and city superintendents of the state have been asked to take part in the program.

Visitors will also have opportunity to attend different classes in the Summer School and see the actual work of the several departments.

A full program will be issued later.

NATIONAL P-T-A SHORT COURSE
June 22 to July 11

(See outline of this credit course under Education).

This course was authorized by the National P-T-A Executive Board and the Field Secretary, Mrs. Arthur C. Watkins, has been designated by the National Board to conduct the course. There will be daily lectures and conferences. The local P-T-A Association and the State Association are fully cooperating with the National Board in bringing to the members of the P-T-A this intensive course for improvement of P-T-A work.

As this is the only National School in the South, it is hoped by the P-T-A authorities that many members will attend from all over this section of the country. A special folder will be issued.

The State Executive Committee urges that each local organization send one teacher and one parent for this course.

Fifth Week
MUSICAL FESTIVAL
July 21 to 26

The special folder regarding the Music Festival will be issued later giving the program for the week an dthe noted artists who will participate.

V. EDUCATION

S-1. History of Education—C. 1 hr., 6 weeks. Mr. Wise.
A study of the development of education as a phase of changing civilization with emphasis on the sources of modern principles and practices.

V. EDUCATION

S-2. Education in the United States—C. 1 hr. Last three weeks. Mr. Alfriend.

European background. transplantings from Europe. early colonial developments, later European influences, evolution of American education, status and tendencies today. Double periods.

S-3. Educational Hygiene—C. 1 hr., 6 weeks. Mr. Furry.

This course considers the relations of individual and social psychology to the problems of education and mental hygiene. It will also deal with the chief facts regarding normal mental and physical development as a basis for the differentiation and study of abnormal cases.

S-4. Educational Psychology—C. 1 hr., 6 weeks. Mr. Furry.

The facts and problems of psychology having a bearing upon education: the laws of learning; principles of economy in learning; reasoning and problem solving; the transfer of training, etc. Adapted to students of the high school.

S-6. Intelligence Tests—C. 1 hr., 6 weeks. Mr. Purdom.

For description of course see Psychology.

S-7. Elements of Sociology—C. 1 hr. Last three weeks. Mr. Alfriend.

A study of fundamentals with emphasis on social education. Double periods.

S-8. Moral Education—C. 1 hr., 6 weeks. Mr. Furry.

Defining education as the making of moral personalities this course will seek to define the moral person, the materials to be utilized in moral education and the methods to be employed.

S-9. Educational Sociology—C. 1 hr., 6 weeks. Mr. Alfriend.

Social origins and functions of Education; individual versus social aims; education for democracy; vocational and cultural education; socialization of education.

S-10. Principles of Teaching High School Pupils—C. 1 hr., 6 weeks. Mr. Alfriend.

This course is designed for persons now teaching or preparing to teach in the high school. After a brief survey of the development of th high school and its place in the American school system the course will deal with the content, methods and technique of teaching the high school subjects.

S-11. High School Organization and Administration—C. 1 hr., 6 weeks. Mr. Hunter.

A practical course dealing with the organization and management of modern high schools. A number of practical problems relating to the administration of a secondary school, such as organization, curricula. teaching staff, community relationships. part-time education, etc.. will be considered. A specific problem will be assigned for individual investigation by each student electing the course.

S-12. Educational Measurements—C. 1 hr., 6 weeks. Mr. Purdom.

A study of the more important standards and methods of measuring results of teaching with main emphasis on high school subjects.

S-13. Intelligence Tests and Educational Measurements—C. 1 hr., Last three weeks. Mr. Purdom.

An extension of S-6 or S-13. Double periods.

S-35. Administration and Supervision of City Schools—C. 1 hr., 6 weeks. Mr. Hunter.

A practical and systematic course treating the problems of organization and administration in city and town school systems. Among the problems considered will be modern curricula construction: selection, supervision and rating of teachers: city school surveys; school publicity: school boards; business administration: the school budget; and other major problems dealing with the intelligent administration of a modern school system.

S-36. The School Principal—C. 1 hr., 6 weeks. Mr. Wise.

A practical course designed especially for elementary school principals. dealing with the problems of organization and administration of a single school as a distinct unit and its relationship to larger units of which it is a part, covering supervision of instruction, community relationship, etc.

29

V. EDUCATION

S-50a. Principles and Technique of Teaching—C. 1 hr., 6 weeks. Mr. Wise.

À discussion of the teaching problems of the upper grammar grades and the high school.

Text: Holley, "The Teacher's Technique."

S-50b. Project Methods in Elementary Schools—C. 1 hr., 6 weeks. Miss Schweppe.

This course is designed to bring progressive practice in the teaching of history, geography, and civics to the teachers of the elementary grades. A careful study will be made of the materials assigned to the grades, and successful plans for the teaching of these. The use of the recitation period, of tests, of excursions, of maps, of pictures, of exhibits and of dramatizations are studied. The general course in these studies will be discussed.

S-51. Educational Psychology—C. 1 hr., 6 weeks. Mr. Purdom.

For teachers of the elementary grades and Junior High Schools.

S-52. The Junior High School—C. 1 hr., 6 weeks. Mr. Hunter.

This course will deal with the development, organization and administration of the junior high school. Methods of teaching, curriculum, types of buildings, etc., will be considered. Particularly designed for those who are candidates for high school certificates, or expect to become supervising principaals, or teachers in junior high schools.

S-14. Materials and Methods Courses—C. 1 hr., 6 weeks.

These are departmental courses given in their respective departments, not in the School of Education, hence not credited as education courses, but as departmental courses in their respective departments. All but 14-c will be for high school teachers. 14-c will be for elementary and junior high school teachers. They will however meet the requirements for professional state certificates.

Something of the selection and review of the material, text-books appropriate, and special methods will enter into each course.

14-a. English, The teaching of	Mr. Sanford.
1-4b. History, Civics, The teaching of	Mr. Payne.
14-c. Social Science, The teaching of	Miss Schweppe.
14-d. Mathematics, The teaching of	Mr. Stephens.
14-e. Physical Science, The teaching of	Mr. Hendren.
14-f. Biological Science, The teaching of	Mr. Krafka.
14-g. Latin, The teaching of	Mr. Hooper.
14-h. French, The teaching of	Mr. Lustrat, Miss Jack.
14-k. History and Geography. Advanced Methods.	Mr. Bocock.

S. The Organization and Conduct of Parent-Teacher Associations— C. ½ hr. Mrs. Florence Van A. Watkins.

Credit only if taken with some other course in Education. June 22 to August 10. Peabody Hall. Students should register for period desired at the beginning of the summer session. 9:20 to 10:10, one hour **lectures** on the various forms of associations, their legitimate fields, their relations to the State and National, their value to both parents and teachers. 10:20 to 11:00, **round tables** on subjects related to Parent-Teacher work. Experts on many of these subjects will speak at this time. 11:20 to 12:00 discussion period on how to organize a local association, organization problems, programs for different local groups, parliamentary procedure in local groups, and duties of officers and committee chairmen. For those who are unable to take any of the morning courses, a one-hour period from 2:30 to 3:30 will be conducted twice a week. All periods are conducted daily during the three weeks.

An exhibit of the many varieties of free, published helps of the National and of various State associations will be open to principals, superintendents, teachers, and parents.

NOTE:—See also courses in Education under Agriculture and in the Normal School division.

VI. ENGLISH

S-11. Shakespeare—C. 1 hr., 6 weeks. Mr. Park.

Midsummer Night's Dream, Julius Caesar, Macbeth, Hamlet and The Merchant of Venice will be studied. Lectures: written reports. Twelve other plays of Shakespeare will be used as collateral reading.

S-2a. The Study of Poetry—C. 1 hr., 6 weeks. Mr. Park.

Lectures on Poetics. The reading and intepreting of standard English poems, representing the various types of poetry. Special study of the lyric.

S-2b. Present Tendencies of Fiction—C. 1 hr., 6 weeks. Mr. Sanford.

The purpose of this course is to give the student a general knowledge of American fiction: (a) types, (b) excellence in a limited field, (c) wholesome outlook upon life.

S-14a. High School English (Seminar)—C. 1 hr., 6 weeks. Mr. Sanford.

This course will be based on the College Entrance Requirements and similar lists. It will consider the purpose to be kept in view in studying literature in high school, the best way to plan and present for class study various kinds of reading, and some of the recent movements in the teaching of literature. It will attempt to show the relation of the literature work to composition, grammar and other English work of the class, bringing the units of the instruction and practice in connection with all the exercises of the school.

S-1. Advanced English Grammar—C. 1 hr., 6 weeks. Mr. Sanford.

This is a course which will devote its whole time to a study of English Grammar. Sanford's English Grammar, The Modern Course in English, Book III, will be the chief text.

S-3a. Studies in Victorian Literature—C. 1 hr., 6 weeks. Mr. Simmons.

The chief figures will be Tennyson and Browning. Representative pieces will be interpreted and discussed in the class-room, and others will be designated for outside reading. The work may be pursued with profit by any person who has had a survey course in English Literature.

S-3b. Literary Voices from the South—C. 1 hr., 6 weeks. Mr. Simmons.

The time allotted to this course will be devoted chiefly to those writers who have represented most typically the Old South, the South of the Civil War, and the New South. Lectures, class-room readings, and reports on assigned topics.

S-1c. Processes and Problems of Writing Prose.—C. 1 hr., 6 weeks. Mr. Simmons.

A study of fundamental processes in the art of composing, and an inquiry into the capital secrets of effectiveness in the transmission of thought and feeling. Lectures, discussions, conferences.

S-4. Contemporary Poetry—C. 1 hr., 6 weeks. Mr. Melton.

The technique and spirit of contemporary verse. Under technique, there will be considered: The pattern of a poem; Organic rhythm; Images and symbols; Diction; Conversative and radical poets. Under spirit, there will be considered: Democracy and the new themes; Patriotism and the late war; Love and religion; Nature and personality. Textbook, New Voices, by Marguerite Wilkinson, (The Macmillan Company.)

S-5. Georgia Literature—C. 1 hr., 6 weeks. Mr. Melton.

This course includes a study of the principal poets, short story writers, and novelists of Georgia. Textbook to be made in class. by professor and students.

A review course in High School English.

JOURNALISM

S-1. Principles of Journalism—C. 1 hr., 6 weeks. Mr. Sanford.

Fundamentals of newspaper reporting and editing. Practical work in reporting for the Summer Session edition of the Summer School Iitems. This course will help teachers who supervise the work of students on high school publications.

NOTE:—See Oratory and Dramatic Art Division for additional courses.

NOTE:—Courses S-11. S-2a may apply on Sophomore or Junior credit; S-1 on Freshman credit: S-3a. 3b. on Junior credit: S-4, S-5 on Junior credit; S-1 Journalism on Freshman credit; Public Speaking S-2 on Freshman. Sophomore or Junior credit: S-1 on Sophomore or Junior credit; S-3 on Junior credit; S-4 on Junior credit.

VII. GRADUATE

The University permits a graduate student, eligible to candidacy for a second degree, to secure the Master's degree upon the successful completion of graduate courses pursued during four Summer Sesions. The student will pursue two half-minor courses or one minor each summer. During the year following each Summer Session the student will have the benefit of the guidance of the professors under whom courses have been pursued in the previous summer.

A thesis is required by the Faculty in connection with each Major course offered in the Summer School.

The right is reserved to withdraw any course for which there are not three or more applicants.

COURSES FOR 1925

BOTANY

S-111. Genetics and Eugenics. Mr. Reade.

The principles of genetics and indication with a discussion of their bearing on industry, society, and government. Babcock and Clausen and other texts. Minor. Five lectures a week for six weeks, and laboratory work. The student will give his whole time to this study. Prerequisite or parallel course: Botany 11.

It is hoped and expected to offer a course in ANGIOSPERMS in the summer of 1926. Prospective students will kindly confer in advance by correspondence or interview with Professor Reade, LeConte Hall.

EDUCATION

S-107. The Philosophy of Education. Mr. Hutchinson. Prerequisite: two courses in Education, preferably one in Psychology and one in Sociology.

This course plans the consideration of foundation material for the construction of a philosophy of education. It is divided into three parts:
 a. Physical and Biological Factors.
 b. Sociological Factors.
 c. Psychological Factors.
These separate parts will be given in successive summers, any two constituting a minor, and all three, with a thesis, a major. Combinations with a part of 102 or 104 may be permitted. For 1925 the course will be:

S-107b. Sociological Factors.

 1. Distinction between Original Nature and Human Nature.
 2. An analysis of the social process and of the social adjustments by virtue of which original nature has developed into human nature.
 3. Social adaptation as a community problem.
 4. The relation of the school to the community.

S-102. Public School Administration. Mr. Hutchinson. (Minor). Prerequisite: Education 10, 11, 12; Psychology, one year; Sociology, one semester, or the equivalent of the above. Combinations with part of 104 or 107 may be permitted.

This course is divided into two parts:
 a. Curriculum Making.
 b. The Organization and Administration of the School and Supervising the Instruction. For 1925 the course will be:

VII. GRADUATE

S-102b. The Organization and Administration of the School and Supervising the Instruction.

1. The Superintendent's Philosophy and Its Significance.
2. Function of the Superintendent. School Board, etc.
3. Distinction between administrative and supervisory functions of the Superintendent.
4. Selection of teachers, measuring the results of teaching, and of supervised study as aids to supervising the instruction.
5. The control of extra curricular activities.

ENGLISH

S-103. Modern English Grammar. Mr. Sanford.

A series of selected topics will be studied. Text-books: Jespersen, Modern English Grammar; Lounsbury, The Standard of Usage; Bradley, The Making of English; Smith, The English Language; Mencken, The American Language; Oliphant. The New English; Greenough and Kittredge, Words and Their Ways in English Speech. Prerequisite: English 1 and 2 or the equivalent. Five hours a week. Half Minor.

S-106. Early Eighteenth Century Literature. Mr. McWhorter.

English Literature, literary characteristics, and literary movements from 1700-1744: DeFoe, Addison, Steele, Swift and other prose writers; Pope, Prior, Gay, Thomson, Young, and minor poets. The Drama. Literary criticism. One-half of this minor course will be given in 1925. Prerequisite: English 1 and 2 and one Junior or Senior College course in English. Six weeks.

FRENCH

S-103. Mr. Lustrat.

Translation into French, composition, conversation, lectures on rhetoric and grammatical difficulties. Reading: Balzac, Eugenie Grandet; Hugo, Ruy Blas; Loti, Pecheurs d'Islande; Daudet, Tartarin de Tarascon; Corneille, Polyeucte, Moliere, Le Tartuffe; Racine. Audromaque; Coppee, Pour la Couronne; Zola, La Debacle; Voltaire, "Prose__ (a book of selections); Rostand, La Princesse Lointaine. Reports on this reading will be made in French. One half of this minor course will be given in 1925, one half in 1926. Prerequisite: French 2 or 21.

HISTORY

S-102b. English History, 1815-1914. Mr. Payne.

A narrative study of events from the fall of Napoleon to the outbreak of the World War. Parliamentary progress, diplomatic development, economic and social legislation emphasized. Biographical studies used freely. Selections from standard authors read. A half minor; thirty recitations. Prerequisite: six hours of College history.

LATIN

S-102. The Roman Drama. Mr. Hooper.

Platus, Terence, Seneca. Relationship of the Roman to the Greek drama on the one hand, to the English on the other. Prerequisite: Latin 4. One half of this minor, 1925, one half, 1926.

MATHEMATICS

Mr. Stephens   Mr. Cumming

One of the following courses will be given if at least three students elect it. Two of the courses constitute a minor; three with a thesis, constitute a major.

101. Differential Equations.

An elementary course in ordinary and partial differential equations, with special reference to the equations occurring in the physical sciences. Text: Cohen or Murray.

VII. GRADUATE

102. Vector Analysis.

An elementary course in vectors which develops a system of coordinates and illustrates their use in certain mathematical and physical problems. Reference Text: Coffin.

103. Projective Geometry.

A course in pure geometry based upon one of the following texts with the others as references: Holgate's Reye, Cremona, Veblen and Young.

104. Theory of Functions.

An introductory course to the theory of functions of a real and a complex variable. Reference works: Harkness and Morley, Durege, Gousat.

105. Analytical Geometry.

An advanced course based on Salmon or other texts of a similar character.

ZOOLOGY

It is hoped and expected that graduate work in Zoölogy will be given in the summer of 1926. Prospective students will kindly confer in advance by correspondence or interview with Professor Joseph Krafka, LeConte Hall, stating whether they would prefer a course in the teaching of Zoölogy or a technical course (in Embryology for example).

Academic Building

VIII. HISTORY AND SOCIAL SCIENCES

S-14c. Social Studies in the Junior High School—C. 1 hr., 6 weeks. Grades seven, eight, and nine. Miss Schweppe.

This course is directed toward the improvement of instruction in history, geography and civics in the Junior High School. Progressive practice will be made concrete through the discussion study of and the planning of series of lessons. The best materials: books, maps, pictures, charts, graphs, cartoons, and examinations will be studied. Suggestions as to how the courses in history, geography, and civics can be given as one general course will be made.

S-14k. Methods of Correlating the Study of History and Geography —C. 1 hr., 6 weeks. Mr. Bocock.

This course will use as a basis of instruction a sketch of the causes, course, and consequences of the Great War. Members of the class should have maps of pre-war and post-war Europe.

S-5-6a, b and c. American History. College credit for History 5-6. Based on the Epochs of American History, three volumes.

S-5-6a. The Colonial Period, 1750 to 1829—C. 1 hr., 6 weeks. Mr. McPherson.

Text: Thwaites' Colonies.

S-5-6b. The Formative Period, 1750 to 1829—C. 1 hr., 6 weeks. Mr. McPherson.

Text: Hart's Formation of the Union.

S-5-6c. The Jacksonian Era, the Slavery Struggle, the War of Secession, Reconstruction and the Modern Period—C. 1 hr., 6 weeks. Mr. McPherson.

Text: Woodrow Wilson's Division and Reunion.

S-22. American Government—C. 1 hr., 6 weeks. Mr. McPherson.

Text: Magruder's American Government in 1923.

Modern European History.

A double course meeting two hours a day. A study of European development from 1789 to the present. Especial emphasis on events leading to the World War.

S-8. The French Revolution and Napoleon—C. 1 hr., 6 weeks, 1½ hrs., 9 weeks. Mr. Payne.

S-9. Europe Since 1815—C. 1 hr., 6 weeks, 1½ hrs., 9 weeks. Mr. Payne.

Either or both of the courses may be taken, and work may be equivalent to "History 2" or "History 8-9" in regular session.

S-14b. The Teaching of History. (Seminar)—C. 1 hr., 6 weeks. Mr. Payne.

. This course for teachers will be a study of the problems of history teaching in the high schools; the relation of history to allied studies; the history curricula in the schools of Europe and the United States in the past; the more recent ideas in the presentation of history by charts, diagrams, maps, pictures, text-books and lectures. Practical exercises in historical methods will be required. The teaching of civics will be studied in like manner. Teachers who contemplate taking this course should bring all available text-books in history.
A review course in High School History.

IX. HOME ECONOMICS

HOME ECONOMICS

S-1. Food Study and Cookery—C. 1½ hrs., 9 weeks. Miss Burson.

Composition, selection and cooking of typical foods, to give a working knowledge of the principles underlying food preparation. Sophomore credit. Prerequisite: General Chemistry. Fee, $3.50. First half-term.

S-2. Home Cookery and Table Service—C. 1½ hrs., 9 weeks. Miss Burson.

Practice in manipulation of foods in family sized quantities; practice in planning, preparing and serving meals. Sophomore credit. Prerequisite: Home Economics 1. Fee, $3.50. Second half-term.

IX. HOME ECONOMICS

S-5. Food Preservation—C. ½ hr., 9 weeks. Second-half term. Misses M. Creswell and Dowdle.

A laboratory course for teachers and Home Demonstration Agents. Canning in tin and glass, preserving, jelly making, brining, pickling, and vinegar making, standard packing. Junior. Prerequisite: Bacteriology 1. Laboratory daily. Fee, $3.00.

S-8. Advanced Cookery—C. 1 hr., 6 weeks. Miss Newton.

Offered for students desiring advanced work in the preparation of food. Junior. Prerequisite: Chemistry 1, Home Economics 1-2. Fee, $3.50.

S-26. Elementary Clothing—C. 2 hrs., 9 weeks. Miss Rathbone.

Fundamental principles related to garment construction and dress making; patterns, machines, factory production of clothing; clothing budgets. Freshman. Fee. $4.00.

S-27. Textile Problems—C. 1 hr., 9 weeks, following Home Economics 26. Miss E. Creswell.

Clothing and household materials; characteristics of the different standard fabrics and their use and care; wet and dry cleaning of all types of clothing. Freshman. Fee, $2.00.

S-32. Advanced Dressmaking—C. 3 hrs., 9 weeks. Misses Rathbone and E. Creswell.

Practice in original designs in modeling and draping; in technique of finishing and decoration; shopwork in all types of clothing for women and children; how to use these methods in secondary classes. Junior. Prerequisite: Home Economics 26. Fee, $3.50.

S-46. Home Equipment and Management—C. 3 hrs., 9 weeks. Miss E. Creswell.

Treated from vocational standpoint including the following topics; (a) Economics of household and of household purchasing. (b) Organization of work. (c) Sanitation, care and renovation. Senior credit, three hours laboratory informal. Residence in Home Management Apartment. Fee, $7.00.

S-53. Home Economics Education—Education of Women—C. 1½ hrs., 6 weeks, and Home Study. Miss Newton.

A brief historical review of the education of women among the leading nations; based on their social and economic status; a survey of the development of Home Economics Education, its social and economic importance.

S-40. Health Education: Personal Hygiene and Home Nursing—C. 1 hr., 6 weeks. Miss Newton.

This course presents health in its personal, social and economic aspects and shows how health and efficiency are improved by hygienic living. The fundamentals of First Aid and Home Nursing are included. Prerequisite: Physiology, Bacteriology, Ag. Chemistry 1. Senior.

S-59. Home Economics Education—Teaching Relationships—C. 1 hr., 6 weeks. Miss Burson.

This course is organized around the needs of the teachers; problems of instruction, management, professional and personal qualifications, school community and promotional relationships; the course of study adapted to community needs. Junior.

See course Art Structure and Design under Arts and Crafts and the course in Household Engineering under Agriculture.

JOURNALISM

See English Division.

X. LATIN

S-5a. Rapid Reading of Latin Authors—C. 1 hr., 6 weeks. Mr. Hooper.

The aim of this course is to develop facility in the reading of Latin without the use of a dictionary. The selections read are varied from year to year to meet the needs of particular classes.

X. LATIN

S-5b. Latin Writing—C. 1 hr., 6 weeks. Mr. Hooper.

This course will include the orderly presentation of the essential facts of the grammar, the translation of connected English into idiomatic Latin, and the study of style and the structure of Latin discourse. It is designed for teachers and others desiring a rapid and comprehensive review of the grammar, and for candidates for a teacher's recommendation in Latin. For the latter class special work will be provided.

Provision will also be made for students of elementary Latin composition.

S-14g. Methods of Teaching High School Latin—C. 1 hr., 6 weeks. Mr. Hooper.

Aims of Latin study; its place and value in the curriculum. The course and materials of study; varying types of textbooks; relative emphasis on various phases of the subjects, such as vocabulary, grammatical forms, syntax, translation, interpretation. The teaching of Latin composition. Oral reading of prose and verse. Features of classroom practice; methods of arousing interest; correlation with other subjects. Reading and discussion of significant articles on the teaching of Latin. References to useful books and illustrative material.

S-5c. Teachers' Course in Cicero—C. 1 hr., 6 weeks. Mr. Hooper.

Selected orations. The course will include a study of Cicero's career as an orator and man of affairs, with particular reference to the literary and artistic qualities of his orations. The historical setting of the period will be considered, with some study of the essential features of the republican constitution.

S-5d. Teachers' Course in Vergil.

On the same general plan as the course in Cicero, dealing however with the writings of Vergil.

NOTE:—Of courses S-5a, S-5b, and S-5c, 5-d, the three courses elected by the largest number of students will be given.

NOTE:—A correspondence study course in Latin Prose Composition will be offered next year. This course may be combined with any two hours of summer work to constitute a year or 3 hour course in Latin.

A review course in High School Latin.

XI. LAW

The following courses are offered in the Law School during the summer of 1925. These are open to regularly registered students (including women) in the Law School and to new students who meet the entrance requirements and to teachers and others not studying for a degree who wish some work in law.

NOTICE:—Beginning with September, 1925, the entrance requirement to the Law School will be raised from one year of college work to two years of college work, amounting to thirty hours. Persons intending to enter the Law School in 1925 may enter the University this summer for the six weeks course on the basis of the present one college year requirement.

Law students by taking work three summers will also shorten the three-year requirement.

Fees for the law courses are $15.00 for each course, or 6 courses for $60.00.

S-1. Municipal Corporation Law—by Cooley. 6 weeks. Mr. Upson.

S-2. Law of Bailments—by Dobie. 6 weeks. Mr. Upson.

S-3. Criminal Law. Mr. McWhorter.

Common-law and statutory offenses; parties in crime; classification and elements of the specific offenses; offenses against the government, jurisdiction.

S-4. Domestic Relations. Mr. McWhorter.

Contracts to marry; marriage; effect of marriage, common law marriages, modifications of the common law imposed by statutes, the wife's separate property, separation and divorce. Parent and Child: Duties of parents; rights of parents. Guardian and Ward: Selection and appointment of guardian; rights, duties and liabilities of guardians; termination of guardianship; infants; persons non compotes mentis and aliens. Master and servant. General principles.

XI. LAW

S-5. Contracts. Mr. Cornett.
Text: Lawson. The essential principles of a contract, the agreement, the competency of parties, the form, the consideration, the consent of parties and the legality of the object of agreement.

S-6. Sales. Mr. Cornett.
Text: Tiffany. Sale and contracts to sell, statute of frauds, warranties, conditions and penalty fo rbreach, deliveries and acceptances, seller's lein, and stoppage in transitu.

S-7. The Constitution of the United States. Judge Cobb.

S-8. The Constitution of the State of Georgia. Judge Cobb.

Dean Sylvanus Morris of the Law School will deliver two public lectures: The Study of the Law. The Application of Principles.

XII. LIBRARY SCIENCE

This course is planned for the need of teacher-librarians and will enable teachers to learn the fundamental principles of library organization, management, book selection, etc., from the standpoint of the school library.

The school library with its book list of over 500 volumes, and this list growing steadily needs expert organization and management.

The Boards of Education should assign some teacher to study the problem and properly organize the library.

S-3. Book Selection and Library Administration from the Point-of-View of the School Library—C. 1 hr., 6 weeks. Miss Archer.
Lectures on school library loan records, equipment, book-buying, school library standards, library furniture and equipment, handling of pamphlets and clippings, binding and mending, cataloging, alphabeting. Two periods.

XIII. MATHEMATICS

S-14d. Teaching High School Mathematics—C. 1 hr., 6 weeks. Mr. Stephens.
Ths course will present and illustrate modern methods of mathematics teaching. The report of the National Committee on Mathematical Requirements will be avaliable for study. Those planning to take this course should bring standard texts in school mathematics with them.

S-1. Trigonometry—C. 1 hr., 6 weeks, 1 hr., 9 weeks. Mr. Cumming or Mr. Stephens.
A standard course in Plane and Special Trigonometry covering the usual subject with solutions of triangles and manipulation of formulas.

S-2. Elementary Analysis—C. 2 hrs., 9 weeks. Mr. Cumming.
A study of Coordinates; plotting of Algebraic and Transcendental curves; discussion of the straight line and circle analytically; functional relations. Six hours per week for six weeks, and twelve hours a week for nine weeks.

S-3. Introduction to Calculus—C. 1½ hrs., 9 weeks. Mr. Cumming.
An elementary course, explaining differentiation and integration and a few applications. Six hours per week for nine weeks.

S-4. College Algebra—C. 1½ hrs., 9 weeks. Mr. Stephens.
This course will take up the following topics: Complex Numbers, Determinants, Partial Fractions, Series, Theory of Equations. Six hours per week for nine weeks.

S-d. Review of Algebra and Geometry. 6 weeks. Mr. Bennett.
Arranged for those teachers who need to validate their high school crdits in Mathematics or who desire a review of these subjects to aid them in their teaching. No credit.

XIV. MODERN LANGUAGES

FRENCH

S-14h. Methods of Teaching French—C. 1 hr., 6 weeks. Mr. Lustrat.

Advanced course for teachers of French in High Schools and Colleges. Methods of teaching; Explanation of texts and grammatical difficulties; Pronunciation will be stressed; Lectures in French on Literary subjects; Reading of difficult French in and outside of the classroom; Reports in French of texts read by the student and lessons on rhetoric; Conversation.

Texts: "Lee Oberle" by Bazin; "Eugenie Grandet" by Balzac; "Andromaque" by Racine; and other texts if time permits.

S-14h. Elementary Methods for French Teachers—C. 1 hr., 6 weeks. Miss Jack.

Review Course. This course is intended for teachers or others having completed at least two years of high school French. It will consist of a systematic review of French. Grammar and Syntax; Translation from English into French; Reading of standard texts; Writing of letters and short essays in French; Conversation. A brief outline of the best methods of teaching will also be given. Pronunciation will be strongly stressed in this course.

French 20—C. 3 hrs., 9 weeks. Miss Jack.

A beginners course equivalent to Junior French. Two periods daily.

French 21—C. 1½ hrs., 6 weeks. Miss Jack.

A half year course with parallel reading between two consecutive summer schools. Senior course.

NOTE:—Miss Jack will conduct French table talk at Lucy Cobb.

SPANISH

S-20. Spanish—C. 3 hrs., 9 weeks. Mr. Chance.

A course similar to French 20.

S-21. Spanish—C. 1½ hrs., 6 weeks. Mr. Chance.

A course similar to French 21.

XV. MUSIC
George Folsom Granberry, Director
PROFESSIONAL TRAINING FOR MUSIC TEACHERS

History:

The department was established by George Folsom Granberry, director of the Granberry Piano School, Carnegie Hall, New York, who remains in charge. In its two sessions the department has established itself as an enthusiastic, genuine and practical success. Teachers completing the course have been able to achieve better results immediately and some have been able to secure better and more profitable positions.

Certificate:

XV. MUSIC

The University through the Summer School grants a certificate to those who complete the course for the Professional Training of Music Teachers. Two Summer Sessions with independent study during the winter are necessary for the accomplishment of the requirements.

Requirements for a Certificate:

"Musical Development through Sight, Touch and Hearing," (by George Folsom Granberry, published by A. P. Schmidt Co., 120 Boylston St., Boston). These four volumes cover the **Presentation of the Elements of Music, the Essentials of Theory and History, Elementary and Intermediate Technique, and Ear Training.** Five periods each week through two summer sessions.

Harmonic, Tonal and Formal Analysis:

Pieces and studies selected from the works of **Bach, Clementi, Bertini, Kohler, Czerny, Elsenheimer,** and **Gurlitt.** Two periods each week through two summer sessions.

Transposition and Intermediate Piano Technique:

Material selected from Sight, Touch and Hearing and works by standard composers. Three periods each week through two summer sessions.

Piano Ensemble Playing:

Orchestra, Operatic and Chamber music arranged for four, six and eight hands, analyzed and performed. Two periods each week of one summer sessions.

Piano Playing:

Individual lessons in Piano Playing are not required for the Professional Music Teachers' Certificate, but a **Playing Test** is required, the material for which is outlined following and may be prepared outside of the summer session. Teachers finishing all other requirements may pass their playing test any time before the close of the following Summer School, at which time they will receive their certificates.

Appreciation of Music:

A written test on the volume, "Music: an Art and a Language," by Walter Raymond Spalding, (A. P. Schmidt, Boston). Ten questions are given on the evolution and development of **Musical Forms** and the **Masters of Music** as given by Spalding. This preparation should be outside the summer session and the test taken with the playing test.

PLAYING TEST

Bach—Two numbers selected from the Little Preludes and Fugues or the Two or Three-part Inventions, or one larger work.

One selection from any of the following composers:

Clementi—One of the later sonatas. **Haydn**—Sonata. **Mozart**—Sonata. **Beethoven**—One of the earliest sonatas.

One selection each from two of the following composers:

Schumann—Scenes from childhood, op. 15. Fantasy Lyrics, op. 12. Four sonatas for Young People, op. 118. Album Leaves, op. 124.

Greig—Lyrical Pieces, op. 12—op. 54—op. 17—op. 68—op. 43.

MacDowell—Etudes for Technic and Style, op. 39. Woodland Sketches, op. 5. Sea pieces, op. 55.

Debussy—"Coin des Enfants." "Arabesques."

Students who are registered for private lessons with Mr. Gran-

XV. MUSIC

berry may take the playing test in place of one of their lessons. Others must register for the playing test at a fee of $5.00.

Tuition:

The tuition for the Professional Training Course, ten periods each week, for the Summer Session of six weeks:

First year, without ensemble classes_____$30.00
Ensemble classes _____ 9.00
Appreciation of Music _____ 9.00

*Mr. Granberry will accept only a limited number of private pupils and only those who are engaged in professional work.

Piano:

Interpretation. Advanced Technique, Repertory, Teaching Literature, etc. Tuition. twelve half-hour lessons:

*Mr. Granberry _____$48.00
Mr. Clement _____ 24.00
Mrs. Rowe _____ 24.00

Piano Ensemble:

The Reading at Sight and Study including Analysis of the Form, Tonal Structure, History and Meaning, of works most of which are outside the realm of piano music: Operatic, Orchestral. Chamber, Choral etc. Many of the numbers are prepared for finished performance and are given at the various public gatherings of the Summer School. The classes are conducted by Mr. Granberry.

Tuition two hours lessons weekly_____$ 9.00

Pipe Organ:

Pedaling, Registration, Church Literature, Concert Repertory. Tuition, twelve three-quarter hour lessons:

Mrs. Granberry _____$48.00

Voice:

(a) Private lessons. (b) Italian diction with special reference to needs of the singing student. in class. (c) Special course in professional training for voice teachers. open only to advanced pupils. Weekly normal lectures on "Tone Placing," Automatic Breach Control, Program Making.

Signora De Fabritis:
(a) 12 half-hour private lessons _____$48.00
(b) Italian diction in class, 1 hour lessons weekly_____ 9.00
(c) Open to (a) and (b) pupils after conference.

Miss Bennett:
12 half-hour private lessons _____$24.00
12 class lessons of one hour, four students in a class each student _____ 12.00

Violin:

Mr. Austin J. Wight:
(a) 12 half-hour private lessons _____$24.00
(b) 12 class lessons, one hour weekly _____ 9.00

Violin:

(a) A thorough, sound and comprehensive training. Instruction in violin pedagogy. Suggestions concerning teaching material and how to practice. Control of the bow. Traditions of the great masters of violin playing.

Violin Playing:

(b) Duets. trios, quartets (including the Belgian Class System. for advanced students). Violin and Piano Sonatas of Bach. Handel, Mozart, Beethoven Rubinstein and Grieg.

Harmony:

Individual lessons with Mr. Granberry or Mr. Clement are at the rate for private lessons, as given above.

Tuition, twelve hour class lessons _____$ 9.00

Musical Appreciation:

Mr. Granberry gives a course of twelve hour lessons. The work is designed not only to make the ear accurate. but to establish taste by acquainting the student in the most elemental way with the best in music. The material used in developing tonal and rhythmical perception and understanding is taken only from the greatest masters. from Wagner's Nibelungen Laid and the stand symphonies, principally those of Beethoven.

Tuition. two hour class lessons weekly _____$ 9.00

XV. MUSIC

PUBLIC SCHOOL MUSIC
(Regular Summer Course)

S-1—Public School Music Course for Grades 1-6—N. 1 hr. Kate Lee Haralson.

The work requires observation, the preparation of lessons, plans and practice in teaching a class:
1. Practice in the choice, singing and presenting of rote songs.
2. Material and plan for teaching the first steps in notation.
3. Sight-singing, study of fundamental problems in pitch and rhythm.
4. Music appreciation, the use of the phonograph and material for each grade.

S-2—Public School Course for Grades 6-9—N. 1 hr. Kate Lee Harralson.

Methods and material in sight-singing, ear-training, oral and written dictation, elementary theory and harmony, music appreciation, class instruction in voice and chorus work.

S-3—Music Expression—N. 1 hr. Kate Lee Harallson.

Conducting class and the organization and conducting of High School Choruses, Glee Clubs, Vocal Class Study, Orchestras and Elective Music including credits for outside Music Study under private teachers.

S-4—Music Appreciation. ½ hr. Kate Lee Haralson.

Appropriate courses for Elementary School, Junior High School and High School including the use of the phonograph.

S-5—Harmony. ½ hr. Kate Lee Haralson.

Introductory harmony and harmonic dictation, including scales, intervals, triads, inversions, dominant seventh chords and their applications in melody harmonizing and original composition.

Choral Music:

The Council of the Summer School earnestly desires to promote good singing and for this reason a Choral Club under the direction of Mrs. Granberry is to be instituted. Qualified students of the Summer School are free to join this club, which will meet regularly and will prepare for participation in public programs. Students who are approved by the Music Department, to the number of thirty, and who are willing to give regular attendance in the choir at the morning services and at certain public affairs in the evenings, will receive, at the close of the Summer School, a refund to the value of their general registration fee. Those who wish to avail themselves of this refund should write to the office of the Summer School asking that they be enrolled for trial.

Community Singing:

A large part of each daily assembly will continue to be given to general singing: patriotic songs, famous ballads, sacred selections, glees, rounds and nonsense jingles. Mr. Granberry will conduct this music at the University and Miss Haralson at the Normal School.

Orchestra:

Mr. Wight conducts a Summer School orchestra. He has had much experience in developing school orchestras. All Summer School students playing orchestral instruments are invitedd to bring them and to register for participation in the orchestral practice and performance.

State License or Certificate:

Those completing the requirements for the University Summer School Certificate in Music, may also secure a State Certificate in Music by presenting a diploma from a recognized high school and credit for two years college work.

Books and Music:

Each teacher registered for the music course should allow at least $8.00 for music and books which are required for the course. A larger sum than this could be advantageously used in procuring new and refreshing teaching material and works of reference.

A Music Festival:

The fifth week of the Summer School, which has been known as Music Week, will this season see the inauguration of the Summer School Music Festival. A Grand Opera will be presented and there will be vocal and instrumental recitals, and concerts of varied vocal and instrumental combinations.

XVI. ORATORY AND DRAMATIC ART

ORATORY AND DRAMATIC ART

Courses in this department are designed to cover three phases of activity in this field of education: (1) instruction in the theory of expression, in the principles of speech improvement and correction, and in methods of teaching; (2) instruction and training in speech-making; (3) instruction and training in oral interpretation of literature and in dramitics. Students who wish to teach these subjects should have some knowledge of each of these three phases mentioned above. Students especially interested in spech-making are advised to take some work in oral interpretation or dramatics, while those chiefly interested in oral interpretation or dramatics should take some work in speech-making. It is advisable during the same session to take courses along these two lines rather than along one line only. The work will be progressive in nature so that students may continue their studies for several years. These courses are exchanged in credit at the University or at Emerson College of Oratory. Students will be grouped, as far as possible, according to individual needs or previous study.

S-2b. Play Production—C. 1 hr., 6 weeks. Mr. McCabe, Miss Cobb.
A study of the problems involved in producing school and community plays. Selection of plays; choosing and training a cast; the stage and stage settings; principles of acting; costuming and make-up; organization and business management; modern plays presented from the platform and for the public. Intended for advanced students and graduates who are interested in the educational and social service aspects of dramatic production. Open to those who receive permission from the instructor.

See also the courses by Miss Vance at the State Normal in **Story Telling, Expression for Teachers** and **Dramatics for the Grades.** Junior credit.

Dr. Park's course in Shakespeare and other English courses will supplement the work in Oratory.

Students should endeavor to take one of Miss Baum's courses in Aesthetic dancing, etc.

'Prunella" by Grantville Barker and Lawrence Houseman will be produced by the department this summer.

S-1. Literary Interpretation. 1 hr., 6 weeks. Miss Cobb.
The "Evolution of Expression," Vols. I, II, III, and IV, used at Emerson Colege of Oratory are the text books for this course. Lectures on the basic principles of Expression embraced in these volumes will be suplemneted by practical work in applying these principles to the interpretation of the printed page varied literary forms being used as material. The student will have daily practice with personal attention and individual criticism for the purpose of developing and guiding his own powers of expression. Lectures will be given on the pedagogical methods of teaching the fundamentals of Expression in the study and interpretation of literature. The work in literary and dramatic interpretation may be applied in the schools from the kindergarten through the High School and College. Sophomore or Junior credit.

Voice—Position, breathing, tone placing, tone support, articulation and enunciation, diction.

Body—Pantomime, to aid in overcoming self-consciousness and timidity, and to substitute freedom and self-confidence. Elementary gesture.

Two sections, (a) more elementary, (b) for those actively engaged in teaching or have completed most of the work in this subject.

S-1a. Public Speaking—C. 1hr., 6 weeks. Mr. McCabe.
The subjects will be treated from the two-fold view-point of speech structure and speech delivery. Types determined by the underlying purpose of the speech will be considered. Toward the last of the course work will be done in fine points of shading and line reading. The extemporaneous speech, the speech from a prepared outline, and the memorized manuscript speech will be covered in theory and practice.

The history of Oratory will be sketched with illustrative examples from c.assic, medieval, and modern orations analyzed and delivered in class.

The work for debates and contests in declamation should develop from a regular course in Public Speaking. This would bring results far superior to the old method of mechanical coaching of a single speech for a set occasion. It would eliminate affectation and what is stilted and studied and substitute simplicity and truthfulness. Normal work is included in his course, Freshman credit.

Voice—Fundamentals of tone production, articulation, tone radiation, pronunciation, diction.

Elementary, gesture to aid the student to acquire ease of bearing.

XVI. ORATORY AND DRAMATIC ART

For students desiring it an opportunity will be sought for experimental work in speaking outside the class in addition to the daily work in the class room.

S-2. **Dramatic Interpretation—C.** 1 hr., 6 weeks. Miss Cobb, Mr. McCabe.

Material will be chosen from classic and modern drama. The one act play will be studied. Expressional reading of principal scenes. The reading of the line and the analysis and interpretation of character will be emphasized. Characters assigned to members of class and scenes presented from the platform. Junior credit.

Pantomime, gesture, voice.

Lectures on modern Little Theatre movement and educational and community dramatics.

Mr. McCabe will present ' Beau Brummell" one evening, and the department will offer "Prunella." by Sackville Barker, during the sixth week.

XVII. PHYSICAL EDUCATION

PHYSICAL EDUCATION FOR WOMEN

Medical Examinations. Medical examinations may be obtained by appointment with the University Physician. Members of the Department of Physical Education reserve the right to require medical examination of students entering their classes. All students taking S-5 are required to take this examination.

The regulation gymnasium costume and shoes will be required for all floor work.

Students wishing to take work in the Physical Education Department must record these courses on the study-lists which they file with the Registrar.

S-3. **Aesthetic Dancing—C.** 1 hr., 6 weeks. Miss Baum.

Technical combinations of steps; Port de Bras and Plastic Exercises; Simple and Intermediate Aesthetic; National and Character Dances.

S-5. **Basketball—C.** 1 hr., 6 weeks. Miss Grote.

Indoor Baseball, Volley Ball. Tennis and Track Athletics Preparatory for State Tests for High School Pupils. Rules. duties of officials, organizations of squads and teams. equipment, methods of coaching, conduct of tournaments. Actual experience in the playing and conduct of the games. Extra practice for those who wish to increase their own practical skill.

S-6. **Technique of Swimming—C.** ½ hr., 6 weeks. Miss ————.

Principles and methods of teaching swimming. diving. life saving. training and coaching, rules of events. American Red Cross Live Saving Test is given.

44

XVII. PHYSICAL EDUCATION

Swimming Practice.

For those who swim and for those who wish to practice swimming. There will be no instruction in the art of swimming at this hour but the pool will be under supervision whenever swimmers are admitted. 1 period daily through the session: 3:00-3:50, 3:50-4:40, 4:40-5:30.

Those who wish to secure the privileges of the swimming pool for the term will present themselves at the proper time and secure appointments for some regular hours each day. For the use of locker and towels a charge of $1.00 is made.

S-7. Technique of Games—C. 1 hr., 6 weeks. Miss Grote.

Games suitable for playgrounds, elementary and secondary schools, ranging from simplest primary school games to organized team games, such as volley ball, captain ball, etc., will be offered.

S-11. Tactics and Calisthenics—C. 1 hr., 6 weeks. Miss Grote.

Graded course in tactics and calesthenics, apparatus work for grades and high schools. Prerequisite: Physical Education 1-2.

S-12. Singing Games and Folk Daancing—C. 1 hr., 6 weeks. Miss Baum.

This course will comprise dances from Russia. Lithuania, Italy, France, Belgium, Scandinavia. Also English and American country dances. Progressive combinations of simple steps to be taught before presenting the dance. Characteristic movements of the dance peculiar to the country from which it comes. Dances suitable for all grades.

FESTIVALS—One complete festival which will be presented at the end of the course. Material for one other festival. Costuming, Pantomime, Music, Dancing. Miss Baum' and other athletic teachers.

HORSEMANSHIP
Men and Women

Equitation. 6 weeks.

It is proposed by the Summer School authorities to use the horses and equipment of the Cavalry R. O. T. C. Unit for this instruction. An army officer will be in charge. Each student will ride twice each week.

There will be two classes, as follows:

E-1—Beginners.

E-2—Students who have ridden before.

Classes will be divided into two sections and held on the Cavalry Drill Grounds. near Memorial Hall. The course will include, saddling. unsaddling, the aids, the gaits. changes of direction, suppling exercises, riding without stirrups. jumping low hurdles, and cross-country riding. A horse show will be held at the conclusion of the course and suitable prizes awarded.

Students will be required to furnish their own riding habits. Riding breeches: flannel shirt, or coat; boots, or leggins with high shoes; cap or sport hat; riding gloves.

Permission to ride will be secured from the Physician of the Summer School before admission to the clases. Absences will be excused only by the officer in charge or the Physician of the Summer School. Fee. $3.00 for 12 lessons of an hour and a half each. Picnics and excursions on horseback will be arranged during the course. The horses are well trained cavalry mounts. This course was a great success and very popular last summer. A credit of ½ hour will be given to each student satisfactorily completing the course.

SCHEDULE FOR HORSEMANSHIP

Time	Mon.	Tues.	Wed.	Thu.	Fri.	Sat.	Remarks.
8:30 to 9:30 A.M.	E-1a	E-2a		E-1a	E-2a		E-1a. Beginners, 1st Section.
4:00 to 5:30 P.M.	E-1b	E-2b		E-1b	E-2b		E-1b. Beginners. 2nd Section. E-2a. Ridden before. 1st eSction. E-2b. Ridden before. 2d Section.

45

XVII. PHYSICAL EDUCATION

RIFLE PRACTICE

Men and Women

Rifle Markmanship.   6 weeks.

There will be three sections in Rifle Markmanship, each section firing twice a week as per schedule below. The course will include the aim and position, the trigger-squeeze exercises and firing on target "L"— distance 50 feet, with caliber .22 ammunition. A competition between the three sections will be held at the conclusion of the course and a suitable prize awarded. Instruction will be given by Regular Army personnel.

SCHEDULE FOR RIFLE MARKSMENSHIP

Time	Mon.	Tues.	Wed.	Thu.	Fri.	Sat.	
4:00 to 5:00 P.M.	R-1	R-2	R-3	R-1	R-2	R-3	R-1, R-2 and R-3 refer to the three sections.

PHYSICAL TRAINING FOR MEN

The Summer School management is pleased to offer to the High Schools of Georgia and neighboring states a four weeks course in athletic coaching for men.

More or less, interscholastic athletics have been introduced into all of our high schools. It is necessary that the men in charge of this work should know both the theory and practice, the hygiene and ethics of good sports. It would be a fine thing for inter- scholastic athletics for a hundred or more of the leading coaches in this section of the South to come together for training under these men of reputation and advance the standards of athletic sports and at the same time form friendships and establish athletic ideals that may permeate the school life of the South.

In addition to the registration fee, a fee of $5.00 will be charged for work in this department. This fee will cover all incidentals, including gymnasium fee, towel fee, locker fee, and swimming pool.

Inquiries concerning these courses may be sent to the Director of the Summer School.

The instruction this year will be in charge of Coach Frank W. Thomas, former Notre Dame quarterback and basketball player. Mr. Thomas has been Assistant Coach at the University of Georgia for the past two seasons, and a great deal of the success of last year's football team was due to Mr. Thomas' intimate knowledge of the famous Notre Dame system of football.

P-1. Basketball Theory.   11:40 to 12:30 daily.   Instructor to be announced.
First four weeks—Woodruff Hall.

P-2. Basketball Practice.   12:30 to 1:30 daily.   Instructor to be announced.
First four weeks—Woodruff Hall.

P-3. Football Theory.   3:50 to 4:40 daily.   Mr. Thomas.
First four weeks—Woodruff Hall.

P-4. Football Practice.   4:40 to 5:30 daily.   Mr. Thomas.
First four weeks—Woodruff Hall.

P-5. General Athletics for High Schools.   8:30 to 9:30 daily.
First aid instruction in physical training for high schools; various rec- reational games; physical standards for students; physical requirements for students; physical drills outlined and explained; treatment of in- juries; first aid; correct bandaging, etc. Woodruff Hall.

46

XVIII. PSYCHOLOGY

S-1. General Psychology—C. 1 hr., 6 weeks. Mr. Patrick.

What Psychology is and does. Reactions; structure and functions of the nervous system; reflex, instinct, and habit; sensation; attention and perception. This course is planned to parallel the correspondence course (C-1.)

S-2. Completion of S-1—C. 1 hr., 3 weeks. Mr. Patrick.

Learning and memory; imagery and memory, association and laws of association; reasoning and imagination; feelings, emotions and sentiments; will and control of action; intelligence and individual differences; personality; language; work, rest and sleep. This course parallels correspondence course C-2.

S-4. Educational Psychology—C. 1 hr., 6 weeks. Mr. Furry.

A course for beginners requiring no previous work in psychology. The nature and objectives of education; the hereditary, hygienic and social bases of education; the psychology of learning; perception, thinking and study; memory; transfer of training; moral education. This course parallels correspondence course, C-4, and can be continued in correspondence course C-5 for one hour additional credit.

S-6. Mental Tests—C. 1 hr., 6 weeks. Mr. Purdom.

An intensive study in the laboratory of a few tests. Material will be used and discussions had of the problems of mental testing and its place in education. The tests will be given scored, interpreted, etc., and the n ples of mental testing worked out. Educational measurements will b ven parallel with this course.

XIX. SCIENCES

BOTANY

S-3. Plant Biology—C. 4 hrs., 9 weeks. Mr. Reade.

A beginner's course in college botany or biology. The class meets four hours every day for laboratory work. As that progresses time is taken out of the four hours for quizes, discussions and reports of reading. This course is supposed to take most of the student's time and energy. Text: Smith et al, A Text-Book of General Botany.

S-11. Genetics—C. 3 hrs., 9 weeks. Mr. Reade.

An introduction to the study of heredity. The class meets for two hours every day, the last period of the morning and the laast one of the afternoon. Lectures, reading and discussions. Botany 3 or its equivalent is prerequisite. Text: Babcock and Clausen, Genetics.

Bird Study

On Friday morning of each week at 6:00 o'clock, Dr. Wheeler will conduct a bird study walk through the grounds and farm of the Agricultural College. The class will assemble at the Memorial Hall.

Similar studies and walks will be conducted at the State Normal School by Dr. Pound. Miss Rainwater, supervisor of Nature Study in Atlanta Public Schools will give several studies on birds with interpretation of bird songs.

Mr. Burleigh in his study of trees and shrubs, each afternoon, will also point out the relation of birds to plant life.

The Biology Department has a collection of mounted birds which will be available for study.

It is hoped in these ways that teachers may become acquainted with the native birds.

CHEMISTRY

S-1. Elementary Chemistry—C. 4 hrs., 9 weeks. Mr. Brockman.

Fundamental course in general chemistry required of Agricultural and Home Economic students and valuable for teachers. Laboratory fee, $3.00. Breakage fee, $3.00.

Organic and Biological Chemistry. (See Agriculture.)

Qualitative Analysis. (See Agriculture.)

Quantitative Analysis. (See Agriculture.)

Also a review of High School Science.

XIX. SCIENCES

S-1. General Science—N. 6 weeks. Mr. Earnest.
(See Normal School.)

PHYSICS

S-1. College Physics—C. 3 hrs., 9 weeks. Mr. Dixon.
An elementary course in Physics equivalent to Physics 1 offered in the regular session. Time required. One period each morning recitation and lecture, and three periods each afternoon recitation and laboratory work with the necessary outside preparation. Laboratory fee, $3.00.

S-2. College Physics—C. 4 hrs., 9 weeks. Mr. Hendren.
An elementary course in Physics equivalent to Physics 2 as offered in the regular session. This course satisfies the requirements of medical colleges of a standard four hour credit course in Physics. Two periods recitation and lecture six days a week and a two hour laboratory period five days a week. Laboratory fee, $3.00.

S-14e. High School Physics for Teachers—C. 1 hr., 6 weeks. Mr. Hendren.
This course is especially designed to meet the needs of the High School teacher in Physics, who, having a good knowledge of the subject matter of Physics, wishes to study modern methods of presenting the subject.
Prerequisite: The completion of a standard college course in Physics with individual laboratory work or its equivalent in terms of experience in teaching Physics in high school.

ZOOLOGY

*Arranged especially to meet the biological requirements for entrance to medical schools.

S-31. General Zoology—C. 4 hrs., 9 weeks. Mr. Krafka.
A course dealing with the general physiology, anatomy, and development of the various animal types, supplemented by a consideration of heredity, variation and evolution. Two recitations and a laboratory period daily for nine weeks. Laboratory fee, $3.50.

S-14f. Teaching of Biology (Seminar)—C. 1 hr., 6 weeks. Mr. Krafka.
A course designed primarily for the discussion of methods of teaching the 2nd Year High School Science. It is proposed to consider such course types as "Nature Study," "type dissection courses," "Civic Biology," "Farm Yard Biology" and Project Method.

XX. SOCIOLOGY

S-10. Modern Social Problems.
S-10a. Rural Sociology—C. 1½ hrs., 9 weeks. Mr. Hutchinson.
A study of the facts of rural and village societal relations, a systematization and interpretation of these facts with a view to stimulating the student of a more comprehensive interest in the problems that confront his own community and wherever possible with a view to offering suggestions for improvement.

S-10b. Community Organization and Child Welfare—C. 1½ hrs., 9 weeks. Mr. Hutchinson.
An analysis of the democratic community, the principles by which such a community is to be arrived at and its importance to all sound social reconstruction. Problems of Child Welfare with special reference to the situation here in this state. Some of the leading social welfare workers of the state will be present at times during the term to address the students in regard to the work that is being done in the state.
NOTE:—Students who register for only six weeks may take one or both parts of Sociology S-10 and complete the work by Correspondence-Study.

Announcement

of the

University of Georgia

For the Session 1926-1927

With a Register of Officers and Students for the
Session 1925-1926

———

Chartered A. D. 1785

CONTENTS

Part I
THE UNIVERSITY
Historical Sketch

Support

Government

Board of Trustees

University at Athens

Administrative Officers

Officers of Instruction

CALENDAR, 1926-1927

1926

June 21, Monday:	Opening of the Summer School.
July 31, Saturday:	Close of the six weeks session Summer School.
August 21, Saturday:	Close of nine weeks session Summer School.
September 11:	Meeting of the Faculty.
September 13:	First day of Registration.
September 13-16:	Examinations for Entrance.
September 15:	Opening of the First Term.
October 1:	Last day of Registration for Graduate Students.
November 1:	Last day on which a programme for a Master's Degree may be handed to the Dean of the Graduate School.
November 25:	Thanksgiving Day.
December 22:	Close of the First Term.

1927

January 3:	Registration for the Second Term.
January 19:	Birthday of General R. E. Lee.
February 21:	Exercises in commemoration of the 126th Anniversary of the Demosthenian Society and the 107th Anniversary of the Phi Kappa Society.
February 22:	Washington's Birthday.
March 19:	Close of the Second Term.
March 28:	Registration for the Third Term.
April 30:	Last day on which graduate theses may be handed in to professors.
May 14:	Last day on which graduate theses may be handed by professors to the Dean of the Graduate School.
May 20:	Last day for submission of prize essays.
May 21:	Last day on which reports of written examinations on minor courses may be made to the Dean of the Graduate School.
May 28:	Last day on which reports of written examinations on major courses may be made to the Dean of the Graduate School.
June 6:	Meeting of the Board of Visitors.
June 9:	Annual Session of the Board of Trustees.
June 8-11:	Examinations for entrance.
June 10, Friday:	4:00 P. M., Military exercises and drill.
June 12, Sunday:	11:00 A. M., Baccalaureate sermon.
June 13, Monday:	10:30 A. M., Exercises of the undergraduates representing the branches of the University.
June 14, Tuesday:	10:30 A. M., Business meeting of the Alumni Society. 12 M., Oration before the Alumni Society.
June 15, Wednesday:	Commencement Day. Close of the 126th annual session.

HISTORICAL SKETCH

In February, 1784, forty thousand acres of land were set aside by the Legislature of Georgia for "the endowment of a college or seminary of learning." In January, 1785, "An Act for the more full and complete establishment of a public seat of learning in this state" was approved. This Act is known as the Charter of the University of Georgia.

Abram Baldwin, the author of the charter, was elected President at the first meeting of the Trustees, in 1786, and directed the disposal of the lands, so as to bring about an income for the University.

In June, 1801, Jackson County was chosen for the location of the University, which was open for students in August.

The tablet on the building, now known as "Old College," states, "The site of this building was chosen on the VI day of July, in the XXVI year of the independence of the United States of America. George Walton, Abram Baldwin, John Milledge, John Twiggs, and Hugh Lawson, a committee of the Senatus Academicus, and for the benefit of the institution the adjacent land was on that day given by John Milledge." The town which began to grow up around this site was named Athens.

In November, 1803, President Meigs reported that three dwelling houses, three stores, and a number of other valuable buildings had been erected. There were between 30 and 45 students enrolled. The college "was organized as other literary institutions in America and in Europe into four classes" and was called Franklin College.

In 1822 the University had two large dormitories and recitation halls, a chapel, and several other buildings on the campus; it had a President, two professors, and three tutors as its faculty; while its student body consisted of 41 Freshmen, 42 Sophomores, 17 Juniors, and 20 Seniors, and its income amounted to $12,000 a year.

Until after the War Between the States, Franklin College remained the only department of the University. Most of the men who afterwards added to the distinction and glory of the state in peace and war, received their training at this college. It had indeed been a fond mother of her great men, though the General Assembly failed to continue the liberal policy begun so wisely with the founding of the state.

In 1872, the funds arising from the Morrill Fund for the establishment of the Land-grant colleges were transferred to the Trustees

o the University and the College of Agriculture and the Mechanic
Arst was established as a co-ordinate department of the University.

In August, 1867, the Lumpkin Law School at Athens (incorporated in 1859) was merged into and became the Law School of
the University.

In 1872, The North Georgia Agricultural College at Dahlonega
became a department through a contract made by the local Trustees,
and in 1873, by arrangement with the local Trustees of the Georgia Medical College (founded in 1829) at Augusta, this institution
became the Medical Department of the University.

By the Constitution of Georgia (adopted in 1877), the appropriation of public funds for education other than "the elementary
branches of an English education" was permitted to the University
only. The following institutions have been ectablished by legislative enactments as departments or branches of the University and
placed under control of its Board of Trustees (each being maintained in whole or in part by annual appropriations from the State
Treasury): The Georgia School of Technology, Atlanta, established
in 1885; The Georgia Normal and Industrial College for Girls, at
Milledgeville, (now the Georgia State College for Women), estab-.
lished in 1889; The Georgia Industrial College for Colored Youths,
near Savannah, established in 1890; The State Normal School at
Athens, established in 1895; the South Georgia Normal School at
Valdosta, (now the Georgia State Woman's College), established
in 1906; The Bowdon State Normal College, at Bowdon, established
in 1919; The South Georgia Agricultural and Mechanical College,
at Tifton, established in 1924.

Somewhat of the growth of the University at Athens may be
seen from the number of departments which have been established
there in recent years: The School of Pharmacy, established in 1903;
The Summer School, authorized by an act of the General Assembly
in 1897, and put on a permanent foundation by an appropriation of
the General Assembly in 1904; The School of Forestry, established
in 1906 through the generous aid of Mr. George Foster Peabody;
The School of Education, established in 1908; The School of Commerce, established in 1912; The School of Journalism, established
in 1915.

In the summer of 1906, the Legislature differentiated the Georgia
State College of Agriculture and directed the Governor to appoint
Trustees charged with its management. At the same session of
the Legislature an industrial and agricultural school was established
in each of the congressional districts of the State as a branch of
this college and under the general supervision of its board of trustees. These are located at Statesboro, Tifton, Americus, Carrollton,

Monroe, Barnesville, Powder Springs, Madison, Clarkesville, Granite Hill, Douglas and Cochran. The General Assembly of Georgia during its session in 1924 converted the district school of Statesboro into the Georgia Normal School and the district school at Tifton into the South Georgia Agricultural and Mechanical College.

In 1918, by resolution of the Board of Trustees, women were admitted to the College of Agriculture and the Mechanic Arts and to the Peabody School of Education.

During the administrations of Chancellor Hill and Chancellor Barrow the lands of the University have been increased to over a thousand acres to provide for the Agricultural College. The original plan of supervising and organizing the high schools was renewed and there are now 275 affiliated four year high schools graduating more than 8,000 pupils a year.

The General Assembly of 1920 submitted an amendment to the Constitution which required the legislature to make appropriations for the support of the University and high schools. This amendment was ratified in November, 1920.

SUPPORT

The University is supported partly by taxation of the people of the State, partly by the income from federal grants, and partly by income from private gifts.

The federal government has made four grants for the support of the College of Agriculture and the Mechanic Arts; the original land grant of 1862; the grant of 1887 for the support of agricultural experiment stations in connection with the College of Agriculture; and the supplementary grants of 1890 and 1907.

In 1895 the State appropriated $29,000 for the erection and equipment of Science Hall. Since that time it has appropriated money for five other buildings, adding greatly to the efficiency of the institution. For maintenance the State pays the sum of $145,000 annually, and has added an annual appropriation of $10,000 for the Summer School. In addition, the sum of $110,000 is appropriated annually for the maintenance of the State College of Agriculture; with $35,000 for State Extension Work, and $2,250 for Farmers' Institutes; also the sum of $128,000 per annum to meet the Federal appropriation to Georgia under the terms and provisions of the act of Congress, approved May 8th, 1914, known as the Smith-Lever Act.

The most considerable gifts that have come to the University are:
The original donation of 35,000 acres of public land by the State.

The donation of 660 acres of land to the University by Governor John Milledge, on which a part of the city of Athens now stands.

The Moore College building, costing $25,000, the gift of the city of Athens.

The Charles F. McCay fund, available about 1970, estimated to amount ultimately to one million dollars.

The Charles McDonald Brown fund of $50,000, the gift of Governor Joseph E. Brown, for aid of male students. This fund now amounts to $264,282.31.

The William Terrell fund of $20,000 for the support of a chair of Agricultural Chemistry.

The George R. Gilmer fund of $15,000 for the training of teachers, income from which now goes to the State Normal School.

The Library building, costing $50,000, the gift of George Foster Peabody, of New York.

The Alumni fund, amounting to nearly $60,000. This fund was secured through a canvass made from 1898 to 1901 and with the money the basement story of Memorial Hall was erected.

In 1921 another canvass was made among the alumni and friends of the University and more than one million dollars in subscriptions was secured. With this money a substantial permanent endowment will be established and a splendid building program is now being carried out.

A fund of approximately $30,000, contributed by friends of the University (1906) for the purchase of land for enlarging the campus, and an equal amount contributed subsequently.

The Alumni Library Endowment Fund, made up of gifts by various alumni and friends of the institution, now amounting to over six thousand dollars.

The Denmark Fund of $4,000, given by the late Brantley A. Denmark in memory of his son, William Starke Denmark, now amounts to $570.59.

A gift of $25,000 from the city of Athens (1908) for the development of the greater campus.

A gift of $40,000 from the Peabody Fund, for the erection of a building, to be known as the "George Peabody Hall," for the School of Education.

-A gift of $12,500 from the Phelps-Stokes Fund, for the permanent endowment of a Fellowship, now amounting to $13,224.77. This fund is open to women.

A gift of $500 by Dr. M. M. Hull ('91) for the establishment of the A. L. Hull Memorial Fund, for aiding students. This fund now amounts to $570.59.

A gift of $600 by Mr. Preston Arkwright ('90) for the same

purpose and under the same conditions as those of the Charles McDonald Brown Fund, now amounting to $926.73.

A gift of $1,000 by the family of Mr. Bert Michael (1912) for the establishment of a scholarship in the Junior class. This fund is open to women.

A gift of $500 by Messrs. Eugene Dodd ('93) and Harry Dodd ('97) for the same purpose and under the same conditions as those of the Charles McDonald Brown Fund, now amounting to $742.32.

A gift of $5,200 by Justice Joseph Henry Lumpkin ('75) for the establishment of the Joseph Henry Lumpkin Scholarship Fund, for the same purpose and under the same conditions as those of the Charles McDonald Brown Fund, now amounting to $7,744.11.

A gift by the Hon. Charles H. Brand of an annual scholarship of $150 during his life, with provision for its perpetuity, now amounting to $990.00.

A gift by Mr. F. A. Lipscomb of an annual scholarship of $200, with provision for its perpetuity, in honor of his father, who was Professor in the University from 1869 until his death in 1873, now amounting to $1,653.41.

A gift by Mrs. Bernice F. Bullard of $10,000 for the same purpose and under the same conditions as those of the Charles McDonald Brown Fund, in memory of her husband, the late Bernice F. Bullard, now amounting to $13,002.16. This fund is open to women.

A fund of approximately $30,000.000 arising from the estate of the late Brantley A. Denmark and known as the Brantley A. and Thomas N. Denmark Memorial Fund, this income being used for general maintenance.

A fund of $5,600 contributed by the Georgia Bankers' Association as a loan fund for the State College of Agriculture. This fund is open to women. An additional fund of $1,000 per annum is being contributed by the Georgia Bankers' Association to be lent to members of the Boys' and Girls' Clubs who may attend the State College of Agriculture.

Ten loan funds of $150 each for Freshmen in College of Agriculture, given by the Georgia Railway & Power Co.

A loan fund for the benefit of twenty-five Freshmen in the College of Agriculture, by the Rotary Educational Foundation.

Thomas J. and Rebecca J. Treadwell Memorial. The amount of this fund cannot as yet be stated. It is for the purpose of educating poor and deserving boys, the scholarship not to exceed $200.00 a year.

The A. F. Churchill Memorial Fund, a gift of $15.000 given by Mrs. Lois Churchill and Miss Lottie Churchill in memory of the late

Captain A. F. Churchill of Savannah, for the aid of worthy students. This fund now amounts to $16,850.00. It is open to women.

A gift of $600 each year for twenty years, given by the family of the late Captain Henry W. Brown who lost his life during the World War. These sums are cumulative and the interest is to be lent to worthy students. This fund now amounts to $3,850.08.

The Horace B. Russell Fund of $1,500, given by the late Judge Horace B. Russell, of New York. The interest provides for prizes in Psychology and Ethics.

The Daughters of the American Revolution Fund of $5,000, given by the Georgia D. A. R. as a loan fund in memory of the University of Georgia boys who fell in the World War, now amounting to $5,700.00.

An annual gift of $100 by the Elijah Clarke Chapter of the Daughters of the American Revolution, as a loan fund for girls.

The William Wilson Findley Fund of $1,000 given to the State College of Agriculture by the Southern Railway Company, the interest thereon to be lent to students residing along the lines of that Railway system.

The Students' Loan Fund, amounting to $709.58.

A gift of $2,000 from the family of Captain Joseph Brown Connally, who lost his life in the Great War. The interest is used to provide a scholarship of $100 per annum for proficiency in Georgia History.

A gift of $5,000.00 by Mrs. Nettie Elsas Phillips establishing in memory of her husband, Benjamin Z. Phillips, the Benjamin Z. Phillips Law Scholarship Fund. Loans from the income of this fund will be made to that member of the second year law class selected by the Law Faculty. This fund is open to women. It now amounts to $5,700.00.

Unless otherwise specified, income from loan funds is used for the aid of male students only.

GOVERNMENT

By an act of the General Assembly, approved August 23, 1889, the government of the University is vested in a Board of Trustees, appointed by the Governor for a term of eight years, and confirmed by the Senate. The Board consists of one member from each Congressional District of the State, four from the State at large, and three from the city of Athens, four additional members elected by the Alumni Society of the University of Georgia under the provisions of the Act of 1925, and the following are ex-officio members: the Governor of Georgia, the Chairman of the Board of Trustees of the North Georgia Agricultural College, the Chairman of the Board of Directors of the Georgia State College for Women, the President of the Commissioners of the Industrial College for Colored Youths, the Chairman of the Board of Trustees of the College of Agriculture, the Chairman of the Board of Trustees of the State Normal School, the President of the Board of Directors of the Medical College, the President of the Board of Trustees of the Georgia State Woman's College, the President of the Board of Trustees of Bowdon State Normal College, the Chairman of the Board of Trustees of the South Georgia Agricultural and Mechanical College, and the State Superintendent of Schools.

Under a special act of the General Assembly, Hon. George Foster Peabody, of New York, is a life trustee.

The immediate control and management of each of the departments of the University situated elsewhere than at Athens is entrusted (subject to general control by the University Trustees) to a "Local Board" or "Commission," of which the number of members, mode of appointment, and terms of office vary.

The University Trustees meet in stated session on the Thursday preceding the Commercement Sunday, and at other times at their pleasure.

The present organization of the board is as follows:

HIS EXCELLENCY GOV. CLIFFORD M. WALKER, Atlanta.
Ex-officio.

GEORGE E. MADDOX, Rome.
From State at Large   Term expires Aug. 13, 1931.
SANDERS McDANIEL, Atlanta,
From State at Large   Term expires Aug. 13, 1933.
WILLIAM E. SIMMONS, Lawrenceville,
From State at Large   Term expires Aug. 13, 1927.
JAMES B. NEVIN, Atlanta,
From State at Large   Term expires Aug. 13, 1929.
ALEXANDER A. LAWRENCE, Savannah,
1st Congressional District   Term expires Aug. 13, 1929.
J. ROBERT POTTLE, Albany,
2nd Congressional District   Term expires Aug. 13, 1929.
L. G. COUNCIL, Americus,
3rd Congressional District   Term expries Aug. 13, 1929.
W. C. BRADLEY, Columbus,
4th Congressional District   Term expires Aug. 13, 1927.
CLARK HOWELL, Atlanta,
5th Congressional District   Term expires Aug. 13, 1927.
LOYD CLEVELAND, Griffin.
6th Congressional District,   Term expries Aug. 13, 1927.

THE UNIVERSITY AT ATHENS

I. **Franklin College.** (The College of Arts). Chartered 1785, offering the Degree of Bachelor of Arts, and including:
1. General Courses in the Liberal Arts.
2. Special Courses.

II. **The Georgia State College of Agriculture and the Mechanic Arts.** Offering the Degree of Bachelor of Science, and including the following:
(a) In the College of Science and Engineering:
1. The General Science Course.
2. The Civil Engineering Course.
3. The Electrical Engineering Course.
4. The Pre-Medical Course.
(b) In the College of Agriculture:
5. The Full Agricultural Course.
6. The Forest Engineering Course.
7. The Veterinary Medicine Course.
8. The Course in Home Economics.
9. The Course in Physical Education.
10. The Winter Course in Agriculture.
11. The Experiment Station (at Experiment).
12. The Farmers' Institutes, and Extension Service.

III. **The School of Education.** Offering the Degree of Bachelor of Arts in Education, Bachelor of Arts in Social Science.

IV. **The School of Commerce** Offering the Degree of Bachelor of Science in Commerce.

V. **The Henry W. Grady School of Journalism.** Offering the Degree of Bachelor of Arts in Journalism.

IV. **The Graduate School.** Offering the following Degrees:
1. Master of Arts.
2. Master of Science.
3. Master of Science in Agriculture.
4. Master of Science in Forestry.
5. Master of Science in Economics.
6. Civil Engineering.
7. Master of Science in Home Economics.

VII. **The Lumpkin Law School.** Offering the Degree of Bachelor of Laws. A three years' course.

VIII. **The School of Pharmacy.** Offering the Degree of Graduate in Pharmacy. A two years' course.

IX. The University Summer School.

Six and nine weeks' sessions, embracing work in the University, the College of Agriculture and the State Normal School. Elementary, High School, College Credit and Graduate courses designed especially for teachers and college students.

I. ADMINISTRATIVE OFFICERS

DAVID CRENSHAW BARROW, LL.D.,
Chancellor Emeritus.

CHARLES MERCER SNELLING, A.M., Sc.D.,
President of Franklin College, and Acting Chancellor.

ANDREW McNAIRN SOULE, B.S.A., F.R.S.A., LL.D., Sc.D.,
President of the College of Agriculture and the Mechanic Arts.

THOMAS WALTER REED, A.M., LL.B.,
Secretary and Treasurer.

SARA COBB BAXTER,
Secretary to the Chancellor.

JULIUS TOWNSEND DUDLEY,
Secretary to the President of Franklin College.

ETHEL REESE,
Secretary to the President of the State College of Agriculture and the Mechanic Arts.

DUCHESS WILLIAMS,
Secretary to the Treasurer.

II. THE UNDERGRADUATE, GRADUATE AND PROFESSIONAL SCHOOLS

CHARLES MERCER SNELLING, A.M., Sc.D.,
Dean of the University.

ANDREW McNAIRN SOULE, B.S.A., F.R.S.A., LL.D., Sc.D.,
Dean of the College of Agriculture.

WILLIS HENRY BOCOCK, A.M., LL.D.,
Dean of the Graduate School.

THOMAS JACKSON WOOFTER, Ph.D., LL.D.,
Dean of the Peabody School of Education.

GEORGE F. GOBER, A.M., LL.D.,
President of the Lumpkin Law School.

SYLVANUS MORRIS, LL.B., LL.D.,
Dean of the Lumpkin Law School.

JOHN MOORE READE, Ph.D.,
Director of the Biological Laboratories.

ROBERT PRESTON BROOKS, Ph.D.,
Dean of the School of Commerce.

ROBERT CUMMING WILSON, Ph.G.,
Dean of the School of Pharmacy.

JAMES PHILANDER CAMPBELL. B.S.A.,
  Director of Extension.
ANNE WALLIS BRUMBY, A.B.,
  Dean of Women.
MARY ETHEL CRESWELL, B.S.H.E.,
  Director of Home Economics.

III. THE AUXILIARY DIVISIONS

DUNCAN BURNET,
  Librarian of the University.
NELL MAY REESE,
  Librarian of the College of Agriculture.
ANNIE CARLTON,
  Librarian, Memorial Hall.
JAMES EDWIN WARE, Lieutenant Colonel, U. S. A., Retired,
  Commandant of the Reserve Officers' Training Corps.
JOSEPH SPENCER STEWART, Ped.D.,
  Director of the Summer School; Inspector of High Schools.
HAROLD IRWIN REYNOLDS, A.B., M.D.,
  Surgeon to the University.
LILLIAN WYNN,
  Superintendent of the Crawford W. Long Infirmary.

OFFICERS OF INSTRUCTION

THE FACULTY

DAVID CRENSHAW BARROW, LL.D.,
  Chancellor Emeritus.
CHARLES MERCER SNELLING, A.M., Sc.D.,
  President of Franklin College and Acting Chancellor.
ANDREW McNAIRN SOULE, B.S.A., F.R.S.A., LL.D., Sc.D.,
  President of the College of Agriculture and the Mechanic Arts.

EMORY DEWITT ALEXANDER, B.S.A., M.S.A.,
  Farm Crops Specialist.
THOMAS LYNN ASBURY, B.S.A.,
  District Supervisor of County Agents.
STANLEY GEORGE BACKMAN,
  Captain Infantry, U. S. A., Assistant Professor of Military
  Science and Tactics.
DuPRE BARRETT, B.S.F.,
  Field Agent in Forestry.

DAVID FRANCIS BARROW, Ph.D.,
Professor of Mathematics.

FREDERICK WILLIAM BENNETT, B.S.A.,
Associate Professor of Dairy Husbandry.

A. LAURA E. BLACKSHEAR,
Illustrator.

WILLIS HENRY BOCOCK, A.M., LL.D.,.
Milledge Professor of Ancient Languages.

WILLIAM BRADFORD, A. B., M.D.,
Assistant State Supervisor of Agricultural Clubs.

WILLIAM EARLE BROACH, B.S.A.,
Field Agent in Agricultural Engineering.

GEORGE MARION BROADHURST, B.S.C.,
Adjunct Professor of Secretarial Studies.

CHARLES JOSEPH BROCKMAN, A.M., Ch.Eng.,
Adjunct Professor of Chemistry.

ROBERT PRESTON BROOKS, Ph.D.,
Professor of Economics and Finance.

WALTER SCOTT BROWN, B.S.A.,
District Supervisor of County Agents.

MALCOLM H. BRYAN, A.M.,
Adjunct Professor of Economics.

WALTER CLINTON BURKHART, D.V.M.,
Associate Professor of Veterinary Medicine.

THOMAS DEARBORN BURLEIGH, B.S., M.S.,
Associate Professor of Forestry.

DUNCAN BURNETT,
Librarian of the University.

SUSIE BURSON, B.S.H.E.,
Teacher in Winterville Practice School.

MATILDA CALLAWAY, B.S.H.E.,
Teacher in Childs Street Practice School.

JAMES PHILANDER CAMPBELL, B.S.A.,
Director of Extension Work.

EPSIE CAMPBELL, B.S,.
State Supervisor of Vocational Home Economics.

JAMES WILLIAM CANTRELL, A.B.,
Associate Professor of Physics.

LEONIDAS MYERS CARTER, B.S.,
Professor of Agricultural Chemistry.

CLAUD CHANCE, A.B.,
Adjunct Professor of Romance Languages.

PAUL W. CHAPMAN, B.S.A.,
State Supervisor of Vocational Agriculture.

ROSS RENFROE CHILDS, B.S.A., M.S.A.,
Professor of Agronomy, in charge of Cotton Industry.

WALTER PAGE CLARKE, B. S.,
Field Agent in Poultry Husbandry.

WYATT ARNTON CLEGG, B.S.A.
Associate Professor of Agricultural Engineering.

WILLIAM OLIN COLLINS, B.S.A.,
Associate Professor of Soil Chemistry.

WALTER GROVER CORNETT, LL.B.,
Professor of Law.

ELLIS MERTON COULTER, Ph.D.,
Professor of History.

GEORGE ARTHUR CRABB, B.S.A.,
Professor of Agronomy, in charge of Soils.

EDITH VAUGHAN CRESWELL, B.S.H.E.,
Adjunct Professor of Home Economics.

MARY ETHEL CRESWELL, B.S.H.E.,
Director of Home Economics.

FORREST CUMMING, A.M.,
Adjunct Professor of Mathematics.

GEORGE VIVIAN CUNNINGHAM, B.S.A.,
State Supervisor of Agricultural Clubs.

URIAH HARROLD DAVENPORT, B.S.,
Professor of Electrical Engineering.

LESLIE VINCENT DAVIS, B.S.A.,
Supervisor of Fertilizer Investigations.

ELLIS HOWARD DIXON, A.B., A.M.,
Adjunct Professor of Physics.

LOIS PAULINE DOWDLE, B.S.H.E.,
State Supervisor of Girls' Clubs.

JOHN ELDRIDGE DREWRY, A.B., B.J., A.M.,
Adjunct Professor of Jurnalism.

MARION DERRELLE DuBOSE, A.M.,
Associate Professor of English.

AUSTIN SOUTHWICK EDWARDS, Ph.D.,
Professor of Psychology.

LULA EDWARDS, B.S.H.E.,
District Supervisor Home Demonstration Work.

EDWIN MALLARD EVERETT, A.M.,
Instructor in Mathematics.

JOHN RICHARD FAIN, B.S., Sc.D.,
PProfessor of Agronomy and Supervisor Rehabilitation Work.

MARY FERGUSON, A.B.,
Instructor in Romance Languages.

GEORGE HENRY FIROR, B.S.A.,
  Field Agent in Horticulture.
JOHN WILLIAM FIROR, B.S.A.,
  State Agent in Marketing.
FRANK WILLIAMS FITCH, B.S.A.,
  Field Agent in Dairy Husbandry.
GLENN LOREN FULLER, B.S.,
  Soil Specialist in State Survey.
JOHN KYRGESS GILES, B.S.A.,
  Assistant Director of Extension.
GEORGE F. GOBER, A.M., LL.D.,
  Professor of Law.
ERNEST LEE GRIGGS, Graduate of V. M. I.,
  Professor of Civil Engineering and Drawing.
HARLOW WILLIAMSON HARVEY, B.S.A.,
  Specialist in Landscape Gardening.
HAROLD MILTON HECKMAN, B.S.C., A.M.,
  Professor of Accounting.
LINVILLE LAURENTINE HENDREN, Ph.D.,
  Professor of Physics and Astronomy.
THOMAS SCOTT HOLLAND, A.B.,
  Associate Professor of Romance Languages.
WILLIAM DAVIS HOOPER, A.M.,
  Professor of Latin.
JOHN A. HOSCH, B.S.C.,
  Instructor in Economic Geography.
GEORGE ALEXANDER HUTCHINSON, Ph.D.,
  Professor of Philosophy and School Administration.
NANNIE ELLA IVEY, B.S.H.E.,
  Assistant Manager College Cafeteria.
MILTON PRESTON JARNAGIN, B.S.A., Sc.D.,
  Professor of Animal Husbandry.
JOHN WILKINSON JENKINS, A.M.,
  Professor of Business Administration.
JAMES AUGUSTUS JOHNSON, B.S.A.,
  District Supervisor of County Agents.
ROBERT WALLACE JONES, D.V.M.,
  Associate Professor of Veterinary Medicine.
RUFUS LAFAYETTE KEENER, B.S.A.,
  Associate Professor of Horticulture.
CHARLES EDWARD KELLOGG, B.S.,
  Associate Professor of Animal Husbandry.
JOSEPH KRAFKA, Jr., Ph.D.,
  Professor of Zoology.

KATHERINE LANIER, B.S.H.E.,
District Supervisor Home Demonstration Agents.

JULIAN GORDON LIDDELL, B.S.A.,
Field Agent in Swine Industry.

MARION WAYNE LOWRY, B.S.A., M.A.,
Associate Professor of Soil Chemistry.

MARY ELLA LUNDAY, A.B., A.M.,
Physical Director for Women.

JOSEPH LUSTRAT, Bach. ès Lett., Officer d'Academie, Lett. D.,
Professor of Romance Languages.

SAMUEL PATTERSON LYLE, B.S., M.S.,
Professor of Agricultural Engineering.

LEO HARTLAND MARLATT,
Field Agent in Cheese Production.

SUSAN MATTHEWS, B. S.,
Food and Nutrition Specialist.

JULIAN HOWELL MILLER, B.S.A.,
Associate Professor of Botany.

FRANK ELIJAH MITCHELL, B.S.A.,
Field Agent in Poultry Husbandry.

WILLIAM ARTHUR MINOR, B.S.A.,
Farm Management Specialist.

LEILA RITCHIE MIZE, B.S.H.E.,
State Agent Home Demonstration Work.

MAYOR DENNIS MOBLEY, B.S.A.,
Associate Professor of Agricultural Education, in Charge of
Practice School.

JOHN MORRIS, A.M.,
Professor of Germanic Languages.

SYLVANUS MORRIS, LL.B., LL.D.,
Professor of Law.

JENNIE BELLE MYERS,
Social Director.

MARTHA McALPINE, A.B.,
Specialist in Parent Training.

FREEMAN CHEYNE McCLURE, A.B.,
Instructor in Romance Languages.

ROSA McGEE, B.S.H.E.,
District Supervisor Home Demonstration Work.

THOMAS HUBBARD McHATTON, B.S., Sc.D., M.Hort.,
Professor of Horticulture.

HADEN MAYO McKAY, B.S.A., M.S.A.,
Field Agent in Horticulture.

WALTER FLOY McLENDON, D.V.M.,
  Adjunct Professor of Veterinary Medicine.
JOHN HANSON THOMAS McPHERSON, Ph.D.,
  Professor of History and Political Science.
ROBERT LIGON McWHORTER, A.M.,
  Professor of English.
ROBERT LIGON McWHORTER, A.B., LL.B.,
  Professor of Law.
CATHERINE NEWTON, B.S.H.E., M.S.,
  Associate Professor of Foods and Nutrition.
IRA C. NICHOLAS, Captain Infantry, U. S. A., Assistant Professor
  of Military Science and Tactics.
JONAS GRANBURY OLIVER, B.S.A.,
  State Supervisor of County Agents.
ROBERT EMORY PARK, A.M., Litt.D.,
  Professor of English.
WILLIAM OSCAR PAYNE, A.M.,
  Professor of History.
HERMAN VICTOR PERSELLS, D.V.M.,
  Associate Professor of Veterinary Medicine.
EDWIN DAVIS PUSEY, A.M.,
  Professor of Education.
ROSALIE VIRGINIA RATHBONE, B.S.,
  Associate Professor of Clothing and Textiles.
JOHN MOORE READE, Ph.D.,
  Professor of Botany and Director of Biological Laboratories.
THOMAS WALTER REED, A. M., LL.B.,
  Registrar.
WILLIAM WALTER REITZ, M.S.,
  Associate Professor of Agricultural Education.
WALDO SILAS RICE, B.S.A.,
  Associate Professor of Animal Husbandry.
ALBERT G. G. RICHARDSON, D.V.M.,
  Professor of Veterinary Medicine.
SAMUEL LOGAN SANDERSON, A.M.,
  Instructor in English.
STEADMAN VINCENT SANFORD, A.B., Litt.D.,
  Professor of English Language and Journalism.
LESTER E. SAWYER, B.S.F.,
  Adjunct Professor of Forestry.
ALFRED WITHERSPOON SCOTT, A.B., Ph.D.,
  Associate Professor of Chemistry.
RHEA CLARKE SCOTT, B.S.,
  Associate Professor of Institutional Management.

JULIUS EUGENE SEVERIN, D. V. M.,
  Associate Professor of Veterinary Medicine.
LAFAYETTE MILES SHEFFER, B.S.,
  Associate Professor of Agricultural Education.
LOUIS IRVING SKINNER, B.S.A.,
  District Supervisor of County Agents.
W. MASON SMITH, B.S.C., M.B.A.,
  Adjunct Professor of Finance and Accounting.
LAWRENCE C. SMITH, 1st Lieut., Cavalry, U. S. A., Assistant
  Professor of Military Science and Tactics.
ROBERT MURRAY SOULE, B.S.A.,
  Associate Professor of Agricultural Chemistry.
HERMAN JAMES STEGEMAN, Ph.B.,
  Associate Professor Physical Education for Men.
ROSWELL POWELL STEPHENS, Ph.D.,
  Professor of Mathematics.
JOSEPH SPENCER STEWART, Ped.D.,
  Professor of Secondary Education.
CHARLES MORTON STRAHAN, C., and M.E., Sc.D.,
  Professor of Civil Engineering.
CHARLES WILLIAM SUMMEROUR, B.S.A.,
  Editor, College of Agriculture.
PAUL TABOR, B.S.A., M.S.A.,
  Associate Professor of Agronomy, in Charge of Farm Crops.
JAMES RALPH THAXTON, A.B.,
  Adjunct Professor of Romance Languages.
KENNETH TREANOR, B.S.A.,
  Farm Management Specialist.
RICHARD B. TRIMBLE,
  Captain, Cavalry, U. S. A., Assistant Professor of Military
  Science and Tactics.
LUCILLE TURNER, B.S.H.E.,
  District Supervisor of Home Demonstration Agents.
STEPHEN CUMMINS UPSON, LL.B.,
  Professor of Law.
ELKIN VOGT, B.S.,
  Instructor in Zoology.
JOHN DONALD WADE, Ph.D.
  Associate Professor of English.
ROOSEVELT PRUYN WALKER, A.M.,
  Professor of English.
FRANK WARD, B.S.A.,
  Pure Seed Specialist.

JAMES EDWIN WARE,
Lt. Colonel U. S. A., Retired. Professor of Military Science and Tactics.

WALTER PRESTON WARREN, A.B., LL.B.,
Assistant Registrar.

EDISON COLLINS WESTBROOK, B.S.A.,
Cotton and Tobacco Specialist.

JOHN TAYLOR WHEELER, B.S.A., M.S.,
Professor of Agricultural Education.

HENRY CLAY WHITE, Ph.D., Sc.D., D.C.L., LL.D.,
Professor of Chemistry and Terrell Professor of Agricultural Chemistry.

FREDERIC WALDO WHITNEY, Major, Calvary, U.S.A., Assistant Professor of Military Science and Tactice.

CECIL NORTON WILDER, B.S.A., M.S.A.,
Associate Professor of Agricultural Chemistry.

ROBERT CUMMING WILSON, Ph.G.,
Professor of Pharmacy.

JAMES HERBERT WOOD, B.S.A.,
Professor of Poultry Husbandry.

HAROLD OLIVER WOODWARD, B.S.A.,
Adjunct Professor of Poultry Husbandry.

THOMAS JACKSON WOOFTER, Ph.D., LL.D.,
Professor of Philosophy and Education.

Tutors

DOLAN E. BROWN, Pharmacy.
THOMAS F. GREEN, JR., Mathematics.
POPE R. HILL, Mathematics.
WALTER EDWIN SEWELL, A.B., Mathematics.
WILLIAM TATE, A.B., English.

Fellows

CHARLES H. BAKER, Commerce.
JAMES RUEY PATRICK, Education.
ROBERT T. SEGREST, Commerce.

Student Assistants

ERNEST L. GRIGGS, JR., Civil Engineering.
BUREN L. JONES Physics.
LOURA K. LEWIS, Latin.

Library Staff

SARAH LAMAR, Assistant.
LOUISE HOLLINGSWORTH, Assistant.
HAZEL PHILBRICK, Assistant.

A. H. PARHAM, Law Librarian.
C. S. FAIN, Student Assistant.
R. H. FREEMAN, Student Assistant.
MAYBELLE STITH, Student Assistant.
FLORENCE LESTER, Student Assistant.
CALLIE McWHIRTER, Student Assistant.
MARJORIE HODGSON, Student Assistant.

Other Officers

PHARES OBADIAH VANATTER, Superintendent of Field Experiments.
AMBROSE PENN WINSTON, Foreman College Farms.
CHARLES BOWDEN SWEET, Superintendent of College Green. house and Grounds.
EDGAR LEE SECREST, A. B., Secretary University Y. M. C. A.

Clerical Force

MRS. H. T. AIKEN, Vocational Home Economics.
CALLIE ANTHONY.
LOLLIE BARNETT, Home Economics.
SUE BELL, Mailing Clerk.
REBA BURKHALTER, Assistant Mailing Clerk.
ALBERTA CHURCH, Home Economics.
JESSIE MAY COMPTON, Agricultural Education.
MRS. W. F. DOBBS, Horticulture.
LUCILE EPPS, Secondary Education and Summer School.
MOZELLE JARRETT, Agricultural Extension.
ALICE JONES, Extension.
ANNE RUTH MOORE, Publicity.
ADA PATAT, Editorial and Veterinary.
WESSIE PENLAND, Audit Clerk.
WILLIE SMITH, Agronomy and Animal Husbandry.
MATTIE THOMPSON, Agronomy and Dairy.
VIRGINIA THORNTON, Extension Division.
MRS. W. C. THORNTON, Poultry Husbandry.
SAPELO TREANOR, Administration.
MRS. L. E. WOLFE, Agricultural Engineering.
MRS. OSCAR WOODY, Administration.

Part II

THE UNDERGRADUATE SCHOOLS

The College of Arts

The College of Science and Engineering

The College of Agriculture

The Peabody School of Education

The School of Commerce

A. General Information Concerning Undergraduate Schools

B. Degree Requirements

C. Subjects of Instruction

A. GENERAL INFORMATION CONCERNING UNDERGRADUATE SCHOOLS

ADMISSION

Entrance to the University may be secured (a) by examination, (b) by certificate.

Entrance by Examination

Examinations are held at the University in June and September of each year. These are in writing, and two hours are allowed to each unit upon which examination is offered. Examinations will be offered in each of the entrance subjects as requested, according to a schedule, on the last four days of the week in June preceding Commencement and the first four days of the opening week in September. All students planning to enter by examination must arrange to be present upon these dates, since other dates can be arranged only by special action of the faculty.

The applicant must pass in the required units in at least four groups of studies. Satisfactory certificates may be accepted in additional units to make 15.

Entrance by Certificate

Certificates for admission will be accepted from graduates of accredited secondary schools when made on official blanks and properly signed by the Superintendent or Principal, provided the applicant has the necessary 15 units indicated. Diplomas will not be accepted on promises to file certificates. Certificates will not be accepted for less than one year's attendance in the school issuing the certificate.

Before certifying to the work done in his school, the Principal should satisfy himself of the previous high school training of the pupil, if a part was done in another school. Subjects in which an examination has been passed for admission to the school, or for which regular certificates from recognized schools were received, may be included in the certificate, provided the official records from the school or of the examinations are given. Work done in the grammar grades or high school reviews of such work cannot count as units of high school training.

Each year notice will be sent to the Principal showing the college standing of all students who are admitted by certificate to the colleges which have adopted the University of Georgia system.

The certificate should be mailed directly to the University of Georgia, care of the Entrance Committee, by the school official authorized to sent it.   All subjects not certified should be crossed out.

Admission to the University admits only to those degrees which would be possible with the preparation offered.

CONDITIONS

Conditions in Greek, French, Spanish and German may be made up in the University in classes provided for the purpose, provided the applicant submits fifteen units for entrance. No other conditions are provided for.

UNITS

The requirements for admission are stated in terms of units.

A unit represents a year's study in any subject in a secondary school, constituting approximately a **quarter** of a full year's work. This statement is designed to afford a standard of measurement for work done in secondary schools.   It takes the four-year high school course as a basis and assumes that the length of the school year will be approvimately thirty-six weeks, that a period is at least forty minutes, and that the study is pursued four or five periods a week; but, under ordinary circumstances, a satisfactory year's work in any subject cannot be accomplished in less than one hundred and twenty sixty-minute hours, or their equivalent.   Schools organized on a different basis can, nevertheless, estimate their work in terms of this unit.   Less than forty minutes for recitations or too many subjects a day will reduce the unit value.   The subject may cover more than one year according to the pleasure of the teacher in arranging courses.   The time element counts on the certificate as well as the quantity and quality of work.   As a general rule, four units a year is as much as the average pupil can prepare adequately. Two hours in manual training or other laboratory or industrial work are equivalent to one hour in the class room.

Physical science covers about 300 minutes a week and manual training, agriculture, home economics or other industrial work about 360 minutes a week for one unit valuation.

Units Recognized by the University

Each subject named below is valued at a specific number of units if the proper time has been devoted to its preparation, but its value cannot rise above that number of units although additional time may have been given to it.

English Grammar 1, Rhetoric 1, Classics 1 or 2
American History or American History and Civil Government -- 1 unit
Ancient History (Greek and Roman) and Medieval History to Modern Times ------------------------------------ 1 unit
Modern History (General History may be counted as a unit, but not in addition to Ancient and Medieval and Modern History) ---------------------------------- 1 unit
English History -- 1 unit
Algebra (to quadratics ------------------------------------ 1 unit
Algebra (quadratics and beyond) -------------------½ or 1 unit
Geometry (Plane) -- 1 unit
Geometry (Solid) -- ½ unit
Trigonòmetry -- ½ unit
Latin --1, 2, 3 or 4 units
Greek ---1, 2 or 3 units
German -- 1 or 2 units
French --1 or 2 units
Spanish --1 or 2 units
(Not less than one unit of any foreign language will be accepted).
General Science --------------------------------------½ or 1 unit
Physics --½ or 1 unit
Chemistry -- 1 unit
Zoölogy --½ or 1 unit
Botany --½ or 1 unit
Physical Geography --------------------------------½ or 1 unit
Physiology ⎫ Any two of these
Zoölogy   ⎬ may be counted together
Botany   ⎭ as ------------------------------------ 1 unit
Biology -- 1 unit
Agriculture ---1 to 3 units
Free-hand Drawing ⎫ The Entrance Committee, may after
Manual Training   ⎬ investigating each claim, grant a
Commercial subjects ⎭ total credit not exceeding ----- 3 units
Home Economics ⎫
Music   ⎭---------------------------------1 to 3 units
For detailed information regarding the subject matter of the above units teachers should consult standard texts and bulletins on the subject.

REQUIREMENTS FOR ENTRANCE TO THE DEGREE COURSES OF THE UNIVERSITY OF GEORGIA

For unconditional admission the candidate must secure credit by examination or acceptable certificate as follows:

DEGREE	Age	English	History	Mathematics	Foreign Language	Modern Language	Elective (1)	TOTAL	R
Bachelor of Arts	16	3	2	2.5	5		2.5	15	Either 1.75 (2 Spanish, or to 3 of Latin.
Bachelor of Arts in Social Sciences	16	3	2	2.5	3		4.5	15	Latin.
Bachelor of Arts in Education	16	3	2	2.5	2*		5.5	15	Latin 3. or M
Bachelor of Journalism	16	3	2	2.5	2		5.5	15	3 Latin, or Language.
Bachelor of Science (General)	16	3	2	2.5		2	5.5	15	French or German
Bachelor of Science in C. E. or E. E.	16	3	2	2.5		2	5.5	15	French or Spanish r German
B.S. in Agriculture B. S. Forestry, D.V.M., B.S. Home Econ. B.S. Phys. Education	16	3	2	2.5			7.5	15	As many as 3 units in agricu are allowed from the District cultural Schools.
Bachelor of Science in Commerce	16	3	2	2.5	2		5.5	15	3 Latin, or 2 Modern Langu
Bachelor of Laws	18	3					12	15	Also two years in under special condit
Graduate in Pharmacy	18	3					12	15	
Bachelor of Science in Medicine	16	3	2	2.5	2		5.5	15	
Pre-Medical Course	16	3	1	2	2		7	15	1 Algebra, 1 Geome ry, 2 from s language.

ENTRANCE WITH ADVANCED STANDING

Students entering from another college or university must present an official certificate adopted by the Georgia colleges, or its equivalent, showing in detail, entrance units, college work already accomplished and honorable dismissal. This official certificate should be accompanied by a current catalogue describing the courses for which credit is sought.

Such advanced students must in general enter the University not later than the beginning of the Senior year. In determining their position in the University, however, the value of the work done at such college, as well as the work offered for entrance at that college, will be measured by University standards. No credit will be allowed for courses not offered at the University.

No advanced credit, except by examination, will be given for work done at any institution not offering two full years work beyond the standard four-year high school work, or for work done at any institution in a course to which students are admitted who have not completed the equivalent of 15 high school entrance units.

A student admitted to advanced standing with a low record at previous institutions or who fails to maintain his advanced work may be required to repeat a course in the discretion of the professor.

Correspondence with reference to credits for advanced standing should be addressed to Committee on Advanced Credits, L. L. Hendren, Chairman.

SPECIAL STUDENTS

Sometimes a person of mature years, not a candidate for a degree, but with a definite aim or for purposes of general culture, desires to take a course in the University without meeting the full entrance requirements. Such special students may be admitted under the following conditions: (a) they must be not less than twenty years of age; (b) they will not be admitted to classes for which entrance examinations are required, unless they pass such examination; (c) they must give evidence of adequate preparation for the courses sought, to the individual professor in charge; (d) their names are printed separately in the catalogue. Students not less than eighteen years of age may be accepted as special students in the School of Forestry, upon the recommendation of the professor in charge.

An application for admission as a special student should be addressed to the Entrance Committee on a blank furnished by the Committee.

Should a student admitted as a special student become a candidate for a degree, he will be required to satisfy the full fifteen units of entrance requirement.

SHORT COURSES

Students taking the short courses in Agriculture, Horticulture, and Dairying are exempt from the entrance requirements.

ADMISSION TO LAW SCHOOL

Requirements for admission to the first year class include two years of college work. A student twenty-one years of age, who is partly deficient in literary work will be allowed to make this up. This being a state institution the trustees no not think it right to refuse admission to mature students who are qualified to pursue the couse. The curriculum is as high as that of any other school and will be so maintained; it is higher than that of many others.

ADMISSION TO THE GRADUATE SCHOOL

Admission to the Graduate School is granted to graduates of colleges of good standing. Other persons of suitable age and attainments may also be admitted by special permission of the Committee on Graduate Courses. Admission to the Graduate School does not necessarily involve admission to candidacy for a degree. Application for admission should be made by correspondence or at the office of the Dean of the Graduate School.

A student who is in any wise doubtful as to his eligibility for admission to the Graduate School, previously to his coming to Athens, should correspond with the Dean of the Graduate School.

METHODS OF ENTRANCE

Note All applicants must have been successfully vaccinated or must be vaccinated before they register.

Freshman Week. Plans are under way for the inauguration of Freshman Week at the opening of the University in September. These plans will necessarily change the announcements herein as to the time students shall report for registration, the time for entrance examinations, and the like. A supplement to these announcements will be attached to each copy of this catalogue before it is mailed out and special attention is called thereto.

Entrance Following Examination. Those who plan to enter by examination will receive entrance cards from the Entrance Committee in the Faculty Room, Academic Building, as soon as they have made the necessary units.

Entrance in Advance. Applicants planning to enter by certificate will be saved much trouble and annoyance and possible delay by having *their certificates mailed by the Principal of the school in advance* to the Entrance Committee as soon as they have decided to make application. All preliminary adjustments can be made by correspondence, at the close of which the successful applicant will need merely to present his entrance card to the Dean of the College or department in which he wishes to enroll.

Entrance on Registration Days. All new students, whether they have filed certificates or wish to take the examinations, will report to the Entrance Committee in the Faculty Room, Academic Building. As soon as the entrance requirements are met, entrance cards will be issued, which the applicant will present to the proper Dean for registration. Applicants are not admitted on "probation" or "trial," or on "the promise of certificates later," or on "diplomas" or general "letters of commendation." They must stand the examinations or submit the official certificates. Applicants from a distance should, before coming to the University, await assurance that their credentials will be accepted and are sufficient for admission.

SCHOLARSHIP AND LOAN FUNDS

(Unless otherwise specified all loan and scholarship funds are open to males only).

Charles McDonald Brown Scholarship Fund. This endowment was established in 1881, by the Hon. Joseph E. Brown, ex-Governor of Georgia, in memory of his son, of the class of 1878, for the purpose of aiding young men in defraying the expenses of their education. The interest on this fund is lent to worthy young men on condition that they obligate themselves to return it with four per cent interest. Young men who are preparing for the ministry are required to return but one-half of the amount borrowed, with interest.

The colleges participating in the benefits of this fund are: the colleges at Athens, (including the Law Department), the Medical College at Augusta, and the North Georgia Agricultural College at Dahlonega.

A special circular of information concerning the fund and blank forms of application will be supplied on request. Applications for loans from this fund must be made on these forms and must be in the hands of the Chancellor by June 1st. The grants are made in June by the Board of Trustees. Only $100.00 a year, in ten monthly installments, is allowed a borrowing student.

The Honor Graduate of an Accredited High School, on presentation of an official certificate by the Principal, is awarded a scholarship at the University for one year in the Academic courses. This exempts him from the payment of matriculation fee.

Exemption from matriculation fee for one member of the Citizens Military Training Camp of this area.

The Bert Michael Scholarship. Sixty dollars a year, the income of a fund given by the family of the late Bert Michael, of the class of 1912, to be given to a member of the Junior class, selected by a committee of the Faculty. Open tomales and females.

The Arkwright Fund. The income of a fund given by Preston S. Arkwright, to be lent on the same terms as the Charles McDonald Brown Scholarship Fund.

The Joseph Henry Lumpkin Scholarship Fund. The income of a fund given by Joseph Henry Lumpkin, to be lent on the same terms as the Charles McDonald Brown Scholarship Fund.

The Dodd Fund. The income of a fund given by Eugene and Harry Dodd, to be lent on the same terms as the Charles McDonald Brown Scholarship Fund.

The Brand Fund. The sum of $150.00 a year, during the life of Hon. C. H. Brand, with provision for perpetuity.

The Lipscomb Fund. The sum of $200.00 a year, during the life of Mr. Frank A. Lipscomb, with provisions for perpetuity.

The Daughters of the American Revolution. The income of a fund of $5,000 given by the Georgia Division of the Daughters of the American Revolution, to be lent on the same terms as the Charles McDonald Brown Scholarship Fund.

The Joe Brown Connally Scholarship in Georgia History. In 1922 the family of Captain Joe Brown Connally, a graduate of the University who lost his life in the Great War, established in his memory a permanent scholarship to be awarded at every Commencement to a member of the Junior class for proficiency in Georgia History. The scholarship yields $100 annually.

The Elijah Clarke D. A. R. Scholarship. One hundred dollars per annum to be lent some worthy young woman student.

The Bernice F. Bullard Fund. The income of a fund of $10,000 given by Mrs. Bullard in memory of her husband, the late Bernice F. Bullard of Savannah, Georgia, to be lent on the same terms as the Charles McDonald Brown Fund, except that this fund is open to women.

Thomas J. and Rebecca J. Treadwell Memorial. The amount of this fund cannot as yet be stated. It is for the purpose of educating poor and deserving boys—the scholarship is not to exceed $200 a year.

Aaron F. Churchill Fund. Mrs. Lois Churchill and Miss Lottie Churchill gave in 1922 to the University of Georgia the sum of $15,000 as a memorial to the late Captain A. F. Churchill of Savannah. The interest from this fund is to be lent to worthy students, male or female.

Henry W. Brown Fund. The Henry W. Brown memorial fund consists of annual payments of $600.00 for twenty years by the family of the late Captain Brown who lost his life during the World

War. These sums are cumulative and the interest is to be lent to worthy students.

The Georgia Bankers' Association has established a student loan fund. For some time this fund was administered by the Agricultural Committee of the Bankers' Association. Since the beginning of the Collegiate year 1921-22, this fund has been in the hands of the Board of Trustees of the Agricultural College as a trust fund. Application, therefore, should be made to President Soule not later than May 1st and the application should be endorsed by a local banker. There are certain rules and regulations that the Georgia Bankers' Association has requested be observed in making these loans, that will be furnished the applicant. Open to males and females.

The Georgia Bankers' Association also contributes the sum of one thousand dollars per annum to provide loans to members of the Boys' and Girls' Clubs of the State College of Agriculture, under certain rules as to appointment.

William Wilson Findley Foundation. The Southern Railway Company has given the sum of $1,000 to be known as the Southern Railway Loan Fund, William Wilson Findley Foundation, in the Georgia State College of Agriculture. This fund is to be administered on the principle of the Brown fund and the Georgia Bankers' Association fund. Naturally, only one appointment can be made under this foundation for the college year 1926-1927. The only restriction placed upon this fund is that students benefiting by it live in counties traversed by the Southern Railway, Augusta Southern, Tallulah Falls Railway, Georgia Southern and Florida Railway, Macon and Birmingham Railway, or Hawkinsville and Florida Southern Railway.

A loan of $100 will be made each year for ten years by the Atlanta Union Stockyards to the most deserving student making the highest average in all livestock subjects for the first three years in the College of Agriculture.

Twelve hundred and fifty scholarships valued at $15 each to Boys' Short Course at Camp Wilkins in the summer of 1926.

Five hundred and twenty-five scholarships valued at $15 each to Girls' Short Course at Camp Wilkins in the summer of 1926.

These short course scholarships are given by the Georgia Bankers' Association, the Southeastern Fair, by various railroads, boards of trade, chambers of commerce, women's clubs, patriotic citizens and boys' clubs.

Ten loan funds of $150 each have been given by the Georgia Railway and Power Company for the benefit of Freshmen.

A loan fund for the benefit of twenty-five members of the Freshman class has been established by the Rotary Educational Foundation.

A scholarship of $400 will be awarded to the boy fulfilling the entrance requirements of the college who produces the largest yield of corn on an acre using nitrate of soda as the sole source of ammonia. Offered by the Chilean Nitrate of Soda Company.

Junior Scholarship—$75 in gold to the student showing the greatest proficiency in all agricultural subjects for the college year 1926-1927.

Sophomore Scholarship—$60 in gold to the student showing the greatest proficiency in all agricultural subjects for the college year 1926-1927.

Freshman Scholarship—$40 in gold to the student showing the greatest proficiency in all agricultural subjects for the college year 1926-1927.

The Phelps-Stokes Fellowship

This fellowship has been endowed under the following resolutions of the Trustees of the Phelps-Stokes Fund:

"Whereas, Miss Caroline Phelps-Stokes in establishing the Phelps-Stokes Fund was especially solicitous to assist in improving the condition of the negro, and

Whereas, It is the conviction of the Trustees that one of the best methods of forwarding this purpose is to provide means to enable southern youth of broad sympathies to make a scientific study of the negro and his adjustment to American civilization:

"Resolved, That twelve thousand five hundred dollars ($12,500) be given to the University of Georgia for the permanent endowment of a research fellowship, on the following conditions.

"1· The University shall appoint annually a fellow in Sociology, for the study of the Negro. He shall pursue advanced studies under the direction of the Departments of Sociology, Economics, Education or History, as may be determined in each case by the Chancellor. The Fellowship shall yield $500, and shall, after four years, be restricted to graduate students.

"2. Each Fellow shall prepare a paper or· thesis embodying the result of his investigation, which shall be published by the University with assistance from the income of the fund, any surplus remaining being applicable to other objects incident to the main purpose of the Fellowship. A copy of these resolutions shall be incorporated in every publication issued under this foundation.

"The right to make all necessary regulations, not inconsistent with the spirit and letter of these resolutions is given to the Chancellor and Faculty, but no changes in the conditions of the foundation can be made without the mutual consent of both the Trustees of the University and of the Phelps-Stokes Fund.''

OPPORTUNITIES FOR SELF-HELP

A considerable number of students secure remunerative employment to aid them in their education. Usually the students of Agriculture are able to secure work on the farm for which they are paid. In a few instances other departments need the services of students. Usually these places go to those who have been in attendance for some time, and who are known to be willing, capable, and trustworthy. The University does not assume any responsibility whatever in this matter. As a matter of accommodation the committee on Self-Help coöperate as far as possible with students. The Y. M. C. A. offers its services in helping young men to secure employment. Very much depends, however, on the individual's power of initiative. Students should not come to the University expecting others to find places for them.

It seems necessary to warn students on this subject. The average young man cannot ordinarily do much more than earn his living when he has nothing else to do. To earn a living and at the same time carry the work of a college course planned to occupy a student's full time is more than most students can accomplish. In a few instances they have succeeded, but as a rule students who attempt more than partial self-support should expect to lengthen their term of study.

HONORS AND APPOINTMENTS

Sophomore Declaimers. In April of each year ten members of the Sophomore class are selected to compete for a declamation prize. The contest is held in May.

Junior Speakers. Six members of the Junior class are selected on the basis of original speeches to represent the class in exercises held at the chapel in May.

Senior Speakers. The Senior class is represented on Commencement Day by two orators, the selection being made on the merits of original speeches. No student who fails to receive his degree may appear among the speakers.

Speakers from the Lumpkin Law School. Two members of the Lumpkin Law School are selected by the Faculty to represent that school on Commencement Day.

Valedictorian At the regular Faculty meeting, on Monday before the third Wednesday in May, the Faculty nominates not more than five members of the Senior class who stand first in scholarship. The names are submitted in alphabetical order to the Sneior class. and they elect from them a valedictorian, with the understanding that he shall maintain his standing in scholarship, but need not be the first honor man.

No student is allowed to appear at Commencement either as speaker or declaimer who is not a member in good and full standing of one of the literary societies, and who has not taken instruction in declamation in this or some other institution—in either event to the satisfaction of the Professor of Englsh.

The Debaters' Medals. Six gold medals are offered by the Board of Trustees, to be awarded as prizes to members of the Freshman and Sophomore classes for excellence in debating. A medal is awarded to each of the debaters representing the Literary Society which. wins a debate.

The Ready Writers' Medal. To encourage the art of composition the Board of Trustees award a gold medal for the best essay written by any student of the University upon a theme announced after the competitors enter the room.

The Wilcox Prize. Two prizes, in French and German, of $50.00 (gold) each, have been offered for competition in the Senior class in French and in German. These prizes were founded in 1896 as a memorial to their lamented father, by the sons of the late Prof. Cyprian Porter Wilcox, A.M., LL.D., who, from 1872 until his death in 1895, filled with great distinction the chair of Modern Languages in the University. In 1918 the prize in German was discontinued.

The Freshman Prize. The "Hamilton McWhorter Prize," as of the class of 1875, for general excellence in the Freshman class, is awarded to the member of that class who stands first in scholarship.

The Bryan Prize. The Hon. W. J. Bryan gave the sum of two hundred and fifty dollars, the income of which is given annually as a prize to the writer of the best essay on our form of government.

The Philosophy Prize. Two prizes of fifty dollars each were founded in 1902 by Judge Horace Russell, of New York. These prizes, named by the Board of Trustees the "Horace Russell Prize in Psychology," and the "Walter B. Hill Prize in Ethics," are awarded to the writers of the best essay on subjects assigned by the Professors of Philosophy and Psychology.

The Military Prize. A prize is annually awarded to the best drilled member of the R. O. T. C. in a competition held during Commencement.

The R. E. Park, Jr., Prize. Prof. R. E. Park offers a gold medal for the best oration by a member of the Junior class.

The L. H. Charbonnier Prize. Twenty-five dollars in gold is offered by Mrs. Jas. F. McGowan, of Augusta, in honor of her father, who for more than thirty years served the University with distinction as Professor of Engineering, Commandant of Cadets and Professor of Physics and Astronomy. The prize will be given to the member of the graduating class whose record in the School of Physics has been most creditable.

Trustees' Prize—$25 in gold from the Board of Trustees to the student writing the best essay on "Development Programme for Georgia."

Alpha Zeta Prizes. A gold medal given by the Georgia Chapter of the Alpha Zeta Fraternity to the members of the Freshman Agricultural class making the best record in all required subjects.

A gold medal to the member of the Sophomore Agricultural class making the best record in all required subjects.

$10 in gold given by H. G. Hastings & Company to the student writing the best essay on "The Economic Importance of the Home Garden."

$10 in gold given by H. G. Hastings & Company to the student writing the best essay on "Relative Value of Prolific and Single-eared Types of Corn on Upland Soil."

The **Georgia Cracker** Poetry Prize of $25 is offered by that magazine for the best poem written by an undergraduate.

The **Georgia Cracker** Short Story Prize of $25 is offered by that magazine for the best short story written by an undergraduate.

Mu Beta Chapter of Chi Omega Sorority offers a prize of twenty dollars to the woman student of the University of Georgia who has the highest scholarship average. A student must be taking fifteen hours of college work in order to be eligible for this prize.

The **Alpha Mu honorary** society offers a prize of fifteen dollars to the home economics student making the highest scholastic average. A student must be taking fifteen hours of college work to be eligible for the prize.

B. DEGREE REQUIREMENTS

FRANKLIN COLLEGE—The College of Arts

This is the original foundation, chartered in 1785, and named in honor of Benjamin Franklin. It has become merged with the general organization, giving the courses in liberal arts and participating also in the instruction of graduate students.

BACHELOR OF ARTS
REQUIREMENTS FOR THE DEGREE

Freshman

	Hrs.
English 1 _ _ _ _ _ _ _ _	3
Greek 1, or French 1, or German 1, or Spanish 1 _ _ _ _	3
History 22, 3 _ _ _ _ _ _ _	3
Latin 1 _ _ _ _ _ _ _ _ _	3
Mathematics 1, 2 _ _ _ _ _ _	3
	15

Sophomore

	Hrs.
English 2, or Psychology 1, 2, 3 _ _ _ _ _ _ _ _ _	3
Greek 2, or French 2, or German 2, or Spanish 2 _ _ _ _	3
History 2 or 4 _ _ _ _ _ _ _	3
Latin 2 _ _ _ _ _ _ _ _ _ _	3
Mathematics 3, 4, or Physics 2 _ _ _ _ _ _ _ _ _ _	3 or 4
Military Science or Elective _	3
	18 or 19

The three hour credit for Military Science which may be elected in the Sophomore year is based on completion of all the Military Science prescribed for Freshmen and Sophomores.

JUNIOR

Required

	Hrs.
Group I—One Course	
English Language 1 _ _ _ _ _	3
French 20 _ _ _ _ _ _ _ _ _	3
German 20 _ _ _ _ _ _ _ _	3
Spanish 20 _ _ _ _ _ _ _ _	3
Greek 20 or 3 _ _ _ _ _ _ _	3
Latin 3 _ _ _ _ _ _ _ _ _	3
Group II—One Course	
History 4; 5-6 _ _ _ _ _ _ _	3
Commerce 5 _ _ _ _ _ _ _ _	3
Philosophy 3-4-5, 3-4-6 _ _ _	3
Psychology 1, 2-3 _ _ _ _ _	3
Sociology 5-6-7; 9 _ _ _ _ _	3

Electives

	Hrs.
Any course in Group I not taken as required course _	3
Any course in Group II not taken as required course _	3
One course in Group III not taken as required course _ _ _ _ _ _ _ _	3 or 4
Astronomy 1-2 _ _ _ _ _ _ _	3
Commerce 6, 26, 34, 51, 60, 80 _ _ _ _ _ _ _ _ _ _	3
Education 1-2-3; 7-8-9; 10-11-12; 14 _ _ _ _ _ _ _	3
English 3; 4; 5; 6; 9; 11; 12; 13 _ _ _ _ _ _ _ _ _ _	3

Group III—Two Courses

Math. 3-4 or Physics 2
(must be taken) _ _ 3 or 4
Botany 3 _ _ _ _ _ _ _ _ 4
Zoölogy 31 _ _ _ _ _ _ _ _ 4
Chemistry 2; 21 _ _ _ _ 3 or 4
Physics 4 _ _ _ _ _ _ _ _ 4
Psychology 7-8-9 and 71, 81,
91 _ _ _ _ _ _ _ _ _ _ _ 4

English Language _ _ _ _ _ 3
French* _ _ _ _ _ _ _ _ _ 3
German* _ _ _ _ _ _ _ _ _ 3
Greek* _ _ _ _ _ _ _ _ _ _ 3
Greek and European Litera-
ture _ _ _ _ _ _ _ _ _ 3
History or Political Science
5-6; 8-9; 10-15 or 13-14;
11-12 _ _ _ _ _ _ _ _ _ 3
Italian* _ _ _ _ _ _ _ _ _ 3
Journalism 1; 4-8-9; 7 _ _ _ _ 3
Law* _ _ _ _ _ _ _ _ _ _ 6
Mathematics 5; 6-11 and any
two of 7; 8; 9 _ _ _ _ _ _ 3
Military Science* _ _ _ _ _ 3
Psychology 4-5-6; 17-18-19 _ 3
Spanish* _ _ _ _ _ _ _ _ _ 3

SENIOR

Required

Hrs.

Group I—One Course
English Language 1 _ _ _ _ _
French 21 _ _ _ _ _ _ _ _
German 21 _ _ _ _ _ _ _ _
Greek 3 or 4 or 21 _ _ _ _ _
Spanish 21 _ _ _ _ _ _ _ _
Latin 4 _ _ _ _ _ _ _ _ _ 3
Group II—One Course
Commerce 5 _ _ _ _ _ _ _ _
History 8-9 _ _ _ _ _ _ _ _ 3
History 10-15 or 13-14 _ _ _ 3
Political Science 11-12 _ _ _ 3
Philosophy 3-4-5; 7 _ _ _ _ _ 3
Sociology 5-6-7; 9; 19 _ _ _ 3
Group III—One Course
Botany 3; 4; 5; 6; 9; 11 _3 or 4
Chemistry 2; 3; 4; 5; 8 _ 3 or 4
Physics 4; 5; 6 _ _ _ _ 3 or 4
Psychology 7-8-9 and 71, 81,
91 _ _ _ _ _ _ _ _ _ _ _ 4
Psychology 10-11-12 _ _ _ _ 4
Zoölogy 31; 4 _ _ _ _ _ _ _ 4

Electives

Any course in Group I not
taken as required course _ _ 3
Any course in Group II not
taken as required course _ _ 3
Any course in Group III not
in same department as re-
quired course taken _ 3 or 4
Astronomy 1-2 _ _ _ _ _ _ _ 3
Commerce 6, 26, 34, 51, 60,
80 _ _ _ _ _ _ _ _ _ _ _ 3
Education 1-2-3; 7-8-9; 10-
11-12; 14 _ _ _ _ _ _ _ _ 3
English 3; 4; 5; 6; 9; 11; 12;
13 _ _ _ _ _ _ _ _ _ _ _ 3
English Language _ _ _ _ _ _ 3
French* _ _ _ _ _ _ _ _ _ _ 3
German* _ _ _ _ _ _ _ _ _ 3
Greek* _ _ _ _ _ _ _ _ _ _ 3
Greek and European Litera-
ture _ _ _ _ _ _ _ _ _ _ 3
History or Political Science,
5-6; 8-9; 10-15 or 13-14;
11-12 _ _ _ _ _ _ _ _ _ 3
Italian* _ _ _ _ _ _ _ _ _ 3
Journalism 1; 4-8-9; 7 _ _ _ 3
Law* _ _ _ _ _ _ _ _ _ _ 6
Mathematics 5; 6-11; any two
of 7; 8; 9 _ _ _ _ _ _ _ _ 3
Military Science _ _ _ _ _ _ 3
Psychology 4-5-6; 17-18-19 _ 3
Spanish* _ _ _ _ _ _ _ _ _ 3

Electives to complete the requirement of not less than sixty-six hours for those taking Greek or sixty-nine hours for those not taking Greek must be taken. Not more than one course may be taken as electives in any subject during one collegiate year, except that two courses in Education may be taken as electives one year and one course in Education as an elective the other year, and not more than three courses may be taken as electives in Psychology, Philosophy, Sociology and Education during any two collegiate years.

The requirements for the State Professional Certificate for teachers include at least nine hours of courses in Education.

*Any French, German, Greek, Italian, Latin or Spanish course offered in the University may be taken as a general elective. Not more than one X course may be counted for a degree.

*Advanced Military Science may be taken on recommendation of the Professor of Military Science and Tactics and with the approval of the Curriculum Committee. Credit of not more than three hours each for Junior and Senior years.

*Six hours of academic credit are allowed for studies in the Law School taken in the Junior or Senior year. The Law course designated are: Law I, consisting of (1) Elementary Law, (a) Blackstone 1, 2, 3; (b) American Elementary Law; (2) Torts; (3) Criminal Law.

No course of less than three hours can be used as an elective to satisfy the requirements of this degree.

BACHELOR OF ARTS IN THE SOCIAL SCIENCES

Requirements for the Degree

English, 3 hours; Latin, 3 hours; Mathematics, 3 hours; additional foreign language, 6 hours; natural sciences, 6 hours in two; and with majors and minors distributed as follows:

I. With major in Philosophical-Social Science: in history-political science, 9 hours; in philosophical-social science, 12 hours. Or,

II. With major in History-Political Science: in philosophical social science, 9 hours; in economics, 3 hours; in history-political science, 12 hours.

Electives must then complete a minimum total of 69 hours with 69 points of quality credit, or 66 hours with 66 points when Greek is taken as the elective language.

With the major in Philosophical-Social Science, the courses must be selected under the direction and with the approval of the Dean of the School of Education.

With the major in History-Political Science, the courses must be selected under the direction and with the approval of the head of the department of History and Political Science.

Men must satisfy the military requirements and women must meet the requirements in health education.

Note—For the teacher's college State Professional Certificate 9 hours in education are required. See School of Education.

BACHELOR OF ARTS IN EDUCATION

Requirements for the Degree

A statement of the requirements for this degree will be found under "The Peabody School of Education," page 64.

THE COLLEGE OF SCIENCE AND ENGINEERING

The College of Agriculture and the Mechanic Arts was established in 1872, from the proceeds of the quota of the landscrip funds assigned to this state under the Morrill Bill. In accordance with the act of Congress, the "leading object" in this college is, "without excluding the scientific and classical studies, and including military tactics, to teach such branches of learning as are related to agriculture and the mechanic arts." In 1906 the Legislature appointed a separate Board of Trustees charged with especial oversight of the College of Agriculture, and the institution was organized with two departments, the College of Science and Engineering and the College of Agriculture, the President of the College also being made the Dean of the College of Agriculture. Each remains an integral part of the University organization.

In this College but one degree is given, that of Bachelor of Science. It is believed that this degree should be, in all cases, the certificate of satisfactory completion of a proper course of mental training which, although given by divers arrangements of studies, should be equally severe and, therefore, without discrimination as to title.

The undergraduate degrees offered by the College of Science and Engineering are: Bachelor of Science (General); Bachelor of Science (Civil Engineering); Bachelor of Science (Electrical Engineering); Bachelor of Science (Architecture); Bachelor of Science (Commerce); Bachelor of Science (Medicine).

General provision, applicable to all courses and classes: In all Science or Engineering courses laboratory work (two hours for one) may be substituted for lecture or recitation hours, at the option of the professor.

BACHELOR OF SCIENCE (General)

Freshman

	Hrs.
Mathematics 1-2	3
English 1	3
Latin 1 or French 1 or German 1 or Spanish 1	3
Physics 1	3
Graphics 12	2
History 3	1
Total	15

Sophomore

	Hrs.
History 2 or 4	3
Mathematics 3-4	3
Latin 2 or French 2 or German 2 or Spanish 2	3
Any two of Chemistry 21; Chemistry 22; Zoölogy 31; Zoölogy 32; Botany 3; Physics 4	8 or 9 or 10
Military Science or Elective	3
Total	20, or 21 or 22

The three hours credit for Military Science given in the Sophomore year is based on the completion of all the Military Science prescribed for Freshmen and Sophomores.

The student must select one science department from the Sophomore group (Mathematics, Physics, Chemistry, Zoölogy, Botany), in which to take his major course. This consists of three courses totalling not less than nine hours in the same department, exclusive of Freshman courses, preferably begun in the Sophomore year and continued through Junior and Senior years, but in some departments a major may be completed in two years by taking two courses in the same year.

Selection of the major must be made (not later than the beginning of the Junior year and preferably earlier) after consultation with the head of the department chosen, who thereupon becomes the official advisor of the student and must approve the selection of all his other subjects.

The total science group requirements in the Sophomore, Junior and Senior years are seven courses, totalling not less than twenty-three hours. After a student has selected his major course, of the remaining four required courses, not more than two shall be from the same department.

Of the total science group requirements from the Sophomore, Junior and Senior years at least one course must be selected from the department of Chemistry and one course from either the department of Botany or the department of Zoölogy.

JUNIOR

Required

	Hrs.
Group I—Two Courses	
Botany 3; 4; 5; 6; 9; 11	3 or 4
Chemistry 3; 31; 4; 5; 8; 21	3 or 4
Mathematics 5; 6-11	3
Physics 4; 5	4
Psychology 7, 8, 9 and 71, 81, 91	4
Zoölogy 1-2; 31; 4; 5	3 or 4
Astronomy 1-2	3
Group II—One Course	
English Language 1	3
French 20	3
German 20	3
Spanish 20	3
Group III—One Course	
Commerce 5, 6, 26, 30-31, 51, 75	3
*English 2; 3; 4; 5; 6; 9; 11; 12; 13	3

Elective

General electives from any course offered in the University to complete the requirement of not less than sixty-nine hours.

Not more than one X course may be counted for a degree.

Advanced Military Science may be taken on recommendation of the Professor of Military Science and Tactics and with the approval of the Curriculum Committee. Credit of not more than three hours each for Junior and Senior years.

Six hours of academic credit are allowed for studies in the Law School taken in the Junior or Senior year. The law course designated is: Law 1, consisting of (1) Elementary Law, (a) Blackstone 1, 2, 3; (b) Ameri-

History 4; 5-6; 8-9 _ _ _ _ _ _
Sociology 5-6-7 _ _ _ _ _ _ _ 3

can Elementary Law; (2) Torts; (3) Criminal Law.

No course of less than three hours can be used as an elective to satisfy the requirements of this degree.

SENIOR

Required

Hrs.

Group I—Two Courses
Botany 3; 4; 5; 6; 9; 11 3 or 4
Chemistry 3; 4; 5; 8; 9; _ 3 or 4
Mathematics 5 or any two or
7; 8; 9 _ _ _ _ _ _ _ _ _ _ 3
Physics 4; 5; 6 _ _ _ _ _ 3 or 4
Psychology 10-11-12 _ _ _ _ 4
Zoölogy 31; 4; 5 _ _ _ _ _ _ 4
Astronomy 1-2 _ _ _ _ _ _ _ 3
Group II—One Course
English Language 2 _ _ _ _ _ 3
French 21 _ _ _ _ _ _ _ _ _ 3
German 21 _ _ _ _ _ _ _ _ _ 3
Spanish 21 _ _ _ _ _ _ _ _ _ 3
Group III—One Course
Commerce 5, 6, 26, 34, 51,
60, 80 _ _ _ _ _ _ _ _ _ 3
Education 1-2-3; 4-5-6; 10-11-
12 _ _ _ _ _ _ _ _ _ _ _ 3
*English 3; 4; 5; 6; 9; 11;
12; 13 _ _ _ _ _ _ _ _ _ _ 3
History 5-6; 8-9; 10-15; 13-
14 _ _ _ _ _ _ _ _ _ _ _ 3
Political Science 11-12 _ _ _ 3
Philosophy 3-4-5; 3-4-6, 7 _ _ 3
Psychology 1-2-3 _ _ _ _ _ _ 3
Sociology 5-6-7; 9, 10 _ _ _ _ 3

Elective

General electives from any course offered in the University to complete the requirement of not less than sixty-nine hours.

Not more than one X course may be counted for a degree.

Advanced Military Science may be taken on recommendation of the Professor of Military Science and Tactics and with the approval of the Curriculum Committee. Credit of not more than three hours each for Junior and Senior years.

Six hours of academic credit are allowed for studies in the Law School taken in the Junior or Senior year. The Law course designated is: Law 1, consisting of (1) Elementary Law, (a) Blackstone 1, 2, 3; (b) American Elementary Law; (2) Torts; (3) Criminal Law.

No course of less than three hours can be used as an elective to satisfy the requirements of this degree.

BACHELOR OF SCIENCE (Civil Engineering)

The degree of Bachelor of Science in Civil Engineering is given on completion of the four years course outlined below. The studies required have been chosen so that the student will receive a sound, broad mental development in addition to his special knowledge of engineering. The instruction in engineering subjects includes a large amount of field practice and office drafting and computation. Thorough application of principles to designing, laying out, and erecting engineering structures is required.

---

* In addition to the three hours of English required in Freshman year, a student must elect in either Junior or Senior year a three hours course in English.

Freshman

	Hrs.
Graphics 12 _ _ _ _ _ _ _ _	2
English 1 _ _ _ _ _ _ _ _ _	3
Mathematics 1, 2 _ _ _ _ _ _	3
Physics 2-3 _ _ _ _ _ _ _ _	5
French X or 1 ⎫	
German X or 1 ⎬ one_ _ _ _	3
Spanish X or 1 ⎭	

16

Sophomore

	Hrs.
Civil Engineering 1 _ _ _ _ _	3
Graphics 14 _ _ _ _ _ _ _ _	2
Mathematics 3, 4 _ _ _ _ _ _	3
Physics 4 _ _ _ _ _ _ _ _ _	4
Chemistry 21 or 22 _ _ 4 or 5	
French 1 or 2 ⎫	
German 1 or 2 ⎬ one _ _ _ _	3
Spanish 1 or 2 ⎭	

19 or 20

See note under Electrical Engineering.

Junior

	Hrs.
Chemistry 4 _ _ _ _ _ _ _ _	3
Civ. Eng. 2, 3, and 4 _ _ _ _ _	6
Graphics 15 _ _ _ _ _ _ _ _	2
Electrical Engineering 1 _ _ _	4
Mathematics 5 _ _ _ _ _ _ _	3

18

Senior

	Hrs.
Astronomy 1 _ _ _ _ _ _ _	1½
Geology _ _ _ _ _ _ _ _ _	1½
Civil Eng. 5-6, 7-8 _ _ _ _ _	6
Graphics 16 _ _ _ _ _ _ _ _	2
Electrical Engineering 3 _ _	4
Mathematics 7-9 or Civil	
Engineering 9 _ _ _ _ _	3

18

BACHELOR OF SCIENCE (Architectural Engineering)

Freshman

	Hrs.
Graphics 12 _ _ _ _ _ _ _ _	2
English 1 _ _ _ _ _ _ _ _ _	3
Mathematics 1, 2 _ _ _ _ _ _	3
Physics 2-3 _ _ _ _ _ _ _ _	5
French X or 1 ⎫	
German X or 1 ⎬ one_ _ _ _	3
Spanish X or 1 ⎭	

16

Sophomore

	Hrs.
Civil Engineering 1 _ _ _ _ _	3
Graphics 14 _ _ _ _ _ _ _ _	2
Mathematics 3, 4 _ _ _ _ _ _	3
Physics 4 _ _ _ _ _ _ _ _ _	4
Chemistry 21 or 22 _ _ 4 or 5	
French 1 or 2 ⎫	
German 1 or 2 ⎬ one _ _ _ _	3
Spanish 1 or 2 ⎭	

19 or 20

See note under Electrical Engineering.

Junior

	Hrs.
Chemistry 4, 5, or 8 _ _ _ _	3
Mathematics 5 _ _ _ _ _ _ _	3
Graphics 15 _ _ _ _ _ _ _ _	2
French 2 or 3 _ _ _ _ _ _ _	3
Architecture 10 _ _ _ _ _ _	3
Civil Engineering 2 _ _ _ _ _	3

17

Senior

	Hrs.
Astronomy 1 _ _ _ _ _ _ _ _	1½
Geology _ _ _ _ _ _ _ _ _	1½
Graphics 16 _ _ _ _ _ _ _	2
French 3 _ _ _ _ _ _ _ _	3
Civil Engineering 5 and 6 _	3
Civil Engineering 11 _ _ _	3
Civil Engineering 9 _ _ _ _	3

17

BACHELOR OF SCIENCE (Electrical Engineering)

The course in Electrical Engineering is especially designed to give to those who contemplate making this subject their life-work a broad and well-rounded academic training, supplemented by a course in Electrical Engineering proper, which is as full and thorough as the time allowed will permit. Students are strongly urged to lay a broad foundation for electrical work, and to finish their course at some higher institution, after which they are advised to enter the shops of some electrical company before entering upon their profession. While some of the men trained here have entered upon a successful career in electrical work without studying further elsewhere, we believe the best and most lasting results will be obtained by following the plan outlined above.

Freshman

Hrs.

Graphics 12	2
English 1	3
Mathematics 1, 2	3
Physics 1-3	5
French X or 1 / German X or 1 / Spanish X or 1 } one	3

16

Junior

Chemistry 4, 5, or 8	3
Civil Eng. 2, 3, and 4	6
Electrical Eng. 1, 2	6
Mathematics 5	3

18

Sophomore

Hrs.

Civil Engineering 1	3
Graphics 14	2
Mathematics 3, 4	3
Physics 4	4
Chemistry 21 or 22	4 or 5
French 1 or 2 / German 1 or 2 / Spanish 1 or 2 } one	3

19 or 20

Senior

Astronomy 1	1½
Geology	1½
Civ. Eng. 5, 6, 7, 8	3
Graphics 15	2
Electrical Eng. 3, 4	5
Mathematics 7, 9	3

16

Note: For the degrees in Civil Engineering, Electrical Engineering and Architectural Engineering:

A student who offers no modern language for entrance must take two consecutive years in French, German or Spanish.

A student who offers one or more units of modern language for entrance and who wishes to continue the same language will take the advance course listed above in the language chosen.

A student who offers two units of modern language for entrance will be permitted to take History 2 and English 2 in lieu of the two-year language options.

A student who chooses a language option must continue the same language through two years, except that when Spanish 2 can be taken in the Freshman year it may be followed by English 2 in the Sophomore year.

Military Science and Tactics are required for two years; a credit of three hours is allowed for this work, as a substitute for the language requirements in the Sophomere year.

PRE-MEDICAL COURSES

For entrance to the Medical Department of the University at Augusta, or other acceptable medical school, preliminary collegiate work of specified character, covering two full academic years, is required. (Three summer terms are the equivalent of one yar). To meet this requirement the following course of instruction is arranged. For admission to this course the entrance requirements are those of the degree course in Bachelor of Arts, Bachelor of Arts in Social Sciences, or Bachelor of Science (General).

First Year

English; Chemistry 22; Zoölogy 32; French, or German, and one of the following: Mathematics; Latin; History.

NOTE:—A knowledge of Plane Trigonometry is a prerequisite or Physics 2, and a student should take Mathematics 1 in his Freshman year if he has not previously completed a course in Trigonometry.

Second Year

Chemistry 3; Botany 3 or Zoölogy 4 or 5; Physics 2; French, or German, and one of the following: Psychology 7-8-9; Economics; English; History; Botany 11.

Except when specifically indicated by number, any course offered in the University in the subject may be taken.

In addition, instruction in theoretical and practical military science is required of all students.

BACHELOR OF SCIENCE IN MEDICINE

The degree of Bachelor of Science in Medicine will be conferred on those completing satisfactorily the following four-year course:

1st Year
Mathematics 1-2
English 1
Language (3 hrs.)
Physics 2
History 2 or 4
Military Science.

2nd Year
Chemistry 22
English 2
Language (3 hrs.)
Zoology 32
General Elective (3 hrs.)
Military Science.

3rd Year
Chemistry 3
Botany 3
Language (3 hrs.)
Pychology 7, 8, 9, 71, S1, 91
General Electives (3 hrs.)

4th Year
One year at the Georgia Medical College, Augusta, Ga., (a branch of the University of Georgia.)

THE COLLEGE OF AGRICULTURE

Historical Statement

The Georgia State College of Agriculture was organized in accordance with an act of the General Assembly of the State passed July 21, 1906. It is an outgrowth of the State College of Agriculture and Mechanic Arts established as a department of the University of Georgia on May 1, 1872, by the Trustees of the University who accepted for the purpose, funds arising from the landscrip. From time to time support was received from the federal government, until the State, realizing that agriculture represents its principal industry, decided by legislative enactment to differentiate and specifically support an agricultural college.

The act of 1906 establishing the present College and better known as the "Conner Bill," contains the following preamble which sets forth reasons for enlarging the work of the State College of Agriculture along both educational and research lines:

"Agriculture is the principal industry of the State, and the main source from which the material prosperity of the State must come. Experience has demonstrated the great value of agricultural education in permanently improving the soil, multiplying its yield and increasing the value of its products. There is a growing demand by the people of the State for agricultural education, and for the practical benefits of scientific research in this line, and for improved methods in farming."

This act provides that the State College of Agriculture shall be under the direction of a Board of Trustees, consisting of eleven men three selected from the trustees of the University proper, three from the directors of the Georgia Experiment Station, including the Commissioner of Agriculture, and five from the State at Large. The Board has the same functions and exercises the same authority as that of similarly organized and co-ordinated divisions of the University, but is subject, in accordance with the provisions of the constitution of the State, to the general control of the University trustees.

The Georgia State College of Agriculture constitutes an integral part of the University System of Georgia, and while it has certain buildings, lands and equipment set aside for the special use of its corps of instructors and students, its work in general is closely associated with the University proper, so that agricultural students enjoy all the advantages which a great university system affords. These advantages include instruction and advice from the professors in other colleges, use of the general libraries and scientific laboratories, and membership in the various class and society organizations.

This is most desirable, since classroom training is but a part of a person's education.

For detailed information concerning the College of Agriculture send for regular catalogue of that institution, addressing President Andrew M. Soule, Athens, Ga.

BACHELOR OF SCIENCE IN AGRICULTURE

Introduction

The four-year Bachelor of Science course provides for a liberal and thorough training along scientific lines in agronomy, soil fertility, animal husbandry, veterinary medicine, dairy husbandry, horticulture, forestry, agricultural engineering, cotton industry, agricultural chemistry, poultry husbandry, and agricultural education. The course is practical.

General training in chemistry, physics, botany, biology, English and mathematics is also provided. Certain fundamental studies are prescribed, and the largest liberty of selection commensurate with the best interest of the student, is permitted. In this way the student is enabled to select a course which is in keeping with his taste, and at the same time obtain sufficient special training to fit him for the kind of work he desires to pursue after graduating.

Outline of Course

Freshman	Credit Hrs.	Sophomore	Credit Hrs.
Farm. Crops 1	2	Animal Husb. 2, 3, 4 and 5	3
Agr. Eng. 1, 2, 3, 4	3	Botany 1	4
Horticulture 1, 2 and 3	3	Agr. Chemistry 2b	3
Poultry Husb. 20 and 21	2	English 2	3
English 1	3	Physics 1	3
Chemistry 1	4	Soils 1, 2	3
Mathematics 1	1½		
	18½		19

The division of the time in the junior and senior years shall be as follows:

Major	12
Minor, group 1	6
Minor, group 2	6
Gen. Elective	12
	36

Total requirements for degree will be *73½ hours credit. Not more than 21 hours can be taken from any one division in the Junior and

*The Student who completes the military training offered in the Freshman and Sophomore years receives a three-hour credit, which may count as a general elective toward his degree.

Senior years. Major courses may be selected from the divisions of agronomy, animal husbandry, horticulture, agricultural chemistry, agricultural engineering, agricultural education and poultry husbandry.

ELECTIVE COURSES. It is urged that the student give particular attention to his elective courses, selecting those courses that give the broadest training commensurate with special work in a division.

Group 1 (6 hours required)

Agricultural Chemistry
Botany
Zoölogy

Physics
Mathematics
Geology

(Note:—Bacteriology and Entomology are placed in Group I for those majoring in agricultural education.)

Group 2 (6 hours required)

Six hours in any subjects of Junior or Senior rating offered in the College of Agriculture; must be approved by the head of the division in which the student is majoring.

Not later than the beginning of the junior year the student must submit a program written on a prescribed form for the schedule of work in the junior and senior years, showing his majors and minors, as well as his general electives. This program must be approved by the head of the department in which he takes his major.

LABORATORY PERIODS. Two laboratory hours count as one hour of recitation, and are included on that basis in the number of hours required.

BACHELOR OF SCIENCE IN FORESTRY

All students wishing to take the degree of Bachelor of Science in Forestry must be sixteen years of age and must present credit for 15 entrance units as specified under "Terms of Admission" on page —. The degree of B.S.F. is conferred on those completing the four-year course.

In the four-year professional course, opportunity is given to specialize in certain main lines. For those students desiring to specialize in city forestry an opportunity is offered for the election of landscape gardening and allied subjects; for those desiring to specialize in technical forestry with the object of entering the federal or state service, the election of advanced courses in botany and forestry; for those desiring to specialize in lumber salesmanship and mill superintendency, the election of courses in economics and business administration; for those desiring to specialize in dendropathology, the election of advanced courses in botany, and plant pathology.

OUTLINE OF COURSE

Freshman Year

Subject	Credit Hrs.
Chemistry 1, Elementary Chemistry	4
Botany 1, Plant Biology	4
English 1, English Composition	3
Math. 1, Trigonometry	1
Forestry 19, Principles of Forestry	1
Agr. Eng. 29, Elementary Surveying	1½
Agr. Eng. 1, 2, Forge Work, Drawing	2

Summer Term

Forestry 7, Cruising and Scaling	2
Forestry 12, General Forestry	4

22½

Sophomore Year

Ag. Chemistry 2b, Qualitative Analysis	3
Forestry 4, Dendrology	3
Physics 1, College Physics	3
Agronomy, Soils (1, 2)	3
Ag. Eng. 5, Surveying	3
Forestry 27, Mensuration	3

Summer Term

Forestry 7a, Forest Increment	2
Forestry 16, Forest Practice	4

24

Junior and Senior Years

Not later than the beginning of the junior year the student is required to designate his specialization and must select, with the advice and approval of the head of the department, the course of study he desires to pursue during the following two years. The major and one minor must be selected from technical forestry subjects, one minor may be selected from Departments in Group I, and twelve hours of general electives from Departments in Group II. Whether or not a student will be permitted to elect more than eighteen hours of work a year will depend upon his class record.

DIVISION OF TIME

Major, Forestry	12
Minor, Forestry	6
Minor, Group I	6
Gén. Electives, Group II	12

36

Group I

Agri. Engineering
Agri. Chemistry
Horticulture

Botany
Plant Pathology
Civil Engineering

Group II

General electives may be chosen from any department of the College of Agriculture or from any college or school of the University.

DOCTOR OF VETERINARY MEDICINE

A four-year course in veterinary medicine leading to the degree of Docter of Veterinary Medicine (D.V.M.) is offered. The demand for veterinarians is increasing in the southern states and there has been a general decrease in attendance at veterinary colleges throughout the country in recent years. There are excellent opportunities in veterinary medicine at the present time.

Outline of Course

Freshman

Subject	Hrs.
Anatomy 7, 8	4
Animal Husbandry 2, 3, 4, 5	3
English 1	3
Anatomy 5 (Histology)	2
Zoölogy 3	4
Chemistry 1	4

20

Sophomore

Subject	Hrs.
Anatomy 9, 10	4
Anatomy 6 (Embrylogy)	1
Animal Husbandry 8a, 9a	3
Bacteriology 1, 2	3
Agri. Chemistry 1 (Organic)	3
Vet. Physiology 1	4

18

Junior

Subject	Hrs.
Infectious Diseases	3
Pathology 1, (General)	4
Surgery 1	3
Pharmacy 1	1
Materia Medica 2	2
Therapeutics	1
Clinical Diagnosis	1
Parasitology	2
Horseshoeing	1
Clinics	3

21

Senior

Subject	Hrs.
Hygiene and Sanitation	1½
Infection and Immunity	1½
Surgery 2	3
Pathology 2 (Special)	3
Non-infectious Diseases	3
Pathology 3 (Food Insp'n)	2
Opththalmology	1
Obstetrics	2
Jurisprudence	1
Clinics	3

21

Junior Elective
Dairy Bacteriology (Bac. 3) 1½

Senior Elective
Surgical Exercises _ _ _ _ _ ▲

SIX-YEAR COURSE IN AGRICULTURE AND VETERINARY MEDICINE

On account of the demand and need for a combined course in Agriculture and Veterinary Medicine and the many opportunities open for men trained in both subjects, a six-year course leading to the degrees of B.S.A. and D.V.M. is offered. Men who take this combined course are especially well fitted to become managers of large stock farms and plantations and to occupy positions as field veterinarians in educational and experimental work and for investigational and experimental work in connection with experiment stations and other establishments where such work is conducted.

Freshman

	Hrs.
Agronomy (Farm Crops) 1	2
Agri. Eng. 1, 2, 3, 4 _ _ _ _	3
Chemistry 1 _ _ _ _ _ _ _	4
English 1 _ _ _ _ _ _ _ _ _	3
Horticulture 1, 2, 3 _ _ _	3
Mathematics 1 _ _ _ _ _ _	1½
Poultry Husbandry 20, 21 _	2

18½

Sophomore

	Hrs.
An. Husbandry 2, 3, 4, 5 _ _ _	3
Soils 1, 2 _ _ _ _ _ _ _ _ _ _	3
Agr. Chemistry 2b _ _ _ _ _ _	3
English 2 _ _ _ _ _ _ _ _ _	3
Physics 1 _ _ _ _ _ _ _ _ _ _	3
Botany 1 _ _ _ _ _ _ _ _ _ _	4

19

Junior Agr. & Vet. Freshman

	Hrs.
Agronomy (Farm Eco. 2) _	3
Agr. Chemistry 1 _ _ _ _ _ _	3
An. Husbandry 6, 7 _ _ _ _	3
Anatomy 7, 8, 5 _ _ _ _ _ _	6
Bacteriology 1 _ _ _ _ _ _ _	1½
Horticulture 13 _ _ _ _ _ _	1½
Zoölogy 31 _ _ _ _ _ _ _ _	4

22

Senior Agr. & Vet. Sophomore

	Hrs.
An. Husbandry 8, 9, 14 _ _	6
Agronomy (Farm Crops 2)	3
Anatomy 9, 10, 6 _ _ _ _ _ _	7
Bacteriology 2 _ _ _ _ _ _	1½
Vet. Physiology _ _ _ _ _ _	4

22½

NOTE:—For description of courses in Animal Husbandry, Biology, Chemistry and English, consult the various department descriptions.

NOTE:—The above is a tentative outline with respect to the agricultural subjects included in the course. Considerable latitude in the selection of these subjects will be permitted, the major portion, however, must be along the lines of Animal Husbandry and General Agriculture. No latitude is permitted with respect to the veterinary subjects.

NOTE:—The degree of B.S.A. (Bachelor of Science in Agriculture) is to be conferred at the completion of the fourth year. The degree of D.V.M. (Doctor of Veterinary Medicine) to be conferred upon the completion of the entire course.

Junior Veterinary	Hrs.	Senior Veterinary	Hrs.
Clinics	3	Clinics	3
Horseshoeing	1	Food Inspection	2
Infectious Diesases 1	3	Jurisprudence	1
Materia Medica	2	Non-Infectious Diseases	3
Pharmacy	1	Ph. Path. and Lab. Diag.	3
Pathology 1	3	Surgery 2	3
Physical Diagnosis	1	Obstetrics	2
Parasitology	2	Ophthalmology	1
Surgery 1	3	Hygiene and Sanitation	1½
Therapeutics	1	Infection and Immunity	1½
	20		21

Electives

Bacteriology 3, ane and one-half hours, juniors.

Surgical Exercises, one hour, seniors.

BACHELOR OF SCIENCE IN HOME ECONOMICS

The four-year degree course in Home Economics is arranged to meet the needs of the women students seeking the following:

1. Higher education for the profession of home-making which includes general culture and preparation in the broadest sense for participation in municipal and rural community building along lines of health sanitation and economic and social welfare.

2. Preparation for positions as county and supervising home demonstration agents or specialists in extension work in Home Economics.

3. Preparation for teaching and supervision in Vocational Home Economics.

4. Training in institutional management: of schools, hospitals, hotels, from standpoint of diet and feeding; lunch rooms, cafeterias, tea rooms, etc.

5. Lines of special technical and research work in which women can engage for the state and federal governments.

6. Editorial work in Agriculture and Home Economics.

To the Junior Class. For admission to the junior class, graduation from a junior college is required. Women without such graduation may be admitted provided they present certificates of equivalent work done in institutions of high rank in this state or elsewhere. In any case the work done must consist of 36 hours of standard college work. Women of sufficient maturity may enter as special students in courses for which they have prerequisites.

The two years college work must include six hours English; six hours home economics; four hours chemistry; three hours physics; three hours educational psychology; two hours elementary drawing and design; one and one-half hours of physiology; three hours of history, and four and one-half hours of electives. All science must carry standard laboratory work.

For electives the following courses may be offered: Foreign Language; Mathematics; Manual training; History, and Agriculture.

The three hours Agriculture may be a survey course and must include stundard laboratory or field work.

Two years physical education is required.

A student presenting 30 hours of college work may receive junior rating and is permitted to carry junior subjects for which she can offer prerequisites.

OUTLINE OF COURSE

A total of 69 hours is required for the B.S. degree in Home Economics.

Freshman

	Hrs.
English 1 _ _ _ _ _ _ _ _ _	3
Chemistry 1 or 2 _ _ _ _ _	4
Horticulture 3 _ _ _ _ _ _ _	1
Home Economics 26 _ _ _ _	2
Home Economics 22 _ _ _ _	2
Home Economics 27 _ _ _ _	1
History 22 _ _ _ _ _ _ _ _	1½
Physiology _ _ _ _ _ _ _ _	1½
Physical Education 1 _ _ _ _	1½
Total hours _ _ _ _ _ _ _	17½

Sophomore

	Hrs.
English 2 _ _ _ _ _ _ _ _	3
Psychology 1, 2, and 3 _ _ _	3
Home Economics 29 _ _ _ _ _	2
Physics 1 _ _ _ _ _ _ _ _	3
Home Economics 1, 2 _ _ _ _	3
History or Language _ _ _ _	3
Physical Education 2 _ _ _ _	1½
Total hours _ _ _ _ _ _	18½

Junior and Senior Courses

Upon completion of freshman and sophomore work, the student may select courses conforming either to the Home Demonstration or Vocational Home Economics groups. The division of time in the junior and senior years shall be as follows:

Home Demonstration

	Hrs.
Major _ _ _ _ _ _ _ _ _ _	12
Minor, Group 1 _ _ _ _ _ _	6
Minor, Group 2 _ _ _ _ _ _	6
Minor, Group 3 _ _ _ _ _ _	6
General Elective _ _ _ _ _ _	3
	33

Vocational Home Economics

	Hrs.
Major _ _ _ _ _ _ _ _ _ _	12
Minor, Group 1 _ _ _ _ _ _	6
Minor, Group 2 _ _ _ _ _ _	*
Minor, Group 3 _ _ _ _ _ _	9
General Elective _ _ _ _ _ _	6
	33

Group 1
Chemistry
Botany
Zoology
Bacteriology
Physiology

Group 2
Agriculture

Group 3
History
Education
English
Economics
Sociology

* Minor Group 2 is included in general electives.

Group 2 may include any six hours of junior or senior subjects in the College of Agriculture not including Home Economics to be approved by the Head of the Division of Home Economics.

The student who wishes a minor in Physical Education may take 7, 8 and 9 in her junior year and 10, 11 and 12 or other Physical Education courses for which she has the prerequisites in her Senior year instead of the general electives.

The student's program may include college credit courses offered in the Summer School.

The teacher training course in Vocational Home Economics consists of four years totalling 69 hours as now required for the B.S.H.E. degree. Under the requirements of the State Vocational Board such a course will be required of students qualifying to teach Vocational Home Economics. Upon graduation from this course the State Board for Vocational Education grants a teacher's certificate.

Suggested Vocational Home Economics Course

Junior	Hrs.	Senior	Hrs.
Home Economics 32 _ _ _ _	3	Home Economics 12-13 _ _ _ _	3
Home Economics 23-24-11		Home Economics 45-31 _ _ _	3
or Home Economics 10 _ _ _	3	Home Economics Education	
Agricultural Chemistry 1 _ _	3	53-57 _ _ _ _ _ _ _ _ _ _	3
Bacteriology 1-5 _ _ _ _ _ _	3	Electives _ _ _ _ _ _ _ _ _	6
Home Economics Education		Home Economics 40 _ _ _	2
50, 54 and 55 _ _ _ _ _ _ _	3	Horticulture 10 _ _ _ _ _	1
Electives _ _ _ _ _ _ _ _ _	3	English _ _ _ _ _ _ _ _ _	3
		Home Economics 46 _ _ _	3
		Sociology _ _ _ _ _ _ _ _	3
Total _ _ _ _ _ _ _ _ _ _	18	Total _ _ _ _ _ _ _ _ _ _	15

Suggested Home Demonstration Course

Junior	Hrs.	Senior	Hrs.
Home Economics 12-13 _ _ _	3	Home Economics 32 _ _ _ _	3
Home Economics 45-31 _ _ _	3	Home Economics 23-24-11	
Poultry Husbandry 30-31 _ _	2	or Home Economics 10 _ _	3
Horticulture 10 _ _ _ _ _ _	1	Agricultural Chemistry 1 _ _ _	3
Animal Husbandry 16 _ _ _	1½	Bacteriology 1-5 _ _ _ _ _ _	3
Home Economics Educa-		Home Economics Educa-	
tion 53 _ _ _ _ _ _ _ _	1½	tion 51 _ _ _ _ _ _ _ _ _	1
Electives _ _ _ _ _ _ _ _	6	Elective _ _ _ _ _ _ _ _ _	5
	15		18

The division of time in the four years shall be as follows:

	Per Cent.
Home Economics, technical _ _ _ _ _ _ _	25-35
Related Science and Arts _ _ _ _ _ _ _	25-25
Professional _ _ _ _ _ _ _ _ _ _ _ _ _	28-15
Humanistic _ _ _ _ _ _ _ _ _ _ _ _ _ _	22-25

EXTENSION DIVISION

Under the terms and provisions of the Smith-Lever Act, approximately 250 county agents, home demonstration agents and specialists are employed to carry information in agriculture and home economics to the farm home. This work is known as extension service.

The farmer, his wife and his children are enrolled in a big extension school. The boys and girls are enrolled in clubs. Thus it may be seen that by far the larger part of the student body of the Georgia State College of Agriculture is not in Athens but is located in all parts of the state. The institution has a state for its campus and some of its greatest service work in done with the farmer, his wife and children on the farm and in the farm home itself.

Rulings passed by the Extension Division pertaining to county agents in Georgia make it necessary that the applicant be between twenty-two and fifty years of age. He must have a degree from a standard agricultural college, or a Bachelor's degree from some other institution and one year's work in an agricultural college. He is furthermore required to have farm experience.

The requirements for home demonstration agents state that the applicant should be a graduate of a standard four years' graduate course with a Major in Home Economics and Minors in Science, Agriculture and Education, or at least two years' training in college with a minimum of two years' successful teaching experience plus approved college work of Junior and Senior grade in Home Economics, Science and Agriculture.

In order that the young men and women of Georgia may meet these requirements, there are offered at this time at the Georgia State College of Agriculture certain six weeks short courses for both men and women who are now employed as county or home demonstration agents. These six weeks courses are restricted to individuals already occupying one of the above positions and are offered that present incumbents may attain to the qualifications as laid down by the Extension Division. These six weeks courses are offered as necessity demands and in such lines as the students require. Three credit hours are all that a student may carry during the six weeks.

For young men desiring to become county agents. a general course of study has been approved to fill their needs. This course embraces all of the subjects that county agents find essential and necessary in the proper conducting of their office. For women see course in Home Economics.

BOYS' AND GIRLS' SHORT COURSES AT CAMP WILKINS

A short course of one week is given every summer for the boys and girls who have won scholarships in the different agricultural and home economics clubs of the state. This course is also open to boys and girls who do not win schouarships.

Scholarships for the short courses are given by fair associations, chambers of commerce, women's clubs, banks, and other public-spirited organizations and individuals who are interested in stimulating education in agriculture and home economics among boys and girls.

Every year more than 1,000 boys and girls take advantage of this elementary instruction which is made very practical indeed and is visualized as far as possible by application and illustration.

CORRESPONDENCE COURSES

In order to meet the increasing demand for correspondence courses in the College of Agriculture the following courses are offered for the year 1926-1927. The fee will be $6.50 per hour of College credit, or $18.00 for a three-hour course. A special circular giving detailed information may be obtained by writing the President, Georgia State College of Agriculture.

AGRICULTURAL CHEMISTRY 21. The chemistry of plant and animal growth and metabolism. *Professors Carter* and *Lowry*.

AGRICULTURAL CHEMISTRY 22. Soil Chemistry. *Professors Carter* and *Lowry*.

AGRICULTURAL CHEMISTRY 23. Fertilizers. *Professors Carter* and *Lowry*.

AGRICULTURAL EDUCATION 16. Community Problems. *Associate Professor Reitz.*

AGRICULTURAL EDUCATION 18. Rural Social Problems. *Associate Professor Reitz.*

AGRICULTURAL ENGINEERING 7. Farm Building. *Professor Lyle.*

AGRICULTURAL ENGINEERING 10. Farm Buildings. *Professor Lyle.*

AGRICULTURAL ENGINEERING 25. Farm Sanitary Equipment. *Professor Lyle.*

FARM CROPS 1. Field Crop Production. *Associate Professor Tabor.*

ANIMAL HUSBANDRY 2, 3, 4. Breeds of Livestock. *Associate Professor Rice.*

ANIMAL HUSBANDRY 6. Livestock Production. *Associate Professor Kellogg.*

FORESTRY 4a. Dendrology. *Professor Burleigh.*

HOME ECONOMICS 44. Home Planning and Furnishing. *Miss Edith Creswell.*

HOME ECONOMICS 53. History and Development of Education in Home Economics. *Miss Newton.*

HORTICULTURE 10. Landscape Gardening. *Dr. McHatton.*

HORTICULTURE 13. Economic Entomology. *Dr. McHatton.*

POULTRY HUSBANDRY 20. General Poultry. *Professor Wood.*

POULTRY HUSBANDRY 23, 24, 25. Incubation and Brooding, Marketing Standard Judging. *Professor Wood.*

POULTRY HUSBANDRY 27. Feeds and Feeding. *Professor Wood.*

POULTRY HUSBANDRY 28. Advance Judging. *Professor Wood.*

POULTRY HUSBANDRY 41. Poultry Hygiene. *Dr. Richardson.*

ZOOTECHNICS AND HYGIENE.__*Dr. Richardson.*

BACHELOR OF SCIENCE IN PHYSICAL EDUCATION

This course is designed for the technical and professional training of teachers or supervisors of physical education, leaders of playgrounds and recreation centers and specialists in nutrition and health education.

A minor in physical education provided for students who wish to prepare to combine leadership in physical education and health education activities with the teaching of other subjects in the high school or girls camp.

The regulation gymnasium costume of black serge bloomers, all white middies, black tie, black hose, and white tennis shoes should be procured in Athens.

Physical Education 1 and 2 are general courses open to all students. Lectures in health education are required of all freshman women.

The prescribed subjects for the freshman and sophomore years are selected to furnish a basis of general education and to give the prerequisite sciences necessary for the technical courses comprising the major. A total of 69 hours is required for the degree.

Freshman	Hrs.	Sophomore	Hrs.
English 1 _ _ _ _ _ _ _ _ _	3	English 2 _ _ _ _ _ _ _	3
Zoology 31 _ _ _ _ _ _ _ _	4	Physics 1 _ _ _ _ _ _ _ _	3
History 4 or Language _ _	3	Psychology 1-2 _ _ _ _ _ _ _	2
Chemistry 1 _ _ _ _ _ _ _ _	4	Language or History 4 _ _	3
History 22 _ _ _ _ _ _ _ _	1½	Physiology and Anatomy _ _	4
Physical Education 1 _ _ _ _	1½	Physical Edu. 7-8-9 _ _ _ _	2½
		Physical Edu. 2 _ _ _ _ _ _	1½
Total hours _ _ _ _ _ _	17	Total hours _ _ _ _ _ _ _	19

Not later than the beginning of the junior year the student shall submit a program for the work of the junior and senior years written on the prescribed form and conforming to the following division of time.

	Hrs.
Major	12
Minor, Group 1	6
Minor, Group 2	6
Minor, Group 3	6
Electives	6
Total	36

GROUP 1

Botany
Agricultural Chem. 1
Bacteriology
Zoology
Physics

GROUP 2

Psychology
Education
Sociology

GROUP 3

Home Economics 1-2
Home Economics 45, 31
Home Economics 12, 13

THE PEABODY SCHOOL OF EDUCATION
INCLUDING PHILOSOPHICAL SOCIAL SCIENCE

HISTORICAL BRIEF

In June 1908, the trustees adopted a plant to convert the chair of Philosophy and Education into a School of Education, to provide a special building, and to enlarge the staff of instruction. The trustees of the Peabody Education Fund gave the funds for the special building which was completed in 1913, and named George Peabody Hall, in honor of George Peabody who, in 1867, created this Fund as an aid to the cause of education in the South.

This building contains well equipped class rooms, offices, library, rest room, and laboratories for psychology and home economics. It is one of the best adapted and most artistic buildings on the campus.

In September 1918, the trustees of the University passed a resolution opening this school to women.

LABORATORIES

The Psychological Laboratory occupies several rooms in the first floor of George Peabody Hall and is equipped with the latest psychological instruments for qualitative and quantitative studies of such mental phenomena as the senses, feeling, memory, attention, etc. There is full equipment for experimental pedagogy, and educational and mental tests and measurements.

The Home Economics Laboratories include a large kitchen laboratory, pantry, dining rooms, class room, clothing and textile room, all well equipped with modern furnishings.

SCOPE OF THE SCHOOL

Developing from the chair of Philosophy and Education this School has two collegiate divisions, the Division of Education and the Division of Philosophical-Social Science.

1. The Division of Education has for its special function the preparation of teachers for high schools, normal schools, and special subjects; of principals, superintendents and educational administrators. This work differentiates from that of the normal schools in that the latter prepare primarily for the elementary schools.

Courses in education are also given for all students, since education is such a great factor in every social order or community.

The Departments of this Division are the following:

I. The History of Education and Educational Philosophy.

II. Educational Psychology.

III. Secondary Education and School Administration.

IV. The Principles and Practice of Teaching.

2. **The Division of Philosophical-Social Science** offers studies in human nature, human development, social institutions, social progress, and philosophical theory. Its Departments are the following:

I. Philosophy.　　II. Psychology.　　III. Sociology.

CURRICULA

There are two degrees offered with the major courses in this School. These are the degrees, Bachelor of Arts (Education) and Bachelor of Arts (Social Science), the curricula for which are as follows:

I. BACHELOR OF ARTS IN EDUCATION

Requirements for the Degree

This degree is offered for study in the human and social sciences with special opportunity for preparation for educational work.

The following are the minimum requirements expressed in year hours. These are to be multiplied by two for value in semester hours.

English, 3 hours; mathematics, 3 hours; history, government, economics, 6 hours; zoology, botany, physics, chemistry, 6 hours; education, 12 hours; foreign language, Greek literature, 9 hours; psychology, sociology, philosophy, 6 hours.

In addition, any requirements in health education must be met by women, and military requirements must be met by men.

The above must be understood as minimum requirements. All elections must be made and requirements met subject to the approval of the Dean of the School of Education. More than the minimum may be required in some subjects in accord with elections approved.

Notes on the Degree Requirements

1. Foreign Languages

The foreign language requirements may be met in any one of several combinations as follows:

Option 1. Latin three hours and six hours of a modern language.

Option 2. Six hours of a modern language and three hours of Greek Literature. (See Greek 5, "European Literature.")

Option 3. Latin three hours, Greek Literature three hours and three hours of a modern language.

Option 4. Six hours of Latin and three hours of a modern language.

Option 5. A total of twelve hours in two modern languages. This may be six in each or nine in one with three in the other.

Any one of these Options may be selected. In construing the above, an "X" course may be counted provided it is not the only course taken in the language. If only one course is taken in a language it should be one numbered "20" or "1."

Greek 5, Greek Literature, is a study in translations which does not involve a study of the Greek language.

2. Natural Sciences

For the foundation of studies of human development and of educational theory and practice the biological sciences have some preference. It is recommended that for the first year Introductory Biology, a course including both Botany and Zoology when such a course is offered, shall be elected, and that for the second year Genetics (Botany 11), or one other natural science be elected. At least one of the courses must include the laboratory work.

3. English.

In English the student must be proficient in the use of the English language, which proficiency is generally attained through courses in grammar and composition and rhetoric. The student must also give evidence of a good knowledge of English literature. The character of work done in the high school will determine which course or courses will be assigned to meet the degree requirements. If proficiency is shown in English 1, Journalism 1, may be taken as a practice course in writing.

4. Teaching Specialties.

At the beginning of the junior year or earlier the student must select two preferred subjects as teaching specialties. In the junior and senior years academic courses must be taken in these preferences as far as needed to complete from nine to twelve hours of credits in the major preference, and from six to twelve hours in the minor preference, this total in each case being somewhat dependent upon the courses offered in the departmnts involved.

II. BACHELOR OF ARTS IN SOCIAL SCIENCE.

With Major in Philosophical Social Science

The requirements for this degree are much the same as for Bachelor of Arts in Education, the following being the exceptions:

(1) The foreign language option must include Latin 1.

(2) Instead of the major of twelve hours in Education, twelve hours must be chosen from courses in Psychology, Sociology, and Philosophy.

(3) From courses in History, Government, Economics, nine hours must be completed.

General Requirements

In accordance with the general requirements of the University, 69 hours with 69 points must be completed for either of the above degrees. For recommendation to teach, the scholarship grades should run the points up to a much larger number than 69.

There is a State law requiring that all graduates of public schools or colleges show a satisfactory acquaintance with the constitution of the United States and of the State of Georgia. This may be satisfied by examination based on high school courses, or by taking in course History 22.

SUGGESTED FRESHMAN COURSES

The special courses in education, philosophy, psychology, and sociology are not open to Freshmen. It is best to begin with other rquired courses as follows:

English 1 or English 2.

History 2 or 22-3.

Mathematics 1-2.

A Modern Language X or 1, or Latin 1.

A Natural Science, preferably Biology.

Military or Health Course.

In the Sophomore year, Psychology 1-2-3 and Education 1-2-3 may be taken.

COLLEGE PROFESSIONAL CERTIFFICATE

The requirements for the degree Bachelor of Arts in Education will satisfy the requirements of the State Department of Education for the College Professional Certificate. With any other bachelor of arts degree or with the bachelor of science general degree nine hours in Education must be elected. These must be taken from the courses listed under Education and should include Education 10-11-12 with other courses as advised by the Dean of the School of Education in accordance with the specific requirements of the State Department of Education.

SCHOOL OF COMMERCE

The School of Commerce was organized in 1913 in response to a demand for courses designed to prepare students for business careers. The work of the School embraces the general field of theoretical and practical Economics, Business Administration and Accounting. The cultural aspects of education, however, have been kept in mind in arranging the curriculum of the School, fewer than half of the required hours being given to courses of a technical nature.

Candidates for the B. S. in Commerce degree are required to complete 69 hours of work. Of this total, 30 hours (or 31, depending upon the choice between Physics 1 and Physics 2) are in cultural courses—6 hours of English, 9 hours of Modern Language, 3 hours of Physical Science, 6 hours of History and 6 of Mathematics. One of the mathematics courses, however, Statistics and the Mathematics of Investments, is primarily a business course, as is one of the history courses, Industrial History of Europe and America. Twenty-seven hours of purely business subjects are required—33, if the mathematics and history courses just referred to be included. The remaining 11 (or 12) hours are free electives. Some or all of them may be in business courses.

The requirements in the Freshman and Sophomore years are fixed. In the Freshman year the work is similar to that of the A. B. degree, except that Latin is not required. In the Sophomore year, the requirements are still largely cultural. The Principles of Economics is a course suitable for any degree. Only the Accounting course is specifically a business course. The technical business training is confined almost wholly to the Junior and Senior years; and the program of study must be prepared in consultation with the Dean of the School.

Students in Other Departments

Courses offered in the School of Commerce are open as general electives to students working in other departments. Commerce 5, Principles of Economics, is probably the best course for such students, though other subjects may be taken with approval of the Dean.

The following are the courses of the Freshman and Sophomore years:

Freshman

English 1 (Rhetoric and Composition) _____ 3
Mathematics 1, 2 (Trigonometry and Analytical Geometry) ____ 3
Modern Language (French, German or Spanish) _____ 3
Commerce 1 (Geography and Industry) _____ 3
History 2 (Modern European) _____ 3
                                                          ―――
        Total _____15

Sophomore

English 2 (English Literature) _____ 3
Physics 1 or Physics 2 _____3 or 4
Commerce 5 (Principles of Economics) _____ 3
Commerce 6 (Elementary Accounting) _____ 3
Modern Language (French, German or Spanish) _____ 3
History 44 (English and American Industrial History) _____ 3
                                                      ――――――
        Total _____18 or 19

THE HENRY W. GRADY SCHOOL OF JOURNALISM

The Department of Journalism was authorized by the Board of Trustees in 1915, and was changed to the Henry W. Grady School of Journalism in 1921. This school was created in response to a demand for courses designed to aid students in a journalistic career.

The degree of Bachelor of Arts in Journalism will be given upon the satisfactory completion of the four-year course outlined below.

Requirements for the Degree

1. The students must satisfy the full entrance requirements for the Bachelor of Arts, the Bachelor of Arts in Social Sciences, or the Bachelor of Science degrees.

2. He must complete a total of not less than eighteen hours in Journalism.

3. He must satisfy the typewriting test.

4. He must complete a total of 71 hours.

Special Requirements

At the beginning of the Junior year, if the college work of the student is deficient in any respect, he cannot continue his work as a candidate for the degree of Bachelor of Journalism in four academic years. No student will be recommended for the degree of Bachelor of Arts in Journalism unless his English is satisfactory.

The Language Requirements

The language requirements for this degree may be satisfied as follows: six hours of Latin or Greek, or nine hours of modern languages, six hours of which must be taken in the same subject, and not more than one X college course may be counted.

For the benefit of those who take this course and who may intend teaching at any future date, attention is called to the fact that the requirements for the State Professional Certificate for teachers include nine hours of courses in Education.

Students in Other Departments

Courses offered in the Henry W. Grady School of Journalism are open as general electives to students in other departments.

Outline of Course of Study

Freshman

	Hrs.
Journalism _ _ _ _ _ _ _ _ _	3
English 1 _ _ _ _ _ _ _ _ _	3
Mathematics 1-2 _ _ _ _ _ _	3
History 22 and 3 _ _ _ _ _	3
Commerce 1 or 5 _ _ _ _ _ _	3
Modern Language or Latin or Greek _ _ _ _ _ _ _ _ _ _	3

Total _ _ _ _ _ _ _ _ _ _ _18

Sophomore

	Hrs.
Journalism 2 _ _ _ _ _ _ _ _	3
English 2 or Psychology 1-2-3 _ _ _ _ _ _ _ _ _ _	3
Mathematics 3-4 or 6-11 or Science with lab. _ _ _3 or 4	
History 2 or 4 _ _ _ _ _ _ _ _	3
Commerce 92 _ _ _ _ _ _ _ _	1
Modern Language or Latin or Greek _ _ _ _ _ _ _ _ _ _	3
Military Science or Elective _	3

Total _ _ _ _ _ _ _ _19 or20

Junior

	Hrs.
Journalism 5-11-12 _ _ _ _ _	3
Journalism 4-13 _ _ _ _ _ _	3
History 5-6 or 11-12 _ _ _ _	3
Science (with Laboratory) _ _	4
*Modern Language _ _ _ _ _ _	3
Electives _ _ _ _ _ _ _	3 or 6

19 or 22

*If Latin or Greek, instead of a modern language is selected, then the student must select in his Junior year six hours of electives.

Senior

	Hrs.
Journalism 3-15 _ _ _ _ _ _ _	3
Journalism 7 or Journalism 8, 9, 14 _ _ _ _ _ _ _	3
English Language 3 or English 4 _ _ _ _ _ _ _ _ _ _	3
Electives _ _ _ _ _ _ _ _ _	6

Total _ _ _ _ _ _ _ _ _ _ 15

In the Junior and Senior years all elections must be made in accordance with the advice and approval of the head of the school.

C. SUBJECTS OF INSTRUCTION OFFERED BY THE FACULTIES OF THE UNDERGRADUATE SCHOOLS

(Lecture periods and recitation periods are one hour each. Laboratory periods are two hours each. One hour credit is given for each lecture period once a week for the entire year. One hour credit is given for each laboratory period, once a week for the entire year.)

AGRICULTURAL CHEMISTRY

1. ORGANIC AND BIOLOGICAL CHEMISTRY. A systematic study of the classification and relation of the carbon compounds; study of digestion and metabolism and the chemical composition of foods. Prerequisite: Inorganic Chemistry 1 or 2 with laboratory. Two lectures and one laboratory. Three hours credit. Junior or Senior. Fee, $7.50. Breakage deposit, $3.00. M. F., 9:20; lab., Th. F., 2:30-4:20. *Professor Carter* and *Associate Professor Wilder*.

2b. QUALITATIVE ANALYSIS. In this course a study is made of the characteristic properties and reactions of the common metals and acid radicals. Prerequisite: Inorganic Chemistry 1 or 2 including work in laboratory. One lecture and two laboratory periods during the sophomore year. Three hours credit. Fee, $7.50. Breakage deposit, $3.00. M., 10:15; labs: Sec. 1, M., 11:10-1:00, W., 2:30-4:20; Sec. 2, W., 11.10-1:00, F., 11:15-1:00. *Associate Professor Wilder*.

3. QUANTITATIVE ANALYSIS. The object of this course is to prepare the student for special work in agricultural chemistry as well as to teach the method of quantitative analysis. The methods of both gravimetric and volumetric analysis will be treated in lectures and carried out in the laboratory. Two lectures and recitations and four laboratory periods for three terms. Six hours credit. Fee, $7.50. Breakage deposit, $5.00. Time will be arranged. *Associate Professor Wilder*.

3b. QUANTITATIVE ANALYSIS. Same as Course "3", except that students not specializing in chemistry, have one hour of lectures and recitations and two laboratory periods. Three hours credit. Optional for juniors and seniors. Fee, $7.50. Breakage deposit, $5.00. T., 9:20; lab., T., 11:10-1:00; S., 11:10-1:00. *Associate Professor Wilder*.

4. ADVANCED QUANTITATIVE ANALYSIS. Methods employed in soil investigation, the analysis of soils, fertilizers, feeds, water, etc. Students taking this course must have had Agricultural Chemistry "3." Work for laboratory will be outlined and standard references given. Two hours of lectures and recitations and four laboratory periods for three terms during senior year. Six hours credit. Fee, $7.50. Breakage deposit, $5.00. Time will be arranged. *Professor Carter*.

4b. QUANTITATIVE ANALYSIS. Same as course "4," except that students not specializing in chemistry have one hour of lectures and recitations and two laboratory periods. Three hours credit. Optional for seniors. Fee, $7.50. Breakage deposit, $5.00. Time will be arranged. *Professor Carter.*

ADVANCED COURSES are given in the Graduate School.

AGRICULTURAL EDUCATION

10. INTRODUCTION TO VOCATIONAL EDUCATION. The place of Vocational Education in a system of education; vocational needs of the several groups of society; schools as vocational training institutions; development of vocational education in America; some problems of vocational guidance, etc. Third term. Three hours per week. One hour credit. Juniors or Seniors. T. Th. S., 12:05. *Professor Wheeler.*

11. ADMINISTRATIVE PROBLEMS. Deals with the administrative problems of the agricultural teacher; the place, function and organization of the rural high school, and how vocational training in agriculture may be fitted into the curriculum; problems of consolidation. Third term. Three hours per week. One hour credit. Prerequisites: Courses 10, 12, 13. Senior or Junior. T. Th., 10:15; ,S., 11:10. *Professor Wheeler.*

12. INTRODUCTION TO EDUCATION. The meaning and view point of education; original nature, the raw material for education; the relation of education to human behavior; nature of learning and its processes. Three hours per week. First term. One hour credit. Junior year. T. Th. S., 12:05. *Associate Professor Reitz.*

13. VOCATIONAL PSYCHOLOGY. Psychology of motive, acquisition ownership, responsibility, co-operation, competition; vocational aspect of attitude, habit formation, and motor learning; application of principles of learning to the practice of teaching agriculture, etc. Three hours per week. Second term. One hour credit. Junior. T. Th. S., 12:05. *Associate Professor Reitz.*

14. TEACHING AGRICULTURE. The instructional problems of the vocational teacher are treated in this course: Selecting subject content; organizing subject content for teaching; directing teaching activities. etc., with all day, part time, and evening classes. First and second terms. Three hours per week. Two hours credit. Prerequisite: Courses 10, 12, 13 or parallel these courses. Senior. Laboratory fee, $2.00. T. Th. S., 11:10. *Professor Wheeler.*

15. SUPERVISED TEACHING. Arrangements are made with all Senior students in this division to plan and carry out observation, participation and teaching practice under supervision. Through the year, one to three credits by arrangement. Prerequisite: Course 14. *Professor Wheeler* and *Associate Professor Mobley.*

16. COMMUNITY PROBLEMS. This course deals directly with the com-

munity problems of the teacher of agriculture (correlating with Course 14); school survey, agricultural survey, analyzing and charting survey data. First and second terms. Two classes and. one laboratory period per week. Two hours credit. Prerequisite: Courses 10, 12, 13. Senior. Laboratory fee, $2.00. M. W., 10:15; W., 2:35-4:25. *Associate Professor Reitz.*

17. RURAL JOURNALISM. Deals with the development of a program of promotional work for the agricultural teacher; emphasis is given to writing news and feature stories for country weekly, metropolitan daily, and farm publications. Third term. Two classes and one laboratory period per week. One hour credit. Senior M. W., 10:15. Laboratory arranged. *Professor Chapman.*

18. RURAL SOCIAL PROBLEMS. Factors, forces and agencies molding the country dweller and the rural community. Special attention will be given to Georgia conditions and problems. First and second terms. Two class periods and one laboratory period per week. Two hours credit. T. Th. S., 11:10. Junior and Senior. *Associate Professor Reitz.*

19. VISUAL MATERIALS. This course deals with special problems in chart making, and educational photography. Open only to Seniors in this division. Offered each term. One lecture and two three hour laboratory periods per week. Laboratory fee, $5.00. Time to be arranged. *Professor Wheeler.*

ADVANCED COURSES are given in the Graduate School.

AGRICULTURAL ENGINEERING
SHOP

1. (a) *WOOD WORK. The use, care and sharpening of hand tools. Study of the characteristics and strength of woods used in farm carpentry. . Rafter cutting and farm building construction. (b) FORGE WORK. Forging and welding of iron and steel. Making, hardening and tempering small tools. Repair of farm equipment. First term. Required of Freshmen. One hour credit. Two three-hour laboratory periods per week. *Associate Professor Clegg.*

2. *DRAWING. Freehand lettering. Plotting and charting agricultural statistics. Study of working drawing so student may be able to make and read blue prints. Pictorial drawing and sketching. Second term. Required of Freshmen. One hour credit. Two three-hour laboratory periods. *Associate Professor Clegg.*

3. *FARM MACHINERY. A study of the construction, adjustment, care and use of field machinery. Special attention, is given materials and design. Course includes hitches, belt lacing and rope splicing. Field work in season. First half of third term. Required of Freshmen.

---

* Laboratory fee for courses 1, 2, 3, and 4. or 1, 2 and 29. $5.00.

One half hour credit. Two three-hour laboratory periods. *Associate Professor Clegg.*

4: *FARM MOTORS. A study of the construction, adjustment, care and use of the internal combustion motor. Special attention is given to lubrication, ignition, timing and carburetion. Last half of third term. Required of Freshmen. One-half hour credit. Two three hour laboratory periods. Agricultural Engineering 1, 2, 3, and 4: Section 1, T. F., 2:35-5:20; Section 2, T. Th., 10:15-1:00; Section 3, Th., 2:35-5:20; S., 10:15-1:00. *Associate Professor Clegg.*

26. †ADVANCED FARM SHOP. Repair and care of hand tools used in the farm shop. Construction of appliances for use on the farm. Study of labor-saving devices and equipment for swine production. Prerequisites: Agricultural Engineering 1, 2, 3, and 4. Two lectures and one laboratory period. First term. Junior or Senior year. One hour credit. *Associate Professor Clegg.*

27. †ADVANCED FARM SHOP. A study of equipment and actual construction of devices and machines used on dairy farms, poultry yards and orchards. Exercise and field trips. Prerequisites: Agricultural Engineering 1, 2, 3 and 4. One lecture and two laboratory periods per week. Second term. Junior or Senior. One hour credit. *Associate Professor Clegg.*

28. †ADVANCED FARM SHOP. Sheet metal work, ropes and belts. Harness repair. Repair and care of farm machinery. Prerequisites: Agricultural Engineering 1, 2, 3, and 4. One lecture and two laboratory periods per week. Third term. Junior or Senior year. One hour credit. Agricultural Engineering 26, 27 and 28: M., 4:25; M. W., 2:35-4:25. *Associate Professor Clegg.*

MACHINES AND MOTORS

11. *FARM MACHINERY. An advanced course in field machinery. Special attention is given to power machinery, the measurement and transmission of power. Construction, repair and design. Prerequisites: Agricultural Engineering 1, 2, 3, and 4, and Physics 1. One lecture and two laboratory periods. First half year. Junior or Senior year. One and one-half hours credit. *Associate Professor Clegg.*

12. *FARM MOTORS. Sources and application of power adaptable to agricultural purposes. The horse as a motor, windmills, water wheels, steam, oil and gasoline engines and electric motors. Study of belt and power traction. Tractor field work. Prerequisite: Agricultural Engineering 11. One lecture and two laboratory periods per week. Second half year. Junior or Senior year. One and one-half hours ·

---

† Laboratory fee for courses 26, 27 and 28. $5.00.
* Laboratory fee for courses 11 and 12, $4.50.

credit. Agricultural Engineering 11 and 12. S., 12:05; T. Th., 11:10-1:00. *Associate Professor Clegg.*

SURVEYING

29. FORESTRY SURVEYING. Elementary training in the use of the level. transit and other surveying equipment. Prerequisite: Mathematics 1. One lecture and two laboratory periods. Required of forestry students in second half of Freshman year. One and one-half hours credit. Laboratory fee, $2.00. (Time to be arranged.) *Professor Lyle.*

5. ADVANCED FORESTRY SURVEYING. A course in the use of compass, level, plane table and transit, with the uses of these instruments in topographic and reconnaissance work. Prerequisites: Agricultural Engineering 1, 2 and 29. One lecture and two laboratory periods throughout the year. Required in the Sophomore year for forestry students. Three hours credit. Laboratory fee, $3.00. M., 4:25; M. W., 2:35-4:25. *Professor Lyle.*

22. †AGRICULTURAL SURVEYING. Training in the use, care and adjustment of the level, transit and other surveying equipment, with field problems in leveling and land measurement. Prerequisites: Agricultural Engineering 1, 2, 3, and 4, and Mathematics 1. One lecture and two laboratory periods. First term. Junior or Senior year. One hour credit. *Professor Lyle.*

23. †DRAINAGE AND TERRACING. A study of land drainage by field tile, ditches, and levees, and of terracing and the prevention of soil erosion, with field problems. Prerequisite: Agricultural Engineering 22. One lecture and two laboratory periods. Second term. Junior or Senior year. One hour credit. *Professor Lyle.*

24. †RURAL ROADS AND PAVEMENTS. Location, grading and drainage of roads and highways; road surfacing and paving materials; construction and maintenance; culverts and bridges. Prerequisites: Agricultural Engineering 22 and 23. One lecture and two laboratory periods. Third term. Junior or Senior year. One hour credit. Agricultural Engineering 22, 23 and 24. M. W. F., 11:10-1:00. *Professor Lyle.*

BUILDINGS AND SANITATION

7. *FARM BUILDINGS. Locating and planning of farmsteads and farm buildings. A practical study in design of farm structures and their cost. Prerequisites: Agricultural Engineering 1, 2, 3, and 4, and Physics 1. One lecture and two laboratory periods. First term. Junior or Senior year. One hour credit. *Professor Lyle.*

† Laboratory fee for courses 26. 27. 28. $5.00.
* Laboratory fee for courses 7. 10 and 25. $5.00.

10. *FARM BUILDINGS. The selection and economical use of building materials; architectural details; planning the farm home; special problems. Prerequisite: Agricultural Engineering 7. One lecture and two laboratory periods. Second term. Junior or Senior year. One hour credit. *Professor Lyle.*

25. *FARM SANITARY EQUIPMENT. A study of heating, ventilating, lighting, waterworks, and plumbing systems for farm buildings, and of farm power plants and home conveniences. Prerequisite: Agricultural Engineering 10. One lecture and two laboratory periods. Third term. Junior or Senior year. One hour credit. Agricultural Engineering 7, 10 and 25. T., 10:15; T. Th., 11:10-1:00. *Professor Lyle.*

HOUSEHOLD MECHANICS

18. HOME DESIGNING. This course is offered for Home Economics students. Location of homes with reference to sanitary, convenient and attractive surroundings; planning for comfort, convenience and beauty at reasonable cost. One lecture and two laboratory periods. First term. Junior or Senior year. One hour credit. Laboratory fee, $1.00. (Time to be arranged.) *Professor Lyle.*

19. HOME EQUIPMENT. This course is supplemental to 18, and takes up home conveniences, water supply, sewerage disposal, lighting, heating and ventilation. Prerequisites: Agricultural Engineering 18. and Physics 1. Second term. One hour credit. Laboratory fee, $1.00 *Professor Lyle.*

20. HOUSEHOLD MECHANICS. Selection, installation, operation and maintenance of mechanical equipment in the modern home. Prerequisite: Physics 1. Two lectures and one laboratory period. First term. Junior or Senior year. One hour credit. Laboratory fee, $2.00. T. Th., 9:20; S., 8:25-10:15. *Professor Lyle.*

21. ADVANCED HOUSEHOLD MECHANICS. Electric motors. Pumps, water systems, unit light plant and other household machinery. Construction, care, use and repair of automobile. Ignition, lubrication, carburetion, battery and tires. Second term. Junior or Senior year. Fee, $2.00. One lecture, two laboratory periods. *Professor Lyle.*

ADVANCED COURSES are given in the Graduate School.

AGRONOMY
FARM CROPS

1. FIELD CROP PRODUCTION. A study of the principal factors of crop production and their effect on the crops of Georgia such as cotton, corn, small grain, peanuts, cowpeas, soy beans, tobacco, and sugar cane. First and second terms. Freshman. Two hours credit. Laboratory

---

* Laboratory fee for courses 7, 10 and 25, $5.00.

fee, $1.50. T. Th., 8:25 or 9:20. Lab., M. W. or F., 2:35-4:25. *Associate Professor Tabor.*

2. FORAGE CROPS. A general study of the forage crops of this country, with especial attention to those adapted to the cotton belt. Prerequisite: Farm crops 1. Junior and Senior. Two lectures and one laboratory period. Three hours credit. Laboratory fee, $2.50. T., 2:35, Th., 4:25. Lab. T., 3:30-5:20. *Associate Professor Tabor.*

3. CEREALS. A general study of the principal cereal crops, such as corn, oats and wheat, and their requirements for profitable yields. Prerequisite: Farm Crops 1. Junior and Senior. Two lectures and one laboratory period. Three hours credit. Laboratory fee, $2.50. M. W., 10:15. Laboratory F., 10:15-12:05. *Associate Professor Tabor.*

6. WEEDS AND SEEDS. Study of identification, distribution and means of control of common weeds for half year, and the identification, analysis and qualities of seeds for the remaining half year. Junior and Senior. Prerequisites: Farm Crops 1 and Botany 1. Two lectures and one laboratory period. Laboratory fee, $3.50. M., 11:10, F., 9:20. Laboratory W., 11:10-1:00. *Associate Professor Tabor.*

SOILS

1 and 2. PRINCIPLES OF SOIL MANAGEMENT. Origin, formation and physical properties of soils. Chemical properties of soils, uses of lime and other soil amendments. Drainage and tillage practices. Commercial fertilizers and maintenance of soil fertility. Prerequisite: Chemistry 1. Sophomore. Two lectures and one laboratory period. Three hours credit. Laboratory fee, $3.50. M. F., 9:20; lab., T. W. or Th., 2:30-4:25. *Professor Crabb.*

3. *SOIL FORMATION. Rock disintegration and geological agencies relating to origin and formation of soils. Soil provinces, series and types, of the United States. Practice in soil survey and preparation of maps and reports. Prerequisite: Soils 1 and 2. Juniors and Seniors. Two lectures and one laboratory period. Three hours credit. Laboratory fee, $5.00. M. F., 11:40; lab., F., 2:35-4:25. *Professor Crabb.*

3a. SOIL SURVEY. Required of students specializing in soils. Field survey of soils. Soil mapping and the preparation of base maps and soil survey reports. Prerequisites: Soils 1, 2 and 3. Three months in summer between Junior and Senior years. Three hours credit. *Professor Crabb.*

5. *ADVANCED SOIL MANAGEMENT. Occurrence and properties of predominant soils of the south. Practices and management to increase fertility and crop· production. Prerequisite: Soils 1 and 2. Juniors and Seniors. Three hours credit. Two lectures and one laboratory

---

* Soils 3, 5 and 6 will not be given unless at least five apply.

period. Laboratory fee, $3.50. Alternates with Soil 6. Course given 1927-1928. T. S., 11:10; lab., Th., 11:10. *Professor Crabb.*

6. *FERTILIZERS AND MANURES.* History of fertilizer industry. Composition of farm crops. Source, manufacture and use of fertilizer materials. Soil conditions affecting value of fertilizers. Value and care of farm manures. Prerequisites: Soils 1 and 2. Juniors and Seniors. Two lectures and one laboratory period. Three hours credit. Laboratory fee, $3.50. Alternates with Soils 5. Courses given 1926-1927. T. S., 11:10; lab., Th., 11:10-1:00. *Professor Crabb.*

COTTON INDUSTRY

1. COTTON INDUSTRY. Special students will be given an opportunity to become familiar with the literature of cotton. Course given only on permission from the professor in charge. Three hours lectures. Three hours credit. Fee, $3.50. Time will be arranged. *Professor Childs.*

3. PRODUCTION OF COTTON AND OTHER FIBER CROPS. A study of all phases of cotton production. Junior or Senior entire year. Two lectures, one laboratory period. Three hours credit. Fee, $3.50. T. Th., 10:15; lab., T., 2:35-4:25. *Professor Childs.*

4. PLANT BREEDING. A general course in the principles of breeding. Prerequisite: Botany 1. Two lectures and one laboratory period. Junior or Senior. Three hours credit. Fee, $3.50. T. Th., 12:05; lab., S., 11:10-1:00. *Professor Childs.*

7. RESEARCH PLANT BREEDING. Cotton Industry 4 is prerequisite for this course. An advanced course in breeding. Entire year, Senior. One lecture, two laboratory periods. Three hours credit. Fee, $3.50. M., 11:10; lab., W. F., 11:10-1:00. *Professor Childs.*

9-10. COTTON INDUSTRY. Cotton grading, warehousing and marketing. Experimental cotton breeding. Prerequisite: Cotton Industry 3 or 4. Given only as summer course. Thirty hours laboratory work per week, for six weeks. Three hours credit. Fee, $15.00. *Professor Childs.*

11. COTTON GRADING. A study of the grades of cotton, warehousing, and marketing. One lecture and two laboratory periods. Junior or Senior. Laboratory fee, $15.00. Will not be given unless as many as ten men register for the work. Three hours credit. F., 2:35; lab., M. W., 2:35-4:25. *Professor Childs.*

FARM ECONOMICS

1. AGRICULTURAL ECONOMICS. A general study of the principles of agricultural economics with a general survey of agricultural condi-

---

* Soils 3, 5 and 6 will not be given unless at least five apply.

tions in this and other countries. Junior. Three lectures per week. Three hours credit. M. W. F., 12:05. *Dr. Fain.*

2. ELEMENTARY FARM MANAGEMENT. The application of the general principles of economics to an individual farm will be considered in this course with especial reference to conditions in Georgia. Junior. Two lectures and one laboratory period. Three hours credit. Laboratory fee, $3.50. T. Th., 9:20; lab., S., 9:20-11:10. *Dr. Fain.*

3. *ADVANCED FARM MANAGEMENT. A continuation of the study of the individual farm as begun in Farm Economics 2. A special study will be made of the farm records that have been secured in the state. Senior. Prerequisite: Farm Economics 2. One lecture and two laboratory periods. Three hours credit. Laboratory fee, $3.50. M. W. F., 2:35-4:25. *Dr. Fain.*

4. MARKETS. A general survey will be made of market conditions and general factors that will have to be considered in getting the most for the farm crops. Prerequisite: Farm Economics 2. Senior. Two lectures and one laboratory period. Three hours credit. Laboratory fee, $3.50. M. F., 11:15; Th., 2:35-4:25. *Dr. Fain.*

ADVANCED COURSES are given in the Graduate School.

ANIMAL HUSBANDRY

2. *HORSES, MULES AND BEEF CATTLE. The origin, history and development of the various breeds of horses and beef cattle are studied. The adaptation of the various breeds and types of different conditions of soil, climate and environment is considered. Prerequisite: Animal Husbandry 1. Two recitations each week. First term. Sophomore, W. F., 10:15. *Dr. Jarnagin.*

3. *DAIRY CATTLE. The origin and utility of the several breeds of dairy and dual-purpose cattle are studied. Their adaptation to the production of milk, butter, cheese, or to both milk and beef making are carefully considered. Prerequisite: Animal Husbandry 1. Two recitations each week. Second term. Sophomore. W. F., 10:15. *Dr. Jarnagin.*

4. *SHEEP AND SWINE. A study of the history and development of the various breeds of lard and bacon hogs. The history of the various breeds of sheep is taken up and comparison of the several classes made. Prerequisite: Animal Husbandry 1. Two recitations per week. Third term. Sophomore. W. F., 10:15. *Dr. Jarnagin.*

5. *STOCK JUDGING. Practical work in comparative judging and show-ring placing of various breeding and market classes of horses, dairy and beef cattle, bacon and lard hogs, fine, medium and long wool sheep. Prerequisite: Animal Husbandry 1. Fee, $3.50. One laboratory

---

* Courses 2, 3, 4 and 5 constitute a year's work. Three hours credit.

period per week. First, second and third terms. Sophomore. M. or F., 2:35-4:25. *Dr. Jarnagin and Associate Professor Kellogg.*

6. LIVE STOCK PRODUCTION. The principles of breeding, feeding and general management of sheep, beef cattle and hogs are studied. The laboratory work consists of advanced live stock judging and preparation of livestock for the show or the sale ring. Prerequisite: Animal Husbandry 2, 3, 4 and 5. Fee, $3.50. Two recitations and one laboratory period per week. Junior. Three hours credit. M. F., 9:20; lab., W., 11:10-1:00. *Associate Professor Kellogg.*

8. PRINCIPLES OF BREEDING. This course includes the study of the fundamentals of genetics and their application to practical livestock breeding, a consideration of methods that the founders of the several breeds used as well as methods now being applied by successful present day constructive breeders. An intensive study is made of pedigrees of the leading breeds of each class of livestock. Prerequisite, Animal Husbandry 6. Three recitations. Senior year. Three hours credit. T. Th. S., 9:10. *Associate Professor Kellogg.*

8a. PRINCIPLES OF BREEDING. For Sophomore veterinary medicine students. Deals with heredity, selection, atavism and variation. The pedigrees of phenomenal animals and methods and principles followed by the best breeders are studied. Three recitations per week. First term. Sophomore. One hour credit. T. Th. S., 10:15. *Associate Professor Kellogg.*

9. ANIMAL NUTRITION. A study of the gross anatomy and physiology of the digestive system is included. The theoretical and practical side of compounding balanced rations for maintenance, milk and butter production, fattening and growth are fully explained. Three recitations per week. Three hours credit. Senior. M. W. F., 12:05. *Dr. Jarnagin.*

9a. ANIMAL NUTRITION. For sophomore veterinary students. It deals with feeding problems and the underlying principals of animal nutrition. Second and third terms. Two hours credit. Three recitations per week. T. Th. S., 10:15. *Associate Professor Kellogg.*

10. ADVANCED WORK IN ANIMAL NUTRITION. For advanced students in animal husbandry. The results of feeding tests at the various experiment stations and agricultural colleges. Three one-hour recitations per week. Prerequisite: Animal Husbandry 9. First term. Senior. One hour credit. Time will be arranged. *Dr. Jarnagin and Associate Professor Kellogg.*

11. FEEDING PROBLEMS. Qualified students are allowed to assist in conducting feeding tests, keeping records and summarizing results of experimental feeding conducted by the division of animal husbandry. Prerequisite: Animal Husbandry 9. Three one-hour recitations per

week. Second term. One hour credit. Time will be arranged. *Dr. Jarnagin* and *Associate Professor Kellogg.*

12. ECONOMICS OF ANIMAL PRODUCTION. The various types and breeds of live stock are considered in their relation to the utilization of various farm crops, the productiveness of the soil and the creation of wealth in general. Prerequisite: Animal Husbandry 8 and 9. Three recitations per week. Third term. One hour credit. Time will be arranged. *Dr. Jarnagin* and *Associate Professor Kellogg.*

13. RESEARCH WORK IN ANIMAL HUSBANDRY. Qualified students are allowed to carry on investigations in animal husbandry under the approval and direction of the professor in charge of the department. Three hours per week. Senior. Three hours credit. Time will be arranged. *Dr. Jarnagin* and *Associate Professor Kellogg.*

17. FEEDS AND FEEDING. (Smith-Hughes Vocational Students.) Feeds and feeding; the practical problems of feeding farm animals. The students will be required to carry out feeding demonstrations with animals on the College farm. Fee, $3.50. Two recitations per week and the necessary time in the barn. Three hours credit. M. W. F., 11:10. *Dr. Jarnagin.*

18. MARKETING LIVE STOCK. A study of live stock products; advertising and selling pedigreed live stock; freight and insurance rates in transit; liability of carrier and shipper; trade terms and practices; sales methods; commission firms; cooperative live stock shipping and selling associations. Prerequisite: Animal Husbandry 1 to 6 inclusive. Two recitations and one laboratory period per week. Second term. Senior elective. Hours to be arranged. *Dr. Jarnagin* and *Associate Professor Kellogg.*

19. ADVANCED STOCK JUDGING. Three laboratory periods per week. Third term. Prerequisite: Animal Husbandry 1, 2 and 3. One hour credit. Fee, $3.50. *Dr. Jarnagin, Associate Professor Kellogg* and *Associate Professor Rice.*

20. ADVANCED STOCK JUDGING. Three laboratory periods per week. First term. Prerequisite: Animal Husbandry 19. One hour credit. Fee, $3.50. *Dr. Jarnagin, Associate Professor Kellogg,* and *Associate Professor Rice.*

21. ADVANCED FIELD WORK IN STOCK JUDGING. A field trip during first term equivalent to thirty-six laboratory periods. One hour credit. Prerequisite: Animal Husbandry 20. *Dr. Jarnagin, Associate Professor Kellogg,* and *Associate Professor Rice.*

29. FARM MEATS. Killing, cutting and curing of farm meats. Second term. One lecture and two laboratory periods per week. Junior or senior elective. One hour credit. Fee, $2.00. *Associate Professor Rice.*

DAIRYING

7. PRINCIPLES OF DAIRYING. The study of milk production and various methods of manufacturing and market demands. Prerequisite: Animal Husbandry 2, 3, 4 and 5. Fee, $3.50, combined with Animal Husbandry 14. One lecture and two laboratory periods per week. First term. One hour credit. M., 10:15; labs., M. and F., 11:10-1:00. *Associate Professor Bennett.*

14. DAIRY MANUFACTURING. A continuation of "7." It includes butter making with power machinery, ice cream manufacturing, butter judging, creamery machinery and creamery- management. Prerequisite: Animal Husbandry 7. Fee, $3.50, combined with Animal Husbandry 7. Two laboratory periods and one recitation. Second and third terms. Junior. Two hours credit. M., 10:15; labs., M. F., 11:10-1:00. *Dr. Jarnagin* and *Associate Professor Bennett.*

15. MILK PRODUCTION AND DAIRY AND FARM MANAGEMENT. Advanced judging of dairy cattle, the breeding, feeding and management of dairy cattle and marketing of dairy products. Fee, $3.50. Two recitations and one laboratory throughout the Senior year. Three hours credit. W. F., 10:15; lab., Th., 2:35-4:25. *Associate Professor Bennett.*

16. ANIMAL HUSBANDRY. For students in home economics. Production and handling of milk and its products in the home. Farm butter making and the making of various kinds of soft cheese will be taken up. Fee, $3.50. One lecture and two laboratory periods. Second half year. One and one-half hours credit. Time will be arranged. *Associate Professor Bennett.*

22. CREAMERY BUTTER MAKING. An advanced course in creamery organization, equipment, theory and practice of cream separation, butter manufacture, and pasteurization of dairy products under commercial conditions. Prerequisite: Animal Husbandry 7, 14. Fee, $3.50. Two laboratories and one recitation. First term. Senior. One hour credit. W.,11:10; lab., M. W., 2:35-4:25. *Associate Professor Bennett.*

23. CHEESE MAKING. An advanced study of essentials in the establishment of a cheese factory; practical and experimental work in making, curing, and storing cheese. Prerequisite: Animal Husbandry 7, 14. Fee, $3.50. One recitation and two laboratories. Second term. Senior. One hour credit. W., 11:10; labs., M. W., 2:35-4:25. *Associate Professor Bennett.*

24. ICE CREAM MAKING. The manufacture, handling, and judging of ice cream; laboratory tests essential in the ice cream factory. Prerequisites: Animal Husbandry 7 and 14. Fee, $3.50. One recitation and two laboratory periods per week. Third term. Senior. One hour credit. W., 11:10; labs., M. W., 2:35-4:25. *Associate Professor Bennett.*

25. MARKET MILK. An advanced course dealing with the food value

of milk, its relation to public health, and problems in producing and distributing milk. Prerequisite: Animal Husbandry 7, 14. General Bacteriology 1-3. Fee, $2.00. Two recitations and one laboratory period. First term. One hour credit. *Associate Professor Bennett.*

26. DAIRY PRODUCTS INSPECTION. Advanced judging of dairy products; market grades; principal bacteriological and chemical tests used in determining quality and detecting adulteration and preservatives. Prerequisite: Animal Husbandry 7, 14, General Bacteriology 1, 3, Agricultural Chemistry 1. Fee, $2.00. One recitation and two laboratory periods. Second term. One hour credit. *Associate Professor Bennett.*

27. DAIRY PLANT MANAGEMENT. Organization of ownership; essentials in construction; selection and care of dairy machinery; principles of plant operation; purchasing raw materials; advertising and marketing dairy products. Prerequisite: Animal Husbandry 7, 14. Fee, $2.00. Two recitations and one laboratory. Third term. One hour credit. *Associate Professor Bennett.*

ADVANCED COURSES are given in the Graduate School.

BOTANY

A. LESSON WITH PLANTS. Three lessons a week. First term. One hour credit. T. Th. S., 9:20. *Associate Professor Miller.*

1. INTRODUCTORY BOTANY FOR AGRICULTURAL STUDENTS. Three hours lectures or recitations and one laboratory period per week. Three terms. Four hours credit. Fee, $3.50; breakage deposit, $1.00. Lecture, T. Th. S., 12:05; lab., Sec. 1, M., 2:35 and 3:30; lab., Sec. 2, F., 2:35 and 3:30. *Professor Reade* and *Associate Professor Miller.*

2. LOCAL FLORA. Given by special arrangement only. Three laboratory periods per week. Three hours credit. *Professor Reade.*

3. INTRODUCTORY PLANT BIOLOGY. Three hours lectures or recitations one laboratory period per week. Three terms. Four hours credit. Fee, $3.50; breakage deposit, $1.00. Sec. 1, M. W. F., 10:15; lab., T., 2:35 and 3:30. Sec. 2, T. T. S., 11:10; lab., Th., 2:35 and 3:30. *Professor Reade* and *Associate Professor Miller.*

4. LIVERWORTS TO ANGIOSPERMS. Comparative morphology and phylogeny. Two hours of recitations and two laboratory periods per week. Three terms. Four hours credit. Prerequisite: Botany 3. Fee, $3.50, breakage deposit, $1.00. Not given in 1926-1927. *Professor Reade.*

5. BACTERIA. Three laboratory periods per week. Three terms. Three hours credit. Prerequisite: Botany 3. Fee, $5.00; breakage deposit, $5.00. Not given in 1926-1927. *Professor Reade.*

6. TRUE FUNGI. Laboratory and field work and reading. Three laboratory periods per week. Three terms. Three hours credit. Prerequisite: Botany 1 or 3. Fee, $5.00; breakage deposit, $5.00. M. W.

F., 11:10 and 12:15. *Professor Reade* and *Associate Professor Miller.*

9. PHYSIOLOGY. Laboratory work and reading. Three laboratory periods and one conference hour per week. Three terms. Four hours credit. Fee, $5.00; breakage deposit, $5.00. Prerequisite; Botany 1 or 3. M. W. F., 9:20 and 10:15. *Associate Professor Miller.*

7. PHYTOPATHOLOGY. Three laboratory periods per week. Three terms. Three hour credit. Prerequisite: Botany 6. Fee, $5.00; breakage fee, $5.00. Not given in 1926-1927. *Professor Reade.*

11. GENETICS. Three hours lectures per week. Three terms. Three hours credit. Prerequisite: Botany 1 or 3, Zoology 31. T. Th. S., 9:50. *Professor Reade.*

ADVANCED COURSES are given in the Graduate School.

CHEMISTRY

1. ELEMENTARY CHEMISTRY. Three hours a week of lectures and recitations and one laboratory period. Three terms. Four hours credit. Fee, $2.50, and breakage fee, $5.00. Sec. 1, M. W. F., 9:20; Sec. 2, M. W. F., 12:15. Lab., Sec. 1, M., 2:35; Sec. 2, T. 11:05 to 1:00; Sec. 3, Sec. 8:30 to 10:15. *Associate Professor Scott* and *Adjunct Professor Brockman.*

2. INORGANIC CHEMISTRY. Three hours a week of lectures and recitations. Three terms. Three hours credit. Not open to Freshmen. T. Th. S., 12:15. *Professor White.*

21. INORGANIC CHEMISTRY. Three hours a week of lectures and recitations and one laboratory period. Three terms. Four hours credit. Not open to Freshmen. Fee, $2.50. Breakage fee, $5.00. T. Th. S., 12:15; lab., Sec. 1, T., 2:35; Sec. 2, W., 2:35. *Professor White* and *Adjunct Professor Brockman.*

22. INORGANIC CKEMISTRY. Three hours a week of lectures and recitations and two laboratory periods. Three terms. Five hours credit. Mainly for pre-medical students. Fee, $5.00. Breakage fee, $5.00. Sec. 1, T. Th. S., 12:15; Sec. 2. M. W. F., 9:20 Lab Sec 1, M W 2:35, Lab. Sec. 2, T. and Th., 2:35. *Associate Professor Scott* and *Adjunct Professor Brockman.*

3. ORGANIC CHEMISTRY. Three hours a week of lectures and recitations and one laboratory period. Three terms. Open to students who have completed Courses 21 or 22. Fee, $2.50. Breakage fee, $5.00. M. W. F., 12:15; lab. Sec. 1, Th. 9:20 to 11:10, Sec. 2, Th. 2:35. *Professor White* and *Associate Professor Scott.*

31. ADVANCED ORGANIC PREPARATIONS. Six hours a week of lectures and laboratory work. Three terms. Prerequisite: 21 (or 22) and 3. Fee, $10.00. Breakage fee, $10.00. Three hours credit. *Associate Professor Scott.*

4. INDUSTRIAL (including Agricultural) CHEMISTRY. Three hours a

week of lectures and recitations. Three terms. Three hours credit. Open to students who have completed Courses 21 or 22. M. W. F., 10:15. *Profssor White.*

5. PHYSICAL CHEMISTRY. Three hours a week of lectures and conference and one laboratory period. Three terms. M. W. F., 11:10; lab., M., 2:35. Four hours credit. Open only to students by special arrangement. Prerequisite: Courses 21 or 22 and 3. Fee, $2.50. Breakage fee, $5.00. *Adjunct Professor Brockman.*

8. ANALYTICAL CHEMISTRY. Qualitative. Three laboratory periods a week. Three terms. Three hours credit. Prerequisite: Courses 21 or 22. Fee, $10.00. Breakage fee, $10.00. Sec. 1, M. W. F., 10:15; Sec. 2, M. W. F., 2:35. *Adjunct Professor Brockman.*

9. ANALYTICAL CHEMISTRY. Quantitative. Three laboratory periods a week, Three terms. Three hours credit. Prerequisite: Course 8. Fee, $10.00. Breakage fee, $10.00. *Professor White* and *Adjunct Professor Brockman.*

91. ANALYTICAL CHEMISTRY. Advanced. Continuation of Course 9. Three laboratory periods a week. Three hours credit. Fee, $10.00. Breakage fee, $10.00. *Professor White, Associate Professor Scott and Adjunct Professor Brockman.*

92. ANALYTICAL CHEMISTRY. Advanced. Continuation of Course 91. Three laboratory periods a week. Three hours credit. Fee, $10.00. Breakage fee, $10.00. *Professor White. Associate Professor Scott and Adjunct Professor Brockman.*

ADVANCED COURSES are given in the Graduate School.

CIVIL ENGINEERING

1. ELEMENTARY SURVEYING. Three hours a week. Three terms. Three hours credit. Field practice required. Text: Breed and Hosmer. M. W. F., 11:10. *Professor Griggs.*

2. MATERIALS OF CONSTRUCTION AND FOUNDATIONS. Three hours per week. Three terms. Three hours credit. Lectures, library work, essays and laboratory. Prerequisite: Course 1. M. W. F., 12:05. *Professor Strahan.*

3. RAILWAY ENGINEERING. Three hours per week. First and second terms. Two hours credit. Prerequisite: Course 1. Allen's Railroad Curves and Earthwork. Field practice. T. Th. S., 9:10. *Professor Griggs.*

4. HIGHWAY ENGINEERING. Three hours per week, third term. One hour credit. Baker's Roads and Pavements. Laboratory. Prerequisite: Courses 1 and 3. T. Th. S., 9:10. *Professor Griggs.*

5. APPLIED MECHANICS, BRIDGES, ETC. Three hours per week. First and second terms. Two hours credit. Spofford's Theory of Structures. Prerequisite: 2, 3 and 4. M. W. F., 10:15. *Professor Strahan.*

6. SANITARY ENGINEERING AND SEWERAGE. Three hours per week. Third term. One hour credit. Lectures. M. W. F., 10:15. *Professor Strahan.*

7. HYDRAULICS. Three hours per week. First and second terms. Two hours credit. Russell's Hydraulics. Lectures. T. Th. S., 9:10. *Professor Strahan.*

8. WATER SUPPLY ENGINEERING. Three hours per week. Third term. One hour credit. Lectures. T. Th. S., 9:10. *Professor Strahan.*

9. REINFORCED CONCRETE AND ARCHES. Three hours per week. Three terms Three hours credit. Text: Taylor and Thompson. M. W. F., 11:10. *Professor Strahan.*

10. ELEMENTS OF ARCHITECTURE. Three hours per week. Three terms. Three hours credit. Hamlin's History of Architecture; Ware's Vignola. Prerequisite: Courses 12 and 14. M. W. F., 10:15. *Professor Griggs.*

11. ARCHITECTURAL DESIGN. Three hours per week. Three terms. Three hours credit. Prerequisite: Courses 9 and 10. T. Th. S., 10:15. *Professor Griggs.*

ADVANCED COURSES are given in the Graduate School.

Drawing

12. ELEMENTARY GRAPHICS. Two laboratory periods per week. Three terms. Two hours credit. French's Engineering Drawing. M. W. Th. F., 2:35-4:25. *Professor Griggs.*

14. DESCRIPTIVE GEOMETRY. Recitations and drafting. Two recitations and one laboratory period per week. Three terms. Two hours credit. Prerequisite; Course 12. Text: Phillips and Millar. M. W. F., 10:15. *Professor Griggs.*

15. TOPOGRAPHY AND PERSPECTIVE. Two hours per week. Three terms. Two hours credit. Lectures. Prerequisite: Course 14. T. Th., 10:15-11:40. *Professor Griggs.*

16. GRAPHIC STATICS AND STRUCTURAL DESIGN. Two hours per week. Three terms. Two hours credit. Lectures. Thompson's Bridge and Structural Design. Prerequisite: Courses 12, 14. T. Th., 12:05. *Professor Strahan.*

ADVANCED COURSES are given in the Graduate School.

COMMERCE
Accounting

6. ELEMENTARY ACCOUNTING. Foundation for advanced Accounting courses. Three hours per week. Three terms. Three hours credit. Required of Sophomores. M. W. F., 11:10 and 12:05; T. Th. S., 8:25. *Professor Heckman* and *Adjunct Professor Smith.*

11. ADVANCED ACCOUNTING. Three hours per week. Three terms. Three hours credit. Prerequisite: Commerce 6. T. Th. S., 10:15. *Professor Heckman.*

12. AUDITING. Detailed and balance sheet audits; practical auditing work required. Three hours per week. First half year. One and one-half hours credit. Prerequisite: Commerce 6, 11. M. W. F., 10:15. *Professor Heckman.*

13. COST ACCOUNTING. Practice in constructing systems that show costs. Prerequisite: Commerce 11. Three hours per week. Second half term. One and one-half hours credit. M. W. F., 11:15. *Professor Heckman.*

14. ADVANCED ACCOUNTING PROBLEMS. Miscellaneous and selected Certified Public Accounting Problems. Three hours per week, first half year. One and one-half hours credit. Prerequisite: Commerce 11. M. W. F., 10:15. *Professor Heckman.* (Not offered in 1926-27.)

15. INCOME TAX ACCOUNTING. Three hours per week, second half year. One and one-half hours credit. Prerequisite: Commerce 11. M. W. F., 10:15. *Professor Heckman.* (Not offered in 1926-27.)

Business Law

20a. CONTRACTS AND AGENCIES. Three hours per week. First term. One hour credit. T. Th. S., 11:10. *Professor Heckman.*

20b. SALES AND NEGOTIABLE INSTRUMENTS. Three hours per week. Second term. One hour credit. T. Th. S., 11:10. *Professor Heckman.*

20c. PARTNERSHIPS AND CORPORATIONS. Three hours per week. Third term. One hour credit. T. Th. S., 11:10. *Professor Heckman.*

Banking and Finance

26. MONEY AND BANKING. Principles of money, credit and banking. Special study of the Federal Reserve System. Three hours per week. Three terms. Three hours credit. M. W. F., 10:15. *Professor Brooks.*

30. CORPORATION ORGANIZATION AND FINANCE. Three hours per week. First half year. One and one half hours credit. M. W. F., 11:10. *Adjunct Professor Smith.*

31. INVESTMENTS. Fundamentals in the analysis of securities. Three hours per week, second half year. One and one-half hours credit. M. W. F., 11:10. *Adjunct Professor Smith.*

34. PUBLIC FINANCE. American Public Finance, federal, state and local. Three hours per week. Three terms. Three hours credit. M. W. F., 12:05. *Professor Brooks.* (Not offered in 1926-27.)

MATHEMATICS OF INVESTMENT. (Mathematics 11). This course, covering the mathematics of annuities, bonds and insurance, is offered by the Department of Mathematics. Three hours per week. First or second half year. One and one-half hours credit. Prerequisite: Mathematics 1, 2. Required of Juniors in School of Commerce. T. Th. S., 10:15; 12:05. *Professor Stephens.*

Economics

1. INDUSTRIAL AND COMMERCIAL GEOGRAPHY. The geography of economic resources and trade. Three hours per week. Three terms. Three hours credit. Required of Freshmen. M. W. F., 10:15, 12:05; T. Th. S., 9:20, 10:15, 12:05. *Professor Jenkins.*

5. ECONOMIC PRINCIPLES. An introductory course in economic theory. Prerequisite to all advanced courses. Three hours per week. Three terms. Three hours credit. Required of Sophomores. M. W. F., 9:20; 10:15; 12:05. *Professor Brooks* and *Adjunct Professor Bryan.*

36a. SOCALISM. The rise and spread of socialist doctrines and their effects upon recent legislation. First term. Three hours per week. One hour credit. T. Th. S., 11:10. *Adjunct Professor Bryan.*

36b. LABOR PROBLEMS. Labor Legislation, unemployment, woman and child labor, cooperation. Three hours per week. Second term. One hour credit. M. W. F., 12:05. *Adjunct Professor Bryan.*

36c. SOCIAL INSURANCE. The workingmen's insurance movement in Europe and the United States. Three hours per week. Third term. One hour credit. M. W. F., 12:05. *Adjunct Professor Bryan.*

37a. LIFE INSURANCE. Principles and Practices. Three hours per week. First term. One hour credit. T. Th. S., 9:20. *Adjunct Professor Smith.*

37b. FIRE INSURANCE. Contracts, rates, reserve, settlement of losses, etc. Three hours per week. Second term. One hour credit. T. Th. S., 9:20. *Adjunct Professor Smith.*

37c. CASUALTY INSURANCE. Marine, automobile, title, credit, corporate bonding. Three hours per week. Third term. One hour credit. T. Th. S., 9:20. *Adjunct Professor Smith.*

ELEMENTARY STATISTICS. (Mathematics 6). This course in the of Statistics is offered by the Department of Mathematics. Three hours per week. First or seocnd half year. One and one-half hours credit. Prerequisite: Mathematics 1, 2. Required of Juniors. T. Th. S., 10:15 and 12:05. *Professor Stephens.*

Business Administration

51a. BUSINESS ADMINISTRATION. The manager's administration of production, finance, marketing, risk-bearing and personnel. Three hours per week. First term. One hour credit. T. Th. S., 9:20. *Professor Jenkins.*

51b. INDUSTRIAL MANAGEMENT. The administration of industrial enterprises, with particular attention to factory practice. Physical equipment, scientific management, and labor relations are considered. Three hours per week. Second term. One hour credit. T. Th. S., 9:20. *Professor Jenkins.*

51c. PERSONNEL MANAGEMENT. The principles of personnel relations in industry, taking up such phases as cooperative management, profit sharing, pension plans, training, and supervision. Three hours per week. Third term. One hour credit. T. Th. S., 9:20. *Professor Jenkins.*

Marketing

60a. MARKETING. A general course emphasizing the principles that guide the varied marketing institutions. Three hours per week. First term. One hour credit. T. Th. S., 12:05. *Professor Jenkins.*

60b. SALESMANSHIP. The formation of sales and price policies; the appropriate organization of a sales department; the technique and routine of sales administration. Three hours per week. Third term. One hour credit. T. Th. S., 9:20. *Professor Jenkins.*

60c. ADVERTISING. A study of the nature and scope of advertising, its service to producers and consumers, and modern advertising practice. Three hours per week. Second term. One hour credit. T. Th. S., 9:20. *Professor Jenkins.*

Transportation and Utilities

75a. RAILROAD TRANSPORTATION. The historical development of steam railways and the elements of transportation economics. Three hours per week. First term. One hour credit. M. W. F., 9:20. *Professor Jenkins.*

75b. HIGHWAY TRANSPORTATION. An introduction to highway economics, including a general survey of automotive transportation and of city and rural traffic problems. Three hours per week. Second term. One hour credit. M. W. F., 11:10. *Professor Jenkins.*

75c. WATER TRANSPORTATION. The principles of ocean transportation. Inland waterway and coastwise shipping. Port problems. Three hours per week. Third term. One hour credit. M. W. F., 11:10. *Professor Jenkins.*

76a. RAILROADS AND GOVERNMENT. The relation of American Government to railroad rates, service and management, with comparisons from other nations. Three hours per week. First term. One hour credit. M. W. F., 11:10. *Professor Jenkins.*

·76b. TRAFFIC MANAGEMENT. A study of traffic administration from the standpoint of the shipper. Three hours per week. Second term. One hour credit. M. W. F., 11:10. *Professor Jenkins.*

76c. SOUTHERN MARKETING AND TRANSPORTATION PROBLEMS. A close study of Southeastern rate cases, the Southern Basing Point System, the present rate structure in the South and needed adjustments. Three hours per week. Third term. One hour credit. M. W. F., 11:10. *Professor Jenkins.*

77. PUBLIC UTILITY REGULATION. A study of the principles and prob-

lems of public service regulation, including: the growth of state commissions, and the extent and limitation of their jurisdiction; bases of rate making, theories of value, and valuation of intangibles; nature, kinds, and rates of depreciation; reasonableness of operating expenses. Full year, three hours. M. W. F., 12:05. *Professor Jenkins.*

80a. FOREIGN COMMERCE ECONOMICS. An introductory course in the principles of foreign trade, including a study of international commercial policies. Three hours per week. First term. One hour credit. T. Th. S., 12:05. *Professor Jenkins.*

80b. U. S. FOREIGN TRADE. The nature and origin of American imports. The character and destination of our exports. Three hours per week. Second term. One hour credit. T. Th. S., 9:20. *Professor Jenkins.*

80c. IMPORTING AND EXPORTING TECHNIQUES. Technical procedure attending export and import shipments; packing, shipping, customs regulations, insurance and financing. Three hours per week. Thrid term. One hous credit. T. Th. S., 9:20. *Professor Jenkins.*

Secretarial Courses

91. SHORTHAND. Elementary course in theory and practice of Gregg Shorthand. Three hours per week. Three terms. Two hours credit. M. W. F., 12:05 and 2:35. *Adjunct Professor Broadhurst.*

92. TYPEWRITING. Touch system of typewriting. Three hours per week. Three terms. One hour credit. M. W. F., 11:10; T. Th. S., 11:10; 12:05 and 2:35 Fee $10.00. *Adjunct Professor Broadhurst.*

96a. OFFICE ORGANIZATION. A study of office organization with relation to personnel, equipment and the establishment of routine processes. Consideration is given to the types of organization, layout and equipment. Three hours per week. First term. One hour credit. T. Th. S., 10:15. *Adjunct Professor Broadhurst.*

96b. OFFICE MANAGEMENT. The conduct of a modern office with consideration of the problems of standardization, incentives; relations between employer and employe; order and billing systems; filing systems and devices. Three hours per week. Second term. One hour credit. T. Th. S., 10:15. *Adjunct Professor Broadhurst.*

96c. BUSINESS CORRESPONDENCE. Training in business letter composition; a study of the fundamental principles of business correspondence. Specific types of letters considered both as to content and appearance. Written exercises and problems. Three hours per week. Third term. One hour credit. T. Th. S., 10:15. *Adjunct Professor Broadhurst.*

It is recommended that students should have a knowledge of touch typewriting before undertaking Course 96c.

ADVANCED COURSES are given in the Graduate School.

EDUCATION

A. HISTORY AND PHILOSOPHY OF EDUCATION

1-2-3. INTRODUCTORY STUDIES IN EDUCATION.

1. INTRODUCTION TO EDUCATION. A study of selected educational classics. First term. T. Th. S., 9:20. Credit one hour. *Associate Professor Brumby.*

2. HISTORY OF EDUCATION. A brief survey of the forces and events which have contributed to the shaping and directing of educational progress. While the main emphasis is given to modern times, the course furnishes the historical background necessary to a study of the rise of present day state school systems. Second term. T. Th. S., 9:20. Credit one hour. *Associate Professor Brumby.*

3. EDUCATIONAL HYGIENÉ. A study of the importance and place of health as an aim in education; physical hygiene and mental efficiency; Mental hygiene; conservation of human life; hygiene of the school room, the school grounds, and the home. Third term. T. W. S., 9:20. Credit one hour. *Associate Professor Brumby.*

3. EDUCATIONAL HYGIENE. A study of the importance and place of health as an aim in education; physical hygiene and mental efficiency; mental hygiene; conservation of human life; hygiene of the school room, the school grounds, and the home. Third term, T. Th. S., 9:20. Credit one hour. *Associate Professor Brumby.*

7-8-9. EDUCATIONAL SOCIOLOGY AND PHILOSOPHY.

7. EDUCATIONAL SOCIOLOGY. Social origin and function of education; individual versus social aims; determination of objectives; vocational and cultural education; vocational guidance; socialization of aims, management, and the school generally. First term. T Th S., 11:10. Credit one hour. *Professor Woofter.*

8-9. DEVELOPMENT OF EDUCATIONAL THEORIES AND PRACTICES. In the United States, the South, and Georgia. Education for citizenship in a democracy. Second and third terms. Credit two hours. T. Th. S., 11:10. *Professor Woofter.*

15. ADVANCED HISTORY AND PHILOSOPHY OF EDUCATION.

1. The approach to contemporary educational problems through the history of education in its relations to human development.

2. Modern educational policies and practices as developed in relationship to the political, economic, and social life of some of the great nations of the world, England, Prussia, France, and the United States. Three terms, credit three hours.

It is contemplated that this course may be taken for undergraduate credit on approval; also that it is intended as three-fourths of a Graduate Minor, the other one-fourth to be assigned as additional work

to accompany this course. See Graduate Education 101. Probably not
given 1926-27. *Professor Woofter.*

B. EDUCATIONAL PSYCHOLOGY AND HYGIENE

4-5-6. INTRODUCTORY EDUCATIONAL PSYCHOLOGY.

4-5. A study of inherited nature, habit and learning, the psychology
of school subjects, transfer, and diagnosis. First and second terms.
(6). Third term. The nature and problems of adolescence and the
education of the adolescent. Credit three hours. M. W. F., 10:15.
Professor Edwards.

17-18-19. PHYSICAL AND MENTAL HYGIENE: SCHOOL HYGIENE. Physical hygiene and mental efficiency; mental hygiene and conservation of
human life; hygiene of the school child and of the school plant. Not
given 1926-27.

26-27-28. EXPERIMENTAL EDUCATION. Experimental studies of individual differences, habit formation and learning, tests for defects,
transfer of learning, problems of perception, imagery, association, attention, memory, and special types of learning and study. Not given
1926-27.

23-24-25. CHILD STUDY. See Psychology 23-24-25.

102. GRADUATE COURSE. See Graduate School.

C. SECONDARY EDUCATION AND SCHOOL ADMINISTRATION

10-11-12. TEACHING IN THE HIGH SCHOOL.

This is a practical course which should be taken by all those who
wish recommendation for the College Professional Certificate. It is
a full session course, credit three hours. For convenience it is described in separate parts, as follows:

10. METHODS OF TEACHING IN THE HIGH SCHOOL. OBSERVATION AND
PRACTICE TEACHING. A course in general method with special application to high school teaching. First term. M. W. F., 9:20. One
hour credit. *Professor Pusey.*

11. CLASS MANAGEMENT. OBSERVATION AND PRACTICE TEACHING. A
study of the general principle of class management including such
topics as discipline, incentives, daily schedules, course of study, supervised study, and aims and methods of the recitation period. Work in
observation and practice teaching is the laboratory part of this course.
Second Term. M. W. F., 9:20. One hour credit. *Professor Pusey.*

12. EDUCATIONAL TESTS AND MEASUREMENTS. A critical study of the
more important methods and devices used in measuring objectively
the results of teaching, followed by practical work in giving and
scoring tests. This will be accompanied by a brief course in diagnosis.
Third Term. M. W. F., 9:20. One hour credit. *Professor Pusey.*

20-21-22. SECONDARY EDUCATION AND SCHOOL ADMINISTRATION.

This is a full session course, credit three hours, divided as follows:

20. THE JUNIOR HIGH SCHOOL. The place of the junior high school in the school system. The functions of the junior high school. Short courses and their value. The arrangement of the subject matter in these courses. Extra-curricular activities and guidance. First Term. M. W. F., 12:05. One hour credit. *Professor Pusey.*

21. THE SENIOR HIGH SCHOOL. The functions of the senior high school. Curriculum making and curriculum adjustment. The school plant, the selection of teachers, marking systems and classification of pupils. Extra-curricular activities and guidance. Placement of graduates. Second Term. M. W. F., 12:05. One hour credit. *Professor Pusey.*

22. SCHOOL ORGANIZATION AND ADMINISTRATION. A practical study of school problems, administrative in character, in town and in rural schools. School laws, regulations of boards of education, the relationship of various school operatives to one another, to the pupils and to the community. Special attention will be given to the duties of the principal in organizing and in conducting a school. Third Term. M. W. F., 12:05. One hour credit. *Professor Pusey.*

16. PRINCIPLES OF SECONDARY EDUCATION. Development of the American high school, its function and types; the high school pupil, problems of growth physical and mental, testing for physiological age, individual differences and their treatment; principles underlying the curricula, psychology of the high school subjects and methods based thereon; vocational, moral, and cultural functions of the high school. Not given 1926-27.

16b. PRINCIPLES OF ELEMENTARY EDUCATION. Given if sufficient demand. M. W. F., 11:10. See *Professor Pusey.*

104. GRADUATE COURSE: SCHOOL ADMINISTRATION. See Graduate School.

D. THEORY AND PRACTICE OF TEACHING

10-11-12. TEACHING IN THE HIGH SCHOOL. See Secondary Education.

14. TEACHING THE MAJOR SUBJECTS. This is a group of departmental courses offering studies in special methods of teaching. Each course is a term course or its equivalent, credit one hour.

Every student preparing to teach must select some major subject for teaching, and should complete twelve hours in this subject. The course in special methods for the major subject, if offered, should be elected. With the approval of the Dean of the School of Education, this course may be combined with other courses in education to make a unit course in any degree.

The instructor giving each course must be consulted for permission to register for his course and for the schedule hour which must be agreed upon with him.

Following is a list of these courses:

S-14a. THE TEACHING OF ENGLISH IN THE HIGH SCHOOL. (In summer session only).

,14b. THE TEACHING OF HISTORY AND CIVICS. This course for teachers will be a study of the problems of history teaching in the high schools; the relation of history to allied studies; the history curricula in the schools of Europe and the United States in the past; the more recent ideas in the presentation of history by charts, diagrams, maps, pictures, text-books and lectures. Practical exercises in historical methods will be required. The teaching of civics will be studied in like manner. Second term, credit one hour. *Professor Payne.*

14c. THE TEACHING OF SOCIAL SCIENCE. The nature and importance of social science in the high school, methods of teaching, examination of texts and library references, and discussion of other practical phases. This course does not include methods in history teaching.

14d. TEACHING SECONDARY MATHEMATICS. Methods of presentation. Content and justification of courses. Special references to Report of Committee on Reorganization of Mathematics in Secondary Schools. Three hours per week. Third term. One hour credit. *Professor Stephens.*

14e. THE TEACHING OF HIGH SCHOOL PHYSICS. A course devoted to a consideration of the organization of the subject matter and materials of a standard high school Physics course and to a study of methods of conducting the course. Some laboratory work will be required in glass blowing and the devising and mounting of typical laboratory experiments and projects. A complete syllabus for a year's course will be worked out and discussed. The following texts will be used in connection with the lectures as a basis for discussion. Rusk—"How to Teach High School Physics", Mann—"Physics Teaching". Prerequisite: A standard college course in Physics or two years' teaching experience in Physics in a standard high school. Offered during the second half-year if as many as three qualified students apply. Two hours per week for a half-year. Credit, one hour. *Professor Hendren.*

14f. THE TEACHING OF BIOLOGICAL SCIENCE. A course designed to consider the methods of presentation of biological materials in the High Schools of Georgia, including an historical development of course types, such as "dissection" courses, "type" courses, "principle" courses "project" courses; review of the contents of present day outlines and their adaptability to our equipment; relation to nature study and college courses; note book demands, grading systems; equipment costs; library necessities, etc. Prerequisites; a knowledge of Biology such as would be obtained in Botany 3, Zoology 31 or experience in teaching the subject in the High School. Three hours per week, third term. Credit one hour. *Professor Krafka.*

S-14g. THE TEACHING OF LATIN. (Summer term only). The course is based on The Classical Investigation, Part I, General Survey, and discusses the objectives of the study, the examination of various text books used in the secondary school, the problems of teaching in each of the four years of the study. It also covers rapid review of grammar, and exercises in translations from English into Latin. One term credit one hour. *Professor Hooper.*

14h. THE TEACHING OF FRENCH. A study of aims, general method, difficult points in teaching, text books to be used, and an exemplification of methods with these texts together with some practice and discussions of other practical helps. Prerequisite, at least two college years, preferably three, above French X. Second term, credit one hour. *Associate Professor Brumby.*

E. ELEMENTARY AND RURAL EDUCATION

Courses in Elementary and Rural Education are given in the summer session, rarely in the regular nine months.

34. ADMINISTRATION OF STATE AND COUNTY SCHOOLS. State and county systems and their relations; readjustments, consolidation, equalization of opportunities, securing and holding good teachers, finances, and other pressing practical problems. Summer session.

35. SUPERVISION. The improvement of teaching through supervision; general supervisors; special supervisors; health inspectors, the school visitor, the attendance officer, and other problems of rural supervision. Summer session.

36. THE SCHOOL PRINCIPAL. The main stress of this course will be on the principal of the small town, rural, or consolidated school, his problems, preparation, etc. Summer session.

40. PRINCIPLES AND METHODS OF TEACHING IN RURAL ELEMENTARY SCHOOLS.

41. RURAL SCHOOL MANAGEMENT. A course for teachers.

42. RURAL LIFE AND EDUCATION. Rural life conditions, sociological problems, education as adapted to rural life and betterment.

50. TECHNIQUE OF TEACHING. A study of principles and methods for use in the general elementary grades. The project method and other progressive practices applied.

51. SCHOOL MANAGEMENT. A course for elementary teachers considering problems of discipline, classification, attendance, records, equipment, school occasions, community interests, etc.

52. PRINCIPLES OF ELEMENTARY EDUCATION.

For Graduate courses, see Graduate School.

For Correspondence Courses, see Correspondence Division.

ELECTRICAL ENGINEERING

1. ELECTRICAL MACHINERY AND APPARATUS. A study of the theory of direct currents and their application to electrical machinery and engineering auxiliaries—meters, storage batteries, transmission lines, distribution systems, electric lights, etc. Three hours lecture and quiz and one laboratory period each week. Required of Juniors in the Civil Engineering and Electrical Engineering courses. Fee, $5.00. Three terms. Four hours credit. M. W. T., 11:10; lab., 2:35. *Professor Davenport.*

2. MECHANICAL ENGINEERING OF POWER PLANTS. A study of Prime Movers and Power Plant Auxiliaries—steam engines and boilers steam turbines, gas and oil engines, waterwheels and windmills, condensers, economizers, feed water heaters, pumps, piping, etc. A limited amount of laboratory work with steam, gas, and gasoline engines will be required. The course will include visits to plants where the various types of prime movers will be found in operation. Two hours per week. Three terms. Two hours credit. Required of Juniors in the Electrical Engineering course. T. Th., 11:10. *Professor Davenport.*

3. ELECTRICAL MACHINERY AND APPARATUS—ALTERNATING. A continuation of Course 1. A study of the theory of alternating currents and their application to electrical machinery and engineering auxiliaries, transformers, meters, lights, transmission lines, distributing systems, etc. Three lectures and one laboratory period each week. Three terms. Four hours credit. Required of Seniors in the Civil Engineering and the Electrical Engineering courses. Fee, $5.00. M. W. F., 12:15; lab., W., 2:35. *Professor Davenport.*

4. ELECTRICAL ENGINEERING OF POWER PLANTS. A study of electrical machinery and auxiliaries, its operation and control, switchboards and measuring devices, distribution, transmission, and utilization. Typical installation, both hydro-electric and steam-electric, will be studied in detail and visits will be made to such plants as are available for study. Construction drawing and diagrams of these plants will be used where they are available. Two hours per week. Three terms. Two hours credit. Required of Seniors in Electrical Engineering Course. T. Th., 12:15. *Professor Davenport.*

TheElectrical Engineering Laboratory, occupying the basement of the Moore Building is equipped with direct current motors and generators of various types; with alternators, both single phase and polyphase; with synchronous motors, synchronous converters, induction motors, series alternating current motors, etc.; with specially constructed experimental machines; with transformers and storage batteries, a farm lighting outfit, gas engines, a 20 H. P. semi-Diesel Type, Fairbanks-Morse Oil Engine, a 10 H. P. steam engine, and with all the necessary meters, lamp banks, distribution circuits and control devices.

The equipment is modern, and, for a limited number of students furnishes all the apparatus necessary for a full and thorough course of instruction and laboratory work in electrical machinery.

ENGLISH

All courses run three hours a week. Each course is valued at three hours credit. English 1 and English 2 are prerequisite to all other courses in English.

1. RHETORIC AND COMPOSITION. Required of Freshmen. M. W. F., 8:25, 9:20, 10:15, 11:10, 12:05, 2:35; T. Th. S., 8:25, 9:20, 11:10, 12:05. *Professors Park, Sanford, Walker. McWhorter, Associate Professors Wade, DuBose, Mr. Sanderson. Mr. Tate.*

2. SURVEY OF ENGLISH LITERATURE. For Sophomores. M. W. F., 9:20, 10:15, 11:10, 12:05; T. Th. S., 9:20, 10:15. *Professors Park, Walker, McWhorter, Associate Professors Wade, DuBose. Mr. Sanderson.*

Elective Courses

3. AMERICAN LITERATURE. This course attemps to give a comprehensive account of American literature. M. W. F., 10:15; T. Th. S., 9:20. *Associate Professor Wade.* (Given in alternate years. Omitted in 1926-1927.)

4. THE NOVEL. The development of the English novel. T. Th. S., 9:20. *Professor Sanford.*

5. CONTEMPORARY DRAMA. M. W. F., 9.20. *Professor Park.* (Given in alternate years. Omitted in 1926-1927.)

6. EIGHTEENTH CENTURY LITERATURE. T. Th. S., 12:05. *Professor McWhorter.*

9. VICTORIAN LITERATURE. M. W. F., 10:15. *Associate Professor Wade* and *Professor Walker* jointly. (Given in alternate years. Omitted in 1927-1928.)

11. SHAKESPEARE. T. Th. S., 11:10. *Professor Walker.* (Given in alternate years.Omitted in 1926-1827.)

12. POETRY. The technique of English verse with the study of outstanding examples. M. W. F., 9:20. *Professor Park.* (Given in alternate years. Omitted in 1927-1928.)

13. THE ENGLISH THEATRE. T. Th. S., 11:10. Fee for equipment, $5.00. *Professor Walker* and *Associate Professor Wade* jointly. (Given in alternate years. Omitted in 1927-1928.)

ADVANCED COURSES are given in the Graduate School

ENGLISH LANGUAGE

1. ANGLO-SAXON. Phonology, Inflections, and Translations. Textbooks: Smith's "Old English Grammar," and Bright's "Anglo-Saxon Reader." Three hours a week. Optional for Juniors. T. Th. S.. 12:15. *Professor Sanford.*

2. MIDDLE ENGLISH. Chaucer's Prologue and Knight's Tale with lectures based on Ten Brink's "Chauser's Sprache and Verskunst," and Morris' "Organic History of English Words," Part II. Three hours a week. Optional for Seniors. M. W. F., 9:20. *Professor Sanford.*

4. ENGLISH SYNTAX. This course will deal with the structure of the English sentence. Optional for Juniors and Seniors. Three nours a week. Hours to be arranged. *Professor Sanford.*

FORESTRY

1. FOREST POLICY. A consideration of the forest laws and legislation of the various countries and states. The development of a policy. Three hours lecture and recitation. First term. Open to Juniors. One hour credit. M. W. F., 2:35-3:30. *Adjunct Professor Sawyer.*

2. FARM FORESTRY. Forestry as an adjunct to agriculture. Forest influences, nursery practice, field plantings, thinnings and improvement cuttings, protection, estimating timber, wood measurements, seasoning and preservative treatment of wood, financial results. Three recitation periods, second half-year. Open to Juniors in agriculture. One and one-half hours credit. Fee, $1.00. M. W. F., 9:20-10:15. *Professor Burleigh.*

4. DENDROLOGY. Comprehensive study of forest trees of North America. Taxonomy, botanical and silvical characteristics, range, winter and summer identification. One lecture and two laboratory periods, entire year. Three hours credit. Fee, $3.50. W., 4:20; F., 2:30-5:20. *Professor Burleigh.*

4a. TREE AND SHRUB IDENTIFICATION. Systematic study of the local flora. Winter and summer characteristics. Practical field identification. Three laboratory periods. Second half-year. One and one-half hours credit. Fee, $1.50. Time will be arranged. *Professor Burleigh.*

5. SILVICULTURE. Collection and testing of seeds. Location and construction of seed beds. Transplanting. Silvicultural systems of management. Three laboratory periods the entire year. Collateral reading. Open to Juniors. Fee, $3.50. T. Th., 2:35-5:20. *Professor Burleigh.*

6. FOREST PROTECTION. Methods of preventing, fighting and controlling forest fires. Control of forest diseases and injurious insects. Three lectures and recitation periods. Entire year. Three hours credit. Open to Juniors. T. Th. S., 9:20. *Professor Burleigh.*

7. CRUISING AND SCALING. Freshman summer camp. Use of volume tables, estimating standing timber, log rules. Two hours credit. Time will be arranged. Fee, $7.00. *Adjunct Professor Sawyer.*

7a. FOREST INCREMENT. Sophomore summer camp. Formation of volume tables, growth tables, yield tables. Two hours credit. Fee, $7.00. Time will be arranged. *Adjunct Professor Sawyer.*

8. FOREST MANAGEMENT. First term, forest organization. Second term, forest finance. Third term, working plans. One lecture and two laboratory periods, entire year. Open to Seniors. Three hours credit. Fee, $2.00.M. 2:30-5:20, T. 11:10. *Adjunct Professor Sawyer.*

9. LUMBERING AND LOGGING. Systematic study of logging operations in different sections of North America. Three recitation periods, entire year. Three hours credit. Open to Juniors. M. W. F., 10:15. *Adjunct Professor Sawyer.*

10. FOREST HISTORY. An analysis of the economic conditions which have resulted in the development of forestry. The influence of form of government and property rights. Three recitations, first term. Open to Juniors. One hour credit. M. W. F., 9:20. *Adjunct Professor Sawyer.*

11. FOREST ECONOMICS. The relation existing between the practice of forestry, industry, and the prosperity of a country. Three recitation periods, second term. Open to Juniors. One hour credit. M. W. F., 9:20. *Adjunct Professor Sawyer.*

12. GENERAL FORESTRY. Elementary forest field work in dendrology, surveying, logging, camping and packing. Text, lecture, field work. Freshman, summer camp, two months. Four hours credit. Fee, $3 00. *Adjunct Professor Sawyer.*

14. FOREST ADMINISTRATION. Contracts, agency, appropriation of water for power and irrigation, affidavits, bonds, commercial paper. Three recitation periods, third term. Open to Juniors. One hour credit. M. W. F., 9:20. *Adjunct Professor Sawyer.*

15. WOOD TECHNOLOGY. Structure of wood tissue; classification of fibres, identification of woods, generic and specific. Three laboratory periods first half year. Open to Juniors. One and one-half hours credit. Fee, $2.00 M. W. F., 11:10-1:00. *Professor Burleigh.*

15a. WOOD IDENTIFICATION AND USE. Structure and properties of wood. General characteristics. Practical means of identification. Three laboratory periods, first half-year. Open to Juniors in Agriculture and home economics. One and one-half hours credit. Fee, $1.50. *Professor Burleigh.*

16. FIELD WORK. Field work in forest surveying, silviculture, logging, engineering, and advanced timber estimating. Lecture and field work. Sophomore, summer camp, two months. Four hours credit. Fee, $3.00. *Adjunct Professor Sawyer.*

17. SEMINAR. Systematic review, special investigative studies, research. Three hours, entire year. Three hours credit. Open to Seniors. T. Th. S., 12:05. *Professor Burleigh.*

18. THESIS. Either original research or simply investigative. Three hours credit. Open to Seniors. *Professor Burleigh.*

19. PRINCIPLES OF FORESTRY. Forest influences. Relation of forestry to agriculture and industry. Results of general deforestation. Three recitation periods, third term. Open to freshmen. One hour credit. M. W. F., 10:15. *Professor Burleigh.*

20. FOREST SURVEYING. Methods of survey, mapping, and reporting adopted by the United States Forest Service. Topographic mapping and map reading. Working plan maps. One lecture and three laboratory periods. Four hours credit. Open to Juniors. Fee, $3.00. Th., 11:10; W. F., 2:35-5:20. *Adjunct Professor Sawyer.*

22. FOREST BY-PRODUCTS. Turpentine orcharding, maple sugar, tan bark and extract wood, gums and resins, wood distillation. Recitation, collateral reading. Second half year. One and one-half hours credit. Open to Juniors. M. W. F., 11:10. *Adjunct Professor Sawyer.*

23. GRADES AND GRADING. A detailed study of the grading rules of the various associations. Practice work in grading. Lecture, collateral reading, field work. Three hours, one term. One hour credit. Open to Juniors. M. W. F., 10:15. *Adjunct Professor Sawyer.*

24. MILL ORGANIZATION. The development of the modern sawmill and its equipment. Labor efficiency. Various systems of management. Lecture, collateral reading. Three hours, one term. One hour credit. Open to Juniors. T. Th. S., 9:20. *Adjunct Professor Sawyer.*

27. FOREST MENSURATION. Timber estimating and scaling. Methods used in the construction of volume, growth and yield tables. Two recitations and one laboratory period the entire year. Three hours credit. Required of Sophomores. Fee, $3.50. T. Th., 10:15; lab., S., 10:15-12:05. *Adjunct Professor Sawyer.*

28. TREE SURGERY. The causes and treatment of three injuries. One lecture and two laboratory periods, the entire year. Three hours credit. Open to juniors. Fee, $3.00. Th., 11:10; laboratory, T. Th., 2:35-4:25. *Adjunct Professor Sawyer.*

ADVANCED COURSES are given in the Graduate School.

GERMANIC LANGUAGES

X. A course for beginners. Three hours per week. Three terms Three hours credit. Sec. 1, M. W. F., 9:20; Sec. 2, T. Th. S., 12:15. *Professor Morris.*

1. Continuation of X; grammar completed; translation of about 200 pages of modern narrative prose. Three hours per week. Three terms.

Three hours credit. T. Th. S., 9:20. Optional for Freshmen and Sophomores. *Professor Morris.*

2. Conversation and sight reading with the object of giving a practical mastery of the language. Optional for Sophomores. Three hours per week. Three terms. Three hours credit. M. W. F., 10:15. *Professor Morris.*

20. Elementary course offered as one of the Junior language options. Conducted exclusively in German. Optional for Juniors and Seniors. Three hours per week. Three terms. Three hours credit. M. W. F., 11:10. *Professor Morris.*

21. Continuation of 20. Translation of about 600 pages of modern prose. Optional for Seniors. Three hours per week. Three terms. Three hours credit. T. Th. S., 10:45. *Professor Morris.*

ADVANCED COURSES are given in the Graduate School.

GREEK

X. FOR BEGINNERS. Three hours per week. M. W. F., 9:20. Three hours credit. *Professor Bocock.*

1. XENOPHON'S ANABASIS. Geography, and some work in the history of Greece. Three hours per week. M. W. F., 10:15. Three hours credit. *Professor Bocock.*

2. HOMER, ILIAD OR ODYSSEY; Xenophon's Hellenica or Lysias. History of the literature. Three hours per week. T. Th. S., 11:10. Three hours credit. *Professor Bocock.*

3. SELECTIONS FROM PLATO; Introduction to the study of Greek tragedy; Euripides. Three hours per week. W. M. F., 12:15. Three hours credit. *Professor Bocock.*

4. SELECTIONS FROM THE TRAGIC POETS, Herodotus, Thucydides, Plato, Demosthenes. Three hours per week. Three hours credit. Hours to be agreed upon. *Professor Bocock.*

20. A BEGINNING COURSE FOR UPPER CLASSMEN. Three hours per week. M. W. F., 9:20. Three hours credit. *Professor Bocock.*

21. SECOND YEAR GREEK FOR UPPER CLASSMEN. In addition to the Greek read a good deal of Greek literature will be read in translation. Three hours per week. M. W. F., 10:15. Three hours credit. *Professor Bocock.*

ADVANCED COURSES are given in the Graduate School.

Greek Literature

5. EUROPEAN LITERATURE. (a) The Principles of the Study of Literature, (b) The development of European Literature, (c) Greek Literature in translations. Select readings. Three hours per week. Optional for Juniors and Seniors. T. Th. S., 9:20. Three hours credit. *Professor Bocock.*

HISTORY AND POLITICAL SCIENCE

2. RECENT EUROPEAN HISTORY. After a review of the French Revolution and the Napoleonic era, political, social, and economic developments are traced to the present time. Sophomore. Three hours per week. Three terms. Three hours credit. Section 1. M. W. F., 11:10; Section 2, T. Th. S., 9:20. *Professors McPherson and Coulter.*

Either History 2 or 4 may be taken to satisfy the Sophomore requirement in History.

22. AMERICAN GOVERNMENT. An introductory course covering essential facts of federal, state and local government in the United States. Required of Freshmen in course in Bachelor of Arts, three hours per week during first half-term. T. Th. S., 10:15. One and one-half hours credit. *Professors McPherson and Coulter.*

3. HISTORY OF GEORGIA. A course designed to give an interpretation of the social, economic, and political life of the people of the state. Freshmen. Section 1, two hours per week through second half-year. W. F., 10:15. One hour credit. Sec. 2, three hours per week through first half-year. T. Th. S., 10:15. Sec. 3, three hours per week through second half-year. T. Th. S., 10:15. One and one-half hours credit. *Professor Coulter.*

4. ENGLISH HISTORY. Emphasis is laid on constitutional development. Contemporary European developments are kept constantly in view. Sophomores. Three hours per week. Three terms. Sec. 1, M. W. F., 11:10; Sec. 2, T. Th. S., 9:20. Three hours credit. *Professor Payne.*

44. ECONOMIC HISTORY OF EUROPE. A survey of modern European economic history, agricultural, commercial and industrial. Sophomores B.S., Commerce. Three hours per week. Three terms. M. W. F., 12:05. Three hours credit. *Professor Payne.*

5. AMERICAN POLITICAL HISTORY. A general course covering the political history of the United States. Juniors and Seniors. Three hours. first and second terms. T. Th. S., 11:10. Two hours credit. *Professor McPherson.*

6. AMERICAN CONSTITUTIONAL HISTORY. An historical and interpretative study of the origin and growth of the American Federal and State Constitutions. Juniors and Seniors. Three hours, third term. T. Th. S., 11:10. One hour credit. *Professor McPherson.*

8. FRENCH REVOLUTION. An advanced and intensive study of the Revolutionary Period. Juniors and Seniors. Three hours, first half-year. M. W. F., 3:30. One and one-half hours credit. *Professor Payne.*

9. NAPOLEON I. An advanced and intensive study of Napoleon and his times. Juniors and Seniors. Three hours, second half-year. M. W. F., 3:30. One and one-half hours credit. *Professor Payne.*

10. THE ANTE-BELLUM SOUTH. The social, economic, and political de-

velopment, with particular reference to slavery and states rights. (This course and History 13 alternate yearly, the former being given in 1925-1926). Three hours per week during the first half-year. M. W. F., 9:20. One and one-half hours credit. *Professor Coulter.*

11. POLITICAL SCIENCE. An introduction to the theory of Political Science, comprising a study of the origin, nature, organization and functions of the state. Juniors and Seniors. Three hours, first term. M. W. F., 10:15. One hour credit. *Professor McPherson.*

12. AMERICAN GOVERNMENT AND POLITICS. An advanced study of the American system of government, federal, state and local. Juniors and Seniors. Three hours, second and third terms. M. W. F., 10:15. Two hours credit. *Professor McPherson.*

13. CIVIL WAR AND RECONSTRUCTION. A course dealing with the diverging political and economic doctrines leading to civil war, and the remaking of the nation in a social, economic and constitutional sense. (This course and History 10 alternate yearly, the former being given in 1926-1927). Three hours per week during the first half-year. M. W. F., 9:20. One and one-half hours credit. *Professor Coulter.*

14. RECENT AMERICAN HISTORY. This course begins with the pacification of the South and continues to the present time, emphasizing the broader aspects of national development. (This course and History 15 alternate yearly, the former being given in 1926-1927). Three hours per week during the second half-year. M. W. F., 9:20. One and one-half hours credit. *Professor Coulter.*

15. LATIN-AMERICAN HISTORY. A general course in the development of Latin-American countries with emphasis on their relations with the United States. (This course and History 14 alternate yearly, the former being given in 1925-1926). Three hours per week during the second half-year. M. W. F., 9:20. One and one-half hours credit. *Professor Coulter.*

16. CONTEMPORARY WORLD HISTORY. A study of current world affairs. Open to Seniors with a credit average of three hours. (Not given in 1925-1926). Three hours credit. *Professor Coulter.*

ADVANCED COURSES are given in the Graduate School.

HOME ECONOMICS

Foods and Cookery

1. FOOD STUDY AND COOKERY. Composition, selection and cookery of typical foods, to give a working knowledge of the principles underlying food preparation. One lecture and two laboratory periods, first half-year. Sophomore. One and one-half hours credit. Prerequisite: General Chemistry. Fee, $3.50. M. W., 2:35-5:20; S., 12:05. *Miss Scott.*

2. HOME COOKERY AND TABLE SERVICE. Practice in the manipulation

of foods in family sized quantities; practice in planning, preparing and serving breakfasts, dinners, luncheons, suppers. One lecture and two laboratory periods, second half-year. Sophomore, one and one-half hours credit. Prerequisite: Home Economics 1. Fee, $3.50. M. W., 2:35-5:20; S., 12:05. *Miss Scott.*

5. FOOD PRESERVATION. Advanced canning of fruits and vegetables; drying fruits and herbs; making fruit juices; jelly making; preserving. Junior, one lecture and two laboratory periods, last half of third term. Credit, one-half hour. Fee, $2.50. M. W.F., 11:10-1:00. *Miss Newton.*

10. INSTITUTIONAL COOKING AND MANAGEMENT. Plans for organization and equipment of kitchens, dining rooms, lunch rooms; practical work in marketing, cooking, serving; catering for special occasions. Junior or Senior. Prerequisites: College courses Home Economics 1-2. Credit, three hours. Three laboratory periods. Fee, $3.50. M. W. F., 11:10-1:00. *Miss Scott.*

11. The course is divided into three parts, as follows. (a) The more complex processes of cookery and wider variety of seasonings and flavorings. (b) Experimental cookery in which each student or group of students carries on individual cookery investigations. (c) Advanced table service including planning and serving more elaborate meals. One and one-half hours credit. First half year. Prerequisite: Home Economics 2. Fee, $3.50. M. W. F., 11:10-1:00. *Miss Newton.*

12. NUTRITION. A study of the fundamental principles of human nutrition, the chemistry and physiology of digestion and metabolism. Senior, first half-year. Two laboratories and one lecture. Credit one and one-half hours. Prerequisite: Organic Food Chemistry; Physiology; Bacteriology 1. Fee, $3.50. T. Th. S., 11:10-1:00. *Miss Newton.*

13. DIETETICS. Nutritive requirements for individuals; relative cost of foods; dietary calculations. Seniors, second half-year. Two laboratory periods and one lecture. Credit, one and one-half hours. Prerequisites: Agricultural Chemistry 1, Bacteriology 1; Home Economics 12. Fee, $3.50. T. Th. S., 11:10-1:00. *Miss Newton.*

17. CATERING. This course is especially designed for advanced undergraduate students who are preparing to be dietitians or for the commercial fields. It includes special problems in the preparation of food and service for luncheons, dinners, teas, and banquets. One lecture and two informal laboratory periods. Second half-year. Credit, one and one-half hours. Prerequisite: Home Economics 10. *Miss Scott.*

NOTE:—The uniform for cookery laboratory consists of a wash dress, preferably white, a white apron with holder and hand towel, a hair net or a white cap.

Related Art and Clothing Group

22. DRAWING AND DESIGNING. Fundamental principles governing correct drawing; representation of object and nature. Motifs, composition and color harmonies, use of different media. First and second terms. Freshman. Three laboratory periods. Two hours credit. Fee, $4.00. Section 1, T. Th., S., 11:10-1:00. Section 2, M. W., 2:35-5:20. *Miss Rathbone.*

23. PATTERN DESIGNING. Making plain foundation waist and skirt patterns, fitting and altering patterns and making original designs, using plain foundation patterns; a study of different type figures and pattern designing for them. One lecture and two laboratory periods. First term. Junior. One hour credit. Fee, $2.00. T. Th., 2:35-5:20. *Miss E. Creswell.*

24. MILLINERY. Study of becoming shapes and styles for different types; making and covering wire and solid frames; making and placing, decorations; renovation of materials. Home millinery problems emphasized. Two laboratory periods and one lecture, following 23 One-half hour credit. First half of second term. Fee, $1.50. T. Th., 2:35-5:20. *Miss E. Creswell.*

26. ELEMENTARY CLOTHING. The fundamental principles related to garment construction and dressmaking; patterns, machines. Factory production of clothing; clothing budget. Two laboratory periods and one lecture. Two hours junior credit. First and second terms. Fee, $4.00. Section 1, M. W., 2:35-5:20. Section 2, T. Th. S., 11:10-1:00. *Miss E. Creswell.*

27. TEXTILE PROBLEMS. This course deals with textile problems of interest to the consumer. Clothing and household materials; characteristic of the different standard fabrics and their uses; their use and care; wet and dry cleaning of all types of clothing. Three laboratories, third term. Freshman. One hour credit. Fee, $2.00. T. Th. S., 11:10-1:00. *Miss E. Creswell.*

29. ADVANCED DESIGN. Principles of composition, line and dark and light, and color harmony; applications to decorations; textile design, costume designing; illustration work with ink, charcoal, colored crayons and water color. Prerequisite: Home Economics 22. Sophomore or Junior elective. Three laboratory periods per week, first and second terms. Two hours credit. Fee, $4.00. T. Th., 2:35-5:20. *Miss Rathbone.*

31. COSTUME DESIGNING. Studying and drawing foundation figures; designing costumes and accessories for different types. Color texture combinations. Media; crayon, crayola, water-color. One and one-half hours credit. Three laboratories last half year. Prerequisite: Home Economics 32 and 22. Fee, $3.50. T. Th., 2:35-5:20. *Miss Rathbone.*

32. ADVANCED DRESSMAKING. Practice in original designs in modeling and draping; in technique of finishing and decoration; shopwork in all types of clothing for women and children. Prerequisite: Home Economics 22 and 26. Two laboratory periods and one lecture. Three hours credit. Fee, $3.50. T. Th. S., 9:20-11:10. *Miss Rathbone.*

Home Administration Group

40. HEALTH: VOCATIONAL HOME-MAKING RELATIONSHIP. Personal hygiene, child and adult; illness, preventive and curative measures in the home. Community hygiene. Three lectures per week. Senior, first and second terms. Two hours credit. T. Th. S., 10:15. Prerequisite: Bacteriology 1, Physiology, Agricultural Chemistry 1. *Miss Lunday.*

45. HOME FURNISHING AND DESIGNING. Location, structure and strucural sanitation; application of principles of design and color to furniture and house furnishings. Three lectures, second half-year. One and one-half hours credit. M. W. F., 11:10. *Misses Rathbone and Campbell.*

46. HOME EQUIPMENT AND MANAGEMENT. Treated from vocational standpoint: (a) Economics of household and household purchasing. (b) Organization of work. (c) Sanitation, care and renovation. Fee, $7.00. Senior credit, three hours. Laboratory informal. M. W. F., 10:15. *Miss E. Creswell.*

Education Group

50. METHODS AND MATERIALS IN VOCATIONAL HOME ECONOMICS. Principles of teaching home economics; general consideration of methods of presentation. The influence of the community on the work. Surveys leading to the organization of courses of study. Junior. First term. Three lectures. One hour credit. M. W. F., 10:15. *Miss Rathbone.*

51. ORGANIZATION OF HOME DEMONSTRATION WORK. Survey of conditions, social and economic; factors and forces in county and community; methods of organization; social outgrowths; community fairs; recreation and dramatic expression; field work under supervision, summer preceding senior year. Junior, three lectures and recitations. One hour credit. Informal. *Miss Mary E. Creswell.*

52. ORGANIZATION OF HOME DEMONSTRATION WORK. Continuation of Course 51. Senior, second term. One hour credit. Informal. *Miss Mary E. Creswell.*

53. HISTORY AND DEVELOPMENT OF EDUCATION IN HOME ECONOMICS. A survey of the development of home economics in education; home-making as a vocation; social and economic aspects, the influence of vocational education upon it. Junior or Senior, last half-year. One and one-half hours credit. M. W. F., 10:15. *Miss Newton.*

54. TEACHING CLOTHING AND HOME MANAGEMENT IN VOCATIONAL SCHOOLS. Vocational courses studied with reference to content, time allotment, and adaptation to demand for such. Junior, third term. Three lectures. One hour credit. M. W. F., 10:15. *Miss Rathbone.*

55. TEACHING FOODS AND COOKERY IN VOCATIONAL SCHOOLS. A survey of the present status of the teaching of foods and cookery in secondary schools; an analysis of the essential elements in standardizing courses of study; methods of presentation of subject matter, etc. Junior, three lectures. Second term. One hour credit. M. W. F., 11:10. *Misses Newton* and *Campbell.*

57. PRACTICE TEACHING IN VOCATIONAL SCHOOLS. A minimum of one and one-half hours is required of Seniors selecting the Vocational 'Home Economics group. Prerequisite: 54 and 55. One lecture. Laboratory to be arranged. One and one-half hours credit. S., 12:05. *Misses Burson* and *Callaway.*

60. This course is designed to give an understanding of child psychology and a knowledge of child training and. care through a study of family relationships; the educational importance of the pre-school years; the needs and problems of the pre-adolescent and of the adolescent years; how the new schools and homes are attempting to meet these needs; organization of child study groups. One hour credit. Junior or Senior. Prerequisites: Psychology 4, 5, 6, or equivalent. First half second term. Daily 8:25. *Miss McAlpine.*

Collegiate Winter Courses

A course of three months is offered in which students qualifying as juniors can receive college credit for a term's work. This course is planned especially to aid the county agent who desires advanced study but can be absent from her work for a limited space of time.

7. READINGS IN FOOD AND NUTRITION. To give the student an opportunity to become familiar with the results of modern investigation in food preservation and nutrition. Lectures, readings and reports on certain deficiency diseases such as scurvy, pellagra, and rickets; neuritic and anti-scorbutic properties of food. Six recitations a week. One hour credit. Time will be arranged. *Miss Newton.*

9. DEMONSTRATION COOKERY. An advanced course with problems selected from the general field of food preparation. Special emphasis placed upon skillful manipulation and clear presentation of the subject. Juniors or Seniors. One lecture and five laboratories. One hour credit. Fee, $3.50. Time will be arranged. *Miss Newton.*

14. WORK WITH BATTERS AND DOUGHS. The leavening agents, composition, reactions, and residues; use of various fats and flours showing the difference in quality, quantity and cost. Products will be used

in the College cafeteria. Three laboratories and two lectures per week. One hour credit. Fee, $1.50. Time will be arranged. *Miss Scott.*

25. MILLINERY. Making wire frames from measurements and illustrations for foundation molds. Molding in net, buckram and willow. Study of difficult frames and crowns. Discussion of stable milinery materials and findings. Bow making and hand made trimmings for home millinery. Individual problems given attention. Four laboratories and one lecture. Credit, one hour. *Miss E. Creswell.*

56. DEMONSTRATION IN CLOTHING. The study of special methods in presenting lectures and demonstrations in clothing and related fields. Single lessons and series will be planned for different types of classes and groups of people. The typical illustrative material will be worked up to use in such classes. Two lectures and three laboratories. One hour credit. Time will be arranged. *Miss Rathbone.*

44. HOME PLANNING AND FURNISHING. Application of principles of design and color to house furnishings, to finishes for walls and floors, selection and arrangement of rugs, draperies, and furniture with view to beauty, economy and the sanitary needs of the modern house. Five lectures. Junior. One hour credit. *Miss Campbell.*

47. HOME MANAGEMENT. Efficiency in equipping and organizing the work in the home; independent water; electric lighting and sewerage systems for the rural home; kitchen and laundry equipment; laundering and cleaning of floors, walls and furnishings. Five lectures. One hour credit. *Miss E. Creswell.*

58. GIRL'S CLUB CLOTHING PROGRAM. Discussion of the principles and processes involved in hand and machine sewing; selection of material and suitability of textiles to projects; methods in presentation of subject matter, illustrative material. Junior. Prerequisite: Home Economics 26. Credit 1 hour. Fee, $1.50. Three lectures, three laboratories. *Miss E. Creswell.*

ADVANCED COURSES are given in the Graduate School.

HORTICULTURE

1. *ELEMENTS OF HORTICULTURE; FRUIT GROWING. A general study of location, site, frost, planting, varieties, tillage and management. Three lectures per week. First term. Freshman. One hour credit. *Dr. McHatton.*

2. *PRUNING AND PROPAGATION. A course in grafting, budding and other methods of propagation, with a study of pruning and its practice and effect. Three laboratory periods per week. Second term. Freshman. One hour credit. *Dr. McHatton.*

3. *ELEMENTS OF HORTICULTURE; TRUCK GARDENING. A study of the

---

* Laboratory fee for Courses 1, 2, and 3, $3.50.

11

main truck crops as to planting, tillage, marketing, etc. Also a study of hotbeds and their management. Three laboratory periods per week. Third term. Freshman. One hour credit. Hort., 1, 2, 3. T. Th., 10:15-1:00; T. F., 2:35-5:20; S., 10:15; Th., 2:35. Section for women M. W., 2:35-5:20. *Dr. McHatton.*

4. SMALL FRUITS. Fruit Harvesting, Storing and Marketing. A study of the various small fruits of interest to the horticulturist for the first half of the term, second half of the term given to fruit handling, storing and marketing. Prerequisite: Horticulture 1, 2 and 3. By special permission Horticulture 1, 2 and 3 may be carried parallel with the junior course. Three lectures per week. First term. Junior or Senior year. One hour credit. Hort., 4, 6, 10. T. Th. S., 10:15. *Associate Professor Keener.*

5. †POMOLOGY AND GARDEN SEEDS. A course in systematic pomology and the testing of garden seeds. Prerequisite: Horticulture 1, 2, 3 and 4, the latter course being taken parallel. Three laboratory periods per week. First term. Junior or Senior year. One hour credit. Hort., 5, 7, 9. T. Th., 2:35-5:20. *Associate Professor Keener.*

6. GREENHOUSE MANAGEMENT AND FLORICULTURE. A study of the management of the various flower and vegetable crops grown under glass. Prerequisite: Horticulture 1, 2 and 3. Three lectures per week. Second term. Junior or Senior year. One hour credit. *Associate Professor Keener.*

7. †GREENHOUSE CONSTRUCTION AND MANAGEMENT. A study of different types of greenhouse heating, construction, etc. Visits to commercial florists with maps, plans and elevations of greenhouses and heating systems required. Practical work in greenhouses. Second term. Junior or Senior year. Laboratory, three periods per week. One hour credit. *Associate Professor Keener.*

9. †SPRAYING. A study of the history and chemistry of spraying. Practice in the making and application of material. Prerequisite: Horticulture 1, 2 and 3. Three laboratory periods per week. Third term. Junior or Senior year. One hour credit. *Associate Professor Keener.*

10. LANDSCAPE GARDENING. A study of the various schools of landscape architecture. The plants used in producing the various effects. This course is especially adapted for Smith-Hughes and Home Economics students. Prerequisite: Horticulture 1, 2 and 3, or equivalent. Three lectures per week. Third term. One hour credit. *Dr. McHatton.*

11. ADVANCED POMOLOGY. A course in the detailed study of the practical and scientific phases of fruit growing. Prerequisite: Horticulture 1 to 10 inclusive. Three lectures per week throughout the

† Laboratory fee for Courses 5, 7 and 9. $3.50.

year. Senior year. Three hours credit. M. W. F., 10:15. *Dr. Mc-Hatton.*

12. THESIS. A problem relative to any of the following courses 11, 14, 15 and 16 will be assigned to the student for study. At the end of the year a thesis stating the problem, results, etc., will be required. Three laboratory periods per week throughout the year for Seniors. Course 12 must be taken by students majoring in horticulture. Three hours credit. Laboratory fee, $3.50. M. W. F., 11:10-1:00. *Dr. Mc-Hatton.*

13. ECONOMIC ENTOMOLOGY. A course in practical entomology designed especially for use upon the farm. Special attention is paid to the identification of insects and their control. Last half year. Junior or Senior. Two laboratory periods and one lecture per week. One and one-half hours credit. Laboratory fee, $2.50. W. S., 9:20; lab., W., 2:35. *Dr. McHatton.*

14. ADVANCED OLERICULTURE. A study of the problems of vegetable culture, both outdoors and under glass. Prerequisite: Horticulture 1 to 10 inclusive. Three lectures per week given throughout the year to Seniors. Three hours credit. M. W. F., 10:15. *Dr. McHatton.*

15. ADVANCED FLORICULTURE. A study of the more practical and scientific problems of flower growing, both under glass and outdoors. Prerequisite: Horticulture 1 to 10 inclusive. Three lectures per week. Open to Seniors. Three hours credit. M. W. F., 10:15. *Dr. McHatton.*

16. ADVANCED LANDSCAPE GARDENING. An advanced course in the study of the various schools of landscape art considering composition, materials, etc. Prerequisite: Horticulture 1 to 10 inclusive. Three lectures per week. Seniors. Three hours credit. M. W. F., 10:15. *Dr. McHatton.*

23. HOME ORCHARDING. The problem of a home orchard, its size, varieties and species of fruits. Offered only to the women of the six weeks short course. This course will be accepted as one hour of the six hours of Agriculture required in the B.S. Home Economics degree. Four lectures and two laboratory periods per week for six weeks. One hour credit. Laboratory fee, $1.50. M. T. Th. S., 9:20; lab., W. F., 9:20-11:10. *Associate Professor Keener.*

24. HOME VEGETABLE GARDENING. The problem of a home vegetable garden, its site, varieties, etc. It is offered only to the women of the six weeks short course. This course will be accepted as one hour of

---

NOTE:—The professor in charge will not be required to give Courses 11, 14, 15, or 16 to less than five students unless the whole senior class in horticulture is less than five in which case he may put all the members in the course most acceptable to them. Special arrangements may be made for especially desirable, mature and sufficiently prepared students who wish to enter any of the above courses.

NOTE:—Juniors and Seniors specializing in Horticulture will be expected to make one inspection trip each year to certain designated points in the state.

the six hours of Agriculture required in the B.S. Home Economics degree. Four lectures and two laboratory periods per week for six weeks. One hour credit. Laboratory fee, $1.50. M. T. Th. S., 9:20; lab., W. F., 9:20-11:40. *Associate Professor Keener.*

ADVANCED COURSES are given in the Graduate School.

JOURNALISM

1. NEWSPAPER REPORTING AND CORRESPONDENCE. The work of the reporter and the correspondent; gathering news; writing news; news values. Three terms. Three hours a week. T. Th. S., 11:10. *Professor Sanford,* and *Adjunct Professor Drewry.*

2. COPY READING. Editing newspaper copy and writing newspaper headings; writing and re-writing from assignments. Three hours a week. Three terms. M. W. F., 10:15. *Adjunct Professor Drewry.*

3. FEATURE WRITING AND SPECIAL ARTICLES. Practice in writing articles of a varied character to suit the miscellaneous needs of the newspaper. Special study is devoted to the short story and the feature story. Two terms. Three hours a week. M. W. F., 9:20. *Professor Sanford.*

4. HISTORY AND PRINCIPLES OF JOURNALISM. Journalism in various periods and conditions; the aims of journalism. First term. Three hours a week. M. W. F., 12:05. *Adjunct Professor Drewry.*

5. THE EDITORIAL. The theory and practice of editorial writing, interpretation and comment; preparation and presentation of the editorial page. Open to Juniors and Seniors. Third term. Three hours a week. T. Th. S., 10:15. *Professor Sanford.*

6. THE COMMUNITY PAPER. The purpose of this is to open the whole field of the problems and possibilities of the country field. Open to Juniors and Seniors. One term. T. Th. S., 10:15. Three hours a week. *Professor Sanford.*

7. NEWSPAPER ADVERTISING. Special attention to selling plans and special campaigns; preparation of copy; booklets, posters, etc. Three terms. Three hours a week. M. W. F., 12:05. *Professor Sanford.*

8. TLE MAGAZINE. A study of the development and influence of the magazine. Students will be required to submit two original magazine articles a month and to indicate a list of publications that might consider such an article. One term. Three hours a week. T. Th. S., 12:05. *Adjunct Professor Drewry.*

9. CLASS PUBLICATIONS. A study of religious, scientific, agricultural, educational publications; the assembling, preparation, and presentation of news. One term. Three hours a week. T. Th. S., 12:05. *Adjunct Professor Drewry.*

10. RURAL JOURNALISM. (AGRICULTURAL EDUCATION 17.) Study of rural publicity report writing, press work; special work in the com-

pliation and arrangement of statistical data. Two lectures and one laboratory period, third term, one hour credit. M. W. F., 10:15. *Professor Chapman.*

11. NEWSPAPER ETHICS. Canons of Journalism. Ethical vs. unethical partisanship. Propaganda. Journalism as a profession. One term. Three hours a week. T. Th. S., 10:15. *Professor Sanford.*

12, THE LAW OF THE PRESS. Three hours a week. One term. T. Th. S., 10:15. *Professor Sanford.*

13. PUBLIC OPINION OF THE PRESS. (Pre-requisite, Journalism 4, to be taken first term of same year in which this course is taken in the last two terms.) Attention will be given to the problems involved in the newspapers and magazines. A considerable amount of comparative reading is required. One term. Three hours a week. T. Th. S., 12:05. *Adjunct Professor Drewry.*

14. LITERARY CRITICISƆ. A study of the methods and standards in the preparation of critical reviews of books and other publications for newspapers and magazines. This is followed by practical exercises in the compositions of such review, with guidance and comment by the instructor. One term. Three hours a week. T. Th. S., 12:05. *Adjunct Professor Drewry.*

15. GEORGIA LITERATURE. A study of Sidney Lanier and Joel Chandler Harris, and of Harry Stilwell Edwards and other contemporary writers. One term. Three hours a week. M. W. F., 9:20. *Professor Sanford.*

LATIN

1. The reading of a play of Terence, and of selections from Livy. Review of grammar and exercises in translations into Latin. Three hours a week. Three terms. Three hours credit. Sec. 1, T. Th. S., 8:25; Sec. 2, M. W. F., 11:10. *Professor Hooper.*

2. Reading of Horace, selected odes, and Cicero de Officiis. Book 1. Metres and weekly exercises. Three hours per week. Three terms. Three hours credit. Sec. 1, M. W. F., 9:20; Sec. 2, T. Th. S., 12:05. *Professor Hooper.*

3. Reading of Horace, Satires and Epistles; Tactitus, Annals; Pliny, selected letters. Three hours per week. Three terms. Three hours credit. M. W. F., 10:15. *Professor Hooper.*

4. Reading of plays of Terence and Plautus, and selections of authors not read in the lower classes. Three hours per week. Three terms. Three hours credit. T. Th. S., 10:15. *Professor Hooper.*

MATHEMATICS

1. TRIGONOƆETRY. Plane. Three hours per week, first term. One hour credit. M. W. F., 10:15, 11:10, 12:05, 2:35; T. Th. S., 8:25, 9:20, 11:10, 12:05. *Professors Stephens, Barrow and Adjunct Professor Cumming, Messrs. Everett Sewell, Hill and Green.*

1a. TRIGONOMETRY. Plane and spherical. Three hours a week for half-year. One and one-half hours credit. M. W. F., 10:15. Sec. 1 until first mid-term. M. W. F., 11:10. Sec. 2, last half year.

2. ANALYTICAL GEOMETRY. Elementary course. Three hours per week, second and third terms. Two hours credit. M. W. F., 10:15, 11:10, 12:05; T. Th. S., 8:25. 9:20, 11:10, 12:05. *Professors Stephens, Barrow,* and *Adjunct Professor Cumming, Messrs. Everett, Sewell, Hill* and *Green.*

3. CALCULUS. An introductory course. Three hours per week, first half-year. One and one-half hour credit. Prerequisite: Courses 1, 2, M. W. F., 9:20, 10:15, 12:05. *Professors Stephens* and *Barrow,* and *Adjunct Professor Cumming.*

4. ALGEBRA. Three hours per week, second half-year. One and one-half hours credit. Prerequisite: Courses 1. 2. M. W. F., 9:20, 10:15, 11:10; T. Th. S., 12:05. *Professors Stephens* and *Barrow,* and *Adjunct Professor Cumming.*

5. CALCULUS. Differential and integral. Three hours per week. Three terms. Three hours credit. Prerequisite: Courses 3, 4. M. W. F., 9:20. *Professor Barrow.*

6. STATISTICS. Three hours per week, first or second half-year. One and one-half hours credit. Prerequisite: Courses 1, 2. T. Th. S., 10:15; 12:05. *Professor Barrow.*

7. DIFFERENTIAL EQUATIONS. Three hours per week, first half year. One and one-half hours credit. Prerequisite: Course 5. T. Th. S., 11:10. *Professor Stephens.* (Not given unless elected by three or more).

8. ANALYTICAL GEOMETRY. An advanced course. Three hours per week for half-year. One and one-half hours credit. Prerequisite: Course 5. (Not given unless elected by three or more). *Professor Barrow.*

9. THEORETICAL MECHANICS. Three hours per week, second half-year. One and one-half hours credit. Prerequisite: Course 5. (Not given unless elected by three or more). T. Th. S., 11:10. *Professor Stephens.*

10. TEACHING HIGH SCHOOL MATHEMATICS. Three hours per week for second term. One hour credit. (Not given unless elected by three or more). *Professor Stephens.*

11. THEORY OF INVESTMENT. Annuities, bonds, and insurance. Three hours per week, first or second half-year. One and one-half hours credit. Prerequisite: Courses 1, 2. T. Th. S., 10:15, 12:05. *Professor Stephens.*

ADVANCED COURSES are given in the Graduate School.

PHILOSOPHY

4-5. INTRODUCTION TO PHILOSOPHY AND LOGIC.

4. LOGIC. An introduction to the methods of reflective thinking, particularly to scientific and mathematical thinking, a study of formal logic and its application in reflective thinking. First half year. One and one-half hours credit. M. W. F., 9:20. *Professor* ——————.

5. INTRODUCTION TO PHILOSOPHY. An introduction to the nature and scope of the field of Philosophy together with a study of the changing concepts in Philosophy and of present interest in philosophical problems. Second half year. One and one half hours credit. M. W. F., 9:20. *Professor* ——————.

7-8. HISTORY OF PHHILOSOPHY.

7. ANCIENT AND MEDIAEVAL PHILOSOPHY. A historical survey of Greek and Roman philosophy and of Scholasticism in the Middle Ages.

8. MODERN PHILOSOPHY. The historical development of the trends of thought in modern Europe and their influence upon early American thought. Three terms, three hours credit. M. W. F., 11:10. *Professor* ——————.

9. AMERICAN AND CONTEMPORARY THOUGHT. A survey of the trends of thought in the development of present philosophical tendencies in America and of the interaction between America and contemporaneous European thought. Open to students who have had at least three hours in Philosophy. (This course alternates yearly with Philosophy 10). Three terms. Three hours credit. *Professor* ——————.

10. ETHICS. An advanced course in the origin and growth of ethical ideals. Systems of personal and social ethics and their philosophical implications. Open to students who have at least 3 hours in Philosophy. Three hours credit. *Professor* ——————.

101. CURRENT PHILOSOPHY. Present philosophical tendencies. For graduate students. Prerequisite six hours in philosophy or its equivalent. Minor. *Professor* ——————.

102. SOCIAL PHILOSOPHY. For graduate students. *Professor* ——————

PHYSICAL EDUCATION FOR WOMEN
Suggested Course

Junior	Hrs.	Senior	Hrs.
Physical Edu. 6-10-11-12-22	4	Physical Education	
Physical Edu. 13-15	3	Health 40 and 20	3
Agricultural Chemistry 1	3	Physical Edu. 15-16-17	3
Sociology	2	Bacteriology 1-5	3
Physical Edu. 43	1	Phys. Education 44-45	3
Home Economics 1-2	3	Home Economics 12-31	3
Electives	3	Electives	3

Botany 11
Language
Education
English 4
Public Speaking

English 5
History
Sociology
Home Economics
Education

1. PHYSICAL EDUCATION. This course includes athletics, dancing, swimming and natural gymnastics. Special classes in individual gymnastics are offered for those having weak hearts, faulty posture, underweight, etc. One and one half hours credit. *Misses Lunday and*

2. PHYSICAL EDUCATION. Athletics, individual gymnastics, more advanced dancing, swimming and natural gymnastics are offered. Some choice in the type of work taken will be permitted. Prerequisite Physical Education 1. One and one-half hours credit. *Miss Lunday.*

4. HORSEMANSHIP. Will include saddling and unsaddling, the aids, gaits, changes of direction, suppling exercises, riding without stirrups, jumping and cross country riding. The students will be required to furnish their own riding habits, breeches, flannel shirt or coat, boots or leggins with high shoes, and cap or sport hat.

Written permission from parents or guardian and physician's certificate will be required. Seven weeks, winter term. Section 1, T. and Th., 9:20; Section 2, M. and W., 2:35. *Major Whitney.*

6. SWIMMING. Principles and methods of teaching swimming, diving, life saving, training and coaching, rules of events. American Red Cross Life Saving Test is given. Three recitations per week first term. Junior or Senior. One-half hour credit. *Miss ——————*

7. GAMES. This course includes games suitable for playgrounds, elementary and secondary schools, ranging from simplest primary school games to organized team games such as dodge ball, captain ball, etc. The psychology of play, selection, adaptation and relative value of material will be discussed. Three recitations per week. Sophomore first term. One hour credit. Fee, $1.50. *Miss Lunday.*

8. MINOR SPORTS. This course involves technique of field ball, soccer, tennis and volley ball. Rules, methods of coaching, organization of tournaments, etc., will be studied with practice in coaching under supervision. A study will be made of motor efficiency tests including practice in testing and scoring. Three periods per week. Sophomore second term. One hour credit. Fee, $1.50. *Miss Lunday.*

9. FIRST AID. Course of instruction, treatment of accidents and emergencies and the development of habits and attitudes of health. A Red Cross diploma in first aid is available for those passing the examination. Three periods per week. First-half third term, Sophomore year. One-half hour credit. *Miss ——————*

10. MAJOR SPORTS. The technique of hockey, basketball, field and

track. Study of rules, duties of officials, instruction and practice in coaching and refereeing. Three hours a week. First term. Junior year. Prerequisite Physical Education 8. One hour credit. *Miss Lunday.*

11. TACTICS AND GYMNASTICS. Graded course in tactics and gymnastics including natural and formal drill and the use of various forms of apparatus. Three classes a week. Second term Junior year. One hour credit. *Miss ————*

12. FOLK DANCING AND SINGING GAMES. Representative national dances and singing games suitable for all grades will be presented. Three hours per week. Third term Junior year. One hour credit. Fee for 10-11-12, $6.00. *Miss Lunday.*

13. KINESIOLOGY. A study of the anatomical mechanism involved in bodily movements and development. Three recitations per week. Junior first half year. Prerequisite Zoology 31, Physiology and Anatomy. Credit one and one-half hours. *Miss ————*

15. INDIVIDUAL GYMNASTICS. Presentation of the more common postural and foot defects and discussion of measures for their correction. Lecture and laboratory work under supervision. Junior or Senior two lectures and one laboratory. Second half year. Prerequisites: Physical Ed. 13. Credit one and one-half hours. Time to be arranged.

20. DANCING. The work of this course includes appreciation and interpretation of music and pantominic dancing through natural and full bodily movement. A special costume is required. Prerequisite Physical Education 1 and 2. Junior or Senior two periods per week three terms. One hour credit. Fee, $2.00. *Miss ————*

22. CLOGGING. This course will include representative clog and character dances. Three hours per week. Junior or Senior. One half hour credit. *Miss ————*

39. ORGANIZATION LEADERSHIP. Scouting and other organizations for the adolescent girl. This course includes training for girl scout leadership under trained directors. Three hours per week. Third term, Junior or Senior. One-half hour credit. *Miss ————*

40. HEALTH. The principles of personal and general hygiene will be presented. The various aspects of community hygiene will be considered. Three lectures per week. Senior, first and second terms. Prerequisite: Physiology, Bacteriology 1 Ag. Chem. 1. Two hours credit. *Miss Lunday.*

43. HISTORY OF PHYSICAL EDUCATION. The course will include study of historical conditions influencing physical education as well as its modern tendencies and advancements. Three hours a week. One hour credit. Third term Junior year. *Miss ————*

44. THEORY AND PRINCIPLES OF PHYSICAL EDUCATION. Includes discussion of ideals, aims and objectives of physical education and prac-

tice in the selection and use of suitable teaching materials. The material considered will include games, athletics, dancing and formal gymnastics.

45. PRACTICE TEACHING. A minimum of one and one-half hours is required of seniors majoring in Physical Education. One lecture. Laboratory to be arranged. Prerequisite Senior standing in Physical Education. One and one-half hours credit. *Miss* ——————

PHYSICAL EDUCATION FOR MEN

1. FIRST YEAR PROGRAM. Three terms. Required of all male Freshmen.

First Term Courses: 1, Freshman football; 2, basketball; 3, cross country; 4, tennis; 5, golf; 6, swimming; 7, boxing and wrestling; 8, gymnasium work.

Second Term Courses: 1, basketball; 2, cross country; 3, swimming; 4, class basketball; 5 fraternity basketball; 6, dormitory basketball; 7, boxing and wrestling; 8, gymnasium work.

Third Term Courses: 1, Freshman baseball; 2, Freshman track; 3, golf; 4, tennis; 5, spring football; 6, swimming.

2. SECOND YEAR PROGRAM. As prerequisite to three hours of credit in Physical Education. Varsity candidate for two squads or Varsity candidate for squad for two years.

3. THIRD OR FOURTH YEAR PROGRAM. Class work. Theory and practice of coaching. Prerequisite: full second year work, candidate for any two squads in one year or candidate for any squad for two years. Three hours credit.*

INTRA MURAL PROGRAM, Under direction of the department. No football.

Basketball—(a) campany teams; (b) class teams; (c) inter-fraternity teams; (d) dormitory teams; (e) department teams; (f) faculty teams.

Baseball—(a) company teams; (b) class teams; (c) inter-fraternity teams; (d) dormitory teams; (e) department teams; (f) faculty teams.

Track—Inter-class track meet; inter-fraternity track meet; military physical fitness meet for student body.

ADVANCED COURSES are given in the Graduate School.

PHYSICS AND ASTRONOMY

PHICS 1. ELEMENTARY PHYSICS. An introductory course, descriptive rather than analytical in character, emphasizing the practical applications. This course, although of college grade, does not satisfy the requirements for entrance of the leading Medical Schools of a

————
* This credit will not be allowed any student electing advanced military science.

standard four hour college course. Two hours a week recitation and lecture, and one laboratory period per week. Credit, three hours. Three terms. Fee, $3.00. Recitation, Sec. 1, M. W., 10:15; Sec. 2, M. W., 11:10; Sec. 3, T. Th., 8:25; Sec. 4, T. Th., 11:10. Laboratory, three sections meet each day, except Saturday at the following hours: 9:20, 11:10, 2:35. *Associate Professor Cantrell, Adjunct Professor Dixon,* and *Messrs. Carter* and *Mote.*

PHYSICS 2. ELEMENTARY PHYSICS. An introductory course, covering the same subject matter as Physics 1, but more analytical in charter. This course meets the requirements for entrance of the leading Medical Schools of a standard four hour college course. It is desirable that students who intend to pursue scientific work of any kind or who desire a four hour standard college course take this course rather than Physics 1. Prerequisite: Plane Trigonometry. In special cases students who have not completed a course in Plane Trigonometry will be permitted to enter Physics 2 if they are taking Mathematics 1 as a parallel course. Three hours a week recitation and lecture, and one laboratory period per week. Credit, four hours. Three terms. Fee, $3.00. Recitation: Sec. 1. (for Engineering students only), M. W. F., 9:20; Sec. 2, M. W. F., 12:05; Sec. 3, T. Th. S., 10:15; Sec. 4, T. Th. S., 12:05. Laboratory, three sections meet each day on M. T. W. Th., at the following hours: 9:20, 11:10; 2:35. *Professor Hendren, Associate Professor Cantrell, Adjunct Professor Dixon.*

PHYSICS 3. A course to accompany and supplement Physics 2. Required of Engineering students. In this course a large number of problems are solved illustrating the fundamental principles studied in Physics 2. An elementary study of the theory of measurements is made, also the theory of the slide rule is studied and practice is required in its use. One hour per week recitation. Three terms. Credit, one hour. T., 9:20. *Associate Professor Cantrell.*

PHYSICS 4. GENERAL PHYSICS, covering Mechanics in the first term and Electricity in the second and third terms, wtih a brief discussion of the theory of heat and the wave theory of light. Prerequisite: Physics 1 and Mathematics 1. Required parallel course Mathematics 3. Three hours per week recitation and lecture, and one laboratory period per week. Three terms. Credit, four hours. Fee, $3.00. Sec. 1, (exclusively for elective students) M. W. F., 12:05; Sec. 2, (exclusively for Engineering students) T. Th. S., 10:15. Laboratory, Sec. 1, W., 2:35; Sec. 2, Th., 2:35. *Professor Hendren, Associate Professor Cantrell* and *Adjunct Professor Dixon.*

PHYSICS 5. GENERAL PHYSICS, covering Sound and Light the first term, Heat and Moulecular Physics the second term, and the History of Physics the third term. Prerequisites: Physics 2 or Physics 4 and Mathematics 1-3. Three terms. Credit, four hours. Fee, $3.00. M.

W. F., 10:15, or by arrangement; laboratory Tuesday afternoon or by arrangement. *Professor Hendren.*

PHYSICS 6. ADVANCED ELECTRICITY. The first and second term will be devoted to an analytical study of the basic principles of electricity and magnetism accompanied in the laboratory by a series of standard electrical measurements; the third term will be devoted to an elementary study of the electron theory and the theories of atomic structure accompanied by a series of laboratory exercises on the discharge of electricity through gases, radioactivity and spectrum analysis. Prerequisites: Physics 4 and Mathematics 5. Three hours per week recitation and one laboratory period per week. Credit, four hours. Fee, $3.00. Schedule by arrangement. *Professor Hendren.*

ASTRONOMY 1-2. INTRODUCTION TO ASTRONOMY. Astronomy 1 is given the first half-year and is primarily descriptive Astronomy. Astronomy 2 is given the second half-year and is primarily devoted to laboratory exercises in Astronomy and an extension of the work in descriptive Astronomy given the first half-year. Two hours per week recitation and lecture, and one laboratory period per week. T. Th. S., 9:20. Credit, three hours. Fee, for Astronomy 2, $3.00. *Professor Hendren.*

ADVANCED COURSES are given in the Graduate School.

POULTRY HUSBANDRY

20. GENERAL POULTRY. Study of breeds and varieties; culling, judging and exhibiting; poultry house construction; feeds and feeding; egg production; parasites and diseases. Two lectures and one laboratory period. First term. Freshman. One hour credit. Fee, $2.00. T. Th., 8:25 or 9:20; lab., W., 2:35-4:25; S., 8:25-10:15; S., 11:10-1:00. *Adjunct Professor Woodward.*

21. GENERAL POULTRY. A continuation of Poultry Husbandry 20. Mating and breeding; incubation and brooding; care of growing stock; caponizing, fattening and killing; advertising and marketing. Two lectures and one laboratory period. Second term. Freshman. One hour credit. Fee, $2.00. Same hours as Poultry Husbandry 20. *Adjunct Professor Woodward.*

22. UTILITY JUDGING. Entire time to be devoted to judging and scoring birds for egg production; study and practice of common culling methods. Prerequisite: Poultry Husbandry 20 and 21. Two lectures and one laboratory period first term. Junior or Senior elective. One hour credit. Fee, $2.00. *Adjunct Professor Woodward.*

23. INCUBATION AND BROODING. Embryology of the chick, theory and practice of incubation; types and construction of incubators and brooders, and their operation; care and management of baby chicks. Prerequisites: Poultry Husbandry 20 and 21. Two lectures and one laboratory period. Second term. Junior or Senior elective. One hour credit. Fee, $2.00. *Adjunct Professor Woodward.*

24. POULTRY MARKETING. Candling, grading, packing and marketing eggs; fattening, killing, picking and dressing fowls; caponizing; study of markets, and cooperative marketing. Prerequisites: Poultry Husbandry 20 and 21. Two lectures and one laboratory period. Third term. Junior or Senior elective. One hour credit. Fee, $2.00. Poultry Husbandry 22, 23 and 24. M. W., 11:10., lab., Th., 2:35-4:25. *Professor Wood.*

25. STANDARD JUDGING. Entire term to be devoted to studying the Standard of Perfection and practice work in judging and placing birds for standard requirements. Both score card and comparison judging will be stressed. Prerequisites: Poultry Husbandry 20 and 21. Two lectures and one laboratory period. First term. Junior or Senior elective. One hour credit. Fee, $2.00. *Professor Wood.*

26. POULTRY BREEDING. The laws and principles of breeding, heredity; mendelism as applied to poultry; line breeding; mating and selection, care of breeding stock, etc. Prerequisites: Poultry Husbandry 20 and 21. Two lectures and one laboratory period. Second term. Junior or Senior elective. One hour credit. Fee, $2.00. *Adjunct Professor Woodward.*

27. POULTRY FEEDS AND FEEDING. Study of the comparative value of different poultry feeds. Mixing feed and methods of feeding. Crops and rotations. Prerequisites: Poultry Husbandry 20 and 21. Two lectures and one laboratory period. Third term. Junior or Senior elective. One hour credit. Fee, $2.00. Poultry 25, 26 and 27. T. Th., 11:10; lab., F., 2:35-4:25. *Adjunct Professor Woodward.*

28. ADVANCED JUDGING Study of the American Standard of Perfection with practice in judging. Trips will be made to nearby poultry shows. Prerequisites: Poultry Husbandry 20, 21 and 25. Two lectures and one laboratory period. First term. Senior. One hour credit. Fee, $2.00. *Professor Wood.*

29. POULTRY FARM MANAGEMENT. Capital and labor requirements; business management; operation details; records and accounts; advertising and correspondence. Prerequisites: Poultry Husbandry 20, 21, 22 and 3 inclusive. Two lectures and one laboratory. Second and third terms. Senior. Two hours credit. Fee, $4.00. Poultry 28, 29, M. W., 10:15; lab., W., 2:35-4:25. *Professor Wood.*

10. SEMINAR AND PROJECT. The student is assigned a project on which to pursue a definite line of investigation. At the end of the year a thesis is required stating the problem results, etc. Prerequisites: Poultry Husbandry 20, 21 and 23 to 27 inclusive. Three terms. Senior. Three hours credit. Fee, $4.00. Hours to be arranged. *Professor Wood.*

30. GENERAL POULTRY. Junior and Senior elective for Home Demonstration Agents and County Agents. Statistical study of poultry

industry; breeds and varieties; standard selection; utility judging; poultry house construction; feeds and feeding; management of the layers; artificial illumination; sanitation; diseases, parasites and their control. Five one-hour lectures and one two-hour laboratory period per week for six weeks. One hour credit. Fee, $2.00. Hours to be arranged. *Professor Wood* and *Adjunct Professor Woodward.*

31. ADVANCED GENERAL POULTRY. Junior and Senior elective for Home Demonstration Agents and County Agents. Principles of poultry breeding; management of the breeding stock; natural and artificial incubation and brooding; care of the growing stock; caponizing, fattening, killing and dressing; candling, grading and packing eggs; records, accounts and advertising. Five one-hour lectures and one two-hour laboratory period per week for six weeks. One hour credit. Prerequisite: Poultry Husbandry 30. Fee, $2.00. Hours to be arranged. *Professor Wood* and *Adjunct Professor Woodward.*

41. POULTRY HYGIENE. The anatomy and physiology of the domestic fowl. Sanitation and disinfection in relation to the control and eradication of external and internal parasitisms and the contagious diseases of the fowl. Feeds in their relation to nutritional diseases and the common non-infectious diseases. Prerequisites: Poultry Husbandry 20 and 21. Three lectures per week the year. Three hours credit. Junior or senior elective. *Dr. Richardson.*

ADVANCED COURSES are given in the Graduate School.

PSYCHOLOGY

NOTE: Courses in Psychology are not open to Freshmen.

1-2-3. INTRODUCTORY GENERAL AND SOCIAL PSYCHOLOGY. Especially adapted for students in the Arts dgeree.

1-2a. ELEMENTS OF PSYCHOLOGY. A study of mental life and behavior as treated in current texts, with applications to every day living. First half-year, T. Th. S., 10:15. One and one-half hours credit. *Professor Edwards.*

2b-3. SOCIAL PSYCHOLOGY. A study of mental interactions in group life, the psychology of social life, and the expressions of the larger mind in social organization, institutions, democracy, tradition, public opinion, trend of sentiment, and the public will. Second half-year. T. Th. S., 10:15. One and one-half hours credit. *Professor* ————

4-5-6. EDUCATIONAL PSYCHOLOGY. See Education 4-5-6.

7-8-9. PRINCIPLES OF PSYCHOLOGY. Especially adapted for students who plan to take advanced work in psychology and for pre-medical students. A year-course for beginning students; 7 and 8 (first and second) general; 9 (third) applications of psychology to medicine. M. W. F., 9:20. Three hours per week. Three terms. With psychology 71-81-91, this course may be taken as a science with four hours credit. Credit must not be given for both Psychology 1, 2, and 7, 8. *Professor Edwards.*

71-81-91. LABORATORY WORK. One laboratory period of two hours per week may be taken in connection with Psychology 7, 8, 9. Credit, one hour. W., 4:25. This course is generally taken in connection with 7-8-9, but may be taken as a separate course with special permission for one hour credit. *Professor Edwards.*

10-11-12. EXPERIMENTAL PSYCHOLOGY. A year course for students who have a satisfactory knowledge of beginning psychology, preferably a year course. A study of scientific methods in psychology; experiments and discussions in the fields of sensation, perception, memory, affective processes, action, tests and measurements. This course may be counted as a science in Group I. Three laboratory periods and one class conference per week. Three terms. M. W. F., 2:35. Four hours credit. *Professor Edwards.*

23-24-25. CHILD STUDY AND THE STUDY OF A SPECIAL SUBJECT. (Not given in 1926-1927).

31-32-33. THE PSYCHOLOGY OF MENTAL DEFICIENCY, OF SUPERNORMALITY, AND OF INDIVIDUAL DIFFERENCES. (Not given 1926-1927).

ADVANCED COURSES are given in the Graduate School.

ROMANCE LANGUAGES

French

X. A course for beginners who are conditioned in French and wish to substitute both French and German for Greek. Three hours a week. Three terms. Three hours credit. T. Th. S., 8:25, 12:05; M. W. F., 9:20. *Associate Professor Holland, Adjunct Professor Chance and Miss Ferguson.*

1. A continuation of French X. A study of grammatical difficulties, idioms, and provincialisms. Reading of from 600 to 1,000 pages of prose and poetry. Three hours a week. Three terms. Three hours credit. T. Th. S., 9:20; M. W. F., 12:05. *Associate Professor Holland. Adjunct Professor Thaxton, Adjunct Professor Chance.*

2. Continuation of French 1. Reading of from 1,000 to 2,000 pages of standard French, classical and modern. Study of French literature through texts and lectures in French. Optional for Sophomores. Three hours per week. Three terms. Three hours credit. T. Th. S., 11:40. *Associate Professor Holland.*

3. Prerequisites 1 and 2. Optional for Juniors and Seniors. Lectures in French and French Literature. Collateral reading of 3,000 pages of classical texts. Three terms. Three hours a week. Three hours credit. *Professor Lustrat.*

2. An elementary course offered as one of the Junior language options. About 200 pages of easy French prose are read and there is practice in conversational French. Three hours per week. Three

terms. Three hours credit. Optional for Juniors. M. W. F., 11:10. *Professor Lustrat.*

21. A continuation of French 20. French composition. Reading of about 1,000 pages of standard authors, classical and modern; parallel reading. Three hours per week. Three terms. Three hours credit. Optional for Seniors. T. Th. S., 10:15. *Professor Lustrat.*

Italian

1. Three hours per week. A one-year course is offered in this subject. It is realized that a good reading knowledge of Italian can be acquired by properly trained students in one year. Three hours per week. Three terms. Three hours credit. *Professor Lustrat.*

Spanish

X. Elementary courses for students not offering Spanish for entrance. Three hours per week. Three terms. Three hours credit. M. W. F., 9:20, 12:05; T. Th. S., 8:25, 12:05. *Mr. McClure.*

1. Intermediate course. Prerequisite: Spanish X. Three hours a week. Three terms. Three hours credit. M. W. F., 12:05; T. Th. S., 9:20. *Adjunct Professor Thaxton. Adjunct Professor Chance, Mr. Mr. McClure.*

2. Advanced course. Prerequisite: Spanish 1. Three hours per week. Three terms. Three hours credit. T. Th. S., 11:40. *Adjunct Professor Thaxton.*

20. A course similar to French 20. Three hours per week. Three terms. Three hours credit. M. W. F., 10:15. *Adjunct Professor Chance.*

21. A course similar to French 21. Three hours per week. Three terms. Three hours credit. T. Th. S., 10:45. *Adjunct Professor Chance.*

SOCIOLOGY

The work in this department is divided into three groups. Courses numbered 1 to 9 are general elementary courses. Courses numbered 20 to 29 ar more advanced courses in the principles of sociology and are basic to graduate work in pure sociology. Courses numbered 10 to 19 are advanced courses dealing with problems of social reconstruction, the application of sociology to business and professional life and with problems and methods of social welfare work.

1-2-3. INTRODUCTION TO SOCIAL SCIENCE. This is a general course designed to orient the student with reference to the problems of human life, the college courses that deal with such problems and the methods they employ. (Not offered in 1926-27).

5-6-7. ELEMENTS OF SOCIOLOGY: SOCIAL ADAPTATION AND SOCIAL EVALUATION.

5. SOCIAL ADAPTATION. A study of social behavior as it manifests it-

self in outward social interactions. Conscious behavior as a backward, a present, and a future reference, and its significance in social causation. Suggestion and imitation as the medium for non-voluntary social interaction. The use of the hypothesis and the introduction of the contractual order in the higher social processes. Prerequisite: Psychology 1-2-3. First term. T. Th. S., 11:10. One hour credit. *Professor Hutchinson* or *Professor* —————.

6-7. SOCIAL EVALUATION: ETHICS AND RELIGION. A study of social interaction, social tradition and social evaluations in their relation to the growth and development of moral and religious ideals and values. The methods by which new moral and religious values are arrived at by society and by the individual, or, the problems and methods of moral and religious education. Second and third terms. T. Th. S., 11:10. Two hours credit. *Professor Hutchinson* or *Professor* —————

10. MODERN SOCIAL PROBLEMS (1) An inquiry into the scope and methods of sociology as an applied science. (2) The underlying principles to be observed in gathering social facts and the significance of social facts to the business and professional man. (3) An intensive study of the normal and pathological aspects of two major problems. Lecture, recitation and seminar. Open to Juniors and Seniors who have had three approved hours in Sociology. (This course and Sociology 11 will alternate yearly, Sociology 10 being given in 1926-27). Three terms. M. W. F., 10:15. Credit three hours. *Professor Hutchinson.*

10a. FIELD WORK, a laboratory course to accompany Sociology 10 to give the student a training in gathering and using social data. The problem assigned to each student will be one that includes facts that relate to his dominant interest, whether it be business, professional or philanthropic. Three terms, one hour credit. *Professor Hutchinson* and —————.

11. RURAL SOCIOLOGY AND COMMUNITY ORGANIZATION. Present tendencies in the rural as distinct from the urban social process. The community as a fundamental factor in all social progress. The technique of community organization and the theory underlying this technique. Open to Juniors and Seniors who have had three approved hours in Sociology. (This course and Sociology 10 alternate yearly, the former being given in 1926-27). Three terms, three hours credit. *Professor Hutchinson* and —————.

11a. FIELD WORK, a laboratory course to accompany 11 that is similar to 10a in its relation to 10. (This course and Sociology 10a alternate yearly, the former being given in 1926-27). Three terms. One hour credit. *Professor Hutchinson* and —————.

12. SOCIAL PATHOLOGY. Poverty and pauperism, vagrancy, crime and other adult pathological conditions and the methods of correcting them. Also a more detailed study of pre-pathological tendencies as

they manifest themselves in the backward, the unstable and the delinquent child together with the steps necessary to prevent these tendencies from developing into pathological conditions. This course is essentially a course in "case method" in which the family or the individual child becomes a particular case to be dealt with. Text and library assignments, observation of typical cases, class room discussion, and field practice. Open to Juniors and Seniors who have had Sociology 10 or 11 and their prerequisites or to Seniors who are taking Sociology 10 or 11 at the same time. Three terms. Three hours credit. (Not given in 1926-27). *Professor Hutchinson and* ————

20. SOCIAL ANTHROPOLOGY. A study of primitive peoples, their traditions and customs as an aid to understanding present race characteristics and modern race problems. Prerequisite Sociology three approved hours. (Combined with Sociology 21 this course and Sociology 24 alternate yearly, the latter being given in 1926-27). First and second terms. Two hours credit. *Professor* ——————.

21. RACE RELATIONS. The Problem of Americanizing the European immigrant. The problem of race relations between the White and the Negro, the Indian, the Japanese, etc., as distinct from the problem of assimilating the European immigrant. Prerequisite Sociology 20. Spring term. One hour credit. *Professor* ——————.

24. PRINCIPLES OF SOCIOLOGY. Advanced course. (1) An introductory survey of the philosophical presuppositions of Sociology as a science. (2) The origin and development of Society and an analysis of social institutions, customs, etc., as factors in social control. (3) The distinction between the realistic and the pragmatic, humanistic interpretation of the social process. (This course alternates yearly with Sociology 20, 21. It will be given in 1926-27). Three terms. Three hours credit. *Professor* ——————.

VETERINARY MEDICINE

Comparative Anatomy

5. HISTOLOGY. A study of the microscopic structure of animal tissues. The preparation and mounting of sections will be taken up if time permits. Freshmen. First and second terms. One lecture and two laboratory periods. Two hours credit. Fee, $3.50. T., 9:20; labs., M. T., 2:35-4:25. *Dr. Jones.*

6. EMBRYOLOGY. A study of reproduction and the development of the embryo. Prerequisite: Anatomy 7, 8, and 5 and Physiology 1. Sophomores. One hour credit. Time to be arranged. Fee, $2.00. *Dr. Krafka.*

7. OSTEOLOGY AND ARTHOLOGY. A study of the bones and joints. Freshmen. First term. Three laboratory periods. One hour credit. Fee for this and the following course, $10.00. T. Th., 10:15-1:00; S., 10:15-12:05. *Dr. Jones.*

8. MYOLOGY AND SPLANCHNOLOGY. The study of the muscles and viscera. Prerequisite: Anatomy 1. Freshmen. Second and third terms. Three laboratory periods. Three hours credit. T. Th., 10:15-1.00; S., 10:15-12:05. *Dr. Jones.*

9. ANGIOLOGY AND NEUROLOGY. The study of the organs of circulation and the nervous system. Prerequisite: Anatomy 7 and 8. Sophomore. First and second terms. Three laboratory periods. Three hours credit Fee for this and the following course, $10.00. M. W., 10:15-1:00; S., 10:15-12:05. *Dr. Jones.*

10. COMPARATIVE ANATOMY. Consists of the study of the variations in form and structure of corresponding organs and parts of the various domestic animals. Dissections of the hog, ox and dog will be made. Prerequisite: Anatomy 7, 8 and 9. Sophomores. Third term. Three laboratory periods. One hour credit. M. W., 10:15-1:00; F., 10:15-12:05. *Dr. Jones.*

Veterinary Physiology

1. A study of the normal function of the animal body. Three lectures and one laboratory period. Prerequisites: Anatomy 5, 7, 8. Sophomores. Entire year. Four hours credit. Fee, $10.00. F., 2:35-4:25. *Dr. Persells.*

Bacteriology

1. GENERAL. Treats of the biological, physiological and morphological features of bacteria. One lecture and recitation and two laboratory periods, first half year. Sophomores in Veterinary degree course only. One and one-half hours credit. Fee, $5.00. Breakage fee, $5.00 W., 9:20; labs., M. W., 2:35-4:25. *Dr. Burkhart.*

2. PATHOGENIC. A study of the pathogenic bacteria. Prerequisite: Bacteriology 1. Sophomore Veterinary students only. Last half year. One lecture and two laboratory periods. One and one-half hours credit. Fee, $5.00. Breakage fee, $5.00. W., 9:20; labs., M. W., 2:35-4:25. *Dr. Burkhart.*

3. DAIRY. (See description on page 49).

4. INFECTION AND IMMUNITY. A detailed study of infection and theories of immunity. The various paths of entrance and elimination of infection into and from the body are fully discussed. Prerequisite: Bacteriology 1 and 2. Veterinary Seniors. One lecture and two laboratory periods, half-year. One and one-half hours credit. Fee, $5.00; breakage fee, $5.00. *Dr. Burkhart.*

Pharmacy and Materia Medica

1. PHARMACY. This course is preliminary to the study of Materia Medica. Various pharmaceutical processes are considered. Juniors in Veterinary Degree Course. Three hours, first term. One hour credit. T. Th. S., 11:10. *Professor Wilson.*

2. MATERIA MEDICA. This course will embrace the study of the physical and chemical and general therapeutical actions of drugs from the vegetable, animal and mineral kingdoms. Prerequisite: Course 1. Juniors in Veterinary Degree Course. Three hours, second and third terms. Two hours credit. T. Th. S., 11:10. *Professor Wilson.*

Veterinary Therapeutics

VETERINARY THERAPEUTICS. A study of the uses of drugs. Prerequisite: Courses in Pharmacy and Materia Medica. Juniors in Veterinary Degree Course. Three hours, third term. One hour credit. T. Th. S., 11:10. *Dr. Burkhart.*

Pathology

1. GENERAL PATHOLOGY. The cause of disease, pathological phenomena in general are considered. Prerequisite: Physiology 1-2, Anatomy 5, and Bacteriology 1-2. Two lectures and two laboratory periods. Juniors. Fee, $5.00. Four hours credit. T. Th., 9:50; labs., M. W., 9:20-11:10. *Drs. Richardson and Jones.*

2. SPECIAL PATHLOGY. Autopsies and laboratory diagnosis. A consideration of pathological conditions of the various organs and parts of the body. Autopsies of animals with be conducted. Prerequisite: Pathology 1. Three hours credit. Senior year. Laboratory fee, $5.00. M. W. F., 4:25. *Dr. Persells.*

3. FOOD INSPECTION. A course designed to cover in a broad way the subject of food inspection as it concerns meat and milk inspection. Prerequisites: as for Pathology 2. Seniors. Two lectures and one laboratory period. First and second terms. Two hours credit. M. W. F., 12:05. *Dr. Persells.*

4. PARASITOLOGY. A study of the animal parasites infesting farm animals and fowls. Juniors. Second and third terms. Three lectures. Two hours credit. F. S., 9:50; Th., 12:05. *Dr. Richardson.*

Comparative Medicine

1. INFECTIOUS DISEASES. In this course the various infectious diseases of animals are studied. Juniors. Three hours of lectures and recitations. Entire year. No fee. Three hours credit. T. Th. S., 10:15. *Dr. Burkhart.*

2. NON-INFECTIOUS DISEASES. All the diseases not classed as infectious and which affect the domestic animals will be considered in this course. Seniors. Three hours of lectures and recitations. No fee. Three hours credit. M. W. F., 11:10. *Dr. Richardson.*

3. HYGIENE AND SANITATION. Physiological aspects of feeding and feeding methods; water supply; tables; pastures; sheds and paddocks;

care of the skin, hoofs and claws; burying, cremation, chemical disinfection; federal and state livestock sanitary laws; transportation of animals. Half-year. One and one-half hours credit. Senior. M. W. F., 9:20. *Dr. Persells.*

Surgery

1. GENERAL SURGERY. Wound dressing, suturing, local and general anaesthetics, asepsis and surgical conditions in general are studied. Juniors. Three hours of lectures and recitations per week, entire year. Three hours credit. M. W. F., 11:10. *Dr. Severin.*

2. SURGERY. A consideration of the surgical diseases of the various regions of the body. Dentistry and lameness are included. Seniors. Three hours per week of lectures, recitations and laboratory exercises, entire year. Three hours credit. T. Th. S., 10:15. *Dr. Severin.*

3. CLINICS. Daily clinics will be held at the hospital, and junior and senior students will be assigned to the care of patients and required to diagnose cases and to recommend and administer treatment under the supervision of the professor in charge and to assist at all operations. Juniors and Seniors. Two hours daily, entire year. Three hours credit. No fee. No text required. M. T. W. Th. F., 2:35-4:25. *Dr. Severin.*

4. CLINICAL DIAGNOSIS. A systematic study of the methods used to recognize or identify diseases in the living animal. Juniors. Three hours of lectures and demonstrations for one term. One hour credit. Fee, $5.00. T. Th. S., 8:25. *Dr. Severin.*

5. HORSESHOEING. A special study of the foot of the horse, and the methods of shoeing and balancing used to overcome abnormal conditions. Juniors. Three hours of lectures, recitations and demonstrations for one term. One hour credit. No fee. T. Th. S., 8:25. *Dr. Severin.*

6. SURGICAL EXERCISES. Elective senior year. One hour credit. This is a laboratory course in which students will be required to perform all the more common surgical operations upon properly anaesthetized large and small animals. Fee, $10.00. T. Th. S., 9:20. *Dr. Severin.*

7. OPHTHALMOLOGY. A study of the eye and its appendages. Seniors Three hours per week of lectures, recitations, clinics and demonstrations and surgical exercises for one term. One hour credit. M. W. F., 10:15. *Dr. Severin.*

8. OBSTETRICS. A course of study in the anatomy and physiology of the organs of reproduction of the female, the diseases incident to pregnancy and parturition and diseases of new born animals. Seniors. Lectures, demonstrations and clinics constitute the work of the course. Three hours per week for two terms. Two hours credit. Fee, $3.50. M. W. F., 10:15. *Dr. Severin.*

Veterinary Jurisprudence

A course of lectures on law as it applies to the veterinarian as a practitioner. Legal principles, federal, state and municipal laws, acts and ordinances affecting the veterinarian receive the necessary attention. Seniors. Three hours per week, one term. One hour credit. *Dr. Richardson.*

Zootechnics and Animal Hygiene

ZOOTECHNICS AND ANIMAL HYGIENE. The exterior of the horse will be studied in its relation to age, soundness and utility. The various animal plagues will be discussed as to their cause, prevention and economic importance. The common non-specific diseases and the injuries of farm animals will be discussed from the viewpoint of prevention and first aid to the injured. Entire year. Three hours credit. T. Th. S., 12:35. Fee, $3.50. *Dr. Persells.*

ZOOLOGY

1. ELEMENTARY HUMAN ANATOMY. Three hours of lectures per week. First half-year. One and one-half hours credit. Required of Junior Pharmacy students. M. W. F., 9:20. *Adjunct Professor Vogt.*

2. PHYSIOLOGY. Three lectures per week, second half of year. One and one-half hours credit. M. W. F., 9:20. *Adjunct Professor Vogt.*

31. INTRODUCTORY ZOOLOGY. Organization and general physiology of animals, with consideration of the ontogenic and phylogenic factors in their development. Three recitations and one laboratory period per week for three terms. Four hours credit. Fee, $3.50. M. W. F., 10:15; T. Th. S., 8:25; lab., M., 11:10; M. W. or T., 2:35. *Professor Krafka* and *Adjunct Professor Vogt.*

32. INTRODUCTORY ZOOLOGY. Organization and general physiology of animals, with consideration of the ontogenic and phylogenic factors in their development. Three recitations and two laboratory periods per week for three terms. Five hours credit. Fee, $3.50. M. W. F., 10:15; or T. Th. S., 8:25; lab., M. W., 2:35 to 4:25, or T. Th., 2:35 to 425. *Professor Krafka* and *Adjunct Professor Vogt.*

4. VERTEBRATE MORPHOLOGY. A comparative study of the various vertebrate types from a developmental and structural standpoint. Two reciataions and two laboratory periods per week for three terms. Four hours credit. Zoölogy 31 is prerequisite. Fee, $5.00. T. Th., 9:20. *Professor Krafka.*

5. HISTOLOGY AND EMBRYOLOGY. The first term is occupied with the aistological study of the principal types of tissue; the second term with the early embryonic development of the frog; the third term with the advanced embryonic development of the chick. The student is

required to make his own preparation for study. Two lectures and two laboratory periods per week for three terms. Four hours credit. Zoölogy 31 is prerequisite. Fee, $5.00. *Professor Krafka.*

6. MORPHOLOGY AND CLASSIFICATION OF INSECTS. A study of the anatomy, physiology, ecology and life histories of the insect groups; with extensive collection and classification of the local fauna. Two lectures and two two-hour laboratory periods per week. Laboratory fee, $2.50. M. W. F., 11:10-1:00. *Professor Krafka.*

ADVANCED COURSES are given in the Graduate School.

Part III
THE GRADUATE SCHOOL

THE GRADUATE SCHOOL

DAVID C. BARROW, LL.D., Chancellor Emeritus.
C. M. SNELLING, Sc.D., Chancellor of the University.
W. H. BOCOCK, LL.D., Dean of the Graduate School.

HISTORICAL

Although the first statutes of the University contemplated resident graduate students,* it was the custom here (as it was elsewhere, and perhaps still is in some universities) to confer the degree of Master of Arts upon any Bachelor of Arts of good character who, three years or more after graduation, should formally aopply for the degree and pay a fee therefor.† In 1868 a course of study was laid down which candidates for the Master's degree were to pursue. From 1869 until 1890 the regulations required the candidate successfully to complete the most advanced course in each of the academic (non-professional) schools. In 1892 the requirements for the degrees became what they have since substantially remained; slight modifications have been made from time to time.

The degree of Master of Science was first offered in 1890, M.S. in Agriculture in 1910,‡ M.S. in Forestry in 1917, M.S. in Economics in 1923, M.S. in Home Economics in 1924.

The graduate work of the University has been supervised by the Faculty, chiefly through its Committee on Graduate Courses. In 1910 the work was set apart by the Board of Trustees as the Graduate School, with its own Dean.

ADMISSION

Admission to the Graduate School is granted to graduates of colleges of good standing. Other persons of suitable age and attainments may also be admitted by special permission of the Committee on Graduate Courses. Armission to the Graduate School does not necessarily imply admission to candidacy for a degree. Application for admission should be made by correspondence or at the office of the Dean of the Graduate School.

---

* "Masters and Bachelors of Arts, who shall signify to the President their purpose of residing at the lCollege or in Athens with a view of pursuing literature, under his direction, and under the government of the College, and give a sufficient bond to the Board of Trustees for the payment of their quarter bills shall be considered as resident Graduates and students of the College." Laws of the College of Georgia, 1803, Chap. II., Sec. IV. So also Code of Laws for the government of Franklin College, 1816. Chap. II, Sec. XVI.
† Code of 1803. Chap. XII. Secs. II and IV. Code of 1816, Chap. II, Sec. XVI and Chap. VIII, Sects. II and IV.
‡ The degree of Master of Agriculture had been offered from 1876 to 1879.

Should a student desire to take a graduate course for which his undergraduate work has not offered sufficient preparation, he will be rekuired to pursue the requisite studies. The professor who conducts a graduate course undertakes to see that every student who is admitted to his course has satisfied the prerequisites or is satisfying them according to his directions.

DEGREES

The degrees conferred in the Graduate School are Master of Arts, Master of Science, Civil Engineer, Master of Science in Agriculture, Master of Science in Forestry, Master of Science in Economics, Master of Science in Home Economics.

Candidates must have received a baccalaureate degree from this or some other institution of reputable standing, and must pursue here and complete satisfactorily a major and two minor courses. But graduate work done at a reputable university elsewhere may be credited here (to an amount not exceeding one quarter of the programme) in the following way: the candidate will submit an outline of the course taken elsewhere (and such other information as may be required) to the professor here in whose department the course lies. If the course meets with the approval of the professor and of the head of the department, the course is adopted by the department, and if it covers different ground from one of the previously approved courses it is submitted to the Faculty for approval; and in all cases the professor subjects the candidate to a written and presents him for an oral examination in the usual way.

The programme of study must not include any course that forms a part of the candidate's programme of study or of his curriculum for any other degree conferred or to be conferred; it should be submitted early in the session (not later than November 1st,) to the Dean of the Graduate School for the approval of the committee on Graduate courses and of the Faculty.

Candidates are expected to show correctness and good taste in their use of English, both oral and written, and, as a rule, a reading knowledge of French or German is required of a candidate for any graduate degree except Master of Science in Agriculture and Master of Science in Home Economics.*

A thesis or essay required in connection with a graduate course must show independence of judgement in the treatment of some definite problem from the sources. A bibliography must be added covering all literature used, and specific acknowledgements made. Assignment of

---

* "Any student who shows notable weakness in English, either oral or written, in his work in any course in the University of Georgia, shall, at the request of any instructor, be required to do special work under the direction of the department of English." Faculty Minutes, Sept. 20th, 1915.

subject must be made to the candidate and reported to the Dean of the Graduate School not later than January 1st, and the thesis must be handed to the professor not later than May 1st, and by him to the met certain requirements for liberal as well as technical courses, the Dean of the Graduate School not later than May 15th. If the thesis be approved by the professor and by the Faculty, a bound copy must be delivered before the second Wednesday in June to the Dean of the Graduate School for deposit in the Library.

After the professors under whom the candidate has pursued an approved programme of study have reported in writing to the Dean that he has satisfactorily pursued the required courses and has passed written examinations upon them, he will be orally examined by a committee of the Faculty.* If the course has included a thesis, the oral examination will not be held until the committee appointed to examine the thesis has made a favorable report to the Dean. Reports of written examinations on minor courses must be made not later than three weeks before Commencement Sunday, and reports on major courses not later than two weeks before Commencement Sunday. In making reports the professor will transmit a copy of the written examination (questions and candidate's papers) for the use of the examining committee of the Faculty. This committee is appointed by the Chancellor and consists of not less than five members of the Faculty. All other members of the Faculty are invited to attend the examination. After the professor who has given the course has finished his questioning, an equal amount of time, or more, will be at the disposal of the other members of the committee.

Examinations, both oral and written, on a major course may go outside of the formal limits of the course and include fundamental matters that may have been treated in undergraduate courses. This regulation applies also, though in less degree, to examinations on minor courses. Where a graduate minor is based on an advanced undergraduate course, the student may at the option of the instructor take the undergraduate examination for each term, but it is expected that each graduate course shall be subject to one written examination covering the entire course.

MASTER OF ARTS. Prerequisite degree, Bachelor of Arts or Bachelor of Science. The major course and at least one minor must be selected from the following departments of study: Philosophy, Education, History, Political Science, Economics, Rhetoric, English Literature, the English Language, German, Latin, Greek, Romance Languages, Mathematics.

MASTER OF SCIENCE. Prerequisite degree, Bachelor of Science or

---

* Attendance on certain general lectures (on graduate study, on the use of the library, and on similar subjects) is also required of all candidates, and the subject matter of such lectures may be included in the oral examinations.

Bachelor of Arts. In special cases the committee on Graduate Courses is authorized by the Faculty to accept the degree of B.S. in Engineering or B.S. in Agriculture when the undergraduate curriculum has minimum requirements being an equivalent of our French 1 or German 1, and at least three 3-hour college courses in the fields of the English Language and Literature, History, and Political Economy. The major course and at least one minor must be selected from the following departments of study: Mathematics, Chemistry, Geology, Physics, Astronomy, Physiology, Zoölogy, Botany, Psychology.

CIVIL ENGINEER. Prerequisite degree, Bachelor of Science in Civil Engineering or Bachelor of Science in Electrical Engineering. The major course must be in the department of Civil Engineering and the minors may be minor graduate courses, or certain undergraduate courses offered in other departments of the University. The choice of minors is subject to the approval of the Professor of Civil Engineering.

MASTER OF SCIENCE IN AGRICULTURE.* A reputable baccalaureate degree prerequisite. The major and at least one minor must be selected from courses offered in the College of Agriculture. One minor may be chosen from graduate courses offered in other departments of the University or from certain undergraduate courses. The choice of courses is subject to the approval of the professor in charge of the department in which the major course is selected.

MASTER OF SCIENCE IN FORESTRY. Prerequisite degree, Bachelor of Science in Forestry or Forest Engineer. The major course must be in Forestry; one minor may be selected from any department of the College of Agriculture; and one minor from any department or college of the University, but choice of courses is subject to the approval of the Professor of Forestry.

MASTER OF SCIENCE IN ECONOMICS. Prerequisite degree: Bachelor of Science in Commerce, or Bachelor of Science, or Bachelor of Arts, or Bachelor of Arts in the Social Sciences. The major course must be selected from courses offered by professors in the School of Commerce. One minor must be taken from courses offered by professors in the School of Commerce or by professors in the department of History and Political Science. The choice of courses is subject to the approval of the Dean of the School of Commerce.

MASTER OF SCIENCE IN HOME ECONOMICS.* Prerequisite degree:

---

* Professors under whom graduate study is pursued for the degree of Master of Science in Agriculture or Forestry or Home Economics constitute a council of advisors to the candidate under the chairmanship of the professor of the major study. This council (1) passes on the preparation of the candidate for graduate study and holds a qualifying examination to that end: (2) considers the programme of the candidate, determining the scope of work to be covered in each subject, and reporting the approved programme to the Chairman of the Committee on Graduate Work of the College of Agriculture and to the Dean of the Graduate School of the University; (3) follows the progress of the student's work and his preparation for the final examinations, for that purpose holding a preliminary oral examination not later than sixty days prior to the completion of graduate courses in the regular session and not later than two weeks prior to the completion of a course in the Summer quarter. A written report of this examination is made to the Chairman of the Committee on Graduate Courses.

Bachelor of Science in Home Economics. The major study must be in Home Economics and one minor may also be taken from that department. Minors will be selected with distinct reference to the major. The choice of courses is subject to the approval of the head of the department of Home Economics.

COURSES 1926-1927

EXPLANATION. Courses of instruction are classed as majors or minors according to the estimated amount of work required, and to some extent according to the nature of the subject. A major course will require half of the work of a candidate for the Master's degree in residence for one year. A minor course will require a quarter of his time.

A major course is based upon and presupposes the Senior or most advanced undergraduate course of a department. No student will be admitted to a major course who has not had at least two years of undergraduate work in the same or a closely related subject. A minor course is also generally based upon the most advanced undergraduate course of a department, but extensions of certain advanced undergraduate courses may also be rated as minor graduate courses provided at least one lecture hour a week is devoted to strictly graduate work. No student, however, will be admitted to a graduate minor unless he has had at least one year of undergraduate work in the same subject. A candidate for a degree will not be permitted, as a rule, to offer more than one minor that is not based upon the most advanced undergraduate course of a department. All courses are submitted for approval and rating to the Committee on Graduate Courses, and are finally passed upon by the Faculty.

AGRICULTURAL CHEMISTRY

101. AGRICULTURAL CHEMICAL ANALYSIS. This course will be based on the work offered Seniors and will be limited to the types of soils of the state of Georgia. Analysis will be made of at least five types as unlike as can be obtained, and a special study will be made of the nature and character of the organic matter contained. The geological formation in the localities in which these soils are found will be studied. Work will be done towards improving a few of the methods by which it is now difficult to duplicate results, such as that for determining humus. Parallel reading and an acquaintance with work being carried on in other laboratories will be required. This reading will be Stockbridge's Rocks and Soils; Hopkins's Fertility; Hall's Soils; Hilgard's Soils, and the Bulletins bearing on the subject. Wiley's Principles and Practice of Agricultural Analysis, Vol. I, and Bulletin No. 107, Official and Provisional Methods of Analysis, will be used as reference books. Three conference hours and six laboratory periods per week. Major. *Professor Carter.*

102. ADVANCED AGRICULTURAL ANALYSIS. One conference and two laboratory periods per week, with readings and reviews of such chemical literature as applies most directly to the line of laboratory work elected and approved by the faculty. Latitude will be allowed in the work undertaken, in order to meet the needs of the individual student. Outlines of specific courses, elected by students, will be submitted to the faculty at the time of registration for the course. Prerequisites: Agricultural Chemistry 1, 2b, and 3b, or equivalent. Minor. *Professor Carter.*

AGRICULTURAL EDUCATION

101. PROBLEMS IN VOCATIONAL TEACHING. An advanced course in vocational education involving educational aims, educational and sociological values of vocational subjects; means of measuring values, educational needs of the several vocational groups of society; school organization to meet these needs, curricula; relations of school activities and work activities; where vocational education can best be done; vocational methods; the vocational teacher. Readings: Bagley, Dewey, Snedden, Strayer, Eliot, Thorndike, Davenport, Prosser, and others. Prerequisite: Undegraduate Courses 10, 12 and 13, or equivalent. Two hours a week. Minor. *Professor Wheeler.*

102. TEACHER-TRAINING IN AGRICULTURE. Government agencies affecting the development of agricultural education in the United States; national and state legislation; types of schools affected; organization and course of study; organization and administration of teacher-training under the "National Vocational Education Act;" national and state policies, laws and plans for teacher-training; review of the Federal Act. Report of National Committee on Vocational Education; Bulletins and Proceedings of the National Society for Vocational Education; state laws for carrying out the provisions of the Federal Act. Prerequisite: Undergraduate Courses 10-14 inclusive, or their equivalent. Three hours a week. Major. *Professor Wheeler.*

103. PROBLEMS OF TEACHING COLLEGE AGRICULTURE. Bases for course development and construction, steps in course organization, bases of method, development of special methods for special subjects. A problem in course organization is required to be worked out. Prerequisite: Undergraduate Courses 10, 12 and 13, or equivalent. Two conferences a week. Minor. *Professor Wheeler* and *Associate Professor Reitz.*

104. VOCATIONAL EDUCATION. An advanced course in vocational education administration involving the administration of vocational education in the United States under the Smith-Hughes Law; examples of state organization; specific examples of the administration of the separate phases of vocational education; Agriculture, Home Economics, Trades and Industry, and Commerce; the problems of financing voca-

tional education; the problem of overcrowding the separate vocations, etc. Prerequisite: Undergraduate Courses 10-15 inclusive, or equivalent. Two conferences a week. Minor. *Professor Wheeler.*

NOTE: 101 and 104 may be combined to form a major.

AGRICULTURAL ENGINEERING

102. FARM BUILDING CONSTRUCTION. A course in the structural design of farm buildings. Plans, bills of material, and specifications are required. Prerequisites: Agricultural Engineering 1, 2, 3, 4, 7, 10, and 25. Texts: Strength of Materials, Boyd; Concrete Construction, Seaton; Reinforced Concrete, Hool; Estimating and Contracting, Radford; Bulletins on Building and Sanitation Codes, United States Bureau of Standards. Handbooks: Kidder-Nolan, Southern Pine, Merriman, Marks. One conference and two laboratory periods a week. Minor. *Professor Lyle.*

103. SOUTHERN FARM BUILDINGS. A course in the design of buildings for farms in the southern states. A series of plans accompanied by statements concerning their suitability for southern farms is required. Prerequisites: Agricultural Engineering 1, 2, 3, 4, 7, 10, and 25. Texts: Farm buildings, Foster-Carter; Household Mechanics, Keene; United States Department of Agriculture, State Extension and Commercial plans and bulletins. One conference and two laboratory periods. Minor. *Professor Lyle.*

Courses 102 and 103 together form a Major course.

104. AGRICULTURAL ENGINEERING RESEARCH. Major or Minor. Original investigation of an approved problem pertaining to one or more of the following major phases of Agricultural Engineering: Farm Machinery; Farm Power; Farm Buildings; Land Reclamation; with thesis. Outlines of problems selected will be submitted to the faculty. Major. Two conferences and four laboratory periods each week. Minor. One conference and two laboratory periods each week. Prerequisites: the most advanced undergraduate course in the phase selected. *Professor Lyle.*

AGRONOMY

Farm Crops

101. CEREALS a. Minor. Prerequisite: Farm Crops 1, or equivalent, and one course in Botany.

Undegraduate Farm Crops 3, with one additional conference devoted to a study of selected bulletins and papers from state experiment stations and U. S. Department of Agriculture. Three conferences and one laboratory period each week. *Associate Professor Tabor.*

101a. CEREALS b. Major or minor. Prerequisite: Farm Crops 1 and 3, or equivalent, and one course in Botany.

A study of the factors of production, harvesting, and storing and shipping of one or more of the cereal crops, and critical review of the experimental literature of the selected crop or crops. Original investigations of an approved problem and report of same in theses required in major. Two conferences and one laboratory period each week with minor. Three conferences with three laboratory periods with major. *Associate Professor Tabor.*

101b. FORAGE CROPS. Major or minor. Prerequisites: Farm Crops 2, or equivalent, and one course in Botany.

A study of factors of production, use, harvesting, and shipping of one or more forage crops, and a critical review of the experimental literature of the crop or crops studied. Original investigation of an approved problems and report of same in thesis required in major. Two conferences and one laboratory period each week with minor. Three conferences with three laboratory periods with major. *Associate Professor Tabor.*

Cotton Industry

101. COTTON PRODUCTION. A study of all phases of cotton production. Species, varieties, climates, soils, factors affecting growth, fertilization, cultivating, insect enemies, diseases and marketing are some of the factors considered. Selected readings from the following books: The World's Cotton Crops, Todd, The Development and Properties of Raw Cotton, Balls; Wild and Cultivated Cotton plants of the World, Watt. Office of Experiment Station, Bulletin 33; Cotton Seed Products, Lamborn. Cotton Trade Guide and Students' Manual, Miller. In addition extensive use is made of all publications of the U. S. Department of Agriculture and the various State Experiment Stations. Prerequisites: Farm Crops, 1; Botany. 1; Cotton Industry, 3, and Soils 1 and 2, or their equivalent. A laboratory fee of $15.00 charged for that part of the course in grading and marketing. Major or minor. Major, three conferences and three laboratory periods per week. Minor, two conferences and one laboratory period per week. *Professor Childs.*

Soils

102. FERTILIZERS. This course is based on Undergraduate Courses 1, 2, and 6, and will consist of a study of the manufacture and use of commercial fertilizers. The principles involved in the application of fertilizers to crops and the study of experimental methods for determining values of fertilizer materials to crop growth. Specific problems will be studied in the greenhouse and field. Parallel readings and acquaintance with the subject matter and the work as carried on by investigators will be required. These readings will include: The

Manufacture of Chemical Minerals, by Fisch; Fertilizers and Crops, by Van Slyke; Manures and Fertilizers, by Wheeler; Fertilizers, by Hall; Principles and Practice of Agricultural Analysis, Vol. II, by Wiley; Bulletins from the United States Department of Agriculture and State Experiment Stations. Minor. Two conferences and one laboratory period each week. *Professor Crabb.*

103. SOIL FERTILITY. The work of this course will consist of the study of crop requirements and the investigation of some problem definitely related to plant growth. Conferences, parallel readings and laboratory work will be required. The parallel readings will be based on Plant Pathology, by Duggar; Soil Conditions and Plant Growth, by Russell; Soil Fertility and Permanent Agriculture, by Hopkins; Fertilizers and Crops, Van Slyke; Manures and Fertilizers, by Wheeler; Soil Fertility and Fertilizers, by Halligan; Manures, by Aikman; Agriculture, by Storer; The Soil Solution, by Cameron; Bulletins of the United States Department of Agriculture, and of State Experiment Stations. Prerequisites: Soils 1-2 and 5, or equivalents. Minor. Two conferences and one laboratory period each week. *Professor Crabb.*

NOTE: 102 and 103 may be combined to form a major.

104. SOIL TYPES. a.   A general study of the origin and formation of the soil of a given area. b. Examination and investigation of the occurrence of soil series and soil types in the field. The course will consist of conferences and assigned readings of Geology, by Chamberlain and Salisbury; Physical Geology, by Chamberlain and Salisbury; Physical Geology, by Pierson and Schuchert; Rocks, Rock Weathering and Soils, by Merrill; Soils and Agriculture of the Southern States, by Bennett; Soil Survey Reports, Bureau of Soils; U. S. Department of Agriculture; Geological Survey Reports of Georgia and U. S. Geological Survey. At least two field excursions will be required of the area studied. Prerequisites: Soils 1, 2, and 3, or equivalent courses. Major and Minor. When taken as a major, the entire state of Georgia will be studied and a thesis will be required. When taken as a minor, either the northern half or the southern half of the state will be studied.   Major, three conferences per week. Minor, two conferences per week. A minor of north Georgia and a minor of south Georgia may be combined as a major. *Professor Crabb.*

Farm Economics

101. A study of the business status, living conditions, and systems of farming followed by land-owner, tenant, and share-cropper in a restricted area. Not less than fifty farms are to be studied. The data are to be secured by the survey method, and are to be classified and tabulated in such a way as to bring out the findings most clearly Such surveys as are already available are to be utilized. Details of

each survey are to be submitted to the committee on Graduate Courses. Prerequisites: Courses 1-2, and 3. Major for M.S. Agr. *Professor Fain.*

ANIMAL HUSBANDRY

101. FEEDING PROBLE 1 S. This course will include a study of feeding stuffs most generally available under cotton belt conditions and their adaptation to the various classes of farm animals. Feeding tests with a sufficient number of animals to give reliable results and covering periods of from 90 to 150 days will be required. Accurate and detailed records of kind and amounts of feed will be kept together with records of production. Prerequisite: Undergraduate Course 9, and Veterinary Medicine 3, 4 (Animal Physiology). Parallel reading; Armby's Principles of Animal Husbandry; Henry's Feeds and Feeding; Sinclair's Heavy Horses; Gay's Productive Horse Husbandry; Wing's Modern Sheep Breeding and Management; Mumford's Beef Production; State and U. S. Government Bulletins. Two conferences per week and sufficient time in laboratory to conduct feeding tests. Minor. *Professor Jarnigan.*

102. SWINE PRODUCTION. This course is a continuation of Undergraduate Course 6. Students will be required to conduct feeding experiments with swine. Methods of breeding, feeding and management will be studied. Prerequisites: Undergraduate Courses 8 and 9, and Veterinary Medicine 3, 4 (Animal Physiology). Parallel reading: Coburn's Swine Industry; Dietrich's Swine; Dawson's Hog Book, College Experiment Station and Government Bulletins. Two conferences per week and sufficient time in laboratory to conduct feeding test and tabulate results. Minor. *Professor Jarnagin.*

103. SHEEP PRODUCTION. This course will include a historical study of breeds of sheep with reference to their adaptability for early spring lamb production. Breeding and feeding records of the College flocks of Southdown, Shropshire and grade ewes will be studied and tabulated. Economic production of spring lambs under Georgia conditions will be emphasized.

Parallel readings will include Productive Sheep Husbandry, Coffey; Sheep Management, Kleinheinz; Sheep Manual, Stewart; Sheep Farming, Craig; Sheep Breeds and Management, Wrightson; Modern Sheep Breeds and Management, the Shepherd Boy, and Government and Experiment Station bulletins on phases of sheep production. Prerequisites, Animal Husbandry 6, 8 and 9. Two conferences per week and four laboratory periods per week throughout the year. Thesis required. Major. *Professor Jarnagin.*

BACTERIOLOGY

101. The nature of the course will be based, upon one of the following divisions of Bacteriology: Pathogenic Bacteriology and Immunity, Agricultural Bacteriology and Industrial Bacteriology.

The minimum qualifications of a student pursuing advanced work in Pathogenic Bacteriology and Immunity are Agricultural Chemistry 1 and Bacteriology 1, 3 and 4. In Agricultural and Industrial Bacteriology the minimum qualifications of a student are Agricultural Chemistry 1 and Bacteriology 1, and 3 or 5. Parallel reading and individual laboratory work will be required.

An outline of the course for each student will be submitted at the time of registration.

Major, one conference hour and four laboratory periods per week. Minor, one conference and two laboratory periods per week. *Associate Professor Burkhart.*

BOTANY

101. MYCOLOGY. Course 6 with extension (two hours graduate laboratory). Three other suitable undergraduate courses in Botany are prerequisite. Minor. *Professor Reade.*

105. MYCOLOGY. An extension of the graduate work of 101. Course 6 and two other undergraduate courses in Botany are prerequisite. Minor. Three hours per week. *Professor Reade.*

103. MYCOLOGY. 105 with the addition of a thesis. Prerequisite; 6 and three other suitable undergraduate courses. Major. Four hours per week. *Professor Reade.*

104. SYSTEMATIC SPERMATOPHYTES. Work in field and herbarium under supervision. Prerequisite: Four suitable undergraduate courses in Botany. Three hours per week. Minor. *Professor Reade.*

111. GENETICS AND EUGENICS. Botany 11, extended by the study of Parts II and III of Babcock and Clausen, the examination of library files of the literature of Genetics, and the completion of laboratory experiments to the value of 36 hours. Minor. *Professor Reade.*

Note:—It cannot be guaranteed that all the graduate courses in Botany will be given in any one year, and no course will be given unless two or more students apply for it.

CHEMISTRY

Opportunity is offered to a limited number of qualified students to pursue advanced work in Chemistry. The minimum qualification for entrance to a course and the nature of the advanced work will be determined by individual conference.

CIVIL ENGINEERING

101. Baker's Masonry Construction. Irrigation, based on Wilson, Newell. Land Drainage, Elliott, and United States Irrigation Papers. Hydraulic Concrete, Turneaure, Taylor and Thompson. Hydraulics. Russell, Merriman. Lectures. Various essays and designs are required of the students. Six hours per week. Major. *Professor Strahan.*

COMMERCE

101. STUDIES IN INDUSTRIAL AND ECONOMIC GEOGRAPHY. Intensive study of selected commodities, and also of the international exchange of goods. Prerequisite: Commerce 1, 60, a, b, c; 75, a, b, c; 80, a, b, c. Three hours per week. Major. *Professor Jenkins.*

105. HISTORY OF ECONOMIC THOUGHT. A general study of the development of economic thought from ancient times to the present, with emphasis on the English classical economists. Prerequisite: Economics 5. Three hours per week. Minor. *Professor Brooks.*

112-113. AUDITING AND COST ACCOUNTING. This course is the third year of Accounting. It is open to either seniors or graduate students. Prerequisites: Commerce 6 and 11. When taken by graduate students, one hour per week of strictly graduate work will be required. Four hours per week. Minor. *Professor Heckman.*

114-115. ADVANCED ACCOUNTING PROBLEMS AND INCOME TAX ACCOUNTING. Montgomery, Income Tax Accounting; Prentice Hall, Federal Tax Course; Finney, Consolidated Statements; Gordon and Lockwood, Modern Accounting Systems. Prerequisites: Commerce 6 and 11, and prerequisite or parallel, 14-15. Three hours per week. *Professor Heckman.*

134. PUBLIC FINANCE. Bastable, Public Finance; Henry C. Adams, Public Finance;; Select chapters from Adam Smith's Wealth of Nations, Seligman's Essays in Taxation, Bulloch's Selected Readings in Public Finance, and the Proceedings of the National Tax Association. A specific study will be made of Georgia problems. Parallel course, Commerce 34, with one hour per week exclusively graduate work. Minor. *Professor Brooks.*

151. BUSINESS ADMINISTRATION. Diemer, Factory Organization and Administration; Marshall, Business Administration; Federated Engineering Societies, Waste in Industry; Tead & Metcalf, Personnel Administration; Farquhar, Factor Storekeeping; Ronald Press, Management and Administration; A. W. Shaw Co., System. Parallel course, Commerce 51, a, b, c, with one hour per week of exclusively graduate work. Minor. *Professor Jenkins.*

EDUCATION

101. EDUCATION IN THE UNITED STATES (Education 24). In the main this course is historical: (1) Early transplanting from Europe. (2) Developments more distinctly American. (3) Evolution of various phases of education; elementary, secondary, higher, technical, professional, and special. (4) Influences of Rousseau, Pestalozzi, Fröbel, Herbart, Spencer, and others. (5) Prominent American leaders. (6) Development of administration and supervision. (7) Educational philanthropies. (8) Reorganization and expansion of education demanded by modern conditions, with special attention to the South. Coördination of state, county, national, and private endeavor. Prerequisite: Education 11, or equivalent. Three hours a week. With a thesis, major; without a thesis, minor. *Professor Woofter.* Not offered in 1926-1927.

104. PUBLIC SCHOOL ADMINISTRATION. (Minor.)

104a. CURRICULUM MAKING. An inquiry concerning the principles to be observed in selecting and organizing the public school curriculum; the articulation of the curricula of the elementary school with the junior high school; the junior high with the senior high school or the elementary with the four year high school and the articulation of the high school with the curricula of higher institutions; the adaptation of the curricula to existing social conditions and present social tendencies. A study of local and state surveys as a means of discovering the present social status and existing tendencies. The Psychology of the Child as a factor in determining the curricula. Other factors.

Bobbitt: The Curriculum; Sleight: The Organization and Curricula of Schools; Johnston, Newlin, Pickell: Junior Senior High School Administration; The New York State Survey; The Portland Survey; Various local surveys and current literature.

Half minor. Prerequisite: Education 10, 11, 12; Psychology, one year, Sociology, one semester; or the equivalent of the above.

104b. THE ORGANIZATION AND ADMINISTRATION OF THE SCHOOL AND SUPERVISING THE INSTITUTION. (1) The superintendent's philosophy of life and its significance. (2) Function of the superintendent. (3) Function of the School Board. (4) Selection of teachers as a preliminary to supervising the instruction. (5) Measuring the results of teaching as a further preliminary. (6) Helping tht teacher to discover herself in the methods of teaching. (7) Supervising study. (8) The control of extra curricular activities.

Adams, The Evolution of Educational Theory; Cubberly, Public School Administration; Cubberly, The Principal and His School; Chadsey, The Teacher's Technique; Miller, Directing Study.

Half minor. Prerequisite: Education 10, 11, 12; Educational Psychology and Tests and Measurements, or their equivalent.

(Note:—Education 104 may be combined with Education 107 or with Educational Psychology 102 or 120, to make a major.) *Professor Hutchinson.*

103. EDUCATIONAL SOCIOLOGY. See Sociology 103.

ADVANCED EDUCATIONAL PSYCHOLOGY. Major or minor. See Psychology 102. *Professor Edwards.*

ENGLISH

101. OLD AND MIDDLE ENGLISH. Phonology, Inflections and Translation. Text-books: Smith's Old English Grammar; Chaucer's Prologue, Knight's Tale, with lectures based on Morris's Organic History of English Words, Part I (K. J. Trübner), Part II (Ms.). Three hours per week, first and second terms. Minor. *Professor Morris.*

102. HISTORICAL ENGLISH SYNTAX. (a) General Linguistic development. (b) The Syntax of Old, Middle; and Modern English. Prerequisite: Course 101 or the equivalent.

Maetzner, English Grammar, Volumes II and III; Kellner, Historical English Sxntax; Emerson, English Language; Whitney, Life and Growth of Language; Nesfield, Historical English, Jespersen, Modern English Grammar; Horn, Historische neuenglishche Grammatik.

Three hours per week, second and third terms. Minor. *Professor Sanford.*

105. THE ENGLISH NOVEL; History and Technique. The course includes the reading of twenty-seven works of prose fiction from Sir Thomas Malory to Kipling.

Text-books: J. G. Dunlop's History of Prose Fiction; F. M. Warren's History of the Novel Previous to the 17th Century; Bliss Perry's Art of Prose Fiction. And for reference: Jusserand's English Novel in the Time of Shakespeare; Walter Raleigh's English Novel.

Prerequisite: English 4, or the equivalent. One hour per week, first term; three hours, second term; two hours, third term. Minor. *Professor Sanford.*

106. EARLY EIGHTEENTH CENTURY LITERATURE. English literature, literary characteristics, and literary movements from 1700 to 1744. Detailed study of life and times and principal works of De Foe, Addison, Steele, Swift, Lady Mary Wortley Montague, Bishop Berkeley. and other prose writers; of Pope, Prior, Gay, Thomson, Young, and minor poets. Early eighteenth century drama. Early eighteenth century criticism. Lectures and recitations, with papers required regularly.

Text-books: "Cambridge History of English Literature"; Dennis, "The Age of Pope"; Gosse, Saintsbury, Morley, Stephen; historical, biographical, and critical material in the library.

Prerequisite: English 1 and 2 and one Junior-Senior course in English. Minor. Two hours per week. *Associate Professor McWhorter.*

FORESTRY

101. SILVICULTURE. An investigation into the factors of site as they relate to the commercial production of forest products. A specialized problem will be worked out during the year, such as: (a) The germination and development of forest seedlings as influenced by the quality of site, from the commercial point of view. (b) The information of a yield table for a particular forest species, based upon quality of site. (c) Growth table for a particular forest species, based upon quality of site. (d) Quality increment in a particular forest species, based upon quality of site. Parallel reading (with special emphasis on readings dealing with selected problem): Research Methods, Clements; Physiology and Ecology, Clements; Oecology of Plants, Warming; Files of Forest Quarterly and Proceedings of Society of American Foresters: Forest Service Nurseries; Germination of Forest Seedlings, Boerker. Prerequisite: Botany 1 and Forestry 4 and 5. One lecture and not less than six laboratory (field) hours per week. Major. (This course may also be taken, reduced by half, as a minor). *Associate Professor Burleigh.*

102. ADVANCED DENDROLOGY. A specialized development of the prerequisite undergraduate course, Forestry 4. A detailed study of minor characteristics in the identification of trees and shrubs, special emphasis being placed on winter characteristics. The study will include the silvical as well as dendrological characteristics. Complete herbarium specimens will constitute a portion of the required report. Parallel reading and reference: Manual of Trees, Sargent; Trees, Rogers; North American Trees, Britton; Key to Trees, Collins and Preston; Studies in Trees, Levison; Key to Buds and Bark, Nebraska University; Pennsylvania Trees, Illick; Michigan Trees, University of Michigan; New Mexico Trees and Shrubs, Agricultural Experiment Station; Minnesota Trees and Shrubs, Clements; Vermont Trees, University of Vermont; Texas Trees, University of Texas; Forest Service Bulletins and Circulars. Two lectures per week, six hours field and laboratory work. Minor. *Associate Professor Burleigh.*

GERMAN

101. THE GERMAN CLASSICS. Selections from the following: Goethe: Werther, Faust I, Poems, Egmont, Iphigenie, Wilhelm Meister. Schiller: Kabale and Liebe, Fiesco, Don Carlos, Jungfrau von Orleans, Wallestein, Wilhelm Tell, Poems. Lessing: Emilia Galotti, Minna von Barnhelm, Nathan der Weise, Hamburgische Dramaturgie, Laokoon, Controversial Writings.

Commentaries: Bellermann, Minor, Hettner, Braun, Bulthaupt, Fischer.

Major. About eleven hundred pages. Four conferences weekly *Professod Morris.*

102. A minor course in the *German Classics.* About seven hundred pages. Prerequisite: German 2 or 21. Two conferences weekly. *Professor Morris.*

103. GERMAN COMPOSITION. Practice in speaking and writing German. Prerequisite: German 21 or 2. Two hours per week. Minor. *Professor Morris.*

104. German 2 with an extension of one hour a week of practical exercises in written and off-hand oral translation from English into German, with the necessary syntactical study. Minor. *Professor Morris.*

GREEK

101. (a) Selections from Homer, Herodotus, the dramatists, Thucydides, Plato, and Demosthenes.

(b) Brief introduction to Historical Grammar. Classical Greek Syntax: Gildersleeve, and other works. Oral and written exercises in Attic Greek. Recitation of the more familiar metres. Readings in the History of Greece. Prerequisite: Greek 4. Three lectures per week. Major. *Professor Bocock.*

HISTORY

101. THE ENGLISH CONSTITUTION TO THE REIGN OF HENRY VII. A course comprising a thorough study of the foundations of Anglo-Saxon institutions, and their development to 1485, based upon a critical study of Stubbs's Constitutional History of England. Minor. Three hours a week, first half-year. *Professor Payne.*

102. THE ENGLISH CONSTITUTION SINCE THE REIGN OF HENRY VII. A course based upon the constitutional histories of Hallam and May, and covering the later phases of the development of English institutions. Three hours a week, second half-year. Minor. *Professor Payne.*

102a. POLITICAL HISTORY OF TUDOR AND STUART TIMES. A course on the political and constitutional history of England from 1485 to 1689, with constant reference to the development of Continental Europe during the same period. Three hours a week, second half-yar. Minor. *Profssor Payne.*

Courses 101 and 104 or 101 and 102a are together rated as a major. Each includes parallel reading, tested by frequent examinations.

103. CIVIL WAR AND RECONSTRUCTION. An extension of History 13. Graduate students will take this course with the undergraduate class and will be required, in addition to meeting the requirements of His-

tory 13, to write a topic from the original sources, so far as they are available.

In addition to attending History 13, there will be one conference hour weekly for instruction in historical method, and for seminar work. Half Minor. *Professor Coulter.*

103a. RECENT AMERICAN HISTORY. An extension of History 14. The same requirements hold as for History 103. Half Minor. *Professor Coulter.*

104. THE FRENCH REVOLUTION AND NAPOLEON I. Not offered in years in which Course 101 and 102, or 102a is given). An advanced course in the topical study of European History from 1789 to 1815, based on some of the standard authorities for this period. Emphasis is placed upon the constitutional experiments of the French Revolution, and the problems raised by the Napoleonic wars. Conferences two hours per week. Minor. *Professor Payne.*

105. THE ANTE-BELLUM SOUTH. An extension of History 10. The same requirements hold as for History 103. Half Minor. (This course and History 103-103a alternate yearly). *Professor Coulter.* Not offered in 1926-1927.

Prerequisites for all graduate students in History: two college years of history.

HOME ECONOMICS

131. COSTUME DESIGNING. Designing modern costumes for special types, occasions, fancy dress, pageants, etc., using historical costumes and literature as inspiration and background for original work. A study of the history of costume from Egyptian through Greek, Roman, French and English to modern costume, of the influence of economic and political conditions in the manners and dress of peoples; of factors influencing modern costumes. References: Traphagen, Costume Design and Illustration; Boehn, Modes and Manners of the 19th Century; Hughes, Dress Design; Racinet, Le Costume Historique; historical novels describing the manners and life of peoples of different periods (Dumas, Thackeray, etc.). Plays chosen for wealth of setting and costuming. Each student is required to plan in its entirety and partially execute costumes for pageant, play or other important costume function. Prerequisite: Home Economics 22, 30, 31, 32. Regular session, two conferences and two laboratory hours per week. Minor, or with another prescribed minor, a major, for the degree of Master of Science in Home Economics. *Associate Professor Rathbone.*

112. FOOD INVESTIGATION by means of animal feeding experiments. Laboratory study of typical Georgia foods by feeding them to standard laboratory animals, the albino rat for vitamines A and B, the guinea

pig for vitamin C. Problems dealing with the effect on vitamin content of temperature, aging, dying and various methods of storing and preserving food. Study of cereal literature of food investigation. Prerequisite: 13. Minor, one conference, four laboratory periods. *Associate Professor Newton.*

113. DIETETICS. Investigations dealing with dietary habits of individuals on groups, for example, a study of diets of (1) school children, white or colored, (2) normal adults, (3) abnormal adults, (4) abnormal children. Problems for investigation will be chosen by the student and worked out under the supervision of the instructor. Prerequisite: 13. Minor, one conference, four laboratory periods. *Associate Professor Newton.*

112 and 113 constitute a major in nutrition.

HORTICULTURE

101. Junior courses Nos. 5, 7, and 9 with extension. Selected reading from the following: The American Fruit Culturist, Thomas; Fruit and Fruit Trees of America, Downing; Cyclopedia of Hardy Fruits, by Hedrick, and other allied promological books and bulletins from the College Experiment Stations and United States Government. Minor. *Professor McHatton.*

102. POMOLOGY. This course is open to students who have specialized in Horticulture, and is based upon Bailey's Evolution of Our Native Fruits. Selected reading from the following, to be mainly along the lines of origins of varieties of plants and the histories of various fruits: Plant Breeding, Bailey; Species and Varieties, Their Origin and Mutation, DeVries; Animals and Plants Under Domestication, Darwin; Fruits and Fruit Trees of American, Downing; American Fruits and Their Culture, Hume; The Grapes of New York, Hedrick; Foundations of American Grape Culture, Munson; The Apples of New York, Beach; Journals, Bulletins, etc. Three conference hours or equivalent in laboratory periods. Minor. *Professor McHatton.*

103. POMOLOGY. Course 102, with the addition of a thesis on some horticultural subject. The thesis is to call for not less than three laboratory periods per week and is to consist of reasearch work to be chosen by the student with the assistance of the instructor. Major. *Professor McHatton.*

104. LANDSCAPE GARDENING. (This course is open to students who have made a specialty of Horticulture). The history of the various schools of landscape art, a study of the fundamental principles involved, and the adaptability of the various types form the basis of the course. Selected readings from the following: Landscape Gardening. Kemp; English Pleasure Gardens, Nichols; American Gardens. Lowell; Art and Craft of Garden Making, Mawson; Cottage Gardens, Thornger;

Landscape Beautiful, Waugh; Town Planting, Webster; Landscape in History, Geike; and other publications. A thesis on some definite Georgia landscape will be required. Two conference hours and four laboratory periods per week. Major. *Professor McHatton.*

LATIN

101. READING COURSE, designed to supplement the undergraduate course, and therefore somewhat general in nature. It comprises the reading of considerable portions of Catullus, Lucretius, Juvenal, Seneca, and the Younger Pliny, with readings in Dill, Mommsen, and Ferrero; a review of grammar, from the comparative and historical point of view; exercise in Latin writing; reading in the history of the literature, and an introduction to epigraphy and paleography. Four hours per week. Major. *Professor Hooper.* Not offered in 1926-1927.

102. THE ROMAN DRAMA. This is a minor course, consisting of lectures on the subject, and reading of a number of representative plays of Plautus, Terence, and Seneca. Especial attention is paid to the relationship of the Roman drama to the Greek drama on the one hand, and the English drama on the other. Prerequisite: Latin 4. Two hours per week. *Professor Hooper.* Not offered in 1926-1927.

MATHEMATICS

Of the following courses the requirement for a major will be two lectures per week in each of any three, together with an original paper covering an investigation of some related topic to be assigned by the department. Two of the courses constitute a minor. Prerequisite: Mathematics 5 (Advanced Calculus). *Professor Stephens* and *Associate Professor Barrow.*

101. DIFFERENTIAL EQUATIONS. An elementary course in ordinary and partial differential equations, with special reference to those equations occurring in the physical sciences. Text: Cohen and Murray.

102. VECTOR ANALYSIS. An elementary course in vectors which develops a system of coördinates and illustrates their use in certain mathematical and physical problems. Reference text: Coffin.

103. PROJECTIVE GEOMETRY. A course in pure geometry based upon one of the following texts with others as reference: Holgate's Reye, Cremona, Veblen and Young.

104. THEORETICAL MECHANICS. An analytical treatment of certain problems in statics and dynamics with the aid of the Calculus. Many problems will be used. Text: Ziwet and Field or Jeans.

105. THEORY OF FUNCTIONS. An introductory course to the theory of functions of a real and complex variable. Reference works: Harkness and Morley, Durege, Goursat.

106. ANALYTICAL GEOMETRY. An advanced course based on Salmon or other text of similar character.

PHILOSOPHY

101. SOCIAL PHILOSOPHY. A study of present philosophical tendencies in their relation to the development of Social Theory; the beginnings of the development of a technique for research in Social Science. Texts: Perry, Present Philosophical Tendencies; Lichtenberger, Development of Social Theory; current periodical literature. Prerequisites: One year of Philosophy and one of Sociology; a year of Psychology is much to be desired. Minor. (Combinable with Sociology 101 to make a major in Sociology). Two hours per week (or four hours per week for a half-year). *Professor Hutchinson.*

PHYSICS

105. ADVANCED SOUND, LIGHT AND HEAT. HISTORY OF PHYSICS. An extension of Physics 5, the extension consisting of one hour in conference work each week devoted to a discussion of parallel reading or of one afternoon per week of advanced laboratory work. Three terms. Prerequisite courses: Physics 4, Mathematics 3-4; parallel or prerequisite course, Mathematics 5. Minor. *Professor Hendren.*

106. ADVANCED ELECTRICITY AND MAGNETISM AND THE ELECTRON THEORY. An extension of Physics 6, the extension consisting of one hour or of one afternoon per week of advanced laboratory work. Three terms. Prerequisite courses: Physics 4 and Mathematics 5. Minor. *Professor Hendren.*

107. THE ELECTRON THEORY. A study of electricity, light, heat, radioactivity and radiation according to the modern electron theory. Use will be made of Campbell's Modern Electrical Theory and of current scientific publications. Two hours per week lecture and recitation, one hour per week laboratory conference and three hours per week laboratory work. Three terms. Prerequisite course: Physics 5 or 6 and Mathematics 5.

Parallel courses: if Physics 5 has not been taken as a prerequisite. Physics 105 will be required as a parallel minor course. If Physics 6 has not been taken, Physics 106 will be required as a parellel minor course. If Differential Equations has not been taken, Mathematics 101 will be required as a parallel course. Major. *Professor Hendren.*

* Note:—It is not guaranteed that more than one of these courses will be given in 1926-1927, and a course will not be given unless two or more students apply for it.

POULTRY HUSBANDRY

101. An extension of Undergraduate Courses 2, 4, 6, and 7. The research problem will be concerned with the cost of producing market

eggs (one or two additional conference hours per week). Minor. *Professor Wood.*

PSYCHOLOGY

PSYCHOLOGY 101; SYSTEMATIC PSYCHOLOGY. (May not be offered for 1926-1927.)

PSYCHOLOGY 102; EDUCATIONAL PSYCHOLOGY.

PSYCHOLOGY 120. An advanced and intensive study of the Psychology of High School subjects. Each student will be expected to do special work on some high school subject selected in conference with the instructor and, in addition, to take Psychology 20, 21, and 22. The latter course takes up the psychology of high school subjects, the special problems of learning and teaching them and the problems of the teaching and supervision of study in the high school. Prerequisite: one year of Psychology. Minor. One conference a week of strictly graduate work, and Psychology 20, 21 and 22, three times a week. *Professor Edwards.* Not offered in 1926-1927.

SOCIOLOGY

101. MODERN SOCIAL PROBLEMS. A study of the various theories of social reform and of the philosophy underlying these theories, with an intensive study (preferably combined with field work) in some specific field. Prerequisite: Two years in Sociology or one year in Sociology, and one year in other Social Sciences. Minor. Two hours per week. *Professor Hutchinson.*

103. EDUCATIONAL SOCIOLOGY. This course considers the function of education, the educational situation, educational problems, methods and solutions, all from the standpoint of the needs of the state, or the social group.

1. Biological-sociological factors:—the meaning of evolution, natural selection, variations, heredity, eugenics, recapitulation, long period of human infancy, types of ancient man, etc.

2. Approach through social organization, social adjustment, and social problems to-day, and the place of education therein.

3. Education in a democracy, cultural and practical values, administration factors, school subjects, and the socialized school.

4. Incidentally, as time permits, some readings about the social conditions and movements of the times.

Three hours a week, minor; with additional thesis or equivalent assignments, major. Prerequisites: Three hours of Sociology and three hours of Education, subject to approval.

BIBLIOGRAPHY. 1. Newton, Evolution and Eugenics. Osborne, Men of the Old Stone Age. Conklin, The Direction of Human Evolution.

2. Cooley, Social Organization. Nearing, Social Adjustment. Ellwood, The Social Problem.

3. Smith, Educational Sociology. Snedden, Educational Sociology.

4. Ross, Sin and Society; Changing America. Stoddard, The Rising Tide of Color; The Revolt of the Under Man. Current news. *Professor Woofter.* Not offered in 1926-1927.

PHELPS-STOKES FELLOWSHIP

The work of the Fellow for 1925-1926 was under the direction of *Professors Edwards, Hutchinson,* and *Fain.*

ZOOLOGY

104. VERTEBRATE MORPHOLOGY. Special problems for individual investigation are assigned to each student. A thesis is required, satisfactorily presenting the results of the investigation, together with a complete bibliography. Four conference hours and eight laboratory hours per week. Prerequisites: Zoölogy 3, 4, and 5. Major. *Professor Krafka.*

EXPENSES

Residents of Georgia pay no tuition fees. Students who are residents of other states pay a tuition fee of $100.00 per annum. The following estimate of expenses for a student rooming in a dormitory and boarding at Denmark Hall includes all necessary items except clothing and railroad fare:

Matriculation fee (paid on entrance)	$ 50.00
Library fee (paid on entrance)	5.00
Board (monthly, in advance, $16.00), Denmark Hall	144.00
Furnishing room in dormitory (estimated)	14.00
Laundry (estimated at $2.00 per month)	18.00
Room rent, fuel, lights and attendance, ($5.00 per month)	45.00
Books and stationery, (estimated)	20.00
Fee for Infirmary, Gymnasium and Athletics	21.00
Laboratory fees, (estimated)	9.00
Fee for Student Council	.50
Fee for "Georgian"	1.00
Fee for Student Activities	3.00
	$330.50

GRADUATE COURSES IN THE SUMMER SCHOOL

The University permits a graduate student, eligible to candidacy for a second degree, to secure the Master's degree upon the successful completion of graduate courses pursued during four Summer Sessions. The student will pursue two half-minor courses or one minor each summer. During the year following each Summer Session, the student will have the benefit of the guidance of the professors under whom courses have been pursued in the previous summer.

A thesis is required by the Faculty in connection with each Major course offered in the Summer School.

COURSES FOR 1926

The right is reserved to withdraw any course for which there are not five or more applicants.

EDUCATION

S-104. School Administration.   Mr. Pusey.

For county and city school superintendents and for principals of independent school districts.

The course will be given in two parts, each a half minor, as follows:

104-a.

Organization of a school system and its relation to a general state system; duties of the superintendent and his relationship to the board of education; financing a school system, budget making, sources of revenue, school bookkeeping, salary schedules; school architecture, care of school plant and equipment; consolidating schools, school building programs.

104-b.

The school population, census and attendance; progress of pupils through the grades, pupil accounting; courses of study; supervision; qualifications of teachers, training of teachers in service; school reports; statistical methods; auxiliary agencies.

Each part constitutes a course of six weeks, and both parts are essential to complete a minor. Both may be taken together, but if only one is taken, the other should be completed the next session of attendance.

Prerequisites: Education 10, 11, 12; Psychology, one year; Sociology, one semester. Equivalents may be offered.

ENGLISH

S-105.   The English Novel.   History and Technique.   Mr. Sanford.

The course includes the reading of twenty-seven works of prose fiction from Sir Thomas Malory to Kipling. One half of this course will be given in 1926 (thirty lectures).   Text-books: J. G. Dunlop's History of Prose Fiction; E. M. Warren's History of the Novel Previous to the 17th Century; Bliss Perry's Art of Prose Fiction. And for reference: Jusserand's English Novel in the Time of Shakespeare; Cross's Development of the English Novel; George Saintsbury's English Novel; Walter Raleigh's English Novel. Prerequisite, English 4, or the equivalent. Minor.

S-106.   Early Eighteenth Century Literature.   Mr. McWhorter.

English Literature, literary characteristics, and literary movements from 1700-1744: DeFoe, Addison, Steele, Swift and other prose writers: Pope, Prior, Gay, Thomson, Young, and minor poets. The Drama. Literary criticism. One-half of this minor course (poets) will be given in 1926. Prerequisite: English 1 and 2 and one Junior or Senior College course in English. Six weeks.

HISTORY

S-102-a. Tudor Times, 1485-1603.   (First half.)   Mr. Payne.

A study of the political and constitutional history of England from 1485 to 1603, with constant refrence to the development of Continental Europe for the same period. Readings, reports, and tests, based upon selections from Gasquet, Dixon, Bacon, Froude, Innes, Hallam, Brown, Johnson, Cambridge Modern History, Dictionary of National Biography, of England, 1485-1547; Pollard, Political History of England, 1547-1603; Seebohm, Era of the Protestant Revolution. A half minor: five classes a week for six weeks. Prerequisite, six hours of college history.

S-104-a.   **The French Revolution, 1789-1799.**   (First half of 104.)
Mr. Payne.

A topical study of European history from 1789 to 1799, with special emphasis upon French history. A seminar course based upon the standard authorities for this period. A half minor; thirty recitations. Prerequisite: Six hours of college history.

Authorities to be used in S-104-a: Mignet. Thiers. Carlyle. Tocqueville, Taine. Aulard. Madelin. Anderson. Young. Stryienski, Stephens, Bourne, Rose. Mahan, and Cambridge Modern History.

HOME ECONOMICS

S-112. Miss Newton.

Food investigation by means of animal feeding experiments. Laboratory study of typical Georgia foods by feeding them to standard laboratory animals; for vitamins A and B the albino rat. for C, the guinea pig. Problems dealing with the effect on vitamin content of temperature, aging. dyeing, and various methods of storing and preserving food. Study of current literature on food investigation. Reference will be made to various technical journals; prerequisite: Home Economics 13. Half Minor, nine weeks.

MATHEMATICS

Mr. Stephens.

One of the following courses will be given if at least five students elect it. Two of the courses constitute a minor; three with a thesis, constitute a major.

101. Differential Equations.

An elementary course in ordinary and partial differential equations, with special reference to the equations occuring in the physical sciences. Text: Cohen or Murray.

102. Vector Analysis.

An elementary course in vectors which develops a system of coordinates and illustrates their use in certain mathematical and physical problems. Reference Text: Coffin.

103. Projective Geometry.

A course in pure geometry based upon one of the following texts with the others as references; Holgate's Reye, Cremona, Veblen and Young.

104. Theory of Functions.

An introductory course to the theory of functions of a real and a complex variable. Reference works: Harkness and Morley, Durege, Goursat.

105. Analytical Geometry.

An advanced course based on Salmon or other texts of a similar character.

PSYCHOLOGY

S-102a-102b. Mr. Edwards.

102a deals with the normal mind. integration, mental hygiene. the more advanced problems of learning with their educational applications. 102b deals with the psychology of the abnormal as it relates to education and with diagnosis and treatment in education. It is advised that both half minors be taken together in one summer; if only one is taken the other should be completed the following summer. Given as parallel courses the first six weeks. Prerequisite. one year of psychology and such other study and experience as will satisfy the instructor that the student can do the work of the course.

Part IV

THE PROFESSIONAL SCHOOLS
The Lumpkin Law School
The Pharmacy Department

THE LUMPKIN LAW SCHOOL

TRUSTEES OF THE UNIVERSITY
Committee on Law Department

Hon. RICHARD B. RUSSELL, Chief Justice of the Supreme Court, Chairman.

Hon. SANDERS McDANIEL, Vice Chairman_____Atlanta
Hon. WILLIAM E. SIMMONS_____Lawrenceville
Hon. MARION SMITH_____Atlanta
Hon. J. R. POTTLE_____Albany
Hon. A. A. LAWRENCE_____Savannah
Hon. F. D. FOLEY_____Columbus
Hon. A. S. HARDY_____Gainesville
Hon. H. J. ROWE_____Athens

FACULTY

DAVID C. BARROW, LL.D., Chancellor Emeritus.
CHARLES M. SNELLING, A.M., Sc.D., Chancellor.
GEORGE F. GOBER, A.M., LL.D., President and Professor of Law.
SYLVANUS MORRIS, A.M., B.L., LL.D., Dean of the Law Department and Professor of Law.
WALTER G. CORNETT, LL.B., Professor of Law.
STEPHEN C. UPSON, A.B., LL.B., Professor of Law.
ROBERT L. McWHORTER, A.B., LL.B., Professor of Law.

In the development of our State and to keep time to its future progress, the teaching of the Law becomes important. Nothing has shown more the wisdom of our law makers than the establishment of the Lumpkin Law School as a Departmnt of the University which was done more than fifty years ago. It is not enough that students of the Law should be taught, but at the same time they should be imbued with the spirit and traditions of our State's past history, with the lives and works of these great men who have gone out from the University and added lustre to its name. Lawyers who graduated from this school are practising their profession in every part of the State; they occupy places in all the Courts from the Chief Justice of the Supreme Court down through all the other courts; in the office of Governor, Attorney General, and in the Congress of the United States; and as heads of great industries. The Lumpkin Law School proudly points to its past history and the success of its graduates as a vindication of its teaching and as an earnest of its present and future work.

It is not enough that a student of the Law should serve a term on the tread mill of years to be a successful practioner. He must be grounded in basic principles and understand their application; he must learn that the Science of the Law must be applied in a practical way and that it undertakes to govern the people in their every day affairs. Knowledge of the Law cannot be gotten solely from text books based in the main on the law of other jurisdictions with few references to Georgia decisions; to rely on these in the Georgia Courts the lawyer when he enters on his profession finds he has to unlearn much that is confusing, and must be thrown aside.

The Trustees of the University have recognized these conditions and have placed in the teaching force men of experience as teachers and as successful practitioners and with long service in the administration and enforcement of the law as judges and prosecuting attorneys. These teachers do their work under the supervision of the Board of Trustees who insist on thorough work and the maintenance of the highest standard. The School belongs to the State and every aspiring youth has the right to pursue his law course in it and have the benefit of what it offers.

During the 1925-26 session many lectures by distinguished lawyers have been delivered before the Law School. The subjects discussd were of a practical character and intended to present to the students a broad view of their professional work. Lectures are expected during the session of 1926-27 from:

Hon. Clifford Walker, Governor of Georgia.

Chief Justice Richard B. Russell, of the Supreme Court and Chairman of the Board of Trustees.

Justice Samuel Atkinson, of the Supreme Court.

Justice Alexander Stephens, of the Court of Appeals.

Hon. George M. Napier, Attorney General of Georgia.

Hon. J. J. Brown, Commissioner of Agriculture.

Hon. T. R. Bennett, Superintendent of Banks.

Hon. John T. Boufeuillett, Public Service Commission.

Hon. Samuel H. Sibley, Judge of the United States District Court.

Hon. Blanton Fortson, Judge of the Superior Court.

Hon. J. D. Bradwell, Judge of the City Court of Athens.

Hon. Hugh M. Dorsey, Former Governor of Georgia.

Hon. John M. Slaton, Former Governor of Georgia.

Hon. T. W. Hardwick, Former Governor of Georgia.

Other lectures will be delivered by different members of the Board of Trustees of the University, many of whom are active and successful lawyers.

The next session of this Department begins September 15th, 1926. The time requisite for graduation is three years. The fees are $75.00 per year, of which $40.00 is due at the opening of the University and $35.00 at the opening of the University after the Christmas holidays. Students entering as late as January 1st pay $50.00 for the remainder of the session instead of the full $75.00.

On arrival here, report to the Dean, in the Lumpkin Law School Building.

ENTRANCE REQUIREMENTS

GENERAL. Students in the Department must not be less than eighteen years old, and must be of good moral character.

FIRST YEAR CLASS. Requirements for admission to the first year class include two years of college work. A student twenty-one years of age, who is partly deficient in literary work will be allowed to make this up. This being a state institution the trustees do not think it right to refuse admission to mature students who are qualified to pursue the course. The curriculum is as high as that of any other school and will be so maintained; it is higher than that of many others.

SECOND YEAR CLASS. Applicants for the second year class, in addition to the general requirements must have completed one year's course of study in a standard law school, or must have read law under advice and direction in a law office for one year and must stand satisfactory examinations on the work of the first year.

SECOND YEAR ENTRANCE EXAMINATIONS

Examinations for students applying to enter the second year class will be held beginning Monday, September 6th, 1926.

Examinations begin at nine o'clock A. M. each day.

Applicants are particularly urged to bear this in mind.

TRANSFERS. Students transferring from the Academic Departments must obtain the written permission of the Chancellor and certificates from the proper officer of the University showing that they have been satisfactory students in those departments.

ELECTIVES. Students not applying for the degree may enter upon complying with the general requirements.

A student may present, among the general options taken for A. B. and B. S. General, six hours from the curriculum of LL.B,. provided the courses taken and the time value of each be approved by the Curriculum Committee.   z

DEGREE

Students who continue in actual attendance upon the exercises of this Department during three years, and those who are admitted to the second year of the course, and continue in actual attandance for two years, and complete successfully the required course of study, receive the degree of Bachelor of Laws of the University of Georgia.

ADMISSION TO THE BAR

Under the law of the State the graduates of the Lumpkin Law School are admitted to the bar, without examination, on the presentation of the diploma.

Under a rule of the United States Court for the Northern District of Georgia, graduates of the Lumpkin Law School who have been admitted to the State Bar will be admitted to the District Court of the United States without examination.

Those desiring more detailed information as to the Law School should request from President George F. Gober, Athens Ga., or from Dean Sylvanus Morris, Athens, Ga., a special Law School Bulletin.

COURSE OF STUDY

The course in this Department is completed in three years, consisting of six terms. The exercises of the University, including this Department, begin on the third Wednesday in September of each year and end at the annual Commencement on the third Wednesday in June.

The autumn term commences with the college year and closes the day before Christmas.

The spring term commences the day following New Year and closes at Commencement.

Three courses of instruction are pursued, to-wit: the Study Course, the Lecture Course, and Case Study.

The classes meet the professors of law daily (except Sunday), according to schedule between the hours of 8:35 A. M. and 5:00 P. M., with the previously assigned part of the text-book then being read. The professor delivers lectures explanatory of the text, discusses cases bearing on the text, and questions the members of the class on the text, the cases, and the lecture of the previous meeting. The third year is devoted chiefly to the study of cases, and to instruction in practice.

First Year

Prof. Gober. Four periods a week.
CONSTITUTIONAL LAW; UNITED STATES, GEORGIA.
Prof. Morris. Six periods a week.
ELEMENTARY PRINCIPLES OF LAW. TORTS.
Prof. McWhorter. Four periods a week.
CRIMINAL LAW. DOMESTIC RELATIONS.
Prof. Cornett. Three periods a week.
CONTRACTS. QUASI CONTRACTS.
Prof. Upson. Three periods a week.
MUNICIPAL CORPORATIONS. BAILMENTS. CARRIERS.

Second Year

Prof. Gober. Four periods a week.

EVIDENCE. CONFLICT OF LAWS.

Prof. Morris. Six periods a week.

COMMON LAW PLEADING. GEORGIA PROCEDURE. EQUITY. EQUITY PLEADING.

Prof. McWhorter. Four periods a week.

CORPORATIONS. INSURANCE. PERSONALTY.

Prof. Cornett. Three periods a week.

SALES. AGENCY. PARTNERSHIP.

Prof. Upson. Three periods a week.

NEGOTIABLE INSTRUMENTS. BANKING. SURETYSHIP.

Third Year

Prof. Gober. Four periods a week.

PRACTICE IN STATE COURTS. ROMAN LAW. INTERNATIONAL LAW.

Prof. Morris. Five periods a week.

PUBLIC UTILITIES. CASES ON TORTS. CASES ON CORPORATIONS.

Prof. McWhorter. Four periods a week.

REALTY. ABSTRACTING. LEGAL ETHICS.

Prof. Cornett. Three periods a week.

FEDERAL PROCEDURE. CASES ON CONTRACTS. LEGAL BIBLIOGRAPHY.

Prof. Upson. Three periods a week.

WILLS. BANKRUPTCY.

METHODS OF INSTRUCTION

READING. The best features of the lecture and the recitation are secured by the method of instruction pursued in this Department. Reading is daily assigned in the text-books, the professor comments on the same, and the student is reequired to recite thereon. By this means each part of the subject is explained to the student, is then read by him, and he is either questioned, or hears others questioned.

From experience, as well as from observation, it is believed that the "lecture system" alone, as pursued in so many similar institutions, does not meet all the necessities of the case. However learned the lecturer and however attentive the student, the impression left upon the beginner's mind is not so permanent as that produced by his own study of the subject, reinforced by the oral recitations and by the explanations of the professors. Under the plan of instruction outlined, the student studies with the incentive of desire to learn, and with the knowledge that his fellow students will hear his oral examinations. Ample explanations and illustrations together with incidental lectures arising out of the subject of the lesson, from the professors, aid the student's own labor. The consequence is that the student, from pride as well as ambition, learns each lesson, and his knowledge thus acquired is permanently fixed in his mind. The act of reciting fixes in the mind that which is recited. Moreover, the professor is, by this means, enabled to ascertain those points which are not understood by each student, and to adapt his explanations to the need of the entire class.

LECTURES. With this system of daily drilling in the recitation rooms, and with the proper study which it enforces, the student is given a sufficient knowledge of the subject to prepare his mind for the incalculable benefit to be derived from lectures. It is believed that a knowledge of the law cannot well be obtained under either system unaided by the other; the effort is thus made to derive all the benefits of both. All the good features of the "recitation system" are thus combined with the "lecture system," and the attempt made to reap the fruits of both the general plans of professional education.

CASE STUDY. The study of cases illustrative of the principles under discussion is being steadily developed. The facilities for this work are greatly increased by the additions to the library. Special emphasis is laid upon the study of Georgia cases, but the adjudications of courts of last resort throughout the country are examined and discussed. The student is shown how to find and select authorities upon the questions under investigation. He is directed to trace the adjudications of questions from their inception in court, through the development up to the crystallization of the settled doctrine as announced in the ruling case, and thus to observe the growth of law. This is more important in our State than elsewhere because the doctrine announced by the Supreme Court is frequently embodied in the Code, and thus becomes positive statute.

CASE METHOD. Frequently the question is asked, is the case method used in this Department In answering, exclusively not, the reasons can be no better stated than in the language of Dr. Joseph Redlich, of the University of Vienna, in his report to the Carnegie Foundation: "First, before the student enters upon the case method of study, he ought to have a certain foundation upon which to build, which should give him a prospectus and should acquaint him with the elementary ideas and the fundamental concepts common to all branches of the law. Similarly, at the end of the term of study, an effort should be made to give the student a comprehensive view of the law as a whole, and of its relation to the administration of justice. Second, the law school course should be lengthened to cover a period of four years."

PLEADING. In addition this course offers exceptional advantages in the frequent exercises in the actual drafting of pleadings and other legal papers, thus practically impressing on the mind of the student the principles involved by putting them into actual use.

EXAMINATIONS

There are two kinds of examinations—oral and written. Each professor daily examines orally on the prescribed reading. Written examinations are held at the conclusion of each text-book or branch of study. These examinations are made very searching, and the student is given abundant time to write out his answers without assistance, thus impressing upon his mind what he has learned and disclosing accurately and impartially his progress.

DEGREE

Students who continue in actual attendance upon the exercises of this Department during the three years, of two terms each, and those who are admitted to the second year of the course, and continue in actual attendance for two years, of two terms, to-wit: the autumn and spring terms, and complete successfully the required course of study, receive the degree of Bachelor of Laws, of the University of Georgia.

ADMISSION TO THE BAR

Under the law of the State the graduates of this Department are admitted to the bar, without examination, on presentation of the diploma.

Under a rule of the United States Court for the Northern District of Georgia, graduates of this Department who have been admitted to the State Bar will be admitted to the District Court of the United States without examination.

HONORS

Two members of the Law Department are allowed places among the Senior speakers on Commencement Day, and one representative of the Department on University Day. The speakers from the Law Department are chosen by the Faculty of the Law Department for general excellence in all the exercises and branches of study in the Department. Those of the third year class only are eligible to those places, who have attended the full three years course in this Department, and have incurred no conditions.

MOOT COURTS AND LEGAL EXERCISES

After the students are sufficiently advanced, moot courts are held in which one of the professors presides, the juries being taken from the students in other departments of the University. The law students are assigned to act as counsel in the cases on trial. In these courts the students are taught the actual practice of law, such as pleading, drawing orders, moving for new trials, advocacy before the court and jury, the use of reports and text-books as authority; in short, all the elements of actual court house practice.

Second year students are given practical work in practice and procedure two hours each month throughout the year.

Throughout the course exercises are given in pleading and drawing deeds, wills and mortgages, and all kinds of legal documents, including commercial paper. It is the purpose of the Department to equip its graduates for active practice of the profession.

A moot parliament is conducted by students under the direction of the instructor, wherein actual practice is had in parliamentary law.

A class in public speaking is conducted by one of the professors.

SOCIETIES

Literary

There are two literary societies in connection with the University, viz., the Demosthenian and Phi Kappa Societies. The former was founded in 1801, the latter in 1820. The members of the societies meet in their respective halls every Wednesday. Debates on interesting subjects are held at each meeting. At these debates the student learns self-reliance, readiness of expression, rapidity of thought. To the lawyer, perhaps one of the most valuable accomplishments is the ability "to think on his feet," and these societies afford a good field for the acquirement of this habit.

JEFFERSONIAN LAW DEBATING SOCIETY

The law students conduct a successful and beneficial society, which meets once a week, and they debate questions of law. All students of the Department are eligible to membership in the society. The society is one of the most useful features of the law course.

DISCIPLINE

In matters of discipline the students of the Law Department are governed by the same rules and regulations prescribed for other students of the University.

LIBRARY

The General Library of the University contains more than 59,500 volumes, and is housed in a handsome modern building. About 1,000 volumes are added yearly, and the Library subscribes for nearly 200 popular and professional periodicals. A number of local and metropolitan papers are received through gift or subscription. The hours of the week-day opening are from 8:30 A. M. until 10 P. M., with half-hour recess at dinner and supper time. The Sunday hours are from 3 to 6 P. M. The Library is in charge of a trained Librarian and permanent staff of three regular assistants and several student assistants. All students have library privileges.

The Library of the Law Department is in charge of a librarian, and is open for the use of law students on every working day of the session. Within the last two years, books costing $8,000.00 have been added. The library now contains complete sets of the State Reports of Courts of Last Resort, of the Reports of the United States Supreme Court, of the American Reports, American Decisions, American State Reports, Lawyers' Reports Annotated, Federal Reporter, with complete digests, Statutes of the State and of the United States, and valuable text-books. Standard magazines and other law publications are in the library. These purchases have been made so judiciously and upon such advantageous terms that the actual cost is far below the value of the books.

Through the action of the authorities of the State Library in replacing text-books, many valuable reference books have been acquired by the law library.

The University is indebted to the widow of the late Brantley A. Denmark for the handsome and valuable library of her husband and of her son, the late Thomas N. Denmark, both loyal sons of the institution. Valuable text-books were recently donated to the University by Hon. Alex C. King, of Atlanta. The Reports of the State Supreme Court and of the Court of Appeals, the Acts of the Legislature, Codes and other public books are furnished to the library by the State.

Recently Mr. W. M. Davis, of Macon, gave to this Department the splendid law library collected by his father, the late Hon. Buford M. Davis, '69, and by his brother, the lamented Bryan B. Davis, '97. This collection of several hundred volumes contains valuable text-books, reports and digests.

Hon. H. S. West, of Athens, has recently donated a valuable collection of text-books and reference books to the Department.

During the year 1914 several hundred volumes were added by the gift to the University of the Horace B. Russell library.

The widow of Hon. W. S. Basinger donated more than a hundred valuable volumes of her husband's library to the Department in 1915.

During the year 1920 Hon. Hamilton McWhorter made a handsome gift to the school of a set of the Federal Reporter and a number of other valuable volumes.

Mr Garrard Glenn, of New York, also donated fifty volumes of the Georgia Reports.

Through the instrumentality of Hon. R. Toombs DuBose the school received from the State two sets of Georgia Reports, two sets af Appeals Reports, and two sets of Park's Codes.

Many valuable books of reference were donated in 1923 by Hon. A. J. Cobb and Hon. Peyton L. Wade.

The Hon. Henry R. Goetchius who for a long while was a valuable member of the Board of Trustees of the University, has died since the last annual commencement. He was a great scholar and a distinguished lawyer. Before his death he expressed an intention to donate his law library to the Lumpkin Law School. This intention was carried out by his wife and she sent to the library about eight hundred volumes which are valuable books. This gift is most highly appreciated.

FOUNDATION AND GROWTH

More than half a century ago three distinguished Georgians founded a law school which exists today as the Law Department of the University of Georgia. While methods of legal study and education have, in these years, changed, nay undergone a revolution, the great underlying principles of the founders are today the inspiration of the teachers and the norm of the progress of this school. No men were by temperament and training better fitted to impress on the students the due relation of principle and practice, the accurate adjustment of the laws to the law. Thus this school seeks to instill those unchangeable principles of the law which must animate all philosophically framed rules of conduct, and at the same time give actual practice as far as possible, in the application of those rules. While it strives to attain a standard of excellence in the academic training of the lawyer, it keeps always in view the fact that, to the lawyer, law is a business, the most intensely practical of all human pursuits.

The high standard of professional honor and courtesy set by the founders is the priceless heritage of the school today. Unceasing effort in all the work of the school, is made to impress the student with the solemn responsibility of the lawyer, and the sacredness of the trust imposed upon him. The ideals of the school are high and clean.

PROGRESS AND IMPROVEMENT

For many years the school has been moving forward steadily, and as rapidly as the conditions in the State allow. More than ten years ago the Law Department became in reality an integral part of the University, and the transfer from the Academic to the Law School of any but worthy men ceased. The adoption of the two years' course soon followed. The wisdom, if not the necessity, of that action was never doubtful. The efficiency of the work was more than doubled. The approval of the State Bar Association has been repeatedly expressed. The election of additional teachers has been an untold advantage. The requirement of fifteen academic units for entrance went into operation with the opening of the session of 1908, and has borne good fruit in the better class of students admitted.

Beginning with the autumn term of 1919, the course for graduation has been extended to three years. The successful inauguration of this change is evidenced by the gratifying attendance upon the first year course. Beginning with September, 1925, the entrance requirement is two years of college work.

Among the many advantages offered by the school most worthy of note is the connection with the University. The advantages of this connection at once occur to the student. Access to the academic schools, the libraries, debating societies, participation in literary and other University activities, wider acquantanceship with the young men of the State University fellowship are invaluable to the lawyer.

HISTORICAL NOTE

At the regular meeting of the Trustees of the University of Georgia in 1859, the board determined to reorganize the University, and in the plan that was then adopted it was determined to establish a law school, "in which facilities for the best legal education would be afforded." In pursuance of the plan, on August 4, 1859, on motion of Governor Herschel V. Johnson, Joseph Henry Lumpkin (the first Chief Justice of Georgia), William Hope Hull and Thomas R. R. Cobb were elected professors, and the law school opened in the autumn of that year. On December 19, 1859, by an Act of the General Assembly of Georgia, the Lumpkin Law School was incorporated, and these three gentlemen were both the incorporators and the professors. From that time to the death of Judge Lumpkin in 1867 (Mr. Cobb having died in 1862), the Law Department of the University was conducted under the name of the Lumpkin Law School, and the graduates were awarded their diplomas by the Trustees at the regular Commencement. The exercises of the law school were suspended during the War between the States.

In August, 1867, Benjamin H. Hill and William L. Mitchell were elected by the Board of Trustees to the two vacancies in the Law Department, and from that time forward the Law School has been conducted under the name of the *Law Department of the University.*

From the time of Mr. Hill's election to the United States Senate in 1877, his connection with the school was nominal, and the classes were under the sole care of Mr. Mitchell until 1881, when Pope Barrow and George Dudley Thomas were elected professors of law. Dr. Mitchell died in 1882 and Mr. Barrow resigned in 1883. In 1884 Andrew J. Cobb was elected, and from that time until 1890 Mr. Thomas and Mr. Cobb filled the chairs.

In 1890, Howell Cobb was elected. In 1893, Mr. Thomas and Mr.

Andrew J. Cobb having resigned as regular professors, and became lecturers, Sylvanus Morris was elected.

The chair of lecturer on Medical Jurisprudence was filled by Dr. R. D. Moore from 1873, to 1879 by Dr. R. M. Smith, from 1880 to 1883 by Dr. John Gerdine, and in 1883 Dr. S. C. Benedict was elected. In 1907, Dr. Benedict having resigned, T. F. Green was elected Lecturer on Medical Jurisprudence. In 1908, Mr. Green having resigned, Dr. James C. Bloomfield was elected Lecturer on Medical Jurisprudence.

From 1873 to the time of his death in January 1888, Chancellor P. H. Mell delivered lectures on Parliamentary Law to the class in connection with the Senior class in other departments of the University. In 1894 John D. Mell was elected Lecturer on Parliamentary Law.

Dr. J. H. T. McPherson was elected Lecturer on Roman Law in 1899.

In 1900 Sylvanus Morris was elected Dean.

In 1901 the Course of Study was extended from one to two years.

In 1906 Thomas F. Green was elected Lecturer on Federal Procedure.

In 1908 Hon. Andrew J. Cobb was elected Lecturer on Procedure and Constitutional Law.

In 1909, Hon. Howell Cobb having resigned as regular professor and having been made professor emeritus, Mr. Thomas F. Green was elected regular professor of law.

Hon. Howell Cobb died during the year 1909.

In 1909, John D. Mell resigned as Lecturer on Parliamentary Law.

In 1912, Joseph S. Stewart was elected Lecturer on Parliamentary Law.

In 1913, H. Abit Nix was elected Instructor in Law.

In 1916, the Chair of Medical Jurisprudence was abolished.

In 1918, Messrs. Green and Nix resigned and Messrs. Walter G. Cornett and Henry G. Howard were elected Instructors in Law. Mr. Howard was called to the military service, and resigned. Mr. Stephen C. Upson was elected to the vacancy in 1919.

In 1919, the building, the "Lumpkin Law School," was formally opened.

In 1920, the course was extended to three years.

In June, 1921, the Faculty was reorganized, the three members in office being retained, Professors Cornett and Upson being made regular professors and Hon. Andrew J. Cobb being elected a regular prfessor. In 1923, R. L. McWhorter was elected professor.

In 1924, entrance requirement of one year of college work was adopted.

In 1925, Hon. Andrew J. Cobb died and Hon. George F. Gober was elected as President and Professor of Law.

In 1925 entrance requirement of two years of college work became effective.

TUITION AND EXPENSES

The tuition in the Law Department is $75.00 per annum, divided as follows: $40.00 for the autumn term, to January first, and $35.00 for the spring term, from January first to Commencement. Tuition is payable in advance at the beginning of each term.

No matriculation or library fee is required in this Department. The students in law are entitled to the privilege of all other departments of the University, at Athens, without extra charge.

The expenses of the course are as follows:

Tuition, per annum _____$75.00
Initiation fee, literary society _____'_____ 2.00
Infirmary fee _____ 5.00
Visit from Physician at Room. Privileges of Infirmary and nurse. Prescriptions. Typhoid Inoculation. Physical Examination.
Gymnasium fee _____ 5.00
Classes in Gymnastics. Privileges of the Building and Swimming Pool.
Athletic fee _____ 11.00
Admission to all Contests held in Athens.
Student Activities _____ 3.00
Georgia Cracker _____ 1.00
Student Council _____ .50
Board, per month _____ 16.00
Room rent, light, heat, etc., per month_____ 5.00
Stationery for the year _____ 2.00
Text-books can be had for about (each year) _____ 75.00

The incidental expenses of a student are just what he makes them, and the patrons of the University are urged to take into their own hands the control of a matter which no college regulations can reach.

Excellent table board on the cooperative plan can be had in the Denmark Dining Hall at $16.00 per month; elsewhere at $20.00 per month and upwards. In all the dormitory buildings the rooms contain bedsteads, washstands, tables and chairs. The student furnishes pillows and the necessary linen. On account of the large demand for these rooms, application should be made as far in advance as possible.

If dormitory rooms cannot be obtained, or are not desired, the next cheapest plan is to rent a furnished room in some residence near the Dining Hall. Many such rooms are for rent, on the campus and elsewhere. The prices range from $10.00 per month, ($5.00 for each occupant of a room), upwards, including rent of furniture and bedding, attendance and lights, but not usually including fuel.

If preferred, the student can obtain board and lodging in private houses, at prices ranging from $25.00 upward per month.

LOAN FUNDS

Law students are admitted to participate in the benefits of the "Brown Fund" and the "Lumpkin Fund' and other loan funds. Those who wish information in regard to these funds should write to Chancellor Charles M. Snelling, Athens, Ga.

BENJAMIN Z. PHILLIPS FUND

Mrs. Nettie Elsas Phillips has generously donated $5,000, the income to be lent to a student in the Law Department, the award to be made by the law faculty. The gift is a memorial of her late husband, Benjamin Z. Phillips, a graduate and loyal alumnus of the Department.

THE PHARMACY DEPARTMENT

FACULTY

DAVID C. BARROW, LL.D., Chancellor Emeritus.

CHARLES M. SNELLING, A.M., Sc.D., Chancellor.

THOS. W. REED, A.M., LL.B., Registrar and Treasurer.

ROBERT C. WILSON, Ph.G., Professor of Pharmacy and Materia Medica; Dean of the School of Pharmacy.

HENRY C. WHITE, Ph.D., Professor of Chemistry.

WILLIAM D. HOOPER, A.M., Professor of Pharmaceutical Latin.

L. L. HENDREN, Ph.D., Professor of Physics.

JOHN M. READE, Ph.D., Professor of Botany.

A. W. SCOTT, Ph.D., Associate Professor of Chemistry.

J. W. CANTRELL, A.B., Associate Professor of Physics.

C. J. BROCKMAN, A.M., Ch. Eng., Adjunct Professor of Chemistry.

D. E. BROWN, Tutor in Pharmacy.

ANNOUNCEMENT

The next session of this Department begins coincident with the opening of the University September 15th, 1926. The time to complete the course is two years of three terms each, or eighteen months. The first term begins with the opening of college in September and the third term ends in June.

It is the aim of the University in maintaining the Department of Pharmacy to give to the profession of pharmacy men qualified to hold position of trust and responsibility. It believes that it can best accomplish this mission by giving educated men.

While it is recognized that pharmacy of today is largely mercantile in character, still it cannot be denied that it is also professional. It is the belief of the University that a man's best business asset is a thorough and broad education; thorough in the sense that he may be able to interpret properly the fundamental principles underlying the practice of any profession, and broad in the sense that he may not become narrowed in his views and that he may cope intelligently with men in other walks of life.

With a view to a thorough comprehension of the course in pharmacy involving a study of the allied sciences upon which pharmacy rests, the following

ENTRANCE REQUIREMENTS

have been adopted, corresponding to the requirements of the American Conference of Pharmaceutical Faculties:

1. The applicant must be of good moral character, not less than 17 years of age.

2. The applicant must present certificate from an accredited high school showing that he has completed at least four years of high school work. The required fifteen entrance units may be complied with as follows: English 4, History 4, Mathematics 2, Electives 6; Total 15.

The above is in force as regards applicants for admission to the Junior Class as candidates for a degree. Applicants for registration in the Senior Class or for advanced standing, must present certificate showing completion of at least one year in a School of Pharmacy, whose entrance and scholastic requirements and length of term compare favorably with those of the University.

It is the desire of the University authorities that every man who enters will graduate, but it has been our experience that men, who have not had the necessary preliminary training, find it difficult to carry the work outlined for our students. Hence we have established as a minimum entrance requirement completion of not less than four years of high school work.

DEGREES

1. Completion of the work of the Junior and Senior years entitles the student to receive the degree of Graduate in Pharmacy, Ph.G., of the University of Georgia.

2. Under certain restrictions candidates for a baccalaureate degree in the University may obtain permission to enter the classes in Pharmacy and Materia Medica and receive the degree in Pharmacy at the same time as the baccalaureate degree.

GOVERNMENT

Students of Pharmacy are governed by the same rules and regulations as laid down for other students of the University, except that they are not required to drill.

MILITARY INSTRUCTION

Pharmacy students are not required to drill, yet are urged to take at least one year of such training.

THE CURRICULUM

Junior Year

	Hrs. Rec.	Hrs. Lab.	No. weeks	Total hrs.
Inorganic Chemistry _ _ _ _ _ _ _ _	3	2	36	180
Materia Medica and Botany _ _ _ _ _	3	-	36	108
Physics _ _ _ _ _ _ _ _ _ _ _ _ _ _	3	2	36	180
Physiology _ _ _ _ _ _ _ _ _ _ _ _ _	3	-	36	108
Arithmetic of Pharmacy _ _ _ _ _ _	3	6	12	108
Galenical Pharmacy _ _ _ _ _ _ _ _	3	6	24	216
Pharmaceutical Latin _ _ _ _ _ _ _	2	-	12	24
				—— 924

Senior Year

	Hrs. Rec.	Hrs. Lab.	No. weeks	Total hrs.
Organic Chemistry _ _ _ _ _ _ _ _	3	2	36	180
Analytical Chemistry _ _ _ _ _ _ _	-	6	36	216
Materia Medica _ _ _ _ _ _ _ _ _	3	-	36	108
Pharmacy _ _ _ _ _ _ _ _ _ _ _ _	6	9	36	540
Accounting _ _ _ _ _ _ _ _ _ _ _ _	3	-	12	36
				——1080

Total number hours for the degree _ _ _ _ _ _ _ _ _ _ _ 2004

The above represents the amount of time required to complete the course leading to a degree. Students who may be somewhat slow in performing the laboratory work required frequently put in from 10 to 50 per cent additional or extra work.

In addition to these subjects, it is recommended that Junior Pharmacy students take up also Freshman English, and the Seniors register for the course in Business Administration or Business Law.

CHEMISTRY

The courses in Chemistry offered to students in Pharmacy cover two years. The first year is devoted to the study of General Inorganic Chemistry and the second year to the study of Qualitative Analysis and Organic Chemistry. Each student receives his own set of equipment and performs his experiments individually. A laboratory fee covers the cost of chemicals required and a breakage fee is deposited with the Registrar to cover the cost of apparatus which may be broken or damaged during the course of the work.

GENERAL INORGANIC CHEMISTRY. This course is an elementary study of the non-metallic and metallic elements and their compounds. Lectures on the fundamental theories of Chemistry are illustrated by experiments, diagrams, working drawings, and specimens from the Departmental museum. This course consists of three hours of lecture-recitation each week supplemented by two laboratory periods of two hours each. In the laboratory each student with his own apparatus and reagents performs carefully chosen experiments to illustrate and prove the theories which are mentioned in the lecture-recitation, Laboratory space permits each student to perform individual experiments without over-crowding.

QUALITATIVE ANALYSIS. In this course the student makes a series of identifying tests which prove the presence or absence of metal and acid ions in solutions or in the solid form. Attention is also given to making mixtures similar to the materials which the graduate will have occasion to meet in his professional work. The qualitative analysis of salts, alloys and some minerals is studied. In the lecture-recitation periods the scientific laws which are fundamental in the prosecution of the actual analytical work are studied. Three periods of two hours each per week are devoted to this work.

ORGANIC CHEMISTRY. This is a study of the typical compounds of carbon, their classification, general relations and methods of preparation. The origin and nature of many of the drugs from the animal and vegetable kingdoms are made clear. The more important compounds are prepared and studied in the laboratory. Three hours of lecture-recitation and one period of two hours a week in the laboratory are required.

PHYSICS

Junior Year

ORGANIC PHYSICS. Physics 1. In this course especial emphasis is placed on the application of the principles of Physics to practical life. Two hours per week recitation and two hours per week individual laboratory work.

Second year Pharmacy students may obtain permission to take up some advanced work after completion of this course.

PHYSIOLOGY

Junior Year

In this course the student masters, as far as practicable, the gross anatomy of the human body, with frequent reference to the anatomy of lower animals. On completion of this, a short course in Histology is given, after which the subject of Physiology is taken up. This course is based in part upon the text, but is largely extended by lectures and demonstations according to a syllabus which is furnished each student. Three hours per week. Lectures and recitations.

LATIN

This course will be given during the Junior year and will consist of recitations and lectures in the rudiments of Latin with special reference to medical and pharmaceutical nomenclature. The common Latin phrases and abbreviations as they relate to prescriptions will be covered in detail. Previous knowledge of Latin is not required.

BOTANY AND MATERIA MEDICA

Junior Pharmacy students are given a short course in Botany from September until December, involving a study of the gross anatomy of plants with the end in view of laying the foundation for the study of vegetable Materia Medica. Following this course in Botany and beginning in January of the Junior year, the study of Materia Medica of vegetable drugs is taken up and is continued until December of the Senior year. Classification is made of these drugs from the standpoint of families, from the standpoint of parts used and from the standpoint of active constituents, including also the animal drugs of the U. S. P. Following this course and beginning in January of the Senior year, the various medicinal agents, vegetable, animal, mineral and synthetic are classified according to their medicinal action. As a part of this study the subject of posology and toxicology receive ample attention. The Materia Medica cabinet contains unground and ground specimens of most of the official vegetable drugs and many non-official as well as a complete collection of inorganic drugs. These various specimens are utilized for identification tests. The student is required to be able to identify from 150 to 200 drugs by microscopic and chemical tests.

In addition to the stock materia medica cabinets already mentioned, three individual Sharp & Dohme's materia medica cabinets and one Eli Lilly's are available at all times for individual study.

In the stock room and laboratory will be found specimens of practically every official drug or preparation of that drug, many of the National Formulary and many non-official.

Texts for the past year: Bailey's Botany, Culbreath's Materia Medica, Wilcox's Materia Medica and Therapeutics.

JUNIOR PHARMACY

First Term from September to December. Pharmaceutical Arithmetic.

In this course, a close study of the various systems of weights and measures is made, their history, their application in Pharmacy and their relationship to each other. The importance of the metric system is stressed in its many advantages both as regards metric pre-scriptions and manufacturing.

The conversion of weights to volumes, volumes to weights, re-ducing and enlarging formulas, proportions, percentage solutions, concentration and dilution and alligation, including many original problems in addition to those of the text, constitutes the work of the course in collaboration with laboratory exercises which impress the principles involved. The various styles of balances in use in actual practice are demonstrated and discussed, the principles upon which they operate and the proper precautions which should be taken in their care. Text: Strumer's Arithmetic of Pharmacy, Arny's Prin-ciples of Pharmacy.

As an addition to the laboratory. work during this time, students are required to familiarize themselves, by actual experiments, with the various pharmaceutical processes; i. e., methods for the regula-tion of heat by use of the various baths, comparison of the various thermometer scales with problems for conversion, calcination, igni-tion, deflagration, carbonization, torrefaction, fusion, evaporation, dessication, exiccation, granulation, distillation, sublimation, tritura-tion, elutriation, solubility, decantation, filtration, precipitation, crystallization, maceration and percolation, etc. Text: Arny's Phar-macy. Laboratory Notes. Second and Third terms, January to June. Galenical Preparations.

Reasons for the classification of pharmaceutical preparations into Waters, Solutions, Spirits, Syrups, Tinctures, etc., are brought out. Their distinguishing characterictics as regards solvent, keeping qual-ities, medicinal and pharmaceutical uses are pointed out by lecture, recitation and laboratory work and observation. Beginning with the simpler preparations and going gradually to the more complex, most of the Waters, Spirits, Solutions, Mucilages, Syrups, Elixirs, Glycer-ites, Collodions, Oleates, Infusions, Vinegars, Mixtures, Emulsions Liniments and Powders of the U. S. P. and many of the N. F. and incidental formulas are manufactured by each student as well as many Tinctures, Fluidextratcts, Extracts, some one or more Resins and Oleoresins. The laboratory reports on the manufacture of these preparations insure a thoroughly study of each individual preparation from every standpoint. A knowledge of all principles involved is stressed and the ability to interpret properly the directions of the U. S. P. or other formularies. Calculations as to reducing or en-larging or converting the formula as well as cost are required in most cases. Text: Arny's Pharmacy, U. S. P., N. F. and Dispensa-tories.

SENIOR PHARMACY

September to December.

During this period a study of the more difficult U. S. P. and N. F. preparation is taken up, including the manufacture of Ointments, the value, uses and advantages of the various bases; the manufacture and close study of Cerates, Cataplasms, Plasters; the manufacture and study of allied preparations, salves, cold creams, skin-foods, lotions, jellies, petroxylins, etc.; the manufacture of suppositories by hand and the various molds with a study of the various bases in common use. The subjects of pill making, compressed and tablet triturate manufacture, pastilles and troches receive a large amount of attention. The choice of excipient to insure proper disintegration of the pill with strict regard for the chemical or physical character of the material in hand, constitutes the important factor in the study of pills. Each student makes several hundred pills of the U. S. P. and from various prescriptions. Compressed and tablet triturates are made and a study is made of their comparative solubility.

January to June.

During this period the chemistry of medicinal and pharmaceutical products is taken up, many are manufactured, identity tests, impurity tests and quantitative tests are made in many cases. The incompatibilities of all the more important products are studied closely, and an effort is made to correct such incompatibility.

Many of the preparations of the U. S. P. and N. F. involving chemical reactions in their manufacture are made and studied, and it is pointed out how these preparations may be made to advantage in the retail store when a proper knowledge of the principles involved is at hand. The work involves products of the vegetable, animal and mineral kingdoms as well as the more important synthetics of the market.

The work is made intensely practical, nothing being required which can not be advantageously applied in the retail store. It is endeavored to develop a correct technic of operation and at the same time a correct scientific attitude of mind to the problem in hand, in so far as principles are involved.

In the latter part of the course the subject of prescriptions is considered from every standpoint. We have on hand several thousand original prescriptions, which are read and criticized as to method of filling, character of finished product, dose and action, cost and selling price.

The problems and cares of actual prescription practice are demonstrated in the free dispensary in charge of the Pharmacy Department. From five hundred to one thousand prescriptions for the student body of the University are filled annually by members of the Senior class, under direct supervision of the Instructors in Pharmacy.

On the whole, it is endeavored in this course to make direct application of the principles of all the allied sciences, to present conditions in pharmaceutical practice.

Texts: Arny's Principles of Pharmacy, Scoville's Art of Compounding, U. S. P. and N. F.

References: Ruddiman's Incompatibilities, United States and National Standard Dispensatories, Leach Food and Drug Analysis, Merck's Report, Remington's Pharmacy, Caspari's Pharmacy, Advanced Texts in Organic and Physiological Chemistry.

ACCOUNTING

Since the practice of Pharmacy involves, in addition to its professional side, a knowledge of fundamental business principles, we have instituted, as a requirement for Seniors, a course in accounting

The subject of book-keeping, leases, banking, etc., will be handled in this course and the Graduate in Pharmacy from the University will then be prepared to handle or direct both the professional and the mercantile side of his or her employer's business.

Three hours per week recitations and laboratory practice throughout the first term. Text to be announced.

TEXT BOOKS

The following text-books were used the past year, but it is suggested that students do not provide themselves with text-books before coming to College because of the fact that these texts may be changed before the opening of College in September.

Noyes' Text-Book of Chemistry, Stoddard's Organic Chemistry, Noyes' Qualitative Analysis, Bailey's Botany, Culbreath's Materia Medica, Wilcox's Materia Medica and Therapeutics, Mann and Twiss'• Physics, Hough and Sedgwick's Physiology, Arny's Principles of Pharmacy, U. S. Pharmacopoea, National Formulary, Scovill's Art of Compounding, Sturmer's Pharmaceutical Arithmetic, Sturmer's Pharmaceutical Latin, Laboratory Manuals in Physics, Chemistry and Pharmacy are furnished.

If text-books in chemistry, physiology, physics, botany, materia medica or pharmacy are already on hand or if a Pharmacopoeia, Dispensatory or National Formulary, are procurable, it is well to bring these along for reference purposes.

EQUIPMENT FOR GENERAL USE IN PHARMACY LABORATORY

1 E. & A. Analytical Balance sensitive to .1 mgm. or 1/640 of a grain.

4 Becker's Balances sensitive to 1 mgm. or 1/64 of a grain.

5 Trip Scales for coarse weighing with metric weights from 1 gm. to 500 gm., and avoirdupois weights from ⅛ oz. to 2 lbs.

1 No. 3 Whitall Tatum & Co.'s Suppository Machine.

1 No. 25 Whitall Tatum & Co.'s Compressed Tablet Machine.

1 No. 1 Whitall Tatum & Co.'s Emulsifier (2 gallons.)

1 No. 10 Whitall Tatum & Co.'s Tablet Triturate Machine.

1 No. 4 Whitall Tatum & Co.'s Suppository Mold.

1 No. 7 Whitall Tatum & Co.'s Suppository Mold.

2 Automatic Water Baths.

1 Automatic Water Still.

Hydrometers, Alcoholmeters and Specific Gravity Bottles. Individual equipment includes the following:

1 Balance sensitive to .01 gm.

1 Set Weights 1 mgm. to 500 mgm.

1 Set Weights 1 gm. to 50 gms.

1 Set Weights ½ gr. to 5 grains.

1 Set Weights ½ scruple to 2 drachms.

Pill tile, spatula, beakers, flasks, test tubes, clamps, funnels, metric and apothecary graduates, evaporating dishes, thermometers, pipettes, percolators, watch glasses, separatory funnels, burettes, glass tubing, glass rod, mortars and pestles, crucibles, retort stands, copper waterbaths, bunsen burner, rubber tubing. powder papers, filter papers, and many smaller items. These items are lent to students to be kept in individual lockers for the year. Those items which are misplaced or damaged are to be paid for by the student.

All materials (pharmaceutical or chemical) are furnished.

There will be found in the laboratory or stock room practically every preparation of the U. S. P. and many of the N. F.

EXPENSES

Junior, or First Year

Tuition, one-half payable at beginning of term, balance payable at the opening of college in January_____$ 50.00

Literary Society Fee _____ 2.00

Infirmary, Gymnasium, Athletic Fees _____ 21.00

Student Council Fee _____ .50

Georgia Cracker Fee _____ 1.00

College Co-op Fee _____ 1.00

Student's Activities Fee _____ 3.00
Materia Medica Fee _____ 1.00
Pharmacy Laboratory Fee _____ 12.50
Chemistry Laboratory, including breakage deposit_____ 6.00
Physics Laboratory Fee _____ 3.00

As stated above, $25.00 of this amount can be paid at the opening of college in January.

Senior or Second Year

Tuition, payable as above _____$ 50.00
Literary Society _____ 2.00
Infirmary, Gymnasium, Athletic _____ 21.00
Student Council _____ .50
Georgia Cracker _____ 1.00
College Co-op _____ 1.00
Student Activities _____ 3.00
Materia Medica Laboratory _____ 1.00
Pharmacy Laboratory _____ 12.50
Chemistry Laboratory, Organic (including breakage deposit) 5.00
Chemistry, Qualitative (including breakage deposit) _____ 15.00

$112.00

As stated above, $25.00 of this amount can be paid at the opening of college in January.

Expenses of Students When Rooming in a Dormitory and Boarding

at Denmark Hall

Board (paid monthly in advance, 9 months at $16.00)____$144.00
Laundry (estimated at $2.00 per month)_____ 18.00
Room Rent, light, heat and attendance, $5.00 per month__ 45.00
Deposit Fee in Dormitory and Dining Hall_____ 5.00
Books and Stationery, estimated, for one year_____ 35.00

$247.00

The individual expenses of a student are just what he makes them, as no college regulation can control this matter.

No graduation or diploma fees.

A student should come prepared to spend $150.00 during the first thirty days for registration, books, board in advance and small incidentals.

DORMITORIES

There are four dormitories, Old College for Juniors and Seniors, New College, Candler Hall and Milledge Hall for lower classmen.

Rooms in the dormitories are lighted with electricity, and are furnished with chairs, bed, table and washstand. A charge of $5.00 per month per man, where there are two in a room, and $4.00 per month per man, where there are more than two in a room, is made for each room occupied, to cover the expense of janitors, fuel, water and lights.

Where two occupy the same room, each occupant shall pay on matriculation $17.50, and on January 1st, $27.50—making a total of $45.00 for the session.

Where more than two occupy the same room, each occupant shall pay on matriculation $14.00 and on January 1st, $22.00—making a total of $36.00 for the session.

A deposit of $2.00 is required of every student before assignment is made. This fee is a charge against damage to the property, and the balance is returned at the end of the year. The dormitories are in charge of a Committee from the Faculty. The rules and regulations prescribed by this Committee are enforced through Proctors placed over each division of the dormitories.

Those desiring dormitory rooms should apply in person, or by letter, to T. W. Reed, Treasurer, Athens, Ga. No assignment will be made until the required deposit fee is paid. Applications should be made early as only about three hundred can be accommodated.

If dormitory rooms cannot be obtained, or are not desired, the next cheapest plan is to rent a furnished room in some residence near the Dining Hall. Many such rooms are for rent on the campus and elsewhere. The prices range from $10.00 per month ($5.00 for each occupant) upwards, including rent of furniture and bedding, attendance and light, but not fuel.

If preferred, the student can obtain board and lodging in private houses at prices ranging from $25.00 per month upward.

CURRENT DRUG TOPICS

Monthly conferences will be held during the coming year on the principal topics of the day of interest to druggists, as gleaned from the pharmaceutical and chemical publications.

The following publications are on hand and are accessible to students at all times:

American Journal of Pharmacy, Monthly.
The National Druggist, Monthly.
The Journal of the N. A. D. R., Weekly.

The Spatula, Monthly.
The Southern Pharmaceutical Journal, Monthly.
Meyer Brothers' Druggist, Monthly.
The Pharmaceutical Era, Monthly.
The Bulletin of Pharmacy.
The Midland Druggist, Monthly.
Merck's Report, Monthly.
The Druggists' Circular, Monthly.
The Journal of the American Pharmaceutical Association, Monthly.
The American Druggist, Monthly.
Journal of Industrial Chemistry, Monthly.
Industrial and Engineering Chemistry, Monthly.
Chemical Abstracts (American Chemical Society), Semi-Monthly.
Bulletins of Hygienic Laboratory.
Journal of American Medical Association.

INFIRMARY

A resident nurse is in charge, whose services are available at all times. A physician has offices at the Infirmary, and his services are at the command of students.

In collaboration with the Infirmary, the Pharmacy Department is operating a free dispensary, where prescriptions for the student body are filled free of charge.

These prescriptions are handled by members of the Senior class under the supervision of members of the Faculty. They are studied closely from every standpoint, and afford wonderful opportunity for actual drug store practice. Plans are on foot to increase materially the scope of this work.

PHARMACY AS A PROFESSION FOR WOMEN

Women have found a demand for their services by the larger drug stores of the country. The result is that many women are being licensed each year by the State Board of Pharmacy to practice Pharmacy on an equal basis with men. Salaries are attractive, and women are particularly fitted for this work. Many women are entering the various Schools of Pharmacy each year. All departments of the University are open to them.

PRIVILEGES AND ADVANTAGES

Students in this department of the University are accorded all the privileges extended to other students, and likewise all the many advantages of the institution, including the gymnasium, athletics in general, literary societies, public speaking. military and college activities, and opportunity to take other courses than those required.

THE RECORD OF OUR GRADUATES BEFORE THE BOARD OF EXAMINERS

It has been our endeavor to teach PRINCIPLES underlying the practices of Pharmacy and the wisdom of this course is evidenced by the record of our graduates before the State Board of Examiners.

Our graduates have established what is probably a world's record, in the fact that with two exceptions every one who has taken the State Board Examination has been accorded a license. A number have received Pharmacist's license, and more Pharmacist's licenses have been issued our graduates in the past five years than have gone to the graduates of all other schools combined. From the records of the Secretary of the State Board of Pharmacy, it is shown that only about 50 per cent of those taking the examination receive a license, whereas the percentage of our graduates is practically 100.

The University has endeavored to make the course in Pharmacy measure up to the high standard maintained in its other departments and to make it thorough both from theoretical and practical standpoints, as is evidenced by the fact that all of our graduates have passed the State Board and are occupying positions of trust and responsibility in some of the most prominent drug stores of this and other states.

PHARMACY AS A PREPARATION FOR MEDICINE

By a slight modification of the courses in Pharmacy and by taking some additional work during the year, with possibly some summer work, it is possible for a student in the Pharmacy Department to complete within two years all the work required for entrance into the Medical College.

No other course offers better opportunities as a foundation for the study or practice of medicine as a thorough course in Pharmacy with its allied studies.

Direct all correspondence concerning the School of Pharmacy to

ROBERT C. WILSON, Dean,

Athens, Georgia.

Part V
THE AUXILIARY DIVISIONS

A. The Department of Military Science and Tactics

B. Home Study

C. The University Summer School

D. The University Library

E. The University Health Service and the Crawford W. Long Infirmary

F. Accredited Schools

MILITARY SCIENCE AND TACTICS

JAMES EDWIN WARE, Lieutenant Colonel, U. S. Army, Retired, Professor.

FREDERIC WALDO WHITNEY, Major, Cavalry, U. S. Army, Assistant Professor.

RICHARD B. TRIMBLE, Captain, Cavalry, U. S. Army, Assistant Professor.

IRA C. NICHOLAS, Captain, Infantry, U. S. Army, Assistant Professor.

STANLEY G. BACKMAN, Captain, Infantry, U. S. Army, Assistant Professor.

LAWRENCE G. SMITH, 1st Lieutenant, Cavalry, U. S. Army, Assistant Professor.

Clerical Force

JOHN DOZIER SMITH, Staff Sergeant, (Captain, Quartermaster Corps Reserve). Store Keeper.

CLIFFORD HAYES, Sergeant, Chief Clerk.

ROBERT M. PROCTOR, Sergeant, Property Clerk.

HARRIS B. AVRETT, Private First Class, Record Clerk.

Reserve Officers Training Corps

ESTABLISHMENT. Under the provisions of Special Regulations No. 44, War Department, Washington, August 19, 1919, units of Infantry, and Cavalry of the Senior Division Reserve Officers' Training Corps. are established at the University of Georgia, and all students are allowed full privileges of the organization.

PROVISIONS OF THE LAND GRANT ACT. Unless specially excused by the head of the institution, upon the recommendation of the Professor of Military Science and Tactics, all physically fit male students, except graduates and those in the Law and Pharmacy Departments, are required to take two years work in the Department of Military Science and Tactics. This work entitles the student to a credit of three hours toward graduation.

OBJECT. The primary object of the Reserve Officers Training Corps is to provide systematic military training at civil educational institutions for the purpose of qualifying selected students of such institutions as reserve officers in the military forces of the United States. It is intended to attain this object during the time that students are pursuing their general or professional studies with the least parcticable interference with their civil careers, by employing methods designed to fit men, physically, mentally, and morally, for the pursuits of peace as well as pursuits of war. It is believed that such military training will aid greatly in the development of better citizens as well as provide a large number of educated men physically efficient and fitted to lead intelligently the units of the armies upon which the safety of the country will depend.

COURSES. The course in the Reserve Officers' Training Corps is divided into two periods. The Basic Course consists of the first two years. The Advanced course consists of the last two years, with a period at summer camp, held usually at the end of the third or Junior year. Attendance at the Advanced Camp is compulsory for those students who receive commutaion of subsistence as hereinafter described.

In the case of either camp, the student receives from the government, mileage at the rate of five (5) cents per mile to and from camp, quarters, food, uniforms, equipment, medical attention and all other necessities while there. Students at the Advanced Summer Camp receive while at camp, in addition to the above the pay of a soldier of the seventh grade, now seventy (70) cents per day.

These summer camps are instructive and attractive. The student enjoys for six weeks a vigorous, outdoor life, meets students from other institutions in various activities and competitions, and is given opportunity for travel in various parts of the country, all without cost to himself.

COMMUTATION OF SUBSISTENCE. When any member of the Reserve Officers' Training Corps has completed two academic years of service in the Senior Division or has taken a course in a Junior Division substantially equivalent to the Basic Course of the Senior Division, and has been selected by the Chancellor of the University and the Professor of Military Science and Tactics as qualified for further training, he may be admitted to the Advanced Course of the Senior Division. Any member of the Senior Division who has been admitted to the Advanced Course and who executes the proper written agreement, will be entitled to commutation of subsistence, except while at the summer camp where he will be furnished subsistence in kind.

The rate of commutation of subsistence is fixed from time to time by the Secretary of War and is based on the cost of the garrison ration of the army. The present rate is thirty cents per day. The commutation is payable for not to exceed two years, including the summer vacation period but excepting the time while at summer camp.

UNIFORM. The uniform of the Basic Course Reserve Officers' Training Corps is that of the United States Army with a distinctive sleeve insignia added. This uniform is furnished free to each student in the R. O. T. C., but remains the property of the United States and must be returned to the Supply Officer when the student leaves the institution. In addition, each student attending camp is issued a summer uniform for his use there.

Each student in the first year Advanced Course is required to deposit thirty (30) dollars with the Registrar, all of which is returned to him after deducting for cost of clothing or equipment, at the end of the session, second year Advanced Courst students are required to deposit ten dollars.

One (1) dollar will be deducted from the military deposit of each student in the Reserve Officers' Training Corps each year for space in the "PANDORA," the student annual. Each student's picture appears in his organization group.

The students of the Advanced Course now enjoy the advantage of commutation of uniforms. This enables us to furnish each student with a uniform made to his measure.

The uniform adopted for students of the Advanced Course, R. O. T C., is the same as that of the Regular Army officer, but with different insignia. The coat will have the new roll collar.

It consists of cap, coat, breeches, leather leggins, woolen shirt, web belt and black tie, all of excellent material, which with reasonable care will last two years or more.

The uniform will cost about $35.00 complete, (price varies slightly each year and is determined by competitive bids from about a dozen makers).

The Government allowance is $30.00 for the first year and $6.00 for the second year, total for the two years of $36.00.

FINANCIAL BENEFITS TO STUDENTS. Each student who takes the full course as outlined herein receives from the government in clothing subsistence and money an average of more than $100 per year for the last two years; this is an important item to students who are partly or wholly making their own way.

EQUIPMENT. In addition to the clothing mentioned above, a complete set of arms and equipment is issued to each student in the Military Department. The University is accountable to the Federal Government for the clothing and equipment issued to the students. Each student in the Basic Course of the Reserve Officers' Training Corps is required to deposit $10.00 with the Registrar. Upon leaving the University this deposit fee of $10.00 will be returned to the student after deducting therefrom the cost of any clothing or equipment lost.

COURSES OF INSTRUCTION

FOR UNITS OF ALL ARMS. Organization; military courtesy and discipline; drill, close and extended order; care and use of arms and equipment; target practice; personal hygiene, first aid and sanitation; guard duty; minor tactics; morale; physical training; topography; field engineering; administration; military law, military history and policy of the United States; map problems; ceremonies.

INFANTRY SPECIAL. Bayonet and hand grenades; automatic rifle; machine guns; trench mortars; one pounder gun; marching; tactical walks.

CAVALRY SPECIAL. Selection and care of animals; hippology; feeding and grooming; care and treatment of minor injuries and ailments; shoeing; equitation; packing; pistol practice; sabre practice; development and employment of Cavalry; Cavalry minor tactics; machine guns; cross country riding; polo.

CREDITS ALLOWED. Academic credits toward graduation are allowed physically fit male students as follows:

a. In any course except Law, Medicine and Pharmacy, three hours for two years successful work. (Freshman and Sophomore). The work is compulsory, under the Land Grant Act.

b. In any course except Engineering, Law, Medicine and Pharmacy, advanced Military Science and Tactics is an elective and three hours credit is given for the work of each year. (Junior and Senior).

It is seen that a student in certain courses may obtain a total credit of nine hours for work in the Military Department.

Students taking the above excepted courses may take work in the Military Department providing their schedule can be arranged; but no academic credits are allowed them.

BENEFITS RECEIVED BY STUDENTS IN RESERVE OFFICERS TRAINING CORPS

1. Just enough physical exercise at drill, in the first period of the day, to put the student in good condition for the day's work.

2. It helps to form habits of punctuality, neatness and courtesy.

3. It trains men to respect regularly constituted authority.

4. In inculcates patriotism, love of country, and loyalty to our country's Flag.

5. A total of three (3) hours credit is given for satisfactory completion of Basic Course, and six (6) hours for the Advanced Course.

6. A good serviceable uniform is furnished without expense to the student. This makes a considerable saving on his clothing bill. The uniform should be worn only on drill days.

7. It affords an opportunity to go to R. O. T. C. summer training camps without expense to the student.

8. Students in the Advanced Course get thirty (30) cents per day for about two (2) years.

9. Upon graduation the student receives a commission as Second Lieutenant in the Officers' Reserve Corps of the United States Army.

10. The uniform for the Advanced Course is made to measure, and is of same cloth, style and finish as worn by regular army officers, except insignia. This uniform can be worn by graduates after they get

their Reserve Commissions, thus saving the cost of a new officers' uniform. The coat has the new roll collar.

11. From three to five honor graduates of the DEPARTMENT OF MILITARY SCIENCE AND TACTICS are, each year, offered a commission as Second Lieutenant in the Regular Army or Marine Corps, with no examination other than physical.

12. The University of Georgia is rated by the War Department as a Distinguished College. We expect to keep that rating.

13. An opportunity to visit one or more State Fairs or Horse Shows as a member of the R. O. T. C. Bare-back Riding Squad. This has been a popular trip for the last two years.

14. The opportunity for all students of the Cavalry Unit and selected students of the Infantry Unit, after the first year, to learn and play the game Polo, "The Sport of Kings," with little expense to the students. These most proficient will be selected for teams.

15. An opportunity of becoming an expert pistol or rifle shot.

16. We have an annual R. O. T. C. Horse Show by the Cavalry Unit. Many handsome silver cups and ribbons are awarded to students. These trophies are donated by local business firms and individuals. The Horse Shows are well attended.

DIVISION OF HOME STUDY

GEO. A. HUTCHINSON, Director.
R. WARNER JONES, Secretary.
—. —. —————, Asst. Secretary.

This Division was organized for the purpose of rendering a service to those who are unable to pursue a university course in residence. At present, two types of courses are being offered: One, extension courses in which a member of the faculty meets a group of students twice a month for a lecture and discussion and combines this with outlined home-study work, tests and examinations. In the other, straight correspondence-study courses are offered to individuals who are not accessible to these study groups. The number of study groups that may be arranged for will be restricted by the capacity of our faculty to meet such groups. It will also, of course, be restricted by distance from the University. The courses offered by correspondence-study and in extension are offered by the regular faculty of the University of Georgia and are made as nearly as possible the equivalent of the courses here at the University. The consensus of opinion among the correspondence students with whom I have talked is that there is a value to be derived from correspondence work that is not often derived from residence work. On the other hand, however, the personal stimulus of the instructor is lost in correspondence work. For this reason, it is better when the student can do it to do a summer term's work under an instructor and follow that up with correspondence work under him.

INSTRUCTIONS

All correspondence, including lesson reports, should be directed to the University of Georgia, Division of Home Study. When so directed, should the director be away your correspondence will come to the office and be properly cared for instead of being forwarded to him.

All checks for fees and books should be made payable to Geo. A. Hutchinson, Director.

New courses are being added to the list already offered. If you do not find in the list what you need, write us and we shall gladly do all we can to meet your needs. We have organized this work to serve you and we can best do that if you will let us know your needs. We cannot agree to offer every course asked for, but when there is a sufficient demand to justify it we shall put forth every effort to put the course on. Any suggestions as to how we may increase the efficiency of the department will be cheerfully received. Any information not included in this statement will be cheerfully given if you will write and ask for it.

REGULATIONS

Rule I. Courses offered are open to all qualified students. A student in attendance in any educational institution is thereby disqualified for correspondence-study work, unless he has the approval of the proper officials of that institution.

Rule II. No preliminary examination is required for admission to correspondence-study, but the applicant must furnish such evidence as is needed to demonstrate his fitness to undertake such work. Should a student desire university credit, this fact should be stated in advance, and the 15 units entrance requirements must be satisfied before coming up for a degree.

Rule III. Students may begin correspondence-study courses at any time, except in July and August. (See note I below).

Rule IV. A student may register for one, two or three courses at the same time, depending upon the amount of other work the student has to do. It is generally better to concentrate upon one course at a time and move forward as rapidly as possible.

Rule V. A student who has satisfactorily completed a part of a course in residence may complete the remainder by correspondence, provided the course is given as a correspondence-study course.

Rule VI. The examination at the end of a course is optional, but is required where credit is sought. The examination may be taken at the University or under conditions approved by the University.

Rule VII. The fee for a correspondence course to teachers in this State is $6.00 per credit hour, plus 50c to pay postage on lesson reports returned to the student. To all others, it is $8.00 per hour, or $21.00 for three hours registered for at one time, plus 50c per hour postage. Where a student registers for more than one hour and decides not to pursue the course, the balance of the fee, after deducting for the first hour, may be refunded, provided application is made for the refund within three months from date of registration and before completion of the first hour.

Rule VIII. The time limit of a course unit is six months and of a three hour course is one year from date of registration. An extension of this time limit may be granted upon the payment of an extension fee of $1.00. To be of most value, a three hour course should be completed in about nine months, i. e., about one lesson each week. Either a pronounced shortening or extension of the time is inadvisable and whenever in the judgement of the instructor offering the course such a shortening or extension of the work is hindering the student in his mastery of the work the student may be required to conform more nearly to this standard. It is only extreme variations from this standard, however, that are likely to call forth a protest from the instructor.

Rule IX. Some colleges rate credit by an hour of recitation per week for a term or quarter, others rate by an hour for a semester, or half year; still others use an hour for the scholastic year of nine months. The University of Georgia uses the year hour. This should be kept in mind in comparing institutions. A credit is the equivalent of an hour of college credit.

Rule X. Credit to an amount not exceeding one-third of the hours required for graduation may be obtained through correspondence-study courses. This does not modify the regulation requiring at least one year's residence for any degree.

Rule XI. A three hours course designated by three numerals, as "Education 1, 2, 3", indicates that each unit is separate and complete in itself. Other courses require two or three units to complete. A course must be complete before the credit received may be counted toward a degree.

Rule XII. One year of residence is required for any degree. This is interpreted to mean not less than 30 weeks, completing at least 15 college credit hours in the Upper Devision, Junior-Senior years. Only in cases of peculiar merit will attendance in summer terms be accepted to satisfy the minimum residence required, and such cases must come up on the recommendation of the head of the college concerned, and be approved by the faculty, upon recommendation of the Curriculum Committee. A student who offers as many as 15 hours of the requirements for a degree through correspondence or extension courses must satisfy the one year residence in the regular session.

Rule XIII. Text books to be used in the correspondence and extension courses may be bought from the Department of Correspondence-study at the publishers' list price. Then upon completion of the course we will usually repurchase the books at approximately two-thirds of the price for which we sell them, provided the books are returned in good condition. Students desiring to return the texts should indicate their desire in their application in order that we may sent them second-hand copies, if we have them on hand.

NOTES. 1. Many professors have vacation during July and August; hence we cannot guarantee that a student may begin in these months, though it might be possible.

2. Should a professor have vacation before any course under his instruction is completed, the vacation period will not count as part of the student's six-month limit, unless the course is carried on by another instructor.

3. Should the number of students in any course at any time be as large as the instructor can keep up with, other applicants may be asked to defer the course a short while, or to substitute another in its stead.

4. Credit received for work done by correspondence-study and extension courses, and validated by an examination, is entered on the University records as so much college credit and will be accepted as such by the University toward a degree and by the State Department of Education toward certification.

COURSES GIVEN

The following courses of study have been arranged for this department, the numbers corresponding to those in the department in which they are given.

1. AMERICAN ECONOMIC HISTORY, Economics 2. College credit, 3 hrs. *Adjunct Professor Bryan.*

2. COMMERCIAL LAW, Commerce 20. College credit, 3 hrs. *Professor Heckman.*

3. ECONOMICS, Introductory Course, Economics 5. College credit, 3 hrs. *Adjunct Professor Bryan.*

4. EDUCATION 1, 2, 3, History of Education. College credit, 3 hrs. *Adjunct Professor Brumby.*

5. EDUCATION 4, 5, 6, Educational Psychology. College credit, 3 hrs. *Professor Edwards.*

6. EDUCATION 7, 8, 9, Educational Philosophy — Sociology. College credit, 3 hrs. *Professor Woofter.*

7. EDUCATION 10, 11, 12, Principles of Teaching and Management. College credit, 3 hrs. *Professor Pusey.*

8. EDUCATION 19, Hygiene and Education. College credit, 1 hr. *Professor Edwards.*

9. EDUCATION 40, 41, Rural Education. College credit, 2 hrs. *Professor Woofter.*

10. EDUCATION 50, 51, 52. College credit, 3 hrs. *Professor Pusey.*

11. ELEMENTARY ACCOUNTING, Commerce 6. College credit 3 hrs. *Adjunct Professor Smith.*

12. ENGLISH 1, Rhetoric and Composition. College credit, 3 hrs. *Professor Park.*

13. ENGLISH 2, English Literature. College credit, 3 hrs. *Professor Park.*

14. ENGLISH 11, Shakespeare. College credit, 3 hrs. *Professor Walker.*

15. HISTORY 2, Modern Europe (Beginning Course). College credit, 3 hours. *Professor Coulter.*

16. HISTORY 4, History of England. College credit, 3 hrs. *Professor Payne.*

17. HISTORY 5-6, American History. College credit, 3 hrs. *Professor McPherson.*

18. HISTORY 8-9, Modern Europe. College credit, 3 hrs. *Professor Payne.*

19. HISTORY 14b, Teaching History in High School. College credit, 1 hr. *Professor.*

20. HISTORY 44, Economic History of Modern Europe. College credit, 3 hrs. *Professor Payne.*

21. INDUSTRIAL & COMMERCIAL GEOGRAPHY, Economics 1. CollegeCredit, 3 hrs. *Professor Jenkins.*

22. JOURNALISM 1, Newspaper Reporting and Correspondence. College credit, 3 hrs. *Adjunct Professor Drewry.*

23. JOURNALISM 8, The magazine. College credit, 1 hr. *Adjunct Professor Drewry.*

24. LATIN, Prose Composition. College credit, 1 hr. *Professor Hooper.*

25. MATHEMATICS 1, Plane Trigonometry. College credit, 1 hr. *Adjunct Professor Cumming.*

26. MATHEMATICS 2, Analytical Geometry. College credit, 2 hrs. *Professor Barrow.*

27. MATHEMATICS 3, Calculus. College credit, 2 hrs. *Professor Barrow.*

28. MATHEMATICS 4, College Algebra. College credit, 1 hr. *Adjunct Professor Cumming.*

29. PHILOSOPHY 7, 8, Social Philosophy. College credit, 3 hrs. *Professor Hutchinson.*

30. PSYCHOLOGY 1, 2, 3, Introductory Psychology. College credit, 3 hrs. *Professor Edwards.*

31. SHORTHAND, Gregg System, Commerce 91. College credit, 2 hrs. *Adjunct Professor Broadhurst.*

32. SOCIOLOGY 9, Principles of Sociology. College credit, 3 hrs. *Professor Hutchinson.*

33. SOCIOLOGY 10, Modern Social Problems. College credit, 3 hrs. *Professor Hutchinson.*

Other courses in the several departments will be added from time to time as the demand justifies. Correspondence is invited concerning courses needed.

An effort is being made to organize courses that will supplement the Summer School work so that those students who do two hours of a three hour course in six weeks summer session may complete the remaining hour by correspondence. At present such courses are orgainzed in History C-8c-9c, Modern Europe; in Latin C-1c, Latin Prose Composition and in Sociology C-10c, Modern Social Problems.

Other such courses will be organized and announced during the summer session.

SPECIAL BULLETIN

A special Bulletin will soon be issued, presenting in detail the courses offered and the credits given for each course, and useful suggestions are made therein as to the selection of courses looking to the completion of the requirements for the several degrees offered by the University.

Those who are interested in the work offered by the department should correspond with Dr. Geo. A. Hutchinson, Director, Division of Home Study, Peabody Hall, Athens, Ga.

THE UNIVERSITY SUMMER SCHOOL

CALENDAR

Saturday, June 19th: Dormitories open. Faculty Meeting 5 P. M., at Memorial Hall.

Monday, June 21st: Registration 8:30 to 6:00.

Tuesday, June 22nd: Classes begin as scheduled.

June 28th to July 3rd: Woman's Club Institute.

July 12th to 16th: County and City Superintendents' Week.

July 19th to 23rd: Music Festival Week.

July 26th to 31st: Vocational Agricultural Teachers' Short Course Close of Six Weeks Term.

August 3rd to 15th: Boys' and Girls' Short Course.

August 21st: Closing of Nine Weeks Term.

SUMMER SCHOOL BOARD

CHARLES M. SNELLING, Dean of the University and Acting Chancellor.

JERE M. POUND, President State Normal School.

ANDREW M. SOULE, President Agricultural College.

THOMAS J. WOOFTER, Dean Peabody School of Education.

F. E. LAND, State School Superintendent.

ADMINISTRATIVE COUNCIL

CHAS. M. SNELLING   JERE M. POUND
ANDREW M. SOULE

JOSEPH S. STEWART, Director of Summer School.

THOMAS W. REED, Registrar and Treasurer.

H. I. REYNOLDS, Physician to the Summer School.

LUCILLE EPPS, Secretary to the Director.

GENERAL INFORMATION

The University Summer School was authorized by the General Assembly in 1903. It is an integral part of the University, the Agricultural College, and the State Normal and its courses coordinate with these as indicated in the outline of courses.

There will be two terms, one for six weeks and the other for nine weeks. They both begin on June 21st, the first ends on July 31st, and the longer term on August 21st.

The laboratories, libraries, gymnasiums, dormitories and other equipment of the three institutions are available during the summer.

Nearly every department offers courses in the summer, under-graduate and a number of graduate courses, equal in quality and valued in terms of the regular year.

LOCATION

Athens, a city of over 20,000 people, is situated in the Piedmont region of North Georgia. The climate is excellent. The University and Agricultural College are situated on one body of land of over 1,000 acres and the Normal School has about 50 acres. This give ample opportunity for walks, rides and picnics.

Excursion parties will be organized for the purpose of visiting points in and near Athens. Excursions will be run every other Saturday to Tallulah Falls, about fifty miles distant, and into the heart of the Blue Ridge Mountains at Franklin, N. C.

SPECIAL OPPORTUNITIES IN THE SUMMER SCHOOL

In addition to the regular undergraduate work in the three institutions opportunities are offered:

(1). Teachers who wish to advance in special lines of work, increase their professional skill or qualify in new subjects.

(2). Candidates for State certificate who need special courses in Education and other subjects.

(3). Those who wish to work towards a degree.

(4). Directors of physical training and coaches of athletics in the high schools and playground work.

(5). Supervisors and teachers of Music, Oratory, Vocational Home Economics and Agriculture and other special lines of work.

(6). County Superintendents who desire to study problems of Rural School Organization and Management.

(7). Principals of Elementary and High Schools who wish to acquaint themselves with recent progress in education or to study special problems.

(8). Pre-Law, Pre-Medical, and Pre-Dental students who wish to save time in preparation for these courses.

(9). Graduates of college who wish to specialize in some field of work and study for a Master's Degree.

(10). Members of P.-T. A. and Woman's Clubs and other Social workers who wish to better prepare for their duties.

(11). Properly recommended high school graduates who are about to enter upon regular University courses and who desire to broaden their preparation for University work.

(12). Students registered in the three institutions here or in other colleges who wish to shorten the time required for graduation by completion of work in the summer.

(13). Serious minded men and women in any occupation who wish to broaden their culture and use part of their vacation to secure it while enjoying the delightful associations among a student body of over 2,000.

REGISTRATION

The regular time for registration for both terms will be Monday, June 21st. All students of the Summer School should register on that day. Registration after June 30th for credit will not be permitted except by vote of the Council.

Registration may be grouped in the following classes:

(1). HIGH SCHOOL GRADUATES UNDER 20 YEARS OF AGE.

a. Those desiring entrance to freshman class should file their entrance certificates with Dr. W. D. Hooper, Chairman of the Entrance Committee.

b. If advanced credit is desired the official college record should be filed with Dr. L. L. Hendren, Chairman of Advanced Credit Committee.

(2). AUDITORS.

Any adult of good moral character is permitted to attend all the regular exercises of the Summer School as an auditor, by paying the registration fee. An auditor does not participate in recitations, does not take examinations and hence does not receive credit.

(3). STUDENTS OVER 20 YEARS OF AGE.

The Summer School does not attempt, in general, to make inquiry concerning the educational qualifications of applicants for admission who are over 20 years of age. In granting admission to these, the Summer School assumes that the applicant possesses the usual educational qualifications for college or normal work or in lieu of these, that he has maturity and special fitness which are likely to lead to success in the work to be undertaken. Entrance requirements must be satisfied before graduation, however.

(4). HIGH SCHOOL PUPILS NOT YET GRADUATED.

The Summer School has no preparatory department. Instruction is provided in certain letter courses, found elsewhere in this bulletin. These courses may be taken by pupils on the special recommendation of the high school principal. A blank form for the principal's use may be obtained from the Summer School office. Teachers who have not credit for their high school work may also register for these courses and validate their former work.

(5). GRADUATE STUDENTS.

Those desiring graduate work should correspond with Dean W. H. Bocock and as far as possible adjust their credits before the opening of the Summer School.

Often the matter of advanced credit may be more satisfactorily adjusted after study at the Summer School and the ability and attainment of the student has been determined by the department concerned. The applicant should collect, as far as possible, previous credits and be prepared to submit these during the summer to the Advanced Credit Committee. Where the applicant has already submitted and had approved his college credits by the state certification departments and is studying only to complete these requirements, the former credits need not be submitted here. Applicants are requested to write to the Director or the professor in whose department work is desired if additional information is needed.

FEES

A registration fee of $3.00 is charged every student on registering. A fee of $12.00 is charged for three credit hours or courses and $5.00 for each additional hour or course, with a maximum of $30.00 for seven hours in the nine weeks term. One physical training course will be allowed without extra charge. The fee for a graduate course is $15.00 for one minor or two half minors. There are special fees in the music department, in law and a few others, which will be indicated in connection with the course. Certain courses carry laboratory fees. All entertainments are free to Summer School students.

DORMITORIES

The effort has been made this year to increase the dormitory facilities to accommodate as many as may come and add to their pleasure and comfort.

STATE NORMAL SCHOOL. At the State Normal School five dormitories are available which will furnish superior accommodation for 550 women. These are Bradwell, Gilmer, Senior, Winnie Davis, and Miller Halls. One dormitory is reserved for men and wives. The charge is $32.50 for room and board for six weeks. Apply to Mr. A. Rhodes for reservation.

UNIVERSITY OF GEORGIA. At the University, Old College, New College, Candler Hall and John Milledge Dormitory will be available, which will accommodate 350 women. Room rent is $5.00 per person for six weeks and $2.00 for the last three weeks. Apply to T. W. Reed for reservation. Send reservation fee of $5.00, which pays rent. This is refunded, for cause, if desired before June 21st.

COLLEGE OF AGRICULTURE. Soule Hall at the College of Agriculture will accommodate 70 women. Room rent is $10.00 per student, two in a room. A room reservation fee of $5.00 to be refunded when the room is surrendered in good condition is required and should accompany application. Apply to Miss Mary Creswell for reservation.

CHAPTER HOUSES. A number of fraternity houses will be open for the six weeks term, some for men and some for women, accommodating 250 students. Room rent is $8.00 for the six weeks term.

Many prefer private homes or private board. Arrangements have been made to accommodate as many as desire to live in private homes. Apply to T. W. Reed.

Students should have their mail addressed to the dormitory in which they have made reservation.

Students occupying rooms in any of the dormitories should bring with them at least the following articles: *1 pillow, 2 pairs of pillow cases, 2 pairs of sheets, 2 counterpanes, half dozen towels.*

SELECTION OF DORMITORY

It is important that those making application for reservation of rooms keep in mind the fact that courses for primary and elementary work will be given at the State Normal School and all teachers who register for these primarily will find it convenient to room there. Likewise for home economics the Agricultural dormitory will be most convenient; for University courses select the University dormitories or chapter houses, though students may live at any of these places or in private homes and be accessible to their work. The street car company gives a dollar ticket good for seven days for as many trips per person as desired.

DINING HALLS

DENMARK HALL, at the University, can accommodate 350 women and men at $30.00 for six weeks; $45.00 for nine weeks; for one week, $6.00; for less than one week, 40 cents each meal. Students rooming in the University are expected to eat at Denmark Dining Hall.

THE AGRICULTURAL COLLEGE CAFETERIA can accommodate 150 men and women at $35.00 for six weeks, and a like rate per week for the nine weeks.

THE STATE NORMAL DINING HALL can accommodate 550 at $30.00 for six weeks.

Some of the CHAPTER HOUSES provide board as well as room. Table board may also be had in private homes, cafeterias, tea rooms, the hotel coffee shops, at from $5.00 to $7.00 a week. Many students live in private homes and eat at the college dining halls. The Summer School has no trouble finding accommodations for 2,000 students.

RAILROAD RATES

A round trip rate of a fare and a half has been granted by the railroads on the identification certificate plan. These certificates may be obtained from the Director and *must be presented to the ticket agent when ticket is purchased* or no reduction will be granted. The selling dates are June 19-28, inclusive, and July 3-5, 10-12, 17-18, 24-26, July 31-August 2, 7-9 and 14-16, final limit of all tickets to be validated by the regular ticket agents of the Athens terminal lines before return jouney is commenced. Round trip tickets will be sold from stations in Alabama, Georgia, Florida, South Carolina and Tennessee.

Send to Dr. J. S. Stewart, Director, Athens, Ga., for Summer School Bulletin and descriptive folders of special courses.

THE UNIVERSITY LIBRARY

LIBRARY STAFF

LOUISE HOLLINGSWORTH
SARAH BAILEY LAMAR
HAZEL PHILBRICK
STUDENT ASSISTANTS
CLARENCE S. FAIN
ROBERT H. FREEMAN
FLORENCE W. LESTER
CALLIE T. McWHIRTER
MAYBELLE STITH

The General Library was founded November 27, 1800, and is the oldest department of the University. The present building, a gift of George Foster Peabody, was completed in 1905. It contains 60,000 volumes, 85,000 pamphlets, as well as maps, manuscripts, archives, etc.

Within its limits it is a good modern working library, still the best for purposes of undergraduate instruction in Georgia. It contains many rareties, and has received notable gifts during past years.

The library is carefully classified, its contents are made readily available through modern card catalogues, periodical and special indexes and other guides.

Through the income of the Alumni Endowment Fund a selection of the best books published each year is purchased for the purposes of cultural and recreative reading.

LIBRARY HOURS

Week days, 9:00 A. M. to 6:00 P. M.; 7:00 to 10:00 P. M.
Sundays, 3:00 to 6:00 P. M.
Holidays, 3:00 to 6:00 P. M.
Vacations, 10:00 to 12:00 A. M., every other week day.

MEMORIAL HALL LIBRARY

In Memorial Hall a branch library has been installed and this library is in charge of Miss Annie Carlton, as librarian, who also has general charge of the first floor of that splendid building and such portions as are devoted to the entertainment of students and visitors.

UNIVERSITY HEALTH SERVICE AND CRAWFORD W. LONG INFIRMARY

HAROLD I. REYNOLDS, A.B., M.D., Physician to the University.
MISS LILLIAN WYNN, Resident Nurse.

The infirmary is situated on the Lumpkin street side of the campus. It originally consisted of a two room house. In 1914 two wards and several private rooms were added at the instance of Chancellor Barrow and with the aid of the Woman's Club of Athens. A physician and resident nurse were employed to take care of the sick students. Later operating rooms and offices were added so that now the University has a hospital for the care of its sick students. During the past year the building has been enlarged and new equipment added.

The function of the Health Service now includes vaccination against smallpox, which is required on entrance to the University, unless the prospective student has the scar of a successful vaccination; typhoid inoculation, which is elective; a complete physical examination upon entrance, with advice to the students and parent about any physical defect that may be found; and lectures on hygiene and sanitation. In addition an effort is made to keep up with the physical condition of the student during the entire period of his college life.

The annual fee is $5.00 which entitles the student to all of the above. This fee does not cover major surgery and consultations with specialist.

Whenever a student is seriously ill the parents are notified. If an operation is necessary the parents are consulted by telephone or telegraph by the Dean before any procedures are instituted.

During the Summer School and Boys' and Girls' Club meeting the Infirmary is open for the care of the sick. A nominal fee is charged.

THE UNIVERSITY ACCREDITING SYSTEM

In 1903 the University undertook, in a definite way through the Professor of Secondary Education, Dr. Stewart, the building up and accrediting of the High Schools of the State. The first list of accredited schools was issued in 1904-05. There were 7 four-year public schools and 4 four-year private academies, and 39 three-year high schools listed that year. There were graduated from the four-year public schools that year 54 boys and 40 girls, and from the three-year schools, 161 boys and 277 girls. There were 149 teachers in these fifty schools.

Gradually the number of accredited schools has increased until the University list for 1926 show 308 four-year schools.

The accredited system has grown in the confidence of the schools and colleges, until now it is accepted by all as a standard for the State.

In 1921, Chancellor Barrow increased the University Committee on Accrediting to Professors Stewart, Hooper, Fain from the University, and requested the College Association to appoint three members; the High School Association to add its Vice-President and Secretary and the State Department of Education to be represented by the State Supervisor of High Schools. The Commission of nine members is thoroughly representative of all the educational institutions concerned and assures proper consideration of applications.

The Commission for 1926-1927 consists of the following members:

J. S. STEWART, Chairman_____University of Georgia
W. D. HOOPER_____University of Georgia
J. R. FAIN_____State College of Agriculture
J. G. STIPE, Emory University_____College Association
PEYTON JACOBS, Mercer University_____College Association
H. H. CALDWELL, School of Technology_____College Association
J. E. PURKS, Vice-President_____High School Association
F. A. BRINSON, Secretary_____High School Association
E. A. POUND_____Department of Education

The Commission meets usually during the first week in April and passes upon the list of accredited schools for the current year, based upon the applications filed with the chairman, the reports of inspection by the two inspectors, and the records of students in the colleges.

Schools are not added to the list at any other time or except by vote and authority of the Commission.

Entrance by certificate from an accredited school now represents fully 90 per cent of the Freshmen in all of our colleges.

Correspondence relating to accrediting will be addressed, as in the past, to the Chairman and Inspector, Dr. Joseph S. Stewart, University Campus, Athens, Ga. The inspection of schools applying for the accredited list will be made by either Dr. Stewart or Supervisor Pound.

Correspondence relating to high schools in general and to State aided high schools, to teacher-training classes, to class A. B. and C. high schools and Junior high schools should be addressed to Mr. Pound, State Department of Education, Atlanta, Ga.

LIST OF ACCREDITED HIGH SCHOOLS, 1926

NOTE:—A * before the name of the school indicates that it has won a place on the Southern List of Accredited Schools as well as in Group I of the Georgia list. A † before the name of a school indicates that it was placed on the list for the first time this year. A figure (1) after certain schools indicates that they have been warned on account of certain deficiencies of their graduates in Freshman collegiate records. Group I represents the best schools in teaching staff, equipment of laboratory, library, and building, and those that have three-fourths of the academic teachers holding degrees. Group II represents those schools that have inadequate equipmnt in laboratory, library, or that do not have three-fourths of the teachers college graduates, but offer 16 units. Only four-year schools are accredited.

Abbeville High School, I—Supt. L. M. Wilson.
Acworth High School, I—Supt. L. D. Singleton.
Adairsville High School, II—Supt. C. G. Metts.
Adel High School, I—Supt. D. F. Bruton.
Alamo: Wheeler County High School, II—Supt. J. M. Harvey.
Alpharetta: Milton County High School, II—Supt. R. M. Donehoo.
*Albany High School, I—Prin. J. O. Allen.
Americus
  *High School, I—Prin. C. M. Hale.
  3rd District A. & M. School, I—Prin. J. M. Prance.
Arlington High School, II—Supt. D. H. Wood.
*Ashburn High School, I—Supt. Geo. S. Roach.
Athens:
  *High School, I—Prin. E. B. Mell.
  *Lucy Cobb Academy (Private), I—Miss M. L. Rutherford.
  †State Normal School Academy, I—Supt. Kate E. Hicks.
Atlanta:
  *Boys' High School, I—Prin. H. O. Smith.

*Commercial High School, I—Prin. W. C. Lowe.
*Fulton High School, I—Prin. W. F. Dykes.
*Girls' High School, I—Miss Jessie Muse.
*Marist College (1), (Private), I—Rev. D. S. Rankin.
Mozley School for Girls, (Private), II—Mrs. J. W. Mozley.
*North Ave. Presbyterian, (Private), I—Miss Thyrza S. Askew.
†Peacock School, II—Prin. J. H. Peacock.
Sacred Heart, (Private), I—Sr. M. Carmelita.
*Technological High School, (1), I—Prin. W. O. Cheney.
*University School, (1), (Private), II—Pres. R. K. White.
*Washington Seminary, (Private), I—Prin. L. D. & E. B. Scott.
Woodberry Hall, (Private), I—Miss Rosa Woodberry.
†Attapulgus High School, II—Supt. H. G. Guffey.
Augusta:
    Catholic High School, II—Prin. W. A. Murphy.
    *Richmond Academy, I—Prin. Geo. P. Butler.
    Mount St. Joseph, (Private), I—Sr. Rose de Lima.
    *Tubman High School, I—Prin. T. H. Garrett.
*Bainbridge High School, I—Supt. E. G. Elcan.
Baldwin High School, II—Supt. C. S. Hubbard.
Barnesville:
    *Gordon Institute, I—Pres. L. D. Watson, Jr.
    6th District A. & M. School, I—Prin. T. O. Galloway.
Bartow High School, I—Supt. C. E. Anthony.
Barwick High School, II—Supt. J. W. Adams.
Baxley High School, I—Supt. C. V. Brown.
*Blackshear High School, I—Supt. E. D. Whisonant.
Blairsville High School, II—Supt. W. P. Lunsford.
Blakely High School, I—Supt. J. L. Graham.
*Blythe High School, I—Supt. J. H. Morrison.
Blue Ridge: Willingham Ind. Sch., (Pri.), II—Pres. A. B. Greene.
Boston High School, II—Supt. A. H. Stephens.
Bowman High School, II—Supt. D. D. Still.
Braselton High School, II—Supt. T. C. Llewellyn.
†Bremen High School, II—Supt. J. G. Colbert.
†Brinson Consolidated School, II—Supt. I. W. Hughes.
Brooklet High School, II—Prin. J. W. Davis.
*Brunswick: Glynn County Academy, I—Supt. R. D. Eadie.
Buchanan High School, I—Supt. H. L. Lawson.
Buford High School, I—Supt. W. M. Nunn.
Buena Vista High School, I—Supt. Chas. E. Lawrence.
Butler High School, II—Supt. A. E. Shearer.
Byromville High School, II—Prin. C. J. Gearin.
†Byron Consolidated School, II—Supt. N. W. Hurst.

*Cairo High School, I—Supt. O. H. Hixon.
*Calhoun High School, I—Supt. M. C. Allen.
Camilla High School, I—Supt. Eugene Attaway.
*Canton High School, I—Supt. J. P. Cash.
Carrollton:
    High School, I—Supt. Knox Walker.
    4th District A. & M. School, I—Prin. I. S. Ingram.
*Cartersville High School, I—Supt. W. E. Dendy.
Carnesville: Franklin County High School, I—Supt. R. H. Moss.
Cave Spring High School, I—Supt. O. A. Strange.
*Cedartown High School, I—Supt. J. E. Purks.
Chamblee High School, I—Supt. M. E. Smith.
†Chatsworth High School, II—Supt. W. H. Padgett.
†Chauncey High School, II—Supt. O. C. Kibler.
Chickamauga High School, II—Supt. W. M. Patterson.
Chipley High School, I—Supt. R. B. Madre.
Clarkesville: 9th District A. &M. School, I—Prin. W. A. Hatfield.
Claxton High School, I—Supt. H. J. W. Kizer.
Clayton: Rabun County High School, II—Supt. R. C. David.
Clermont: Chattahoochee High School, (Private), II—Supt. W. L.
    Walker.
Cochran:
    *High School, I—Supt. T. M. Purcell.
    12th District A. & M. School, I—Prin. F. M. Greene.
College Park:
    High School, I—Supt. C. R. Brown.
    *Georgia Military Academy, (1), (Private), I—Col. J. C. Wood-
    ward.
†Collins High School, II—Prin. O. F. Helm.
†Colquitt High School, II—Supt. W. H. Drake.
Columbus:
    *High School, I—Prin. T. C. Kendrick.
    Industrial Hall, I—Prin. F. P. Bradford.
Comer High School, II—Supt. O. G. Lancaster.
*Commerce High School, I—Supt. W. H. Martin.
Concord High School, II—Supt. J. M. Cook.
*Conyers High School, I—Supt. R. H. Foy.
*Cordele High School, I—Supt. D. H. Standard.
Cornelia High School, I—Supt. N. V. Dyer.
*Covington High School, I—Supt. A. W. Baldwin.
Crawford High School, II—Supt. L. P. Green.
Crawfordville: Alexander Stephens Inst., I—Supt. J. D. Nash.
Cumming High School, II—Supt. C. H. King.
*Cuthbert High School, I—Prin. R. G. Hall.

Dallas High School, I—Supt. W. C. Sams.
*Dalton High School, I—Supt. U. J. Bennett.
Danielsville: Madison County High School, II—Supt. L. E. Hemrick.
Darien High School, II—Supt. W. A. Branson.
†Davisboro High School, II—Supt. G. F. Tyner.
*Dawson High School, I—Supt. W. E. Monts.
*Decatur High School, I—Supt. G. W. Glausier.
Demorest: Piedmont College Inst., I—Prin. B. H. Crockett.
Doerun High School, II—Supt. J. C. Moore.
Donalsonville High School, I—Supt. W. T. Burt.
Douglas:
    High School, I—Supt. J. T. Henry.
    11th District A. & M. School, I—Prin. J. M. Thrash.
Douglasville High School, I—Supt. E. P. Ennis.
*Dublin High School, I—Supt. H. B. Carreker.
East Point: William A. Russell High School, I—Supt. J. T. McGee.
*Eastman High School, I—Prin. Z. S. Henderson.
Eatonton High School, I—Supt. B. E. Flowers.
Edison High School, II—Supt. B. Rumble.
*Elberton High School, I—Supt. R. M. Grier.
†Eastanollee Vocational High School, II—Supt. M. E. Brand.
Ellaville High School, II—Supt. J. A. Lowry.
Ellijay: Gilmer County High School, II—Supt. R. H. Panter.
Epworth Seminary, (Private), I—Prin. W. H. Patton.
†Fairburn High School, II—Supt. E. W. Martin.
†Fairmount High School, II—Supt. C. M. Copeland.
Fayetteville: Fayette County High School, I—Supt. C. W. Peacock.
*Fitzgerald High School, I—Supt. G. E. Usher.
Folkston: Charlton County High School, II—Supt. John Harris.
Forsyth High School, I—Supt. J. H. Riser.
Fort Gaines High School, II—Supt. W. P. Aiken.
*Ft. Valley High School, I—Supt. J. F. Lambert.
Franklin: Heard County High School, II—Supt. M. E. Howell.
Gainesville:
    *High School, I—Supt. W. P. Martin.
    *Riverside Academy, (1), (Private), I—Pres. Sandy Beaver.
Gibson High School, II—Supt. A. A. O'Kelley.
Glennville High School, II—Supt. F. W. Elarbee.
Gordon High School, I—Supt. H. R. Bowles.
Gore High School, II—Supt. W. M. Putney.
Granite Hill: 10th District A. & M. School, I—Supt. Luther Elrod.
Grantville High School, II—Supt. Young Evans.
Gray High School, I—Supt. Merritt B. Pound.

*Greensboro High School, I—Supt. C. C. Wills.
Greenville High School, II—Supt. J. A. Pendergrast.
*Griffin High School, I—Supt. L. M. Lester.
Guyton High School, II—Supt. J. W. Jones.
†Hahira High School, II—Supt. G. W. Dickinson.
†Hamilton High School, II—Supt. J. B. Munn.
Hampton High School, II—Supt. E. E. Treadwell.
Harlem High School, II—Supt. W. F. Tribble.
*Hartwell High School, I—Supt. J. I. Allman.
*Hawkinsville High School, I—Supt. T. A. Clower, Jr.
Hazelhurst High School, II—Supt. Geo. W. Hulme.
Hephzibah High School, I—Prin. W. G. Robertson.
Hiawassee Academy, II—Supt. H. E. Nelson.
†Hinesville High School, II—Supt. H. A. Bacon.
Hogansville High School, I—Supt. M. V. Braddy.
†Homerville High School, II—Supt. C. M. Williams.
†Ila High School—Mrs. Edythe W. Marion.
Jackson High School, I—Supt. R. I. Knox.
Jefferson: Martin Institute, II—Supt. W. T. Foster.
Jeffersonville: Twiggs County High School, II—Supt. O. W. Johnson.
Jesup: Wayne County High School, II—Supt. C. C. Garris.
Jonesboro High School, II—Supt. A. D. Kean.
†Kingsland High School, II—Supt. W. S. Miley.
†Kite High School, II—Supt. W. T. Chambless.
LaFayette High School, I—Supt. Carl Motsinger.
*LaGrange High School, I—Supt. F. F. Rowe.
Lakeland: Lanier County High School, II—Supt. J. A. Hancock.
*Lavonia High School, I—Miss Mabel Woodward.
Lawrenceville High School, I—Supt. C. O. Stubbs.
Leesburg High School, II—Supt. V. P. Folds.
Leslie: Union High School, II—Supt. W. L. Lamb.
Lexington: Meson Academy, II—Supt. W. A. Haley.
Lincolnton High School, I—Supt. Chas. V. Parham.
Lithonia High School, II—Supt. D. V. Spencer.
*Locust Grove Institute, (Private), I—Supt. Claude Gray.
Loganville High School, II—Supt. J. R. Garrett.
Louisville Academy High School, I—Supt. D. Donaldson.
Lumpkin High School, II—Supt. R. H. Comer.
Lyons Consolidated High School, I—Supt. B. H. Johnson.
Macon
  *Lanier High School for Girls, I—Prin. Walter P. Jones.
  *Lanier High School for Boys, I—Prin. Walter P. Jones.
  Rutland High School, II—Prin. W. H. Sorrells.

Madison:
    *High School, I—Supt. J. H. Purks.
    8th District A. & M. School, I—Prin. B. F. Gay.
Manchester High School, I—Supt. H. R. McLarty.
*Marietta High School, I—Supt. C. A. Keith.
Marshallville High School, I—Supt. E. A. Wight.
Maysville High School, II—Supt. J. B. Brookshire.
McDonough High School, I—Supt. R. O. Powell.
McRae: Acad. of So. Ga. College, (1), I—Supt. Ralph W. Wood.
†Meigs High School, II—Supt. Thomas P. Kimble.
†Menlo High School, II—Supt. J. C. Flanigan.
*Metter High School, I—Supt. R. P. Ford.
Midville High School, I—Supt. J. H. P. Thomas.
Milledgeville:
    *Georgia Military College, (1), I—Supt. E. T. Holmes.
Millen High School, I—Supt. F. A. Brinson.
†Molena High School, II—Supt. I. B. Evans.
*Monroe High School, I—Supt. C. W. Reid.
Montezuma High School, II—Supt. W. E. Queener.
Monticello High School, I—Supt. R. H. Harris.
†Morgan High School, II—Supt. W. S. Banks.
†Morgantown: Fannin County High School—Supt. F. S. Cantrell.
†Morven High School, II—Supt. Sankey Booth.
*Moultrie High School, I—Supt. J. L. Yaden.
*Mount Berry: The Berry Schools, (Private), I—Prin. G. Leland
    Green.
*Mount Vernon: Brewton-Parker Institute, (Private), I—Supt. A.
    M. Gates.
Mount Zion Seminary, (Private), I—Supt. H. N. Howard.
Nashville High School, I—Supt. W. J. Chisholm.
Nelson High School, II—Supt. Clyde M. Carpenter.
*Newnan High School, I—Supt. B. F. Pickett.
Norcross High School, I—Supt. W. H. Maxwell.
*Norman Park Institute, (Private), I—Supt. Leo H. Browning.
†Oakwood High School, II—Supt. L. C. Westbrook.
†Ochlochnee Consolidated School, II—Supt. J. G. Garrison.
Ocilla High School, I—Supt. E. V. Whelchel.
*Oxford: Emory University Academy, (Private), I—Prin. A. W.
    Reese.
Pavo High School, I—Supt. L. R. Towson.
Pearson High School, II—Prin. M. Kirby.
Pelham High School, I—Supt. T. H. Wilkinson.
Pembroke: Bryan County High School, I—Supt. E. N. Smith.
Perry High School, I—Supt. J. M. Gooden.

†Pinehurst High School, II—Supt. W. B. Cornelius.

Plains High School, II—Supt. E. L. Bridges.

Powder Springs: 7th District A. & M. School, I—Prin. D. D. Scarborough.

*Quitman High School, I—Supt. H. D. Knowles.

†Register High School, II—Supt. Frank P. Lee.

Reidsville High School, I—Supt. J. W. Tanner.

Reynolds High School, I—Supt. E. H. Joiner.

Richland High School, I—Supt. Bailey Phillips.

Roberta High School, I—Supt. C. E. Bryson.

Rochelle High School, II—Supt. A. C. Fraseur.

Rockmart High School, II—Supt. T. E. Ford.

Rome:

    *High School, I—Supt. B. F. Quigg.

    *Darlington School, (Private), I—Pres. C. R. Wilcox.

Royston High School, I—Supt. H. K. Adams.

†Sale City High School, II—Supt. W. H. Coleman.

Sandersville High School, I—Supt. W. F. Gunn.

Sautee: Nacoochee Institute, (Private), II—Rev. J. K. Coit.

Savannah:

    *Senior High School, I—Prin. M. M. Phillips.

    *Benedictine School, (1), (Private), I—Rev. Raphael Arthur.

    *Pape School, (Private), I—Miss Nina Pape.

    St. Vincent's Academy, (Private), II—Mother M. Clare.

Senoia High School, II—Supt. J. Wesley May.

Sharpsburg: Starr High School, II—Prin. R. A. Moore.

Shellman High School, II—Supt. W. Rumble.

Smithville High School, II—Supt. J. H. Forbis.

†Snellville Consolidated (Grayson Ga., R. 1), II—Supt. W. C. Britt.

Social Circle High School, II—Supt. W. T. Knox.

Soperton High School, II—Supt. W. D. Reid.

Sparks College Academy, (Private), I—Pres. M. S. Hale.

Sparta High School, II—Supt. C. C. Chalker.

Springfield: Effingham Academy, II—Supt. W. R. Koon.

Springplace: Lucy Hill Cons. H. S., II—Prin. W. F. Huffaker.

Stapleton High School, I—Supt. C. O. Lam.

Statesboro High School, I—Supt. R. M. Monts.

Statham High School, II—Supt. J. W. Williams.

Stillmore High School, II—Supt. A. W. Strozier.

†Stone Mountain High School, II—Prin. L. F. Herring.

Summerville High School, I—Supt. R. G. Vinson.

*Summit: Emanuel County High School, I—Supt. Ernest Anderson.

Swainsboro High School, I—Supt. Thomas B. Conner.

†Sycamore High School, II—Supt. J. W. Smith.

Sylvania High School, II—Supt. W. B. Lovett.
Sylvester High School, I—Supt. John Boswell.
†Talbotton Consolidated School, II—Supt. Thos. J. Barrett.
Tallapoosa High School, I—Supt. D. W. Windsor.
Tate High School, II—Supt. R. W. Ransom.
Tennille High School, I—Supt. W. M. Parker.
Thomasville:
    *High School, I—Prin. H. R. Mahler.
    Plunkett School, (Private), I—Supt. F. R. Plunkett.
Thomson High School, II—Supt. E. D. Gunby.
*Thomaston: R. E. Lee Institute, I—Supt. Mark A. Smith.
Tifton:
    *High School, I—Supt. J. C. Sirmons.
    South Georgia A. & M. College—Pres. S. L. Lewis.
Tignall High School, II—Supt. S. V. Savage.
*Toccoa High School, I—Supt. A. M. Stephens.
*Valdosta High School, I—Supt. A. G. Cleveland.
Vidalia High School, I—Supt. W. L. Downs.
Vienna High School, I—Supt. J. H. Jenkins.
Villa Rica High School, I—Supt. G. H. Coleman.
Wadley High School, I—Supt. T. A. Stanton.
Waleska: Reinhardt College Acad., (Pri.), I—Supt. R. C. Sharp.
Walker Park: 5th District A. & M. School, I—Prin. J. H. Walker.
Warrenton High School, I—Supt. M. H. Dillard.
†Warwick High School, II—Supt. H. B. Franklin.
*Washington High School, I—Supt. M. O. McCord.
Watkinsville High School, II—Supt. W. M. Avera.
Waverly Hall High School, II—Supt. J. O. J. Taylor.
*Washington High School, I—Supt. M. O. McCord.
Watkinsville High School, II—Supt. W. M. Avera.
Weverly Hall High School, II—Supt. J. O. J. Taylor.
Waycross:
    *High School, (1), I—Prin. W. D. Miller.
    Piedmont Institute, (Private), I—Supt. W. C. Carlton.
    Wacona High School, R. 1, I—Supt. A. V. Folsom.
*Waynesboro High School, I—Supt. Jack Lance.
*West Point High School, I—Supt. W. P. Thomas.
*Winder High School, I—Supt. W. W. Stancil.
Winterville High School, I—Prin. T. N. Gaines.
Woodbury: Meriwether County High School, I—Supt. H. R. Adams.
Wrens High School, I—Supt. C. C. McCollum.
Wrightsville High School, II—Supt. W. M. Pettis.
Young Harris Academy, (Private), I—Supt. J. A. Sharp.
Zebulon High School, I—Supt. A. J. Hargrove.

NEGRO SCHOOLS

Albany: Georgia Normal & Industrial School, I—Supt. J. W. Holley.

Athens:

High & Industrial School, I—Prin. S. F. Harris.

Knox Institute & Industrial School, (Private), I—Prin. L. S. Clark.

Atlanta:

Atlanta University Academy, (Private), I—Pres. M. W. Adams.

Morehouse High School, (Private), I—Pres. John D. Hope.

Morris Brown University Academy, (Private), I—Pres. J. H. Lewis.

Spellman College High School, (Private), I—Dean Edna E. Lamson.

Augusta: Paine College Academy, (Private), I—Prin. John E. Cade.

Brunswick: *Selden Normal & Industrial Institute, (Private), II— Prin. S. Q. Mitchell.

Forsyth: A. & M. State School, I—Supt. Wm. M. Hubbard.

Macon: Ballard Normal College, (Private), I—Prin. R. G. von Tobel.

Thomasville: Allen Normal & Industrial School, (Private), II—Prin. Mary L. Marden.

Part VI
UNIVERSITY PUBLICATIONS AND SOCIETIES

Literary Societies

The Demosthenian Society was founded in 1801, and the Phi Kappa Society in 1820. The members of the societies meet in their respectiv halls every Wednesday evening at 8 o'clock.

On the evening of February 21st these Societies celebrate together, with public exercises, the anniversary of their founding.

Under the auspices of the Literary Societies intercollegiate debates are held annually.

A Champion Debate between the two literary societies is held some time during May.

Engineering Society

The Engineering Society was organized in 1889. Its object is to create an interest among the students in matters pertaining to civil, electrical, and architectural engineering, and recent development along all lines of scientific research. The society holds fortnightly meetings during the session, at which papers are read and lectures delivered. The society publishes in June "The Engineering Annual."

The Agricultural Club

The young men of the Georgia State College of Agriculture have an organization known as the "Agricultural Club." It meets once each week and the meetings are attended by large numbers of students. Debates are held regularly on subjects of popular and scientific interest and papers are delivered on special subjects of importance to the farming interests of Georgia.

The club publishes the 'Georgia Agriculturist" for distribution to the students, faculty, alumni, and to farmers and business organizations. All of the contributions to the magazine are furnished by the students and they manage its business affairs under the direction of the faculty. The "Agriculturist" furnishes an excellent medium for literary training in writing and editing agricultural material.

The Economics Society

The students of the School are brought together for association and improvement in the Economics Society. The purpose of this organization is two-fold: First, its object is to discuss and study current economic and business problems; and second, to invite men of experience along various lines of business endeavor to speak to the students. This society is not in lieu of the old literary societies but in addition to them.

Jeffersonian Law Debating Society

The law students conduct a successful and beneficial society, which meets once a week, and they debate questions of law. All students of the Lumpkin Law School are eligible to membership in the society.

Henry W. Grady Speaking Club

The law students organized this club and its purpose is to interest its members in the art of public speaking.

The Forestry Club

The Forestry Club is an organization of students interested in forestry, and related subjects. Meetings are held every two weeks in which subjects of interest in forestry are discussed.

The Veterinary Club

The Veterinary Club, which was organized in 1920, is open to students in Veterinary Medicine. Regular meetings are held to discuss problems in Veterinary Science.

The Saddle and Sirloin Club

The Saddle and Sirloin Club was organized in 1919 by the students in Animal Husbandry. This club meets regularly every week in which stock judging, fitting stock for the show ring, and like subjects are discussed. The club holds a contest in fitting livestock for the show ring at the College each year which is very interesting as well as instructive.

The Pioneer Club

Early in the fall in 1919 the Pioneer Club was organized for promoting the welfare of the women at the University, encouraging higher scholarship, and promoting those activities which contribute to the general welfare of the institution. The club was admitted into the Georgia Federation of Women's Club in the spring of 1920.

The Homecon Club

All students majoring in home economics automatically become members of the Homecon Club when registering at the University. This club meets bi-monthly and presents interesting and instructive programs.

The members of the club have the privilege of writing for the home economics section of the Agricultural Quarterly and training in writing and editing home economics material is received in this way.

Alpha Mu

Alpha Mu is the honorary sorority to which students of home economics are eligible for election on a basis of scholarship and student activities.

The Horticultural Club

The Horticultural Club is composed of students interested in the advancement of horticultural science. Prizes are offered each year for essays on horticultural subjects. Regular monthly meetings and one special meeting in which an outside speaker of prominence is brought in are held.

The Poultry Club

The students interested in poultry are organized into a club known as "The Georgia Poultry Scientists." Meetings are held monthly at which topics of interest to the poultry industry are discussed.

The Education Club

The Education Club is an organization composed of students interested in Agricultural Education and the training of High School Teachers of Agriculture. Meetings are held semi-monthly.

The University Y. M. C. A.

The College Young Men's Christian Association holds weekly meetings which are addressed by local or visiting ministers, or by members of the Faculty; prayer-meetings are also held daily.

The Association has its own secretary, whose time is devoted to this work. Attractive reading rooms, containing the current periodicals, are open to all students. The Association also conducts an employment bureau and is of service in arranging boarding places for new students. At the opening of each session, a mass meeting which is largely attended, is held under its auspices.

University Y. W. C. A.

The first organization started for women upon their entrance into University life was the Y. W. C. A., and no organization has served to enrich the lives of the young women students on the whole, as much as this organization. It is primarily a religious organization, but the fact has not been forgotten that development mentally, physically, socially as well as spiritually should be thought of in this organization and any activity that will promote higher and better Christian living among the students has been fostered. Vesper services are held each evening at sunset. Bible study classes meet weekly, and social and athletic meetings are held from time to time.

The Athletic Association

The Athletic Association is a student organization for the encouragement of all athletic sports. Football, baseball, basketball, tennis and track teams are regularly organized. Each student on entering the University is required to pay eleven dollars as an athletic fee, which entitles the student to membership in the Athletic Association, general admission to all athletic contests on Sanford Field, and the Red and Black, the official organ of the Athletic Association. Subject to the direction of the Faculty Chairman of Atheltics, acting as representative of the Chancellor and Faculty, the management of the athletic activities of the University is delegated to the Athletic Association and to the Board of Directors.

Other Student Organizations

Other student organizations are the Sphinx, the Gridiron Club, the Senior Round Table, the Junior Cabinet, the Buccaneers, the Senate, the Thalian Dramatic Club, the Glee and Mandolin Club, the Barristers, the Counsellors, the Cosmopolitan, the Square and Compass, the Sine and Tangent, the Chi Delta Phi, the Aghon, the Zodiac, and the American Legion.

The Debating Council

All work in public speaking and debate is in the hands of the Debating Council. The Council is composed of six men—three chosen from each of the two Literary Societies. The Council operates under the supervision of the Department of English.

PUBLICATIONS OF THE UNIVERSITY

Bulletin of the University of Georgia. Under this general title the University issues a monthly publication, which is sent to regular mailing lists or may be had upon application to the University.

This includes the Register, the General Catalogue of the University system, announcements of the Summer Session, the Lumpkin Law School, the School of Pharmacy, the Graduate School, the Alumni Number, the Catalogue of Trustees, Officers and Alumni, and several numbers of scientific and literary nature.

University Items, a news letter, issued monthly during the session.

The Alumni Record, issued monthly by the Alumni Society.

From the College of Agriculture are issued:

Bulletins of Farmers' Institutes, President Soule, Editor.

Bulletins of the Experiment Station, Director H. P. Stuckey, Editor, Experiment, Ga.

Bulletins of the College of Agriculture.

The publications conducted by the students include:

The Red and Black, a weekly now in its thirtieth volume, the organ of the Athletic Association.

The Georgia Cracker, a monthly literary magazine.

The University Handbooks, issued by Y. M. C. A. and Y. W. C. A.

The Engineering Annual, now in its twenty-fourth volume, issued by the Engineering Society.

The Georgia Agriculturist, published quarterly by the Agricultural Club.

The High School Quarterly, published by Dr. J. S. Stewart, Professor of Secondary Education in the interest of High School Development.

National Honorary Societies

In addition to the various local honorary societies, the following National Societies have Chapters in the University:

The Phi Beta Kappa Society, founded in 1776. Students in the Bachelor of Arts Course, the Bachelor of Science (General) Course, the Bachelor of Arts in Journalism Course, the Bachelor of Arts in Social Science Course, and the Bachelor of Arts in Education Course are eligible for membership. Not more than one-fifth of the graduates in these courses may be selected in any one year. The choice is made on the basis of high scholarship, character, and promise of future success in scholarly pursuits.

The Society of Phi Kappa Phi, founded in 1897, is open to honor students of all departments of the University. The University of Georgia Chapter was established in 1923, and permits the election of not more than one-sixth of the graduating class. The prime object of the Society is "to emprasize scholarship and character in the thought of college students, to hold fast to the original purpose for which institutions of learning were founded, and to stimulate mental achievement by the prize of membership."

Beta Gamma Sigma, founded in 1913 for the purpose of encouraging and rewarding scholarship and accomplishment among students in schools of business administration in American colleges and universities. The Alpha Chapter of Georgia was established May 15, 1918, only students in the School of Commerce being eligible for membership. The qualifications for membership are good moral character, high scholarship, and promise of marked business ability.

Alpha Zeta, established in 1915. for the promotion of scholarship in agricultural colleges. The qualifications for membership are high scholarship and excellence in college activities.

Scabbard and Blade, founded in 1904, and established in the University in 1920 "to unite in closer relationship the Military Departments of American Universities and Colleges, to preserve and develop the essential qualities of good and efficient officers, and to spread intelligent information concerning the military requirements of our country."

Part VII
General Regulations, Financial Obligations and Dormitories

DISCIPLINE AND GENERAL REGULATIONS

· The discipline of the Colleges of Athens is in the hands of the Chancellor of the University, who in its administration may ask advice of the Faculty. The honor system prevails and formal regulations are few and general in character.

The State of Georgia extends the privileges of the University to all persons who are qualified for admission. Thus the University does not receive patronage, but is itself the patron of those who seek its privileges and honors. It is maintained at public expense for the public good. It cannot, however, be the patron of inefficiency, idleness, or dissipation. Its classes have no room except for those who diligently pursue the studies of their choice and are willing to be governed in their conduct by the rules of propriety. Every student owes to the public a full equivalent of expenditures in his behalf, both while in the institution and afterwards.

The Registrar's books will be open Monday, September 15th, and the following rule has been passed by the Board of Trustees relative to registration:

All students registering after Saturday noon following the Wednesday on which the University opens shall pay an extra registration fee of $3.00, unless excused from the payment of the same by the Chancellor.

The annual session of the University is divided into three terms, as follows:

First Term—From the opening in September to the beginning of the Christmas vacation.

Second Term—Beginning at the close of the Christmas vacation and extending to and including the third Saturday in March.

Third Term—Beginning at the close of the second term and extending to and including the Friday before Commencement Day.

EXAMINATIONS

At the end of and within each term a sufficient number of days is set apart for term examinations; two examinations, of not more than three hours duration each, being given on each day, and the examinations for the Senior classes at the end of the third term conclude on the Wednesday preceding Commencement Day.

The term examinations of any session will be open to students who may have failed in the examinations of preceding sessions.

No other examinations (except the regular entrance examinations) will be authorized by the Faculty or held by the officers of instruction, it being understood that this regulation does not forbid written tests within the regular class hour, provided the preparation for such written tests does not involve neglect of other duty.

ADVANCED CREDITS

I. Work done at the University.

(a) By students who have no conditions and who register for the regular number of credit hours prescribed for the year and degree for which they qualify. Credit for such work shall be recorded by the Registrar from the reports of the professors.

(b) By students who are registered for less than the regular number of hours for the year and degree for which they qualify. Credit for such work shall be recorded by the Registrar from reports from the professors only when he is authorized by the Dean to do so. The Dean shall furnish the Registrar with a list of all students who are permitted to register for less than the regular number of hours.

(c) By students who are scheduled for more than the regular number of hours prescribed. Credit for such work, in excess of the regular number of hours, shall be recorded by the Registrar only upon authorization of the Committees on Extra Studies to do so. The Committee on Extra Studies shall furnish the Registrar and the Dean with a list of all students who have been granted permission to schedule extra hours, the number of hours granted, and a schedule of the subjects in which credits may be recorded.

(d) By students who have one or more conditions.

On registration, a student with conditions in an entire course or in part of a course shall be required to register first for these conditioned courses unless given special permission by the Dean to do otherwise, and shall not be permitted to register in excess of the rgular number of hours except by permission of the Committee of Extra Studies. (By "condition" is understood a required subject for a previous year for which the student did not register, or any required subject for which the student was registered and in which he received a grade of less than 60. When a student has more than the number of conditional passes or grade between 60 and 70 allowed under the rules, he shall be required to register for and take over such courses or parts of courses as may be in excess of the number of conditional passes allowed. In the case of students entering with advanced standing a condition may also mean that only a part of the work was done before entering the University.

(1) In case the student attends classes to remove the condition recording the grade shall be governed by rules (a) and (c).

(2) In case the professor agrees that the condition may be removed by work not requiring class attendance or by a limited attendance at class, a statement as to the circumstances of this agreement shall be

filed immediately by the professor with the Registrar who shall make the proper records on his books and transmit a copy of the agreement to the Extra Studies Committee or the Advanced Credit Committee as he case may require.

The Registrar shall not record credits from the reports of professors for any work for which the student is not registered, nor for any work for which he is registered and is excused from the class attendance by the professor without first referring such cases to the Advanced Credit Committee or to the Committee on Extra Studies.

II. Work done at other institutions.

(a) Courses completed at other institutions giving at least two years of college work in advance of the fourth year of high school and whose certificates are acceptable to the departments and to the Advanced Credit Committee. Credit for such work shall be recorded only on reports made by the Advanced Credits Committee to the Registrar.

(b) Courses completed at other institutions giving at least two years of college work in advance of the fourth year of high school but whose certificates are not acceptable. Credit for these courses is to be given only on certificate of examination by the professor of the subject to the Advanced Credit Committee or on a certificate of satisfactory work completed in residence in an advanced course in the same subject. Credit shall be recorded only on reports made as in (a).

(c) Courses completed at institutions offering only one year of work in advance of the fourth year of high school and whose certificates cannot be acepted on account of the action of the Georgia Association of Colleges. Credits for such courses shall be given only on certificate of examination by the professor to the Advanced Credit Committee and shall be recorded only as in (a).

(d) Any course, paralleling a University course required for a degree, completed as a part of the regular four year high school course and in which the student can pass an examination satisfactory to the professor shall be accepted in lieu of that specific requirement but shall not count toward the number of credits required for a degree. Certificates of such examinations shall be filed with the Committee on Advanced Credit and shall be recorded only as in (a). Furthermore they shall be recorded as to indicate their special significance.

(e) Examination for advanced credit may be given only as provided for above except by special action of the Advanced Credit Committee No credit for work done outside the University shall be recorded except from reports submitted by the Advanced Credits Committee.

REPORTS

Five reports of the standing of students are made during the session.

A student's work shall be adjudged satisfactory if he has a grade of 70 or more in at least half of his courses, and no grade below 60 in more than one course, provided the average of all courses is not less than 65.

The mark of a student who changes his course after the middle of a term is that which he received on the mid-term report.

CLASSIFICATION OF STUDENTS

Students having credit in the Registrar's office for as many as twelve session hours shall rank as Sophomores. Those having credit in the Registrar's office for as many as five-sixths of the total number of required hours in their respective degree courses for the Freshman and Sophomore years shall rank as Juniors. Those having credit in the Registrar's office for as many as five-sixths of the total number of required hours in their respective degree courses for the Freshman, Sophomore and Junior years shall rank as Seniors. Students having credit in the Rigestrar's office for less than twelve session hours shall rank as Freshmen. All credits must be unconditioned.

EXTRA STUDIES

1. Any work in excess of the number of hours prescribed in the catalogue for the course and year in which the student qualifies shall be known as "Extra Studies.'

2. No credit shall be given for "Extra Studies" unless permission to register for such work has been granted by the Committee on Extra Studies and field in the Dean's office.

3. No Freshman shall be allowed to register for more hours than those prescribed in the catalogue for the course which he elects.

4. Any student above Freshman rank may register for a total of three-tenths of the number of hours required for the degree for which he is registered, provided: (a) he has a "standing of 2" or higher in the preceding term or year; (b) he has the written consent of the head of the department in which he has selected his Major or of his adviser, as his course of study may require, and provided further, (c) that permission to carry the extra hours has been granted by the committee.

5. Credit received for "Extra Studies" may not operate to shorten the time required for a degre to less than that prescribed in the catalogue unless the student maintains a "standing of 2" while pusuing such "Extra Studies."

6. Exceptional cases, when referred to the Committee on Extra Studies, shall be dealt with on their individual merits.

No student who has been permitted to schedule extra hours may change any part of his schedule without permission from the Committee on Extra Studies.

8. Credit received for "Extra Studies" must be audited and approved by the Committee on Extra Studies before it may be counted toward a degree.

HOURS AND QUALITY CREDITS

Instruction is given in courses to which credit is assigned in accordance with the amount of time given to each. The unit of comparison is one hour of class-room work a week throughout the session of nine months, or its equivalent, and its time credit is one hour. A course which implies three class-room hours a week throughout the session of nine months carries a credit of three hours. A course of three class-room hours a week throughout the term carries a credit of one hour, a course of three class-room hours for two terms a credit of two hours, and so on. Likewise a course of four hours a week throughout the session carries a credit of four hours, and a course of five hours for the session a credit of five hours, and a proportionate credit for courses of four or five hours planned for one term or for two terms or for a semester. Any course is thus ranked by comparison with the unit hour.

Any course is a unit of instruction for the time assigned to it, and no credit is given for a fraction of such course.

Two hours of preparation are expected for each class-room hour.

Two hours of laboratory are counted as equal to one class-room hour.

For an undergraduate degree in the College of Arts or the College of Science and Engineering, including the Peabody School of Education, the School of Commerce, and the Grady School of Journalism, sixty-nine hours of credit* are required as the minimum, but more may be necessary to secure the requisite number of points.

For an undergraduate degree in the College of Agriculture the number of hours required is stated in connection with the outline for the degree.

For the required grouping and selection of courses, see the outlines for the respective degrees.

Marking System

Results of work will be recorded in the Registrar's office as follows:

100-90 Exceptionally high quality, valued at 3 points for each hour.

90-80 Good, valued at 2 points for each hour.

---

*If Greek is taken, sixty-six hours are required as a minimum.

80-70 Fair, valued at 1 point for each hour.

70-60 Conditional pass, valued at—1 point for each hour.

60-0 Below pass.

I Incomplete.

X Failure to take Examination.

Graduation

In order to graduate a student must have attained a minimum standing of one, that is the ratio between his hour and points must be one or higher, provided that not more than two conditional passes may be counted in the Freshman year or in the Sophomore year and not more than one conditional pass may be counted in the Junior year or in the Senior year. Students will be required to graduate under the catalogue of the year in which they enter.

Standing

The standing of a student is defined as the ratio of his total number of points to his total number of hours.

Honors

Students are graduated "With Highest Distinction" (Summa cum laude) who attain a standing of three.

Students are graduated "With High Distinction" (Magna cum laude) who attain a standing of 2.6-3.

Students are graduated "With Distinction" (Cum laude) who attain a standing of 2.3-2.6.

ATHLETICS AND STUDENT ORGANIZATIONS

The University is a member of the Southern Intercollegiate Conference, and all students on its teams are subject to the regulations of that body. The chief regulations are as follows:

1. No person shall participate in intercollegiate athletics at an institution until after the expiration of twelve months of the date of his matriculation there, and until he shall have completed the scholastic requirements of that institution.

2. No person who has participated in any intercollegiate contest as a member of any college team shall be permitted to participate in an intercollegiate contest as a member of a team of another institution.

3. Participation in intercollegiate athletics shall be limited to three years over a five year period, counting from the time of first matriculation. Participation in any intercollegiate contest in any college year shall constitute one year of athletic participation.

4. No student who is found delinquent in his studies by the Faculty shall be permitted to participate in any intercollegiate contest. The following regulations determine delinquency in this institution

under regulation 4, and apply to all members of athletic teams, including student managers and assistants:

(a) A candidate for a team must have a minimum credit for twelve hours of college work at the beginning of the second year; at the beginning of the third year he must have at least twenty-four hours credit, of which twelve hours must have been passed during the second year; at the beginning of the fourth year he must have at least thirty-six hours credit, of which twelve hours must have been passed during the third year.

(b) In order to be eligible for a team, a student must have, *at the end of the half-term*, a mark of 70 or more in at least half of his courses, and no mark below 60 in more than one course, provided the average of all courses is not less than 65.

(c) A graduate student may be a member of team for not more than one year, and must have a satisfactory standing in each course that he is taking.

(d) The regular absence rules apply to members of teams.

(e) Changes in the course of study may be made only with the approval of the Faculty Committee on Athletics.

COMMENCEMENT

The annual Commencement exercises are held on the third Wednesday in June. Other exercises are held on preceding days, and the baccalaureate sermon is preached on the Sunday preceding. The summer vacation extends from Commencement Day to the third Wednesday in September. During this time, however, the Summer Session of the University is held, as indicated in the Calendar. A short recess is given at Christmas, and national and state holidays are observed, as indicated in the Calendar.

STUDENT ADVISERS

Students are assigned in suitable numbers to the several members of the Faculty for special oversight. In case of any proposed change in his course of study, a student must consult his adviser, who will judge the reason for the change and report the case to the Dean for final action.

CHAPEL EXERCISES

Chapel exercises, conducted by the Chancellor or some member of the Faculty, are held every morning except Sunday in the Chapel. On Sunday the students may attend services in any of the Sunday Schools, Churches, and Religious Associations in the city. These are as follows: Baptist, Catholic, Christian, Episcopal, Methodist, Presbyterian, Jewish Synagogue, Young Men's Christian Association, etc.

STUDENT COUNCIL

1. The name of the supreme ruling body of the organization shall be the Student Council of the University of Georgia.

2. The student Council shall be composed of twelve active representatives from departments or groups of departments as hereafter indicated, representation being equal between fraternity men and non-fraternity men in each department or group of departments, which are grouped and have representation as follows:

A.B. and B.S. departments, two representatives.

A.B. Ed. and B.S. Com. departments, two representatives.

A.B. Social Sc., Pre-Med., Pharmacy, C.E., E.E., and Graduate departments, two representatives.

Law department, two representatives.

B. S. Agr. department, four representatives.

The Student Council of the Women of the University of Georgia. The name of the supreme ruling body of the organization shall be the Student Council of the Women of the University of Georgia. The Student Council shall be composed of five active representatives with the power of voting: a president, one Senior and one Junior from the Home Economics department, and one Senior and one Junior from the Academic department. One Sophomore and one Freshman, chosen irrespective of degree, will represent their classs on the Council, without the power to vote.

FINANCIAL OBLIGATIONS

MATRICULATION FEE. A matriculation fee of fifty dollars shall be paid by every student entering the University, excepting those entering the Professional Schools.

MATRICULATION FEE FOR NON-RESIDENT STUDENTS. Students who are residents of other states are charged a tuition fee of one hundred dollars a year, in addition to the regular matriculation fee.

TUITION FEE. The tuition fee in the Lumpkin Law School is $75.00 a year, divided as follows: $40.00 payable at the beginning of the term, and $35.00 payable at the opening of college in January. The tuition in the Pharmacy department is $50.00 a year, divided as follows.: $25.00 payable at the beginning of the term, and $25.00 payable at the opening of college in January.

LIBRARY FEE. A library fee of five dollars shall be paid by every student entering the University, excepting those in the Lumpkin Law School and the School of Pharmacy.

LITERARY SOCIETY FEE. A literary society fee of two dollars shall be paid by every student entering the University.

ATHLETIC, GYMNASIUM, AND INFIRMARY FEE. This fee shall be paid by all students entering the University. The annual fee of $21.00 is divided as follows: Gymnasium, $5.00; Athletics, $11.00; and Infirmary (including medical attention), $5.00.

LATE REGISTRATION FEE. All students registering after Saturday noon following the Wednesday on which the University opens shall pay an extra matriculation fee of $3.00, unless excused by the Chancellor. This rule also applies to late registration after the Christmas and Easter holidays.

DEPOSITS. A deposit fee of ten dollars shall be paid by every student taking part in military drill, basic course, and thirty dollars by every student in Advanced Courses. The fee of basic course students will be returned if no part of the uniform is lost or destroyed. A deposit fee of $2.00 shall be paid by every male student entering the University who occupies a room in one of the dormitories. This fee will be returned unless property is damaged. A deposit fee of five dollars is required of every woman occupying a room in Soule Hall. This fee will be returned unless property is damaged.

LITERARY MAGAZINE FEE. A fee of one dollar shall be paid by every student entering the University for the support of the literary magazine. This fee entitles the student to the *Georgia Cracker* for one year.

STUDENT COUNCIL FEE. A fee of fifty cents shall be paid by every student entering the University. This fee is for the maintenance of the Student Council.

STUDENT ACTIVITIES FEE. A fee of three dollars shall be paid by every student entering the University, to be known as the student activities fee.

DORMITORIES

There are four dormitories, Old College for Juniors and Seniors; New College, Candler Hall and Milledge Hall for lower classmen.

Rooms in the dormitories are lighted with electricity, and are furnished with chairs, bed, table and washstand. A charge of $5.00 per month per man, where there are two in a room, and $4.00 per month per man, where there are more than two in a room, is made for each room occupied, to cover the expense of janitors, fuel, water and lights.

Where two occupy the same room, each occupant shall pay on matriculation $17.50, and on January 1st $27.50—making a total of $45.00 for the session.

Where more than two occupy the same room, each occupant shall pay on matriculation $14.00 and on January 1st, $22.00—making a total of $36.00 for the session.

A deposit of $2.00 is required of every student before assignment is made. This fee is a charge against damage to the property, and the balance is returned at the end of the year. The dormitories are in charge of a Committee from the Faculty. The rules and regulations prescribed by this Committee are enforced through Proctors placed over each division of the dormitories.

Those desiring dormitory rooms should apply in person, or by letter, to T. W. Reed, Treasurer, Athens, Ga. No assignment will be made until the required deposit fee is paid. Applications should be made early as only about two hundred can be accommodated.

DENMARK DINING HALL

The Hall, which is in charge of a member of the Faculty, furnishes excellent table board to those students who desire it at the lowest charge consistent with the current prices of food, labor and necessary equipment. The charge during 1926-1927 will probably be $16.00 per month and will certainly not exceed $18.00 per month.

SOULE HALL

The new women's building, Soule Hall, was first occupied during the Summer School, 1920, and was opened for the regular session in September. It is on a high hill overlooking Athens, and is one of the most pleasant and delightful locations in the city. On the first floor of this building are well equipped laboratories for work in clothing, cooking, nutrition, laundry, as well as a swimming pool and gymnasium. The rest of the building is devoted to residence quarters, including spacious parlors, infirmary, a housekeeping apartment for home management classes, baths, and thirty-five double bed rooms. Each student's room is equipped with two single beds, indivdual wardrobe closets, lavatories with hot and cold running water and other complete and attractive furnishings. This building is one of the most complete and efficiently equipped of its kind in the state and provides for the broadest opportunities for women in university life.

All non-resident women students registered in the College of Agriculture are expected to live here. It is also open to women in other departments of the University as long as there are vacancies.

There is a social director in charge of the physical and social welfare of the girls. She will not only sponsor the social life in the dormitory, but will also see to proper chaperonage for other occasions when it is advisable to have such. She will be one of the agents of the students government by which the activities of the girl are regulated.

Each room is supplied with two single beds, two mattresses ,two pillows, one dresser, one table, and three chairs. Students are to furnish their own bed linen, scarfs and towels.

The room rent is $30.00 per term, per student, paid in advance. All applications should be made to Miss Mary E. Creswell, Director of Home Economics, Georgia State College of Agriculture, Athens, Georgia. Each application should be accompanied by a check for $5.00, made payable to T. W. Reed, Treasurer, University of Georgia. This amount is required as a guaranty against damage and loss of keys and is wholly or in part refunded at the close of the year.

Meals may be had at the College Cafeteria in the Administration Building. Monthly rates in accordance with the current prices will be made to students.

PRIVATE BOARD AND LODGING

The charges for private rooms vary with the character of the furnishings. This is a very popular way of lodging. The students board at the Denmark Dining Hall, the Agricultural Cafeteria, or they can secure private table board. A number of families in the city offer board and lodging. The University cannot agree to engage rooms in private families. A list of those desiring boarders or having rooms to rent, will be given on application, but the student must make his own arrangements.

The officers of the University Y. M. C. A. and the Y. W. C. A. also render every assistance possible to those desiring advice and help in such matters. There need be no anxiety, therefore, in regard to securing accommodations.

EXPENSES

Residents of Georgia pay no tuition fees except in the Law and Pharmacy courses. Students who are residents of other states are charged a tuition fee of $100.00 per annum in academic courses. A fee of $21.00 is required of all students, to cover infirmary (including medical attention), gymnasium, and student activities. The following estimate of expenses includes all necessary items except clothing and railroad fare:

Expenses of Students when Rooming in a Dormitory and Boarding

at Denmark Dining Hall

Matriculation fee (paid on entrance)	$ 50.00
Library fee (paid on entrance)	5.00
Fee of literary society or other literary club (paid on entrance)	2.00
Board (paid monthly, in advance) 9 mos. @ $16.00 per month	144.00
Books and stationery (estimated)	25.00
Laundry (estimated at $2.00 per month)	18.00
Room rent, light, heat and attendance ($5.00 per month)	45.00
Deposit fees in Dormitory and Dining Hall	5.00
Fee for Infirmary, gymnasium, athletics	21.00
Fee for Student Council	.50
Fee for "Georgia Cracker"	1.00
College Co-op. Fee	1.00
Student Activities fee	3.00
Laboratory fees, approximately	20.00

Engineering students must have a set of drawing instruments.

A student, the first year, can scarcely meet his necessary expenses on less than $350 for the scholastic year; usually it will exceed this amount.

NOTE: In order to meet all the necessary expenses of registration, books, uniform and other expenditures incident to securing a room and board, a student should come prepared to expend about $150.00 during the first ten days. After that period his board and room rent will constitute the major part of his expenses.

OPPORTUNITIES FOR SELF-HELP

A considerable number of students secure remunerative employment to aid them in their education. Usually the students of Agriculture are able to secure work on the farm for which they are paid. In a few instances other departments need the services of students. Usually these places go to those who have been in attendance for some time, and who are known to be willing, capable, and trustworthy. The University does not assume any responsibility whatever in this matter. As a matter of accommodation the Committee on Self Help co-operates as far as possible with students. The Y. M. C. A. offers its services in helping young men to secure employment. Very much depends however on the individual's power of initiative. Students should not come to the University expecting others to find places for them.

It seems necessary to warn students on this subject. The average young man cannot ordinarily do much more than earn his living when he has nothing else to do. To earn a living and at the same time carry the work of a college course planned to occupy a students full time is more than most students can accomplish. In a few instances they have succeeded, but as a rule students who attempt more than partial self support should expect to lengthen their term of study.

INCIDENTAL EXPENSES

The incidental expenses of a student are what he makes them, and parents are urged to take into their own hands the control of a matter which no college regulations can successfully reach.

Part VIII
DEGREES, HONORS AND PRIZES, 1925-1926

DEGREES, HONORS AND PRIZES, 1926

MASTER OF ARTS

James Wesley Adams
Lily Wingo Brooks
Esther Bush
Rose Bush

Claude Chance
Alethea Jane Macon
Harry LaFayette Middlebrooks
James Ruey Patrick

MASTER OF SCIENCE

Pope Russell Hill

MASTER OF SCIENCE IN AGRICULTURE

Wyatt Arnton Clegg   Jasper Guy Woodroof

MASTER OF SCIENCE IN ECONOMICS

John Wesley Johnson

BACHELOR OF ARTS

Frances Elizabeth Little
Edna Elizabeth Strauss   } summa cum laude
Grace Evelyn Strauss

Bertram Sidney Boley
Thomas McElmurray Close
Joseph Quinton Davidson
Clarence Samuel Fain   } magna cum laude
John Joseph Hennessy
Helen McDorman*
Walter Preston Warren, Jr.
Edgar Arthur Waxelbaum

Yewly Eugene Bargeron
Harrison Agnew Birchmore   } cum laude
Penelope Griffin
Hugh Smiley Stanley

Margaret E. Acree
Dan Sully Beeland
Charles Allen Bickerstaff
George Slade Cargill, Jr.
James Choice Fanning
Gordon Aulie Franklin
Lucy Booton Frederick
Jones Llewellyn Griffin

Zona Hamilton
Charles Herty Hooper
Lee Roy Leffler
George Dudley Morton
Douglas Milton Orr
Emma Elizabeth Plaster
Mae Belle Sanders
Stephen Parks Shell

Samuel Yoer Tupper, Jr.
Marion Smith, as of the class of 1903

BACHELOR OF ARTS IN SOCIAL SCIENCES

William Robert Humphreys   Marilla Elizabeth Staight

BACHELOR OF ARTS IN EDUCATION
Ruby Anderson,* summa cum laude

Sarah Louise Betts*
Ella Sue Minor* } magna cum laude

Lucile Alexander*
Lunette Mallary Jones*
Bess Ellison Matthews* } cum laude
Norma Claire Parker*
Celia Perry

Dorothy Reed Belcher
Inez Porterfield Brooks
Loyce Furman Cargile
Mary Frances Carmichael
Clara Gibbs Dally
Jewel Davis
Sam Lee Gaulding
John Franklin Graham
Florence Weltner Lester

Anne Roberts Moran
Cassandra Elizabeth Morton
Ruby Louise McMahan
Sarah Louise Stewart
Arnoldina Thornton
Helen Treanor
Frances Walton
Eleanor Ward
Ruth Ethel Weideman

Samuel Wasden Wood

BACHELOR OF ARTS IN JOURNALISM
John Daniel Allen, summa cum laude
Lillian Louise Wade,* magna cum laude
Victoria Billups Cohen,* cum laude

James Calvin Bonner
Rufus Sterling Davis
Ann Louise Moon

Louise Bacon Osborne
Dudley Hilton Taylor
Samuel Hoyt Worley

Murray Ellis Wyche

BACHELOR OF SCIENCE
Martin Edward Kilpatrick, magna cum laude
James Newton Brawner, Jr., cum laude

Robert Edward Anderson
John Herbert Burroughs
David Lewis Earnest, Jr.
Robert Lee Garrett
Thomas Wright Goodwin

John William Gray, Jr.
Edward Waterman Hagler
Bassett Maguire
Gwinn Huxley Nixon
Dill Pittman

George Buford Randolph

BACHELOR OF SCIENCE (Civil Engineering)

Ernest Lee Griggs
Walter Edwin Sewell } summa cum laude

David Stanley Campbell, magna cum laude

George Warren Cumbus
Ralph Kelly Jones } cum laude

Joseph Elder Bishop
Harold Loyd Frederick
James Attaway Kennedy

Richard Gideon Minter
Lamar Cobb Sledge
Charles Houston Starling, Jr.

*Work done partly in other institutions.

BACHELOR OF SCIENCE (Agriculture)

Harvey Walter Rankin*
Pinckney Alston Steiner } with honors

Altus Robert Bennett
Clarence Harvey Brand
Jacob Johnson Butler
Alwin Wimbish David
Garr Samuel Dennis
John Etheredge
Walter Albert Fuller
Thomas Hart Gignilliat
Chandler Balkcom Gladin
William Henry Hardman
William Carl Huggins
Otis Warner Jones

Archie Langley
John Alfred Mauldin
James White Morton, Jr.
Henry Smith Stanhope Munro
Robert Henry McRae
Hubert Bond Owens
William Harris Simpson, Jr.
John Fletcher Smith
James Louis Stephens
Jack Van Houten
Glenn Frederick Wiley
John Harrison Wright

BACHELOR OF SCIENCE (Home Economics)

Wyoline Hester*
Pearl Campbell Moon* } with high honors

Mildred Boley
Anna Dean Bridges
Edith O'Steen Ward* } with honors

Peggy Baker
Bertha Margaret Benson
Annie Mae Wood Bryant
Frances Elizabeth Comer
Frances Lucyle Cook
Elizabeth Curry
Sarah Elizabeth Petty

Mattie Jane Ridgway
Dorothy Rowland
Ellie Smalley
Leona Smith
Martha Jane Smith
Nell Marie Storey
Marian Grace Talmage

BACHELOR OF SCIENCE (Forestry)

Charles Bernard Beale
George Norman Bishop
Raiford Franklin Brown

Charles Patrick Doherty
James Loyd Eaton
John Bullock Gaskins

DOCTOR OF VETERINARY MEDICINE

Douglas LaFayette Davis
Adlai Bee Griner
George Raiford Hatfield

Alvin Lee Odom
Harry Poe
Ezekiel Fred Thomas

BACHELOR OF SCIENCE (Commerce)

Tyler Francis Haygood
Morris Harry Levy
Robert Taylor Segrest } cum laude

Joseph Wilson Berry
Mordaunt Grey Boatwright
Wayland Eugene Boltom
Lewis Pearce Brown
Judson Harrell Drewry
Thomas Stephens Gray
Frank Conley Haralson
James Bruce Harper
James Willis Hay, Jr.
George Saynor Johnson
Marshall Craig Levie
Willoughby Earl Marshall, Jr.
Carlton Newton Mell

James Zeb Morris
Malcolm Nash
Burwell Atkinson Nolan
Hugh Pendleton Nunnally
Myron Isaac Prisant
Thomas Sheftall Russell, Jr.
John B. Satlof
Cecil Wyman Sherlock
Allen Nicholls Smith
Julius Glenn Tatum
Harry Leslie Wesley
John Marvin Wesley
Thomas Edward Winslow

*Work done partly in other institutions.

BACHELOR OF LAWS

John Paxton Erwin, with first honor

Charles Joseph O'Byrne
Julian Davis Wooten   } with honors
Luther Harmon Zeigler

Osmond Reimert Bie
Perry Brannen
Joseph Heyward Cherry
Louis Perry Chick
Robert Shelnut Dennis
Richard Allen Denny, Jr.
Edwin Jacob Feiler
Starkey Sharp Flythe
John Morgan Forrester
Lucius Coleman Groves
Earl Dunbar Harrison
William Julian Hatcher
Henry Olin Hubert, Jr.
Frederick Heber Kent

Dorothy Ida Levy
Freeman Cheyne McClure
James Edwards Manucy, Jr.
John Duncan Odom
Arthur Sears Oldham
Austin Herschel Parham
John Robert Phillips, Jr.
William Tyrus Ray
Herbert Albert Strickland
Harry Lundy Taylor
Mathilde Lumpkin Upson
Minor Lewis Wheaton
Iver Leon Wooten
Luther Mandeville Wyatt

The following degrees have been conferred between Commencement of 1925 and Commencement of 1926.

MASTER OF ARTS

Rose Belle Johnson
James Wilkins Overstreet, Jr.

Harold Telford Patterson
Newman Atkinson Wade

BACHELOR OF ARTS

Lester Hargrett, magna cum laude

BACHELOR OF ARTS IN EDUCATION

Anna King Clark, magna cum laude

Louise Leslie Fant   Florence Alice Simpson

Samp Boon Tolar

BACHELOR OF ARTS IN SOCIAL SCIENCES

H. R. Adams
Dorothy South Fargason

Anne McGaha Griffin
Laura Mae Ware

BACHELOR OF SCIENCE

Thomas Hillyer Whitehead

BACHELOR OF SCIENCE (Agriculture)

Fred Harris Bargeron
Leon Sellers Carter
George Miller Clarke
Ernest Carl Dietz

Ralph Leonard Dolvin
Guy Taylor Gard
John Cooper Morcock
Edwin Francis Shippey

BACHELOR OF SCIENCE (Forestry)

Bishop Franklin Grant

BACHELOR OF SCIENCE (Home Economics)

Edith Carolyn Hanson

---

*Work done partly in other institutions.

BACHELOR OF SCIENCE (Commerce)

Leo William Belcher   Munro de Mere d'Antignac
Charles Franklin Crouch   Mahlon Cooper Garrett
John Wesley Johnson

List of Prizes and Medals

Hamilton McWhorter Prize, for general excellence in the Freshman class.—J. R. Cumming.

Ready Writer's Prize, for the best essay upon a subject announced after admission to the examination room. Gold medal—offered by the Board of Trustees.—Willie Mae Cook.

Cadet Prize, for the best drilled cadet. Gold medal—offered by the Board of Trustees.—W. R. Woodward.

Willcox Prize, for the best French scholar in the Senior class, $50.00 in gold—offered by the sons of the late Professor C. P. Willcox.—D. G. Sullivan.

Horace Russell Prize in Psychology, for the best essay upon a psychological subject. $50.00 in gold—offered by Judge Horace Russell, of New York.—George H. Culpepper.

Walter B. Hill Prize in Ethics, for the best essay upon an ethical subject. $50.00 in gold—offered by Judge Horace Russell, of New York.—Sarah Betts.

W. J. Bryan Prize, for the best essay on "Our Form of Government." $10.00 in gold—offered by Hon. W. J. Bryan, of Nebraska. —Not awarded.

L. H. Charbonnier Prize, for the best scholar in Physics in the Senior class. $25.00 in gold—offered by Mrs. J. F. McGowan, of Augusta.—D. S. Campbell.

Bert Michael Scholarship, to be given to a member of the Junior class, selected by a committee of the Faculty. Sixty dollars, the income of a fund given by the family of the late Bert Michael, of the class of 1912.—Marie Turnipseed.

Joe Brown Connally Scholarship in Georgia History, presented by the family of the late Captain Joe Brown Connally, of the Class of 1896, who lost his life as the result of the Great War. $100.00 for the present to a member of the Junior class for proficiency in Georgia History. J. T. Barrs.

Chi Omega Prize. A prize of $20.00 in gold—offered by Mu Beta Chapter of the Chi Omega fraternity to the woman student of the University who has the highest scholarship average. A student must be taking fifteen hours of college work in order to be eligible for this prize.—Marie Turnipseed.

D. A. R. Prize, $10.00 in gold presented by the Elijah Clarke Chapter to the member of the Freshman class writing the best essay on a topic in Southern History.—A. J. Mathews.

Law School Prize: A set of Corpus Juris to the student in the Senior Class who made the highest grade in the course of Legal Bibliography.—E. J. Feiler.

Scholarship Key awarded by the Delta Sigma Pi (National Commerce Fraternity) to the student in the School of Commerce making the best record for the four year term.—M. H. Levy.

Trustees' Prize, $25.00 in gold, from the Board of Trustees to the student writing the best essay on "A Development Program for Georgia."—S. B. Adair.

Junior Scholarship, $75.00 in gold, to the student showing the greatest proficiency in all agricultural subjects for the college year. —J. W. Fanning.

Sophomore Scholarship, $60.00 in gold, to the student showing the greatest proficiency in all agricultural subjects for the college year. —Robert F. Sikes.

Freshman Scholarship, $40.00 in gold, to the student showing the greatest proficiency in all the required work.—Chesley M. Dellinger.

Two Gold Medals, given by the Georgia Chapter of the Alpha Zeta Fraternity, to be presented at the public meeting of the Agricultural Club in the fall:

To the agricultural student in the Freshman class showing the greatest proficiency in all the required work:

To the agricultural student in the Sophomore class showing the greatest proficiency in all the required work.—Not announced.

Alpha Mu Prize. A prize of $15.00—offered by the Alpha Mu honorary society to the Home Economics student making the highest scholastic average. A student must be taking fifteen hours of college work to be eligible for the prize.—Laura Wilson.

$10.00 in Gold, given by H. G. Hastings & Company, to the student writing the best essay on "The Economic Importance of the Home Garden."—R. M. Fulghum.

$10.00 in Gold, given by H. G. Hastings & Company, to the student writing the best essay on "Relative Values of Prolific and Single-eared Types of Corn on Upland Soil."—R. M. Fulghum.

Part VIII
THE MEDICAL COLLEGE
at Augusta

CALENDAR

1926

September 23rd and 24th, Thursday and Friday_____
_____Entrance Examinations and Re-examinations
September 25th, Saturday_____Registration
September 27th, Monday_____:_____Instruction Begins
November 25th, 26th, and 27th, Thursday, Friday and Saturday,___
    Thanksgiving _____ _____Holidays
December 11th, Saturday_____First Trimester Ends
December 22nd, Wednesday 1:00 P. M._____Christmas Recess Begins

1927

January 3rd, Monday_____Instruction Resumed
January 19th, Wednesday, Lee's Birthday_____Holiday
February 22nd, Tuesday, Washington's Birthday_____Holiday
March 12th, Saturday_____Second Trimester Ends
May 30th to June 4th, inclusive_____Examination Week
June 6th_____Commencement

BOARD OF DIRECTORS

HON. ENOCH CALLAWAY_____President

HON. ENOCH CALLAWAY_____Augusta
HON. WILLIAM H. BARRETT_____Augusta
HON. JOSEPH S. DAVIS_____Albany
HON. WILLIAM H. FLEMING_____Augusta
HON. JAMES B. NEVIN_____Atlanta
HON. ALEXANDER A. LAWRENCE_____Savannah
DR. E. T. COLEMAN_____Graymont
DR. JOHN FLETCHER LUNSFORD_____Preston
DR. HENRY W. SHAW_____:_____Augusta

MR. GEORGE P. BATES,   DR. CARLTON H. MARYOTT,
    Treasurer.   Secretary.

FACULTY

CHARLES MERCER SNELLING, A.M., Sc.D., Chancellor.
WILLIAM HENRY GOODRICH, A.B., M.D., F.A.C.S., Dean.

JAMES MERIWEATHER HULL, M.D., Professor of Opthalmology, Otology, Laryngology, and Rhinology.

THOMAS DAVIES COLEMAN, A.M., M.D., F.A.C.P., Professor of Medicine.

THEODORE EUGENE OERTEL, M.D., F.A.C.S., Professor of Opthalmology.

EUGENE EDMUND MURPHEY, M.D., F.A.C.P., Professor of Medicine.

WILLIAM HENRY GOODRICH, A.B., M.D., F.A.C.S., Professor of Gynecology.

NOEL McHENRY MOORE, M.S., M.D., Professor of Pediatrics.

CHARLES WILLIAMS CRANE, M.D., F.A.C.S., Professor of Surgery.

WILLIAM CRISSY KELLOGG, A.B., M.D., F.A.C.S., Professor of Laryngology.

HENRY MIDDLETON MICHEL, M.D., F.A.C.S., Professor of Orthopedic Surgery.

RICHARD VANDERHORST LAMAR, M.D., Professor of Pathology and Bacteriology.

CARLTON HOWARD MARYOTT, Ph.D., Professor of Chemistry.

WILLIAM SALANT, B.S., M.D., Professor of Physiology and Pharmacology.

ANDREW JONES KILPATRICK, M.D., Professor of Obstetrics.

CARLISLE S. LENTZ, A.B., M.D., Professor of Hospital Administration.

VIRGIL PRESTON SYDENSTRICKER, A.M., M.D., F.A.C.P., Professor of Medicine.

JOSEPH AKERMAN, A.B., M.D., F.A.C.S., Professor of Obstetrics.

LYSANDER PALMER HOLMES, M.D., Professor of Clinical Roentgenology.

ELIOT ROUND CLARK, A.B., M.D., Professor of Anatomy.

HARRY BENJAMIN NEAGLE, A.B., M.D., C.P.H., D.P.H., Professor of Preventive Medicine.

RALPH HILL CHANEY, A.B., A.M., M.D., F.A.C.S., Professor of Surgery.

EDWIN LINTON, A.B., A.M., Ph.D., Honorary Fellow in Parasitology.

WILLIAM ANTHONY MULHERIN, A.M., M.D., F.A.C.P., Clinical Professor of Pediatrics.

GEORGE ALBERT TRAYLOR, B.Sc., M.D., F.A.C.S., Clinical Professor in Surgery.

CHARLES IVERSON BRYANS, M.D., Clinical Professor of Opthalmology and Otology.

ASBURY HULL, M.D., Clinical Professor of Genito-Urinary Diseases.

GUY TALMADGE BERNARD, M.D., F.A.C.S., Clinical Professor of Surgery and Dermatology.

HENRY McE. KNOWER, Ph.D., Visiting Professor of Anatomy.

MISS ALICE F. STEWART, R.N., Director of Nurses.

HINTON JAMES BAKER, M.D., Associate Professor of Pediatrics.

GEORGE TURNER HORNE, M.D., Associate Professor of Gynecology.

ROBERT LEWIS RHODES, A.B., M.D., F.A.C.S., Associate Professor of Surgery.

EVERARD ANSLEY WILCOX, B.S., A.M., F.A.C.S., Associate Professor of Gynecology.

PAUL EATON, M.D., Associate Professor of Preventive Medicine.

WILLIAM JOHNSTON CRANSTON, M.D., Assistant Professor of Medicine.

ALBERT ALONZO DAVIDSON, M.D., Assistant Professor of Medicine.

ARCHIBALD BLACKSHEAR, A.B., B.L., Lecturer on Forensic Medicine.

DR. M. C. BAINES, M.D., Lecturer on Psychiatry.

WILLIAM WHATLEY BATTEY, M.A., M.D., Associate in Surgery.

WILLIAM HENRY ROBERTS, M.D., Associate in Genito-Urinary Diseases.

JAMES HARVEY BUTLER, M.D., Associate in Medicine.

JOHN COSKERY WRIGHT, M.D., Associate in Gynecology.

WILLIAM HENRY SHAW, M.D., Associate in Obstetrics.

ALFRED LARSON, B.A., Ph.D., Associate in Bacteriology.

EDGAR R. PUND, A.B., M.D., Associate in Pathology.

GEORGE LOMBARD KELLY, A.B., M.D., Instructor in Medicine.

PETER BURUM WRIGHT, M.D., Instructor in Surgery.

CHARLES DOUGLAS WARD, B.S., M.D., Instructor in Surgery.

JOHN HAYES SHERMAN, B.S., M.D., Resident Surgeon and Instructor in Surgery.

IRVINE PHINIZY, B.S., M.D., Resident Physician and Instructor in Medicine.

FRANK LANSING LEE, B.S., M.D., Instructor in Medicine.

ANDREW AUGUSTUS WALDEN, M.D., Instructor in Medicine.

FRANCIS XAVIER MULHERIN, M.D., Instructor in Pediatrics.

KING WALKER MILLIGAN, Ph.G., M.D., Instructor in Medicine.

MR. CLAUDE R. SMITH, B.S., Instructor in Chemistry.

HENRY PIERCE HARRELL, M.D., Instructor in Pediatrics.

CLAUDE McKINLEY, BURPEE, B.S., M.D. Instructor in Medicine.

MISS AGNES CAMPBELL, R.N., Instructor in Public Health Nursing.

RICHARD LAMAR HARRIS, M.D., Instructor in Psychiatry.

MR. JACOB ERNEST NADLER, Instructor in Physiology.

MISS E. ALMA BROWN, R.N., Instructor of Nurses.

FRANK CRAWFORD STORY, A.B., Instructor in Anatomy.

JOHN CALVIN SANDISON, A.B., Instructor in Anatomy.

ROY G. WILLIAMS, M.D., Instructor in Anatomy.

WADE RAMSEY BEDINGFIELD, A.B., M.D., Clinical Instructor in Eye, Ear, Nose, and Throat.

HENRY WASHEIM, Jr., B.S., Assistant in Physiology.

MONTIE PRESTON AGEE, M.D., Instructor in Surgery and Gynecology.

WILLIAM D. JENNINGS, M.D., Assistant in Medicine.

ROBERT IRVIN BRYSON, M.D., Assistant in Surgery.

LAURIE LESTER DOZIER, M.D., Deputy Commissioner of Health for Richmond County.

JAMES CLAYTON, METTS, B.S., M.D., Assistant in Medicine.

WILLIAM JOSEPH HUSON, M.D., Assistant in Medicine.

SAMUEL JOSEPH LEWIS, M.D., Clinical Assistant in Eye, Ear, Nose and Throat.

WALTER BYRON JAMESON, M.D., Assistant in Pediatrics.

DAVID MARION SILVER, M.D., Clinical Assistant in Eye, Ear, Nose and Throat.

HUGHES BRANTLEY JENKINS, B.S., Student Assistant in Chemistry.

ALVIN BERNARD DeLOACH, Ph.G., Pharmacist.

LOUIS WARREN FARGO, M.D., Photographer.

OTHER OFFICERS

MISS JANIE TURNER, Secretary.

DR. LOUIS W. FARGO, Secretary of Faculty.

MISS LOUISE MILLIGAN, Registrar of Clinic.

MRS. DAHLIA McFALL, Librarian.

FACULTY COMMITTEES

EXECUTIVE COMMITTEE—Professors Goodrich, Chairman; Maryott, Secretary; Bryans, Murphey, and Clark.

COMMITTEE ON COLLEGE AFFAIRS—This committee is composed of the full time heads of the departments.

STUDENT ADVISORY COMMITTEE—Professors Bryans, Holmes, Asbury Hull, Kelly, Maryott, and Rhodes.

COMMITTEE ON HOSPITAL AND DISPENSARY—Professors Akerman, Chaney, Goodrich, Kellogg, Lentz, Murphey, Rhodes, and Sydensticker.

COMMITTEE ON BUILDINGS AND GROUNDS—Professors Lentz, Maryott, and Neagle.

The Dean is ex-officio member of all committees.

BOARD OF TRUSTEES OF THE UNIVERSITY HOSPITAL
THOMAS BARRETT, Chairman.
MEMBERS OF THE BOARD

THOMAS BARRETT,
J. C. C. BLACK, JR.
HAROLD C. EVE

SAM A. FORTSON
WILLIAM B. BELL
MAYOR WILLIAM P. WHITE

MEDICAL BOARD
ROBERT L. RHODES, M.D., Chairman
EUGENE E. MURPHEY, M.D.
JOSEPH AKERMAN, M.D.
WILLIAM C. KELLOGG, M. C.
VIRGIL P. SYDENSTRICKER, M.D.
RALPH H. CHANEY, M. D.
WILLIAM H. GOODRICH, M.D., Dean of Medical School.
CARLISLE S. LENTZ, M.D., Secretary.

HOSPITAL STAFF
December 31, 1925.
CARLISLE S. LENTZ, M.D., Superintendent.
VIRGIL P. SYDENSTRICKER, M.D., Physician in Chief.
THOMAS D. COLEMAN, M.D., Consulting Physician.
EUGENE E. MURPHY, M.D., Attending Physician.
RICHARD V. LAMAR, M.D., Attending Physician.
WILLIAM J. CRANSTON, M.D., Assistant Attending Physician.
J. HARVEY BUTLER, M.D., Assistant Attending Physician.
RALPH H. CHANEY, M.D., Surgeon in Chief.
ROBERT L. RHODES, M.D., Attending Surgeon.
CHARLES W. CRANE, M.D., Attending Surgeon.
GUY T. BERNARD, M.D., Attending Surgeon.
GEORGE A. TRAYLOR, M.D., Attending Surgeon.
WILLIAM H. GOODRICH, M.D., Attending Gynecologist.
GEORGE T. HORNE, M.D., Assistant Attending Gynecologist.
EVERARD A. WILCOX. M.D., Assistant Attending Gynecologist.
WILLIAM A. MULHERIN, M.D., Attending Pediatrician.
NOEL M. MOORE, M.D., Attending Pediatrician.
HENRY P. HARRELL, M.D., Assistant Attending Pediatrician.
HENRY M. MICHEL, M.D., Orthopedic Surgeon.
ASBURY HULL, M.D., Urologist.
JAMES M. HULL; M.D., Opthalmologist and Laryngologist.
T. E. OERTEL, M.D., Opthalmologist and Laryngologist.
WILLIAM C. KELLOGG, M.D., Opthalmologist and Laryngologist.
CHARLES I. BRYANS, M.D., Opthalmologist and Laryngologist.
L. PALMER HOLMES, M.D., Roentgenologist.
RICHARD V. LAMAR, M.D., Pathologist.

HOUSE STAFF

CLAUDE M. BURPEE, M.D., Assistant Attending Physician.

JOHN H. SHERMAN, M.D., Resident Surgeon.

IRVINE PHINIZY, M.D., Resident Physician.

JAMES C. METTS, M.D., Assistant Resident Physician.

THOMAS G. BROOKS, M.D., Assistant Resident Surgeon.

LEWIS H. WRIGHT, M.D., Assistant Resident Obstetrician.

WILLIAM J. BURDASHAW, M.D., WILLIAM F. DOBYNS, M.D., ANDREW H. FOWLER, M.D., JOHN G. HOOD, JR., M.D., JOHN D. LAMON, JR., M.D., POWELL M. TEMPLES, M.D., RICHARD B WEEKS. M.D., JOHN D. WILEY, M.D., Internes.

WALTER H. ROSE, M.D., Interne in Pathology.

ALICE F. STEWART, R.N., Director of Nurses.

E. ALMA BROWN, R.N., Instructor.

CORA A. BROWN, R.N., Assistant in Charge Operating Room.

LEILA ANDERSON, R.N., Assistant in Lamar Wing.

ELEANOR KEITH, R.N., Head Nurse Barrett-4.

SADIE POWELL, R.N., Head Nurse Barrett-3.

FRANCES KING, R.N., Night Superintendent.

ENNIS STROUPE, Dietitian.

MERNA MONROE, Assistant Dietitian.

JOHN P. HALLINAN, Secretary-Treasurer.

A. B. DeLOACH, Ph.G., Pharmacist.

CARRIE L. GOODRICH, Record Clerk.

A. E. CHEEKS, Chief Engineer.

A. R. JORDAN, Store Keeper.

OUT-PATIENT DEPARTMENT

CARLISLE S. LENTZ, M.D., Director.

JOSEPH AKERMAN, M.D., Chief of Clinic.

MISS LOUISE MILLIGAN, Secretary.

V. P. SYDENSTRICKER, M.D., Medical Department.

W. J. CRANSTON. M.D., Medical Department.

E. E. MURPHEY, M.D., Medical Department.

A. A. DAVISON, M. D., Medical Department.

ANDREW A. WALDEN, M.D.. Medical Department.

J. H. BUTLER, M.D., Medical Department.

KING W. MILLIGAN, M.D., Medical Department.

C. M. BURPEE, M.D., Medical Department.

H. J. BAKER, M. D., Pediatrics.

F. X. MULHERIN, M.D., Pediatrics.

H. P. HARRELL, M. D., Pediatrics.

R. H. CHANEY, M.D., Surgical Department.

C. W. CRANE, M.D., Surgical Department.

W. W. BATTEY, M. D., Surgical Department.
G. A. TRAYLOR, M.D., Surgical Department.
C. D. WARD, M.D., Surgical Department.
P. B. WRIGHT, M.D., Surgical Department.
W. H. GOODRICH, M.D., Gynecology.
GEORGE T. HORNE, M.D., Gynecology.
JOHN C. WRIGHT, M.D., Gynecology.
E. A. WILCOX, M.D., Gynecology.
M. P. AGEE, M.D., Gynecology.
H. M. MICHEL, M.D., Orthopedics.
W. H. ROBERTS, M.D., Urology.
J. M. HULL, M.D., Eye, Ear, Nose and Throat.
T. E. OERTEL, M.D., Eye, Ear, Nose and Throat.
C. I. BRYANS, M.D., Eye, Ear Nose, and Throat.
W. R. BEDINGFIELD, M.D., Eye, Ear, Nose and Throat.
S. J. LEWIS, M.D., Eye, Ear, Nose and Throat.
D. M. SILVER, M.D., Eye, Ear, Nose and Throat.
J. F. BURDASHAW, M.D., Eye, Ear, Nose and Throat.
G. T. BERNARD, M. D., Dermatology.
JOSEPH AKERMAN, Obstetrics.
L. PALMER HOLMES, M.D., Roentgenology.
REGNALD MAXWELL, D.D.S., Dentistry.
H. B. GROSE, D.D.S., Dentistry.

ANNOUNCEMENT FOR SESSION 1926-1927

The ninety-eighth annual session of the Medical Department of the University of Georgia will begin September 23rd, 1926, and end June 6th, 1927.

HISTORICAL NOTE

The Medical Department of the University of Georgia was chartered in 1828 under the title of the Georgia Medical Academy. In 1829 it became the Medical College of Georgia, and continued under this name until 1873 when it became affiliated with the State University as its Medical Department. In 1911, by an act of the legislature, it became legally the Medical Department of the University of Georgia, and passed into the control of the University, its affairs being administered by a Board of Directors appointed in part by the Governor of the State and in part from the University Board by its President.

MEDICAL COLLEGE BUILDING

The Medical College is housed in a four-story brick structure, situated on the College campus covering about forty-five acres. It is near the geographical center, and about one mile from the business center, of Augusta, and is easily accessible by trolley from all parts of the city.

The first floor of the building is used for the out-patient department. It contains thirty rooms which provide for the various clinics, offices, laboratories, and waiting rooms. On the second floor are located the administration offices, the library, and the departments of chemistry, hygiene, and surgery. On the third and fourth floors are the departments of anatomy, pathology and bacteriology, and physiology and pharmacology and an animal room containing fifty individual cement animal cages.

HOSPITALS

The City of Augusta in 1914 built upon the College grounds and in immediate proximity to the College building a hospital plant especially designed as a teaching hospital for the Medical School, and known as the University Hospital. The buildings, equipped, cost nearly a million dollars. They are of modern fire proof construction, and are furnished throughout with standard appliances of the best material and design. Of the total of 250 beds, approximately 175 are available without restriction for teaching purposes.

The University Hospital is maintained by the City of Augusta, but the medical and surgical control is vested entirely in the Medical Department of the University of Georgia. The visiting staff is appointed by the Board of Directors of the Medical School from members of the teaching staff, thus assuring a proper use of the clinical material of the hospital for purposes of teaching.

The Wilhenford Hospital for children, containing fifty beds, and located on the College campus, is under the medical and surgical care of the teaching staff in Pediatrics and is used for clinical teaching without restriction.

The U. S. V. B. Psychiatric Hospital No. 62, located at Augusta, through the courtesy of the Veterans Bureau, affords clinical material for the course in Neuro-Psychiatry. This course is taught by the members of the hospital staff, who give the didactic work at the college and the clinical work at the hospital.

The Georgia State School for Mentally Defective Children, which is operated by the State Board of Health, is located about ten miles from Augusta, and provides occasional demonstrations in this field of study.

CLINICAL MATERIAL

Augusta being preeminently a cotton manufacturing city has a very large negro and mill population, probably more than 35,000. from which the school draws its clinical material, and in relation to which it is very conveniently located. There is, therefore, an abundance of material for clinical teaching in the hospital and out-patient department, at all times.

The school also has the control and care of the bed-sick poor in their homes, which provides opportunity for a selection of cases for admission to the hospital and also makes it possible for third and fourth-year students to visit patients in their homes, and thus secure clinical experience under conditions that more nearly parallel those met with in actual practice. This plan was put into operation beginning with the session 1925-1926.

This school directs the hygienic and sanitary activities of the city and county, and uses them for field work in training its students in this important branch. This also gives full opportunity for properly training prospective county health officers.

AUTOPSIES

The city morgue, with specially designed autopsy and cold storage rooms, is situated adjacent to the University Hospital. Autopsies are conducted by the staff in pathology on material supplied from the wards of the hospital, from the out-patient department, and by the coroner's physician. Students are required to attend the autopsies, particularly those on patients who have died in the hospital, and participate in the work and in the discussions.

LIBRARY

The Library is located in the south wing of the main college building, in quarters that afford ample room, good light and retirement. It is open each day from 9 A. M. to 5 P.M. except Saturdays when it closes at noon. During the school session it is open five evenings a week. A full time Librarian is in charge.

There are in the Library about 5,500 bound volumes and 6,600 pamphlets. The list of books comprises many standard reference works in medicine and surgery, and the fundamental sciences, as well as many of the latest text books and monographs. There are ninety current journals in English, French and German, in the fields of Chemistry, Anatomy, Physiology, Bacteriology, Pathology, Medicine, and Surgery. The files of many of these journals are complete to date. The Library is maintained partly by appropriation from the general funds, and partly by the income from the William J. Young Library Endowment. The income from this endowment amounts to about $1,500 a year, and is used for books and periodicals only.

PHOTOGRAPHY

Many of the illustrative aids to teaching are prepared by a trained and salaried photographer. Charts and photographs of specimens, lantern slides and photomicrographs are made particularly for the Departments of Anatomy and Pathology. Also photographs of selected patients in the out-patient department and hospital are taken upon request of the attending staff. There is a liberal supply of the best optical apparatus and photographic material.

REQUIREMENTS FOR ADMISSION

Each student before admission must submit proper evidence of having had a suitable training both in high school work and in work of collegiate grade.

HIGH SCHOOL REQUIREMENTS. The equivalent of a four years course in an accredited secondary school, covering at least fifteen units of work is required. Eight of the fifteen units must be apportioned in Groups I to IV as follows:

Group I, English_____ 3
Group II, Foreign Language_____ 2*
Group III, Mathematics (Algebra 1, Plane Geometry 1)_____ 2
Group IV, History_____ 1
Group V, Science_____ 1

Three additional units must be taken from the five groups.

The remaining four units may be distributed among any of the subjects counted by the high school toward its diploma.

A unit is the credit value of at least thirty-six weeks' work of four or five recitation periods per week, each period to be of not less than forty minutes duration.

PRE-MEDICAL COLLEGE REQUIREMENTS. In addition to the high school work specified above, each candidate for admission must have successfully completed at least sixty semester hours of collegiate work, extending through two years of thirty-two weeks each in some approved college.

A semester hour is the credit value of sixteen weeks' work consisting of one lecture or recitation period per week, each period to be not less than fifty minutes. At least two hours of laboratory work is to be considered the equivalent of one lecture or recitation period.

A description of the subjects required in the two years premedical college course is given below. The remainder of the course may be selected from the general curriculum of the college, but the work of the two years premedical course must be such as to make it acceptable as the equivalent of the first two years of the course leading to the degree of Bachelor of Science.

SUBJECTS REQUIRED IN THE TWO YEAR PRE MEDICAL COURSE

CHEMISTRY. A total of twelve semester hours is required. Eight semester hours must be in general inorganic chemistry, half of which must represent laboratory work. Qualitative analysis may be counted as general inorganic chemistry. The remaining four semester hours must be in organic chemistry, including at least two semester hours of laboratory work.

---

* Both units of Foreign Language must be offered in the same language.

PHYSICS. A total of eight semester hours is required, of which at least two must be laboratory work. It is strongly urged that this course be preceded by a course in trigonometry.

BIOLOGY. A total of eight semester hours is required, four of which must be laboratory work. The requirement may be satisfied by a course of eight semester hours in either general biology or zoölogy, or by courses of four semester hours each in zoölogy and botany, but not by botany alone.

ENGLISH LITERATURE AND COMPOSITION. A total of six semester hours is required. The usual introductory college course of six semester hours or its equivalent meets this requirement.

NON-SCIENCE SUBJECTS. Of the sixty semester hours required as a measure of the two years of college work, at least twelve, exclusive of the six semester hours of English, should be in other than the physical, chemical, or biological sciences. A reading knowledge of French and German is extremely useful.

The above represents only the minimum requirements. Prospective Medical Students are strongly advised, wherever possible, to take a third collegiate year.

APPLICATIONS FOR ADMISSION

Students desiring admission will be furnished with proper blanks, together with instructions for filling them out. Applications, when properly filled out, should be returned, accompanied by the statutory fee of two dollars, to the Medical Department, at Augusta. Each student must include with his application a statement, signed by a physician in good standing, and by the Secretary of the College from which he comes, testifying to his good moral character.

Owing to the greatly increased number of applicants for admission, the Medical Department has been forced, for the present, to place a limit of thirty-six on the number of students who may be enrolled in any one class. In selecting students preference will be given to residents of Georgia. In case of a surplus of applicants from residents of the state, selection will be made on the basis of ability as demonstrated in the premedical courses. It is necessary, therefore, *that applications be sent in before June 15*, and that each application be accompanied by a letter of recommendation from one of the student's instructors in Biology, Chemistry or Physics.

No student will be admitted with any conditions, and if such exist at the time of application in June, they must be removed before the opening of the Medical Department in the fall, through attendance at a summer school.

Women are admitted on the same basis as men.

In conformity with the state law, all credentials are acted upon by the Professor of Secondary Education, at Athens, Georgia.

All communications should be addressed to the Medical Department, University of Georgia, Augusta, Georgia.

ADMISSION TO ADVANCED STANDING

A student desiring admission to advanced standing is required to present satisfactory evidence that his preliminary and medical education is equivalent to that required of the class to which admission is sought. All high school and college credentials are passed upon in the same manner as those of the applicant for admission to the first year course. Students from accredited medical schools whose record of work is satisfactory may be admitted to advanced standing without examination, though the right of requiring examination is not waived. Students will not be received into any class unless there are vacancies.

REQUIREMENTS FOR GRADUATION

A candidate for the degree of Doctor of Medicine from the University of Georgia must be at least twenty-one years of age, and of good moral character. He must be free from indebtedness to the University. He must have successfully completed four years of medical study in accredited institutions, the last year of which shall have been in this school.

COMBINED DEGREE

The University of Georgia confers the degree of Bachelor of Science in Medicine upon those students who successfully complete a four-year course, three years of which are given at Athens, in the College of Science and Engineering, and the last year of which, given at Augusta, is identical with the first year of the course leading to the degree of Doctor of Medicine. The requirements for admission in this course are given fully in the general catalogue of the University. Those who expect to take this course should address, the Registrar, University of Georgia, Athens, Ga.

SPECIAL STUDENTS

Students desiring to take certain courses only will be registered as special students, upon making satisfactory arrangements with the head of the department in which the work is to be done, and upon payment of the special fees. The work so done will not count towards the degree of Doctor of Medicine.

POST GRADUATE WORK

Graduates in medicine who desire to do post graduate work can make the necessary arrangements for it with the head of the departmnt in which they wish to work. No fees will be charged residents of the State of Georgia or alumni of this school, except a breakage fee of $10.00, which, after deduction for any breakage, will be returned.

EXAMINATION AND PROMOTION

Final examinations are held at the completion of the various courses. A grade of 75 per cent is necessary to secure credit for any course. Grades between 100 and 75 are grouped under the letters A to C. D signifies a condition, requiring reexamination; E failure. The work of each course is so condensed that no part of it can be omitted without serious loss; consequently no "cuts" are permitted, except for illness or other unavoidable cause, and work so lost must be made up. In no case will credit be given in a major course (one occupying 100 hours or more) if absences have exceeded 20 per cent of the class exercises. In a minor course the requirement of 80 per cent attendance may be waived in cases of illness, upon recommendation of the instructor and the committee on college affairs.

If, in a single year, a student fails in all his courses, or if he fails in two major courses and receives the grade of D in the other courses, he is dropped from the rolls without privilege of readmission. If he fails in two major subjects, or if he receives the grade of D in all subjects, he is dropped from the rolls but with the privilege of applying for readmission. However, readmission to the school may be denied if the class is already full. If, after the repetition of one year, a student fails a second time, he must withdraw from the school. If a student fails in one major course he must repeat the course or its equivalent, in a manner satisfactory to the head of the department concerned, before he goes on with the next year's work. A student who has failed in a minor course may be permitted to take a reexamination if the head of the department concerned judges it advisable. Such reexaminations are held the week preceeding the opening of the session in September.

The faculty will terminate the course of any student who manifests distinct moral unfitness for the practice of medicine.

TUITION AND FEES

In conformity with the regulations governing other branches of the University of Georgia, the Medical Department does not require tuition fees of residents of the State. For such residents the laboratory and other fees will be as follows:

Matriculation fee, $5.00, paid but once at the time of first registration.

Laboratory fees, $90.00 each year.

The fees for non-residents $300.00 each year. This sum includes tuition and laboratory fees.

Of each student a deposit of $10.00 is required to cover possible injury to the property of the University. The unused portion of this deposit is returned at the end of the college year.

LATE REGISTRATION FEE. A fee of $10.00 is charged students who register later than the regular registration day.

STUDENTS' AID

The Charles McDonald Brown Scholarship fund was established at the University of Georgia in 1882 by the late Hon. Joseph E. Brown, ex-Governor of Georgia.

The interest on this fund is lent to worthy young men who would not otherwise be able to acquire a university education, on condition that they refund the money as soon as they can, after providing for their own livelihood.

By the rules and regulations for the administration of this fund any student in the Medical Department is eligible to participate in its benefit.

Application must be made to the Chancellor of the University at Athens prior to the first of June each year. Examinations for scholarships are conducted in May, and appointments are made by the Board of Trustees in June.

For further information address the Chancellor, University of Georgia, Athens, Ga.

REGISTRATION

Each student before beginning any class work is required to register at the office. All credentials pertaining to entrance requirements must have been approved. Students will not be permitted to register later than one week after the opening of the session.

STUDENT DISCIPLINE

With the approval and support of the faculty the students of this school regulate their conduct according to an honor system administered by a board elected from the student body by the students themselves. Each student upon entering is required to pledge himself in writing to uphold the system and conform systematically to its requirements.

MEDICAL SUPERVISION OF STUDENTS

During the first month of the college year, the student must file a record of a physical examination made by a member of the teaching staff, who shall be designated by the college.

STUDENT EXPENSES

In addition to the fees payable to the college, from $50.00 to $100.00 a year is required to cover the cost of text-books and instruments used by the student.

Suitable board and room may be obtained in the vicinity of the college for $8.00 to $10.00 a week.

Each student is required to have a suitable microscope of his own, payment for which in installments can be arranged through the office.

GENERAL PLAN OF INSTRUCTION

The medical course extends through four years, of thirty-four weeks each, from the latter part of September to about the first of June. Each year is divided into three terms, or trimesters of approximately equal duration.

The work of the first two years is devoted almost entirely to a study of the fundamental sciences of chemistry, anatomy, physiology, pharmacology, pathology and bacteriology. The instruction is largely practical and most of the time is spent by the student in the laboratory, working under competent supervision. This laboratory work is supplemented by class room courses and conferences, which are designed to explain the fundamental principles of the subjects studied and to emphasize their relation to the study of medicine.

In the third trimester of the second year clinical work is introduced by the courses in physical diagnosis, clinical diagnosis, and minor surgery.

During the third year the student, beside attending lectures and demonstrations, spends a considerable part of his time in the medical and surgical clinics. Here, under the supervision of some one of the attending staff, he examines patients, prepares case records, makes diagnoses, and outlines the indicated treatments.

In the fourth year, instruction is given almost wholly in the wards of the hospital and in the clinics.

Courses in public health are given in each of the four years.

Reductions in the excessive time formerly devoted to Anatomy and Chemistry have made it possible to leave a substantial amount of time for elective work. Better students are encouraged to employ this time for original investigations.

A detailed description of the work in the various years in given under the separate departmental announcements and the arrangement of hours is shown in the schedule.

DEPARTMENTS

ANATOMY

DR. ELIOT R. CLARK, Professor.

DR. HENRY McE. KNOWER, Visiting Professor.

DR. EDWIN LINTON, Honorary Fellow in Parasitology.

DR. ROY G. WILLIAMS, National Research Council Fellow, Instructor.

MR. J. C. SANDISON, Instructor.

MR. F. C. STORY, Instructor.

MRS. F. C. STORY, Technician.

The facilities of the department include a well-lighted dissecting-room, with supply-room, an embalming and storage room for cadavers, laboratory for microscopic anatomy with adjacent preparation room, lecture room with projection apparatus, photomicrographic room with suitable equipment, three private laboratories for staff members, and a research laboratory large enough for six investigators. Material for dissection is plentiful. The laboratories are suitably equipped with apparatus and accessories necessary for teaching and investigation. For embryology, histology and neurology there are satisfactory sets of misroscopic slides which are loaned to students.

The required courses given by the department are designed (a) to enable the student to secure a comprehensive knowledge of the anatomy of the human body, gross and microscopic, its mode of development, and the factors, as far as they are known, which govern the healthy growth and maintenance of its parts; (b) to develop in the student independence and initiative and the ability to make accurate, first-hand observations and records. The course in gross and microscopic anatomy are closely correlated. Elective courses are offered for students who desire to extend their knowledge of anatomy beyond that obtained in the required courses, and for those wishing to undertake serious investigation of anatomical problems.

1. GROSS ANATOMY. The basis of this course consists of the dissection, by each student, of a lateral half of the human body. Personal conferences are held daily with each student, and class conferences, at intervals, in which fundamental principles are discussed. The study of the skelton parallels the dissection of the soft parts, a box containing the various bones being issued to each student. First year, first and second trimester, 20 hours a week, 460 hours. *Professor Clark. Mr. Sandison.*

2a. HISTOLOGY. The study of the elementary tissues is followed by that of the organs, including the special sense organs. This is largely a laboratory course and consists of the microscopic study of fresh tissue, frozen sections, and material from the dissecting room, in addition to the usual prepared sections. The instruction is chiefly individual, supplemented by class conferences.

2b. EMBRYOLOGY. This course covers fertilization, cell division, the formation of the germ layers, histogenesis and organogenesis. Use is made of living and injected chick embryos, of pig embryos for dissection, and of serial sections of rat, pig and human embryos. First year first trimester, 7 hours a week, 77 hours. *Professor Knower* and *Mr. Story.*

2c. NEUROLOGY. This course consists of the study of the gross and microscopic anatomy of the central nervous system, and of the chief fiber tracts. First year, second trimester. Total hours for Histology, Embryology and Neurology, 237. *Mr. Story.*

3. TOPOGRAPHICAL ANATOMY. An opportunity is afforded to a limited number of students to study the exact topographical relations of the organs, either from cross-sections or by making special dissections. *Elective.* Second or third trimester, 10 hours a week. *Professor Clark* and *Mr. Sandison.*

4. APPLIED ANATOMY. Third year, trimester, 2 hours a week, 22 hours. *Dr. Wright.*

5. ADVANCED ANATOMY AND INVESTIGATION. To qualified students and graduates informal advanced courses in the different branches of anatomy are offered. Encouragement and opportunity are given to students and others who have sufficient preparation to undertake the investigation of original problems in anatomy. A reading knowledge of French and German is highly desirable. *Professor Clark.*

CHEMISTRY

DR. CARLTON H. MARYOTT, Professor.
MR. C. R. SMITH, Instructor.
MR. H. B. JENKINS, Assistant.

The work in chemistry necessitates as a prerequisite on the part of the student a familiarity with general inorganic chemistry, qualitative analysis and organic chemistry.

1. QUANTITAVE ANALYSIS. A knowledge of quantitative methods, particularly volumetric, is necessary for the proper performance of the work in physiological chemistry. The course consists primarily of laboratory work in which the important volumetric methods are studied. Sufficient practice is given the student for the attainment of accuracy in the procedures and familiarity with the calculations. First year, second trimester, 4 weeks, 9 hours a week, 36 hours. *Professor Maryott* and *Mr. Smith.*

2. PHYSIOLOGICAL CHEMISTRY. In this course a study is made of the chemical composition and reactions of the carbohydrates, lipins, proteins, and other substances of biological interest. The various tissues

and fluids of the body are covered, and considerable quantitative work is done on food, gastric juice, blood and urine. Nutrition and metabolism receive considerable attention, and metabolism experiments are conducted by members of the class. Frequent references are made to current literature. First year, second trimester, 8 weeks, 9 hours a week. Third trimester, 15 hours a week, 327 hours. *Professor Maryott* and *Mr. Smith.*

3. ADVANCED PHYSIOLOGICAL CHEMISTRY. To students who have had a suitable preparation opportunity is given to pursue chemistry beyond that given in course 2, and to enter upon the investigation of new problems. Hours to be arranged.

PHYSIOLOGY AND PHARMACOLOGY

DR. WILLIAM SALANT, Professor.
MR. J. E. NADLER, Instructor.
MR. HENRY WASHEIM, Jr., B.S., Assistant.
MR. W. C. HEATH, Technician.

The facilities of the department comprise a laboratory accommodating forty students, a demonstration room, three physiological and one chemical laboratory for research, a special room for making observations on animals, a well equipped machine shop, a lecture room, office and library. The equipment consists of apparatus required for animal experimentation, and for the study of human physiology including the special senses.

METHODS OF INSTRUCTION. Physiology and Pharmacology are taught by means of (a) laboratory work, (b) demonstrations, (c) lectures, (d) recitations and conferences. In the laboratory the students, working in sections, carry out experiments on animals under the immediate guidance and direction of the staff. Records are preserved, analysed by the students and discussed in conferences. In addition to the above demonstrations are given by members of the staff, of experiments too difficult to be carried out by students. The lectures, recitations and conferences are designed to cover systematically the subject matter of the two fields, and parallel the respective laboratory courses.

1. PHYSIOLOGY, (a) LABORATORY and (b) DEMONSTRATIONS. The first part of the course is taken up with the study of the physiology of nerve and muscle and is followed by experiments on circulation, respiration, secretion, peristalsis and the nervous system. The final two weeks are devoted to "clinical" physiology, which includes blood pressure, pulse tracings, special senses, etc. Twelve hours a week, twelve weeks, 144 hours. *Professor Salant. Mr. Nadler, Mr. Washeim.*

(c) LECTURES. The scope of physiology and fundamental physiological processes are discussed in several introductory lectures. These are followed by lectures on the physiology of muscle, nervous system, circulation, respiration, the physiology of the alimentary canal, and secretion including the internal secretions. Four hours a week. Twelve weeks. *Professor Salant.*

(d) RECITATIONS AND CONFERENCES. Three hours a week for twelve weeks, and one hour a week for eleven weeks, 47 hours. *Professor Salant, Mr. Nadler.*

2. PHARMACOLOGY. (a) LABORATORY WORK AND (b) DEMONSTRATIONS. The actions of drugs on different organs and systems of the body, are studied by experiments on animals. The action of harmless drugs is also tested on man. One day a week for eleven weeks, 77 hours. *Professor Salant, Mr. Nadler, Mr. Washeim.*

(c) LECTURES. Several introductory lectures on general pharmacology are followed by a systematic treatment of drugs used in medicine. Their therapeutic application is emphasized in both lectures and laboratory. Four hours a week, 44 hours. *Professor Salant.*

(d) RECITATIONS AND CONFERENCES. Two hours a week, 22 hours. *Professor Salant, Mr. Nadler.*

3. RESEARCH IN PHARMACOLOGY AND PHYSIOLOGY. Students and graduates with satisfactory preparation in physics, chemistry and biology are encouraged to engage in research under the immediate direction of members of the department. *Professor Salant and Mr. Nadler.*

PATHOLOGY AND BACTERIOLOGY

DR. RICHARD V. LAMAR, Professor.
DR. EDGAR R. PUND, Associate in Pathology.
ALFRED LARSON, Ph.D., Associate in Bacteriology.
MISS DOROTHY WALL SMITH, Technician.
MISS GLADIS GOODRICH, Technician.

The laboratories are well equipped.

General pathology, general and special morbid anatomy and histology, and bacteriology, are taught in a practical way. Aided by the necessary explanations and demonstrations the student himself is set to work. What he does is supervised. The courses in bacteriology come in the first and second years; those in pathology in the second.

1. AUTOPSIES. The autopsies are done in the morgue. The second class is required, and the third and fourth encouraged, to attend. *Professor Lamar and Dr. Pund .*

2. GENERAL PATHOLOGY. MORBID ANATOMY AND HISTOLOGY. This is a course in the fundamental principles and processes of general pathology; the regressive changes, the progressive changes including tumor, and inflammation. Because the study of pathology differs considerably from that of other subjects much pains is taken to teach the point of view and the manner of study.

At the daily exercise a process is first explained and then illustrated by gross demonstration of selected specimens and by projection demonstration of microscopic slides. The specimens are then distributed for study. The student first studies the specimen; then makes a drawing in the note book; and also permanent notes descriptive of the process as a whole.

The student is taught to regard the structural changes not as the whole of pathology, but rather as examples and illustrations of the effect of morbid processes. Functional changes are explained in lectures and are stressed in the recitations. This course serves not merely to teach the principles of pathology, but also to prepare the student for the later and more comprehensive study of pathology in the clinic and the wards.

The museum is well supplied with selected and attractively preserved specimens. The miscroscopic slides are loaned from a collection. Second year, 15 hours a week, 165 hours. *Dr. Pund.*

3. SPECIAL PATHOLOGY. A course in the diseases of the systems, including Gynecological, Pathology, and Neuropathology.

The plan of the work is the same as in the course in General Pathology, to which indeed this course is directly complementary. Drawings and permanent notes are required as before. Late in the course special attention is given to surgical pathological diagnosis. Second year, 15 hours a week, 165 hours. *Dr. Pund.*

4. CLINICAL-PATHOLOGICAL CONFERENCES. In cooperation with the Department of Medicine conferences are held upon the cases which come to autopsy. That member of the fourth class to whom the case had been assigned in the hospital presents the clinical history from the records. The pathologist then demonstrates the autopsy material, and attempts to explain the case as a whole. Fourth year; Mondays, 11 A. M.

5. BACTERIOLOGY. Lectures upon the historical development of bacteriology, upon the systematic position of the bacteria, their general properties and classification, and their relation to fermentation, putrefaction, and infectious diseases, introduce the subject. While the lectures are still in progress the student begins the practical work in the laboratory. He learns the methods of sterilization and the preparation of culture media. He is taught to cultivate, isolate and identify bacteria, beginning with certain saprophytes. Then the commoner species pathogenic for man are studied in detail. The laboratory exercise is preceded by a lecture in which the object and principle of what the student is about to do is made clear to him. First year, 18 hours a week, 198 hours. *Mr. Larson.*

6. INFECTION AND IMMUNITY. A course of lectures with demonstrations and recitations. History and practical application are made prominent. Second year, two hours a week, 20 hours. *Professor Lamar.*

7. ADVANCED WORK. Encouragement and opportunity are offered to qualify students to follow advanced work, and to a few graduates to learn the common methods of investigation employed in research in

pathology and bacteriology. For these purposes the laboratory is suitably equipped with apparatus and supplied with material.

advanced work is given in physical and medical diagnosis, using chosen cases from the abundant material of the medical out-patient department. During this year a comprehensive survey of medicine is given by means of a quiz course based on Osler's Practice. In the fourth year two hours weekly are devoted to lectures, and the remainder of the students' time to clinical and bedside work. Each medical case entering the hospital is assigned to a student who is made responsible for a thorough study of the present state and future progress of the case. In both recitation and clinical periods due attention is given to applied therapeutics.

1. PHYSICAL DIAGNOSIS. Recitations, demonstrations, and practical exercises in the technique of physical diagnosis. Second year, 12 hours a week, 132 hours. *Professor Sydenstricker.*

2. CLINICAL PATHOLOGY. This course prepares the student for his laboratory work in the clinic and ward. The common methods of making laboratory examinations of material from the sick are taught systematically, beginning with the blood, and comprising the urine, sputum, feces and exudates. The necessary material is supplied by the hospitals and clinics. The student himself makes all of the examinations except the Wassermann in test which is demonstrated in detail. The notebook is required and recitations are held. Third year, nine hours a week, 126 hours. *Dr. Burpee* and *Metts.*

3. MEDICINE. A large part of general medicine is covered in this course by means of recitations based on Osler's Practice of Medicine,

MEDICINE

DR. V. P. SYDENSTRICKER, Professor, Director.

DR. THOMAS D. COLEMAN, Professor.

DR. EUGENE E. MURPHEY, Professor.

DR. WILLIAM J. CRANSTON, Assistant Professor.

DR. A. A. DAVIDSON, Assistant Professor.

DR. J. H. BUTLER, Associate.

MR. A. BLACKSHEAR, Lecturer.

DR. M. C. BAINES, Lecturer.

DR. F. L. LEE, Instructor.

DR. KING W. MILLIGAN, Instructor.

DR. A. A. WALDEN, Instructor.

DR. C. M. BURPEE, Instructor.

DR. R. L. HARRIS, Instructor.

DR. G. LOMBARD KELLY, Instructor.

DR. W. D. JENNINGS, Assistant.

DR. J. C. METTS, Assistant.

DR. W. J. HUSON, Assistant.

A course in physical diagnosis in the second year lays the foundation for the medical courses that are to follow. During the third year with collateral reading. Diseases that can be studied in the clinics are passed over rapidly. Third year, three hours a week, 102 hours. *Dr. Jennings.*

4. CLINICAL MEDICINE. Practical instruction is given to small sections in the out-patient department, covering history taking, physical examination, differential diagnosis and treatment of medical cases. Third year, 12 hours a week, 144 hours. *Professor Sydenstricker* and *Drs. Butler, Milligan* and *Lee.*

5. THERAPEUTICS. This course is designed to give the student a practical knowledge of the treatment of the disease. The general indication for the use of and the means of employment of each drug are fully discussed. The actions of such drugs as are indicated in the various diseases, and the best preparations to be used, are thoroughly considered. Third year, three hours a week, 102 hours. *Drs. Davidson* and *Walden.*

6. LECTURE AND RECITATION COURSES The aim is to give the student a thorough knowledge of the most important internal diseases according to the current classification. Diseases that are thoroughly studied in the clinics are passed over rapidly. Fourth year, two hours a week, 30 hours. *Professor Coleman.*

7. WARD WORK. For a period of eleven weeks one-third of the fourth year class is assigned to duty in the medical wards of the hospital. Each medical case in the ward is assigned to a student, who is required to record the history and the physical findings, and to make the routine laboratory examinations. Each student during the past session has had an average of four patients continually under his care. The student is required to make rounds with the visiting physician daily, and to take notes on the clinical course of the case and the therapeutic measures employed. Fourth year, 10 hours a week, 110 hours. *Professors Murphey, Sydenstricker* and *Lamar; Drs. Cranston* and *Butler.*

8. MEDICAL CLINIC. Third and fourth years. One hour a week. Clinical lecture and demonstration. *Professor Murphey.*

9. WORK IN THE OUT-PATIENT DEPARTMENT. In this course the student is assigned a newly admitted patient. After the student has taken the history and made a physical examination, the physician in charge goes over the case with him, pointing out omissions or defects in his work, and consulting as to the differential diagnosis, the prognosis and treatment. About 3,337 patients were admitted to the medical rooms of the out-patient department during the past session. Third year, 82 hours. *Professor Sydenstricker, Drs. Davidson, Walden Butler, Lee, Milligan* and *Burpee.*

10. OUT-PATIENT SERVICE: FOURTH YEAR, SPECIALTY TRIMESTER. Under the supervision of the City Physicians, fourth year students attend the sick poor in their homes. Histories and physical examinations are

done and recorded. All routine laboratory work is carried out and special examinations made as indicated. Treatment and care are outlined by the student and daily visits made to follow the course of the illness. Daily conferences with the instructors form an important part of this work. *Drs. Kelly* and *Huson.*

11. MEDICAL JURISPRUDENCE. Lecture course on this subject from both the medical and legal aspects. Third year, two hours a week, 36 hours. *Mr. Blackshear.*

12. CLINICAL PATHOLOGICAL CONFERENCE. Clinical and autopsy findings are compared and correlated. The histories and material are from the hospital. Fourth year, one hour a week, 34 hours. *Dr. Lamar* and *Medical Staff.*

SUB-DEPARTMENT OF NEUROLOGY

DR. WILLIAM J. CRANSTON, Assistant Professor.

1. A RECITATION AND LECTURE COURSE ON ORGANIC DISEASES OF THE NERVOUS SYSTEM. Text book of Nervous Diseases,—Dana is studied and supplemented by collateral reading in the standard texts. Third year, three hours a week, 100 hours. *Dr. Cranston.*

2. A LECTURE AND RECITATION COURSE IN NEUROSES AND PSYCHOSES On certain days clinical cases illustrating organic nervous diseases are presented to the class. Fourth year, two·hours a week, 68 hours.

3. CLINICAL PSYCHIATRY. The class is taken for one day each week to the United States Veterans Hospital No. 62, where clinical demonstrations by the staff are given. Fourth year, 30 hours. *Dr. M. C. Baines* and *Dr. R. L. Harris.*

DEPARTMENT OF PEDIATRICS

DR. NOEL M. MOORE, Professor.
DR. WILLIAM A. MULHERIN, Clinical Professor.
DR. H. J. BAKER, Associate Professor.
DR. F. X. MULHERIN, Instructor.
DR. H. P. HARRELL, Assistant.
DR. WALTER B. JAMESON, Assistant.

A thorough understanding of what constitutes the normal baby and child is an essential, upon which the proper teaching of Pediatrics should be based. Accordingly, instructions, pertaining to the normal baby and child are stressed.

Preventive Pediatrics is taught to students as the ideal in the successful practice of Pediatrics. With every ill child, demonstrated in clinics, not only the clinical manifestations and pathological side are presented, but also the preventive aspect of the case is emphasized.

Realizing that only by actual contact and proper study of sick children can the important diagnostic and therapeutic differences, peculiar to this branch of medicine, be mastered, the instructions are essentially practical. The subject is taught during the last twenty weeks of the third year, and throughout the fourth year.

1. During the last twenty weeks of the third year the class is instructed and quizzed on the normal baby, normal development, premature baby, care of newly-born, infant feeding, symptomatology, diagnosis and therapeutics, and diseases of the newly-born. Third year, 2 hours a week, 40 hours. *Professor Baker.*

2. PREVENTIVE PEDIATRICS. As a result of thorough organization and commendable cooperation between the Public Health Department, the Obstetrical Department, and the Pediatric Department, Preventive Pediatrics receives its proper consideration. The Public Health Department with its excellent corps of district nurses, social worker-, and the follow-up system, keeps the "well-"baby clinic" abundantly supplied with excellent teaching material. The Obstetrical Department turns over to the Pediatric Department all babies born in the hospital, as soon as the cord is tied. Also in its out-patient obstetrical service the babies are referred to the "well-baby clinic" as soon as it is practical. Since the Pediatric Department conducts all "well-baby clinics" in the City of Augusta and in Richmond County, it is in a position to give a decidedly practical course in this very important branch of medicine.

By such cooperation between the different departments, the students are able to give prenatal advice, deliver the mother, attend the newly-born, and later care for the baby during infancy in the "well-baby clinic."

In this way the essentials of Preventive Pediatrics, such as maternal feeding, mixed feeding, artificial feeding, hygiene, the administration of toxin-antitoxin, vaccination against small pox, etc., are taught in a most practical manner. Fourth year students, in groups of eight are required to attend. Fourth year, 2 hours a week, 60 hours. *Professors Moore* and *Mulherin, Drs. Harrell,* and *Jameson.*

3. OUT-PATIENT DEPARTMENT. The students of the fourth year class, in small sections, are required to work daily for a period of six weeks in the Pediatric clinic, for sick babies and children. The yearly attendance of patients in this clinic is well over two thousand. The students are required to diagnose and treat all cases coming to this clinic, under the supervision of members of the Pediatric Department. All varieties of children's diseases are seen and treated in this clinic. Cases of special interest are sent into the hospitals, and are used as clinical material before the entire class. Fourth year, 10 hours a week, 60 hours. *Professors Moore, Mulherin* and *Baker, Drs. Harrell,* and *F. X. Mulherin.*

4. During the fourth year the various acute and chronic diseases of infancy and childhood are taught in the Pediatric Ward of the University Hospital and in the Wilhenford Children's Hospital. Material is quite sufficient to demonstrate practically all of the diseases of infancy and childhood. No didactic lectures are given, all the work is clinical throughout the fourth year. Students are assigned cases, to be worked up, as soon as the patients arrive in the Pediatric Ward of the University Hospital. These cases are later used by the Pediatric staff in clinics given before the entire class. Clinics for the entire class are regularly held at the Wilhenford Children's Hospital, where an exceptional variety of diseases, common and uncommon, in infancy and childhood are to be seen. The students practically see all pediatric cases going through the Wilhenford Children's Hospital and the University Hospital. This gives the students an unusual opportunity of studying diseases in the patient as well as in their textbooks. Fourth year, 2 hours a week, 68 hours. *Professors Moore, Mulherin* and *Baker*, and *Dr. Harrell.*

SURGERY

DR. RALPH H. CHANEY, Professor, Director.
DR. CHAS. W. CRANE, Professor.
DR. H. M. MICHEL, Professor.
DR. ASBURY HULL, Clinical Professor.
DR. G. T. BERNARD, Clinical Professor.
DR. G. A. TRAYLOR, Clinical Professor.
DR. R. L. RHODES, Associate Professor.
DR. W. W. BATTEY, Associate.
DR. W. H. ROBERTS, Associate.
DR. PETER B. WRIGHT, Instructor.
DR. CHARLES D. WARD, Instructor.
DR. J. H. SHERMAN, Instructor.
DR. ROBERT I. BRYSON, Assistant.
DR. M. PRESTON, AGEE, Instructor.
MISS JOSEPHINE HATCH, Laboratory Technician.

The endeavor in surgical teaching is to place the greatest stress upon diagnosis. The technical side of surgical training, properly, should be emphasized by graduate study and hospital training. An attempt is made through operative clinics in the hospitals and by the personal experimental work to give the student a general idea of the applicability of operative procedure. Instruction starts in the second year with a course in minor surgery including the application of surgical dressings. During the third year teaching is by recitation and lecture, with individual work in the out-patient department and in the laboratory of surgical research. The fourth year is essentially clinical. The student spends his mornings in the hospital as a clinical clerk or attending clinics, and his afternoons in special departments of the out-patient clinics.

1. MINOR SURGERY. Lecture and recitation course covering the treatment of minor infections and simple injuries, followed by a practical course in bandaging, splint making, and their application. Second year, 5 hours a week, 11 weeks. *Drs. Chaney, Ward* and *Assistants*.

2. SURGICAL DIAGNOSIS. Recitation and quiz course. An intensive course intended to bring the general fundamentals of diagnosis rapidly to the attention of the student. Third year, 1 hour a week, 34 weeks. *Dr. Battey.*

3. PRINCIPLES OF SURGERY. A systematic lecture course running through the entire last two years, covering the field of general surgical diagnosis in a detailed manner. Knowledge gained from text-books is supplemented by information abstracted from the current literature. Third year, 1 hour a week, 34 weeks. *Dr. Chaney.*

4. CLINICAL SURGERY. Instruction in the out-patient department. Under the instruction of the clinical staff, the student is taught diagnosis and treatment of ambulatory conditions and as far as possible is allowed to perform and assist in minor operations. One period a week is devoted to orthopedics. Third year, 12 hours a week, 6 weeks. *Drs. Chaney, Michel, Traylor, Rhodes, Battey, P. B. Wright, Ward.*

5. SURGICAL TECHNIC. A practical course given in the department of surgical research. The students in small groups are required to perform those operations which are suitably done on experimental animals. All work is done under rigid asepsis, the same care being used as is maintained in similar cases in the hospital, the animal being under ether anaesthesia. The course is intended to give the student an early first hand knowledge of surgical instruments, surgical procedure, and aseptic techinque, as well as to form a background upon which later the student may on his own election undertake personal research study. Third year, 6 hours a week, 12 weeks. *Drs. Chaney* and *Agee.*

6. SURGICAL PATHOLOGY. A pathological study of material removed at operation. The gross morbid and microsopic processes of the disease are presented from the pathological point of view, and the clinical course, diagnosis and after results are taken up from the clinical aspect. Third year, 4 hours a week, 11 weeks. *Dr. Chaney.*

7. CLINICAL CLERKSHIPS. The students are assigned in sections to the surgical wards of the hospital for one-third of the year. They are required to make routine histories, physical examinations, and laboratory tests, and, in consultation with the staff, complete the necessary special examinations, which will aid in diagnosis. The student is encouraged to make his diagnosis independently, but at all times is under

the supervision of the house staff. Fourth year, 11 weeks. *Drs. Chaney, Ward, Sherman,* and *Assistants.*

8. WARD CLASSES. Daily the students in the surgical section meet with an instructor for general case discussion, special emphasis being placed on differential diagnosis and therapy. Fourth year, 4 hours a week, 11 weeks. *Drs. Bernard, Traylor, Rhodes* and *Battey.*

9. SURGICAL CLINICS. During the period of assignment to the surgical wards of the hospital, the student is required to attend all operative clinics, at which diagnosis, operative techinc and expected results are brought out in detail. Fourth year, 4 hours a week, 11 weeks. *Drs. Chaney, Crane, Traylor, Bernard, Rhodes* and *Battey.*

10. SURGICAL RESEARCH. This is an elective course open to students having completed course 5 or its equivalent. The endeavor is made to encourage individual, constructive thinking on the part of the student, as well as to obtain solution of surgical problems. Fourth year. Elective. 4 hours a week, 11, 23 and 34 weeks. *Dr. Chaney* and *Assistants.*

11. MEDICAL-SURGICAL CLINICS. A general discussion clinic for the entire fourth year class. A special effort is made to present cases having definite diagnostic problems in which both the medical and surgical aspects are evident. The aim is to show that any sharp division between the fields of medicine and surgery is superficial. Fourth year, 2 hours a week, 34 weeks. *Drs. Sydenstricker, Murphey, Chaney* and *Rhodes.*

12. PRINCIPLES OF SURGERY. Continuation of course 3. Fourth year, 1 hour a week, 34 weeks. *Dr. Chaney.*

13. ORTHOPEDIC SURGERY. A clinical period every Monday, for members of the special section. The time is devoted to operative clinics, ward demonstrations and informal lectures. Fourth year, 11 clinics. *Dr. Michel.*

14. ORTHOPEDICS. A systematic lecture and recitation course, covering the general field of orthopedic surgery. Third year, 2 hours a week, 11 weeks. *Drs. Michel* and *P. B. Wright.*

15. GENITO-URINARY SURGERY. A clinical period is given every Thursday to members of special section. The time is devoted to operative clinics, ward demonstrations, and informal lectures. Fourth year, 11 clinics. *Dr. Asbury Hull.*

16. CLINICAL GENITO-URINARY DISEASES. Continuous service in outpatient department for sections of the fourth year class. Practical training is acquired in the diagnosis and treatment of genito-urinary diseases, including cystoscopy. Fourth year, 10 hours a week, 6 weeks. *Drs. Hull* and *Roberts.*

SUB-DEPARTMENT OF DERMATOLOGY

1. Recitations based on a standard text-book in dermatology are given throughout one trimester. Fourth year, one hour a week, 34 hours. Dr. Bernard.

2. The dermatological clinic is attended by the class during one trimester. Fourth year, two hours a week, 36 hours. *Dr. Bernard.*

SUB-DEPARTMENT OF GYNECOLOGY

DR. W. H. GOODRICH, Professor.

DR. GEORGE T. HORNE, Associate Professor.

DR. E. A. WILCOX, Associate Professor.

DR. JOHN C. WRIGHT, Associate in Gynecology.

DR. M. PRESTON AGEE, Assistant.

1. PRINCIPLES OF GYNECOLOGY. This is a recitation and lecture course in the principles and practice of gynecology. Fourth year, two hours a week, 68 hours. *Dr. Horne.*

2. CLINICAL GYNECOLOGY. This is a course in the clinical examination and diagnosis of cases in the out-patient department. Fourth year, 10 hours a week, 120 hours. *Drs. Goodrich, Wright, Wilcox,* and *Agee.*

3. OPERATIVE GYNECOLOGY. This course consists of work in the hospital wards and operating rooms. The class is divided into sections, each section in turn serving as clinical clerks. Cases are assigned to each clerk who is required to secure a complete history and make such examinations, physical or laboratory, as may be essential. In the event of an operation the student assigned to the case is required to assist and make the records. All major operations performed in the hospitals are attended by the group of students assigned to surgical service. Fourth year, 34 periods. *Professor Horne, Drs. Wright* and *Wilcox.*

OBSTETRICS

DR. JOSEPH AKERMAN, Professor, Director.

DR. ANDREW J. KILPATRICK, Professor.

DR. WILLIAM HENRY SHAW, Associate in Obstetrics.

Instruction is both didactic and practical. It begins in the third year and extends through the third and fourth years. During the third year a course in the physiology of normal pregnancy and labor is given supplemented by demonstrations on the manikin and the living subjects in the prenatal clinic. During the fourth year the whole class meets Professor Kilpatrick once each week for study of the various obstetrical complications. The students are also assigned to practical duty in pairs.

The out-patient obstetrical service has been developed to such an extent that it affords opportunity for each student to attend from fifteen to twenty-four cases. Of these he is required to manage at least twelve. The two students on duty reside in the hospital and are subject to call for ward deliveries as well as out-patient calls.

1. LECTURE RECITATIONS AND MANIKIN DEMONSTRATIONS ON THE PHYSIOLOGY OF PREGNANCY AND LABOR. Third year three hours a week throughout the entire year, 100 hours. *Professor Akerman.*

2. PRENATAL STUDY. This includes practice in history taking, palpation, auscultation and pelvimetry. This course is given to small groups throughout the third year. Ten hours a week for two weeks, 20 hours. *Professor Akerman.*

3. WEEKLY CONFERENCES AND CLINICS OF THE MANAGEMENT OF COMPLICATED CASES. Ward cases in the hospital are used for this course. One hour a week throughout the entire fourth year, 33 hours. *Professor Kilpatrick.*

4. OUT-PATIENT SERVICE. For this course the fourth year class is divided into pairs. Each student serves from twenty-four to thirty days according to the size of the class. During his term of service the student resides in the hospital. For the first half of his term of service he acts as assistant to his predecessor and then delivers at least twelve patients himself, preparing and submitting case histories and data for birth certificates for cases attended. While on this service students are allowed to assist in the management of hospital cases. *Professors Akerman, Kilpatrick* and *Resident Staff.*

5. OPERATIVE CLINICS. Arrangements are made whereby both third and fourth year classes witness operations of unusual interest. *Visiting* and *Residential Hospital Staff.*

OPHTHALMOLOGY AND OTO-LARYNGOLOGY

DR. JAMES M. HULL, Professor.
DR. T. E. OERTELL, Professor.
DR. W. C. KELLOGG, Professor.
DR. C. I. BRYANS, Clinical Professor.
DR. W. R. BEDINGFIELD, Clinical Instructor.
DR. S. J. LEWIS, Clinical Assistant.
DR. MARION SILVER, Clinical Assistant.

1. PRINCIPLES OF OPHTHALMOLOGY AND OTO-LARYNOLOGY. Instruction in these branches is given by means of didactic lectures, clinical lectures, and demonstrations. Diseases of the organs of special sense are taught in a systematic way, special attention being paid to pathology and diagnosis. Fourth year, one hour a week, 20 hours. *Professor Hull.*

2. SURGERY OF THE EYE, EAR, NOSE AND THROAT. A course in the surgical treatment of the diseases of the eye, ear, nose and throat.

Fourth year, three hours a week, 15 hours. *Professors Hull, Oertel, Kellogg* and *Bryans.*

3. CLINICAL. A continuous service in the out-patient department Practical training in diagnosis and treatment of the diseases of the eye, ear, nose, and throat. Instruction is given in the use of special diagnostic instruments. Fourth year. *Professors Hull, Oertel* and *Bryans, Drs. Bedingfield, Lewis* and *Silver.*

4. CLINICAL SURGERY. This course consists of work done in the operating room at the hospital. Operations in this department are attended by the group of the students assigned to the special section. Fourth year, one hour a week, 33 hours. *Professors Hull, Oertel, Kellogg* and *Bryans.*

PUBLIC HEALTH

DR. H. B. NEAGLE, Professor,
Commissioner of Health of Augusta and Richmond County.

DR. PAUL EATON, Associate Professor.

DR. L. L. DOZIER, Deputy Commissioner of Health for Richmond County.

MISS AGNESS CAMPBELL, Instructor, Chief of Bureau of Nursing.

MISS ELLEN MARSH, Technician in charge of Public Health Laboratory.

SPECIAL LECTURERS

DR. L. D. FRICKS

DR. JOSEPH GOLDBERGER

MR. BRUCE MAYNE

MR. L. M. FISHER,

MR. H. C. WOODFALL

The City of Augusta and Richmond county are united under the Ellis Health Law of the State of Georgia in a health program which affords unusual opportunities for teaching. The director of the Department of Public Health in the Medical School is Commissioner of Health of the City of Augusta and Richmond county. Under his direction and control, actual experience in city and county health work is available for medical and graduate students, and for the nurses in the University Hospital training schools. The combination of City and County health work under the supervision of the Director of the Department of Public Health of the University Medical School, offers opportunity for practical work in all fields of public health activity. In the University Hospital are isolation rooms for contagious diseases, and provision is made for the admission of special cases sent in by the Board of Health, which ensures material for teaching purposes. General and special clinics provide ample clinical material. Well-baby clinics are being established in connection with the welfare work at the larger cotton mills. The U. S. V. B. Psychiatric Hospital, with 250 beds, maintained by the government for the treatment of ex-soldiers with psycho-neuroses, and the Gracewood Hospital, 50 beds, for mentally defective children maintained by the State. offer facilities for special study. A staff of nine white and four colored nurses is employed by the Health Department in school, clinic, and general bedside nursing. A full time veterinarian, 'with two assistants, superintends the milk and food supply of the city. Two well equipped pasteurization plants, several bottling works, two large abattoirs, several packing and cold storage plants, offer opportunity for a study of food production and distribution. A corps of sanitary inspectors is available for malarial control and other special measures. A full time County Health Officer and one nurse are employed at present in rural health work.

COURSES FOR MEDICAL STUDENTS

Effective cooperation among the heads of departments in the medical school permits the blending of instruction in the elements of preventive medicine with the teaching of other aspects of disease. The work is distributed through the four years of the medical college, in order to avoid overcrowding or radical. alteration of the regular curriculum.

FIRST YEAR. Instruction in Preventive Medicine is begun in the first year through a course in personal hygiene. This consists of lectures by specialists, quizzes, filling out of the standard periodic examination blanks by students and examiners in conference, and a thesis.

The topics covered by lectures are: 1, hygiene of eye and ear; 2, hygiene of nose and throat; 3, veneral disease (a) personal, (b) community; 4, exercise and rest; 5, food: (a) assimilation, (b) elimination, (c) protection of food and water supply; 6, protection against disease, (a) personal, (b) community; 7, mental hygiene; (a) personal, (b) community. Practical work includes compulsory physical examination of each student, and filling out of the standard periodic examination blank; semi-compulsory vaccination against small-pox and typhoid; visits to abattoirs, cold storage plants, pasturization plants and city water plants.

The course comprises 1 hour weekly for the academic year with several Saturday afternoon trips, a total of 63 hours.

SECOND YEAR. In the second year, the bacteriological work is extended to public health laboratory methods. The functions of a public health laboratory are explained, and the routine activities are actually performed. Community and personal hygiene teaching is extended. In the latter half of the year special public health measures in school work are studied in connection with the course in immunity and serum therapy. Special subjects are assigned to students for original investigations. Topics so assigned include the history, function, and future of vital statistics, (mortality, morbidity, and infant mortality). Special stress is laid upon a complete bibliography of original and recent articles, with reprints attached, whenever available.

The public health laboratory methods which are taught include: diagnostic bacteriology, diagnostic parasitology, and identification of mosquitoes. Under sanitation, a study is made of the breeding of mosquitoes, flies, etc., and the protection and control of water, milk, and food supply, as practiced by the Board of Health, comprising laboratory and field work. Under immunity are included lectures and practical demonstrations, a compulsory Schick test, and voluntary toxin-anti toxin treatment. Lectures are given in serology, and voluntary Wassermann tests are made on members of the class. The course comprises a total of 66 hours.

THIRD YEAR. In the third year the clinical work is extended to the special health functions, such as well-baby clinics and school inspection. Special diseases are assigned to individuals who investigate and report regarding the cause, course, prevention, possibility of transmission to others, and the relation to community or personal hygiene. A summary of recommendations for preventive measures is required. Public health administration lectures are given, and a sense of community responsibility is developed by investigation into every activity of the Department of Public Health. A written report is required of every student after each investigation.

Practical work of this year includes the application of vaccine and serum therapy, as participants in the health activities of the City and County; school inspection, visits to welfare stations, play grounds, and various childrens' institutions; demonstration of the collection and analysis of statistics as practiced by the Health Department. This course comprises a total of 103 hours.

FOURTH YEAR. A thesis on some phase of public health is required for presentation before the class at some period of the year. Lectures on vital statistics are supplemented by practical work in the compilation and analysis of statistics collected by the Board of Health during the current year.

Prenatal visits with the staff of the board of health prepare the students for obstetrical service. Preventive pediatrics is studied in 3 special clinics supplied by material from welfare stations. Attendance at well-baby clinics is compulsory and preparatory for the work as conducted in the special preventive pediatrics clinic and the sick-baby clinic.

Special problems in child welfare, epidemic control, school hygiene, health campaigns, surveys, etc., are worked out as opportunity offers, and a special effort is made to have a number of active workers in the public health field deliver lectures at frequent intervals.

Mental hygiene is emphasized as a community problem and practical experience in its solution is offered by clinics for delinquent children, and visits to the State Home for Mentally Defective, and the Lenwood Hospital.

A summary of public health work, with emphasis on a definite plan for city and county health activities, occupies the last twelve hours of the Spring term. This course comprises a total of 33 hours. The total number of hours assigned to the Department of Preventive Medicine is 298.

PUBLIC HEALTH NURSING

The staff of public health nurses has been strengthened by the addition of a competent supervising nurse and supervisors for county, school, and child welfare work.

Public health nursing is being taught undergraduate nurses along the same lines that have been found successful for medical students.

POST GRADUATE INSTRUCTION

Under the Ellis Health Law, training of prospective county health officers in all branches of health work is provided free of charge to residents of the State of Georgia. Non-residents are charged according to the length of the course pursued. Through special arrangement with the State Board of Health, short intensive course of six to eight weeks are provided for prospective county health officers of Georgia. Students taking these intensive courses are then eligible for county positions, with the understanding that they will supplement the work by further study later, as determined by the Director of the Department and the Commissioner of Health of Georgia.

PUBLIC HEALTH DEGREES

BACHELOR OF PUBLIC HEALTH

Prerequisites: The student must have completed a course of study qualifying him to matriculate as a student of the Medical College. The satisfactory completion of an approved program of at least one year in the school of Public Health will be necessary to obtain the degree of Bachelor of Public Health.

Doctors of Medicine completing a minimum of six weeks intensive training in the School of Public Health, combined with actual experience in City, County, or State Health Department under the supervition of the Director of the School of Public Health and the Commissioner of Health of the State of Georgia, are granted this degree after passing a satisfactory examination.

MASTER OF PUBLIC HEALTH

The Master's degree represents one year's advanced work following the Bachelor's degree in Public Health or its equivalent. The work may be wholly or only partially in the school.

Doctors of Medicine having had six weeks intensive training in the School of Public Health and having completed a satisfactory program of City, County, or State Public Health work under the supervision of the Director of the School of Public Health and Commissioner of Health of the State of Georgia are granted this degree. The program must be presented in writing before being undertaken and its duration will depend upon the qualifications of the candidate and the nature of the work.

DOCTOR OF PUBLIC HEALTH

Doctors of Medicine who have concluded at least one year's training in the School of Public Health or its equivalent and who have spent one year in the completion of an approved program are granted this degree after presenting a thesis and undergoing an oral examination. The program outlined may deal with City, County, or State Health work in any or all their respective phases.

GRADUATING CLASS 1925

Battey, Colden Rhind_____Augusta, Ga.
Bond, Ellis Malcolm_____Danielsville, Ga.
Brown, George Wilmot, Jr._____Lawtey, Fla.
Bryant, Verlin L._____Bartow, Ga.
Burdashaw, William Jennings_____Augusta, Ga.
Dobyns, William Frasier_____Fries, Va.
Fowler, Andrew Herbert_____Woodstock, Ga.
Hood, John G., Jr._____Dacula, Ga.
                B.S. in Medicine, University of Georgia.
Lamon, John Daniel, Jr._____Macon, Ga.
                B.S. in Medicine, University of Georgia.
Morgan, Thomas Edward_____Newnan, Ga.
                B. Com., Oglethorpe University.
Muñoz, Justo Luis_____Baltimore, Md.
Richardson, George Williams_____Savannah, Ga.
                B.S. in Medicine, University of Georgia.
Roberts, Tenny Hugh_____Macon, Ga.

Rose, Walter Henry_____Unadilla, Ga.
Savage, Carl Preston_____Rose Hill, N. C.
Smith, Racy Hawkins_____Harrison, Ga.
     B.S. in Medicine, University of Georgia.
Stephenson, John Ttrantham_____Hartsville, S. C.
     B. S., Clemson University.
Temples, Powell McRae_____Statesboro, Ga.
     B.S. in Medicine, University of Georgia.
Walker, Hugh Capers_____Eatonton, Ga.
     B.S. in Medicine, University of Georgia.
Warren, Earle Loy_____Swainsboro, Ga.
     B.S. in Medicine, University of Georgia.
Weeks, Percy Dell_____Millen, Ga.
Weeks, Richard Bynum_____Harlem, Ga.
Wiley, John Davidson_____Sparta, Ga.
     B. S., Davidson College.
Wilson, James Robert_____Thomson, Ga.
     B.S. in Medicine, University of Georgia.
Wright, Lewis H._____Augusta, Ga.
     A. B., University of Nevada, D. V. M., Cornell.

STUDENTS, 1925-1926

Fourth Year Class

Bartoli, Joseph Faraci_____New York, N. Y.
Blanchard, Hubert Hiram_____Harlem, Ga.
Britt, Reddin_____ Lumberton, N. C.
Brown, Felix Bert_____Sharon, Ga.
Diamond, Harry Joseph _____Patterson, N. J.
Florence, Loree_____Athens, Ga.
     A. B., Shorter, B. S. in Medicine, University of Georgia.

Hardman, William Wallace_____Crawford, Ga.
     B. S. in Medicine, University of Georgia.
Howell, James Russell_____Canton, Ga.
Kandel, Harry Milton_____Savannah, Ga.
Kelley, William Henry_____Columbus, Ga.
     B. S. in Medicine, University of Georgia.
Martin, Carl Turner_____Ashland, Ga.
     B. S. in Medicine, University of Georgia.
Miles, Walter Galliber_____Dalton, Ga.
Mobley, John Williams, Jr._____Milledgeville, Ga.
O'Dell, James Walter_____Athens, Ga.
     B. S. in Medicine, University of Georgia.
Porras, Francisco R. de_____Anãsco, P. R.
Roule, Jules Victor, Jr._____Mansura, La.

Sasser, Thomas Judson_____Statesboro, Ga.
B. S. in Medicine, University of Georgia.
Sandison, James Calvin_____Mobley, Mo
A. B., University of Missouri
Smith, Horace Daniel_____Tennille, Ga.
Story, Frank Crawford_____Doerun, Ga.
A. B., Mercer University
Thurmond, John William, Jr._____Edgefield, S. C.
Walton, John Marshall_____Dublin, Ga.
Wasden, Charles Newton_____Midville, Ga.
Wright, George Washington, Jr._____Augusta, Ga.
B. S. in Medicine, University of Georgia.
Zeagler, George Mingledorf_____Zieglar, Ga.
B. S. in Medicine, Mercer University

Third Year Class

Adams, Tommie Martin_____Elberton, Ga.
Baird, James Mason_____Columbus, Ga.
Baxley, William Ward_____Haphzibah, Ga.
Beeler, Courtland, Jr._____Augusta, Ga.
Bell, Rudolph Foster_____Callison, S. C.
Comas, Arsenio_____Cabo Rajo, P. R.
Davis, Feltz_____Macon, Ga.
Fitts, John Berlin_____Danielsville, Ga.
Golsan, Willard Robert, Jr._____Macon, Ga.
B. S., Mercer University
Hammond, Emily Cumming_____Augusta, Ga.
Jackson, Ole Cleveland_____Augusta, Ga.
A. B., Ohio University.
Jenkins, Hughes Brantley_____Sardis, Ga.
B. S. in Medicine, Mercer University.
Josey, Julian Cleon_____Bartow, Ga.
Lane, Byrl Benjamin, Jr._____Donalsonville, Ga.
Lane, John Dunn, Jr._____Berner, Ga.
Larson, Alfred_____Augusta, Ga.
B. A., Ph. D., University of Wisconsin.
Long, William Harvey_____Darien, Ga.
McDaniel, James George_____Eastman, Ga.
B. S. in Medicine, University of Georgia.
McGibony, John Robert_____Greensboro, Ga.
Mosteller, Malcolm_____Lylerly, Ga.
B. S., Oglethorpe University
Oetjen, Leroy Henry_____Augusta, Ga.
Pewell, Cuthbert Ennis_____Swainsboro, Ga.
Ramos, Jose Lebron_____San Lorenzo, P. R.

Rawls, Lewis Lacey_____Wrightsville, Ga.
Rogers, Charles Morgan, Jr._____Chester, Ga.
Scoggins, Paul Thurman_____Athens, Ga.
Strange, James Lawson_____Oak Park, Ga.
Watson, Otho O'Dell_____Dublin, Ga.
Whitaker, Courtland Daniel_____Harlem, Ga.
Wyman, John Frampton_____Aiken, S. C.
Youmans, Comer Roger_____Lexsy, Ga.

Second Year Class

Anderson, Charles Lee_____Columbus, Ga.
Ansley, Hamilton Goss_____Dectaur, Ga.
Brim, James Croswell_____Dawson, Ga.
B. S. in Medicine, Mercer University.
Byne, James Miller, Jr._____Waynesboro, Ga.
Caldwell, John Mars, Jr._____Augusta, Ga.
B. S. in Medicine, University of Georgia.
Collinsworth, Allen Mansfield_____Clarkston, Ga.
Craig, Henry Roosevelt_____Augusta, Ga.
B. S. in Medicine, University of Georgia.
Crovatt, Joseph Gidiere_____Thomasville, Ga.
Daughtry, Leila Alice_____Portal, Ga.
A. B., Bessie Tift
Ferrell, Thomas Joseph_____Americus, Ga.
Fourcher, Kenneth Rushton_____Augusta, Ga.
Haddock, Samuel Harvey_____Macon, Ga.
Hall, John Iredell_____Macon, Ga.
Harbin, Robert Maxwell, Jr._____Rome, Ga.
B. S. in Medicine, University of Georgia.
Henry, Charles Goodrich_____Augusta, Ga.
A. B., University of Georgia
Hensley, Ernest Albert_____Augusta, Ga.
Heriot, George Washington, Jr._____Savannah, Ga.
Holden, Farish Clay_____Ellijay, Ga.
Kicklighter, Raymond Braxton_____Glennville, Ga.
A. B., Lincoln Memorial
Kilpatrick, Charles McCord_____Augusta, Ga.
Lanier, John Ray_____Graymont, Ga.
Lawless, Thomas Frances, Jr._____East Orange, N. J.
Neville, Rufus Lester_____Statesboro, Ga.
Ph.G., University of Georgia.
Parker, Alton Brooks_____Millen, Ga.
Phillips, Alpheus Maynard_____LaGrange, Ga.
Philpot, William Kuhlke_____Augusta, Ga.
B. S. in Medicine, University of Georgia.

Phinizy, Thomas Burdell_____Augusta, Ga.
B. S., University of Georgia
Roberts, Burch Joiner_____Dawson, Ga.
B. S. in Medicine, Mercer University.
A. B., Mercer University
Schwalb, Otto William_____Savannah, Ga.
Seaman, Henry Ansley_____Waycross, Ga.
Smaha, Tofey George_____Griffin, Ga.
B. S. in Medicine, University of Georgia.
Stanford, James Willingham, Jr._____Cartersville, Ga.
Statham, John Claude_____Leesburg, Ga.
Saurez, Raymond, Jr._____Habana, Cuba
Tousignant, Camille_____Bath, S. C.
Wall, William Henry_____Ellaville, Ga.
Wammock, Hoke_____Sopherton, Ga.
Washeim, Henry, Jr._____Neponsit, L. I., N. Y.
B. S., University of Michigan
Webb, Roy Lee_____Hogansville, Ga.
Wilson, Robert Kemp_____Thomasville, Ga.
Wood, David Lloyd_____Dalton, Ga.
Young, Wilburn Cogdell_____Augusta, Ga.

First Year Class

Adams, Alfred Newton_____East Point, Ga.
B. S., Oglethorpe University
Chance, Francis Sinclair_____North Augusta, S. C.
Daniel, John Wilfred, Jr._____Savannah, Ga.
Davis, Abram James_____Macon, Ga.
Drexel, Adolph Edward_____Augusta, Ga.
D. V. M., University of Georgia
Durham, William Robert_____Maxeys, Ga.
B. A., Oglethorpe University
Elarbee, Harry Moore_____Daisy, Ga.
Evans, George Cone_____Sylvania, Ga.
Frank, Jacob Lyall Louis_____Augusta, Ga.
B. S., M. S. Cornell and University of Georgia.
Gepfert, John Randolph, Jr._____Augusta, Ga.
*Grey, Walter Jacob_____Swainsboro, Ga.
Hewell, Guy Crawford_____Dewey Rose, Ga.
. A. B., Mercer University
Jones, Pratt Elmer_____Columbus, Ga.
Kirkland, Walter Paul_____Pearson, Ga.
Little, Robert Nathan_____Cornelia, Ga.
Massicot, Marie Mildred_____Columbus, Ga.
B. S., University of Maryland

McKemie, Howard Marvin_____Coleman, Ga.
McLaughlin, Charles Keiley_____Isle of Hope, Ga.
Miller, Harold Edgar_____Claxton, Ga.
Miller, Robert P., Jr._____Atlanta, Ga.
Morrison, Howard Jack_____Savannah, Ga.
Moss, Thomas Hudson_____Rome, Ga.
Mulherin, Hugh Gallagher_____Augusta, Ga.
Palmer, Joseph Israel_____Thomasville, Ga.
Perkins, Henry Roscoe_____Augusta, Ga.
Pittman, John Green, Jr._____Gaffney, S. C.
Prather, Willie Thomas_____Augusta, Ga.
Rogers, Hunter Beall_____Macon, Ga.
Rosen, Samuel Frederic_____Savannah, Ga.
Schwall, Edward_____Augusta, Ga.
Simonton, Fred Huie_____Roopville, Ga.
Slappey, Theo Aulton_____Albany, Ga.
Smith, Frank Montague_____Claxton, Ga.
Swilling, Mary Evelyn_____Athens, Ga.
Westbrook, Jesse Lovic_____Ila, Ga.
Woods, Otis Clark_____Kite, Ga.

Special Student

Bailey, Lucius Ashley_____Ellenton, S. C.
* Deceased.

The University Hospital School of Nursing

ALICE F. STEWART, R. N., Director of Nurses.

The University Hospital School of Nursing offers to its pupils unusual facilities for obtaining adequate instruction and training in this most important and attractive field of usefulness for women. Among the advantages offered are opportunities to work under the direction of the specialists in medicine and surgery of the Medical School; and, in such science as bacteriology and clinical microscopy, to receive instruction from members of the college Faculty in the laboratories of the hospital.

Careful teaching in nursing methods and bedside care is given by a well selected staff of graduate nurses, who also supervise the work on the wards. The theoretical work is directed and supervised by a full time instructor who correlates it with the practical work. The University Hospital School of Nursing also offers each nurse a definite period in the out-patient department of the Medical School. There she may see treated diseases of milder form which do not come to the hospital ward, such as ear, eye, nose, and throat diseases and subacute skin diseases. This training is of distinct advantage to those nurses who may later choose the public health field and is filling a long felt want in nurses' training. A course in practical pharmacy has been inaugurated with much success.

There is operated a branch of District Nursing in connection with the out-door service of the Medical School, and pupil nurses will be able to have valuable training in this field during their third year, should they so elect. In this work the student nurse accompanies graduate visiting nurses on their daily rounds, assists in the care of patients, learns to keep records, make reports, etc. This is an unusual opportunity since few schools offer a course in Public Health Nursing included as a part of their three years' training course.

REGISTRATION

The University Hospital School of Nursing is an integral part of the Medical Department of the University of Georgia, operating under its charter, and is registered under the laws of the State of Georgia and New York, thus giving its graduates standing in both states. The School secured its New York registration before training schools were standardized in Georgia, and has been one of the foremost in the struggle for higher standards in nursing education.

PLAN OF INSTRUCTION

The school curriculum conforms to that planned by the Board of Regents of the University of the State of N. Y., Albany, N. Y., and is approved by the best training schools in the United States. The course of instruction is graded and lasts for three years. The first year is devoted to a probational course of two months, a preliminary course in Anatomy and Physiology, Bacteriology, Personal Hygiene, Elementary Chemistry, Nutrition and Cookery, Hospital Housekeeping, drugs and Solutions, Elementary Nursing, Bandaging, Ethics. Pathology, Materia Medica, Diet in Disease, Pharmacy, Massage.

INTERMEDIATE YEAR. Surgery, Medicine, Pediatrics, Orthopedics, Communicable Disease, Gynecology, Obstetrics, Eye, Ear, Nose and Throat, Public Sanitation.

THIRD YEAR. Mental and Nervous Diseases, Occupational, Skin and Veneral Diseases, Emergency Nursing, Electives as follows: Public Health Nursing, Private Nursing, Institutional Work, Laboratory Technique.

During the three years much of the instruction is arranged in lecture courses given by the resident and attending staff. The lectures are followed in each instance by quiz and demonstration classes, thus correlating the scientific and practical sides of the work. Examinations are held periodically, and the standing of the student is based upon the results of examination.

THE HOURS OF STUDY

Hours on duty are arranged as follows: the day staff has an eight hour day, with six hours on Sundays and holidays; the night staff is at present on continuous ten hours duty, though, it is expected that this will be lowered to eight within the next few months. Rest and recreation -hours are allowed so that the actual time a nurse spends on duty is aproximately fifty hours per week. Each nurse is required to serve, during her three years, four terms of night duty of from four to six weeks each.

REQUIREMENTS FOR ADMISSION

Candidates must apply personally or by letter to the Director of Nurses. Those applying by letter should enclose statements from their pastors testifying to their qualifications for undertaking professional work, and from their physicians certifying to sound health and unimpaired faculties. No candidate will be considered who is not in good physical condition. Applicants must be between the ages of eighteen and thirty years, of good physique and at least average height. They must furnish written evidence of at least four years high school work. Preference will be given to women with a preliminary training beyond this minimum requirement. The Director of Nurses decides as to the qualification and fitness of the student, and the propriety of retaining or dismissing her at the end of the term of probation. She may also terminate the connection of a student with the school at any time in case of misconduct, insubordination, inefficiency or neglect of duty.

Student nurses are not permitted to return home in order that they may nurse sick members of their family, as it is the opinion of the school authorities that they must only be permitted to nurse under careful supervision.

EXPENSES

Students receive board and lodging and a reasonable amount of laundry from the date of entrance. An allowance for the first year of $70.00 and $120.00 for each of the two succeeding years is made by the hospital, and the school equips the student with uniforms, after the probationary period. There are no tuition fees; but a charge will be made for breakage and damage to hospital property. Text-books are provided by the hospital to be bought by the student at wholesale cost as she is able to pay for them.

VACATIONS

Vacations are given between the beginning of June and the end of September. A period of two weeks is allowed each student yearly. In sickness all students are cared for without expense to them, but time lost through this, or any other cause, beyond stipulated limits, must be made up.

CLASSES

Classes are admitted in February and September.

Part IX
REGISTER OF STUDENTS

REGISTER OF STUDENTS, 1925-1926

GRADUATE STUDENTS

(An asterisk after a name indicates that the student is not a candidate for a degree. (S) indicates membership in the Graduate School for the Summer Session of 1925; (SR), of both the Summer Session of 1925 and the long session of 1925-1926.)

Abercrombie, Vonnie (S) _____Hiram
    A.B., in Education, University of Georgia, 1925.
    Education, Hutchinson.

Abney, Louise_____Athens
    A.B., Agnes Scott College, 1920.
    Psychology, Edwards.

Adams, Bunice Celia (S)_____Athens
    A.B., in Soc. Sc., University of Georgia, 1922.
    History, Payne; **English,** Sanford.

Attaway, Eugene (S) _____Camilla
    B.Ph., Emory University, 1916; B.S. Agr., University of Georgia, 1920.
    History, Payne; **English,** Sanford.

Baker, Charles Hubert_____Danielsville
    B.S. in Commerce, University of Georgia, 1925.
    Commerce, Brooks, Jenkins.

Bennett, Frederick William_____Athens
    B.S. Agr., University of Georgia, 1925.
    Agricultural Chemistry, Carter.

Bennett, Ulric Joseph (S) _____Dalton
    A.B., University of Georgia, 1909, and B.L., 1914.
    Education, Hutchinson; **History,** Payne.

Betts, Sarah Souise* (SR) _____Athens
    Candidate for A.B. in Educ., University of Georgia, 1926.
    French, Lustrat.

Braddy, Minton Venner* (S) _____Hogansville
    A.B. in Educ., Oglethorpe University, 1924.
    Education, Hutchinson.

Brand, Mena Louise (S) _____Lawrenceville
    A.B. in Soc. Sc., University of Georgia, 1921.
    Education, Hutchinson; **History,** Payne.

Brinson, Lessie Alma Brannen (S) _____Millen
    A.B., Wesleyan College, 1904.
    Education, Hutchinson; **English,** Sanford.

Broach, William Earle_____Athens
    B.S. Agr., University of Georgia, 1918.
    Agricultural Engineering, Lyle.

Brooks, Lily Wingo_____Athens
    A.B., Erskine College, 1916. Columbia University, S., 1922; University
    of California, S., 1924.
    Sociology, Hutchinson.

Brookshire, John Balus (S) _____Bowman
    A.B., Mercer University, 1901.
    Education, Hutchinson; **English,** Sanford.

Brown, Claud Vinson (S) _____Union City
    and English Historical Review. A full reading of Fisher. Political **History**
    Philosophy, Hutchinson; **Sociology,** Hutchinson; **English,** Sanford,
    McWhorter.

Bush, Rose (SR) _____Athens
    A.B., University of Georgia. 1924.
    French, Lustrat.

Butler, Mary Ormond (S) _____Madison
    A.B. in Soc. Sc., University of Georgia, 1923.
    English, McWhorter; History, Payne.

Cantrell, Gertrude Ellington_____Athens
    A.B. in Educ., University of Georgia, 1925.
    English, McWhorter; History, Payne.

Carmichael, Mary Frances*_____Athens
    Candidate for A.B. in Educ., University of Georgia, 1926.
    History, Payne.

Carreker, Homer Beeks (S) _____Dublin
    A.B.. Mercer University, 1900.
    Education, Hutchinson.

Carreker, Nell Wyche (S) _____Dublin
    A.B.. Cox College, 1900.
    English, Sanford; Education, Hutchinson.

Carson, Alberta Reppard_____Savannah
    A.B., Randolph Macon College, 1924.
    English, Sanford; History, Payne.

Chance, Claude (SR) _____Athens
    A.B., University of Georgia, 1924.
    French, Lustrat; Education, Hutchinson.

Chapman, Paul Wilber_____Athens
    B.S. Agr., University of Missouri, 1914, and B.S. Educ., 1917.
    Agricultural Education, Wheeler.

Corry, Annie Irrovia (S) _____Siloam
    A.B.. Maryville College, 1920.
    Education, Hutchinson; English, Sanford.

Cromartie, Arthur Dean (S) _____Vidalia
    B.S.. Davidson College, 1924.
    English, Sanford.

Davis, Alfred Lee (S) _____Rome
    B.S., University of Georgia, 1924.
    Education, Hutchinson.

Downs, Walter Lee (S) _____Vidalia
    A.B., University of Georgia, 1909.
    History, Payne; Education, Hutchinson.

Edwards, Myrtle (S) _____Fairmount
    A.B. in Educ., University of Georgia, 1925.
    Mathematics, Stephens, Barrow.

Ferguson, Mary Olivia_____Athens
    A.B., University of Georgia, 1925.
    French, Lustrat.

Gaines, Thomas Newton (S) _____Winterville
    B.Ph., Emory University. 1912.
    Education, Hutchinson; English, Sanford.

Garrett, James Robert (S)_____Loganville
    B.Ph., Milligan College. 1904.
    History, Payne; Education, Hutchinson.

Haley, Georgia (S) _____Elberton
    A.B., La Grange College. 1920.
    History, Payne; English, Sanford.

Harison, Callie Maye (S) _____Cordele
    A.B. in Engl.. Georgia State College for Women, 1924.
    English, McWhorter; Education, Hutchinson.

Hill, Pope Russell_____Toccoa
    B.S. Agr.. University of Georgia. 1916; Emory University. 1922-1923.
    Mathematics, Stephens. Barrow. Cumming; Commerce. Brooks.

Holliday, Norene (S) _____Athens
    A.B., Radcliffe College, 1914.
    French, Lustrat.

Hosch, John Harrison_____Gainesville
    B.S. in Commerce, University of Georgia, 1925.
    History, Payne.

Johnson, John Wesley_____Dalton
    B.S. in Commerce, University of Georgia, 1925.
    Commerce, Heckman, Brocks; English, Sanford.

Johnson, Rose (S) _____Birmingham, Ala.
    A. B., Brenau College, 1917.
    English, Sanford; History, Payne.

Jones, Robert Wallace*_____Winterville
    D.V.M., Kansas City Veterinary College, 1907.
    Agricultural Education, Wheeler.

Kellogg, Charles Edward_____Athens
    A.B., Doane College, 1912; B.S. Agr., University of Nebraska, 1920.
    Animal Husbandry, Jarnagin.

LaBoon, Brandt (S) _____Monroe
    B.S., University of Georgia, 1910.
    Education, Hutchinson; History, Payne.

Lane, Mary* (S) _____Rockmart
    A. B., La Grange College.
    English, Sanford; History, Payne.

Lanier, William Rufus (S) _____Dublin
    B. S., Mercer University, 1899.
    History, Payne.

Lassiter, Horace Shelby (S) _____Macon
    B.S., Emory University, 1923.
    Education, Hutchinson; Mathematics, Stephens, Barrow.

Lawson, Ulysses Auby (S) _____Gainesville
    A.B. and B.Ph., North Georgia Agricultural College, 1915.
    Mathematics, Stephens, Barrow; Education, Hutchinson.

Lewis, Laura Kate_____Waleska
    A.B., La Grange College, 1915.
    Philosophy, Hutchinson; Sociology, Hutchinson.

Littlejohn, Boyd Bashan (S) _____Pacolet, S. C.
    A.B., Wofford College, 1922.
    English, Sanford; History, Payne.

McClellan, Albert Dalton (S) _____Buchanan
    B.S., University of Chattanooga, 1925.
    Mathematics, Stephens, Barrow.

McMullan, Lois (S) _____Hartwell
    A.B., North Georgia Agricultural College, 1920.
    English, Sanford; History, Payne.

Macon, Alethea Jane (S) _____Brunswick
    A.B. in Soc. Sc., University of Georgia, 1922.
    English, Sanford; History, Payne.

Marchman, Robert Lee (S) _____Marianna, Fla.
    A.B. in Educ., Alabama Polytechnic Institute, 1923.
    Education, Hutchinson.

Mehre, Harry James* (S) _____Athens
    B.Ph. in Journalism, Notre Dame University, 1922.
    English, Sanford, McWhorter.

Middlebrooks, Harry LaFayette_____Eatonton
    B.S., University of Georgia, 1925.
    English, Sanford, McWhorter; History, Payne.

Miller, Mary Edna (S) _____Brunswick
    A.B., Wesleyan College, 1924.
    History, Payne; English, McWhorter.

Miller, Stephens Grady (S) _____Young Harris
    A.B., University of Georgia, 1924.
    History, Payne; Education, Hutchinson.

Miller, Verdie Francis (S) _____Blairsville
    A.B., University of Georgia, 1924.
    English, Sanford; Education, Hutchinson.

Morgan, Vander Valdee (S) _____Columbus
    B.Ph., Emory University, 1902.
    History, Payne.

Morrison, John Haygood (S) _____Blythe
    A.B., Emory University, 1915.
    Education, Hutchinson.

Morton, Frank Edward* (S) _____Griffin
    B.S., Holbrook Normal College, 1895; A.B., Alhambra University, 1896,
    A.M., Mineral Springs College, 1900; University of Oregon, 1902-
    1903; University of Tennessee, S., 1911, S., 1921; Columbia Univer-
    sity, S., 1924.
    Education, Hutchinson.

Mote, John Halon_____Athens
    B.S., University of Georgia, 1925.
    Physics, Hendren; Chemistry, Scott.

Mozeley, Coralee (S) _____Clayton
    A.B., Piedmont College, 1924.
    English, McWhorter; Education, Hutchinson.

Munro, Henry Smith* _____Athens
    Candidate for B.S. Agr., University of Georgia, 1926.
    Agricultural Education, Wheeler; Agronomy, Tabor.

Nixon, Joseph Jefferson (S) _____North Augusta, S. C.
    A.B., Furman University, 1922.
    History, Payne.

O'Steen, Myrtie (S) _____Atlanta
    B.S. in Chemistry, Georgia State College for Women, 1924.
    English, Sanford, McWhorter.

Oxford, Julia Mae (S) _____Concord
    A.B., Bessie Tift College, 1923.
    History, Payne; English, Sanford.

Panter, Robert Harmon (S) _____Ellijay
    A.B., Mercer University, 1917.
    Education, Hutchinson;English, Sanford.

Patrick, James Ruey (SR) _____Athens
    A.B. in Soc. Sc., University of Georgia, 1925.
    History, Payne; Phychology, Edwards; Sociology, Woofter.

Patterson, Harold Alford (S) _____Athens
    B.S., University of Georgia, 1924.
    English, Sanford; Education, Hutchinson.

Prickett, Charles Sanford (S) _____Burwell
    A.B., Wofford College, 1923.
    English, Sanford.

Richardson, Robert James_____Athens
    B.S. Agr., University of Georgia, 1925.
    Poultry Husbandry, Wood.

Roberts, Lucian Emerson (S) _____Dallas
    A.B., University of Georgia, 1924.
    English, Sanford; History, Payne.

Rodgers, Annie Bell* (S) _____Hampton
    A.B., La Grange College, 1917.
    English, Sanford; History, Payne.

Rogers, Mary Lucille (S) _____Baxley
    A.B., Wesleyan College, 1923.
    History, Payne; English, McWhorter.

Sams, William Christopher (S) _____Dallas
  A.B., Mercer University, 1916.
  Education, Hutchinson.
Sawyer, Leslie Erwin_____Athens
  B.S. in Forestry, Michigan Agricultural College, 1924.
  Forestry, Burleigh.
Sewell, Walter Edwin_____Newnan
  A.B., University of Georgia, 1925, and candidate for B.S. in C.E., 1926.
  Mathematics, Stephens. Barrow, Cumming.
Sharp, Joseph Worth (S) _____Young Harris
  A.B., Emory University, 1919.
  History, Payne; Education, Hutchinson.
Singleton, Lee Davis (S) _____Gainesville
  B.S. in Commerce, University of Georgia, 1920.
  Education, Hutchinson; History, Payne.
Stanley, Hugh Smiley* (SR) _____Athens
  Candidate for A.B., University of Georgia, 1926.
  Mathematics, Stephens, Barrow, Cumming.
Stephens, James Louis*_____Mystic
  Candidate for B.S. Agr., University of Georgia, 1926.
  Agronomy, Crabb.
Stith, Gertrude Ernestine_____Vidalia
  A.B., University of Georgia, 1924.
  Mathematics, Stephens, Barrow, Cumming.
Stovall, Grace Katherine (S) _____Gainesville
  A.B., Brenau College, 1924.
  English, McWhorter.
Surrency, Eileen (S) _____Surrency
  B.S., Wesleyan College. 1924.
  English, Sanford, McWhorter.
Tarpley, Hubert Marion (S) _____Vidalia
  B.S., Piedmont College, 1923.
  Mathematics, Stephens, Barrow; Education, Hutchinson.
Tate, William _____Fairmount
  A.B., University of Georgia. 1924.
  History, Payne.
Taylor, Marjorie Hileman* (SR) _____Athens
  Philadelphia Friends' School.
  French, Lustrat.
Terrell, Annie Lou*_____College Park
  Candidate for B.S. in Home Economics. University of Georgia, 1926.
  Sociology, Hutchinson.
Thomas, John Vintson (S) _____Milligan College, Tenn.
  A.B., Milligan College, 1891, and A.M., 1900.
  Education, Hutchinson.
Towson, Frances Holmes (S) _____Pavo
  A.B., Wesleyan College, 1916.
  English, Sanford. McWhorter.
Towson, Lambuth Reilly (S) _____Pavo
  B.S., Emory University. 1915.
  Education, Hutchinson; Mathematics. Stephens. Barrow.
Treanor, Honoria Sapelo* (SR) _____Athens
  Candidate for A.B., University of Georgia. 1927.
  French, Lustrat.
Williams, Ida Belle (S) _____Swainsboro
  A.B., Bessie Tift College. 1906: University of Tennessee. S., 1908; A.M.,
    Cox College. 1915; Johns Hopkins University. S., 1916.
  English, Sanford; McWhorter; Education, Hutchinson.
Woodroof, Jasper Guy (S) _____Experiment
  B.S., Agr.. University of Georgia. 1922.
  Education, Hutchinson.

SENIOR

Acree, Margaret	Arts	Toccoa
Alexander, Lucile	Education	Commerce
Allen, John Daniel	Journalism	Marion, S. C.
Anderson, Ruby	Social Science	Athens
Anderson, Robert Edward	Science	Augusta
Baker, Peggy	Home Economics	Royston
Bargeron, Yewley Eugene, Jr.	Arts	Springfield
Bauer, Eitel	Forestry	Athens
Beale, Charles Bernard	Forestry	Savannah
Beeland, Dan Sully	Arts	Reynolds
Belcher, Dorothy Reed	Education	Athens
Bennett, Altus Robert	Agriculture	Athens
Benson, Bertha Margaret	Home Economics	Marietta
Berry, Joseph Wilson	Commerce	Quitman
Betts, Sara Louise	Education	Athens
Birchmore, Harrison Agnew	Arts	Athens
Bishop, George Norman	Forestry	Athens
Bishop, Joseph Elder	Civil Eng.	Athens
Blitch, James Daniel	Science	Statesboro
Boatwright, Mordaunt Grey	Commerce	Augusta
Boley, Bertram Sidney	Arts	Athens
Boley, Mildred	Home Economics	Athens
Bolton, Wayland, Eugene	Commerce	Parrott
Bonner, John Calvin	Journalism	Carrollton
Brawner, James Newton	Science	Atlanta
Bridges, Anna Deane	Home Economics	Sargent
Broach, Mary Upshaw	Arts Irreg.	Athens
Brown, Hester Virginia	Education	Athens
Brown, Lewis Pearce	Commerce	Athens
Brown, Raiford Franklin	Forestry	Athens
Bryan, Nan Coghlan	Arts	Champaign, Ill.
Bryant, Annie May Wood	Home Econ.	Athens
Burroughs, John Hubert	Science	Ila
Butler, Jacob Johnson	Agriculture	Athens
Campbell, David Stanley	Civ. Eng.	Athens
Cargile, Loyce Furman	Education	Macon
Cargill, George Slade	Arts	Savannah
Carmichael, Mary Frances	Education	Athens
Carter, Howard Alexander	Science	Athens
Close, Thomas McElmurray	Arts	Savannah
Cohen, Victoria Billups	Journalism	Madison
Comer, Frances Elizabeth	Home Econ.	Athens

Cook, Frances Lucyle	Home Econ.	Athens
Cumbus, George Warren, Jr.	Civ. Eng..	Athens
Curry, Elizabeth	Home Econ.	Athens
Dally, Clara Gibbs	Education	Jersey
David, Alwin Wimbish	Agriculture	Cedartown
Davidson, Joseph Quentin	Arts	Fort Valley
Davis, Douglas LaFayette	Vet. Med.	Cornelia
Davis, Jewel	Education	Meigs
Davis, Rufus Sterling	Journalism	Lenoir, N. C.
Dennis, Garr Samuel	Agriculture	Athens
Doherty, Charles Patrick	Forestry	Dorchester, Mass.
Drewry, Judson Harrell	Commerce	Griffin
Driskell, Dorothy	Arts	Sparta
DuPuis, Seth Elroy	Journalism	Warrenton
Earnest, David Lewis, Jr.	Science	Athens'
Eaton, James Loyd	Forestry	Viola, Tenn.
England, Robert Baxter	Agriculture	Blairsville
Eyler, William Andrew	Arts	Savannah
Fain, Clarence Samuel	Arts	Ringgold
Fanning, James Choice	Arts	Thomson
Forbes, James Lauritz	Commerce	Valdosta
Franklin, Gordon Aulie	Arts	Pulaski
Frederick, Harold Loyd	Civ. Eng.	Vidalia
Frederick, Lucy Booten	Arts	Marshallville
Fuller, Walter Albert	Agriculture	Athens
Garrett, Robert Lee	Science	Bowdon
Gaskins, John B.	Forestry	Nashville
Gaulding, Sam Lee	Education	Athens
Gignilliat, Thomas Hart	Agriculture	Pineora
Gladin, Chandler Balkcom	Agriculture	McIntyre
Goodwin, Thomas Wright	Science	Augusta
Graham, John Franklin	Education	Macon
Gray, James William	Science	Beaufort, S. C.
Gray, Thomas Stephen, Jr.	Commerce	Augusta
Beckwith, T. Stanley	Commerce	Augusta
Eaton, Clyde Ross	Forestry	Athens
Fortson, Jessie	Home Economics	Columbus
Graham, J. C.	Commerce	Athens
Griffin, Jones Llewellyn	Arts	Jeffersonville
Griffin, Penelope	Arts	Jeffersonville
Griggs, Ernest Lee, Jr.	Civ. Eng.	Athens
Griner, Adlai Bee	Vet. Med.	Athens
Hagler, Edward Waterman	Science	Augusta

Hall, Frank Herndon	Commerce	LaGrange
Hamilton, Zona	Arts	Thomasville
Haralson, Frank Conley	Commerce	Blairsville
Hardman, William Henry	Agriculture	Commerce
Harper, James Bruce	Commerce	Anderson, S. C.
Hatfield, Georgia Raiford	Vet. Med.	Monticello
Haygood, Tyler Francis	Commerce	Yatesville
Head, Herbert Vandolah, Jr.	Commerce	Athens
Hennessy, John Joseph	Arts	Savannah
Herndon, Elisha Merriman	Science	Social Circle
Hester, Mary Wyoline	Home Econ.	Douglasville
Hollis, Howell Tharpe	Science	Buena Vista
Hooper, Charles Herty	Arts	Athens
Huggins, William Carl	Agriculture	Oliver
Johnson, Daniel Boone	Agriculture	Summit
Johnson, George Saynor	Commerce	Augusta
Jones, Mallary	Education	Athens
Jones, Otis Warner	Agriculture	Atlanta
Jones, Ralph Kelly	Civ. Eng.	Oxford
Jones, Richard Mordecai	Arts	Athens
Kennedy, James Attaway	Civ. Eng.	Baconton
Kilpatrick, Martin Edward	Science	Athens
Lampkin, Lois Cobb	Education	Athens
Lampkin, Lucy Cobb	Education	Athens
Langley, Archie	Agriculture	LaFayette
Leffler, Lee Roy	Arts	Savannah
Lester, Florence Weltner	Education	Augusta
Levie, Marshall Craigg	Commerce	Montezuma
Levy, Morris Harris	Commerce	Savannah
Lewis, Walton Felker	Arts	Monroe
Little, Frances	Arts	Sparta
Logan, Alfred Escoe	Science	Comer
Lucky, Judge Curtis	Commerce	Augusta
Marks, Thomas Donald	Science	Summerville
Matthews, Bess E.	Education	Columbus
Mauldin, John Alfred	Agriculture	Hartwell
Mell, Carlton Newton	Commerce	Athens
Melton, James David	Science	Athens
Minor, Ella Sue	Education	Stone Mountain
Minter, Richard Gideon	Civ. Eng.	Hampton
Moon, Anne Louise	Journalism	LaGrange
Moon, Pearl Campbell	Home Economics	Ben Hill
Moore, Andrew Cecil	Journalism	Athens
Moran, Anne Roberts	Education	Milledgeville

Morris, Anne Lewis	Arts	Athens
Morris, James Zeb	Commerce	Carrollton
Morton, George Dudley	Arts	Athens
Morton, Cassandra Elizabeth	Education	Lumpkin
Morton, James W., Jr.	Agriculture	Athens
Moss, Susan	Social Science	Athens
Mulherin, Phillip Anthony	Arts	Augusta
Munro, Henry Smith	Agriculture	Athens
Myers, Jennie Belle	Home Econ.	Albany
McDorman, Helen	Arts	Athens
McLendon, Clarence Durwood	Agriculture	Sasser
McMahan, Ruby Louise	Education	Athens
McRae, Robert Henry	Agriculture	Mt. Vernon
Nash, Malcolm	Commerce	Atlanta
Nelson, Thomas Manduit, Jr.	Commerce	Albany
Nixon, Gwinn Huxley	Science	Augusta
Nolan, Burwell Atkinson	Commerce	Marietta
Nunnally, Hugh Pendleton	Commerce	Atlanta
Odom, Alvin Lee	Vet. Med.	Lyons
Orr, Douglas Milton	Arts	Athens
Orr, Frederick W.	Arts	Athens
Osborne, Louise Bacon	Journalism	Albany
Owen, Malchus Cobb	Agriculture	Tifton
Owens, Hubert Bond	Agriculture	Canon
Parker, Norma Claire	Education	McRae
Pendergrast, John Heidt	Arts	Reynolds
Perry, Celia	Arts	Sale City
Petty, Sarah Elizabeth	Home Econ.	Palmetto
Pittman, Dill	Science	Athens
Plaster, Emma Elizabeth	Arts	Atlanta
Poe, Harry	Vet. Med.	Vidalia
Prisant, Myron Isaac	Commerce	Albany
Randolph, George Buford	Science	Dalton
Rankin, Harvey Walter	Agriculture	Blackshear
Richards, Ruth	Arts	Athens
Ridgway, Mattie	Home Econ.	Canon
Rowland, Dorothy	Home Econ.	Athens
Rowland, Elizabeth	Physical Ed.	Athens
Russell, Thomas Shetfall	Commerce	Savannah
Sanders, Mabel	Arts	Musella
Satlof, John Boris	Commerce	Columbus
Segrest, Robert Taylor	Commerce	LaGrange
Sewell, Walter Edwin	Civ. Eng.	Newnan
Shattuck, Horace DeWitte	Social Science	LaFayette

Davies, William Edward	Commerce	Atlanta
Davis, Thomas Hartley	Pre-Medical	Sautee
Dismuke, G. W.	Pre-Medical	Ocilla
Dobbs, Emmett Oliver	Arts	Barnesville
Dolvin, John Thomas	Commerce	Siloam
Dopson, Robert Newton	Agriculture	Jacksonville
Dorminy, John Henry, Jr.	Commerce	Fitzgerald
Dorr, Laura Doughty	Arts	Augusta
Dowdy, Mattye	Education	Commerce
Dowis, Ollice Bonnie	Agriculture	Duluth
Downs, Robert Carlton	Commerce	Watkinsville
Downs, Robert Hussey	Commerce	Watkinsville
Doyle, Robert Ober	Commerce	Royston
Drew, Jesse Walter	Commerce	Preston
Dudley, Irene Townsend	Arts	Tampa, Fla.
Dunn, Pat	Commerce	Fitzgerald
Dunwody, Donald	Arts	Atlanta
Dykes, Evelyn	Home Econ.	Cochran
Edwards, William Roquemore	Arts	Dawson
Elkins, Pearce Lester	Agriculture	Cairo
Elliott, Charles Newton	Forestry	Covington
Epps, Elizabeth Allene	Home Econ.	Jefferson
Epps, Mozelle	Commerce	Athens
Estroff, Hyman Barnard	Commerce	Louisville
Eubank, Nathan Bryan	Commerce	Columbus
Felton, William Robinson	Arts	Montezuma
Fleming, Eva Mae	Education	Arnoldsville
Fleming, William Frank	Atrs	Albany
Fortson, Nora Palmer	Arts	Athens
Fowler, Winifred Amanda	Arts	Athens
Frain, William Joseph	Commerce	Savannah
Freeman, Lorimer Bassett	Arts	LaGrange
Freeman, Rush Burton	Commerce	Atlanta
Frier, William Ryan, Jr.	Journalism	Douglas
Frost, Macadjia Carter	Education	Jefferson
Fulton, Arthur Earl	Science	Elberton
Furse, Stephen Smith III.	Commerce	Savannah
Galkin, Harry	Pre-Medical	Macon
Garner, Milliard Luther	Agriculture	Dublin
Garrard, James Aubrey	Agriculture	Washington
Gignilliat, Arthur Mathewson	Arts	Pineora
Gracey, Robert Hall	Commerce	Covington, Tenn.
Green, Estelle Madeline	Education	Augusta
Greenfield, David	Commerce	Atlanta

Griffith, Powell West	Pre-Medical	Eatonton
Gross, Omer Seckinger	Pre-Medical	Glennville
Haddock, Claudia Frances	Home Econ.	Athens
Haley, Lois	Home Econ.	Commerce
Hamilton, Thomas Jefferson, Jr.	Arts	Augusta
Hammond, Louise	Education	Augusta
Hanahan, James Frampton	Science	Augusta
Hankinson, Job LeRoy, Jr.	Science	Augusta
Harden, William Dearing	Arts	Augusta
Hardie, Max Meyerhardt	Agriculture	Gordon
Hardin, James Lee	Arts	Leah
Hardy, Benjamin H.	Journalism	Barnesville
Harper, Lewis Heymes, Jr.	Science	Macon
Harper, William Edward, Jr.	Commerce	Savannah
Harris, George Thomas	Commerce	Wrens
Harris, Herschel Billups, Jr.	Pre-Medical	Watkinsville
Harrold, Thomas Jewell	Agriculture	Atlanta
Hart, Dan R.	Medicine	Statesboro
Hart, Rubye Alline	Education	Milledgeville
Hartman, William Arthur	Commerce	Atlanta
Hatton, LeRoy Alexander	Commerce	Atlanta
Heard, Richard Willis, Jr.	Commerce	Savannah
Henderson, John Horace	Agriculture	Adairsville
Heyman, Joseph Kohn	Arts	Atlanta
Hiers, Jack Sidney	Commerce	Waycross
Hinton, Andrew Hill	Pre-Medical	Summerville
Hirsch, Morris	Commerce	Atlanta
Hixson, Ivy May	Arts	Augusta
Hixson, Onie Elizabeth	Home Econ.	Augusta
Hobart, Claude Douglas	Agriculture	Hawkinsville
Hodges, William Launcelot	Commerce	CCyrene
Holder, Metz Raymond	Commerce	Bainbridge
Holliday, Henry Campbell	Medicine	Athens
Hood, Grace	Home Econ.	Commerce
Horton, Sidney Smith	Agriculture	Rome
Houston, Joe L.		Sylvester
Howard, James Willis	Medicine	Augusta
Huff, Emmett Olin	Commerce	Atlanta
Huguley, Harrell Dallas	Commerce	West Point
Hursey, Thomas Parker	Civ. Eng.	Reidsville .
Jackson, Emmett Harris	Agriculture	Granite Hill
Jackson, Mary Mercer	Education	Valdosta
Jackson, Rollin Ashby	Arts	Tignall
Jenkins, Albert Felton	Education	Danielsville

Jennette, John R.	Science	Goldsboro, N. C.
Jester, John Carlton	Arts	Athens
Jewett, George Bowers, Jr.	Agriculture	Macon
Johnson, David Weems	Commerce	Dalton
Johnson, Elizabeth	Home Econ.	Savannah
Johnson, James Ellis	Arts	Baxley
Johnson, Roy	Commerce	Wrightsville
Johnson, Young Joseph, Jr.	Commerce	Commerce
Johnston, William Robert	Arts	Franklin, N. C.
Joiner, Otis Crittenden	Agriculture	Edison
Jones, George Warren	Agriculture	Sale City
Kain, Thomas Gerald	Commerce	Athens
Keating, Patrick Joseph	Agriculture	Savannah
Kendrick, Thomas Clarence	Commerce	Columbus
Kennedy, Elizabeth Ellis	Home Economics	Clarkesville
Kennon, Howard Thomas	Science	McRae
Kersh, Douglas Russell	Pre-Medical	Atlanta
Keys, Emma Ovelle	Home Econ.	Rome
King, Edna Margaret	Home Econ.	Atlanta
Kingery, Andrew Jackson	Arts	Summit
Kline, William Anderson, Jr.	Arts	Columbus
Landrum, Claud England	Education	Fairburn
Lang, Benjamin Sewell	Arts	Calhoun
Leavy, C. Howard	Arts	Brunswick
Letton, Winsor	Pre-Medical	Atlanta
Lewis, John Robison	Arts	Monroe
Lewis, Keith Bush	Arts	Nahunta
Lind, Hilda	Phys. Educ.	Savannah
Little, Anna Belle	Education	Carnesville
Lockhart, Malcolm Mabry, Jr.	Arts	Decatur
Lokey, Hugh Montgomery, Jr.	Science	Atlanta
Lovell, Edward F. III.	Agriculture	Savannah
Loyless, Augustus Shaw	Commerce	Atlanta
Lund, Adolph	Arts	Athens
Maddox, Gordon Isaac	Agriculture	Winder
Mallery, Sabra Louise	Education	Savannah
Martin, Joe Bernard	Commerce	Hartwell
Massey, Zenas Alonza	Agriculture	Columbus
Mathews, James Crawford	Agriculture	Cuthbert
Maughon, Annette	Arts	Monroe
Maxwell, Lee Osborne	Science	Calvary
Meaders, Georgia Jeanette	Home Econ.	Toccoa
Merritt, Samuel Mickleberry	Commerce	Americus
Minor, Randall Hunter	Pre-Medical	Stone Mountain

Mitchell, Louis Hamburger	Commerce	Columbus
Moore, Katherine Robertson	Arts	Augusta
Morgan, Julius Myers	Commerce	Pembroke
Moss, James Royden	Commerce	West Point
Munn, Lesley	Arts	Savannah
McAfee, Broadus B	Commerce	Aragon
McConnell, Hoyt Eakes	Agriculture	Commerce
McDonald, Alex Jackson, Jr.	Arts	Fitzgerald
McDonald, Frank Barlow, Jr.	Commerce	Waycross
McElroy, Charlie Richard	Pre-Medical	Colbert
McElwaney, Lillie Pearl	Home Econ.	Fayetteville
McGee, Gordon H.	Agriculture	Knoxville
McKenzie, John Thomas	Commerce	Montezuma
McTigue, Robert E.	Commerce	Blackshear
McWhirter, Oscar Marvin	Commerce	Athens
McWhorter, Earl Brown	Agriculture	LaFayette
McWhorter, Myrtus Ray	Pre-Medical	Bowdon
Nash, Thomas Acton	Commerce	Washington
Neal, George Hendree	Civ. Eng.	College Park
Newcomb, Russell Frederick	Forestry	Athens
Newton, Alfred Benjamin	Civ. Eng.	Lyons
Nicholson, Madison Gartrell, Jr.	Civ. Eng.	Athens
Noell, Sarah Mildred	Journalism	Comer
Nunnally, Charles Bowie	Commerce	Atlanta
Oliver, George McGrady	Commerce	Americus
Oliver, Joseph McDonald	Arts	Savannah
Oliver, William Wiley	Arts	Valdosta
Olliff, James Clifton	Pre-Medical	Statesboro
Orsini, Felice Marino	Elec. Eng.	Savannah
Osteen, Andrew Jackson	Vet. Medicine	Pembroke
Osteen, Oswald Lamont	Vet. Medicine	Pembroke
Parker, Walter Ennis	Commerce	Waycross
Parsons, Lyman	Commerce	Portal
Patterson, Robert Lee	Arts	Athens
Pearce, William Wayne	Agriculture	Cairo
Persall, John Thomas, Jr.	Pre-Medical	Cordele
Pitts, Jewell	Home Econ.	Bowman
Post, Allen Williams	Arts	Newnan
Pound, Edwine Aldine	Civ. Eng.	Athens
Preston, Charles McDowell	Science	Macon
Pritchard, George Bernard	Civ. Eng.	Savannah
Pryor, John Gatewood	Arts	Smithville
Pyron, Joe Hicks	Education	Reynolds
Quarterman, Mary Brevard	Education	Winder

Race, Guy Austin	Education	Valdosta
Rackley, Bascom Eugene	Commerce	Statesboro
Raine, Theodore	Commerce	Fitzgerald
Randolph, Hollins Nicholas	Science	Atlanta
Ray, Thomas Seaborn	Education	Maysville
Ray, Virginia	Education	Atlanta
Reeves, Henry Yancey	Commerce	Manchester
Renfroe, Jack	Commerce	Quitman
Rhyne, Walter Percival	Pre-Medical	Smyrna
Roberts, James McMullan	Arts	Monroe
Roberts, John Reed, Jr.	Arts	Buford
Roberts, William Duke	Commerce	Pembroke
Robinson, George Henderson	Civ. Eng.	College Park
Robison, Dorothy Elizabeth	Social Science	Augusta
Rogers, Joseph Mauk	Commerce	Doyle
Rogers, Margaret	Home Econ.	Pittsburg
Rollins, John Daley	Science	Dalton
Rowland, Alice Alden	Education	Athens
Royals, George William	Arts	Albany
Sala, Weldon Lea	Commerce	Atlanta
Sams, Frank	Medicine	Dalton
Sanborn, Willa	Arts	Americus
Sanders, Julia Bennett	Home Econ.	Commerce
Sanders, Mary Agnes	Home Econ.	Musella
Scarbrough, Chestney Warren	Arts	Jackson
Scoggins, Bruce Talmadge	Commerce	Athens
Shearouse, Franklin Hartridge	Science	Springfield
Sikes, Robert Fulton	Agriculture	Sylvester
Simmons, Elliott Bernard	Pre-Medical	Savannah
Simpson, Addison Wingfield	Agriculture	Washington
Slappey, Robert Alleyne	Commerce	Marshallville
Smalley, Mary Rosser	Education	Thomson
Smalley, James Luther	Vet. Medicine	Lincolnton
Smalley, Wayne	Agriculture	Athens
Smith, Charles Rufus	Agriculture	Monticello
Smith, Henry Eugene	Commerce	Columbus
Smith, John Raymond	Pre-Medical	Hahira
Smith, Louise	Education	Athens
Smith, Tom Bush	Commerce	Valldosta
Snelling, John Richards	Commerce	Athens
Snow, Asberry Dewey	Science	Good Hope
Sparrow, John Frank	Agriculture	Hawkinsville
Spiers, Percy Marvin	Vet. Medicine	Lincolnton
Sproull, John Frank, Jr.	Agriculture	Lindale

Stancil, Hallman Luke	Arts	Ball Ground
Staples, Eric P.	Arts	Roopville
Starr, Louis Gordon	Commerce	Greensboro
Starr, Mary Blanche	Journalism	Griffin
Steed, Jennie Claire	Education	Augusta
Steele, Virgil Shellnutt	Commerce	Eastman
Stewart, Franz Hahr	Medicine	Athens
Stewart, Gregory Edward	Commerce	Fitzgeralld
Stinson, Forrest C.	Education	Valley Head, Ala.
Stith, Maybelle	Arts	Athens
St. John, Thomas Franklin	Journalism	Athens
Stokes, Marion Russell	Journalism	Moultrie
Stone, George Henry Clement	Science	Athens
Story, Howard Kuhlman	Science	Ellabelle
Stovall, John Thomas, Jr.	Pre-Medical	Danielsville
Strickland, Hunter Adams	Commerce	Royston
Strickland, Lonnie J.	Agriculture	Waycross
Strickland, Wilburn Lesca	Commerce	Buchanan
Strickler, Cyrus Warren	Science	Atlanta
Taliaferro, John	Journalism	Blue Ridge
Talley, William Edgar	Commerce	Villa Rica
Talmadge, Harry Erwin	Arts	Athens
Talmadge, Thomas Roumalgus	Commerce	Forsyth
Tarver, Malcolm Connor	Arts	Dalton
Tebeau, Edmund Earl	Science	Guyton
Temple, Leo Gillis	Pre-Medical	Statesboro
Thomas, Ernest Henry	Agriculture	Martin
Thomas, Goss	Agriculture	Martin
Thomas, Hue, Jr.	Civ. Eng.	Savannah
Thomas, Maurice Clay	Commerce	Macon
Thomas, Roma D.	Commerce	Patterson
Thompson, Friar Matthews	Agriculture	Griffin
Thurmond, Jack	Forestry	Athens
Tibbettts, Marie Ussery	Education	Athens
Tillman, Mary E.	Education	Monroe
Tillman, Wallace Jerome	Commerce	Valdosta
Touchstone, James Fleming	Agriculture	Griffin
Tucker, William T.	Commerce	Athens
Turk, John Martin	Civ. Eng.	Savannah
Tully, Daniel Curtis	Commerce	Reynolds
Tully, George Emmett	Journalism	Savannah
VanGiesen, George Edward	Commerce	Savannah
Vandiviere, Stuart Pitner	Pre-Medical	Columbus
Varner, Earl Morgan	Agriculture	Walden

Veale, Thomas Murray	Science	Watkinsville
Vining, James Benjamin	Vet. Medicine	Marshallville
Waller, Jack	Commerce	Culverton
Walters, Traul Garland	Agriculture	Lavonia
Walsh, James William	Civ. Eng.	Athens
Ward, George Walter	Commerce	Lumpkin
Ward, William Alton	Commerce	Powder Springs
Watkins, Ed Milton	Commerce	Lexington
Watson, Francis Marion	Pre-Medical	Juincy, Fla.
Watson, Henry Brahe	Science	Augusta
Watson, Judson Durward	Arts	Statesboro
Weatherly, Marion King	Commerce	Athens
Weaver, Maxwell D.	Civ. Eng.	Savannah
Wells, Mary Estelle	Home Econ.	Hapeville
Whatley, Berta	Home Econ.	Carrollton
Wheeler, George W.	Commerce	Brooklyn, N. Y.
White, George Douglas	Commerce	Buford
White, Hettie M.	Home Econ.	Chipley
Whitehead, Hiram Jones	Arts	Comer
Whittle, Charles Albert	Journalism	Atlanta
Williams, Frank Hardee, Jr.	Civ. Eng.	Savannah
Williamson, Ruth	Arts	Miami Beach, Fla.
Wilson, Eugene Boykin	Pre-Medical	Thomson
Wilson, Hattie Laura	Home Econ.	Commerce
Wofford, Hoke Smith	Agriculture	Atlanta
Woodall, Lewis Frederick	Science	Athens
Woodward, William Rogers	Civ. Eng.	Jackson
Wright, Wallace Douglas	Commerce	Savannah

FRESHMAN

Abel, McHatton	Agriculture	Macon
Abelson, H. William	Medicine	Atlanta
Adams, Jim Dozier	Commerce	Bethlehem
Adams, James Lewis	Commerce	Dewy Rose
Adams, James Thomas	Science	Tignall
Adcox, Neil Victor	Commerce	Albany
Aiken, James Edward	Commerce	Statesboro
Albea, Wyatt Bernard	Science	Lincolnton
Alexander, Charles N., Jr.	Agriculture	Little Rock, Ark.
Allison, Guy Pryor	Forestry	Americus
Anderson, Fannie Leonora	Home Econ.	Hawkinsville
Andrews, Rebecca Elizabeth	Arts	Augusta
Ansley, Daniel Henry	Arts	Decatur
Armstrong, Elizabeth Judson	Home Econ.	Woodville

Armstrong, Thomas Jefferson	Commerce	Columbus
Austin, Samuel Yates	Civ. Eng.	Hartsdale, N. Y.
Backus, Henry Lindsley	Forestry	Savannah
Ballard, Howard Roy	Journalism	Thomasville
Barksdale, Hermione	Arts	Washington
Barnett, Reeves Henry	Agriculture	Jefferson
Barrow, Craig, Jr.	Arts	Savannah
Bateman, Needham Bryant	Pre-Medical	Deepstep
Beale, Clyde	Journalism	Savannah
Belflower, Alton Preston	Commerce	Sycamore
Bell, Joseph Columbus	Agriculture	Athens
Bellingrath, Albert Ferdinand	Agriculture	Decatur
Bembry, John Robert	Commerce	Hawkinsville
Bennett, Chester Norton	Agriculture	Waycross
Bennett, Joseph Jacob	Pre-Medical	Waycross
Bethea, Charles Gray	Pre-Medical	Greensboro
Betts, Victoria Elizabeth	Education	Athens
Beusse, Jessie Henrietta	Education	Athens
Bickers, Joe W.	Science	White Plains
Bigham, Richard Kenneth	Journalism	Athens
Biggs, Edward M.	Commerce	Staten Island, N. Y.
Bird, George Walter	Forestry	Metter
Blackshear, Joseph Henry	Commerce	Gainesville
Blalock, John Loyd	Commerce	Adairsville
Blitch, Henry Smits	Commrece	Statesboro
Blount, John Jacob, Jr.	Commerce	Hawkinsville
Blumethal, Judith	Education	Savannah
Boggs, Claud Ezekiel	Agriculture	Jefferson
Boland, Joe	Arts	Atlanta
Bolton, Lee Boykin	Commerce	Athens
Bostwick, John, Jr.	Agriculture	Bostwick
Bottom, Jordan Vaughan	Arts	Atlanta
Boyett, Joseph Edward	Elec. Eng.	Ray City
Boyett, Norman Earl	Commerce	Blakely
Bradley, Albert C.	Commerce	Homestead, Fla.
Bradley, Glenn Walter	Commerce	Tampa, Fla.
Bradwell, Samuel Dowse	Commerce	Athens
Brannon, Marvin Edgar	Commerce	Rome
Brantley, Marvin A., Jr.	Commerce	Juitman
Bray, Claude Alvin	Agriculture	Woodbury
Briant, Fred Lee	Commerce	Winterville
Brice, Robert Samuel	Science	Decatur
Brinson, M. E., Jr.	Commerce	Waycross
Brown, Harley Durel	Commerce	Stillmore

Brown, Joseph Emerson	Arts	Atlanta
Brown, Richard Kyle	Pre-Medical	Dewy Rose
Bryant, Verman Huel	Commerce	LaGrange
Buchanan, John A., Jr.	Civ. Eng.	Atlanta
Buchanan, James H.	Commerce	Jackson
Buffington, Joseph Evan	Agriculture	Union City
Buie, William Ruthven	Commerce	Nashville
Bullard, Walter Daniel, Jr.	Commerce	Albany
Burdick, Gilbert Powell	Commerce	Sparta
Burger, Agnes Sims	Arts	Watkinsville
Burgess, Henry Claude	Commerce	Athens
Burpee, George Towns	Commerce	Athens
Burton, Wynn Taylor	Commerce	Atlanta
Busby, Donald Thomas	Science	Cedartown
Bush, Hoke	Commerce	Colquitt
Bush, James LeSesne	Pre-Medical	Dublin
Butt, Cecil Weaver	Civ. Eng.	Chauncey
Caldwell, Andrew Jackson	ommerce	Marietta
Callaway, Hubert Moses	Commerce	Philomath
Camp, Henry Clay	Medicine	Winder
Candler, John Slaughter II.	Arts	Atlanta
Capps, William Monteith	Science	Athens
Carey, Marian Louise	Education	Augusta
Carnes, Robert Emory	Commerce	Atlanta
Carpenter, Kinch Pinckney	Journalism	Winder
Carr, Ewell Sanford	Agriculture	Cave Spring
Carswell, Harry Meldrim	Pre-Medical	Athens
Carter, Allmon	Agriculture	Bowdon Junction
Carter, Joseph Jefferson	Commerce	Columbus
Casey, Earl Ellis	Commerce	Cave Spring
Cate, Charles M.	Commerce	Athens
Causey, Charles Bartlett	Agriculture	Knoxville
Cawley, Louis Vernon	Agriculture	Augusta
Chafin, Glenn Lee	Commerce	Lindale
Chaille, William Jackson	Journalism	Miami, Fla.
Chambers, Levy Bearden	Commerce	Madison
Chastain, Walter Ralph	Vet. Medicine	Tiger
Clark, Roy	Civ. Eng.	Flowery Branch
Cochran, George M., Jr.	Civ. Eng.	Flint
Cohen, Jeannette	Pre-Med.	Mt. Vernon, N. Y.
Coldbeck, Norman Thomas	Commerce	Athens
Collins, Joe Martin	Commerce	Cartersville
Collins, William Burton	Journalism	Rome
Colvin, Combs Nichols	Arts	Locust Grove

Connally, Lindsay Allen	Science	Atlanta
Conway, Katherine Taliaferro	Arts	Washington, D. C.
Cook, J. Lawson	Commerce	Athens
Cooley, John Rogers	Commerce	Maysville
Copeland, George Perry	Commerce	Carrollton
Courson, Prentiss	Journalism	Vildalia
Courts, Malon Clay	Arts	Atlanta
Cowan, James A.	Arts	Decatur
Cox, Sidney Clarence, Jr.	Commerce	Waynesboro
Crawford, Thurston Carroll	Science	Columbus
Crawley, George D.	Journalism	Hampton
Crawley, George Lee	Science	Waycross
Crowell, William Frances	Commerce	Decatur
Crutchfield, Robert Houston	Science	Round Oak
Culbertson, Eva Mae	Home Econ.	Winterville
Cumming, Joe R.	Arts	Cordele
Daniell, Otis Gerome	Agriculture	Powder Springs
Daniels, Anne Elizabeth	Home Econ.	Hawkinsville
Dart, John McRae	Commerce	Douglas
Dasher, Zeno Vance	Education	Marlow
Davidson, Andilea Durward	Agriculture	Epworth
Davis, Frederick Bush	Arts	Atlanta
Davis, Jefferson Dewey	Agriculture	Cornelia
Davis, James Edward, Jr.	Arts	Atlanta
Davis, Troy Alexander		Athens
Davis, William Garland	Agriculture	Cartersville
Dawson, Oscar Pinkney	Agriculture	Blackwells
DeArmond, Reece Gordon	Elec. Eng.	Atlanta
Dellinger, Chesley Monroe	Agriculture	Calhoun
Dews, Lila Louise	Arts	Decatur
Dismuke, Herman Lamar	Commerce	Ocilla
Dodd, Clair Alpen	Science	Menlo
Douglas, Lamar Ashley	Commerce	Nicholls
Drew, Roy Fletcher	Commerce	Marshallville
Dudley, Frank	Civ. Eng.	Athens
Duncan, Amon Ocyrus	Agriculture	Bowdon Junction
Duncan, William Lester	Commerce ·	Woodbury
Dunn, Eugene Palmer	Commerce	Thomson
Dunson, Linton Reese	Agriculture	Commerce
Dykes, Nellie Lucile	Home Econ.	Cochran
Earnest, Charles Broughton	Agriculture	Bowdon Junction
Edwards, Jules Green, Jr.	Arts	Atlanta
Edwards, Nellie Patrick	Arts	Athens
Elder, Ethel Dodd	Home Econ.	Watkinsville

Elder, Lamar Alexander	Commerce	Bishop
Ellerbee, Gladys Gertrude	Home Econ.	Ashburn
Ellis, Lamar Hamilton	Commerce	Atlanta
Epps, Benjamin Scott	Arts	Athens
Epting, Eugene Albert	Commerce	Athens
Evans, Frances	Arts	Columbus
Evans, Isaac Cuthbert	Commerce	Columbus
Evins, Samuel Nesbitt, Jr.	Arts	Atlanta
Ewing, William Bryan	Commerce	Lawrenceville
Eyler, Armand Tise	Science	Savannah
Falligant, Robert Elliott	Arts	Thunderbolt
Fitts, William Wilson	Architecture	Americus
Fleming, L. E.	Commerce	Athens
Fletcher, Richard Van	Science	Jackson
Flournoy, Thomas Moffett	Commerce	Columbus
Flowers, Julian Carlton	Commerce	Valdosta
Folsom, Martha Jane	Education	McRae
Fordham, J. B., Jr.	Agriculture	Dublin
Forman, George Pinkston, Jr.	Civ. Eng.	Greenville
Franklin, Joseph Neel	Commerce	Sparta
Frankum, Robert Oscar	Pre-Medical	Martin
Freeman, Gus	Science	
Frohberg, James Harry	Journalism	Thomasville
Fulghum, Ralph Morris	Agriculture	Mitchell
Fulller, Harold Ames	Commerce	Gainesville
Fuller, William Harrison	Commerce	Atlanta
Gaissert, William Ludwick	Commerce	Sparta
Gilleland, Clement Eugene	Commerce	Athens
Godwin, Georgia Elizabeth	Commerce	Barnesville
Goldberg, Sidney Martin	Commerce	Athens
Goldstein, Mary	Education	Atlanta
Graham, Russell Eldridge	Commerce	Comer
Gray, Sam William	Agriculture	Mt. Berry
Grayson, Leon Harman	Arts	Savannah
Green, William Louis	Agriculture	Athens
Griffith, Mrs. Lillian Branch	Education	Athens
Grimes, Allen Park	Commerce	Athens
Gurley, Albert Lee	Elec. Eng.	Atlanta
Hagler, Thomas Waterman	Science	Augusta
Haley, Sanford Eugene	Commerce	Dewy Rose
Hall, Adolph Kenneth	Pre-Medical	Hahira
Hall, Califf Cal	Pre-Medical	Nicholls
Hall, Walter Tucker	Arts	Atlanta
Hamby, Ralph Ed	Arts	Clayton

Halton, Jack Anthony	Pre-Medical	Sarasota, Fla.
Hamilton, Guy Crawford, Jr.	Journalism	Dalton
Hanson, Isabel	Science	Smyrna
Hanson, Robert Houghston	Commerce	Rome
Harber, George Washington D.	Arts	Commerce
Hargrove, Alexander Guill	Commerce	Athens
Harmon, Edna	Arts	Hapeville
Harper, Hubert	Commerce	Ambrose
Harris, James Jackson	Civ. Eng.	Athens
Hart, Edwin R.	Commerce	Colbert
Haskin, David	Commerce	Macon
Harvley, Otis Everett	Education	Bartow
Head, Harvey Hatcher	Civ. Eng.	Athens
Heagarty, Edwin Martin, Jr.	Commerce	Waycross
Heagarty, John Patrick	Pre-Medical	Savannah
Henderson, T. M., Jr.	Commerce	Tampa, Fla.
Heriot, James Judson	Arts	Savannah
Heyman, Sarah	Journalism	Savannah
Hicks, Edwin Brown	Civ. Eng.	Reynolds
Hill, Benjamin Harvey	Arts	Atlanta
Hill, John B.	Commerce	Columbus
Hill, Hoke Smith	Science	Canon
Hinds, Emerson Burton		Atlanta
Hodgson, John McCullough	Arts	Athens
Hollingsworth, Virgil	Commerce	Augusta
Hollis, Robert Flewellyn	Commerce	Americus
Holmes, Ernest Dexter	Agriculture	Athens
Holt, Dorris Jack	Arts	Albany
Holt, Lewis Lake	Journalism	Sandersville
Holt, Thomas Jefferson	Pre-Medical	Waycross
Hooks, Robert Greene	Commerce	Americus
Hopkins, Addis Harold	Commerce	Chipley
Hornbuckle, Sheldon Leslie	Education	Valdosta
Horton, Oze E., Jr.	Arts	Atlanta
Horton, Ross L.	Commerce	Laurel, Miss.
Howell, William Walker	Commerce	Athens
Huff, Ethel Mae	Home Econ.	Rockmart
Huger, William Beekman	Science	Savannah
Huggins, Tryon Kenimer	Elec. Eng.	Athens
Huguley, Amos, Jr.	Commerce	West Point
Humphrey, Charles Hubert	Commerce	Barnesville
Hunt, Stephen Fortson	Commerce	Athens
Hyatt, Harold Cooper	Elec. Eng.	Loganville
Inglis, Hugh Alexander	Agriculture	Clarkesville

Irion, Ruth Walker	Arts	Athens
Izlar, Durham Wright	Commerce	Waycross
Jackson, Bruce Rudolph	Arts	Bainbridge
Jacobson, Roy Hildreth	Commerce	Atlanta
Jamerson, William White, Jr.	Commerce	Jackson
Jarnagin, Milton Preston III.	Arts	Athens
Jennings, Rufus Brdiges	Commerce	Dawson
Johnson, Eloise	Journalism	Savannah
Johnson, Herbert Foster	Commerce	Valdosta.
Johnson, Joseph	Commerce	Albany
Johnson, J. Wade, Jr.	Arts	Mt. Vernon
Jones, Bannon	Commerce	Athens
Jones, Emory Estelle	Pre-Medical	Jacksonville
Jones, James Francis	Architecture	Athens
Jones, Richard Warner	Commerce	Athens
Jones, William Curtis	Commerce	Brooks
Kadel, Harry LaFayette	Commerce	Rome
Karesh, Mose	Commerce	Macon
Keen, George L.	Commerce	Atlanta
Keener, Mary Adeline	Education	Rabun Gap
Kemp, Wilson	Commerce	Atlanta
Kennedy, Tom	Vet. Medicine	Bronwood
Kennan, Garda	Social Science	Athens
Kenner, Cecil Ernest	Civ. Eng.	Dalton
Key, William Fred	Commerce	Tate
Kimsey, Joseph Johnson	Journalism	Cornelia
Knight, Harry Exton	Commerce	Columbus
Lanford, Leroy Caruth	Agriculture	Tucker
Lanier, Charles Boles	Commerce	Athens
Lattay, James Boyd	Forestry	Crawford
Lautzenhiser, Glenn Bruce	Commerce	Atlanta
Lawrence, Alexander Atkinson	Arts	Savannah
Layton, Claudius Eloise	Science	Atlanta
Lea, Peter F.	Science	Augusta
Lear, Thomas F.	Elec. Eng.	Tifton
Lee, Robert Earl	Medicine	Augusta
Lee, Sara Fellers	Commerce	Augusta
Leffler, Adolph, Jr.	Commerce	Savannah
Legwen, William Andrew	Civ. Eng.	Augusta
Lester, Jewell Inez	Home Econ.	Rome
Lester, Martha Ruprecht	Education	Augusta
Lewis, Elzie Wilson	Agriculture	Calhoun
Lichtenstein, Jack	Commerce	Atlanta
Little, William Douglas	Commerce	Sparta

Lowry, Josephine Egbert	Home Econ.	Madison
Lumpkin, Frank Grieve, Jr.	Commerce	Columbus
Lundy, Walter Hillyer	Commerce	Sylvester
Mallard, Leo	Agriculture	Statesboro
Manning, Barney Ware	Science	Atlanta
Marsengill, S. C.	Commerce	Athens
Martin, Carter Esmond	Agriculture	Bainbridge
Matheny, James Theodore	Pre-Medical	Augusta
Mathews, Andrew Jackson	Arts	Cuthbert
Mayo, Exum LaFayette	Commerce	Bethel, N. C.
Mayhew, Robert James	Commerce	Atlanta
Meeks, Alton Phinnizy	Pre-Medical	Nicholls
Mendel, Helen	Education	Atlanta
Melton, John William, Jr.	Science	Decatur
Middleton, Harmon Campbell	Pre-Medical	Hazlehurst
Milford, Anna Mae	Home Econ.	Hartwell
Milholllin, J. H., Jr.	Arts	Broxton
Miller, Constant	Commerce	Brunswick
Miller, Sam	Arts	Rome
Mitchell, Roscoe William	Commerce	Lobeco, S. C.
Mitchell, Lathrop	Journalism	Thomasville
Montgomery, Marion Everett	Commerce	Meriwether
Moon, Fauntleroy	Education	LaGrange
Moore, A. C., Jr.	Agriculture	Powder Springs
Moore, Marvin Joseph	Commerce	Gray
Morgan, Sigo Madison	Commerce	Pembroke
Morgan, Will Ellington	Pre-Medical	LaGrange
Morris, Hollis Earl	Commerce	Atlanta
Morton, John Harris	Commerce	Gray
Mulherin, William Butler	Commerce	Augusta
Mullins, Clarence Newton	Commerce	Atlanta
Munday, Addie	Home Econ.	Atlanta
Mundy, William W., Jr.	Commerce	Cedartown
Murphey, Edward Lee	Commerce	Barnesville
Myers, Frances Martha	Education	Athens
Myers, Henry Tift	Commerce	Tifton
McAteer, Halcott Gamaliel	Vet. Medicine	Columbia, S. C.
McClure, Sterling Rutherford	Commerce	Atlanta
McCommons, James Everett	Commerce	Thomson
McCommons, Rollin Merritt	Commerce	Greensboro
McCord, Ralph Butler	Medicine	Rome
McCrary, Herdis Wilburn	Commerce	Atlanta
McCullough, Francis Milner	Arts	Round Oak
McCutchen, Frank Kelley	Civ. Eng.	Dalton

McDonald, Joe Norman	Commerce	Hazlehurst
McDougald, Walter Edwin	Commerce	Statesboro
McElmurray, James Warren	Agriculture	Augusta
McGee, Mary D.	Home Econ.	Roberta
McGinty, Arthur Park	Pre-Medical	Atlanta
McGowan, Virginia	Home Economics	Stilesboro
McKinley, Howard Lindsey	Elec. Eng.	Wheatland, Ind.
McLeroy, Hugh Finley	Civ. Eng.	Athens
McMullan, Frank Alonzo	Arts	Atlanta
McWhorter, Hoke	Commerce	Watkinsville
McRee, Bruce Victor	Commerce	Brookhaven
McWilliams, William Comer	Agriculture	Atlanta
Neisler, Charles Hugh, Jr.	Arts	Reynolds
Nessmith, Gordon	Agriculture	Statesboro
Nix, Carl Augustus	Agriculture	Bowdon Junction
Norris, Sarah Emily	Journalism	Augusta
Norvell, John Thomas, Jr.	Pre-Medical	Augusta
Oakley, Jane	Forestry	Asheville, N. C.
Odom, Thomas Dempsey	Commerce	Valdosta
Oglesby, Thomas Dozier	Commerce	Elberton
O'Kelley, George, Jr.	Agriculture	Wintreville
Owens, John Doster	Pre-Medical	Rochelle
Oxford, James Clay	Commerce	Concord
Palmer, Millard H., Jr.	Commerce	Cheyenne, Wyo.
Palmour, James Ernest, Jr.	Arts	Gainesville
Parker, Carl Oliver	Agriculture	Lavonia
Parker, Hugh Arthur	Forestry	Lavonia
Parker, John Chapman	Commerce	Waycross
Parkman, Bonnie	Home Econ.	Americus
Parks, Willis Cooper	Science	Dalton
Parrish, Robert Leslie	Agriculture	Metcalf
Paschal, Paul Holmes	Commerce	Monroe
Patrick, Cecil	Commerce	Vidalia
Patrick, LaTrelle	Home Econ.	Jefferson
Patton, James Marshall	Commerce	Macon
Pearl, Rosina	Education	Augusta
Peeler, Julian Cheatham	Commerce	Woodland
Pentecost, Annie James	Pre-Medical	Lawrenceville
Perry, Anthony Clark	Pre-Medical	Augusta
Pettus, Francis	Journalism	Savannah
Petty, Harry Symmes	Agriculture	Dawson
Pope, Leonard E.	Commerce	Buchanan
Powell, Alfred Edgar	Arts	Valdosta
Powell, Thomas Roy	Agriculture	Harlem

Prater, Homer Shelton, Jr.	Commerce	Atlanta
Pritchard, Charles Robinson	Commerce	Savannah
Pulliam, Henley Morris	Agriculture	Eastanollee
Pulliam, Rufus D.	Agriculture	Winterville
Pullin, Henry Wilson	Science	Locust Grove
Quarles, John Hinton	Journalism	Rome
Ramsay, Christian Norman	Commerce	Louisville
Ramsey, William Little	Commerce	Louisville
Ray, Charles Hardman	Commerce	Lavonia
Ray, Robert William, Jr.	Commerce	Devereux
Read, Lucia	Home Econ.	Athens
Redmond, D. W.	Science	Cochran
Reed, John E.	Agriculture	Chipley
Reid, C. E., Jr.	Commerce	Montezuma
Renfroe, Riley	Science	Quitman
Reppard, Aaron Harry, Jr.	Commerce	Orlando, Fla.
Richards, Albert Glenn, Jr.	Arts	Athens
Richter, Leroy	Commerce	Cairo
Rigdon, Lewis Elbert	Commerce	Tifton
Ringel, Herbert Arthur	Arts	Georgetown, S. C.
Ritchie, Thomas Evans	Agriculture	Clarkesville
Robertson, Edward Hubert, Jr.	Education	Guyton
Robison, Alice Louise	Arts	Monroe
Rollins, Evart Lane	Commerce	Dalton
Rosenthal, Maxwell	Commerce	Savannah
Rowe, Malcolm Allison	Commerce	Comer
Russell, Fielding Dillard	Medicine	Winder
Samuels, Irving Lewis	Commerce	Atlanta
Sawilousky, Belle	Education	Augusta
Scarborough, Allen Garr	Pre-Medical	Jackson
Scharfman, Ephraim	Pre-Medical	Midville
Scoggins, Allan Hastings	Commerce	Rome
Scott, Thomas Jefferson	Science	Valdosta
Sharpe, William Walter III.	Pre-Medical	Waycross
Shattuck, William Judson	Commerce	LaFayette
Shelor, William Powell	Commerce	Loganville
Shepard, William Raymond	Agriculture	Doerun
Sherman, David Mercer	Journalism	Albany
Sherrod, Robert Lee	Pre-Medical	Thomasville
Shirley, Robert E. Lee	Elec. Eng.	Plains
Shiver, Ivey Merwin	Commerce	Sylvester
Simowitz, Bernard Avrum	Commerce	Augusta
Skelton, William Carey	Arts	Hartwell
Skinner, Frank M.	Arts	Waynesboro

Slade, Wallace Rhodes	Commerce	Cordele
Slappey, Matthew R.	Commerce	Hawkinsville
Sloan, McArthur	Agriculture	Hawkinsville
Sloan, Sam Jones	Journalism	Cartersville
Smith, Conril Bransgrove	Commerce	Atlanta
Smith, Edgar Jackson	Agriculture	Hawkinsville
Smith, Edward Lamar	Commerce	Concord
Smith, Samuel Lamont	Arts	Glennville
Smith, Horace Lynwood	Commerce	Athens
Smith, James Henry, Jr.	Commerce	Griffin
Smith, Robert Hoke	Commerce	Crawford
Smith, Shelby, Jr.	Civ. Eng.	Daytona
Smith, Wiley James	Commerce	Augusta
Spence, Earl Allen	Commerce	Waycross
Spinks, Henry Nelson	Pre-Medical	Greensboro
Stanford, Harwood McCuloch	Pre-Medical	Atlanta
Stark, Olivia	Home Econ.	Commerce
Stephenson, Mell Manley, Jr.	Commerce	Athens
Steves. Wilbert Luther	Commerce	Atlanta
Stokeley, Eunice Farr	Arts	Oglethorpe
Story, Reginald	Journalism	Thomson
Strain, Julius Kirby	Commerce	Calhoun
Strickland, Weyman	Commerce	Chipley
Strong, Frances Katharine	Home Econ.	Newnan
Sutherland, Carl Thomas	Arts	Calhoun
Sweat, Carey McDonald	Commerce	Waycross
Tate, Philip May	Science	Fairmount
Taylor, Ellis Kinchin	Commerce	Americus
Taylor, Eva Mae	Commerce	Columbus
Taylor, John Dodson, Jr.	Arts	Summerville
Tessier, Claude Ed	Pre-Medical	Augusta
Thigpen, Clayton	Pre-Medical	Soperton
Thomas, E. Lewis	Agriculture	Martin
Thomason, Owen Willard, Jr.	Commerce	Columbus
Thomson, Robert Pattillo	Commerce	Savannah
Thornton, J. Ben, Jr.	Commerce	Athens
Thornton, William McWhorter	Elec. Eng.	Athens
Todd, Peyton Henry, Jr.	Arts	Atlanta
Tucker, Harrison	Agriculture	Williamston, S. C.
Tunkle, Sadie	Education	Augusta
Turner, Olynthius William	Journalism	Waycross
Turner, William	Commerce	Jackson
Upchurch, J. C.	Commerce	Athens
Upson, Marie L.	Arts	Athens

Upson, Stephen Lumpkin	Arts	Athens
Vandiver, Comer Lester	Commerce	Helen
Varn, William Morris	Commerce	Crawford
Vaughan, Walter Alexander	Agriculture	Carrollton
Vinson, Benjamin Franklin	Agriculture	Macon
Vinson, T. M.	Commerce	Valdosta
Wade, Dudley Bradstreet	Arts	Albany, N. Y.
Wagoner, Roger Reuben	Pre-Medical	Atlanta
Walden, Spencer C.	Commerce	Albany
Walker, Warren	Pre-Medical	Augusta
Wall, Bevil Clay	Commerce	Augusta
Warthen, Thomas Milton	Commerce	Warthen
Waters, Millard F.	Commerce	Glennville
Watkins, Thaddeus Reese	Journalism	Lexington
Waugh, Richard Gordon	Agriculture	Albany
Webb, Robert D.	Pre-Medical	Smyrna
Westbrook, Almand	Commerce	Columbus
Westbrook, Jesse Thomas, Jr.	Commerce	Cordele
White, Milledge	Agriculture	Sylvester
Whitehead, Katisue	Pre-Medical	Atlanta
Whitley, Martin	Civ. Eng.	Fitzgerald
Wilder, George Aubry	Commerce	Athens
Wiley, Edwin Dewitt	Civ. Eng.	Sparta
Williams, Hoyt Daniel	Civ. Eng.	Auburn
Williams, James Robert	Commerce	Acworth
Williams, Ruth	Education	Hull
Williams, Theodore	Commerce	Cordele
Willis, Clarence Hill, Jr.	Pre-Medical	Barneesville
Wilson, Grady Columbus	Agriculture	Loganville
Wilson, Robert Earl	Pre-Medical	Cave Spring
Wimberly, Sarah Carter	Home Econ.	Cochran
Wingfield, RoberCt Screven	Commerce	Athens
Wise, Elizabeth	Home Econ.	Sumter
Witcher, Thomas Augustus	Arts	Athens
Womack, Charles Hollis	Commerce	DeSoto
Wooten, John A.	Commerce	Eastman
Wright, James Christopher	Pre-Medical	Commerce
Wright, John Goode	Arts	Philomath
Yarbrough, Forney Renfro, Jr.	Science	Atlanta
Yonce, Eugene Martin	Agriculture	Mt. Berry
Youmans, Charles Brooks	Commerce	Adrian
Youmans, Harry Dopson, Jr.	Pre-Medical	Lyons
Young, Willis Erskine	Commerce	Winder

Manucy, James Edwards, Jr._____Savannah
O'Byrne, Charles Joseph_____Savannah
Odom, John Duncan_____Columbus
Oldham, Arthur Sears_____Athens
Parham, Austin Herschel_____Newnan
Phillips, John Robert, Jr._____Louisville
Ray, William Tyrus_____Athens
Strickland, Herbert Albert_____Jesup
Taylor, Harry Lundy_____Athens
Upson, Mathilde Lumpkin_____Athens
Wheaton, Minor Lewis_____Griffin
Wooten, Iver Leon_____Quitman
Wooten, Julian Davis_____Sylvester
Wyatt, Luther Mandeville_____Franklin
Zeigler, Luther Harmon_____Savannah

Barnes, Joseph Mack--Waycross
Block, Richard Nelson--------------------------------------Atlanta
Boyett, Edwin Sanford--------------------------------------Blakeley
Crim, Elmer Barrett--------------------------------------Manchester
Curran, John Philip--Athens
Elmore, Thomas Henry---------------------------------------Claxton
Graves, Robert William---------------------------------------Rome
Hay, Isaac Kline---Covington
Jones, Margaret ---Athens
Lummus, Thomas James--------------------------Miami Beach, Fla.
Patterson, Benjamin Lane--------------------------------------Millen
Smith, Lamar Nevitt--Clayton

LAW—SPECIAL

Broadnax, John Ellis_____Atlanta
Burns, James Calhoun_____Atlanta
Cooper, Martin Milner_____Thomasville
Estes, Roy Edwin_____Athens
Harbuck, James Berry_____Savannah
Malavis, George Stephen_____Columbus
Morris, John Robert_____Douglasville
Tanner, Clyde Hampton_____Douglas
Wilcox, Francis Lamar_____Valdosta
Winston, Edward Thomas_____Atlanta
Young, William Hall_____Columbus

SENIOR PHARMACY

Connally, Ralph Collins_____Dallas
Deen, Thomas Sheldon_____Douglas
Dunaway, William Horace_____Dallas
Herndon, John Walker_____Hartwell
Hillis, Julian Whitehead_____Girard
Lesser, Herman Joe_____Rome
Liberti, Vincent Anthony_____Ansonia, Conn.
Parsons, Annie Elizabeth_____Abiline, Texas
Peterson, Bill Henry_____A   iley
Phillips, John Thomas_____Sparta
Temples, Coy Hudson_____Statesboro

SUMMER SCHOOL STUDENTS

County		County	
Abercrombie, Mrs. Daisy Bullock		Attaway, Eugene _ _ _ Mitchell	
Abercrombie, Vannie _ Paulding		Averett, Nellie _ _ _ _ Bullock	
Abercrombie, Stanley _ _ Clark		Avery, Andrew _ _ _ _ Decatur	
Acree, Margaret _ _ _ Stephens		Baggett, Boyd _ _ _ _ _ Barrow	
Acree, Martha _ _ _ _ Mitchell		Baggett, Lillian _ _ _ _ Barrow	
Adair, Reba _ _ _ _ _ _ _ Hall		Bagley, Helen Elizabeth Coweta	
Adams, Bernice _ _ _ _ _ Clark		Bagley, Louise _ _ _ _ _ Dalton	
Adams, Flora _ _ _ _ _ Elbert		Bagwell, Virginia Johnson _ _	
Adams, Georgia Mae _ Lawrence		_ _ _ _ _ _ _ _ _ _ Gwinnett	
Aderhold, Jetta Mae _ Franklin		Bailey, Blanche _ _ _ Spalding	
Adkins, Lena Grace _ _ Dooly		Bailey, Glen O. _ _ _ _ _ Coweta	
Aikens, Harry Solomon Bullock		Bailey, Mary Dean _ _ _ Walton	
Aikens, Irene _ _ _ _ Laurens		Bailey, Mary Ethel _ _ _ Clarke	
Alexander, Thelma _ _ _ Banks		Baird, Martha _ _ _ _ _ _ Coffee	
Alfriend, Kyle Terry, Jr. Monroe		Baker, Florence Edna _ Fulton	
Alfriend, Malcolm _ _ _ Monroe		Baker, Helen Faustine _ _ _ _	
Alfriend, Mary Watts _ Monroe		_ _ _ _ _ _ _ _ _ Chattooga	
Allen, Julia Mae _ _ _ Richmond		Ballard, Ellen _ _ _ _ _Laurens	
Allen Mrs. J. A. _ _ _ _ _ Pike		Ballard, Edna _ _ _ _ Laurens	
Allison, Donald Glen _ _ DeKalb		Banister, Katie _ _ _ _ Forsyth	
Almon, Lurline _ _ Meriwether		Banks, Gertrude Charlotte, N. C.	
Almond, Jose Francis _ Madison		Bankston, Sara _ _ _ _ Henry	
Amason, Ruth _ _ _ _ Madison		Banner, Therese _ _ _ Muscogee	
Amis, Julius _ _ _ _ _ _ Clarke		Barbre, Margaret _ _ _ _ Dooly	

Belcher, Mrs. L. W. _ _ _ Clarke
Bell, Carrie _ _ _ _ _ _ Butts
Bell, J. C. _ _ _ _ _ _ _Clarke
Bell, Lula _ _ _ _ _ _ _ Hall
Bennett, Elizabeth _ _ Jackson
Bennett, L. L. _ _ _ _ _ _ Hall
Bennett, Ulric Joseph Whitfield
Benns, Margaret _ _ _ Taylor
Benson, Bertha Margaret _ Cobb
Bentley, Mary Willie _ Lincoln
Benton, Sallie Mae _ _ Jackson
Bernstein, Hannah _ _ _ Clarke
Berrong, Susie _ _ _ _ _ Towns
Bethes, Maggie _ _ _ _ Tattnall
Bentley, Mary Evelyn Muscogee
Betts, Sarah Louise _ _ Clarke
Beusse, Henriette _ _ _ Clarke
Biggers, Lillian _ _ _ _ Newton
Bickerstaff, Chas. _ _ _ Clarke
Bingham, Mrs. H. W. _ _ Hart
Bichmore, Harrison _ _ Clarke
Blackwell, J. Wm. _ _ Campbell
Blackshear, Mrs. T. J. Laurens
Blanton, Martha _ _ _ Spalding
Blitch, Marie _ _ _ _ _ Ware
Bohler, Susie _ _ _ _ Columbia
Bowen, Sara C. _ _ Oglethorpe
Bower, Jack _ _ _ _ _ Brooks
Bower, Marie _ _ _ _ _ Brooks
Bowers, Alwayne _ _ _ Mitchell
Boyer, Mrs. F. S. _ _ Chatham
Boyer, Norma _ _ _ _ _ Jenkins
Boyett, Edwin Sanford _ Early
Brackett, Pauline _ _ _ Clarke
Boykin, Lilly _ _ _ _ _ Carroll
Bradberry, Robt. Thornton _
_ _ _ _ _ _ _ _ _ _ Clarke
Bradbury, Ellie _ _ _ _ Clarke
Bradbury, Minnie Louise _ Bibb
Bradbury, Mattie Lou _ Clarke
Braddy, Minton Venner _ Troup
Bradley, Bertha _ _ _ Madison
Bradley, Lurline _ _ _ Bartow
Bradwell, Dowse _ _ _ Clarke
Brake, Clara Emma _ Chatham

Brand, Claurence _ _ _ Walton
Brand, Josephine _ _ Columbia
Brand, Mena Louise _ Gwinett
Brannon, Lena _ _ _ _ _ Henry
Brazier, Florence _ _ Mitchell
Bryant, Jenie Ruth _ Randolph
Breedlove, Louise _ _ _ Coffee
Brewer, Mary Belle _ Whitfield
Bridger, Reba _ _ _ _ Chatham
Bridges, Willi Mae _ _ Calhoun
Bridges, W. _ _ _ _ _ _ Terrell
Brinson, Fred Arthur _ Jenkins
Brinson, E. Rexford _ _ Screven
Britt, William _ _ _ Gwinnett
Brodman, John _ _ _ _ Chatham
Bronson, Pauline _ _ _ _ Bibb
Brooks, Annie Lois _ _ DeKalb
Brooks, Mrs. E. S. _ Albany, Ala.
Brooks, Ilae _ _ _ _ _ Carroll
Brooks, Mrs. J. M. _ _ _ Clarke
Brooks, Josephine Reid _ Clarke
Brookshire, John B. _ _ Elbert
Broome, Lynette _ _ Taliaferra
Brown, Berthe _ _ _ _ _ Polk
Brown, Claud V. _ _ _ Campbell
Brown, Camilla _ _ Washington
Brown, Dorothy Elizabeth _ _
_ _ _ _ St. Petersburg, Fla.
Brown, Foster Talmadge _ _
_ _ _ _ _ _ _ _ _ _ Madison
Brown, Mara _ _ _ _ _ Madison
Brown, Kathryn _ _ _ _ Elbert
Brown, Ruth Kimsey _ Clayton
Brown, Thos. Jefferson _ Elbert
Brown, Virginia _ _ _ _ Clarke
Brumby, Isabella _ _ _ Clarke
Bryant, Ruth _ _ _ _ _ Sumter
Bryan, Elizabeth _ _ _ _ _ Tift
Bryan, Kathleen _ _ _ _ _ Hall
Bryan, Lucy _ _ _ _ _ _ Hall
Bryan, Lynda Lee _ _ _ Talbot
Buchanan, Katherine R. _ _
_ _ _ _ _ _ _ _ _ _ Sumter
Bruce, R. Lee _ _ _ _ Forsyth
Bullock, Atha _ _ _ _ _ Paulding

Bullock, Fannie _ _ _ _ _ Polk
Bullock, Hattie _ _ _ _ Paulding
Bullock, Mattie _ _ Meriwether
Burch, Emily _ _ _ _ _ Laurens
Burgess, Ruth _ _ _ _ _ DeKalb
Burk, Dow C., Mr. _ _ _ Floyd
Burke, Mrs. J. H. _ _ Ben Hill
Burman, Fred _ _ _ _ _ Clarke
Burnet, Robin _ _ _ _ _ Clarke
Burns, Alice Williamson _ _ _
_ _ _ _ _ _ _ _ _ _ Jeff Davis
Burns, Evelyn _ _ _ _ _ _ Hart
Burrough, Emily _ _ _ _ Fulton
Burson, Mrs. Florence P.* _ _
_ _ _ _ _ _ _ _ _ Mitcheld
Burt, Mary _ _ _ _ _ Oglethorpe
Burt, Rachel _ _ _ _ Oglethorpe
Burt, Alexander _ _ _ _ Clarke
Busbin, Fay Belle _ _ Chattooga
Bush, Janie _ _ _ _ _ _ Lamar
Butler, Marjorie _ _ _ Wilkes
Bush, Marianne _ _ _ _ Lamar
Butler, Estes _ _ _ _ _ Madison
Butler, Rose _ _ _ _ _ _ Clarke
Butler, Mary Ormond _ Morgan
Butler, Rubye _ _ _ _ _ Clarke
Butler, Rebecca _ _ _ _ Wilkes
Butts, Miss Johnnie Elizabeth
_ _ _ _ _ _ _ _ _ Dothan, Ala.
Cabaniss, Helen _ _ _ _ _ Clarke
Cargill Francis _ _ _ _ Chatham
Campbell, Margaret Oglethorpe
Camp, Frances _ _ _ Wilkinson
Callaway, Matilda _ _ _ Evans
Califf, Ruth Bell _ _ _ _ Twiggs
Califf, Gladys _ _ _ _ _ Twiggs
Caldwell, Claudia _ _ _ Greene
Caldwell, Barbara Marguerite
_ _ _ _ _ _ _ _ _ _ _ _ Pike
Cain, Frank _ _ _ _ _ Gwinnett
Carithers, Ida Marla _ Madison
Carithers, Louise Payne _ Elbert
Carlisle, Lula Elizabeth DeKalb
Carlton, Ella Ree _ _ _ _ Wilkes
Carmichael, Louise _ _ _ Clarke

Cargile, Loyce _ _ _ _ _ _ Bibb
Carmichael, Mary Frances _ _
_ _ _ _ _ _ _ _ _ _ Clarke
Carr, Lucile _ _ _ _ _ Chatham
Carr, Mrs. Robert _ _ _ Banks
Carr, Richard D., Jr. _ _ Clarke
Carreker, Homer Beeks Laurens
Carrier, Lucile _ _ _ Richmond
Carrier, Chalice _ _ _ _ Clarke
Carruth, Neva Lucile _ Fannins
Carson, Alberta R. _ _ Chatham
Carson, Jessie _ _ _ _ _ Fulton
Canter, Frances _ _ _ _ _ Early
Carter, J. A. _ _ _ _ _ _ Coweta
Carter, Leon S. _ Beaufort, S. C.
Carter, Mary _ _ _ _ _ Schley
Carter, Maude _ _ _ _ _ Hart
Carter, Roley B. _ _ _ _ Elbert
Carter, Seleta _ _ _ Paulding
Caskey, Grandison _ _ _ Clarke
Carteel, Robert _ _ _ _ Wilkes
Castelow, Mamie _ _ _ Brooks
Cate, Charles M. _ _ _ Clarke
Cater, Kathleen _ _ _ _ _ Bibb
Cauthen, Mattie Lee _ _ _ _
_ _ _ _ _ _ _ Leesburg, Fla.
Chadwick, Gladys Beaufort, N. C.
Chalker, F. M. _ _ _ _ Ben Hill
Chambless, Mary L. _ _ Lawens
Chambless, Merle _ _ _ Laurens
Chance, Claude _ _ _ _ Clarke
Chandler, O'Neal W. _ _ Oconee
Chandler, Mattie Ruby Madison
Chandler, Ruby _ _ _ _ _ Polk
Chandler, Winnie _ _ _ _ Hall
Chapman, Bertha Mae Cherokee
Chapman, Eva _ _ _ _ Brooks
Chatfield, Lonne _ _ _ _ Monroe
Chatfield, May Dickey _ Monroe
Cheatham, Lillie _ _ _ Terrell
Cheek, R. F., Jr. _ _ _ Franklin
Chew, Julia Lillian _ _ Jenkins
Chick, Ruth _ _ _ _ _ _ Walton
Childs, Allis Cobb _ _ _ Upson
Childs, Mae _ _ _ _ _ _ Butts

Clack, Troy _ _ _ _ _ _ Macon
Clarke, Geo. Miller _ Richmond
Clarke, Arthur _ _ _ _ _ Elbert
Clarke, Amma King _ _ Clarke
Clarke, May Belle _ _ _ _ Crisp
Clarke, Nenia _ _ _ _ _ Clarke
Clarke, Ruth _ _ _ _ _ _ Hall
Clement, Blanton _ _ _ _ Marion
Claud, Mary _ _ _ _ _ _ Greene
Cobb, Ella Mae _ _ _ Cherokee
Cobb, Martha _ _ _ _ _ Sumter
Cobb, Sarah Tinsley _ _ _ Clarke
Cochran, James Selden, Jr. _
_ _ _ _ _ _ _ _ _ Gwinnett
Cochran, J. M. _ _ _ _ _ _ Hall
Coffee, Mrs. W. G. _ _ Franklin
Cohen, Victoria Billups _ Morgan
Coile, Florence _ _ _ _ _ Clarke
Collier, Priscilla _ _ _ _ _ Pike
Coluitt, Carlton Black _ _ Upson
Colquitt, Susie _ _ _ _ _ Clarke
Combs, Esther _ _ _ _ _ Wilkes
Combs, Mary Will _ _ _ Wilkes
Connell, Idelia _ _ _ _ _ Carroll
Conwell, Mary Lou _ _ _ Elbert
Conway, Cora Lee _ _ _ Clarke
Cooly, Wilson James _ _ Brooks
Cook, Annie Lou _ _ _ _ Miller
Cook, John Homer _ _ _ Gordon
Cook, Willie Mae _ _ _ _ Clarke
Cooke, Bessie _ _ _ _ _ Floyd
Cornett, Walter, Jr. _ _ Clarke
Colton, Ruth _ _ _ _ _ _ Harris
Corry, Annie I. _ _ _ _ _ Greene
Couch, C. E. _ _ _ _ _ _ Hall
Cowan, Mrs. R. W. _ _ _ Floyd
Cox, Chloie _ _ _ _ _ Whitfield
Cox, J. A. E. _ _ _ _ _ DeKalb
Cox, Rebecca _ _ _ _ _ _ Gilmer
Cox, William Crozier _ Calhoun
Cox, Mrs. W. H. _ _ Cherokee
Craft, John Frank _ _ _ Elbert
Crawford, Robert Hewitt _ _
_ _ _ _ _ _ _ _ _ _ Mitchell
Crane, Frances _ _ _ _ _ Clarke

Crain, Wilma _ _ _ _ _ Coweta
Crawford, Corine _ _ _ _ Bartow
Crawford, Custer _ _ _ _ _ _
_ _ _ _ _ _ Haysville, N. C.
Crawford, Hettie _ _ _ _ Elbert
Crawford, Modelyn _ _ _ Fannin
Crawford, William F. _ Franklin
Creswell, Edith _ _ _ _ Clarke
Cromartie, Arthur Deen Toombs
Crouch, Charles Franklin Irwin
Crouch, Marjorie _ _ _ _ Irwin
Crow, Jewell _ _ _ _ _ _ Hall
Crowder, Lillian _ _ _ Spalding
Crowe, Louise _ _ _ _ _ Clarke
Crowell, Mary Ola _ _ Columbia
Crowther, Myrtle _ _ _ _ _ _
_ _ _ _ _ _ Antreville, S. C.
Crozier, Edna Elizabeth _ Clay
Crump, Mr. J. H. _ _ _ Franklin
Crump, Mrs. J. H. _ _ Franklin
Crump, Nena _ _ _ _ _ Franklin
Crymes, Myrtle _ _ _ _ Clarke
Cumming, Maud _ _ _ Spaulding
Curran, Jack _ _ _ _ _ _ Fulton
Currie, Myrtle Mae _ _ _ Coffee
Daker, Halen Little _ _ _ Fulton
Dailly, Clara Gibbs _ _ _ Walton
Daniel, Francis J. _ _ _ Burke
Daniels, Bertha Mae _ _ Calhoun
Daniels, Elsie _ _ _ _ _ Calhoun
Daniel, Susan Elizabeth DeKalb
Darden, Forde Miss _ _ Heard
Daves, Nell _ _ _ _ _ _ Polk
David, Alwin W. _ _ _ _ _ Polk
Davis, Alfred L. _ _ _ _ Floyd
Davis, Effie Estell _ _ Clayton
Davis, Elizabeth Nell _ Randolph
Davis, Gladys Elaine _ _ Pierce
Davis, Jennie _ _ _ _ _ Fayette
Davis, Jewel _ _ _ _ _ Thomas
Davis, James A., Mrs. _ Henry
Davis, Kate Lois _ _ Randolph
Davis, Marie _ _ _ _ _ Floyd
Davis, Max Rubye Olene _ Pike
Davis, Rufus S. _ _ Lenoir, N. C.

Davis, Velma _ _ _ _ _ Stephens
Davis, Zadie A. _ _ _ _ Thomas
Davette, Maude _ _ _ _ _ Polk
Dawson, Louise _ _ _ _ Jefferson
Dawson, Susie _ _ _ _ _ Jefferson
Dean, Lola Baring _ Cherokee
Dean, Maud G. _ _ _ _ _ Pierce
Dees, Mrs. Alfred _ _ Dougherty
Dekle, Laurene Miss _ _ Candler
Dekle, Lolla Cobb _ _ _ _ Crisp
Delay, Louise _ _ _ _ _ Floyd
Dellinger, Willie Miss _ _ Clarke
Dennis, Garr S. _ _ _ _ _ Clarke
Dewberry, Veora _ _ _ _ Monroe
De Wet, C. Isak _ South Africa
Dickerson, Mamie _ _ Franklin
Dickerson, Ruth _ _ _ _ Clinch
Dickerson, Ella _ _ _ _ Clinch
Dickson, Ella _ _ _ _ Jackson
Dietz, Ernest _ _ _ _ _ Clarke
Dill, Mrs. Myrtle _ _ _ _ Ware
Dimmock, Mrs. E. D. _ _ Ware
Dimmock, Harriet _ _ _ _ Ware
Dinsmore, Pauline _ _ _ _ Tift
Dockary, Nettie _ _ _ _ Coffee
Dodd, Mittie _ _ _ _ Chattooga
Dolvin, R. L. _ _ _ _ _ _ Greene
Donovan, Elizabeth _ _ Jefferson
Dorminy, J. H., Sr. _ _ Ben Hill
Dorminy, Lillian _ _ _ Ben Hill
Dornblatt, S. _ _ _ _ _ _ Clarke
Dorsett, Essie _ _ _ _ _ Houston
Dolster, Foye Eleanor _ Mittchell
Dotson, Eva Louise _ _ Chatham
Downs, Walter Lee _ _ Toombs
Dozier, Mrs. H. L. _ _ _ Troup
Drake, Ruth Callaway _ Greene
Drake, W. H. _ _ _ _ _ Miller
Drew, Sarah Frances _ _ _ _
_ _ _ _ _ _ _ _ _ Merriwether
Drewry, J. H. _ _ _ _ Spalding
Drexel, A. E. _ _ _ _ _ Clarke
Driskell, Dorothy _ _ _ Hancock
Driver, Vera _ _ _ _ _ _ Cook
Dubose, August Week Chatham

Dubose, Katherine _ _ _ Clarke
Duggan, Ola _ _ _ Seneca, S. C.
Duke, Audrey _ _ _ _ _ Worth
Dukes, Miss Johnye _ Thomas
Dukes, Willie Frances, Miss _
_ _ _ _ _ _ _ _ _ _ Thomas
Dumas, Marie _ _ _ _ _ Clarke
Dunaway, Frank _ _ _ _ Clarke
Dunaway, Fannie Kate Stewart
Duncan, Jewell _ _ _ _ Schley
Duncan, Marietta _ _ _ _ Barrow
Dunevent, Glenn, Miss _ Twiggs
Dunn, Pat _ _ _ _ _ _ Ben Hill
Dunseith, Madelaine McNeal _
_ _ _ _ _ _ Clearwater, Fla.
Durden, Inez _ _ _ _ _ Emanuel
Durden, Ouida _ _ _ Emanuel
Earnest, Clifford _ _ Seminole
Earnest, Dameris _ _ _ Carroll
Edge, Warnie _ _ _ _ _ Oconee
Edwards, Achsah _ _ _ _ Troup
Edwards, Aline _ _ _ Houston
Edwards, Myrtle _ _ _ Gordon
Elder, Sara _ _ _ _ _ _ Clarke
Eldridge, Jessie _ _ _ _ Cobb
Elliott, Mrs. A. C. _ _ _ Henry
Ellis, Lurlynne _ _ _ Jeff Davis
Emory, Mrs. Walter _ _ Troup
England, R. B. _ _ _ _ _ Union
English, Thelma Joe _ _ Greene
Erwin, Marie _ _ _ _ _ Greene
Estes, Kathleen _ _ Meriwether
Estroff, Hyman _ _ _ Jefferson
Etheredge, John _ _ _ _ _ Tift
Etheridge, Lola Blaine _ Clarke
Evans, Allie _ _ _ _ _ Madison
Eve, Sarah Garland _ Richmond
Exley, Birdie Lee _ _ _ Chatham
Fanning, Annie Sue _ _ McDuffie
Fant, Louise Leslie _ _ _ Clarke
Fargason, Dorothy _ _ Crawford
Farr, Ethel _ _ _ _ _ Franklin
Farr, Eva _ _ _ _ _ _ Franklin
Farr, Ruby _ _ _ _ _ Franklin
Farrar, Clifford Eugene Terrell

Faust, Harriet _ _ Oglethorpe
Faver, Joseph Earl _ _ _ Heard
Ferguson, Berdie _ _ Franklin
Ferguson, Lamar _ _ _ Franklin
Fields, Grace _ _ _ _ _ _ Henry
Fincher, Esther Robin _ _ Troup
Fisher, Loys Eunice _ Franklin
Fitzpatrick, Hettie _ _ Madson
Flanagan, Etta _ _ _ _ Clarke
Flanagan, Grady _ _ _ _ Clarke
Flanagan, Mrs. Wilburn Ira _
_ _ _ _ _ _ _ _ _ _ Clarke
Flanigen, Jean N. _ _ _ Clarke
Flemming, James Laurens, S. S.
Florence, George Eslie _ _ _
_ _ _ _ _ _ _ _ Richmond
Floyd, Theodore C. _ _ _ Troup
Floyd, Mrs. Theodore C. _ Troup
Flynn, Lucy _ _ _ _ _ Columbia
Ford, R. P. _ _ _ _ _ _ _Hart
Foreland, Alton Osboren _ _
_ _ _ _ _ _ _ _ Emanuel
Fort, Theo _ _ _ _ _ _Laurens
Foster, Earl Cooper _ _ Murray
Foster, Louis Napoleon, Jr. _
_ _ _ _ _ _ _ _ _ _ Murry
Fowler, Homer B. _ Oglethorpe
Franklin, Leafy L. _ _ _ Wayne
Franklin, Robt. _ _ _ Stephens
Frazier, J. J. _ _ _ _ Jeff Davis
Freeman, Callie Catherine _ _
_ _ _ _ _ _ _ _ _ Walton
Freeman, Lucille _ _ _ _ Monroe
Freeman, Ruby _ _ _ Madison
Freeman, Mrs. T. A. _ Madison
Freeman, Robt. H _ _ _ Monroe
Freeman, Zenith _ _ Whitfield
Froat, Ora _ _ _ _ _ _ _ Hall
Fuller, Bessie _ _ _ _ _ Clarke
Fuller, Dessa _ _ _ _ _ _ Gordon
Fuller, Water _ _ _ _ _ Clarke
Fulmer, Annie _ _ _ _ _ Toombs
Funderburke, Fannie Muscogee
Furr, Era Mae _ _ _ _ Baxter
Furrer, Marie M. _ _ _ Chatham

Gaines, Blanche _ _ _ _ Elbert
Gaines, Etta Mae _ _ _ Elbert
Gaines, Meta Claire _ _ Gordon
Gaines, Thos. N. _ _ _ _ Clarke
Gaissert, Mrs. John Thomas _
_ _ _ _ _ _ _ _ Dougherty
Gamble, Carrie E. _ _ Chattoga
Gard, Taylor _ _ _ _ Habersham
Gardner, George Lee _ _ Macon
Gardner, Joyce _ _ _ McIntosh
Gardner, Osee Belle _ _ _ Macon
Garner, Florrie _ _ Washington
Garner, M. L. _ _ _ _ Laurens
Garner, William Berry _ _ _
_ _ _ _ _ _ _ Washington
Garrett, James Robt. _ Walton
Gary, Effie Katherine Chattooga
Gaskins, Mrs. Newton Jeff Davis
Gaulding, Sam Lee _ _ Clarke
Gaulding, Wilma Griffeth _ _
_ _ _ _ _ _ _ _ _ Madison
Gay, Mrs. M. C. _ _ _ _ Clarke
Gaylor, Earle _ _ _ _ Chattooga
Gaylor, Winston _ _ _ Chattooga
Geeslin, Frances _ _ _ Laurens
Gibbons, Alma Cheatham _ _
_ _ _ _ _ Abbeville, S. C.
Gibson, H. H. _ _ _ _ ————
Gibson, Wilibel _ _ _ _ Warren
Giddens, Mildred _ _ _ Berrien
Gignilliat, Thomas H. Effingham
Gilbert, D. W. _ _ _ _ Laurens
Gilbert, Mrs. J. J. _ _ Seminole
Glass, Martha _ Edgemoor, S. C.
Gordon, Weston G. _ _ DeKalb
Glenn, Mrs. J. E. _ _ Madison
Glover, Mary Crisp _ _ Sumter
Goggans, Ruby _ _ _ _ Monroe
Gordon, Annie Mae _ _ _ Long
Goss, Gussie _ _ _ _ _ Henry
Goss, Zelva Lucile _ _ _ Peach
Gould, Ada Belle _ _ _ _ Hall
Gould, Jewel _ _ _ _ _ _ Hall
Grace, Farabee _ _ _ _ Telfair
Grace, Zula _ _ _ _ _ _ Telfair

Graham, Bernice B. _ _ _ Hall
Graham, John Franklin _ _ _
_ _ _ _ _ _ _ _ _ Madison
Graham, Nellie _ _ _ _ Greene
Grant, Lula E. _ _ _ _ _ DeKalb
Gray, Loyd H. _ _ _ _ Coweta
Greene, Nannie _ _ _ _ _ Ware
Greene, Velvia _ _ _ _ _ Hall
Greer, Frances E. _ _ _ Newton
Gresham, Mrs. E. T. _ _ Greene
Griffeth, Ellen _ _ _ _ Madison
Griffin, Anne _ _ _ _ Oglethorpe
Griffin, Bobbie M. _ _ Quitman
Griffin, Frances _ _ _ _ Hampton
Griffin, Kathryn _ _ _ Decatur
Griffin, Penelope _ _ _ Twiggs
Griffin, Sara Stubbs _ _ Clarke
Griffin, Thelma _ _ _ _ Henry
Griffin, Willie, Miss _ _ Henry
Griffeth, Arthur Ernest, Jr. _
_ _ _ _ _ _ _ _ _ _ Clarke
Grimes, Chloe _ _ _ _ _ Miller
Griner, Adlai Bee _ _ _ Clarke
Groover, Nettie _ _ _ _ Milton
Griswold, Maude _ _ _ _ Coffee
Groves, Hugh A. _ _ Madison
Guillebeau, Clarice _ _ Lincoln
Grest, Laura _ _ _ _ _ _ Tift
Guill, Doris _ _ _ _ _ Hancock
Guillebeau, Iris _ _ _ _ Lincoln
Gunby, Gladys _ _ _ _ Lincoln
Gunnels, Annie Mae _ _ Elbert
Gunter, Bertha _ _ _ _ Wilkes
Gurley, Clara _ _ _ _ Franklin
Gurley, Maude _ _ _ _ Madison
Guthrie, Oscar R. _ _ _ Fannin
Guye, Rebecah _ _ _ McDuffie
Hackney, Irene _ _ _ _ Fannin
Hackney, Ruth _ _ _ _ Fannin
Haddock, Claudia _ _ _ Clarke
Hailey, Tommy _ _ _ _ Clarke
Hale, Clyde _ _ _ _ _ Clarke
Hale, Emmaline _ _ _ _ Damar
Hale, Pauline _ _ _ Oglethorpe
Haley, Georgia _ _ _ _ Elbert

Haley, Mrs. J. R. _ _ Calhoun
Hall, Bernice _ _ _ _ Habersham
Hall, Dora _ _ _ _ _ _ Elbert
Hall, F. H. _ _ _ _ _ _ Troup
Hall, Kate _ _ _ _ _ _ Wilkes
Hall, Lucy _ _ _ _ _ _ Coffee
Hall, Nan _ _ _ _ _ _ Fulton
Hall, Mary Lee _ _ _ _ Jefferson
Hall, Ruby _ _ _ _ _ _ Macon
Hall, Miss Willie _ _ _ Greene
Hamilton, Zula _ _ _ _ _ Crisp
Hamlin, Adell _ _ _ _ _ Lamar
Hammock, Naomi _ _ Muscogee
Hammock, Thelma _ _ _ Irwin
Hammond, Sarah Elizabeth _
_ _ _ _ _ _ _ _ _ Butts
Hampton, Mary Lou _ _ Clarke
Hancock, Mrs. A. C. _ _ Clarke
Hancock, Elizabeth _ _ _ Upson
Hand, Lillian _ _ _ _ _ Decatur
Haney, Veda _ _ _ _ _ Gordon
Hanson, Edith Carolyn _ Harris
Happoldt, Bessie _ _ Wilkinson
Haralson, Edna Dean _ Walton
Harber, John J. _ _ _ _ Jackson
Hardeman, Nina _ _ _ _ Clarke
Harden, Lillian _ _ _ _ Tattnall
Harders, Supt. J. S. _ Columbia
Hardman, Evie _ _ _ _ Madison
Hardman, Ouida E. _ Madison
Hardy, Eula Mae _ _ Jasper
Hardy, Nancy _ _ _ _ _ ———
Hargrett, Lester _ _ _ _ Tift
Harmon, J. Frank _ Cherokee
Harmon, O. T. _ _ _ _ Jackson
Harper, James P. _ _ _ _ _
_ _ _ _ _ _ Anderson, S. C.
Harper, J. K. _ _ _ _ _ Thomas
Harrell, M. M.* Florence, S. C.
Harrell, Vernice Winnifred _
_ _ _ _ _ _ _ _ _ Decatur
Harris, Gladys _ _ _ _ Barrow
Harris, Mrs. J. L. _ _ Johnson
Harrison, Amanda Washington
Harrison, Callie _ _ _ _ Crisp

Harrison, Harville D. _ _ Harris
Harrison, Louise _ _ _ _ Johnson
Harrison, Sara _ _ _ _ _ Crisp
Hart, Edwin _ _ _ _ _ Madison
Hartley, Mabel _ _ _ _ Mitchell
Hartley, Ruby _ _ _ _ _ Mitchell
Hartsfield, Majoris Dozier _ _
_ _ _ _ _ _ _ _ Union, S. C.
Harvey, Cecil _ _ _ _ _ _ Crisp
Harvey, Edna _ _ _ _ Muscogee
Harvey, Elizabeth _ _ _ Clarke
Hatcher, Catherine _ _ Calhoun
Hatcher, Ruth A. Pauline, S. C.
Hatfield, George R. _ _ Jasper
Hattaway, Susanne _ _ Oconee
Hay, Jarrell W., Jr. _ Paulding
Hay, James Willis _ _ Paulding
Hayden, O. L. _ _ _ _ Laurens
Hayes, Clyda _ _ _ _ _ Mitchell
Haygood, Dorothy H. _ _ Clarke
Haygood, Tyler F., Mr. _ Lamar
Haynes, Frances _ _ _ McIntosh
Hays, Uldene _ _ Abbeville, Ala.
Head, Ruth _ _ _ _ _ _ Jackson
Headden, Marie _ _ _ _ Bartow
Heidler, Mrs. Harrison S. _ _
_ _ _ _ _ _ _ _ _ _ Clarke
Hendrick, Era _ _ _ Oglethorpe
Hendry, Pauline _ _ _ _ _ Cook
Heritage, Fannie B. _ _ Wayne
Herrin, Ethel Lillian _ _ Pierce
Herndon, Naomi _ _ _ _ Hart
Harring, Maude _ _ _ _ Douglas
Hewell, Guy C. _ _ _ _ Elbert
Heyward, Mrs. O. J. _ Lumpkin
Hicks, Annie Mae _ _ _ Macon
Hicks, C. J. _ _ _ _ _ Rockdale
Hicks, Irma M. _ _ _ _ _ Polk
Hicks, Henry L. _ _ _ _ Wilks
Hicks, Kate E. _ _ _ _ Taylor
Higgenbotham, Clarence _ _ _
_ _ _ _ _ _ _ _ _ Franklin
Higgenbotham, Martha Morgan
Higgenbotham, Madge Madison
Hightower, Marie _ _ _ Henry

Hightower, Mageline _ _ Polk
Hilburn, Lucille _ _ _ Laurens
Hilburn, Madge _ _ _ Laurens
Hill, Virginia _ _ Bamberg, S. C.
Hillis, Gertrude _ _ _ _ Burke
Hillis, Julian W. _ _ _ _ Burke
Hinton, Sarah C. _ _ _ Pickens
Hinton, Una _ _ _ _ _ Gwinnett
Hirsch, Morris _ _ _ _ Fulton
Hodges, Elizabeth _ _ Decatur
Hodges, James Arthur _ Screven
Hodges, Wm. L. _ _ _ Decatur
Hodgson, Roy _ _ _ _ Clarke
Hogan, Jessie _ _ _ _ Lincoln
Holder, Metz R. _ _ _ _ Decatur
Holder, Mary _ _ _ _ Fulton
Holland, Mrs. E. M. _ _ Stephens
Holliday, Norene _ _ _ _ Clarke
Holmes, Arthur B. _ _ Carroll
Holmes, Allene _ _ _ _ Clarke
Holmes, Mary _ _ _ Richmond
Holmes, Launette Watson _ _
_ _ _ _ _ _ _ _ _ _ Coweta
Holt, Georgia _ _ _ _ Harris
Hood, Grace _ _ _ _ Gwinnett
Hooks, Blanche _ _ Meriwether
Hope, Nan _ _ _ _ _ _ Clayton
Hopkins, Bessie _ _ Oglethorpe
Hopkins, Connie _ _ Oglethorpe
Hopper, Myrtie _ _ _ _ Wilkes
Hopper, Katie _ _ _ _ Fannin
Harken, Florence _ _ _ Colquitt
Horn, Arthur E. _ _ _ _ Walton
Harrigan, Nan _ _ _ _ Chatham
Horton, Madge _ _ _ _ Floyd
Horton, Sidney _ _ _ _ Floyd
House, Louise _ _ _ _ Barrow
Howard, Winnie _ _ _ _ Long
Hubbard, Bertha _ _ _ Franklin
Hubbs, M. Christine _ Whitfield
Hudjins, Pearl _ _ _ _ _ Hall
Hudson, Miss Johnnie Lee _ _
_ _ _ _ _ _ _ _ _ Meriwether
Huff, Alberta _ _ _ _ _ Clarke
Huff, Elizabeth _ _ _ _ _ Troup

Huff, Florine _ _ _ Oglethorpe
Hughes, Aubie _ _ _ _ Mitchell
Hughes, Mrs. F. W. _ _ Bullock
Hughes, Leona _ _ _ _ Forsyth
Hughes, Martha Wilma _ Bryan
Hughes, Walter P. _ _ _ _ Hall
Humphries, Elizabeth _ _ _ _
_ _ _ _ _ _ _ Dade City, Fla.
Humphries, Mae _ _ _ _ Clarke
Hunt, Lois Mary _ _ _ Whitfield
Humphreys, William Robt. _
_ _ _ _ _ _ _ _ _ _ Colquitt
Hunt, Salome _ _ _ _ Jackson
Hurst, Carrie G. _ _ _ Stephens
Hurst, Marybeth _ _ Meriwether
Huss, Nora _ _ _ _ _ _ Coffee
Hutchins, Gladys _ _ _ Oconee
Hutchins, Mae _ _ _ _ Jackson
Hutchins, Myrtie _ _ _ Clarke
Hutchins, Ozie _ _ _ _ _ Hall
Inglett, Martha Jane Richmond
Ingram, Irvine Sullivan Carroll
Ingram, Lula _ _ _ _ _ Brooks
Iricks, Maggie Lou _ _ Bartow
Iricks, Nancy _ _ _ _ _ Bartow
Ivester, V. Byrd _ _ Habersham
Ivey, Virginia _ _ _ _ _ Turner
Jackson, Corine _ _ _ _ Warren
Jackson, Sara Elma _ _ Turner
Jackson, Elsie _ _ _ _ Gwinnett
Jackson, Elvira _ _ _ _ Turner
Jackson, Frances _ _ _ Clarke
Jago, Anne Re _ _ _ _ _ Clarke
Jackson, Ralph _ _ _ _ Clarke
Jago, Eunice Thornton _ Clarke
James, Nola _ _ _ _ _ _ Rabun
Jarrard, W. C. _ _ _ _ _ Hall
Jarrett, Blanche _ _ _ Jackson
Jay, Emmis Mae _ _ _ _ Elbert
Jeffcoat, Mrs. P. G. _ _ _ _
_ _ _ _ _ _ Leesburg, Fla.
Jenkins, Annie _ _ _ _ Johnson
Jenkins, Dallie _ _ _ _ Wheeler
Jester, Elsie _ _ _ _ _ Clarke
Jenkins, Ruby _ _ _ _ _ **Madison**

Johnson, Anna Kate Richmond
Johnson, Bessie Lou _ _ Macon
Johnson, Eliza Beth _ _ Johnson
Johnson, Estelle _ _ _ Madison
Johnson, Frances Dudley _ _
_ _ _ _ _ _ Pulaski, Tenn.
Johnson, Georgia Daytona, Fla.
Johnson, Ida Mae _ _ _ _ Hall
Johnson, Inez Lafayette Stewart
Johnson, John W. _ Whitfield
Johnson, Mary M. _ _ _ Oconee
Johnson, Ora Gertrude Stewart
Johnson, Rosamond _ Muscogee
Johnson, Rose B. _ _ _ _ _ _
_ _ _ _ _ Birmingham, Ala.
Johnson, Sophie _ _ Jefferson
Johnson, Willie Mae Johnson
_ _ _ _ _ _ _ _ Taliaferro
Johnson, D. B. _ _ _ Emanuel
Johnson, Olo Joe _ _ _ Walton
Joiner, Otis C. _ _ _ Calhoun
Jolly, Carrie _ _ _ _ _ Bartow
Jolly, Dorthy _ _ _ _ _ Bartow
Jones, Annie Laurie _ _ Lamar
Jones, B. L. _ _ _ _ Webster
Jones, Ida _ Water Valley, Miss.
Jones, Elma _ _ _ _ _ _ Polk
Jones, Miss Janie _ _ _ Bullock
Jones, Mallary, Miss _ _ Clarke
Jones, Margaret _ _ _ _ _ _
_ _ _ _ _ Water Valley, Miss.
Jones, Margaret Ammons _ Polk
Jones, Melle _ _ _ _ _ Madison
Jones, Norma _ _ _ _ Spalding
Jones, Otis Warner _ _ _ Fulton
Jones, Pearl _ _ _ _ _ Tattnall
Jones, Ruby _ _ _ _ _ Appling
Jones, William C. _ _ Newton
Jones, W. J. Mrs. _ _ Charlton
Jordan, Adelle _ _ _ _ Elbert
Jordan, Daisy Bertha _ _ _
_ _ _ _ _ _ Charlotte, N. C.
Jordan, Gladys _ _ _ _ Brooks
Jordan, Marie _ _ _ _ Baldwin
Jacks, Annie Lois _ _ _ _ Floyd

Kaigler, Mary _ _ _ _ Stewart
Keen, George Lee _ _ _ Fulton
Keen, Mrs. Marion _ _ _———
Keener, Mary A. _ _ _ Rabun
Keener, Mrs. R. L. _ _ Clarke
Kelly, Ethel _ _ _ _ _ Chatham
Kenneth, Alma _ _ _ _ Cherokee
Kenny, Lawrence _ _ _ Clarke
Kennington, Gladys _ _ Twiggs
Kenyon, Josephine _ _ Webster
Keown, Bessie _ _ _ _ Floyd
Kerr, Miss M. K. _ _ Dougherty
Kerr, Frannie _ _ _ _ Bartow
Kessler, Lucile _ _ _ Effingham
Khoury, Claire _ _ _ _ Dodge
Kidd, Annie Mae _ _ _ Madison
Kimbell, Ada Julia _ _ _ _
_ _ _ _ _ _ _ Cherokee, S. C.
Kimbell, Leila Mae _ _ _ _
_ _ _ _ _ _ _ Cherokee, S. C.
Kimbrough _ _ _ _ _ _ Talbot
King, Cleveland _ _ _ _ Forsyth
King, Blanche _ _ _ _ Jefferson
King, C. H. _ _ _ _ _ _ Forsyth
King, Louise Summerfield, Ala.
King, Sara _ _ _ _ _ _ Henry
Kinney, James Paul _ Lincoln
Kitchens, Geslie _ Washington
Kinght, Lillian _ _ _ _ Walton
Knight, Adah _ _ _ _ _ _ _
_ _ _ _ Safety Harbor, Fla.
Knight, M. Evelyn _ _ _ _ _
_ _ _ _ Safety Harbor, Fla.
Knight, Nancy Lou _ _ _ _
_ _ _ _ Safety Harbor, Fla.
Knight, Mrs. T. H. _ _ Walton
Krumrine, Kathryen _ _ Clarke
Laboon, Brandt _ _ _ _ Walton
Lam, C. O. _ _ _ _ _ Paulding
Lampkin, Lois Cobb _ _ Clarke
Lampkin, Lucy _ _ _ _ _ Clarke
Lancaster, B. A. _ _ _ _ Bibb
Lancaster, O. G. _ _ _ Madison
Landrum, Claud England _ _
_ _ _ _ _ _ _ _ Campbell

Lane, Mary _ _ _ _ _ _ Polk
Langford, Avery _ _ _ Franklin
Langford, Masina _ Oglethorpe
Langley, Archie _ _ _ Walker
Lanier, Blanche _ _ _ _ Bryan
Lanier, Geneve _ _ Montgomery
Lanier, Jewel _ _ _ _ Bullock
Lanier, Lois _ _ _ _ Washington
Lanier, W. R. _ _ _ _ Laurens
Lasseter, Horace Shelby _ Bibb
Lasseter, Maire _ _ _ _ Monroe
Lattay, Maugle _ _ Oglethorpe
Lattner, Leona James _ _ Clarke
Launius, J. K. _ _ _ _ _ Walton
Lawrence, Lorna _ _ _ _ Clarke
Lawson, Delmer Thomas _ Hall
Lawson, Ulyses _ _ _ _ _ Hall
Ledford, Ina _ _ _ _ _ Grady
Lee, Aileen _ _ _ _ _ Calhoun
Lee, John Ed. _ _ _ Gwinnett
Lee, Nellee _ _ _ _ _ Chattooga
Leffler, Lee Roy _ _ _ Chatham
Leonard, Omagene _ _ _ Murry
Leger, J. E. _ _ _ _ _ Thomas
Leslie, Mary Cornelia _ _ Troup
Lester, Betty _ _ _ _ _ Butts
Lester, Flora _ _ _ _ _ Cobb
Lester, Florence _ _ _ Richmond
Lester, R. K. _ _ _ _ _ Clarke
Leverett, Gladys Louise _ _ _
_ _ _ _ _ _ _ _ _ Meriwether
Levy, Morris Hart _ _ Chatham
Lewis, Adex Payne _ Franklin
Lewis, Charlotte _ _ _ _ Bibb
Lewis, Lellia _ _ _ _ _ Greene
Lewis, Walton Felker _ Walton
Lillard, Louise _ _ _ _ Johnson
Lin, Mary _ _ _ _ _ _ Fulton
Linch, Evelyn _ _ _ _ _ Butts
Linton, Annie _ _ _ _ _ Clarke
Little, Corinne _ _ _ _ Franklin
Little, Mary _ _ _ _ Franklin
Little, Martha Rhea _ _ _ White
Little, Pauline _ _ _ _ Franklin
Little, Sara Frances Oglethorpe

Littlejohn, Boyd B. Pacolet, S. C.
Locke, Mrs. Pearl _ _ _ Dooly
Lokey, H. M., Jr. _ _ _ Fulton
Long, Della Mae _ _ _ Wayne
Lott, Aurel _ _ _ _ _ _ Coffee
Lovett, Julia _ _ _ _ _ Ben Hill
Lovett, Willie _ _ _ _ Screven
Lowe, Dorothy _ _ _ _ Oconee
Lowry, Losha _ _ _ _ _ Clarke
Lowe, Eva _ _ _ _ _ Muscogee
Lucas, Ludie _ _ _ _ _ Harris
Lund, Adolph _ _ _ _ _ Clarke
Lyle, Miss Minnie _ _ _ Coweta
Lynn, Mrs. M. _ _ _ _ _ _ Davis
Lyon, J. E., Jr. _ _ Washington
Macon, Alethea Jane _ _ Glynn
Malone, Glayds Lane _ Jasper
Malone, Lucy Katherine Jasper
Malone, Mrs. Ola R. _ _ Newton
Mann, Emmilee _ _ _ _ Coweta
Marchman, Robt. Lee _ _ _ _

_ _ _ _ _ _ _ _ Citrus, Fla.
Marshall, Zola _ _ _ _ Clarke
Marshall, Kathleen Merriwether
Martin, Clara _ _ _ Habersham
Martin, Beamon _ _ _ _ Bulloch
Martin, Lois _ _ _ _ _ Walker
Martin, Nita _ _ _ _ Seminole
Martin, Roselle _ _ _ _ Randolph
Martin, Vetie _ _ _ _ _ Madison
Martin, William Robert _ _ _

_ _ _ _ _ _ _ _ _ Mississippi
Mason, Tommie _ _ _ _ Toombs
Massey, Lois _ _ _ _ Lowndes
Matthews, Bess E _ Muscogee
Mathes, J. T. Mrs. _ _ Stephens
Matthews, Alice Frances DeKalb
Matthews, Sara Vincent _ Clarke
Maughon, Sidney, Jr. Cherokee
Maughon, S. T. _ _ _ Cherokee
Maxwell, Grace _ _ _ _ Talbot
Meaders, Georgia _ _ Stephens
Mehre, H. J. _ _ _ _ _ Clarke
Mell, Carlton _ _ _ _ _ Clarke
Mercer, Gertrude _ _ _ Twiggs

Merck, Sarah _ _ _ _ _ Clarke
Merritt, Nannie Hunt _ Spalding
Methvin, Verna _ _ _ _ Terrell
Merritt, Ruby Deen _ _ Forsyth
Mewborne, Grace _ _ _ Elbert
Michael, Laney _ _ _ DeKalb
Miller, Audrey _ _ _ _ Evans
Miller, Mary Edna _ _ _ _ Glynn
Miller, Stephens _ _ _ _ Towns
Miller, Verdie Frances _ _ Union
Miner, Robt. _ _ _ _ _ _ Clarke
Minor, Marie Elizabeth Baldwin
Mitchell, Frank F. _ _ Bartow
Mitchell, Lillian _ _ _ _ Taylor
Mixon, Susie _ _ _ _ _ Bartow
Mobley, Mrs. M. D. _ _ _ Clarke
Mollenhoff, Dora Burside, Iowa
_ _ _ _ _ _ Burside, Iowa
Monroe, John _ _ _ _ Walton
Montgomery, Carolyn F. Fulton
Moody, Clarence Griffin, Jr. _

_ _ _ _ _ _ _ _ _ Green
Moon Christine _ _ _ _ Clarke
Moon, Louise _ _ _ _ _ Walton
Moon, Pearl _ _ _ _ Campbell
Moon, Sarah Frances _ Clarke
Moore, Alva _ _ _ _ _ Clarke
Moore, Arthur _ _ _ _ Fulton
Moore, Carrie _ _ _ _ Butts
Moore, Helen _ Hanceville, Ala.
Moore, Mrs. J. B. _ _ _ _ Hall
Moore, Marie _ _ _ _ _ _ Hall
Moore, Maryn Julia _ Hancock
Moore, Wm. L. _ _ _ _ Jones
Morgan, V. _ _ _ _ _ Muscogee
Morris, Pauline _ _ _ Habersham
Morris. Willie Frank _ Douglas
Morrison, Alma _ _ Montgomery
Morrison, John Haygood _ _
_ _ _ _ _ _ _ _ Richmond
Morrison, Rubye Emily _ _ _
_ _ _ _ _ _ _ _ Oglethorpe
Morriss, Pierce Avis _ Appling
Morton, Elenda _ _ _ Chattooga

Morton, Frank Everett, Mrs. _
_ _ _ _ _ _ _ _ _ Spalding
Morton, Everett, Mr. _ Spalding
Morton, Elizabeth _ _ Stewart
Mosely, Cue _ _ _ _ _ _ Cobb
Moss, Livingston W., Mrs. _
_ _ _ _ _ _ _ _ _ _ Wilkes
Moss, Lizzie _ _ _ _ _ _ Elbert
Moss, Wm. A. _ _ _ _ _ _ _Hart
Moye, Connie Looma _ _ Harris
Mozeley, Coralee _ _ _ Rabun
Mullins, Patsy Jane _ _ Harris
Mullins, Georgie Lee _ _ Dodge
Mullins, Mary _ _ _ _ _ Dodge
Munro, Henry _ _ _ _ _ Schley
Munro, Maurine _ _ _ _ Schley
Murphy, Alma   _ _ _ Coweta
Murphy, Mary _ _ _ _ Jackson
Murry, Eula Mae _ _ Madison
Murry, Barber _ _ _ Madison
Myers, Frances _ _ _ _ _ Clarke
Myers, Gladys _ _ _ _ Lincoln
Myers, Mrs. Jennie Belle _ _
_ _ _ _ _ _ _ _ Dougherty
McArther, Nell Mallory _ _
_ _ _ _ _ Fayetteville, N. C.
McAlphine, Louise _ Habersham
McCants, Charlotte _ _ Barrow
McClellan, Albert Dalton _ _
_ _ _ _ _ _ _ _ _ Haralson
McCollum, Wm. Bruce Jefferson
McConnell, Hoyt Eakes Jackson
McCook, Sue _ _ _ _ _ _ Bibb
McCranie, Fanny Lee _ _ Cook
McCullough, Ouida _ _ Chatham
McCurdy, Frances _ _ _ Banks
McCutchon, Charles Miami, Fla.
McDaniel, Lucile _ _ Gwinnett
McDonald, Mrs. Annie _ _ Lee
McDougald, Mary Gilmore _ _
_ _ _ _ _ _ _ _ _ Laurens
McGee, Mattie Mark _ _ Troup
McGarrick _ _ _ _ _ _ Carroll
McGukin, Ida Elizabeth _ Hart
McIntosh, Rupert D. Richmond

McKelvey, Pat _ _ _ _ _ Polk
McKenzie, Lillian _ _ _ Crisp
McKibben, Claude A. Muscogee
McKinney, Sophia _ _ _ Fannin
McKimonfi Lila _ _ _ _ Clay
McClean, Lola May _ _ Coffee
McLendon, L. B. _ _ _ Terrell
McLennan, Grance _ _ Wheeler
McLeroy, Hugh Finley _ Clarke
McLeroy, Louise _ _ _ Jackson
McMahan, Nina _ _ _ _ Macon
McMillan, Mrs. Lonnie Gwinnett
McMullan, Lois _ _ _ _ Hart
McMullan, Thomas Leverett _
_ _ _ _ _ _ _ _ _ _ Hart
McNeill, Alice _ _ _ _ _ Crisp
McRae, Dorcas _ _ Montgomery
McRae, Robert Henry _ _ _ _
_ _ _ _ _ _ _ _ Montgomery
McRee, Bruce V. _ _ _ Oconee
McWhirter, Callie _ _ _ Clarke
McWhorter, Mary Lucile Greene
McWhorter, Myrtus Ray Carroll
McWhorter, Sara Mae _ Barrow
McWilliams, Arvella _ _ Brooks
Nash, Malcolm _ _ _ _ Fulton
Neal, M. V. _ _ _ _ _ _ Gordon
Neely, Jessie _ Lumberton, Miss.
Nelms, Dreuwillie _ _ Lincoln
Nettles, Thelma _ _ _ _ Polk
Nichols, Nell _ _ _ _ _ Hart
Nicholson, Madison _ _ Clarke
Nicholson, Paul _ _ _ _ Clarke
Nicholson, R. M. _ _ _ _ Oconee
Nix, Lena _ _ _ _ _ _ Madison
Nix, Lois Sue _ _ _ _ _ Polk
Nix, Lucile _ _ _ _ _ Jackson
Nix, Eliza Beth _ _ _ _ Clarke
Nixon, Joseph Jefferson _ _
_ _ _ _ _ _ _ _ _ Richmond
Nixon, Thelma _ _ _ _ Coweta
Noel, Eudora _ _ _ Oglethorpe
Noell, Sarah _ _ _ _ _ Madison
Nolan, B. Atkinson _ _ _ Cobb
Norden, Ulrich _ _ _ New York

Noruille, Hallie McRae Oconee
Oakley, O. W. _ _ _ _ _ Decatur
Oakley, O. W., Mrs. _ _ Decatur
Odom, Alvin L. _ _ _ _ Toombs
Odom, Alvin, Mrs. _ _ Toombs
Odom, Mary Pacolet Mills, S. C.
Oglesby, Ralph A. _ _ Elbert
Odom, Virginia _ _ _ _ _ _
_ _ _ _ _ Spartanburg, S. C.
O'Kelley, Asa Alexander _ _
_ _ _ _ _ _ _ _ Gwinnett
Oliver, Dorothy _ _ _ Chatham
Oliver, Frederica _ _ _ Chatham
O'Quinn, Harriett Louise _ _
_ _ _ _ _ _ _ _ _ Jeff Davis
Orr, Elizabeth _ Greenville, S. C.
Orr, Frederick, W. _ _ _ Clarke
Osborne, Alma _ _ _ Muscogee
Osborne, F. B. _ _ _ _ Oconee
O'Steen, Myrtie _ _ _ _ Fulton
Otto, Lillian _ _ _ _ Chatham
Overstreet, Kathryn _ Screven
Owen, Elizabeth _ _ _ Henry
Owen, Malchus Cobb _ _ Tift
Owens, Donovan _ _ _ Fulton
Owens, J. H., Mrs. _ _ Lumpkin
Oxford, Julia Mae _ _ _ Pike
Ozburn, Mattie _ _ _ _ Towns
Padgett, Walter Herman Murray
Palmer, Louise _ _ _ Mitchell
Panter, Robt. H. _ _ _ _ Gilmer
Parham A. Herschel _ _ Clarke
Paris, Ruby _ _ _ _ _ _ Polk
Park, Celeste _ _ _ _ _ Greene
Park, Marion _ _ _ _ _ Greene
Parker, H. J. _ _ _ _ _ Appling
Parks, Beatrice _ _ _ _ DeKalb
Park, Rubie _ _ _ _ _ _ Pike
Parrish, Molly _ _ _ _ Morgan
Partee, Leila _ _ _ _ _ Henry
Partridge, Georgia _ _ Columbia
Paschall, Ruth _ _ _ _ Chatham
Passolt, Catherine Howell _ _
_ _ _ _ _ _ _ _ _ _ Coweta
Patman, Annie Elizabeth Clarke

Patman, Clyde _ _ _ _ _ Clarke
Patrick, Jennings Bryan _ Butts
Patrick, James R. _ _ _ Clarke
Patterson, Beatrice _ _ _ Clarke
Patterson, Bess _ _ _ _ _ Crisp
Patterson, Ben Lane _ _ Jenkins
Patterson, Carrie Mae _ Walker
Patterson, Harold Telford Clarke
Payne, Dorothy Reid _ Randolph
Peacock, Clayton Wesley _ _
_ _ _ _ _ _ _ _ _ Fayette
Peacock, Evelyn _ _ _ _ Dodge
Peade, Harriett _ _ _ Chatham
Pearson, Esther _ _ _ Mitchell
Pearson, Mrs. O. P. _ Mitchell
Peavy, Essis _ _ _ _ _ Dooly
Peavy, Ethel _ _ _ _ _ _ White
Peavy, Mrs. T. A. _ _ _ _ Lee
Peeples, Bertha _ _ _ _ Barrow
Penton, Merle _ _ _ _ Decatur
Penton, Mildred _ _ _ Decatur
Perkins, Ruby _ _ _ Jefferson
Perry, Florence _ _ _ _ Macon
Peterson, Lille _ _ _ Jefferson
Petty, Mrs. R. E. _ _ _ Clarke
Petty, Sarah Elizabeth Campbell
Phillips, Lesta Lorine _ _ Long
Phillips, Margaret C. _ _ Floyd
Phillips, Nelle _ _ _ _ _ Fulton
Phillips, Mattylu _ _ _ _ _ Tift
Phillips, Roy Eugene _ _ Walker
Pierce, Willie Fred _ _ Screven
Pike, Mary George _ _ Troup
Pinkenton, Irene _ _ _ Putnam
Pirkle, Golden _ _ _ Gwinnett
Pittman, Marcia _ _ Taliafero
Pitts, Mrs. J. E. _ _ _ _ Cook
Poe, Harry _ _ _ _ _ _ Toombs
Poindexter, Mary Elizabeth _
_ _ _ _ _ _ _ _ _ _ Lowdnes
Pool, Lila _ _ _ _ _ _ Barrow
Pope, Marion _ _ _ _ _ Brooks
Post, Allen William _ _ Coweta
Powell, Alfred Edgar _ Lowndes
Powell, Montine _ _ _ Mitchell

Power, John Bunyan _ _ Fulton

Prather, Willie Thomas _ _ _

_ _ _ _ _ _ _ _ Richmond

Price, Alice _ _ _ _ _ _ Dooly

Price, Ola Mae _ _ _ _ Bartow

Price, Pearl _ _ _ _ _ Douglas

Price, Rosalind _ _ _ _ Clarke

Price, Shade Lester _ Jefferson

Price, W. Newnan _ Washington

Prickett, Chas. Sanford Carroll

Prine, Sallie Mae _ _ Chatham

Pringle, Walter, Jr. _ _ _ _ _

_ _ _ _ _ _ Charleston, S. C.

Pruett, Stella _ _ _ _ _ Fulton

Pullin, Molly _ _ _ _ _ Wheeler

Purcell, Clarence _ _ _ _ Clarke

Purdom, Elizabeth _ _ _ Pierce

Purdom, Lee Smith _ _ Pierce

Pyron, C. L. _ _ _ _ _ _ Taylor

Pyron, Joseph H. _ _ _ _ Taylor

Quillian, Fannie _ _ _ _ _ Hall

Rachels, Zola _ _ _ Richmond

Rader, Logan Carson _ _ Bibb

Radford, Lewis C. _ _ Walton

Raffield, Thelma _ _ _ Laurens

Rainey, Louis, Miss _ _ Houston

Rampley, Martha Ruth _ _ _

_ _ _ _ _ _ _ _ _ Habersham

Ramsey, Mary Sue _ _ _ Newton

Ransom, M. M. _ _ _ Pickens

Radcliff, Lucille _ _ _ _ Pierce

Ray, Nettie Hoge _ _ Richmond

Ray, Samille _ _ _ _ _ Wilkes

Register, Irene _ _ _ _ Berrien

Reid, Octie Belle _ _ _ _ Hall

Reid, Annie Grace _ _ _ Upson

Reid, Bernice _ _ _ _ _ Upson

Reid, Lizzie Maye _ _ Telfair

Reitz, Ruth _ _ _ _ _ _ Clarke

Renfroe, Thelma _ _ _ Treutlen

Reynolds, Emmie _ _ _ Henry

Rhency, Kate _ _ _ _ Jefferson

Rhodes, Inez _ _ _ _ _ Fulton

Rhodes, Ruby _ _ _ _ _ Greene

Rice, Linice Ruth _ _ _ Elbert

Price, Oreita _ _ _ _ Johnson

Rice, Lillie Mae _ _ _ Madison

Richards, Ruth _ _ _ _ Clarke

Richardson, Fillye _ _ Harris

Riddick, Ruth _ _ _ _ Lowndes

Ridley, Grace Helen _ Whitfield

Riley, Louise _ _ _ _ _ Upson

Riley, Romano _ _ _ _ Chatham

Rines, Mrs. Estelle Martin Long

Rish, Ruth _ _ _ _ _ Randolph

Ritchie, Ruth _ _ _ _ _ Rabun

Rives, Rosa _ _ _ _ _ _ Barrow

Roberts, R. E. _ _ _ _ Paulding

Robertson, Gwene _ _ _ _ Fulton

Robinson, Frances _ _ _ Laurens

Roddenberry, Belle _ _ Charlton

Rodgers, Annie Belle _ _ Henry

Rodgers, Dorothy _ _ Colquitt

Rodgers, Flora _ _ _ Houston

Rodgers, Leone _ _ _ _ _ Hall

Rodgers, Louise _ _ _ Hancock

Rodgers, Loys _ _ _ _ Brooks

Rodgers, Mary Lucille Appling

Rollins, E. L. _ _ _ _ Whitfield

Rosansky, Annie _ _ _ Toombs

Ross, Eleanor _ _ _ _ Crisp

Rountree, Clyde Holmes Toombs

Rouse, Evelyn _ _ _ _ _ Worth

Rouse, Mrs. J. H. _ _ _ Worth

Rouseau, Talmadge Henry _ _

_ _ _ _ _ _ _ _ _ Franklin

Rowe, Malcolm _ _ _ Madison

Rowland, Hampton _ _ _ Clarke

Rowland, Julia Etta _ _ _ _

_ _ _ _ _ _ _ _ Habersham

Rowland, Mildred _ _ _ _ Cook

Royal, J. S. _ _ _ _ _ Randolph

Rudeseal, Lillian _ _ Habersham

Russel, Abi _ _ _ _ _ _ Henry

Rustin, Bob F. _ _ _ _ _ Taylor

Rustin, Chambiss Fred _ Taylor

Rylee, Evelyn _ _ _ _ Jackson

Ryon, Frances _ _ _ _ Liberty

Salter, J. J. _ _ _ _ Jefferson

Sammons, Mary _ _ Tampa, Fla.

Sams, Edna Corinne _ Paulding
Sanders, Grace _ _ _ _ Jackson
Sams, William Christopher _
_ _ _ _ _ _ _ _ Paulding
Sanders, Florence _ Jefferson
Sanders, Jetta Elizabeth _ Clay
Sanders, Mary _ _ _ _ _ Clay
Sanders, Joy _ _ _ _ _ Madison
Sanders, Mabel _ _ _ Crawford
Sanders, Leo _ _ _ _ Madison
Sanders, Wm. H. _ Talliaferro
Sanders, Bert Watson _ Madison
Saville, Robbie _ _ _ _ _ Banks
Scarbourough, Ernestine _ _
_ _ _ _ _ _ _ _ _ Pulaski
Scarborough, Elda Mae Madison
Scott, Corinne _ _ _ _ _ Cobb
Scroggs, Jessie Lou _ _ _ Hall
Scruggs, Estill _ _ _ _ Jefferson
Scruggs, Mary _ _ _ _ Lowndes
Seagraves, Carl _ _ Habersham
Seals, Corabel _ _ _ Hancock
Segars, Corinne _ _ _ Franklin
Segars, Lunita _ _ _ _ Wilcox
Segrest, Robert Taylor _ Troup
Sellars, J. C., Mrs. _ _ Sumter
Severin, Julius Eugene _ Clarke
Sewell, Cirl _ _ _ _ _ _ Coweta
Sewell, Gladys Evelyn Franklin
Sharpe, Inez _ _ _ _ _ Toombs
Sharpe, Joseph N. _ _ _ Towns
Shaw, Gladys _ _ _ _ _ Greene
Shaw, Maggie _ _ _ _ _ Bartow
Shaw, Mary _ _ _ _ _ Bartow
Shaw, Mr. M. S. _ _ _ _ Tift
Shell, Stephen Parks _ Campbell
Shelor, Sudie _ _ _ _ Laurens
Shepherd, Rosalind _ _ Jackson
Sheppard, Sara Evelyn _ _ _ _
_ _ _ _ _ _ _ _ _ Washington
Sheridan, Geraldine _ _ Madison
Sherman, Evelyn Hilton _ Early
Sherlock, Cecil W _ _ Richmond
Shumake, Mary H _ _ Richmond
Shields, Sara B. _ _ _ _ McDuffie

Shies, Edna Pauline _ _ _ Bibb
Shippey, Edwin Francis _ Clarke
Silkes, Robt. F. _ _ _ _ _ Worth
Simmons, Josephine _ _ Sumter
Simonton, Richard Caldwell _
_ _ _ _ _ _ _ _ _ Barrow
Simpson, Elma _ _ _ _ Jackson
Simpson, Ludie _ _ _ Gwinnett
Simpson, W. H., Jr. _ _ Clarke
Sims, J. H. _ _ _ _ _ Camden
Sims, J. H., Mrs. _ _ _ Camden
Sims, Sarah Boyd _ _ _ Glynn
Singleton, Lee Davis _ _ Hall
Singuefield, Florence _ Calhoun
Sipple, Erldyne _ _ _ Chatham
Skelton, Grace _ _ _ _ _ Hart
Skinner, Anne Lois _ Richmond
Slappey, Maude _ Quincey, Fla.
Slappey, Theo. Arlton Dougherty
Smalley, Ellie _ _ _ _ Lincoln
Smalley, Eleanor _ _ Richmond
Smith, Edna _ _ _ _ _ Elbert
Smith, Carrie _ _ _ _ _ Greene
Smith, Emily _ _ _ _ _ Troup
Smith, Edward Lamar _ _ Pike
Smith, Frances _ _ _ Jackson
Smith, Gertrude _ _ Washington
Smith, John Fletcher _ Walker
Smith, Mrs. K. I. _ _ _ Burke
Smith, K. I. _ _ _ _ _ Stewart
Smith, Kate _ _ _ _ _ Wayne
Smith, Laura _ _ _ Habersham
Smith, Lena _ _ _ Oglethorpe
Smith, Lequa _ _ _ _ _ Floyd
Smith, Leonell _ _ Clinton, S. C.
Smith, Martha _ _ _ _ Talbot
Smith, Mamie _ _ _ _ Clarke
Smith, Mildred _ _ _ _ Clarke
Smith, Mrs. O. S. _ _ _ Clarke
Smith, Ruby _ _ _ _ _ _ Clay
Smith, Martha Eliz _ _ Clarke
Snelling, Albert _ _ _ _ Clarke
Snelling, Richard _ _ _ Clarke
Snow, A. Dewey _ _ _ _ Walton
Sockwell, Mary _ _ _ _ Newton

Soule, Robt. Murry _ _ Clarke
Spears, Annie _·_ _ _ Newton
Spears, Mary Pauline _ Morgan
Speer, Lota _ _ _ _ _ _ Sumter
Spence, Elizabeth _ _ Mitchell
Spence, Lewis _ _ _ _ Carroll
Spiers, Nina _ _ _ _ _ Lincoln
Spiers, Percy M. _ _ _ Lincoln
Spinks, Lorene _ _ _ _ Clarke
Staight, M. Elizabeth _ _ _ _
_ _ _ _ _ _ _ _ Habersham
Stancil, Grover _ _ _ _ Mitchell
Stancil, Isa _ _ _ _ _ _ Mitchell
Stanford, James Leland _ Harris
Stanford, Stephen _ _ Forsyth
Stanford, Mala _ _ _ _ Laurens
Stanley, Hugh Smiley _ Clarke
Stanton, Mrs. A. J. _ _ Newton
Stapleton, Julia _ _ _ Jefferson
Starling, Almera _ _ _ Lowdnes
Stelling, H. G. _ _ _ Richmond
Stephens, Daisy Marietta Sumter
Stephens, Aetna Eloise _ Banks
Stephens, Sallie Mae _ Stewart
Stephens, Thelma _ Washington
Stery, Norma _ _ _ _ Chatham
Stevens, Delree _ _ _ _ Clarke
Stevens, Homer _ _ _ _ Clarke
Stewart, Franz Hahr _ _ Clarke
Stewart, Dr. J. S., Jr. _ Clarke
Stewart, Sarah Louise _ Fulton
Stith, Estelle _ _ _ _ _ Toombs
St. John Jimmie Stubbs, Mrs.
_ _ _ _ _ _ _ _ _ _ Coweta
Stockton, Forrest T., Mr. and
Mrs. _ _ _ _ _ _ _ _ Telfair
Stokes, James _ _ _ _ Lowndes
Stokes, Luella _ _ _ _ _ Johnson
Storey, Mable _ _ _ _ _ Harris
Stovall, Grace _ _ _ _ _ _ Hall
Strauss, Edna _ _ _ Richmond
Strauss, Grace _ _ _ Richmond
Strickland, Kathleen _ _ Butts
Stripling, Mrs. E. L. _ Muscogee
Stripling, Roro _ _ _ _ Tattnall

Strong, Marjorie _ _ _ _ Ware
Strozier, Clementine _ _ Burke
Stubbs, Charles O. _ Gwinnett
Sturdevant, Lillian _ _ Chatham
Suddath, Sarah _ _ _ Candler
Sullivan, Franklin _ _ Franklin
Sullivan, Heman _ _ _ _ Burke
Surrency, Lucy _ _ _ _ Appling
Swann, Serena _ _ _ _ Henry
Swilley, Anne _ _ _ Lake, Fla.
Swilling, Evelyn _ _ _ _ Clarke
Swindell, Lucille _ _ Habersham
Swinson, Eloise _ _ Wilkinson
Talmadge, Charles _ _ Clarke
Talmadge, Coke _ _ _ _ Clarke
Talmadge, John E. _ _ _ Clarke
Tanner, Cassie _ _ _ Gwinnett
Tanner, Katherine _ _ _ _ _
_ _ _ _ _ Union City, Tenn.
Tappan, Gladys _ _ _ _ Green
Tarpley, Hubert _ _ _ _ Toombs
Tarpley, Kathleen _ _ Campbell
Tarpley, M. Elizabeth _ Fulton
Tatum, Jewell _ _ _ _ _ Dodge
Tatum, Julius _ _ _ _ _ Walker
Tatum, Webb _ _ _ Meriwether
Taylor, Buford _ _ _ _ Dooly
Taylor, Mary Elizabeth _ Lamar
Taylor, Furlow _ _ _ _ Clarke
Taylor, Geo. F. _ _ _ _ Franklin
Taylor, Mrs. H. E. _ _ _ Clarke
Taylor, Kathleen _ _ _ _ Green
Taylor, Nannie Mae _ Randolph
Taylor, Ola _ _ _ _ _ _ Rabun
Taylor, Stewart _ _ _ Mitchell
Taylor, Vanda _ _ _ _ Jasper
Tedder, Ruby _ _ _ _ Terrell
Temples, Clay Hudson _ Bullock
Temples, Ouida Jane _ Bullock
Templeton, Emma _ _ _ Burke
Terrell, Annie _ _ _ _ Fulton
Thacker, Florrie _ _ Habersham
Tharpe, Elizabeth _ _ Colquitt
Terrell, Annie _ _ _ _ Fulton
Thetford, Florrie _ _ Muscogee

Thomas, Eula _ _ _ _ Franklin
Thomas, H. O. _ _ Habersham
Thomas, Jessie _ _ _ Franklin
Thomas, John V. _ _ _ Oconee
Thomas, Robt. D. _ _ Appling
Thompson, Gladys Montgomery
Thompson, Ida _ _ _ Decatur
Thompson, Kathrynn Irma _
_ _ _ _ _ _ _ Oplika, Ala.
Thompson, Lucy _ _ _ Walton
Thompson, Mozelle _ _ Madison
Thompson, Ruth Elizabeth _ _
_ _ _ _ _ _ _ _ Cherokee
Thornton, Arnoldina _ Elbert
Thornton, Bertha _ _ _ Elbert
Thornton, Frances _ _ _ Elbert
Thurman, Mary _ _ _ _ _ Tift
Thurman, Velma _ _ _ Madison
Thurman, Willie Mae _ _ Clarke
Ticknor, Mrs. E. T. _ _ _ Bibb
Tidwell, Ethel _ _ _ _ Douglas
Tillman, Mary Elizabeth Walton
Tinley, Mamie Rebecca Jenkins
Todd, Beulah _ _ _ _ Richmond
Tolar, Samp Boon _ _ _ Towns
Tolbert, Netteo _ _ _ Jackson
Tompkins, Esther _ _ _ Heard
Tompkins, L. R. _ _ _ _ Head
Tompkins, Nina _ _ _ Coweta
Toole, Henrietta _ _ Richmond
Torbert, Vera _ _ _ _ _ _ Clay
Touchstone, Mary _ _ _ Henry
Townsend, Lowell M. _ McIntosh
Towson, L. R. _ _ _ _ Thomas
Towson, L. R., Mrs. _ Thomas
Treanor, Helen _ _ _ _ Clarke
Treanor, H. Sapelo _ _ Clarke
Trippe, Miss Glenna _ _ Bartow
Tuck, Elizabeth _ _ _ _ Clarke
Tucker, Blossom _ _ _ _ Fulton
Tuggle, Martha _ _ _ _ DeKalb
Tupper, Virginia _ _ _ _ _ _
_ _ _ _ _ Charleston, S. C.
Turner, Grover C. _ _ _ Carroll
Tyson, Harvey J. _ _ Richmond

Tyson, Rosa Lawson _ McIntosh
Upchurch, Martha _ _ _ Fulton
Vanlandingham, Emily Seminole
Van Valkenburgh, Minnie _ Bibb
Varner, Nea l_ _ _ _ _ Gordon
Vaughan, Christine _ _ _ Dooly
Vaughan, Flavia _ _ _ Twiggs
Vaughan, Maderia _ _ Franklin
Vaughan, Tempie, Mrs. _ Wayne
Vaughter, Miriam _ _ _ Elbert
Ver Nooy, Montine _ _ Clarke
Voorhies, Elizabeth _ Seminole
Wages, Ruth _ _ _ _ _ Clarke
Wakefield, Helen _ _ _ Chatham
Walden, Gordon _ _ _ Jefferson
Walden, Julia _ _ _ _ _ Clarke
Walker, Adelaide _ _ _ Troup
Walker, Hallie _ _ _ _ Sumter
Walker, Josephine _ _ _ Clarke
Walker, Myralin _ _ _ Richmond
Wallis, Texar _ _ _ _ Forsyth
Walters, Traul G. _ _ Franklin
Walters, Vivian _ _ _ _ Early
Walton, Frances _ _ _ Richmond
Walton, Inez _ _ _ _ _ Macon
Ward, Edith _ _ _ _ _ _ Fulton
Ware, Marguerite Adel _ Fulton
Ware, Carl Claudius _ Franklin
Ware, J. H. _ _ _ _ _ _ Wilcox
Ware, Mora _ _ _ _ _ Wilcox
Warren, W. P. _ _ _ _ _ Clarke
Warren, Mrs. W. P. _ _ Clarke
Waters, Dorothy _ _ _ _ Clarke
Waters, Mamie _ _ _ Candler
Wates, Anita _ _ _ _ Richmond
Watkins, Estelle _ _ _ _ Talbot
Watson, Hazel Claire _ Ben Hill
Watson, Sarah _ _ _ _ Ben Hill
Watson, Nancy _ _ _ _ _ Dooly
Watson, Thos. F. _ _ Stephens
Way, Lucile _ _ _ _ _ _ Glynn
Weathers, Ara_ _ _ Montgomery
Weaver, Kate _ _ _ _ _ Fulton

Webb, Charlie Mae, Miss _ _
_ _ _ _ _ _ _ _ _ _ Laurens
Wehunt, Clyde _ _ _ _ Clarke
Wehunt, Minnie Evelyn _ Clarke
Wessels, Mrs. Fred _ _ Chatham
West, Daisy _ _ _ Habersham
West, Mamie _ _ _ _ McDuffie
Westbrook, Emma _ _ Sumter
Westbrook, Marie _ _ _ _ Hall
Weston, Hamilton _ _ _ Brooks
Whitaker, Georgia _ _ Laurens
White, Evelyn _ _ _ Gwinnett
White, Mrs. H. L. _ _ Franklin
White, Jane Elizabeth _ _ _
_ _ _ _ _ _ Concord, N. C.
White, Lucy Mae _ _ _ Evans
White, Una _ _ _ _ _ Lincoln
Whitlow, Agatha _ _ _ Franklin
Whitlow, Amolee _ _ _ Franklin
Whitlow, Moody Talmage _ _
_ _ _ _ _ _ _ _ _ _ Franklin
Whitmire, Lola _ _ _ _ Jackson
Whittle, Claire _ _ Thomaston
Whitworth, Roy D. _ _ _ Irwin
Wier, Sarah _ _ _ _ _ _ Clarke
Willbanks, Virginia, Habersham
Wilcox, Edna _ _ _ Ben Hill
Wilcox, Frances _ _ _ Lowndes
Wiley, Dona _ _ _ _ Stephens
Wiley, Glenn _ _ _ _ Stephens
Wilhite, Lucile _ _ _ _ _ Clarke
Wilkins, Mildred _ _ _ Madison
Wilkinson, James _ _ _ Coweta
Willcox, Clark _ _ _ _ Bulloch
Williams, Carolyn _ _ _ Crisp
Williams, Duffie _ _ _ _ Toombs
Williams, Henry _ _ _ Putnam
Williams, Ida B. _ _ Emanuel
Williams, Martha _ _ _ _ Tift
Williams, Marion _ _ _ Pierce
Williams, Ruth _ _ _ _ Taylor
Williams, Susie _ _ _ Gwinnett
Williamson, Floreen _ _ Jackson

Williamson, Flo _ _ _ _ Clarke
Willingham, Ivah _ _ _ Barrow
Willis, Alla _ _ _ _ _ _ Floyd
Willis, Mary Jane _ _ Chattooga
Wilson, A. T. _ _ _ _ _ White
Wilson, Earnest _ _ _ Laurens
Wilson, Columbus _ _ _ Walton
Wilson, Pearl _ _ _ _ _ Floyd
Wilson, Ruth _ _ _ _ Stephens •
Wilson, Thelma _ _ _ _ Wilcox
Wilson, Thelma _ _ _ _ Murray
Wimberly, Alma _ _ _ Bleckley
Winston, Edward Thomas _ _
_ _ _ _ _ _ _ _ _ _ Fulton
Winslow, T. E., Jr. _ _ Fulton
Witcher, Gus _ _ _ _ _ Clarke
Wood, Gertrude _ _ _ _ Polk
Wood, Maude _ _ _ _ Candler
Wood, Thelma _ _ _ Chattooga
Woodall, Lewis _ _ _ _ Clarke
Woodcock, Bertha _ _ Bullock
Woodberry, Rosa _ _ _ Fulton
Woodroof, Jasper G. _ Spalding
Woods, Annie _ _ _ _ Murray
Woods, Maggie _ _ _ _ Murray
Wootten, Marie _ _ _ _ Telfair
Worley, Samuel _ _ _ _ Fulton
Wrenn, Annie _ _ _ _ _ Burke
Wright, Sarah _ _ _ _ _ Elbert
Wyatt, Mrs. I. T. _ _ _ Jasper
Wyatt, Lola _ _ _ _ _ Bullock
Wyatt, Leila _ _ _ _ _ Bullock
Wyche, Lillian _ _ Meriwether
Wynne, Sarah _ _ _ _ Morgan
York, Myrtis _ _ _ Habersham
Youmans, Annie _ _ Jeff Davis
Young, Edith _ _ _ _ McIntosh
Young, Frank Marion _ Walker
Young, Irene _ _ _ _ McDuffie
Young, Louise _ _ _ _ Decatur
Young, Mary _ _ _ _ _ Decatur
Yow, Elizabeth _ _ _ Stephens
Zachry, Zelma _ _ _ _ _ Harris

WOMAN'S CLUB INSTITUTE

Summer School, 1925

Beacham, Mrs. W. D. _ Clarke
Hodges, Mrs. W. L. _ _ _ Hart
Stephens, Mrs. R. P. _ _ Clarke
Sanford, Mrs. S. V. _ _ Clarke
Troutman, Mrs. M. L. _ Clarke
• Rogers, Edna _ _ _ _ _ Elbert
Watts, Mrs. H. A. _ _ _ Fulton
Holden, Mrs. H. H. _ _ Clarke
Turner, Mrs. R. F. _ _ _ Clarke
Cloud, Mrs. Joel _ _ Oglethorpe
Talmadge, Mrs. John E. _ Clarke
Cunningham, Mrs. E. T. _ _
_ _ _ _ _ _ _ _ Oglethorpe
Gholston, Mrs. J. W. _ Madison
Stanley, Mrs. T. _ _ _ _ Clarke
Rucker, Mrs. J. H. _ _ _ Clarke
Rowe, Mrs. W. A. _ _ _ Madison
Payne, Mrs. M. T. _ _ _ Madison
Wilkins, Mrs. A. M. _ _ Madison
Rucker, Mrs. Lamar _ _ Clarke
Lewis, Mrs. Lena Felker_Walton
Farmer, Mrs. Ira E. _ McDuffie
Gurr, Mrs. W. H. _ _ Terrell
Maxwell, Mrs. W. H._Oglethorpe
Crawford, Mrs. T. W., Oglethorpe
Bryant, Mrs. Clinton _ _ Clarke
Snelling, Mrs. C. M. _ _ Clarke
McCurry, Mrs. A. D. _ _ Barrow
Warthen, Mrs _ _ _ _ Toombs
Weston, Burton _ _ _ Brooks

Bennett, Mrs. Ulric J., Whitfield
Pittman, Mrs. C. E. _ _Jackson
Johns, Mrs. _ _ _ _ _ _ Barrow
Rambo, Mrs. R. K. _ _ Fulton
McCall, Mrs. Howard _ _ Fultin
Smith, Mrs. T. O. _ _ Gwinnett
Pledger, Mrs. J. H. _ _ Barrow
Harber, Mrs. _ _ _ _ _ Jackson
Hardeman, Mrs. T. C. _ Jackson
Loyd, Mrs. W. D. _ Oglethorpe
Michael, Miss Monia _ _ Clarke
Melton, Mrs. W. F. _ _ DeKalb
Smith, Mrs. W. B. Price _Fulton
Blanchard, Mrs. M. _ Oglethorpe
Carmichael, Mrs. S. J. _ Madison
McMullen, Mrs. Amanda _ Hart
Alford, Mrs. H. P. _ _ _ _ Hart
Smith, Mrs. Mungen _ _ _Hart
McCurry, Mrs. W. B. _ _ Hart
Little, Mrs. George _ Oglethorpe
Wilhoit, Mrs. _ _ _ _ _ Warren
Armistead, Mrs. Walter _ _ _
_ _ _ _ _ _ _ _ _ Oglethorpe
Howard, Mrs. G. A., Jr. _ _
_ _ _ _ _ _ _ _ _ Oglethorpe
Carmichael, Mrs. S. J. _ Madison
McCurry, Mrs. _ _ _ _ _ Clarke
Brantley, Mrs. A. P. _ _ Pierce
Roy, Miss Claire _ _ _ Franklin

AGRICULTURAL CONFERENCE

Aderhold, O. C. _ _ _ _ Jackson
Beall, J. S. _ _ _ _ _ Muscogee
Boland, M. G. _ _ _ _ _ Bryan
Bolton, J. L. _ _ _ _ _ Johnson
Brand, M. E. _ _ _ _ Stephens
Bryant, C. A. _ _ _ _ _ Franklin
Burnett, Rolin _ _ _ _ _ Clarke
Cabaniss, Helen _ _ _ _ Clarke
Callahan, J. K. _ _ _ Jefferson

Chanller, T. V. _ _ _ _ Franklin
Clotfelter, C. F. _ _ _ _ Jackson
Cox, Lemuel E. _ _ _ _ _ Fannin
Davis, E. K. _ _ _ _ _ _ Hart
Derdex, Henry _ _ _ _ Cherokee
Dickerson, Geo. W. _ _ Bullock
Drexel, R. J. _ _ _ _ _ Crawford
Duggan, I. W. _ _ _ _ _ Turner
Elrod, Julius _ _ _ _ _ Wilkes

Eskew, W. R. _ _ _ _ _ _ Hart
Fry, Byard O. _ _ _ _ _ Haralson
Fry, H. L. _ _ _ _ _ _ _ _ _ Hart
Gay, Owen E. _ _ _ _ _ Bullock
Hayden, Otis _ _ _ _ _ Laurens
Hemrick, L. E. _ _ _ _ Madison
Hodgson, Prince _ _ _ _ Johnson
Howell, M. E. _ _ _ _ _ Heard
Hunter, Wilson _ _ _ _ Franklin
Jackson, J. W. _ _ _ _ Laurens
Johnson, A. H. _ _ _ _ _ Rabun
Johnson, O. L. _ _ _ _ Mitchell
Johnson, R. L. _ _ _ _ _ Twiggs
King, Geo. H. _ _ _ _ _ Barrow
Maddox, H. H. _ _ _ _ _ Hart
Martin, W. McKee _ _ _Franklin
Mauy, H. A. _ _ _ _ _ _ Pike
Martin, Geo. J. _ _ _ _ Worth
Maxey, Herbert A. _ _ _ _ Pike
Middleton, J. A. _ _ _ _ Dublin
Middleton, R. M. _ _ _ Stephens
Miller, R. E. _ _ _ _ _ Thomas
Mobley, Mayor Dennis _ Clarke
McMillan, C. A., Jr. _ _ Laurens

Putney, W. M. _ _ _ Chattooga
Reid, J. F. _ _ _ _ _ Mitchell
Reed, C. M. _ _ _ _ _ _ Wilkes
Richards, C. F. _ _ _ _ Mitchell
Rew, L. C. _ _ _ _ _ _ Warren
Sanders, E. I. _ _ _ _ Crawford
Seagraves, Carl _ _ Habersham
Sims, J. H. _ _ _ _ _ Camden
Sorrell, W. H. _ _ _ _ _ _ Bibb
Still, Demis W. _ _ _ _ Jasper
Tatum, Webb _ _ _ Meriwether
Thomas, W. W. _ _ _ _ _ Hart
Thomas, H. O. _ _ _ _ _ Rabun
Thomas, Wallace _ _ _ _ Hart
Westbrook, L. C. _ _ _ _ Hall
White, Raymond F. _ _ Carroll
Whitmire, D. W. _ _ _ _ Hall
Wiley, G. T. _ _ _ _ _ Stephens
Woodruff, H. E. _ _ _ _ _ Cobb
Vandiviere, L. A. _ _ _ Dawson
Veatch, Curry LaF. _ Jackson
Young, E. O. _ _ _ _ _ Elbert
Zeigler, O. J. _ _ _ _ _ Turner

SUPERINTENDENT'S CONFERENCE, 1925

Avera, S. W. _ _ _ _ Oglethorpe
Ammons, Allen J. _ _ _ _ Tift
Andrews, W. J. _ _ _ _ Stephens
Adams, T. L. _ _ _ _ _ _ Pike
Bullard, J. H. _ _ _ _ _ Ben Hill
Brown, Mrs. Kate _ _ _ _ Henry
Bostwick, John _ _ _ _ Morgan
Bowey, Roland _ _ _ _ _ _ _
Benton, T. T. _ _ _ _ _ Jackson
Benton, Otho _ _ _ _ Seminole
Beck, E. H. _ _ _ _ _ Lowndes
Bacon, J. O. _ _ _ _ _ Tattnall
Cadwell, J. J. _ _ _ _ _ Dodge
Cameron, J. W. _ _ _ _ Lanier
Cavender, R. C. _ _ _ _ _ Ware
Clark, F. G. _ _ _ _ _ Colquitt
Collins, Zach _ _ _ _ _ Cherokee
Conger, Miss Elizabeth _ Clarke

Cox, Miss Nina _ _ _ _ Turner
Davis, O. W. _ _ _ Oglethorpe
Dozier, Katherine _ _ _ _ Hall
DuPree, J. T., Jr. _ Wilkinson
Eddie, R. D. _ _ _ _ _ _ Glynn
Edwards, C. H. _ _ _ _ _ White
Elrod, Julius _ _ _ _ _ Wilkes
Fullerton, W. R. _ _ _ _ Pike
Forrester, E. J. _ _ _ Hancock
Fitzgerald, W. A. _ _ _ Stewart
Fitzgerald, B. G. _ _ _ _ Twiggs
Gurr, Mrs. Helen _ _ _ Terrell
Hansard, Mary _ _ _ _ Elbert
Harrison, D. W. _ _ Washington
Herndon, W. M. _ _ _ Laurens
Holliday, W. T. _ _ _ _ Stewart
Hill, H. E. _ _ _ _ _ _ Dodge
Holsenbeck, W. M. _ _ _ Barrow

Hulsey, Julius M. _ _ _ _ Hall	Nunn, W. N. _ _ _ _ _ Gwinnett
Hutchinson, G. L. _ _ _ Dodge	Nelson, J. P. W. _ _ Oglethorpe
Jolly, Robt. F. _ _ _ _ Bartow	Purcell, Mrs. B. D. _ _ Wayne
Kean, A. D. _ _ _ _ _ McDuffie	Powell, S. H. _ _ _ _ _ _ Lee
King, Barrett _ _ _ _ Brantley	Pound, E. A. _ _ _ _ _ _ Fulton
Little, R. L. _ _ _ _ _ Taylor	Peck, Lula _ _ _ _ _ _ _ _ _ _
Lord, Wade Hampton _ Houston	Panter, R. H. _ _ _ _ _ _ Gilmer
Moran, C. W. _ _ _ _ Hancock	Rozar, W. C. _ _ _ _ _ Dodge
Moss, J. R. _ _ _ _ _ _ Wilkes	Sibley, Mrs. J. Hart _ _ _ Greene
Moore, W. R. _ _ _ _ Taliaferro	Sumner, R. L. _ _ _ _ Laurens
Moore, E. T. _ _ _ _ Sumter	Stubbs, Laurie Belle _ Gwinnett
Mams, W. B. _ _ _ _ _ _ Hart	Stubbs, Charles _ _ _ Gwinnett
Manley, J. P. _ _ _ _ Spalding	Trulock, C. M. _ _ _ _ _ _ _ _
McLarty, G. T. _ _ _ _ Douglas	Tucker, Violet _ _ _ _ Rockdale
McDuffie, Edgar _ _ _ Franklin	Underwood, J. D. _ _ _ _ **Hall**
McCord, M. O. _ _ _ _ _ Wilkes	Wells, Jere _ _ _ _ _ _ Fulton
Jones, McArthur _ _ _ _ Early	Wisdom, Tom _ _ _ _ _ Harris

TABLE SHOWING DATA REQUIRED BY RESOLUTION OF THE GENERAL ASSEMBLY, APPROVED AUGUST 13, 1904

Professions of parents of students in the University, 1925-1926 so far as known:

Farmers	403
Merchants	197
Lawyers	74
Physicians	66
Railroad Business	52
Real Estate	46
Bankers	38
Manufacturers	31
Cotton Factors	24
Business Managers	38
Government Officials	23
Teachers	42
County Officers	24
Traveling Salesmen	36
Ministers	14
Editors	11
Mechanics	14
Druggists	15
Lumbermen	10
Accountants	13
Hotel Keepers	12
Contractors	16
Insurance	26
Dentists	11
Various	237

INDEX

The University extends a cordial invitation to all educational, agricultural, commercial, manufacturing, financial and industrial bodies and bodies of like character, having for their object the welfare of the state, to use on special occasions, free of rent, such public buildings of the University as the Chancellor and President of the Agricultural College may approve.

MARCH, 1926

Bulletin of the University of Georgia

Vol. XXVI   Number 3

University of Georgia

SUMMER SCHOOL

University Campus Scene

Athens, Georgia

June 21 to July 31 to August 21

1926

Entered at the Post Office at Athens, Ga., as Second Class Matter, August 31, 1905, under Act of Congress of July 16th, 1904. Issued Monthly by the University.

SERIAL NUMBER 398

THE UNIVERSITY SUMMER SCHOOL

CALENDAR

SATURDAY, JUNE 19TH: Dormitories open.

Faculty Meeting 5 P. M., at Memorial Hall.

MONDAY, JUNE 21ST: Registration 8:30 to 6:00.

TUESDAY, JUNE 22ND: Classes begin as scheduled.

JUNE 28TH TO JULY 3RD: Woman's Club Institute.

JULY 12TH TO 16TH: County and City Superintendents' Week.

JULY 19TH TO 23RD: Music Festival Week.

JULY 26TH TO 31ST: Vocational Agricultural Teachers' Short Course. Close of Six Weeks Term.

AUGUST 3RD TO 15TH: Boys' and Girls' Short Course.

AUGUST 21ST: Closing of Nine Weeks Term.

SUMMER SCHOOL BOARD

CHARLES M. SNELLING____Dean of the University and Acting Chancellor

JERE M. POUND_____President State Normal School

ANDREW M. SOULE_____President Agricultural College

THOMAS J. WOOFTER_____Dean Peabody School of Education

F. E. LAND_____State School Superintendent

SCHEDULE OF ENTERTAINMENTS

FIRST WEEK—JUNE 21-26

Wed., 23—Community Sing.
Thurs., 24—
Fri., 25—Jubilee Singers.

Sat., 26—Assembly and reception, Memorial Hall.

SECOND WEEK—JUNE 28-JULY 4
Women's Club Week

Mon., 28—Lecture, Dr. Soule.
Tues., 29—Hodgson's Concert.
Wed., 30—P.-T. A. Evening.

Thurs., July 1—Woman's Club Evening.
Fri., 2—Evening of Magic—Paul Fleming.

THIRD WEEK—JULY 5-9

Mon., 5—
Tues., 6—Recital, Mrs. Granberry.
Wed., 7—Lecture, L. B. Evans.

Thurs., 8—Lecture. Hon. Hoke Smith.
Fri., 9—Erma Seydel, Violin Concert.

FOURTH WEEK—JULY 12-16
Superintendents' Week

Mon., 12—Lecture, Dr. M. L. Brittain.
Tues., 13—Recital, Mr. Hendricks.
Wed., 14—Governor Walker, Superintendent Land.

Thurs., 15—Coffer-Miller Players .
Fri., 16—Coffer Miller Players.

FIFTH WEEK—JULY 19-21
Music Festival Week

Mon., 19—
Tues., 20—Concert.
Wed., 21—Concert.

Thurs., 22—Concert.
Fri., 21—Opera.

SIXTH WEEK—JULY 26-31

Mon., 26—Oratory.
Tues., 27—Pageant.

Wed., 28—Music.
Sat., 31—Closing six weeks.

SUMMER SCHOOL FACULTY

Administrative Council

CHAS. M. SNELLING, ANDREW M. SOULE, JERE M. POUND

JOSEPH S. STEWART_____Director of Summer School
THOMAS W. REED_____Registrar and Treasurer
H. I. REYNOLDS_____Physician to the Summer School
LUCILLE EPPS_____Secretary to the Director

ALFRIEND, KYLE, T., A.B., A.M._____*Education*
 Dean, Bessie Tift
ALLEN, RUTH_____*Demonstration School*
 Macon, Ga., Public Schools
ARCHER, FRANCES R._____*Librarian*
 Librarian, State Normal School
BAIRD, BESSIE, B.S._____*Home Economics*
 Professor of Home Economics, State Normal School
BALDON, MATTE-CONN._____*Penmanship*
 Field Supervisor, Zaner-Blosser Company
BARROW, D. C., LL.D._____*Lecturer*
 Chancellor Emeritus, University of Georgia
BARROW, D. F., Ph.D._____*Mathematics*
 Professor of Mathematics
BENNETT, F. W., B.S.A._____*Animal Husbandry*
 Associate Professor of Animal Husbandry
BENNETT, U. J., A.B._____*High School Mathematics*
 Superintendent of Schools, Dalton, Ga.
BLACKSHEAR, A. LAURA E._____*Poster Designing*
 Illustrator, Agricultural College
BOCOCK, WILLIS H., A.M., LL.D._____*World War Studies*
 Dean of the Graduate School
BRINSON, F. A._____*High School Mathematics*
 Superintendent of Schools, Millen, Ga.
BRITTAIN, M. L.,LL.D._____*Lecturer*
 President Georgia School of Technology
BROADHURST, G. M., B.S.C._____*Commerce*
 Adjunct Professor of Secretarial Duties
BROCKMAN, CHAS. J., A. M., Ch. Eng._____*Chemistry*
 Adjunct Professor of Chemistry
BROOKS, R. P., Ph.D._____*Economics*
 Professor of Banking and Finance
BROWN, PETER F., A.B., Ped.D._____*Elementary Language, Grammar*
 Professor of English, State Normal School
BURKHART, WALTER CLINTON, D.V.M._____*Veterinary Medicine*
 Associate Professor of Veterinary Medicine, Agricultural College
BURLEIGH, T. D., B.S., M.S._____*Forestry*
 Associate Professor of Forestry
BURNET, DUNCAN_____*Librarian*
 Librarian, University of Georgia
BURSON, SUSIE, B.S.H.E._____*Home Economics*
 In charge of Teacher Training Work
CABANISS, MARY H._____*Art Structure and Design*
 Supervisor of Art in Junior High School. Savannah, Ga.
CALLAWAY, MATILDA, B.S.H.E._____*Home Economics*
 Adjunct Professor. Teacher Training
CALLOWAY, IRIS, B.S., A.M._____*Arithmetic*
 Instructor in Mathematics, State Normal School
CARREKER, H. B., A.B._____*High School Latin*
 Superintendent of Schools, Dublin, Ga.

CARTER, L. M., B.S._____*Agricultural Chemistry*
    Professor of Agricultural Chemistry
CHANCE, CLAUDE, A.B._____*Spanish*
    Instructor in Spanish, University of Georgia
CHAPMAN, PAUL W., B.S.A._____*Vocational Journalism*
    State Supervisor of Vocational Agriculture
CHAPMAN, ANNIE_____*Demonstration School*
    Atlanta Public Schools
CHILDS, R. R., B.S., M.S._____*Cotton Grading*
    Professor of Agronomy, in charge of Cotton Industry
CLEGG, W. A., B.S.A._____*Agricultural Engineering*
    Associate Professor of Agricultural Engineering.
CORNETT, WALTER G., LL.B. _____*Law*
    Professor of Law
CLEMENT, GLENN C._____*Piano*
    Granberry Piano School, Carnegie Hall, New York
COBB, CAROLYN, A.B._____*Expression*
    Reader and Teacher of Dramatic Art, Atlanta
CRABB, GEORGE A., B.S.A._____*Soils*
    Professor of Agronomy, in charge of Soils
CRESWELL, MARY E., B.S.H.E._____*Vocational Home Economics*
    Director Department Home Economics
CRESWELL, EDITH, B.S.H.E._____*Home Economics*
    Adjunct Professor in Home Economics
DIXON, ELLIS, H., A.B., A.M._____*Physics*
    Instructor in Physics
DOZIER, EUGENE_____*Assistant in Dancing*
    Potter-Spiker School, Atlanta.
EARNEST, DAVID L., A.M._____*Elementary Science, General Science*
    Professor of Natural Science, State Normal School
EDWARDS, A. S., Ph.D._____*Psychology*
    Professor of Psychology
EVANS, LAWTON B._____*Lecturer*
    Superintendent of Schools, Augusta, Ga.
FAIN, J. R., B.S., ScD._____*Farm Economics*
    Profesor of Agronomy
FARGUSON, DOROTHY, A.B._____*Demonstration School*
    Teacher in State Normal Training School
GOBER, GEO. F., A.M., LL.D._____*Law*
    President of Lumpkin Law School
GRANBERRY, GEO. F._____*Professional Music Course, Piano*
    Director Granberry Piano School, Carnegie Hall, New York
GRANBERRY, MRS. GEO. F._____*The Organ*
    Organist and Instructor in Organ, New York
HALE, MARY_____*Early Childhood Education*
    Teachers Training School, Atlanta, Ga.
HENDREN, L. L., Ph.D._____*Physics*
    Professor of Physics and Astronomy
HENDRICKS, JOHN_____*Voice*
    Professor of Voice, Brenau College
HALE, KATE E._____*Demonstration School*
    Principal of State Normal Training School
HOOPER, WILLIAM D., A.M., Litt.D._____*Latin*
    Professor of Latin
HUNTER, H. REID, A.M._____*City Administration, High Schools*
    Assistant Superintendent, Atlanta, Ga.
KELLOGG, C. E., B.S._____*Animal Husbandry*
    Associate Professor of Animal Husbandry
KEENER, R. L., B.S.A._____*Horticulture*
    Adjunct Professor of Horticulture
KNIGHT, L. L., LL.D._____*Lecturer*
    Former State Historian
KNOWLES, H. D., B.A._____*High School English*
    Superintendent of School, Quitman, Ga.
KRAFKA, JOSEPH, JR., Ph.D._____*Zoology*
    Associate Professor of Zoology

4

LAND, F. E., A.B._____*Lecturer*
    State Superintendent of Schools
LUNDAY, MARY E., A.B., A.M._____*Physical Training*
    Physical Director for Women
LUSTRAT, JOSEPH, BACH. ES LETT., LETT.D._____*French*
    Professor of Romance Languages
LYLE, SAMUEL P., B.S., M.S._____*Household Mechanics*
    Professor of Agricultural Engineering
MEHRE, H. J., A.B._____*Football and Basketball Coaching*
    Physical Director for Men
MCALPHINE,MARTHA J., A.M._____*Child Training*
    Child Study Specialist
MCHATTON, T. H., B.S., Sc.D._____*Horticulture*
    Professor of Horticulture
MCPHERSON, J. H. T., Ph.D._____*History, Government*
    Professor of History and Political Science
MCWHORTER, R. L., A.M., LL.B._____*Law*
    Instructor in Law
NEWTON, CATHERINE, B.S.H.E., M.S._____*Home Economics*
    Associate Professor of Foods and Nutrition
OSTERMAN, F. J., A.M._____*Industrial Arts*
    Instructor, State Normal School
PARK, ROBERT E., Litt.D._____*English Literature*
    Professor of English Literature
PATRICK, J. R., B.A._____*General Psychology*
    Instructor in Psychology
PAYNE, W. O., A. M._____*History*
    Professor of History
PERSELLS, HERMAN V., D.V.M._____*Veterinary Medicine*
    Associate Professor
PIGUERON, MARY CRAIG_____*Concert Vocalist*
    New York, N. Y.
POUND, E. A., A.B._____*Rural High School Problems*
    Supervisor of High Schools
POUND, JERE M., LL.D._____*Lecturer*
    President State Normal School
PRITCHARD, ELIZABETH_____*Demonstration School*
    Teachers Training School, Augusta, Ga.
PUSEY, E. D., LLD., A.M._____*Educational Psychology*
    Professor of Education and School Administration.
RATHBONE, ROSALIE VIRGINIA, B.S._____*Home Economics*
    Associate Professor of Clothing and Textiles
REESE, NELLIE M._____*Librarian*
    Librarian, State College of Agriculture
REITZ, W. W., M.S._____*Agricultural Education*
    Associate Professor of Agricultural Education
RICE, WALDO S., B.S.A._____*Animal Husbandry*
    Associate Professor
RICHARDSON, ALBERT G. G., D.V.M._____*Veterinary Medicine*
    Professor of Veterinary Medicine
RITCHIE, HORACE B., A.M.   *School Management and Administration*
    Professor of Psychology and Pedagogy, State Normal School
SANFORD, STEADMAN V., A.M., Litt.D._____*English Literature, Journalism*
    Professor of English Language and Journalism
ROWE, MRS. GEO. F._____*Music*
    Supervisor of Public School Music, Richmond. Va.
SELL, E. SCOTT, M.S._____*Elementary Agriculture*
    Professor of Agriculture, State Normal School
SHAW, MRS. OPAL_____*Demonstration School*
    Lee Street School, Atlanta, Ga.
SHEFFER, LAFAYETTE M.,B.S._____*Agricultural Education*
    Associate Professor of Agricultural Edcuation
SHEHEE, LOUISE_____*Swimming*
    Major Student in Physical Training
SIMMONS, JAMES H., A.M._____*English Composition, Literature*
    Professor of English, Brenau College

5

SIMPSON, MRS. IDA, B.S._____U. S. History and Civics
    Instructor Hunter College, N. Y.
SMITH, HON. HOKE_____Lecturer
    Former United States Senator
SMITH, JENNIE BELLE_____Public School Music
    Supervisor of Music, Jacksonville, Fla.
SMITH, W. M., M.B.A._____Commerce
    Adjunct Professor of Commerce
SNELLING, MRS. CHAS. M._____Woman's Club
    President Woman's Club Institute
SNELLING, CHAS. M., A.M., Sc.D._____Lecturer
    Professor of Mathematics, Chancellor
SOLOMON, MAGGIE_____Elementary School Methods
    Supervisor Elementary Schools, Atlanta, Ga.
SOULE, ANDREW M., Sc.D., LL.D._____Lecturer
    President Agricultural College
SPIKER, MRS. B. POTTER_____Dancing
    Director Potter-Spiker Dancing School
SPIKER, MRS. PIERPONT_____Pianist
    Musical Accompanist in Dancing
STEPHENS, R. P., Ph.D._____Mathematics
    Professor of Mathematics
STEWART, J. S., A.M.,Ped.D._____Director of Summer School
    Professor of Secondary Education, High School Inspector
SUTTON, WILLIS A., A.M._____Lecturer
    Superintendent City Schools, Atlanta
SYLVA, MARGUERITE_____Concert Vocalist
    Prima donna
TABOR, PAUL, M.S.A._____Farm Crops
    Associate Professor of Agronomy
THAXTON, J. RALPH, A.M._____Spanish
    Adjunct Professor of Romance Languages
TIGNER, MARY_____Handicrafts
    Instructor of Handicrafts, Columbus, Ga.
TOLAR, S. B., A.B._____Physics
    Professor of Physics, Young Harris College
UPSON, STHEPEN CUMMINGS, LL.B._____Law
    Professor of Law
VANCE, CAROLYN, B.L.I._____Elementary Dramatics, Story Telling
    Department Oratory, State Normal School
WALKER, GOV. CLIFFORD_____Lecturer
    Governor of Georgia
WATKINS, MRS. ARTHUR C._____Parent. Teachers' Course
    Executive Secretary, National Parent-Teachers' Association
WHEELER, JOHN T., B.S._____Agricultural Education
    Professor of Agricultural Education
WIGHT, AUSTIN J._____Violin
    School of Violin Playing, Athens, Ga.
WIGHT, MRS. AUSTIN J._____Assistant in Violin
    School of Violin Playing, Athens, Ga.
WILDER, C. N., B.S.A., M.S.A._____Qualitative Analysis
    Associate Professor of Agricultural Chemistry
WILLINGHAM. RUBY_____Kindergarten
    Director of Kindergarten, Columbus, Ga.
WISE, HENRY A., Ph.D._____Education
    Professor of Education, Converse College
WOOD, JAMES H., B.S.A._____Poultry Husbandry
    Professor of Poultry Husbandry
WOODWARD, HAROLD O., B.S.A._____Poultry Husbandry
    Adjunct Professor
ZEIGLER, MAE, A.B., A.M._____Psychology
    Instructor in Child Study and Psychology, State Normal School

GENERAL INFORMATION

The University Summer School was authorized by the General Assembly in 1903. It is an integral part of the University, the Agricultural College, and the State Normal and its courses coordinate with these as indicated in the outline of courses.

There will be two terms, one for six weeks and the other for nine weeks. They both begin on June 21st, the first ends on July 31st, and the longer term on August 21st.

The laboratories, libraries, gymnasiums, dormitories and other equipment of the three institutions are available during the summer. Nearly every department offers courses in the summer, undergraduate and a number of graduate courses, equal in quality and valued in terms of the regular year.

LOCATION

Athens, a city of over 20,000 people, is situated in the Piedmont region of North Georgia. The climate is excellent. The University and Agricultural College are situated on one body of land of over 1,000 acres and the Normal School has about 50 acres. This gives ample opportunity for walks, rides and picnics.

Excursion parties will be organized for the purpose of visiting points in and near Athens. Excursions will be run every other Saturday to Tallulah Falls, about fifty miles distant, and into the heart of the Blue Ridge Mountains at Franklin, N. C.

SPECIAL OPPORTUNITIES IN THE SUMMER SCHOOL

In addition to the regular undergraduate work in the three institutions opportunities are offered:

(1) Teachers who wish to advance in special lines of work, increase their professional skill or qualify in new subjects.

(2) Candidates for State certificate who need special courses in Education and other subjects.

(3) Those who wish to work towards a degree.

(4) Directors of physical training and coaches of athletics in the high schools and playground work.

(5) Supervisors and teachers of Music, Oratory, Vocational Home Economics and Agriculture and other special lines of work.

(6) County Superintendents who desire to study problems of Rural School Organization and Management.

(7) Principals of Elementary and High Schools who wish to acquaint themselves with recent progress in education or to study special problems.

(8) Pre-Law, Pre-Medical, and Pre-Dental students who wish to save time in preparation for these courses.

(9) Graduates of college who wish to specialize in some field of work and study for a Master's Degree.

(10) Members of P.-T. A. and Woman's Clubs and other Social workers who wish to better prepare for their duties.

(11) Properly recommend high school graduates who are about to enter upon regular University courses and who desire to broaden their preparation for University work.

(12) Students registered in the three institutions here or in other colleges who wish to shorten the time required for graduation by completion of work in the summer.

(13) Serious minded men and women in any occupation who wish

to broaden their culture and use part of their vacation to secure it while enjoying the delightful associations among a student body of over 2,000.

REGISTRATION

The regular time for registration for both terms will be Monday, June 21st. All students of the Summer School should register on that day. Registration after June 30th for credit will not be permitted except by vote of the Council.

Registration may be grouped in the following classes:

(1) **High School Graduates Under 20 Years of Age.**
  a. Those desiring entrance to freshman class should file their entrance certificates with Dr. W. D. Hooper, Chairman of the Entrance Committee.
  b. If advanced credit is desired the official college record should be filed with Dr. L. L. Hendren, Chairman of Advanced Credit Committee.

(2) **Auditors.**
Any adult of good moral character is permitted to attend all the regular exercises of the Summer School as an auditor, by paying the registration fee. An auditor does not participate in recitations, does not take examinations and hence does not receive credit.

(3) **Students Over 20 Years of Age.**
The Summer School does not attempt, in general, to make inquiry concerning the educational qualifications of applicants for admission who are over 20 years of age. In granting admission to these, the Summer School assumes that the applicant possesses the usual educational qualifications for college or normal work or in lieu of these, that he has maturity and special fitness which are likely to lead to success in the work to be undertaken. Entrance requirements must be satisfied before graduation, however.

(4) **High School Pupils Not Yet Graduated.**
The Summer School has no preparatory department. Instruction is provided in certain letter courses, found elsewhere in this bulletin. These courses may be taken by pupils on the special recommendation of the high school principal. A blank form for the principal's use may be obtained from the Summer School office. Teachers who have not credit for their high school work may also register for these courses and validate their former work.

(5) **Graduate Students.**
Those desiring graduate work should correspond with Dean W. H. Bocock and as far as possible adjust their credits before the opening of the Summer School.

Often the matter of advanced credit may be more satisfactorily adjusted after study at the Summer School and the ability and attainment of the student has been determined by the department concerned. The applicant should collect, as far as possible, previous credits and be prepared to submit these during the summer to the Advanced Credit Committee. Where the applicant has already submitted and had approved his college credits by the state certification departments and is studying only to complete these requirements, the former credits need not be submitted here. Applicants are requested to write to the Director or the professor in whose department work is desired if additional information is needed.

Full instructions showing places of registration and the order of procedure in registration will be furnished each applicant on the opening date.

Students desiring college credit ,or credit towards a state certificate, will be required to pass examinations during the closing week of the term on scheduled dates.

In courses giving one hour credit, the student must attend not less than 26 days; for one and a half hours credit not less than 43 days; 3 hours credit not less than 86 class periods. No student will be given credit for a course for which he has not been officially registered.

CREDITS

In order that the Summer School work may be maintained at the same standard as the work of the regular session, the following regulations will be strictly enforced:

No. student can become eligible for a degree from the University unless one year has been spent in residence.

For the present the Faculty has ruled that the minimum residence requirement may be fulfilled by attendance on 30 weeks of college credit work in the Summer School.

(a) For students staying only six weeks the maximum credit possible is four hours, while the normal is three hours. Additional physical training may be permitted.

(b) For students staying nine weeks the maximum credit possible is seven hours provided one of the subjects is a science with laboratory, while the normal is four and one-half hours.

(c) Any work in excess of "the normal" is classed as extra hours.

No student will be registered for extra hours except in the following cases:

(a) His average for the preceding year must be 80 or above.

(b) He must be repeating a course on which he has failed or on which he has partial credit.

(c) He must be more mature than the usual student or must have several years teaching experience.

(d) For extra hours to count toward a degree at the University the student must maintain a "standing of 2;" i. e., must make all grades of 80 or above or for every grade of 70 to 79 he must make an equal number of hours with grade of 90 or above.

Work for college credit may be applied on the State Normal School Diploma or towards the University, Agricultural College or State Normal School degree, according to the requirements of these degrees in the regular catalog. Work may also be credited towards a state certificate according to the requirements of the State Board of Education.

FEES

A registration fee of $3.00 is charged every student on registering. A fee of $12.00 is charged for three credit hours or courses and $5.00 for each additional hour or course, with a maximum of $30.00 for seven hours in the nine weeks term. One physical training course will be allowed without extra charge. The fee for a graduate course is 15.00 for one minor or two half minors. There are special fees in the music department, in law and a few others, which will be indicated in connection with the course. Certain courses carry laboratory fees. All entertainments are free to Summer School students.

RETURN OF FEES

Where students report at the office of the Registrar on or before June 28. that they have discontinued any course for which extra fee was paid, such fee is returned. When reported after that date, no rebate for credit of fees is allowed. Exception to this rule may be made only in case of those who for serious personal illness, certified by the Medical Officer, are obliged to withdraw entirely from the Summer School. Any rebate will be reckoned from the date the Registrar receives the Medical Officer's report. No fees will be refunded after the second week of the session.

MONEY

University bills may be paid by check in exact amount. Money orders, express or travelers' checks should be carried for emergency purposes. It would be advisable for students to bring their money in this form and deposit it in a local bank.

Students should come prepared to pay fees on the day they register. Registration will not be complete until fees are paid.

DORMITORIES

The effort has been made this year to increase the dormitory facilities to accommodate as many as may come and add to their pleasure and comfort.

State Normal School. At the State Normal School five dormitories are available which will furnish superior accommodation for 550 women. These are Bradwell, Gilmer, Senior, Winnie Davis, and Miller Halls. One dormitory is reserved for men and wives. The charge is $32.50 for room and board for six weeks. Apply to Mr. A. Rhodes for reservation.

University of Georgia. At the University, Old College, New College, Candler Hall and John Milledge Dormitory will be available, which will accommodate 350 women. Room rent is $5.00 per person for six weeks and $2.00 for the last three weeks. Apply to T. W. Reed for reservation. Send reservation fee of $5.00, which pays rent. This is refunded, for cause, if desired before June 21st.

College of Agriculture. Soule Hall at the College of Agriculture will accommodate 70 women. Room rent is $10.00 per student, two in a room. A room reservation fee of $5.00 to be refunded when the room is surrendered in good condition is required and should accompany application. Apply to Miss Mary Creswell for reservation.

Chapter Houses. A number of fraternity houses will be open for the six weeks term, some for men and some for women, accommodating 250 students. Room rent is $8.00 for the six weeks term.

Many prefer private homes or private board. Arrangements have been made to accommodate as many as desire to live in private homes. Apply to T. W. Reed.

Students should have their mailed addressed to the dormitory in which they have made reservation.

Students occupying rooms in any of the dormitories should bring with them at least the following articles: **1 pillow, 2 pairs of pillow cases, 2 pairs of sheets, 2 counterpanes, half dozen towels.**

SELECTION OF DORMITORY

It is important that those making application for reservation of rooms keep in mind the fact that courses for primary and elementary work will be given at the State Normal School and all teachers who register for these primarily will find it convenient to room there. Likewise for home economics the Agricultural dormitory will be most convenient; for University courses select the University dormitories or chapter houses, though students may live at any of these places or in private homes and be accessible to their work. The street car company gives a dollar ticket good for seven days for as many trips per person as desired.

DINING HALLS

Denmark Hall, at the University, can accommodate 350 women and men at $30.00 for six weeks; $45.00 for nine weeks; for one week, $6.00; for less than one week, 40 cents each meal. Students rooming in the University Halls are expected to eat at Denmark Dining Hall.

The Agricultural College Cafeteria can accommodate 150 men and women at $35.00 for six weeks, and a like rate per week for the nine weeks.

The State Normal Dining Hall can accommodate 550 at $30.00 for six weeks.

Some of the **Chapter Houses** provide board as well as room. Table board may also be had in private homes, cafeterias, tea rooms, the hotel coffee shops, at from $5.00 to $7.00 a week. Many students live in private homes and eat at the college dining halls. The Summer School has no trouble finding accommodations for 2,000 students.

TIME AND PLACE OF RECITATIONS

Recitations will be given in all courses, Tuesday, June 22nd, at 8:45 A. M. The six weeks courses must run thirty-one days and the nine weeks courses fifty. There will be not classes on every other Saturday. The first Saturday will be a class day.

.RAILROAD RATES

A round trip rate of a fare and a half has been granted by the railroads on the identification certificate plan. These certificates may be obtained from the Director and **must be presented to the ticket agent when ticket is purchased** or no reduction will be granted. The selling dates are June 19-28, inclusive, and July 3-5, 10-12, 17-19, 24-26, July 31-August 2, 7-9 and 14-16, final limit of all tickets to be September 6. 1926, tickets to be validated by the regular ticket agents of the Athens terminal lines before return journey is commenced. Round trip tickets will be sold from stations in Alabama, Georgia, Florida, South Carolina and Tenni Ga., Tennessee.

GEORGIA CO-OPERATIVE ASSOCIATION

A co-operative store for the University is in successful operation on the University Campus where books, etc., may be secured.

In connection with the "Co-op" is a University post-office in which there are about 700 call-boxes.

Baggage. Trunks and other baggage should give the dormitory and room number where reservation has been made prior to coming to the Summer School. In other cases baggage should be left at the railway station until a residence is secured.

Residence. Unless reservation has been made, application for room list should be made at the Residence Bureau in Academic Hall. The Summer School offices will be in Academic Hall, first floor.

Absences. Absences are not excused unless certified by the Summer School Physician.

Weekly Bulletins. Announcements for each week are made in the University Items which is provided for free distribution in all of the buildings, and is edited by the class in Journalism.

BOOKS AND MATERIALS

Students of the Summer School will be expected to provide themselves with all books and materials required for their individual use in the courses pursued. Most of the texts to be used are an-

11

nounced in connection with the description of the various courses. Students may procure their books before coming to the Summer School, or they may get them at the Co-op Book Exchange, at the usual market prices.

Those expecting to pursue courses in Primary School Methods or Grammar School Methods or to take advantage of the observation work in the demonstration classes, may save considerable expense by bringing with them such of the State-adopted books as they have at home.

Students are requested to bring any string or any other musical instrument upon which they play, so that a Summer School orchestra may be organized, and thus add to the pleasure and profit of the Summer School. They should also bring any personal equipment for athletics, or other physical training, such as gymnasium and swimming suits, tennis racquets, ball equipment.

PLAY AND RECREATION

Recreation and play is an important part of Summer School life. All forms of athletics will be carried on during the summer. The tennis lover will find several courts at all three institutions. There are basketball courts on each campus, and provision for quoits, indoor baseball, volley ball and other games for women. Sanford Field provides ample facilities for track, baseball, football, basketball and other games for men. The Cloverhurst Golf Club opens its links to teachers in the Summer School for a nominal fee. Clubs, racquets, suits, etc., should be brought from home.

All three gymnasiums are open to regularly registered students during the session, under the control of competent instructors. No fee is charged for the use of the gymnasium and it is hoped that all will come prepared to avail themselves of this training. The swimming pools and baths will be at the service of the students, certain hours and days being set aside for each sex. A small fee is charged for service.

Arrangements have been made for competitive rifle practice and target shooting under direction of army officers.

DAILY GENERAL ASSEMBLY

Daily from 9:20 to 10:00 at the State Normal School and from 11:15 to 11:55 at the University there will be a period in which the students may have the privilege to assembly for devotional exercises, song service, short addresses on topics of current and general interest, or some other interesting exercise. The Assembly music at the University will be under the direction of Mr. Geo. F. Granberry; at the Normal, of the instructor in public school music.

ENTERTAINMENTS AND LECTURES

Care has been given in providing the best of entertainments and lectures. Almost every evening on one of the campuses, students will gather on the lawn, the weather permitting, or in one of the assembly halls for songs and games or lectures and other entertainments.

During the first three weeks the National P.-T. A. course will bring many prominent women to the Summer School and frequent public lectures and conferences will be given by these.

During the fourth week the county and city superintendents gather for study and conference. This brings together over one hundred prominent officials and speakers.

In the fifth week there will be a great musical festival with artists like Marguerita Sylva, Mary Craig, John Hendricks and others, of New York. Thousands attend this feast of music.

In the sixth week all the vocational agricultural teachers assemble, together with prominent speakers.

Paul Fleming, a magician of national reputation, will give an evening entertainment on July 1st or 2nd.

Miss Irma Seydel, a noted violinist of Boston, will play in concert on July 8th.

Mr. and Mrs. Hugh Hodgson, of Atlanta, will give an instrumental and vocal concert during the second week.

The Athens Jubilee Singers give one concert.

The Coffer-Miller Players, of Chicago, will offer two dramatic performances, one of Sheridan's plays, and one of Shaw's or Moliere's, during the fourth week.

The Oratory Department will give a number of dramatic readings and short one act plays.

There will be many departmental lectures by members of the faculty and outside speakers, followed by a social hour.

Arrangements have been made with the Palace Theatre, probably the most beautiful picture theatre in the state outside of Atlanta, by which each registered Summer School student will secure a ticket for two entertainments a week for the six weeks. This feature proved quite popular with the students last summer.

Excellent Radio equipment will be at the services of the Summer School students at the University and the State Normal School under the direction of Mr. Earnest and Mr. Dixon.

The program for the afternoon lectures will be announced each week in the Summer School Items.

On the first Saturday evening there will be a general assembly of the student body and faculty in Memorial Hall followed by a social hour and refreshments.

The physical training, and several other departments will unite in presenting a pageant in open air theatre at the Agricultural College during the sixth week.

All of the entertainments are free to regular registered students of the Summer School.

Certification of Teachers

I. GENERAL ELEMENTARY

Much of the work of the Summer School has been arranged to meet the requirements of the State Board of Education relating to the certification of teachers. The University will accept only those with such high school training that they will be able to prepare for the first grade certificate.

Practically all of the work at the **State Normal** may be applied towards meeting professional requirements of 18 semester hours necessary for **State Professional Elementary Certificate.** Any of the educational courses at the University or Agricultural College may also be so applied.

Many teachers have not graduated from an accredited school and have trouble in securing their high school credits necessary for a state elementary certificate. The Summer School has arranged with four prominent Superintendents to conduct **review courses in high school subjects.** Teachers may thus. validate their high school work. Many teachers found these classes very helpful in the past.

II. HIGH SCHOOL GRADUATES

Graduates of accredited high schools may begin the study of the required 18 semester hours in Education and Methods this summer and receive a **Provisional Elementary Certificate** good for **three** years. By the expiration of this provisional certificate they can complete the professional subjects and be granted a **Professional Elementary Certificate** good for seven years. The provisional certificate is not renewable.

There are practically 5,000 teachers with provisional certificates. These must complete the required **18 semester hours** during the life of their provisional certificates if they wish to continue to teach. Georgia is insisting on professional preparation of the teachers. The Summer School makes it possible for them to secure this preparation without loss of time from their schools and at minimum cost. Eight semester hours may be completed each summer in the six weeks courses, or twelve semester hours in the nine weeks courses. Teachers should check up what credits they have so as not to duplicate work this summer.

III. NORMAL CERTIFICATES

Normal Professional Certificates are based upon **two years** (60 semester hours) **for Normal or College** work beyond graduation from a four year high school.

The work must include at least 18 semester hours in education. If it does not a **Provisional Normal Certificate** may be granted, good for three years only. It must be of standard college grade.

Teachers may work each summer for this certificate and earn it in five summers while still teaching, or they may finish college or normal courses which they were forced to discontinue. Twelve semester hours may be earned in nine weeks. This certificate enables the holder to teach in a high school.

Teachers may submit a High School certificate and what Normal or College work they have done and then complete the two years of work by Summer School attendance and certain correspondence courses with the required residence.

IV. COLLEGE CERTIFICATES

A graduate of an approved college who did not include the eighteen semester hours in education preparatory to Teaching, Supervision and Administration will find under the division of Education all of the courses necessary for compliance with the state regulation converting a **Provisional College Certificate** into a **Professional** one, by passing up eighteen semester hours in professional subjects.

These **Provisional** Certificates are good for only three years. The state expects every holder of one to convert it into a **Professional** Certificate at the end of that time by offering 18 semester hours in Education and Methods.

Many teachers in the high schools have probably neglected, in the past to secure a state license, but under the new state certification plan no teacher should neglect to apply and secure from the state a certificate. It gives an official rating that cannot be overlooked. The Summer School can help where extra preparation is needed.

Many high school teachers have a general license, but the State Board now makes it possible for them to secure a special subject certificate. Study at the Summer School will make possible an application for such a certificate. The time is passed in our high schools when a teacher will offer to teach any subject in the curriculum. She should begin to specialize in one or at most three departments. About 24 semester hours in a subject like English with experience or practice teaching would entitle one to a special subject certificate on the regular college certificate.

There are many teachers of special subjects that have not secured certificates. By concentrating on these special subjects (music, art, physical training, etc.) they will be eligible to apply to the State Department for a certificate to teach, or these subjects may be listed on the general certificate.

Teachers who have taught ten years and can show professional improvement by attendance on Summer Schools, Normal Schools or Colleges and have 18 semester hours in Education may be granted Life Professional Certificates, either Elementary, Normal or College, according to preparation.

Opportunity is thus afforded the teachers in Georgia to secure a certificate, either provisional, professional or life professional, and have his or her record recorded in the State Department of Education.

The Summer School welcomes the opportunity to cooperate with the State Department in this forward step and has endeavored to make available to the teachers the resources of the institutions cooperating in the Summer School.

Do not be satisfied with one of the old county license, but work to convert this into a **State Certificate**, good anywhere.

In less than two years Georgia may have an equalization fund that will enable the State Department to fix salaries according to preparation. Teachers should use this summer and next to secure the highest certificate possible.

NOTICE

A number of other college courses listed in the general catalog may be offered in the Summer School, provided as many as ten students apply for the same. The Council reserves the right to withdraw any course for which eight do not register, to limit the enrollment in any course or class section, or to fix the time of meeting. Where less than eight register for a course, it may be approved, provided those desiring it make up the cost with the professor to the equivalent of eight. The individual instructors must refer such matters to the Council. The Summer School will not be responsible for bills contracted without written authority of the management.

SPECIAL LETTER COURSES

No special courses preparing for the State examinations for license are offered in the Summer School and no such examinations will be held here. Students wishing such preparation should attend one of the State Teachers Institutes.

The following courses are offered to meet entrance requirements and high school credit by examination:

English A—Grammar and a critical study of specimens of English Literature—third year high school. Credit, one unit 6 weeks. Superintendent Knowles.

English B—Composition and critical study of specimens of English Literature—fourth year high school. Credit, one unit 6 weeks. Superintendent Knowles.

Mathematics A-1—Algebra to Quadratic Equations. Credit, one unit. Superintendent Bennett.

Mathematics A-2—Quadratics, Progressions, and the Binomial formula. First term. Credit,, one unit. Superintendent Brinson.

Mathematics B-1—Plane Geometry. First term. Credit, one unit. Superintendent Bennett.

Mathematics B-2—Solid Geometry. Superintendent Brinson.

Latin C—Cicero's Orations (6); Grammar; Composition. First term. Credit, one unit. Superintendent Carreker.

Latin D—Vergil's Aeneid; Grammar; Composition. First term. Credit, one unit. Superintendent Carreker.

The examinations in each course must be approved by the Committee on Entrance of the University.

They are equivalent to the regular college entrance examinations.

Conner Hall, the administration building, Agricultural College

ELEMENTARY SCHOOL COURSES

The work at the State Normal School for the summer of 1926 has been arranged to meet the needs of teachers of first six grades and the kindergarten. **It will be a technical or professional school for teachers of these grades.** The work is arranged primarily for those who have had academic training equal to that of a high school and are now seeking additional training, particularly; to qualify for the eighteen (18) semester hours in Education and Methods required for a professional state certificate.

The work centers about the Demonstration School of six grades and the kindergarten. There will be technical courses in the presentation and problems of each elementary subject with observation in the Demonstration school and practice teaching in the classroom with fellow students.

There will be a dozen pedagogical courses dealing in the large with problems of elementary education in county and city schools. At least half of the eighteen (18) semester hours should be selected in these. With these as a pedagogical and psychological basis, the selection of applied courses in methods, with observation and practice, should give teachers opportunity for real improvement.

I. METHODS IN ARTS AND CRAFTS

S-1. **Art in the Primary Grades—N.** 1 hr., 6 weeks. Miss Cabaniss.
This course is planned to help teachers of the first four grades with their art work. It includes methods of teaching art, discussion of courses of study, and practice in primary drawing, painting and designs. Fee, $1.50.

S-2. **Blackboard Drawing—N.** 1 hr., 6 weeks. Miss Cabaniss.
Directions and practice in using white and colored chalks and charcoal in drawing on the board. This type of drawing is suitable for teachers of elementary grades who wish to illustrate themes, make borders or calendar panels. Fee, $1.50.

Poster Designing (At Agricultural College.)

Art Structure and Costume Designing (At the University.)

S-3-a-b. **Handicrafts for Grades—N.** 2 hrs., 6 weeks. Miss Tigner.
a. **Handicraft for First, Second and Third Grades.**
Including paper folding, paper cutting, toy making, school room borders, rafia work, cardboard construction.

b. **Handicraft for Fourth, Fifth and Sixth Grades.**
Including paper cutting, toy making, paper flowers, basketry, construction of marionette theatres and costumes, doll millinery.
A small fee to cover cost of material is charged.

S-4-a. **Penmanship in the Grades—N.** 1 hr., 6 weeks. Miss Baldon.
The Teaching and Supervision of Handwriting. The course will include psychology and pedagogy of handwriting, methods of teaching, special teaching, supervision, tests and measurements, plans and courses of study, remedial and corrective teaching, individual and group assignment and instruction.
Students enrolling in this course must take Handwriting 4-b. or meet a standard of handwriting set by the instructor.

S-4-b.—
The primary purpose of this course is to improve the student's writing on blackboard and paper. Instruction will be given in the theory and practice of handwriting, with attention to individual difficulties, their causes and remedies.

S-5. **Industrial Arts for Elementary Grades—N.** 1 hr. Mr. Osterman.
A practical course in handwork with related subject-matter for grade

teachers and supervisors of intermediate grades (fourth, fifth and sixth).
Much attention is given to the selection of materials suitable for actual
school work. The meaning of industrial arts, its relation to the other
school subjects, and the method of using it as a vital part of the curriculum are discussed.

The course includes problems concerned with the making of books,
papermaking, pottery, booklets, desk blotters, folders, card cases, writer's
kits, memory books, coping, saw work, etc.

S-6. Public School Music Course for Grades 1-6—N. 1 hr., 6 weeks.
Miss Smith.

The work requires observation, the preparation of lessons, plans and
practice in teaching a class:
1. Practice in the choice, singing and presenting of rote songs.
2. Material and plan for teaching the first steps in notation.
3. Sight-singing, study of fundamental problems in pitch and rhythm.
4. Music appreciation, the use of the phonograph and material for each
grade.
NOTE:—See other music courses at the University.
Two Sections—
a. For first, second and third grade teachers.
b. For fourth, fifth and sixth grade teachers.

II. EDUCATION AND METHODS; GENERAL

S-1. History of Education—N. 1 hr., 6 weeks. Mr. Ritchie.

A study of the development of ideals, conceptions, organization, and
methods of teaching. The work will begin with the transition to modern
times and will place emphasis upon the modern periods. The doctrines
of Rousseau, Pestalozzi, Froebel, Herbart, Spencer, Mann, Page, Dewey
and other moderns, will be interpreted in a practical way to make this
course helpful to teachers of any grade.

S-2. School Government and Efficiency—N. 1 hr., 6 weeks. Mr.
Ritchie.

A course in modern school efficiency from the standpoint of order, discipline, penalties, reports, supervised study and play, playground equipment and management, interest, attention, and other phases of easy control
and highest efficiency. Text: Sears Classroom Organization and Control.

S-3. Intelligence and Educational Measurements—N. 1 hr., 6
weeks. Mr. Ritchie.

An examination of the various achievement tests in the several school
subjects with emphasis on the elementary subjects. These will be studied
from the standpoint of the actual school room problem. The theory of
measurement and the administration of the tests will be stressed. Studens
will purchase a sample set of the most important tests.

S-4. Introduction to Psychology—N. 1 hr., 6 weeks. Miss Zeigler.

Discussion of habit, mind and body, imagery, association, memory,
thinking, reasoning, feelings, sentiments, action and behavior.

S-5. Child Study—N. 1 hr., 6 weeks. Miss Zeigler.

Special emphasis will be put upon the exceptionally dull and bright
children and their treatment. Child behavior. Training in the concrete
study of child life.

S-6. Psychology of Elementary School Subjects—C. I hr., 6 weeks.
Miss Zeigler.

This course is designed to give the psychology of learning as applied
to the language arts, handwriting, reading, spelling, arithmetic, supervised study.

S-7-a-b. Elementary School Methods—N. 2 hrs., 6 weeks. Miss
Solomon.

In this course the main emphasis will be laid upon the principles
which affect the development of sound methods of teaching and upon
the application of these principles in teaching the various school subjects. Attention will be given to such topics as the following: teaching
how to study, project method, socialized recitation, testing and measuring, pupil activities that will lead to good habits of work.
S-a., for first, second and third grade teachers.
S-b., for fourth, fifth and sixth grade teachers.

S-8. Rural Sociology and Education—N. 1 hr., 6 weeks. Mr. Sell.

This course includes a study of rural social conditions in communities
and the causes which underly social and economic changes. The in-

18

fluence of such factors as production, farm tenancy and educational organizations will be carefully considered. Much of the work will be devoted to the survey of the home community in order that the teacher may be able to correctly evaluate social and economic conditions in the community and thereby better serve society.

S-9-a. Methods in Kindergarten—N. 1 hr., 6 weeks. Miss Willingham.

Play Materials in the Education of Young Children: Selection and methods of use of play materials such as toys, building blocks, picture books, pictures, etc.

Beginnings of Music for Young Children: Study of musical needs of young children; methods of presentation, etc.

Observation in Kindergarten required.

S-9-b. Early Childhood Education—N. 1 hr., 6 weeks. Miss Hale.

This course deals with the education of children from four to eight years of age. An effort will be made to formulate a unified program of teaching in kindergartens and first grades, to show how the fundamentals can be taught in a purposeful way, and to build a curriculum based on the child's own interests, purposes, and activities.

S-9-a-b., with observation in the Demonstration School, are specially planned for kindergarten first grade teachers and will show the interrelation of the work of these grades.

S-10. P.-T. A.—N. 1 semester hr., 3 weeks. Mrs. Watkins.

This course is designed to help those who are actively engaged in Parent-Teacher work. Both parents and teachers are welcome to enroll in the class.

S-11. The Teaching of Reading—.N 1 hr., 6 weeks. Miss Solomon.

This course will consider the aims and principles underlying the teaching of reading from first through the sixth grade. Various methods of teaching will be discussed.

S-12-a. Problems in Home Economics—N. 1 hr., 6 weeks. Miss Baird.

A survey of the field of Home Economics and a clearing house for the problems arising in teaching the subject, including the organization of subject matter, correlation with other subjects, modern methods of teaching, equipment and selection of text and reference books.

S-12-b. Unit Courses in Home Economics—N. 1 hr., 6 weeks. Miss Baird.

This course is planned for those who have had no work in Home Economics and for those who wish to review the subject matter, and includes short units in food, clothing, budgeting, personal hygiene, and recreation, with suggestions for reference material and teaching methods.

These two courses should as a rule be taken together.

III. METHODS IN TEACHING SPECIAL SUBJECTS

S-1—Geography and Nature Study for Grades—N. 1 hr. Mr. Ernest.

This course will include a study of the general principles underlying the selection and organization of subject matter of school geography with special emphasis on home geography and a study of physiographic local conditions and a study of life forms. The course will be taught on the project method with field and laboratory lessons. Teachers taking this course should keep free two hours on Tuesday and Thursday afternoons for field work.

S-2. Primary Number and Projects—N. 1 hr. Miss Calloway.

This course is planned for teachers of the first, second, and third grades. Special study will be given to the psychology of number—the number experience of the child,—the study of number games, and the use of devices and of objective material to making and enriching courses of study for these grades.

S-3. Intermediate and Advanced Arithmetic—N. 1 hr. Miss Calloway.

This course in the teaching of intermediate and advanced arithmetic will cover the following topics: Brief treatment of methods of teaching the fundamental operations and denominate numbers; value and place of drill work; fractions; percentage; arithmetic in its relation to social and industrial life, arithmetical tests; methods of conducting supervising study in arithmetic.

19

S-4. Principles of Economic Geography—N. 1 hr. Mr. Sell.

The project method in the teaching of geography will be used in the study of the physical conditions of the earth and how these relate to the growth, development and welfare of the human race. Such general topics as climate and natural vegetation, land forms, soils, mineral deposits, water and natural environment will constitute a large part of this course. For upper grammar grade teachers.

S-5. Physiology and Hygiene—N. 1 hr. Mr. Earnest.

General, personal and school hygiene; some instruction in anatomy and physiology; cause, transmission and prevention of communicable diseases, with special reference to most common diseases; defects of school children; schoolhouse sanitation; medical inspection; health education programs.

S-6. Methods in Language Lessons and Literature—N. 1 hr., 6 weeks. Mr. Brown.

This is a method course for teachers in the elementary grades. The consideration of the material best suited for language lessons and the proper method of presenting this material, the relation and coordination of oral and written work, and the devices to be used in fixing habits of correct speech in the minds of children will be the subjects of discussion.

Texts: Modern Course in English, Book I and Language Work in Elementary Schools by Leiper.

S-7. Methods in Composition and Grammar—N. 1 hr., 6 weeks. Mr. Brown.

This is a methods course for teachers of the sixth, seventh, and junior high school grades. The proper relation of composition and grammar will be discussed, and the best methods of teaching these two closely related subjects will be presented and illustratd. A graded course in literature will be planned and lessons in it taught.

Texts: Modern Course in English, Book II, and the Teaching of English by Chubb.

S-9. Educational Dramatics and Story Telling—N. 1 hr., 6 weeks. Miss Vance.

Methods of coaching plays for and with children from the dramatized reading lesson to a finished performance. Appropriate plays for all occasions will be studied from the point of casting, staging, and costuming. This course is especially valuable in handling problems for reading and speech in primary grades.

S-10. Expression for the Teacher of Reading—N. 1 hr., 6 weeks. Miss Vance.

With special emphasis on the proper use of the Voice. Just how great an asset a well-modulated, pleasing and expressive voice is to a class room no one knows quite so well as children who have had to listen to the harsh, hoarse, monotonous, breathy, rasping, nasal, high-pitched tones of untrained teachers' voices.

S-11. The Teaching of History and Civics in the Elementary Grades —N. 1 hr., 6 weeks. Mrs. Simpson.

This course includes a detailed presentation of practical effective methods of teaching history in the grades; the place and treatment of biography; and the selection and organization of mateials for class room instruction.

Text: Wayland, John W.: How to Teach American History. The Macmillan Company, New York.

S-12. General World History, a Survey Course for Teachers in the Elementary Schools—N. 1 hr., 6 weeks. Mrs. Simpson.

This course is a rapid survey of World History designed to direct a review which will help teachers who are planning to teach a like course to children. Suggestions on the selection and organization of materials for a course offered to elementary school classes will be given.

Text: Webster, Hutton: World History. D. C. Heath, 1923.

DEMONSTRATION SCHOOL
State Normal School

As abstract theories may be meaningless without concrete illustrations of them, the Demonstration Department of the Summer School was organized in order that teachers may observe the practical application of the most approved educational theories.

This department will consist of kindergarten, and first, second, third, fourth, fifth and sixth grades. Experienced, well trained teachers will be in charge of each grade. In addition to the fundamental subjects which will be taught by the regular teachers, Music, Drawing, Physical Education, Dramatization and Handicrafts will be taught by the teachers of the special departments.

The schedule will be changed frequently in order that students may observe the teaching of all elementary school subjects. If a student, for any special reason, desires to observe the same grade all the time, then the first period should be reserved for observation. The time may be equally divided among all the grades including the kindergarten, and then either the first, second or third periods may be reserved for observation. The latter plan is preferable and students are strongly advised to adopt it as greater inspiration is obtained by observing the teaching in all the different grades.

No text-books will be required for this course, but students will use the Library, and mimeographed material on the best methods of teaching all the subjects will be supplied on the payment of a small fee.

Education credit, one hour, will be given to all students who observe daily, take part in all conferences, make required reports, write required papers and stand the final examination. Students not desiring credit may register for the course and observe the teaching without doing the above additional work.

Teaching Staff

Principal, Miss Hicks; Kindergarten, Miss Willingham; First Grade, Miss Hale; Second Grade, Mrs. Shaw; Third Grade, Miss Ruth Allen; Fourth Grade, Miss Pritchard; Fifth Grade, Miss Farguson; Sixth Grade, Miss Chapman; Playground Director, Miss Lunday.

Special Teachers

Music, Miss Smith; Drawing, Miss Cabaniss; Handicrafts, Miss Tigner; Dramatization, Miss Vance; Reading, Miss Solomon.

Peabody Hall

COURSES OF INSTRUCTION
At the University and Agricultural College

I. AGRICULTURE
AGRICULTURAL CHEMISTRY

S-1. Organic and Biological Chemistry—C. 3 hrs., 9 weeks. Mr. Carter.

A systematic study of the compounds of carbon and their relation to plant and animal life. (See general catalogue for full description.) Prerequisite: Inorganic Chemistry 1 or 2 with laboratory. Fee, $7.50; breakage deposit, $3.50. Junior-Senior elective. Required of Sophomore Veterinary Medicine and Junior Home Economic students.

S-2-b. Qualitative Analysis—C. 3 hrs., 9 weeks. Mr. Wilder.

Prerequisite: Inorganic Chemistry 1 or 2, with laboratory. Fee, $7.50; breakage deposit, $3.00.

OR

S-3. Quantitative Analysis—C. Mr. Carter and Mr. Wilder.

An elementary course in fundamentals of quantitative chemical analysis Gravimetric and volumetric methods will be developed. 6 hrs. for 9 weeks Prerequisites: Chemistry 1 and 2b. Fee, $7.50; breakage deposit, $5.00.

AGRICULTURAL ENGINEERING

S-26, 27, 28. Advanced Farm Shop—C. 3 hrs., 9 weeks. Mr. Lyle and Mr. Clegg.

A course in the use of shop tools and equipment in the construction and maintenance of farm labor saving appliances and equipment adapted to special types of farming, as swine, sheep, cattle, or poultry production, dairying, and fruit growing, with general exercises in sheet metal work, ropes and belting, harness repair, and the repair and care of farm machinery. This course offers special training for teachers and extension workers. (See general catalogue for full description.) Junior or Senior elective. Laboratory fee, $5.00.

AGRICULTURAL EDUCATION

S-1. Vocational Education and Vocational Guidance—C. 1 hr., 6 weeks. Mr. Wheeler.

This course presents the field of vocational education in its general phases, and shows the place of vocational education in a scheme of education. The philosophy of vocational education and guidance runs throughout the course showing its educational values and implications. Vocational guidance, educational guidance, vocational tests, vocational counceling, occupational analysis, self analysis, and the psychological basis of interest, aptitude and vocational abilities will be considered. Junior and Senior Elective.

S-2. Administration of Vocational Education—C. 1 hr., 6 weeks. Mr. Chapman.

A course designed to meet the needs of school officials, superintendants, principals and teachers, who are interested in the development of vocational education in the schools of the state. This course deals with the organization of our National Vocational Education Program, and the administration of vocational education within the state and local schools. Junior and Senior Elective.

S-3. The Rural High School Problems—C. 1 hr., 6 weeks. Mr. Pound and Mr. Sheffer.

This course is designed primarily for school officials, administrators, superintendents, principals and teachers.

It deals with all aspects of the problems incident to the organization of a county high school systems in keeping with the recommendations of the University of Georgia and the State Department of Education. Emphasis is given to the rural junior high school; its organization and control; financing; curriculum building; transportation; housing of teachers; and correlation with senior high schools and accredited institutions.

The method followed in teaching this course will be based on problem study and the use of specific examples of Georgia schools.

22

S-10. Introduction to Vocational Education—C. 1 hr., 9 weeks. Mr. Reitz.
> Educational aims and values: the theory and practice of vocational education.

S-12. Introduction to Education—C. 1 hr., 9 weeks. Mr. Reitz.
> The characteristics of the learning process; application of the principles of education to the practice of teaching, etc.

S-13. Vocational Psychology—C. 1 hr., 9 weeks. Mr. Reitz.
> For vocational Agricultural teachers.

S-14. Methods and Materials in Vocational Agriculture—C. 2 hrs., 9 weeks. Mr. Wheeler.
> For teachers of vocational agriculture.

S-11. Agricultural Education Administration—C. 1 hr., 9 weeks. Mr. Sheffer.
> For teachers of vocational agriculture.

S-16. Community Problems—C. 2 hrs., 9 weeks. Mr. Reitz.
> Further considers problems arising in connection with courses 11 and 14.

S-17. Rural Journalism—C. _1 hr., 9 weeks. Mr. Chapman.
> For teachers of vocational agriculture.

SPECIAL COURSES GIVEN TO TEACHERS IN SERVICE WEEK

Of July 26th to 31st, 1926

This course will be a professional improvement course for our vocational teachers. All will be required to attend and transportation expenses will be paid by the State Board of Vocational Education. The course given will deal with the problems of the teachers.

The complete program for this week will be issued later. For information regarding this course, the applicants should write to Mr. Paul W. Chapman, State Supervisor of Vocational Agriculture, Athens, Georgia. He has already engaged eight lecturers for different phases of work to be brought to the attention of the Vocational teacher.

FORESTRY

S-4-a.. Tree and Shrub Identification—C. 1½ hrs., 6 weeks. Mr. Burleigh.
> A systematic study of the local flora, with emphasis placed on practical field identification. The work will be entirely in the open where the various species of trees and shrubs will be observed under natural conditions, and their characteristics pointed out in more or less detail. Species found in other parts of the state and added from time to time to the college arboretum will be includede in this course. The text book will be the booklet issued recently by this institution, "Common Forest Trees of Georgia." Six laboratory periods, two hours each. Fee, $1.50.

ANIMAL HUSBANDRY

S-2-5. Animal Husbandry—C. 3 hrs., 9 weeks. Mr. Rice.
> Type and breeds of farm animals and stock judging. Fee, $3.50.

S-6. Animal Husbandry—C. 3 hrs., 9 weeks. Mr. Kellogg.
> Live stock production and management will be considered in this course with special emphasis on swine. Prerequisite: 2-5 or its equivalent. Lab. fee, $3.50.

S-8. Animal Husbandry—C. 3 hrs., 9 weeks. Mr. Kellogg.
> The breeding of domesticated farm animals will be studied in this course. Prerequisite: 2-5 or its equivalent.

S-9. Animal Husbandry—C. 3 hrs., 9 weeks. Mr. Rice.
> A study of the underlying principles of animal nutrition, with special application to southern conditions will be given in this course. Prerequisite: 2-5 or its equivalent.

S-7-14. Animal Husbandry—C. 3 hrs., 9 weeks. Mr. Bennett.
> A study of milk production and various phases of manufacturing and marketing. Lab. fee, $3.50.

AGRONOMY

S-1. Farm Crops, Field Crop Production—C. 2 hrs., 6 weeks. **Mr. Tabor.**

A study of the factors of crop production as they occur in the South. Lab. fee, $2.00.

S-3. Farm Crops, Cereals—C. 3 hrs., 9 weeks. **Mr. Tabor.**

A study of the corn and small grain crops, special attention given to analysis of yield and to methods used in producing these crops. Lab. fee, $3.50.

SOILS

S-1-2. Principles of Soil Management—C. 3 hrs., 9 weeks. **Mr. Crabb.**

Origin, formation and physical properties of soils. Factors in crop production. Drainage and tillage practices Commercial fertilizers and maintenance of soil fertility. Prerequisite: Chemistry 1. Lab. fee, $3.50.

S-3. Soil Formation—C. 3 hrs., 9 weeks. **Mr. Crabb.**

Rock disintegration and geological agencies relating to origin and formation of soils. Soil provinces, series and types of the United States. Practice of soil survey and preparation of maps and reports. Prerequisite: Soils 1 and 2. Lab. fee, $5.00.

COTTON INDUSTRY

S-9-10. Cotton Industry—C. 3 hrs., 6 weeks. **Mr. Childs.**

A study of cotton grading, warehousing, and marketing. Experimental cotton breeding. For whole course, prerequisite: Cotton Industry 3 and 4. There is no prerequisite for the grading section of the course. Five hours of laboratory work per day for six weeks. Lab. fee, $15.00.

S-3. Farm Economics—C. 3 hrs., 9 weeks. **Mr. Fain.**

A special study of farm records from Georgia crop data. Prerequisites: Farm Economics 2 and Mathematics 6.

HORTICULTURE

S-1-2-3. Horticulture—C. 3 hrs., 9 weeks. **Dr. McHatton and Mr. Keener.**

This is the course in Horticulture required of all agricultural Freshmen. (See general catalogue for description.) Parallel reading of various Horticultural texts is required. One lecture period and one laboratory period daily. Lab. fee for the course, $3.50.

S-4-6-10 or 5-7-9. Horticulture—C. 3 hrs., 9 weeks. **Mr. McHatton and Mr. Keener.**

These are Junior courses required of students specializing in Horticulture and may be used as a general elective in agricultural courses. 4, 6 and 10 may be used as a 3 hour requirement in Group 2 in the agricultural degree. (For further description see the general catalogue.) 4, 6 and 10 is a lecture course requiring parallel reading of various horticultural texts, 5, 7, and 9 is a laboratory course with a laboratory fee attached of $3.50. Mature and special students may be permitted entrance into these courses. General Horticulture 1, 2 and 3 or its equivalent is required as a prerequisite. 4, 6 and 10 has two lecture hours per day. 5, 7 and 9 is a laboratory course with one 4-hour period per day. Fee, $3.50. Both of these courses will not be offered. the professors in charge having the privilege of giving the one for which there is the greatest demand.

Horticulture 13, Entomology, will be offered during the first 6 weeks of Summer School if applications warrant. Credit 1½ hrs. Lab. fee, $2.50. Mr. McHatton.

This course may be used in Group 2. B. S. in Agriculture, or as a general elective. (For more detailed description refer to general catalogue.)

POULTRY HUSBANDRY

S-20-21-22. Poultry—C. 3 hrs., 9 weeks. **Mr. Wood and Mr. Woodward.**

Work to consist of lectures and laboratory exercises. Lab. fee $2.00.

S-20. General Poultry—

Study of breeds and varieties, selection and judging, poultry house construction, feeding, parasites and diseases. Required of Freshmen. Lab. fee, $2.00.

S-21. General Poultry—

Mating and breeding, incubation and brooding, care of young stock, fattening, killing and marketing. Required of Freshmen.

S-22. Utility Judging—

Entire time devoted to judging and culling for egg production. Junior and Senior elective. Lab. fee, $2.00.

S-3-4-25. Poultry—C. 3 hrs., 9 weeks. Mr. Wood and Mr. Woodward.

Lab. fee, $2.00. Prerequisite: Poultry Husbandry 20-21. Junior and Senior elective. Work to consist of lectures and laboratory practice.

S-3. Incubation and Brooding—

Embryology of the chick, theory and practice of incubation; types and construction of incubators and brooders, and their operation; care and management of baby chicks. Lab. fee, $2.00.

S-4. Poultry Marketing—

Candling, grading, packing and marketing eggs; fattening, killing, picking and dressing fowls; caponizing; study of markets and cooperative marketing. Lab. fee, $2.00.

S-25. Standard Judging—

Entire term to be devoted to studying the Standard of Perfection and practice work in judging and placing birds for standard requirements. Lab. fee, $2.00.

VETERINARY MEDICINE

S-1-3 or 1-5. Bacteriology—C. 3 hrs., 9 weeks. Dr. Burkhart.

Bacteriology 1 and 3, general and dairy bacteriology; for agricultural students. Juniors.
Bacteriology 1 and 5, general and household bacteriology; for students in Home Economics. Juniors.
Fee Bact. 1 and 3, or 1 and 5, $10.00. Breakage deposit, $10.00.

S-11. Poultry, (Poultry Diseases)—C. 1 hr., 9 weeks. Dr. Richardson.

S. Zootechnics and Animal Hygiene—C. 3 hrs., 9 weeks. Dr. Richardson.

The anatomy and physiology of domestic animals are briefly considered as well as the exterior of their bodies in its relation to age, soundness and utility. Important animal plagues will be considered from the view point of their cause and prevention. The common non-specific diseases will be considered as to their cause and first aid to the sick or injured.
Poultry 11 and Zootechnics and Animal Hygiene are courses designed for students specializing in Poultry Husbandry or Animal Husbandry, respectively. For those desiring to become county or home demonstration agents, these courses are especially valuable.

S-Ex.-1. Fundamentals of Extension Work—C. 1 hr. Mr. Campbell and Miss M. Creswell.

This course is planned for rural teachers, principals, superintendents and prospective extension workers. It presents the extension field as handled by the County Agricultural Agents and Home Demonstration Agents, and takes under discussion the organization of the work, its history and development, as well as the problems encountered in the betterment of farms and the organization and betterment of communities. The course will likewise include a discussion of boys' and girls' club work, the materials to be used therein; also educational value, as well as the relationship to the school community, home and farm. This course is offered for the first six weeks of the summer school, and consists of lectures, demonstrations and excursions.

II. ARTS AND CRAFTS

ARTS AND CRAFTS

S-4. Poster Designing—C. 1 hr., 6 weeks. Miss Blackshear.

Posters for Visual Instruction and Advertising.
Government, educators and sellers of merchandise realize the power of the poster to carry messages to their people, pupils and buyers. Advertisers appreciate their power to sell commodities, and they pay large sums for artistic advertisments, hence our billboards and street cars are filled with posters which shout their messages.
The course in poster making includes the "advertising idea" as related to teaching any subject or selling a commodity; the technique of compo-

sition; drawing, color and letting. Through problems and lectures suggestions and arrangements of designs are given for application to various pedagogic subjects, and for professional work where posters, or other graphic forms, are desired.

The "Hambridge Theory of Design" is taught and used in connection with the composition of this work, aso free hand sketching from life and still life.

Five two-hour periods a week for six weeks, 7th and 8th periods. A fee to cover cost of materials will be charged.

PENMANSHIP

S-1. Methods in Penmanship—N. 1 hr., 6 weeks. Miss Baldon.

The penmanship courses has two objects in view. First, to improve the handwriting of the teacher, and, second, to instruct the teacher in the best method of presenting the subject of penmanship o her pupils.

The work done in each class will comprise both the technique of handwriting and methods of teaching. Instruction will combine the best from the leading systems of muscular movement writing, and hence, principles and methods will be stressed rather than systems.

During the last two weeks of the term, demonstration lessons will be given by members of each class under the supervision of the instructor.

S-22. Art Structure and Design—C. 2 hrs., 6 weeks. Miss Cabaniss.

In teaching the underlying principles of art, our aim is to learn to recognize and appreciate things of artistic worth. To accomplish this aim, opportunity is provided for the creation of designs based upon these principles and built up by the use of three elements of art language— line, dark and light and color. Opportunity is provided for the applicant of design in the actual working out of some of the problems of handwork suitable for grammar grades and high school. Double periods.

A fee to cover cost of material will be charged. Given at University.

For elementary drawing and blackboard sketching, see Normal School Division.

S-3. Art in the Junior High School Methods—N. 1 hr., 6 weeks. Miss Cabaniss.

This course aims to give certain skills which would be applied to the upper grammar grades and the junior high school in teaching drawing. Such topics as color theory, design, perspective, representation, illustration, etc. Media: charcoal, water colors, crayons. etc. The methods of presentation in this course is a vital consideration.

PUBLIC SCHOOL MUSIC

S-2. Public School Course for Grades 6-9—N. 1 hr. Miss Smith.

Methods and material in sight-singing, ear-training, oral and written dictation, elementary theory and harmony, music appreciation, class instruction in voice and chorus work.

S-3. Music Expression—N. 1 hr. Miss Smith.

Conducting class and the organization and conducting of High School Choruses, Glee Clubs, Vocal Class Study, Orchestras and Eelective Music including credits for outside Music Study under private teachers.

S-4. Music Appreciation. ½ hr. Miss Smith.

Appropriate courses for Elementary School. Junior High School and High School including the use of the phonograph.

S-5. Harmony. ½ hr. Miss Smith.

Introductory harmony and harmonic dictation, including scales, intervals, triads, inversions, dominant seventh chords and their applications in melody harmonizing and original composition.

III. COMMERCE

COMMERCE

S-5, a, b, c. Principles of Economics—C. 3 hrs., 6 weeks. Mr. Brooks.

This course in economic theory is the foundation on which all advanced courses in the School of Commerce rest. It deals with the production, exchange, distribution and consumption of goods and with the usual problems illustrative of the principles. 3 hrs. daily.

S-6, a, b, c. Elementary Accounting—Cr. 3 hrs., 6 weeks. Mr. Smith.

This is an introductory course designed to give the general business student a thorough knowledge of the fundamental principles of accounting. The course begins with the study of the principles underlying the simple balance sheet and profit and loss statements, and proceeds to the development of the theory of debits and credits as applied to ledger accounts. books of original entry and adjusting and closing entries. A comprehensive study is made of partnership problems—partners' capital and drawing accounts, interest on investment, division of profits, closing of partnership and dissolution. Controlling accounts are studied carefully and problems peculiar to the corporation. joint ventures, single entry bookkeeping, and consignments are worked in class. 3 hrs. daily.

S-91. Elementary Gregg Shorthand—C. 2 hrs., 9 weeks. Mr. Broadhurst.

A course for beginners in shorthand. Drill and theory for beginners in shorthand. Drill and theory work on the principles of shorthand. Reading and writing practice, with emphasis on methods of learning shorthand. Two hours daily.

S-92. Touch Typewriting—C. 1 hr., 9 weeks. Mr. Broadhurst.

Keyboard techinque and drill work for beginners. Special attention given to the psychology of habit formation. Methods of keeping records studied. and learning curves plotted. Two practice periods daily.

S-96. Business Correspondence—C. 3 hrs., 9 weeks. Mr. Broadhurst.

A study of the principles underlying effective business letters. An advanced course for students trained in the essentials of grammar, composition and rhetoric. Prerequisites: First year college course in English and ability to use the typewriter. Two hours daily.

IV. CONFERENCES AND SHORT COURSES

NATIONAL P.-T. A. SHORT COURSE

June 21 to July 9

(See outline of this credit course under Education.)

This course was authorized by the National P.-T. A. Executive Board and the Field Secretary, Mrs. Arthur C. Watkins, has been designated by the National Board to conduct the course. There will be daily lectures and conferences. The local P.-T. A. Association and the State Association are fully cooperating with the National Board in bringing to the members of the P.-T. A. this intensive course for improvement of the P.-T. A. work.

As this is the only National School in the South, it is hoped by the P.-T. A. authorities that many members will attend from all over this section of the country. A special folder will be issued.

This course is designed to help those who are actively engaged in the Parent-Teacher work, to ascertain what the legitimate fields are and how best to conduct the work, so that the most worthwhile results are secured. Both parents and teachers are welcome to the class, and special subjects are discussed of interest to Superintendents and School Principals. A class will be held at the Normal at the third period and at the University at the fifth period. One-half hour credit will be allowed if the entire course is completed and examinations passed. It may be selected without credit in addition to the limitations as to number of courses.

Second Week

GEORGIA FEDERATION OF WOMEN'S CLUBS
June 29 to July 3

This will be the third Institute held in connection with the Summer School. An instructive program of Federation work is being arranged by the National and State committees. A special bulletin will be issued later.

COUNTY AND CITY SUPERINTENDENTS CONFERENCE

July 12 to 16

This short course will be arranged, as in former years, to meet the practical needs of county and city superintendents, with special emphasis on the county superintendents.

The State Superintendent, several of the supervisors and a number of county and city superintendents of the state will take part in the program.

Visitors will also have opportunity to attend different classes in the Summer School and see the actual work of the several departments.

A full program will be issued later.

Fifth Week

MUSICAL FESTIVAL

July 20 to 28

The special folder regarding the Music Festival will be issued later giving the program for the week and the noted artists who will participate.

V. EDUCATION

EDUCATION

S-1. **History of Education**—C. 1 hr., 6 weeks. Mr. Wise.

A study of the development of education as a phase of changing civilization with emphasis on the sources of modern principles and practices.

S-2. **Education in the United States**—C. 1 hr. Last three weeks. Double periods. Mr. Alfriend.

European background, transplantings from Europe, early colonial developments, later European influences, evolution of American education, status and tendencies today.

S-3. **Educational Hygiene**—C. 1 hr., 6 weeks. Mr. Wise.

This course considers the relations of the school to the health of its pupils: Health instruction, school conditions, recreation, etc.

S-4. **Educational Psychology**—C. 1 hr., 6 weeks. Mr. Edwards.

The facts and problems of psychology having a bearing upon education; the laws oflearning; principles of economy in learning; reasoning and problem solving; the transfer of training, etc.

S-5. **Educational Psychology**—C. 1 hr. Last three weeks. Double periods. Mr. Edwards.

Continuation of S-4.

S-6. **Intelligence Tests**—C. 1 hr., 6 weeks. Mr. Edwards and Mr. Patrick.

For description of course see Psychology.

S-7. **Introductory Sociology. Social Problems and Education**—C. 1 hr., 6 weeks. Mr. Alfriend.

A study of social problems and the remedial education needed.

S-8. **Moral Education**—C. 1 hr., 6 weeks. Mr. Patrick.

Defining education as the making of moral personalities. this course will seek to define the moral person, the materials to be utilized in moral education, and the methods to be employed.

S-9. **Educational Sociology**—C. 1 hr., 6 weeks. Mr. Alfriend.

Social origins and functions of Education; individual versus social aims; education for democracy; vocational and cultural education; socialization of education.

S-10. The Improvement of Instruction in Secondary Schools. 1 hr., 6 weeks. Mr. Hunter.

This course is designed to meet the needs of high school principals and teachers who wish to become familiar with the most recent methods, devices, and materials used to produce better results in the teaching of high school pupils. The following are some of the major units of the course: The collection, and tabulation of data which will assist the teacher in diagnosing the capacities and interests of the individual pupil, and also the class as a group; the use of the new-type examination, such as the true-false, completion, multiple response, matching, best answer, and informal tests. The use of graphs and charts to stimulate pupils to higher educational achievement; use of special methods, such as the project method, the socialized recitation, and supervised study recitation; the setting up of standards of achievement; provsions or modification of courses to meet the needs of different ability groups; elementary statistics which enable the teacher to scientifically organize and interpret educational data. The instructor will make available much original material and will demonstrate its practical uses.

S-11. Constructive School Discipline—C. 1 hr., 6 weeks. Mr. Alfriend.

Problems of discipline and general school management as factors in the general process of education, especially in the building of character.

S-12. Educational Measurements—C. 1 hr., 6 weeks. Mr. Pusey.

Use of tests in the teaching process; the scoring of tests and the interpretation of results; how to improve forms of examinations and system of marking; how to measure the pupil's progress; how to measure the teacher's efficiency; the selection of tests appropriate for various purposes.

S-14. Teaching the Special Subjects—C. 1 hr., 6 weeks.
14-a. English, The teaching of. Mr. Sanford.

This course will be based on the College Entrance Requirements and similar lists. It will consider the purpose to be kept in view in studying literature in high school, the best way to plan and present for class study varous kinds of reading, and some of the recent movements in the teaching of literature. It will attempt to show the relation of he literature work to composition, grammar and other English work of the class bringing the unifs of the instruction and practice in connection with all the exercises of the school.

14-b. History, Civics, The teaching of. Mr. Payne.

This course for teachers will be a study of the problems of history teaching in the high schools; the relation of history to allied studies; the history curricula in the schools of Europe and the United States in the past; the more recent ideas in the presentation of history by charts, diagrams, maps, pictures, text-books and lectures. Practical exercises in historical methods will be required. The teaching of civics will be studied in like manner. Teachers who contemplate taking this course should bring all available text-books in history.

S-14-c. Social Studies in the Junior High School, The Teaching of C. 1 hr., 6 weeks. Grades seven, eight, and nine. Miss Simpson.

This course is directed toward the improvement of instruction in history, geography and civics in the Junior High School. Progressive practice will be made concrete through the discussion study of and the planning of series of lessons. The best materials; books, maps, pictures, charts, graphs, cartoons, and examinations will be studied. Suggestions as to how the courses in history, geography, and civics can be given as one general course will be made.

14-d. Mathematics, The teaching of. Mr. Stephens.

This course will present and illustrate modern methods of mathematics teaching. The report of the National Committee on Mathematical Requirements will be available for study. Those planning to take this course should bring standard texts in school mathematics with them.

14-f. The Teaching of Biological Science. Mr. Krafka.

A course designed to consider the methods of presentation of biological materials in the high schools of Georgia, including an historical development of course types, such as "dissection" courses, 'type" courses. "principle" courses, "project" courses; review of the contentns of present day outlines and their adaptability to our equipment: relation to nature study and college courses: note book demands, grading systems; equipment costs; library necessities, etc. Prerequisites: a knowledge of biology suc has would be obtained in Botany 3, Zoology 31 or experience in teaching the subject in the high school.

14-g. Latin, The teaching of. Mr. Hooper.

Aims of Latin study; is place and value in the curriculum. The course and materials of study; varying types of textbooks; relative emphasis on various phases of the subjects, such as vocabulary, grammatical forms, syntax, translation, interpretation. The teaching of Latin composition. Oral reading of prose and verse. Features of classroom practice; methods of arousing interest; correlation with other subjects. Reading and discussion of significant articles on the teaching of Latin. References to useful books and illustrative material.

14-h. French, The teaching of. Mr. Lustrat.

S-21. The Psychology and Problems of Adolescence—C. 1 hr., 6 weeks.

This will be a study of the peculiar nature and problems of the high school age, with special study of the psychology of the junior high school pupil.

S-22. High School Organization and Management for Teachers—C. 1 hr. Last three weeks. Double periods. Dr. Pusey.

A practical course dealing with the organization and management of modern high schools. A number of practical problems relating to the administration of a secondary school, such as organization, curricula, teaching staff, community relationships, part-time education, etc., will be cosidered.

S-50-a. The School Principal—C. 1 hr., 6 weeks. Mr. Wise.

A practical course designed especially for elementary school principals, dealing with the problems of organization and administration of a single school as a district unit and its relationship to larger units of which it is a part, covering supervision of instruction, community relationship, etc.

S-37. The Junior High School. 1 hr., 6 weeks. Mr. Hunter.

This course is designed to meet the needs of teachers and principals who are interested in the development, organization, administration, and the educational philosophy of the Junior High School. The following units of instruction will be considered: Historical development of the Junior High School, its purpose, its peculiar functions, peculiar administration features, guidance program, best text books available, practice materials, buildings. methods of teaching, homogeneous grouping of pupils, and program of studies. This course will be so organized and conducted that it will meet the practical needs of teachers, and principals of the small junior high school, as well as the teacher who is doing departmental teaching in a regular high school.

S-38. Administration of High Schools for Officials—C. 1 hr. Last three weeks. Mr. Pusey.

A course arranged especially for county superintendents, principals.

S-41. Rural School Management for Superintendents, Teachers—C. 1 hr. Last three weeks. Mr. Alfriend.

This is a companion course to 38 for county superintendents.

S-50-a. Principles and Technique of Teaching—C. 1 hr., 6 weeks. Mr. Wise.

A discussion of the teaching problems of the upper grammar grades and the high school.
Text: Holley, "The Teacher's Technique."

GRADUATE COURSES—(See Graduate Division)

S-102-a. Graduate Educational Psychology. Dr. Edwards.
S-102-b. Graduate Educational Psychology. Dr. Edwards.
S-104-a. Graduate Educational Administration. Dr. Pusey.
S-104-b. Graduate Educational Administration. Dr. Pusey.

P.-T. A. COURSE—(See Elementary Section for Description)

See also education under **Elementary Division**, and under **Agriculture** and **Graduate Divisions** and **Home Economics Division**.

VI. ENGLISH

S-11. Shakespeare—C. 1 hr., 6 weeks. Mr. Park.

Midsummer Night's Dream, Julius Caesar, Macbeth, Hamlet and The Merchant of Venice will be studied. Lectures: written reports. Twelve other plays of Shakespeare will be used as collateral reading.

30

S-2-a. The Study of Poetry—C. 1 hr., 6 weeks. Mr. Park.
Lectures on Poetics. The reading and interpeting of standard English poems, representing the various types of poetry. Special study of the lyric.

S-14-a. Methods High School English—C. 1 hr., 6 weeks. Mr. Sanford. See Education.)

S-5. Greek Literature in Translation. 1 hr., 6 weeks. Mr. Bocock.
(a- The principles of the study of literature (b) The development of European literature. (c) Greek literature in translations. Select readings.

S-1. Advanced English Grammar—C. 1 hr., 6 weeks. Mr. Sanford.
This is a course which will devote its whole time to a study of English Grammar. Sanford's English Grammar, The Modern Course in English, Book III, will be the chief text.

S-3-a. Studies in Tennyson and Browning—C. 1 hr., 6 weeks. Mr. Simmons.
Representative pieces will be interpreted and discussed in the class-room. and others will be designated, for outside reading. The work may be pursued with profit by any student who has had, a survey course in English Literature.

S-3-b. The South in American Literature—C. 1 hr., 6 weeks. Mr. Simmons.
The time alloted to this course will be devoted chiefly to those writers who have represented most typically the Old South. the South of the Civil War. and the New South. Lectures, class-room readings, and reports on assigned topics.

S-1-c. The Mechanics of Writing Prose—C. 1 hr., 6 weeks. Mr. Simmons.
A study of fundamental processes in the art of composing. and an inquiry into the capital secrets of effectiveness in the transmission of thought and feeling. Lectures. discussions, conferences.

S-1. The Teaching of English in the Junior High School or Upper Grades—N. 1 hr., 6 weeks. Mr. Brown.
This is a course for teachers of English in the upper grammar grades and the junior high school. It will include a study of grammar. literature and composition. oral and written. for these grades. It will be helpful to teachers in the rural consolidated high schools.

JOURNALISM

S-1. Principles of Journalism—C. 1 hr., 6 weeks. Mr. Sanford.
Fundamentals of newspaper reporting and editing. Practical work in reporting for the Summer Session edition of the Summer School Items.
This course will help teachers who supervise the work of students on high school publications.
NOTE:—See Oratory and Dramatic Art. Division for additional courses.
NOTE:—Courses S-11. S-2a may apply on Sophomore or Junior credit; S-1 on Freshman credit; S-3a. 3b. on Junior credit: S-4. S-5 on Junior credit: S-1 Journalism on Freshman credit: Public Speaking S-2 on Freshman. Sophomore or Junior credit: S-1 on Sophomore or Junior credit; S-3 on Junior credit; S-4 on Junior credit.

VII. GRADUATE

The University permits a graduate student, eligible to candidacy for a second degree, to secure the Master's degree upon the successful completion of graduate courses pursued during four Summer Sessions. The student will pursue two half-minor courses or one minor each summer. During the year following each Summer Session the student will have the benefit of the guidance of the professors under whom courses have been pursued in the previous summer.

A thesis is required by the Faculty in connection with each Major course offered in the Summer School. Attendance on certain general lectures is also required of all candidates for a degree.

The right is reserved to withdraw any course for which there are not five or more applicants.

COURSES FOR 1926
EDUCATION

S-104. School Administration. Mr. Pusey.

For county and city school superintendents, and for principals of independent school districts.

The course will be given in two parts, each a half minor, as follows:

104-a.

Organization of a school system and its relation to a general state system; duties of the superintendent and his relationship to the board of education; financing a school system, budget making, sources of revenue, school bookkeeping, salary schedules; school architecture, care of school plant and equipment; consolidating schools, school building programs.

104-b.

The school population, census and attendance; progress of pupils through the grades, pupil accounting; courses of study; supervision; qualifications of teachers, training of teachers in service; school reports; statistical methods; auxiliary agencies.

Each part constitutes a course of six weeks, and both parts are essential to complete a minor. Both may be taken together, but if only one is taken, the other should be completed the next session of attendance.

Prerequisites: Education 10, 11, 12; Psychology, one year; Sociology, one semester. Equivalents may be offered.

ENGLISH

S-105. The English Novel. History and Technique. Mr. Sanford.

The course includes the reading of twenty-seven works of prose fiction from Sir Thomas Malory to Kipling. One half of this course will be given in 1926. Text-books: J. G. Dunlop's History of Prose Fiction; E. M. Warren's History of the Novel Previous to the 17th Century; Bliss Perry's Art of Prose Fiction. And for reference: Jusserand's English Novel in the Time of Shakespeare; Cross's Development of the English Novel; George Saintsbury's English Novel; Walter Raleigh's English Novel. Prerequisite, English 4, or the equivalent. Thirty lectures. Minor.

S-106. Early Eighteenth Century Literature. Mr. McWhorter.

English Literature, literary characteristics, and literary movements from 1700-1744: DeFoe. Addison, Steele, Swift and other prose writers; Pope, Prior, Gay, Thomson, Young, and minor poets. The Drama. Literary criticism. One-half of this minor course (poets) will be given in 1926. Prerequisite: English 1 and 2 and one Junior or Senior College course in English. Six weeks.

HISTORY

S-102-a. Tudor Times, 1485-1603. (First half.) Mr. Payne.

A study of the political and constitutional history of England from 1485 to 1603, with constant refrence to the development of Continental Europe for the same period. Readings, reports, and tests. based upon selections from Gasquet, Dixon. Bacon. Froude. Innes. Hallam, Brown, Johnson. Cambridge Modern History. Dictionary of National Biography, and English Historical Review. A full reading of Fisher. Political History of England. 1485-1547: Pollard. Political History of England. 1547-1603; Seebohm. Era of the Protestant Revolution. A half minor: five classes a week for six weeks. Prerequisite, six hours of college history.

S-104-a. The French Revolution, 1789-1799. (First half of 104.) Mr. Payne.

A topical study of European history from 1789 to 1799. with special emphasis upon French history. A seminar course based upon the standard authorities for this period. A half minor; thirty recitations. Prerequisite: Six hours of college history.

Authorities to be used in S-104-a: Mignet. Thiers. Carlyle. Tocqueville, Taine. Aulard. Madelin. Anderson. Young. Stryienski. Stephens. Bourne, Rose, Mahan. and Cambridge Modern History.

HOME ECONOMICS

S-112. Miss Newton.

Food investigation by means of animal feeding experiments. Laboratory study of typical Georgia foods by feeding them to standard laboratory animals; for vitamins A and B the albino rat. for C, the guinea pig. Problems dealing with the effect on vitamin content of temperature, aging, dyeing, and various methods of storing and preserving food. Study of current literature on food investigation. Reference will be made to various technical journals; prerequisite: -Home 'Economics 13| Half Minor, nine weeks.

MATHEMATICS

Mr. Stephens.

One of the following courses will be given if at least five students elect it. Two of the courses constitute a minor; three with a thesis, constitute a major.

101. Differential Equations.

An elementary course in ordinary and partial differential equations, with special reference to the equations occuring in the physical sciences. Text: Cohen or Murray.

102. Vector Analysis.

An elementary course in vectors which develops a system of coordinates and illustrates their use in certain mathematical and physical problems. Reference Text: Coffin.

103. Projective Geometry.

A' course in pure geometry based upon one of the following texts with the others as references: Holgate's Reye, Cremona, Veblen and Young.

104. Theory of Functions.

An introductory course to the theory of functions of a real and a complex variable. Reference works: Harkness and Morley, Durege. Gousat.

105. Analytical Geometry.

An advanced course based on Salmon or other texts of a similar character.

PSYCHOLOGY

S-102a-102b. Mr. Edwards.

102a deals with the normal mind. integration. mental hygiene, the more advanced problems of learning with their educational applications. 102b deals with the psychology of the abnormals as it relates to education and with diagnosis and treatment in education. It is advised that both half minors be taken together in one summer; if only one is taken the other should be completed the following summer. Given as parallel courses the first six weeks. Prerequisite. one year of psychology and such other study and experience as will satisfy the instructor that the student can do the work of the course.

VIII. HISTORY AND SOCIAL SCIENCES

S-5-6-a, b, and c. American History. College credit for History 5-6.
Based on the Epochs of American History, three volumes.

a. **The Colonial Period, 1750 to 1829—C.** 1 hr., 6 weeks. Mr. McPherson.
Text: Thwaites' Colonies.

b. **The Formative Period, 1750 to 1829—C.** 1 hr., 6 weeks. Mr. McPherson.
Text: Hart's Formation of the Union.

c. **The Jacksonian Era, the Slavery Struggle, the War of Secession, Reconstruction and the Modern Period—C.** 1 hr., 6 weeks. Mr. McPherson.
Text: Woodrow Wilson's Division and Reunion.

S-22. American Government—C. 1 hr., 6 weeks. Mr. McPherson.
Text: Magruder's American Government in 1923.

Modern European History.
A double course meeting two hours a day. A study of European development from 1789 to the present. Especial emphasis on events leading to the World War.

S-8. The French Revolution and Napoleon—C. 1 hr., 6 weeks, 1½ hrs., 9 weeks. Mr. Payne.

S-9. Europe Since 1815—C. 1 hr., 6 weeks, 1½ hrs., 9 weeks. Mr. Payne.

Either or both of the courses may be taken, and work may be equivalent to "History 2" or 'History S-9" in regular session.

S-14-b. The Teaching of History—C. 1 hr., 6 weeks. Mr. Payne.

S-8-9-a. The Great War and After—C. 1 hr., 6 weeks. Mr. Bocock.

This course will include a brief summary of the chief causes of the war, an outline of its course, and some consideration of the Peace Treaties and the League of Nations. Members of the class should have maps of pre-war and post-war Europe.

IX. HOME ECONOMICS

HOME ECONOMICS

S-1. Food Study and Cookery—C. 1½ hrs., 9 weeks. Miss Burson.

Composition, selection and cooking of typical foods, to give a working knowledge of the principles underlying food preparation. Sophomore credit. Prerequisite; General Chemistry. Fee, $3.50. First half-term.

S-2. Home Cookery and Table Service—C. 1½ hrs., 9 weeks. Miss Burson.

Practice in manipulation of foods in family sized quantities; practice in planning, preparing and serving meals. Sophomore credit. Prerequisite; Home Economics 1. Fee, $3.50. Second half-term.

S-5. Food Preservation—C. ½ hr., 9 weeks. Second half term. Miss Callaway.

A laboratory course for teachers and home demonstration agents. Canning in tin and glass, preserving, jelly making, brining, pickling, and vinegar making. standard packing. Junior. Prerequisite; Bacteriology 1. Laboratory daily. Fee. $3.00.

S-8. Advanced Cookery—C. 1 hr., 6 weeks. Miss Callaway.

Offered for students desiring advanced work in the preparation of food. Junior. Prerequisite; Chemistry 1, Home Economics 1, 2. Fee, $3.50.

S-12. Nutrition—C. 1½ hrs., 9 weeks. Miss Newton.

A study of the fundamental principles of human nutrition, the chemistry and physiology of digestion and metabolism. Senior. First half-term. Prerequisite: Organic Food Chemistry, Physiology, Bacteriology 1. Fee, $3.50.

S-13. Dietetics—C. 1½ hrs., 9 weeks. Miss Newton.

Nutritive requirements of individuals; relative cost of foods; dietary calculations. Senior. Second half-term. Two laboratory periods and one lecture. Prerequisites: Agricultural Chemistry 1, Physiology, Bacteriology 1, and Home Economics 12. Fee, $3.50.

S-26. Elementary Clothing—C. 2 hrs., 9 weeks. Miss Callaway.

Fundamental principles related to garment construction and dressmaking; patterns, machines. factory production of clothing; clothing budgets. Freshman. Fee. $4.00.

S-27. Textile Problems—C. 1 hr., 9 weeks, following Home Economcis 26. Miss E. Creswell.

Clothing and household materials; characteristics of the different standard fabrics and their use and care; wet and dry cleaning of all types of clothing. Freshman. Fee $2.00.

Men in Vocational Agriculture

S-32. Advanced Dressmaking—C. 3 hrs., 9 weeks. Misses Rathbone and E. Creswell.

Practice in original designs in modeling and draping; in technique of finishing and decoraton; shopwork in all types of clothing for women and children; how to use these methods in secondary classes. Junior. Prerequisite; Home Economics 26. Fee, $3.50.

S-43. Home Management—C. 1 hr., 6 weeks. Miss Edith Creswell.

Standards of efficiency in home making; organization of household activities; household equipment; sanitation; problems in accounting and budgeting; teaching aspects in Vocational Schools. Junior.

S-40. Health Education: Personal Hygiene and Home Nursing—C. 1 hr., 6 weeks. Miss Lunday.

This course presents health in its personal, social and economic aspects and shows how health and efficiency are improved by hygienic living. The fundamentals of Home Nursing are included. Prerequisite Physiology, Bacteriology, Ag. Chemistry 1. Senior.

S-22. Art Structure and Design.

See Arts and Crafts.

S-59. Home Economics Education—Teaching Relationships—C. 1 hr., 6 weeks. Miss Burson. Educational credit.

This course is organized around the needs of the teachers; problems of instruction, management, professional and personal qualifications, school community and promotional relationships; the course of study adapted to community needs. Junior.

S-28. Costume Designing—C. 1 hr., 6 weeks. Miss Rathbone.

A general course. No prerequisite. Study of principles of art related to clothing; line, spacing, dominant interest, character and so forth. Junior. Planned for elective credit. No prerequisite.

S-31. Costume Designing—C. 1½ hrs., 6 weeks. Miss Rathbone.

Studying and drawing foundation figures; designing costumes and accessories for different types. Color texture combinations. Media; crayon, crayola, water-color. Senior. Prerequisite; Home Economics 32 and 22. Fee, $3.50.

S-25. Millinery—C. 1 hr., 6 weeks. Miss Creswell.

Making wire frames from measurements and illustrations for foundation molds. Molding in net, buckran and willow. Study of difficult frames and crowns. Discussion of staple millinery materials and findings. Bow making and hand made trimmings for home millinery. Indviduals problems given attention. Fee, $1.50.

S-60. Child Training, Education—C. 1 hr., Junior and Senior. Miss McAlpine. Educational credit.

A course in Child Study and Child Training of special interest to those coming in contact with children.

This course is planned to give an understanding of child psychology and a knowledge of child training and care through a study of family relationships; the educational importance of the pre-school years; the needs and problems of the pre-adolescent and of the adolescent years; how the new schools and homes are attempting to meet these needs; organization and conduct of Child Study Groups—Demonstrations. Prerequisites: Psychology 1 and 2 or 4, 5. 6 or 7 and 8 or 23, 24, 25.

NOTE:—Also courses of the Graduate School as well as Art Courses will be offered for the summer.

X. LATIN

S-5-a. Rapid Reading of Latin Authors—C. 1 hr., 6 weeks. Mr. Hooper.

The aim of this course is to develop facility in the reading of Latin without the use of a dictionary. The selectons read are varied from year to year to meet the needs of particular classes.

S-5-b. Latin Writing—C. 1 hr., 6 weeks. Mr. Hooper.

This course will include the orderly presentation of the essential facts of the grammar, the translation of connected English into idiomatic Latin, and the study of style and the structure of Latin discourse. It is designed for teachers and others desiring a rapid and comprehensive review of the grammar, and for candidates for teacher's recommendation in Latin. For the latter class special work will be provided.

Provision will also be made for students of elementary Latin composition.

S-14-g. Methods of Teaching High School Latin—C. 1 hr., 6 weeks.
Mr. Hooper. (See Education.)

S-5-c. Course in Cicero—C. 1 hr., 6 weeks. Mr. Hooper.

Selected orations. The course will include a study of Cicero's career as an orator and man of affairs, with particular reference to the literary and artistic qualities of his orations. The historical settings of the period will be considered, with some study of the essential features of the republican constitution.

S-5-d. Course in Vergil.

On the same general plan as the course in Cicero, dealing however with the writings of Virgil.

NOTE:—Of courses S-5a, S-5b, and S-5c, 5-d, the three courses elected by the largest number of students will be given.

XI. LAW

The following courses are offered in the Law School during the summer of 1926. These are open to regularly registered students (including women) in the Law School and to new students who meet the entrance requirements and to teachers and others not studying for a degree who wish some work in law.

NOTICE:—Beginning with September, 1925, the entrance requirements to the Law School were raised from one year of college work to two years of college work, amounting to thirty hours.

Law students by taking work three summers will also shorten the three-year requirement.

Fees for the law courses are $15.00 for each course, or 6 courses for $60.00.

S-1. Municipal Corporation Law—by Cooley. 6 weeks. Mr. Upson.

S-2. Law of Bailments—by Dobie. 6 weeks. Mr. Upson.

S-3. Criminal Law. Mr. McWhorter.

Common-law and statutory offenses; parties in crime; classification and elements of the specific offenses; offenses against the government, jurisdiction.

S-4. Domestic Relations. Mr. McWhorter.

Contracts to marry; marriage; effect of marriage, common law marriages, modification of the common law imposed by statutes, the wife's separate property, separation and divorce. Parent and Child: Duties of parents; rights of parents. Guardian and Ward: Selection and appointment of guardian; rights, duties and liabilities of guardians; termination of guardianship; infants; persons non compotes mentis and aliens. Master and servant. General principles.

S-5. Contracts. Mr. Cornett.

Text: Lawson. The essential principles of a contract, the agreement, the competency of parties, the form, the consideration, the consent of parties and the legality of the object of agreement.

S-6. Sales. Mr. Cornett.

Text: Tiffany. Sale and contracts to sell, statute of frauds, warranties, conditions and penalty for breach, deliveries and acceptances, seller's lien, and stoppage in transitu.

S-7. The Constitution of the United States. Judge Gober.

S-8. The Constitution of the State of Georgia. Judge Gober.

Dean Sylvanus Morris of the Law School will deliver two public lectures: The Study of the Law. The Application of Principles.

S-9. International Law. Judge Gober. 2 hrs. a week.

Open to students of the summer school at regular summer school fees and to law students.

XIII. MATHEMATICS

S-14-d. Teaching High School Mathematics—C. 1 hr., 6 weeks. Mr.
Stephens. (See Education.)

S-1. Trigonometry—C. 1 hr., 6 weeks, 1 hr., 9 weeks. Mr. Stephens.

A standard course in Plane and Special Trigonometry covering the usual subject with solutions of triangles and manipulation of formulas.

S-2. Elementary Analysis—C. 2 hrs., 9 weeks. Mr. Barrow.

A study of Coordinates; plotting of Algebraic and Transcendental curves; discussion of the straight line and circle analytically; functional relations. Six hours per week for six weeks, and twelve hours a week for nine weeks.

S-3. Introduction to Calculus—C. 1½ hrs., 9 weeks. Mr. Barrow.

An elementary course, explaining differentiation and integration and a few applications. Six hours per week for nine weeks.

S-4. College Algebra—C. 1½ hrs., 9 weeks. Mr. Stephens.

This course will take up the following topics: Complex Numbers. Determinants, Partial Fractions, Series, Theory of Equations. Six hours per week for nine weeks.

S-5. Methods in Algebra and Correlated Junior Mathematics—N. 1 hr. Miss Callaway. Educational credit.

A course for teachers in the upper grammar grades and the junior high school laying stress upon the material, the methods used and text-books in correlated junior high school mathematics.

XIV. MODERN LANGUAGES

FRENCH

S-14-h. Methods of Teaching French—C. 1 hr., 6 weeks. Mr. Lustrat.

Teachers taking this course are supposed to have already a thorough knowledge of French grammar and syntax and consequently it has not so much for purpose to increase their knowledge of the language as to teach them the best methods to present the subject to their own pupils.

No exensive reading will be required in or outside the class room; a single text will be used for practice in pronunciation and the entire course will be given through lectures either in French or in English according to the preparation of those taking the course. In any case frequent talks will be given in French on current topics or literary subjects to bring the student to understand French when it is spoken.

Stress will be placed on pronunciation and conversational French will form an essential part of the course.

With approval of the Dean of the School of Education, this course may be given 1 hour credit toward certain degrees.

S-20. French—C. 1½ hurs., 6 weeks. Mr. Chance.

A beginners course equivalent to Junior French. Two periods daily.

S-21. French—C. 1½ hrs., 6 weeks. Mr. Chance.

A half year course with parallel reading between two consecutive summer schools. Senior course.

SPANISH

S-20. Spanish—C. 3 hrs., 9 weeks. Mr. Thaxton.

A course similar to French 20.

S-21. Spanish—C. 1½ hrs., 6 weeks. Mr. Thaxton.

A course similar to French 21.

XV. MUSIC

George Folsom Granberry, Director

PROFESSIONAL TRAINING FOR MUSIC TEACHERS

History:

The department was established by George Folsom Granberry, director of the Granberry Piano School, Carnegie Hall, New York, who remains in charge. In its four sessions the department has established itself as an enthusiastic, genuine and practical success. Teachers completing the course have been able to achieve better results immediately and some have been able to secure better and more profitable positions.

Certificate:

The University through the Summer School grants a certificate to those who complete the course for the Professional Training of

Professional Music Class

Music Teachers. Two Summer Sessions with independent study during the winter are necessary for the accomplishment of the requirements.

Requirements for a Certificate:

"Musical Development through Sight, Touch and Hearing," (by George Folsom Granberry, published by A. P. Schmidt Co., 120 Boylston St., Boston.) These four volumes cover the **Presentation of the Elements of Music, the Essentials of Theory and History, Elementary and Intermediate Technique, and Ear Training.** Five periods each week through the summer sessions.

Harmonic, Tonal and Formal Analysis:

Pieces and studies selected from the works of **Bach, Clementi, Bertini, Kohler, Czerny, Elsenheimer,** and **Gurlitt.** Two periods each week through two summer sessions.

Transposition and Intermediate Piano Technique:

Material selected from Sight, Touch and Hearing and works by standard composers. Three periods each week through two summer sessions.

Piano Ensemble Playing:

Orchestra, Operatic and Chamber music arranged for four, six and eight hands, analyzed and performed. Two periods each week of one summer session.

Appreciation of Music:

A written test on the volume, "Music: an Art and a Language," by Walter Raymond Spalding, (A. P. Schmidt, Boston.) Ten questions are given on the evolution and development of **Musical Forms** and the **Masters of Music** as given by Spalding. This preparation should be outside the summer session and the test taken with the playing test.

Piano Playing:

Individual lessons in Piano Playing are not required for the Professional Music Teachers' Certificate, but a **Playing Test** is required, the material for which is outlined following and may be prepared outside of the summer session. Teachers finishing all other requirements may pass their playing test any time before the close of the following Summer School, at which time they will receive their certificates.

38

PLAYING TEST

Bach—Two numbers selected from the Little Preludes and Fugues or the Two or Three-part Inventions, or one larger work.

One selection from any of the following composers:

Clementi—One of the later sonatas. **Haydn**—Sonata. **Mozart**—Sonata. _Beethoven—One of the earlier sonatas.

One selection each from two of the following composers:

Schumann—Scenes from childhood, op. 15. Fantasy Lyrics, op. 12. Four sonatas for Young People, op. 118. Album Leaves, op. 124.

Greig—Lyrical Pieces, op. 12—op. 54—op. 17—op. 68—op. 43.

MacDowell—Etudes for Technic and Style, op. 39. Woodland Sketches, op. 5. Sea pieces, op. 55.

Debussy—"Coin des Enfants.' '"Arabesques."

Tuition:

The tuition for the Professional Training Course, ten periods each week, for the summer Session of six weeks: $30.00.

Musical Appreciation:

Mr. Granberry gives a course of twelve hour lessons. The work is designed not only to make the ear accurate, but to establish taste by acquainting the student in the most elemental way with the best in music. The material used in developing tonal and rhythmical perception and understanding is taken only from the greatest masters, from Wagner's Nibelungen Laid and the stand symphonies, principally those of Beethoven.

Tuition, two hour class lessons weekly _____$ 9.00

Piano Ensemble:

The Reading at Sight and Study including Analysis of the Form, Tonal Structure, History and Meaning, of works of which are outside the realm of piano music: Operatic, Orchestral, Chamber, Choral, etc. Many of the numbers are prepared for finished performance and are given at the various public gatherings of the Summer School. The classes are conducted by Mr. Granberry.

Tuition two hours lessons weekly _____$ 9.00

PIANO

Private Piano Lessons.

Interpretation, Advanced Technique, Repertory, Teaching Literature, etc. Tuition, twelve half-hour lessons:

```
*Mr. Granberry _____$60.00
 Mr. Clement _____ 24.00
 Mrs. Rowe _____ 24.00
```

* Mr. Granberry will accept only a limited number of private pupils, and only those who are engaged in professional work.

VOICE LESSONS
John Hendricks
(National Conservatory of Music, New York; Pupil of Jeane Faure, Antwerp; Anton Dvorak, Emil Fischer and James Huneker, New York; Paul Plancon and Sbrigli, Paris.)

(a) **Private lessons**, twelve half hour lessons _____$ 36.00

(b) **Master classes.** Class lessons of one hour each with four in class. Each pupil recieves a fifteen minutes lesson, besides benefitting from the others during the hour. Twelve lessons. _____$ 18.00

PIPE ORGAN LESSONS
Mrs. George F. Granbery

Private Lessons. Pedaling; Registrative; church literature; concert repertory. Twelve lessons _____$ 48.00

VIOLIN LESSONS
Austin J. Wight

Mr. Wight commenced the study of Violin in Boston, Mass., under Adolph Lowinsky; with six years further study under Emil Mollenhauer, conductor of the Handel & Hayden Society and the

People's Symphony Orchestra of Boston, and later under Ovide Musin at the Belgian Conservatory of Music in the City of New York.

(a) 12 half-hour private lessons ----------------------------------$ 24.00
(b) 6 class lessons (Belgian Class System for advanced
    pupils, one hour weekly --------------------------------- 9.00
(c) Orchestra and String Ensemble Class two one hour
    periods weekly --------------------------------------- 9.00
(d) A thorough sound and comprehensive course of violin instruction from the best Austro-German and Franco-Belgian violin schools leading to public appearance in Orchestra, Operatic, Concert and Choral, also participating in the various public gatherings at the Summer School, pupils studying concert pieces, concertos and the violin and piano sonatas of Bach, Handel, Hayden, Mozart, Beethoven, Rubinstein and Greig, will have the assistance of an experienced accompanist.

PUBLIC SCHOOL MUSIC

(See Arts and Crafts)

Choral Music:

The Council of the Summer School earnestly desires to promote good singing and for this reason a Choral Club under the direction of Mrs. Granberry is to be instituted. Qualified students of the Summer School are free to join this club, which will meet regularly and will prepare for participation in public probrams.

Community Singing:

A large part of each daily assembly will continue to be given to general singing: patriotic songs, famous ballads, sacred selections, glees, rounds and nonsense jingles. Mr. Granberry will conduct this umsic at the University.

State License or Certificate:

Those completing the requirements for the University Summer School Certificate in Music, may also secure a State Certificate in Music by presenting a diploma from a recognized high school and credit for two years college work.

Books and Music:

Each teacher registered for the music course should allow at least $8.00 for music and books which are reguired for the course.

A Musical Festival:

The fifth week of the Summer School is known as music festival week. A Grand Opera will be presented and there will be vocal and instrumental recitals, and concerts of varied vocal and instrumental combinations.

The summer school registration fee of $3.00 is charged all registrants and admits to all entertainments. The private lessons will be given in the Chancellor's old home and there will be found also the pianos for private practice. A small rent fee is charged for these.

XVI. ORATORY AND DRAMATIC ART

ORATORY AND DRAMATIC ART

Courses in this department are designed to cover three phases of activity in this field of education: (1) instruction in the theory of expression, in the principles of speech improvement and correction, and in methods of teaching; (2) instruction and training in speech-making; (3) instruction and training n oral interpretaton of literature and in dramatics. Students who wish to teach these subjects should have some knowledge of each of these three phases mentioned above. Students especially interested in speech-making are advised to take some work in oral interpretation or dramatics, while those chiefly interested in oral interpretation or dramatics should take some work in speech-making. It is advisable during the same session to take courses along these two lines rather than along one line only. The work will be progressive in nature so that students may continue their studies for several years. These courses are exchanged in credit at the University or at Emerson College of Oratory. Students will be grouped, as far as possible, according to individual needs or previous study.

S-2-b. Play Production—C. 1 hr., 6 weeks. Miss Cobb.

A study of the problems involved in producing school and community plays. Selection of plays; choosing and training a cast; the stage and stage settings; principles of acting; costuming and make-up; organization and business management; modern plays presented from the platform and for the public. Intended for advanced students and graduates who are interested in the educational and social service aspects of dramatic production. Open to those who receive permission from the instructor.

Expression for Teachers and **Dramatics for the Grades.** Junior credit.

Dr. Park's course in Shakespeare and other English courses will supplement the work in Oratory.

Students should endeavor to take one of Mrs. Spiker's courses in Aesthetic dancing, etc.

See also the courses by Miss Vance at the State Normal in **Story Telling.**

S-1. Literary Interpretation. 1 hr., 6 weeks. Miss Cobb.

The "Evolution of Expression," Vols. I, II, III, and IV, used at Emerson College of Oratory are the text books for this course. Lectures on the basic principles of Expression embraced in these volumes will be supplemented by practical work in applying these principles to the interpretation of the printed page varied literary forms being used as material. The student will have daily practice with personal attention and individual criticism for the purpose of developing and guiding his own powers of expression. Lectures will be given on the pedagogical methods of teaching the fundamentals of Expression in the study and interpretation of literature. The work in literary and dramatic interpretation may be applied in the schools from the kindergarten through the High School and College. Sophomore or Junior credit.

Voice—Position, breathing, tone placing, tone support, articulation and enunciation, diction.

Body—Pantomime, to aid in overcoming self-consciousness and timidity, and to substitute freedom and self-confidence. Elementary gesture.

Two sections, (a) more elemntary, (b) for those actively engaged in teaching or have completed most of the work in this subject.

S-1-a. Public Speaking—C. 1 hr., 6 weeks. Mrs. Spiker.

The subjects will be treated from the two-fold view-point of speech structure and speech delivery. Types determined by the underlying purpose of the speech will be considered. Toward the last of the course work will be done in fine points of shading and line reading. The extemporaneous speech, the speech from a prepared outline, and the memorized manuscript speech will be covered in theory and practice.

The history of Oratory will be sketched with illustrative examples from classic, medieval, and modern orations analyzed and delivered in class.

The work for debates and contests in declamation should develop from a regular course in Public Speaking. This would bring results far superior to the old method of mechanical coaching of a single speech for a set occasion. It would eliminate affection and what is stilted and studied and substitute simplicity and truthfulness. Normal work is included in this course, Freshman credit.

Voice—Fundamentals of tone production, articulation, tone radiation, pronunciation, diction.

Elementary, gesture to aid the student to acquire ease of bearing.

For students desiring it an opportunity will be sought for experimental work in speaking outside the class in addition to the daily work in the class room.

S-2. Dramatic Interpretation—C. 1 hr., 6 weeks. Miss Cobb.

Material will be chosen from classic and modern drama. The one act play will be studied. Expressional reading of principal scenes. The reading of the line and the analysis and interpretation of character will be emphasized. Characters assigned to members of class and scenes presented from the platform. Junior credit.

Pantomime, gesture, voice.

Lectures on modern Little Theatre movement and educational and community dramatics.

XVII. PHYSICAL EDUCATION

PHYSICAL EDUCATION FOR WOMEN

The various courses in this department are organized to meet three needs: Those of the student wishing to improve individual skills; the student preparing for professional work in Physical Education and Health Education, and the teacher in service desiring further training along these lines.

Medical examinations are required of all students taking practical work. These examinations may be obtained by appointment with the University Physician.

The regulation University Gymnasium costume of black bloomers, black hose and black tie, white middy and white tennis shoes will be required for all floor classes and a simple costume will be needed for dancing S-3. These may be purchased in Athens.

Students wishing to take work in the Physical Education Department must record these courses on the study lists which they file with the Registrar.

Tennis courts are provided for the students' use. The swimming pool will be available for swimming practice one hour daily throughout the session with an instructor in charge. Those wishing to take advantage of this privilege for the term will secure appointments for a regular hour each day. For the use of locker and towels a charge of $1.00 is made.

S-3. Dancing—N. 1 hr., 6 weeks. Mrs. Potter-Spiker.
The work of this course includes interpretation of music and pantomimic dancing through natural and full bodily movements. A special costume is required.

S-5. Basketball—C. 1 hr., 6 weeks. Miss Lunday.
Indoor Baseball, Volley Ball, Hockey, Tennis and Track Athletics preparatory for State Tests for High School Pupils. Rules, duties of officials, organization of squads and teams, equipment, methods of coaching, conduct of tournaments. Actual experience in the playing and conduct of the games.

S-6. Technique of Swimming—C. ½ hr., 6 weeks.
Principles and methods of teaching swimming, diving, life saving, training and coaching, rules of events. American Red Cross Life Saving Test is given.

S-7. Games—Theory and Practice—C. 1 hr., 6 weeks. Miss Lunday.
Games suitable for playgrounds, elementary and secondary schools, ranging from simplest primary school games to organized team games such as volley ball, captain ball, etc., will be presented. The psychology of play, selection, adaptation and relative value of material will be discussed.

S-11. Tactics and Calisthenics—C. 1 hr., 6 weeks. Miss Lunday.
Graded course in tactics and calesthenics, apparatus work for grades and high schools. Prerequisite: Physical Education 1-2.

S-12. Folk Dancing and Singing Games—N. 1 hr., 6 weeks. Mrs Potter-Spiker.
Representative national dances and singing games suitable for all grades will be presented.

S-17. Pageantry—N. ½ hr., 6 weeks. Mrs. Potter-Spiker.
This includes instruction and practice in costumes for festivals, pageants.
Arrangement, costuming and production of pageants. A complete pageant will be presented at the end of the course. Prerequisites: physical Education 3 and 12. Junior and Senior.

S-22. Advanced Dancing—N. ½ hr. Mrs. Potter-Spiker.

S-23. Beginners' Swimming—C. ½ hr., 6 weeks.
The fundamental strokes will be taught.

S-24. Advanced Swimming and Diving—C. ½ hr., 6 weeks.
This course will include form swimming and diving and life saving.

S-40-a. Health—C. 1 hr., 6 weeks. Miss Lunday.
The principles of personal and general hygeine will be presented. Prerequisites: Physiology, Bacteriology 1 and Ag. Chemistry 1. Senior.

PHYSICAL TRAINING FOR MEN

The Summer School management is pleased to offer to the High Schools of Georgia and neighboring states a four weeks course in athletic coaching for men.

More or less interscholastic athletics has been introduced into all of our high schools. It is necessary that the men in charge of this work should know both the theory and practice, the hygiene and ethics of good sports. It would be a fine thing for interscholastic athletics for a hundred or more of the leading coaches

Memorial Hall Pool

in this section of the South to come together for training under these men of reputation and advance the standards of athletic sports and at the same time form friendships and establish athletic ideals that may permeate the school life of the South.

In addition to the registration fee, a fee of $5.00 will be charged for work in this department. This fee will cover all incidentals, including gymnasium fee, towel fee, locker feet, and swimming pool.

Inquiries concerning these courses may be sent to the Director of the Summer School.

The instruction this year will be in charge of Coach Mehre (former Notre Dame quarterback and basketball player.) **Mr.** Mehre has been Assistant Coach at the University of Georgia for the past two seasons, and a great deal of the success of last year's football team was du to Mr. Mehre's intimate knowledge of the famous Notre Dame system of football.

P-1. Basketball Theory. 11:40 to 12:30 daily. Mr. Mehre.

P-2. Basketball Practice. 12:30 to 1:30 daily. Mr. Mehre.

P-3. Football Theory. 3:50 to 4:40 daily. Mr. Mehre.

P-4. Football Practice. 4:40 to 5:30 daily. Mr. Mehre.

P-5. General Athletics for High Schools.

First aid instruction in physical training for high schools; various recreational games: physical standards for students; physical requirements for students; physictl drills outlined and explained; treatment of injuries; first aid; correct bandaging, etc. Woodruff hall.

PSYCHOLOGY

(Note:—No courses in Psychology are open to Freshmen.)

S-1, S-2, S-3. Introductory General and Social Psychology.

An introductory course in which S1 and S2 take up a study of mental life and behavior including such topics as sensation, perception. habit, attention. memory. thinking and reasoning. emotions. reaction, instinct, action and will; the elements of social psychology with a view especially to laying a foundation in psychology for these students who will study sociology.

S-1. First half of S-1, S-2. Credit, 1 hr., 8:45. Mr. Patrick.

S-2. Second half of S-1, S-2. Credit, 1 hr. Given the last **three** weeks, double periods, 8:45-9:35. Mr. Patrick.

S-3. Social Psychology. Credit, 1 hr. 11:55. Mr. Patrick

S-4, S-5, S-6. Educational Psychology. (See Education.)

S-21. **Adolescence.** (See Education.)

S-102. **Graduate Educational Psychology.** (See the Graduate School.)

XVIII. SCIENCES

CHEMISTRY

S-1. **Elementary Chemistry—C.** 4 hrs., 9 weeks. Mr. Brockman.

Fundamental course in general chemistry required of Agricultural and Home Economic students and valuable for teachers. Laboratory fee, $3.00. Breakage fee, $3.00.

Organic and Biological Chemistry. (See Agriculture.)

Qualitative Analysis. (See Agriculture.)

Quantitative Analysis. (See Agriculture.)

GENERAL SCIENCE

S-1. **General Science—N.** 1 hr., 6 weeks. Mr. Earnest.

This course is designed to meet the needs of the High School teacher of general science who, having a good knowlege of elementary science, wishes to study and discuss modern methods of teaching this subject. The general method advocated and discussed will be that of the problem-project method recommended by the science committee of the National Education Association. Educational credit.

PHYSICS

S-1. **College Physics—C.** 3 hrs., 9 weeks. Mr. Dixon.

An elementary course in Physics equivalent to Physics 1 offered in the regular session. Time required. One period each morning recitation and lecture, and three periods each afternoon recitation and laboratory work with the necessary outside preparation. Laboratory fee, $3.00.

S-2. **College Physics—C.** 4 hrs., 9 weeks. Mr. Hendren.

An elementary course in Physics equivalent to Physics 2 as offered in the regular session. This course satisfies the requirements of medical colleges of a standard four hour credit course in Physics. Two periods recitation and lecture six days a week and a two hour laboratory period five days a week. Laboratory fee, $3.00.

ZOOLOGY

Arranged especially to meet the biological requirements for entrance to medical schools.

S-31. **General Zoology—C.** 4 hrs., 9 weeks. Mr. Krafka.

A course dealing with the general physiology, anatomy, and development of the various animal types, supplemented by a consideration of heredity, variation and evolution. Two recitations and a laboratory period daily for nine weeks. Laboratory fee, $3.50.

S-14-f. **Teaching of Biology—C.** 1 hr., 6 weeks. Mr. Krafka. (See Education.)

SOCIOLOGY

S-7. **Introductory Sociology—C.** 1 hr., 6 weeks. Dean Alfriend.

A study of sociology through selected social problems, and a discussion of the related educational problems of remedial character.

S-9. **Educational Sociology—C.** 1 hr., 6 weeks. Dean Alfriend. (See Education.)

Lightning Source UK Ltd.
Milton Keynes UK
UKHW022002140119
335570UK00011B/515/P